CONFLICT OF COMMAND

CONFLICTING WORLDS

New Dimensions of the American Civil War

T. Michael Parrish, Series Editor

CONFLICT OF COMMAND

GEORGE McCLELLAN, ABRAHAM LINCOLN, *and the* POLITICS OF WAR

GEORGE C. RABLE

Louisiana State University Press
BATON ROUGE

Published by Louisiana State University Press
lsupress.org

Manufactured in the United States of America
First printing

Designer: Barbara Neely Bourgoyne
Typeface: MillerText
Printer and binder: Sheridan Books

Cover photograph: Abraham Lincoln on the battlefield at Antietam, Maryland, with George McClellan, October 3, 1862. Photo by Alexander Gardner. Prints & Photographs Division, Library of Congress, Washington, DC.

Library of Congress Cataloging-in-Publication Data
Names: Rable, George C., author.
Title: Conflict of command : George McClellan, Abraham Lincoln, and the politics of war / George C. Rable.
Other titles: George McClellan, Abraham Lincoln, and the politics of war
Description: Baton Rouge : Louisiana State University Press, [2023] | Series: Conflicting worlds : new dimensions of the American Civil War | Includes bibliographical references and index.
Identifiers: LCCN 2023007783 (print) | LCCN 2023007784 (ebook) | ISBN 978-0-8071-7977-2 (cloth) | ISBN 978-0-8071-8103-4 (pdf) | ISBN 978-0-8071-8102-7 (epub)
Subjects: LCSH: McClellan, George B. (George Brinton), 1826–1885—Military leadership. | Lincoln, Abraham, 1809–1865—Military leadership. | United States—History—Civil War, 1861–1865—Campaigns. | Command of troops—History—19th century.
Classification: LCC E467.1.M2 R33 2023 (print) | LCC E467.1.M2 (ebook) | DDC 973.7/3092—dc23/eng/20230420
LC record available at https://lccn.loc.gov/2023007783
LC ebook record available at https://lccn.loc.gov/2023007784

to my students at

Anderson University
(1979–1998)

and at the

University of Alabama
(1998–2016)

CONTENTS

MAPS

ACKNOWLEDGMENTS

Because I have worked on this project for a good many years (with a fair number of self-inflicted interruptions), the obligations both professional and personal have accumulated. I must begin with my longstanding debt to William Marvel, who has, for as long as I have known him, generously shared research materials from his many forays into archives far and wide. In addition, Bill along with another longtime friend, A. Wilson Greene, read the entire manuscript with sharp and critical eyes. Their divergent views on McClellan and Lincoln proved invaluable as I worked on revisions. I have greatly benefited from their many suggestions, several of which elicited much laughter and more importantly serious reflection. I have been greatly blessed to have two such generous, smart, and faithful friends.

John Hennessey, Laura Mammina, T. Michael Parrish, Donald Pfanz, Stephen Sears, the late Roger Spiller, Christopher Stowe, Daniel Stowell, and Frank Wetta shared valuable research materials or helped move the project along in other ways. The insights of Mark Grimsley and Ethan Rafuse, presented not only in their published works but also in a stimulating session on George B. McClellan at the 2016 meeting of the Society of Civil War Historians in Chattanooga, Tennessee, proved invaluable.

During nearly five decades of working on various topics on the Civil War era, librarians and archivists have been unfailingly generous. The recent pandemic and closure of libraries has posed serious challenges to researchers, but the growing volume of digitized collections has been a godsend. I am especially grateful for the Library of Congress's digitized Civil War manuscripts and to Michelle Krowl for updates on each new addition.

It was a pleasure to work once again with the Louisiana State University Press. Mike Parrish and an anonymous reader offered generous assessments and some excellent suggestions for revision. Over many years, Mike has kept me supplied with research materials—often from very obscure sources—but more importantly has often proved to be a wise and patient counselor. I am honored to have this book in his fine series. Rand Dotson offered encouragement from the outset and did not even object too much to the length of the manuscript. I have never had a better copyeditor than Kevin Brock. His careful attention (and knowledge of Civil War history) proved very helpful in countless ways. Mary Lee Eggart expertly and efficiently produced the maps.

Since 1998, my wife, Kay, and I have lived in Tuscaloosa, Alabama, where we have been blessed in so many ways. I was privileged to have a fine group of colleagues and students during my years of teaching at the University of Alabama. The Fellowship Sunday School at Forest Lake United Methodist Church has not only tolerated an LSU fan as their teacher but also encouraged and inspired me in countless ways. The Elders—Ian Brown, Guy Hubbs, and Larry Kohl—made Wednesday breakfasts enlightening and entertaining. Larry Kreiser has kept me up to date on Ohio sports news and more importantly has joined me each week to suffer through several disappointing seasons with our poor Cleveland Browns. The Monday duplicate bridge group has provided keen competition and good fellowship. And especially during the pandemic, playing bridge with the Saylors, the Beckners, the Dudgeons, and the Kreisers has greatly contributed to my mental and emotional health. So, too, did maintaining contact with those dear friends from graduate-school days at LSU. Those friendships are now extending past the fifty-year mark—something to be cherished more and more with each passing year.

As I was wrapping up the final details on this book, Kay and I celebrated our fiftieth wedding anniversary. Out of our love for each other have come two wonderful daughters, Anne and Katie. And I dare not forget to acknowledge our superb sons-in-law, Dave and Eric. Of course, our grandsons, Lincoln and Maddox, will want to be mentioned in grandpa's book, and I am more than happy to accommodate those fine fellows.

CONFLICT OF COMMAND

INTRODUCTION

MENTION GEORGE B. McCLELLAN to students of the American Civil War, and the response is predictable. They know McClellan as a foil to Abraham Lincoln who might be able to organize an army but was reluctant to commit it to combat. As Lincoln once said, McClellan had "the slows." To call him a controversial commander at least in the twentieth or twenty-first centuries is misleading. People have largely made up their mind about McClellan—and not in the general's favor; nor do they seem amenable to rethinking their position. When the historian Mark Grimsley in 2015 and 2017 published two brief pieces in a popular Civil War magazine discussing McClellan's image as a feckless commander and suggested some revisions, the response was unsurprising. In the following issues, the letters appeared, dismissive of Grimsley's efforts and unwilling to consider any other interpretation than the standard one.[1]

In his own day, however, McClellan had many warm friends and political supporters as well as, of course, no shortage of critics and enemies. He had the misfortune to clash with Lincoln, another controversial figure of the time, but one who became the savior of the Union, the great emancipator, and the martyr president in the aftermath of his assassination. The apotheosis of Lincoln hardly helped McClellan's historical standing.

McClellan sought vindication in an autobiography but did not live to complete it. His literary executor, W. C. Prime, only made matters worse by bringing McClellan's partially completed manuscript into print and adding excerpts from letters between the general and his wife, Mary Ellen Marcy McClellan, which have offered fodder for McClellan critics ever since. By 1881, McClellan had largely completed his memoirs, and they were stored in a warehouse. Just as he was returning from a European trip, a fire tore through the building, consuming the manuscript. He began anew but in a desultory fashion, often simply adding healthy chunks of his 1864 report on military operations. When McClellan died on October 29, 1885, this new manuscript had only reached May 1862, so Prime took over the project. Even the title, *McClellan's Own Story,* is misleading because it is McClellan's story only in part since he had not come close to completing an account of his Civil War service. Prime did more than McClellan himself to shape the final product and, it might be added, further damage his friend's historical reputation.[2]

As for the historians, consider this lineup. In the anti-McClellan camp are giants of the Civil War field: Bruce Catton, T. Harry Williams, Stephen Sears, and James McPherson.

For the defense, we have Warren Hassler's mediocre biography, a good unpublished dissertation by Joseph Harsh, Ethan Rafuse's fine revisionist study, and a scattering of articles. And then there is Ken Burns, whose documentary simply followed in the footsteps of Catton and company.[3]

Even the historians most critical of McClellan, however, have praised his organizational abilities, and some have acknowledged his strategic sense.[4] In 1882 Francis Winthrop Palfrey, who had served in the 20th Massachusetts Infantry (the famed "Harvard Regiment"), offered one of the earliest and most judicious assessments. Compared to some other Union generals, he found McClellan to be an impeccable gentleman—obviously an important quality given Palfrey's pedigree. While commending him as organizer and strategist, Palfrey noted the general's failure to deploy his forces with enough speed and vigor to obtain "decisive results," though he might have added that decisive results eluded virtually all Civil War generals. He realized that it might seem strange to praise McClellan as the Army of the Potomac's best commander, but he was carefully weighing the difficulties McClellan faced. For Palfrey, the question of timing was especially important in shaping McClellan's historical image because he had faced the Confederates early in the war and at the height of their strength. Yet he also acknowledged that McClellan's politics and especially early talk of a presidential candidacy made his removal from command likely, particularly given his checkered record and difficulties with Lincoln. Whatever these shortcomings and limitations, Palfrey deemed McClellan's failures "partly his misfortune but not altogether his fault."[5]

That roughly balanced, though not entirely convincing, analysis was generous but not uncritical, even as it recognized McClellan's political liabilities without probing more deeply the political nature of the command relationship. Given the president's position as commander in chief, Lincoln and his advisers had to select and evaluate the Union's military leadership.[6] At the beginning of the war, none of the available generals had commanded large armies in combat, and given the eventual size of Civil War armies and the limits of staff, communications, and transportation, that task often seemed beyond the capabilities of even the better ones. Civil War campaigns sometimes seem like a series of blunders and missed opportunities, with the inability of generals to follow up even after victories a striking feature. McClellan's supporters often stressed the role of interference by the Lincoln administration in the Army of the Potomac's military operations including both the withholding of forces from McClellan on the Peninsula and the ordered withdrawal at the end of the Seven Days Campaign.[7]

Yet to mount a defense of McClellan's military record or a more critical assessment of Lincoln's leadership should hardly mean ignoring the general's shortcomings or failing to see how the president grew in his role as commander in chief.[8] Historians have often emphasized McClellan's slowness and timidity along with his repeated overestimation of enemy numbers. And. for sure, McClellan believed in meticulous preparation for any kind of movement and often seemed oblivious to public impatience; he could also appear uncertain of himself when the moment for decisive action arrived.[9] The stress of command itself may also have contributed to what has often been considered McClellan's extreme caution.[10]

Ironically enough, Lincoln too was slow to tackle the army's command problems and at times dealt with McClellan inconsistently and indirectly. The president certainly overlooked personal slights—including from Little Mac—and could recognize McClellan's ability to organize and sustain morale in the Army of the Potomac.[11] Even as many contemporaries and later historians marveled at Lincoln's patience with him, the replacements for McClellan as both general in chief and as commander of the Army of the Potomac proved less than satisfactory—at least until the successes of Ulysses S. Grant in the western theater reached their culmination at Vicksburg and Chattanooga, and he was brought east to take charge of all military operations.

Lincoln and McClellan came to see the nature of the war in quite different ways; Lincoln's views, however, evolved—albeit haltingly—while McClellan's did not. Lincoln would always maintain that preservation of the Union was the war's primary objective, but he came to embrace the emancipation of the enslaved as a critically important means to that end. McClellan remained fundamentally conservative, both in terms of his own Whiggish background and later his identification as a Democrat aligned with the Stephen A. Douglas wing of the party. He believed in moderation and compromise, and the war did not weaken that faith. He could not embrace either emancipation or hard-war policies and had hoped for a short and decisive military campaign to subdue the southern rebellion. Given his political philosophy and West Point training, McClellan favored maneuvering over fighting and preferred moving along rivers and railroad lines rather than advancing overland.[12]

That McClellan would not throw his troops headlong into battle or assault heavily fortified positions partly explains his popularity in the ranks—indeed, his success in winning the loyalty and even affection of his men was striking. McClellan identified with his soldiers, and many of them identified with him. He was quite visible in camp and became known for looking after his troops' welfare. Newspapers paid much attention to McClellan and early in the war uniformly exalted the "young Napoleon."[13] But who could live up to that moniker? Expectations for success ran so high that they set the general and his most devoted acolytes up for disappointment.

McClellan's elevated standing in the army and on the home front stood in ironic contrast to his sometimes-contemptuous attitude toward volunteer soldiers. McClellan may have been a Democrat, but he was no democrat. At the same time, he often had trouble with superiors, whether military or civilian; frustration and anger boiled over if a proposed strategy or request for more men was not approved. He had little faith in civilian leadership or the northern public.

McClellan prided himself on military professionalism, but the men he commanded were mostly citizen-soldiers. He deplored the influence of politics on the conduct of the war yet could hardly escape from that reality. However much McClellan might wish to insulate himself from Washington politicians, that was simply not possible. Politics became inextricably entangled with the war's conduct. Of course, the Lincoln administration had both to select and to deal with an array of military commanders. Lincoln himself had much to learn, could be oblivious to logistical constraints, and had unrealistic expectations for military success based on the Union's superior resources. He eventually developed a steely eyed resolve in working with generals but paid a price for earlier indecisiveness and allowing generals—including McClellan—to bypass the chain of command.[14]

This was no mere clash of military and political cultures, nor was it simply a conflict between two men of markedly different backgrounds and personalities. Focusing on McClellan's weaknesses and Lincoln's strengths or even revising the standard assessments of each man does not paint a very complete picture, either.[15] The relationship between the two began early in the war and at times dominated the course of the conflict, with many a twist and turn. It is therefore better to explore the slow evolution of that relationship in a broad context that brings in the politicians, the generals, the soldiers, and the often forgotten influencers: journalists.

The men in uniform read newspapers, followed politics, and developed their own ideas on strategy; they often viewed their military superiors and civilian rulers with a critical eye. Unlike many nineteenth-century European armies, American armies did not play an independent political role, but political opinions and partisanship at times loomed large.[16] The soldiers would have their say about McClellan and Lincoln, casting their votes during one of the strangest and most important presidential elections in American history.

In the following chapters, the focus will be on the politics of the Lincoln-McClellan connection. Rather than refighting the military campaigns, the story will center around the relationship between Lincoln as commander in chief and McClellan as both general in chief and commander of the Army of the Potomac. The purpose here is not to present a historical brief on behalf of either the president or the general but instead to understand the political dynamics at work in Washington, in the army, and in the country at large. How the partnership between Lincoln and McClellan developed and ultimately failed had a great influence on the course and ultimate costs of the American Civil War. A broadly conceived political approach to this story will also bring in the Army of the Potomac's officers and enlisted men. Nor will McClellan's removal from command in November 1862 mark the climax of the narrative. Indeed, repeated calls for Little Mac's return kept reaching Lincoln, especially any time another Army of the Potomac commander faltered. In the end, the conflict between

Lincoln and McClellan reached its conclusion when the Democrats chose the general as their presidential nominee in 1864, which meant another faceoff with a president who badly wished to be reelected.

It was certainly ironic that McClellan, who took a jaundiced view of politicians if not of democracy itself, should be nominated for president.[17] He drew a Whiggish distinction between politicians and statesmen, viewing himself as principled and his opponents as conniving.[18] His opinions of Lincoln ran hot and cold, but he often saw the president as an uncultivated teller of droll stories who failed to grasp the most important elements of military strategy. The two men came to regard each other warily. Lincoln only occasionally showed flashes of temper, but McClellan could easily grow testy and bristle with self-righteousness. Through much of his life, Lincoln suffered from bouts of melancholy, and McClellan could fall into the depths of self-pity as well.

But again, to emphasize differences or similarities in temperament—while important—would be to miss a large part of the story. Both Lincoln and McClellan considered the Union to be a sacred trust but could not agree on military strategy. McClellan the engineer favored meticulous preparation and thought the war might be won by overwhelming the Confederates in a single campaign. Such a strategy risked considerable delay, and Lincoln had to respond to political pressures that the general cavalierly dismissed. The president could at times be indecisive, while McClellan was often loath to explain (or even share) his plans with the government.[19] Nor did McClellan recognize how changing attitudes about the role of slavery in the conflict meant that more conciliatory and conservative policies were losing public favor. He remained opposed to both confiscation and emancipation even as Lincoln came to embrace both as necessary means to overcome Confederate resistance.

In a note appearing toward the end of his 1866 poetry collection, *Battle-Pieces,* Herman Melville predicted, "Whatever just military criticism, favorable or otherwise, has at any time been made upon General McClellan's campaigns, will stand." That proved to be mostly true because historians' critical assessments of McClellan's generalship and his dealings with Lincoln have largely followed the arguments first laid out during and shortly after the war. Whether, as Melville put it, the "unmerited disparagement of the man . . . must necessarily die out, though not perhaps without leaving some traces," depends on how "unmerited" is defined. That some soldiers voting for Lincoln's reelection "yet believed, and retain the belief, that General McClellan . . . always proved himself a patriotic and honorable soldier" was indisputably true and shows how McClellan's influence had not disappeared after his removal from command.[20] The affections of the general's more devoted supporters persisted long after the war, and they no doubt influenced those few historians inclined to soften the more searing critiques of McClellan.

It is easy now for Americans to forget how many people lacked confidence in Lincoln's decisions as commander in chief and therefore fail to realize how high McClellan stood in the estimation of many contemporaries. Historical reputations are constantly being revised, but McClellan's appears fairly fixed, even as each generation seems to favor different (albeit mostly positive) versions of the Lincoln saga. This all might have struck both men as ironic, though McClellan lacked any appreciation of irony, whereas Lincoln at times reveled in it. Both men shared a burning ambition to not only succeed during the war but also achieve lasting historical fame—that is where to begin the search for understanding.

1

TWO MEN OF AMBITION

HE WAS YOUNG and eager to make a mark in the world. In some ways, he exuded self-confidence, though at times in an oddly cautious way; he felt ready for a professional career yet worried about embarking on an uncertain course in an age of wrenching economic and social changes.

Public speaking was a way to test not only his ideas but also his mettle. While the mid-nineteenth century was an era that celebrated action and deeds, it was also an age of oratory in which an ambitious young man could gain notice with words. The appetite for speechmaking in the fledgling American republic appeared insatiable.

In this instance, the speaker looked toward the future with hope but also apprehension. His mind was an orderly one that longed for a more orderly society, but at age nineteen, with his country at war with Mexico, that possibility remained elusive. He acknowledged his youth and some uneasiness about the cares of manhood. Already wary of politicians and demagogues, he viewed his own class—the graduates of the U.S. Military Academy at West Point—as the key to national success not only in war but also more broadly. "The great difference between the officer and private is that one is supposed to be an educated and well informed man, whilst the other is a passive instrument in the hands of his superior." Such faith in an elite class, indeed in a natural hierarchy, would hardly sit well in democratic America, but his confidence in the power of superior minds was striking and unequivocal. Achieving greatness not just in the military but in all walks of life required study and determination; natural talent combined with hard work remained the key. The young man spoke as the outgoing president of the Dialectic Society—a group devoted to formal discussion and debate. He lauded his fellow (and presumably likeminded) cadets for appreciating the best literature "essential to the man who would bear the character of an accomplished and polished gentleman." Indeed, without educated officers, armies would become little more than mobs of the "most depraved and wicked men who would spread mindless pillage and devastation." Power based on "the virtue of intellectual superiority is infinitely greater and more lasting than that which is the result of mere physical qualities." Setting his sights still higher, he talked of the great commanders of history, including Napoleon, who recognized the importance of study and self-improvement. Yet he could not ignore the nation's mounting sectional tensions and even alluded to "the horrors of civil war." In such a crisis, the trained officers would "hold the balance in our hands," and therefore the army should "ever incline to the conservative party," whose highest goal must be to preserve the Union.[1]

George B. McClellan had presented a thoroughly conventional but in some ways remarkable vision of his own and the nation's future. Blinkered in some respects and prescient in others, it combined the very elements of thought and personality that would both advance and dog his military career. Less than a decade earlier, another restless, ambitious American had laid out a different yet complementary blueprint for national greatness.

The college literary clubs and debating societies offered an outlet for the privileged to expound their beliefs; the popular lyceum movement did the same for a much larger group. Less-educated young men could address the local lyceum and develop their more rough-hewn talents. In 1833, several men in Springfield, Illinois, had organized a lyceum. More than four years later on a wintry day, a young member of the legislature spoke on the "perpetuation of our political institutions." The opening passages extolling the glories of the republic and singing hymns of gratitude to the founding fathers were jejune, but the address soon took on a more somber tone. This aspiring politician (and lawyer) deplored the "increasing disregard for the law." Like young McClellan, he worried about the prevalence of "wild and furious passions" and specifically pointed to recent incidents of mob violence in Mississippi and Saint Louis. In his view, the only real danger to the American experiment came from within: "If destruction be our lot, we must ourselves be its author and finisher. As a nation of freemen, we must live through all time, or die by suicide." He dreaded a lawless spirit spreading through society like some great contagion, with even the best citizens growing alienated from their government.

In such an atmosphere, there might arise a man of boundless ambition eagerly taking advantage of disturbances and disorder to claim the mantle of savior. "Towering genius disdains a beaten path," the speaker warned. "It seeks regions hitherto unexplored. It sees *no distinction* in adding story to story, upon the monuments of fame, erected to the memory of others. It *denies* that it is glory enough to serve under any chief. It *scorns* to tread in the footsteps of *any* predecessor, however illustrious. It thirsts and burns for distinction; and, if possible, it will have it, whether at the expense of emancipating slaves, or enslaving freemen. Is it unreasonable then to expect, that some man possessed of the loftiest genius, coupled with ambition sufficient to push it to its utmost stretch, will at some time, spring up among us? And when such a one does, it will require the people to be united with each other, attached to the government and laws, and generally intelligent, to successfully frustrate his designs." Logic and reason must prevail over wild passion.[2]

In this address, Abraham Lincoln appeared to be warning of dangers springing from his own tribe—that is, the politicians. Was he taking a partisan swipe at his future rival Stephen Douglas, as some historians have suggested? Or perhaps he was pointing to himself when he spoke of the man who longed for distinction? Or did he see himself as the foil to the man of overweening and dangerous ambition?[3]

There is a strong thread of ambition running through the lives of both George McClellan and Abraham Lincoln. The often striking contrasts in their background and experience should not obscure that common thread. Their paths to power and distinction obviously diverged, but both this divergence and their strong drive to succeed form essential background for understanding their complex and often fraught relationship.

When Lincoln delivered his lyceum address, he was nearly twenty-nine years old. As a member of the Illinois legislature, he had already taken an active role in moving the state capital from Vandalia to Springfield, but his career prospects remained uncertain. A fledgling lawyer, Lincoln still showed signs of being a rustic uncomfortable in what passed for polite society. There was within this young man a deep and at times almost angry determination to escape from the poverty of his Kentucky and Indiana homes. He once remarked to an Illinois neighbor, "I have seen a good deal of the back side of the world." The log cabin where he first saw the world's light became fabled, but it was not the straitened economic circumstances that were the most grinding on a sensitive boy. Rather, the social isolation—the virtual absence of kindred spirits—shaped his early years and nourished a streak of melancholy. He hated farm work and hunting and never took to his family's Hard Shell Baptist faith. Lincoln neither talked with pride about growing up poor nor romanticized the arduous labor—including the famous rail splitting—that he came to despise, nor did he look back nostalgically upon driving hogs or poling a flatboat.[4]

Lincoln never had much to say about his family or his early life. "If he mentioned the subject at all, it was with great reluctance and reserve," his law partner and biographer William Herndon recalled. An autobiographical sketch written for the 1860 presidential campaign was unrevealing, except perhaps in its silences. He did acknowledge that his father, Thomas, had grown up "literally without education" and could barely sign his name. Thomas Lincoln was an often dour and difficult man who drove his son hard but lacked ambition. He beat young Abe for shirking work or sneaking off to read a book. Lincoln was eager to escape Thomas's world even after the family settled in Illinois. Later, upon learning that his father had fallen gravely ill, Lincoln could not take the time to visit him; he did not attend his father's funeral.[5]

The evidence on Lincoln's relationship with his mother is much more equivocal. Was young Abe embarrassed by her somewhat unsavory reputation, or did he see her as a saintly woman who encouraged him to learn? Did her sadness and premature death shape his own often dark view of the world? For sure, when his father remarried, Lincoln developed a loving bond with his stepmother, Sarah Bush Johnston, who cared for the blended family well and recognized something special about her stepson.[6]

But for all her efforts, she could not lift the sense of despair and foreboding that would periodically torment Lincoln. There has been much speculation over whether Lincoln suffered from simple depression, bipolar disorder, or some other malady, and it is impossible to diagnose precisely at such a distance in time. In any case, it hardly matters. The point is that for decades Lincoln fought an uneven and at times losing battle against a deep and disabling melancholy. As he once wrote to an early law partner, "If what I feel were equally distributed to the whole human family, there would not be one cheerful face on the earth." Mired in these episodes, he feared never recovering. During the 1830s, Lincoln variously worked as a general-store clerk, surveyor, postmaster, sometime state legislator, and finally a lawyer—all of these activities accompanied by a certain restlessness and dissatisfaction. The vicissitudes of his legal and political career, a strained engagement with Mary Todd, and even gloomy weather would trigger fresh bouts of misery.[7]

As a young man, George McClellan suffered from no such crippling emotional crises and was quite proud of his parents. A Yale graduate with medical training at the University of Pennsylvania, McClellan's father (also named George) had begun practicing medicine in his early twenties, but his various professional activities made him an often absent patriarch. Fortunately for young George, his mother, Elizabeth Brinton McClellan, poured a great deal of energy into her son's education, and early McClellan biographers cast her as an exemplary woman of refined manners.[8] Both father and mother served as models of behavior and success for a young man growing up in a most nurturing and encouraging environment.

If hardly wealthy, the family lived in reasonable comfort. Early on, young George enjoyed a fine education, first from private tutors and later from two years in preparatory school. At the tender age of thirteen, McClellan entered the University of Pennsylvania. Before the teen was able to graduate, however, his father had persuaded a friendly congressman to secure a West Point nomination.[9]

Rather easily meeting the institution's academic demands, McClellan thrived in this orderly and disciplined environment, and a preference for both qualities would characterize his military career. Perhaps recalling his precocious self, in an essay written after the Civil War, McClellan noted how the French military theorist Antoine-Henri Jomini had "early in life. . . . mastered the principles of the art of war." Indeed, McClellan impressed some West Point classmates as a near-genius who excelled at most subjects and displayed an easy confidence in his own ability.[10]

McClellan attended West Point during a period of increasing military professionalization, and the academy's heavy emphasis on engineering suited his temperament. Under the instruction of Dennis Hart Mahan, he absorbed lessons on the limitations of volunteer soldiers, the importance of entrenchments, and the foolishness of frontal assaults. But this was only part of the story. Classmates remembered him as an unassuming and steadfast friend "full of life and enthusiasm," in Orlando Willcox's recollection. With somewhat less enthusiasm and perhaps soured by later experience, Erasmus Keyes agreed that McClellan had been a fine student with strong attachments to his friends and great pride in being an engineer. McClellan found southern cadets especially companionable because of their "manners, feelings & opinions." As time came for leaving West Point, he grew tired of the routine and was eager to join the Corps of Engineers.[11] Certainly to this point in his life—whatever the mild apprehensions and uncertainties expressed in his Dialectic Address—McClellan had received a good education, his life having proceeded smoothly with few if any hitches. A bright future seemingly awaited.

Young Lincoln had not benefited from a fine education, or enjoyed an easy life, or anticipated much future success. "There was absolutely nothing to excite ambition for education," he recalled of his years in Kentucky and Indiana. "The little advance I now have upon this store of education, I have picked up from time to time under pressure of necessity." With little more than a year of formal schooling, Lincoln had to rely on ability and drive, along with great powers of concentration and memory. Many who met him after his move to New Salem, Illinois, recalled his interest in reading, an intensity at times carried to the point of distraction. Though not much of a churchgoer, Lincoln knew parts of the Bible very well; biblical stories, passages, and cadences cropped up in his conversation and speeches. Shortly after being elected to the Illinois legislature, he borrowed some law books and pored over them in New Salem; with more than a hint of pride, Lincoln later remarked that he "studied with nobody."[12]

His frontier military experience was equally informal and even briefer. Service in the Black Hawk War of 1832, future law partner John T. Stuart recalled, turned into "a sort of frolic," though the men occasionally witnessed some horrific sights in this short but brutal conflict. Stuart described Lincoln as a "clever fellow" who "had no military qualities" but easily "kept the esteem and respect of his men." In a self-deprecating way, Lincoln wryly recounted how his military service had been entirely bloodless other than battles with voracious mosquitos, yet he took pride in being elected captain of his company.[13] Still, brief military service—if it can be even be called that—was worlds away from that of McClellan and the professional army.

But then Lincoln, who had enlisted in part to impress local voters, never intended to pursue a military career. Instead, he turned to the law, a profession more suited to advancing his political ambitions and eventually providing a decent income. Here, too, the drive for self-improvement seemed remarkable, though success seemed neither inevitable nor perhaps even likely. Lincoln read law off and on for almost four years while serving in the Illinois General Assembly and working at various odd jobs. Slowly and carefully, he not only absorbed the main ideas from standard works such as William Blackstone's *Commentaries* but also learned about the forms of filing and various other practical matters by dealing with smaller cases before being licensed in 1836. He would eventually have the good fortune of working with two established Springfield attorneys—first Stuart and later Stephen Logan—who recognized talent in the rough, and they especially appreciated their protégé's persuasive powers with juries. In 1844, Lincoln invited a younger man, William Herndon, to become his partner. Billy Herndon was an enthusiastic and sentimental frontier intellectual who absorbed the latest ideas from back east along with copious amounts of alcohol. He perhaps knew Lincoln as well as anyone, though not nearly so well as he thought. But for whatever reason, this odd partnership worked.

It would be easy to mistake Lincoln's love of colorful (and sometimes off-color) stories for the antics of a cracker-barrel rustic. Indeed, in court he deployed a homely appearance, careless dress, and folksy manner to his advantage, though in fact much of Lincoln's practice involved routine cases, most of which never reached a jury. Debt collections, contracts, property disputes, and the occasional criminal case made up the bulk of his work, at least until the 1850s, when he began taking on more lucrative railroad litigation. Tales of a few dramatic pleas to juries or some clever legal stratagems became the stuff of courthouse legend, but in truth Lincoln was a fairly ordinary lawyer, quite successful but not truly distinguished.

Like many other attorneys, Lincoln had to "ride the circuit," in this case the Eighth Judicial Circuit, encompassing fifteen counties over a vast stretch of central Illinois. The search for paying clients drove these men to travel from county seat to county seat each spring and fall, but Lincoln enjoyed the male camaraderie and seemed to thrive despite the bad roads, poor accommodations, and worse food. Besides being good for business, this tiring and often tedious work helped Lincoln gain important political contacts; it seemed to some contemporaries that he preferred life on the road to life at home. Slowly but surely, Lincoln and Herndon developed a successful practice in both state and federal courts; Lincoln himself held that sheer "diligence" was the key to success in the law.[14]

If Abraham Lincoln was the frontier lawyer who seldom stood on ceremony, the young George McClellan was quite a different story. The new officer often stood on ceremony—he once complained to his mother about an overly familiar visitor to West Point who kept calling him "George"—and easily took offense. His sense of professionalism could be punctilious. Still smarting over not having graduated at the top of his West Point class, McClellan was proud of being the only engineer from his cohort heading off to Mexico, where he was determined "to show them"—the pronoun lacked an antecedent but perhaps referred to some West Point administrators or faculty—that "I can nevertheless do something." The prospect of war, success, and fame excited McClellan: "War at last sure enough! Ain't it glorious!" Not exactly the language of drawing-room conversation back in Philadelphia, but then he would soon discover that service in Mexico was not all that glorious. The freshly commissioned officer arrived too late to participate in Major General Zachary Taylor's northern campaigns and quickly fell ill with malaria and dysentery. He eventually arrived in Tampico and served with Major General Winfield Scott in the Vera Cruz Campaign. All the while, the impatient young McClellan freely criticized fellow officers, Mexicans, and anyone who did not quite live up to his exacting standards of military professionalism or gentlemanly behavior.[15]

Especially in their evaluation of enlisted men, McClellan's letters from Mexico mirrored his Dialectic address. While still at West Point and shortly before being commissioned as brevet second lieutenant, McClellan had already complained to his sister about "these wretched Dutch and Irish immigrants" who would likely fill the ranks in Mexico. By the time he had reached the Rio Grande, McClellan felt at least some sympathy for the enlisted men, who "literally die like dogs," but firmly believed that the government should create a large regular army and dispense with volunteers altogether. Not surprisingly, McClellan echoed the widespread contempt of American soldiers for Mexicans, but in his view the volunteers "who carry on in the most shameful and disgraceful manner" were almost as bad. Their distinctly unmilitary appearance and bearing—one can only imagine what McClellan would have thought of Lincoln in the militia—

elicited many a scornful remark in his diary and in letters home. He found American romanticism of the common soldier positively baffling:

> We hear resounding from one end of the Union to the other the cry—The Volunteers are the right arm of the nation, to them will we commit our honor and our fame! Every one believes, or what is practically the same thing, pretends to believe, that although a long course of study is necessary to fit a man for the pursuit of any civil profession, yet any one can become a good officer by putting on a military coat—that the change of dress can produce as wonderful an alteration in the character of the man more wonderful than that of the colors of the chameleon.[16]

McClellan considered himself to be a thoroughgoing professional and, during Scott's campaigns, preformed capably. Despite earning two brevet promotions and notice in official reports, McClellan confessed to being both embarrassed and exasperated at not having compiled a more lustrous war record. Nevertheless, he enjoyed the company of other junior officers, a conviviality well lubricated by "champagne suppers," brandy, rum, and even commissary whiskey. On these occasions, the men smoked cigars, passed along the latest scuttlebutt, and freely criticized various generals.[17]

McClellan's resentments are revealing. As a quite junior officer, it galled him to be outranked by volunteer officers. He feared not gaining promotion during the war, much less in peacetime, and talked of resigning his commission. Although McClellan appreciated General Scott treating him with kindness, he did not relish the commander's invitations to dine and claimed to "prefer keeping clear of generals." This peculiar attitude appeared at odds with a deep respect for military professionalism, but the young McClellan was still finding his way in the world, and his insecurities often welled to the surface. Yet the war with Mexico had offered him considerable opportunity. He naturally learned a great deal from Scott's campaigns, though the lessons largely reinforced those taught in Professor Mahan's West Point classroom. McClellan shared Scott's disdain for President James K. Polk's interference with military strategy, an opinion conveniently filed away for future use.[18]

Impatience with the army and with military politics persisted after McClellan's return to West Point. Although he enjoyed military service "in the abstract," he found American democracy incompatible with his professional ideals:

> Our Government may be a very fine one for civilians; it was not intended for military men. The more truly one likes his profession, the more soldierly pride he has, the more disgusted is he with our service. Could I sink down at once with indifference, stolidity, and foggyism, I would be perfectly content with the Army. As it is, it is a continual heaping of coals on one's head. I am almost afraid to read history or anything appertaining to my profession because the more I know, the more are my eyes opened to our own wretched condition.

Restless and unable to get along with West Point superintendent Henry Brewerton, McClellan could not just settle back into familiar surroundings.[19]

McClellan's performance in Mexico and his brief tenure at West Point likely attracted more notice than he realized; both William T. Sherman and Oliver Otis Howard recalled that, by the late 1840s, McClellan had acquired a notable reputation as both a soldier and student of the military art.[20] Ordered to Fort Delaware in 1851, after a few months he was sent to Washington, where he prepared a bayonet manual and developed a yet-more-jaundiced view of the political class. Posted to Arkansas in early 1852, McClellan served under Captain Randolph B. Marcy, who grew quickly to like and respect his young assistant—for once the feeling was mutual. McClellan enjoyed the work but was soon transferred to Texas, inspecting forts and later surveying rivers and harbors. Once these jobs were done, McClellan reported to Washington territorial governor Isaac Stevens, who would head a survey of possible railroad routes from the Washington coast east through the Cascade Mountains. McClellan's group found few if any promising passes through which to lay track, and he had a falling out with Stevens. All told, McClellan had not distinguished himself for thoroughness and had been excessively cautious during this assignment; he wrote a typically well-crafted report and blamed others for his shortcomings.[21]

Lieutenant McClellan remained conflicted about military life and declared he would surely resign if he thought there would not soon be another war. In March 1854, Secretary of War Jefferson Davis sent him to Santo Domingo to investigate possible locations for a coaling station and naval base. Having gained increasing confidence in the young officer (finally promoted to captain in March 1855), Davis dispatched him as part of a three-man commission to investigate European military policy and operations during the Crimean War. McClellan traveled all over the continent, was especially impressed by Prussian and Russian officers, and finally was able to visit the Crimea once the Russians gave up Sevastopol. A preface to his report—commercially published in the fall of 1861—claimed that the young captain had been sent to Europe "on account of the brilliant military qualities he had already displayed." In that document, McClellan offered critical commentary on military operations in the Crimea, extensive descriptions of terrain and fortifications, a manual for cavalry, and not surprisingly a recommendation that the United States needed a larger regular army. The report won him additional recognition in Washington and in the army. But seeing little prospect for further advancement or professional achievement, in November 1856 McClellan resigned his commission.[22]

While McClellan's military service after the Mexican War may have proven disappointing, it had provided an unexpected opportunity for courtship. Mary Ellen Marcy was the oldest daughter of Randolph Marcy, and in the spring of 1852, McClellan saw a picture of this most attractive sixteen-year-old. He would not meet her for another two years, when he was in Washington working on reports from his western surveys, but by that time his mother had already laid the groundwork back in Philadelphia through social contacts with Mary Marcy, Nelly's mother. McClellan confessed to Mary Marcy that he had quite fallen in love with Nelly and was "determined to win her." Two months later he proposed marriage but was turned down. The newly minted captain was then twenty-seven and she was eighteen, and though her parents liked McClellan, the young woman had a mind of her own. Yet he was not easily discouraged and kept up a steady correspondence with Mary Marcy on the assumption that the best way to the daughter's heart might well be through her mother. For his part, Randolph Marcy was determined that his daughter not marry a military man, so McClellan's departure from the U.S. Army helped his cause.[23]

Suitors had never been in short supply for the lovely Nelly, and at least nine marriage proposals (including one from future Confederate general A. P. Hill) had come her way. In the end, McClellan's quiet persistence—not to mention the steady support from his future mother-in-law—paid off. In October 1859, he met the Marcys in Chicago on a train bound for Saint

Paul, Minnesota, and proposed to Nelly again. This time she accepted, and her parents quickly approved.[24]

During a seven-month engagement, McClellan wrote daily letters. The surviving fragments of this correspondence reveal a man with his eyes on the future. McClellan marveled to Nelly over how "our aspirations, thoughts & desires have been changed" because now each of them "lived for the other." He became increasingly religious, likely under the prodding of Nelly, or as he called her, "my little Presbyterian." For her part, Nelly seemed to be channeling McClellan's life in a new direction, though as with many another smitten man, claims expressed in love letters (along with the usual flights of romantic fancy) require some discounting. His goals now sounded decidedly ordinary and modest. McClellan dreamed of a house built to their exact specifications. "My idea of happiness used to be *rank* and *name*," he confessed. "Now it is domestic happiness with my wife."

Like many a couple in love, they speculated about all kinds of things. Should something happen to her, he could not think of remarrying and believed that, in any case, their relationship would endure into the next life. With Nelly by his side, McClellan had no doubt about their future happiness, a prospect that inspired him to work still harder. But it was also occasionally apparent that earlier ambitions had not been entirely snuffed out. McClellan acknowledged that, given her background, there might still be some attraction to military life, then revealed that his desire for martial glory had not vanished: "It is war on a large scale that interests me & that alone would tempt me into service again."[25]

On May 22, 1860, George B. McClellan and Mary Ellen Marcy wed at Cavalry Church in New York City. By all accounts, the marriage was a loving and successful one. Both husband and wife were attractive, devoted to each other, and deeply religious. They soon came to view the world, with all its opportunities and perils, in remarkably similar ways. While this made for harmony at home and helped them endure separations, it did not always make for smooth or easy relationships outside the family. If not exactly at war with the world, both were quick to take offense and could be touchy over perceived slights, especially from those considered their intellectual, moral, or social inferiors.

In his relations with women, Lincoln enjoyed none of McClellan's advantages. Besides his humble background and ungainly appearance, young

Lincoln much preferred the company of men. Perhaps his mother's early death had contributed to an unease around women, but whatever the cause, contemporaries in New Salem and in Springfield recalled him as a socially awkward man who was no great favorite with the ladies. Upon meeting Anne Rutledge in 1834 and beginning to walk with her in the evenings, Lincoln managed to overcome some of his shyness with this attractive and intelligent young woman. When she suddenly died the following year, the grief threw Lincoln into one of his deepest periods of depression. His odd courtship of Mary Owens, a less attractive but intellectually lively young woman, revealed that he remained self-conscious, reticent, and indecisive.[26]

It would be easy to see the spirited Mary Todd as an even odder match for Lincoln (and Lincoln as a peculiar choice for her), but they did have some things in common. Both had lost their mothers at young ages. Their childhoods (Mary used the word "desolate" to describe hers) were at times quite lonely, though they were equally determined to rise in the world. But then there were the obvious contrasts. Born into a prominent Lexington, Kentucky, family, Mary had received a fine education by the standards for women at the time. Upon moving to Springfield, she never had trouble attracting young men, showed an early interest in fashion, and became a lively conversationalist. She also showed a strong interest in Whig politics and a great admiration for Lincoln's hero, Henry Clay. Mary likely met the socially awkward Lincoln in her brother-in-law Ninian Edwards's parlor, a place crawling with marriage prospects. Given their differences in temperament and background, the courtship proceeded by fits and starts, barely surviving at least one great crisis.[27]

Despite enjoying early success in law and politics, Lincoln nevertheless worried about money and perhaps whether two people of such seemingly disparate upbringings and temperaments could make a go of it. For her part, Mary could see beneath his unkempt appearance and social clumsiness. In any case, the two came to an understanding, became engaged, but then near the end of 1840, Lincoln broke it off. Once again, he had trouble dealing with a woman, and Mary's volatile personality may well have given him pause. Unraveling the psychological dynamics at work baffled contemporaries and has led historians to offer widely divergent theories. In any event, there followed for Lincoln yet another period of enervating depression, but he eventually renewed the relationship with Mary Todd. On November 4, 1842, in Edwards's home, they were hastily married.[28]

Only a week after the wedding, with tantalizing ambiguity, Lincoln termed the marriage a "matter of profound wonder." Some writers have argued that he had been driven by guilt over the previous breakup with Mary into finally marrying her.[29] Mary always claimed that "Mr. Lincoln," as she called him, was her one true love, though Herndon (who never much cared for her) thought she mostly loved "power and prominence." They began married life in a single room in the humble Globe Tavern, however, where they each no doubt discovered more about their differences. Lincoln's dark moods persisted throughout his life, but Mary could be mercurial as well. He could be withdrawn and even cold; she could be demanding and emotionally needy. Lincoln appeared oblivious to everything, from his appearance to coming home from the office on time for meals. He preferred the world of the judicial circuit and politics, while she sought to make a mark in society. Family, friends, and neighbors recalled Mary's outbursts of temper, though whether certain dramatic incidents that provided much grist for gossip typified the relationship is certainly open to question. The two were indulgent parents, but Mary was most involved in raising their four sons, whom some people in Springfield and later in Washington considered to be spoiled hellions. Like many parents of the time, the Lincolns had to face the death of children—in their case two sons.[30] Yet the marriage endured and to some degree grew stronger as two difficult people adjusted to each other and perhaps altered their expectations.

In the vast Lincoln literature, Mary Lincoln often comes off as the party more responsible for the difficulties in the marriage. While that may have been true, Lincoln himself hardly made life easy for his wife. He shared relatively little of himself with anyone, including Mary. Herndon thought Lincoln "the most secretive—reticent—shut-mouthed man that ever existed." He had few close friends and confided in them only haphazardly and guardedly.[31]

Herndon did know one thing for sure: Lincoln was very ambitious. "That man who thinks Lincoln calmly sat down and gathered his robes about him, waiting for the people to call him, has a very erroneous knowledge of Lincoln," Herndon wrote in a much-quoted passage. "He was always calculating, and always planning ahead. His ambition was a little engine that knew no rest." In a less-quoted letter, Herndon was even more pointed: "His ambition was never satisfied; in him it was a consuming fire which smothered his finer feelings." Lincoln studied a question, listened carefully, but less often asked for advice. There was about him a quiet, though in some ways steely, self-confidence that belied his popular image as the humble rail-splitter. Despite periodic moods of depression and seeming apathy, Lincoln often acted like a driven man. He set his sights not only on political success but also on lasting influence, at times appearing to see himself as destined for some great work.[32]

"Every man is said to have his peculiar ambition," Lincoln noted in an election announcement for his first (and unsuccessful) run for the Illinois General Assembly. He defined his own ambition as simply to be "esteemed of my fellow men," but there was much more to it than that. Lincoln could afford to appear before voters as a self-effacing man of modest attainment and background because he had considerable faith in his own abilities and judgment. Even as a young man in New Salem, he talked of one day being "distinguished." Whether in state politics, in the Black Hawk War, in Congress, or as a nationally known politician and possible presidential candidate, Lincoln—much like McClellan—strove to make his mark in the world.[33]

Lincoln had learned and practiced the arts of small-bore politics in the Illinois legislature. The process was often messy, involving vote swapping, patronage quarrels, and no few appeals to politicians' vanity and self-importance. Lincoln could skewer an opponent with words and did not eschew underhanded tactics or outright deception. As a Whig leader in the Illinois House, he worked hard to make Springfield the capital and to advance an overly expansive program of internal improvements. A reputation for being a religious skeptic proved a temporary handicap, but other attributes helped win over voters. Early on he had proven his physical prowess—no small thing on the Illinois frontier—and humor softened some of Lincoln's rougher edges. Self-deprecating references to his unattractive appearance and indifferent attire proved especially appealing; a sense of tragedy and melancholy may well have fueled his frequent resort to storytelling in tense situations. So, too, Lincoln learned to keep the peace among warring politicians and even subordinate his own ambition for the good of his party.[34]

Lincoln's single term in Congress and scathing criticism of President Polk amid what proved to be a popular war against Mexico won him few friends back home. He had enjoyed life in Washington much more than Mary did but ever after remained defensive about accusations of not properly supporting American troops. After his term was over, Lincoln campaigned hard for presidential candidate Zachary Taylor in 1848 but failed to win an acceptable appointment from the new Whig administration.[35]

With his political career seemingly stalled, he returned to the law. The death of the Lincolns' son Edward in 1850 further deepened his melancholy. Lincoln's achievements in life to this point had been modest for a man of overweening ambition. Success as an attorney had not brought much satisfaction or a sense of accomplishing any truly worthwhile purpose. To describe the period between 1849 and 1854 as a midlife crisis for Lincoln overstates the case, but not by much. Life in Springfield and on the judicial circuit went on, with the fires of political ambition tamped down until the slavery question—supposedly settled by the famous Compromise of 1850—burst forth once again.[36] The Kansas-Nebraska Act abrogated what many Americans believed to be the sacred Missouri Compromise, seemingly opening up new territory to slavery. This stirred Lincoln from his torpor.

In 1854, the Kansas question greatly upset the usual partisan calculations and struck politicians and many of their constituents like a great thunderclap. The repeal of the Missouri Compromise, Lincoln later recalled, "aroused him as he had never been before." By autumn, he was giving speeches at a furious pace, excoriating the author of the obnoxious measure, Stephen A. Douglas, for being morally indifferent to the evils of slavery. Yet Lincoln failed to win a U.S. Senate seat that eventually went to an antislavery Democrat, Lyman Trumbull. Amid what amounted to a great shakeup of political parties, Lincoln remained a loyal Whig, deploring the rise of the nativist, anti-Catholic American (Know Nothing) Party while wary of its popular appeal. The slavery question helped kill off the Know Nothings (as it had the Whigs) but also revived Lincoln's political career. He had long regretted his old hero Clay's failure to win support for a plan of gradual emancipation in Kentucky and, by 1855, wondered if the "peaceful extinction of slavery" could ever be achieved. Recognizing the seriousness of the crisis, both political and moral, Lincoln confessed to his friend Joshua Speed, who continued to hold slaves, "how much the great body of the Northern people do crucify their feelings [about slavery], in order to maintain their loyalty to the constitution and the Union."[37]

However reluctant he was to give up on the Whigs, Lincoln eventually helped establish the Republican Party in Illinois. According to Herndon, following the new party's first presidential contest in 1856 and after garnering some votes for vice president at the convention, Lincoln "could not help feeling he was now the leading Republican in his State, and he was therefore more or less jealous of his prerogative." He especially resented the praise heaped on Democrat Douglas by the famous editor Horace Greeley after the Little Giant had broken with President James Buchanan over Kansas policy. By this point, Lincoln and Douglas already knew each other all too well. Lincoln followed Douglas's career with intense interest—and more than a touch of envy. On the slavery question, he dismissed Douglas as a "veritable dodger" and resented the Little Giant's reputation as a commanding politician and, as some even said, statesman.[38]

Considering Douglas neither truthful nor reliable, Lincoln discovered a still larger character flaw. Young John Hay recalled Lincoln in 1854 bursting into an office "waving a newspaper, and fairly quivering with excitement," barely able to contain his ire. "This will never do!" Lincoln exclaimed. "Douglas treats it as a matter of indifference morally, whether slavery is voted down or voted up. I tell you it will never do!" In his famous 1858 "House Divided" speech, Lincoln ridiculed Douglas's claim that his beloved doctrine of popular sovereignty—in this case allowing the voters of Kansas to determine the status of slavery—would end agitation of the subject. Not only had the "agitation . . . not ceased, but [it] has constantly augmented." In the great debates with Douglas, a U.S. Senate seat at stake, Lincoln treated his rival with no little disdain and occasional ridicule. Indeed, he could never quite fathom why Douglas remained so popular with Democrats given the disastrous consequences of Kansas-Nebraska. That made Lincoln's loss in their storied clash all the more painful.[39]

Once again, Lincoln's political ambitions had been thwarted; it hurt, and he admitted it hurt. Despite a certain amount of brooding, if not despair, he soon tried to put the best face on the situation in reassuring notes to political confidants. The debates had certainly given Lincoln "a hearing on the great durable question of the age, which I could have had in no other way." Even though he might now "sink out of view," he had perhaps "made some marks which will tell for the cause of civil liberty long after I am gone." Striking one last blow against his erstwhile foe, Lincoln tartly observed that when Douglas had sung the siren song of "popular sovereignty," he had "managed to be supported both as the best means to *break down*, and to *uphold* the slave power. No ingenuity can long keep those opposing elements in harmony. Another explosion will come before a great while."[40]

In this great crisis, Lincoln was thinking as much about himself as about the country. He longed for a life of lasting significance, hoping to be honored by future generations. And here was Douglas again standing in his way. Back in 1856, though the date is only approximate, Lincoln had drafted a brief document on his relationship with Douglas that spoke volumes about this complicated and psychologically fraught rivalry. Even as young men, he admitted, "we were both ambitious; I, perhaps, quite as much so as he." Conditional in this acknowledgment, a bit grudging perhaps, Lincoln quickly revealed the pain of frustrated hopes. "With *me*, the race of ambition has been a failure—a flat failure; with *him* it has been one of splendid success. His name fills the nation; and is not unknown, even, in foreign lands." The jealousy and resentment were palpable, yet Lincoln added, "I affect no contempt for the high eminence he has reached"—not exactly true, given *how* Douglas had supposedly reached such a lofty standing. Lincoln hinted that his rival's prominence had been acquired by ignoring the "oppressed of my species." He claimed he would pursue just the opposite course, preferring that path to "wear[ing] the richest crown that ever pressed a monarch's brow."[41]

The problem was that Lincoln by the late 1850s had found his path still treacherous if not blocked. "I am ambitious and would like to be president," he remarked to longtime political associate Jesse Fell. Among the possible candidates for the 1860 Republican nomination, William H. Seward of New York or Salmon P. Chase of Ohio seemed far more likely prospects to Lincoln and to many other Republicans. But in 1859 and into 1860, Lincoln delivered a series of speeches, including the celebrated Cooper Union address, which kept his name in the newspapers and before Republicans across the country.[42] He even alluded occasionally, as in a March 1859 speech in Chicago, to the senatorial contest against Douglas: "For myself I am also gratified that during that canvass and since, however disappointing its termination, there was among my party friends so little fault found in me as to the manner in which I bore my part. I hardly dared hope to give as high a degree of satisfaction as it has since been my pleasure to believe I did in the part I bore in the contest." He had perhaps not meant to sound so defensive, but the ache of unfulfilled ambition would not go away. Lincoln remained obsessed with his old rival. By the middle of 1859, he worried that the idea of popular sovereignty was gaining ground, even among some Republicans, and that Douglas, "the most dangerous enemy to liberty," was being aided by "our friends thus magnifying him and his humbug." By the end of 1859 and early in 1860, there was talk—mostly from fairly obscure quarters—of Lincoln as a possible presidential candidate. He scoffed at such reports, declared himself ill-suited to the office. He even deflected his own ambitions onto his wife. "Mary insists, however, that I am going to be Senator and President of the United States, too," newspaper reporter Henry Villard recalled Lincoln saying. "Just think of such a sucker [that is, a citizen of Illinois] as me as President." Yet all the leading candidates—including Seward and Chase—had weaknesses, both ideological and regional. For his part, Lincoln positioned himself to take advantage if any of the prominent candidates' stock fell. By April 1860, he had to admit some interest in the presidency, "The taste *is* in my mouth a little." He still tried to sound modest, but his words seemed quite disingenuous as he handicapped other Republican contenders and was clearly keeping track of who supported him and who did not.[43]

McClellan had become vice president of the Illinois Central Railroad, and in 1858 he had arranged for a private car to transport Douglas to one of the debate sites. McClellan later wrote that the senator far outshone Lincoln in oratorical ability, but he may have acquired some appreciation for Lincoln's legal talents. Needing the income from his law practice as his political career advanced by fits and starts, Lincoln had handled over forty cases for McClellan's railroad.[44]

McClellan had been working for the Illinois Central since 1857, when he had been hired as the chief engineer. His future father-in-law, Randolph Marcy, had agreed that this new opportunity would be far preferable to "garrison duty or hunting Indians in time of peace." Marcy forecast a "brilliant future" for his young protégé, who should be more than equal to any new responsibilities. One can only wonder if anyone had ever predicted a brilliant future for Abraham Lincoln. However that might be, McClellan appeared to thrive and had been quickly promoted to vice president. Yet despite having more than doubled his army salary, he harbored regrets over leaving the army and had yet to achieve the longed-for distinction. His job soon became exciting enough as the Panic of 1857 did what nineteenth-century financial crises often did—throw the railroad business into a tailspin. The Illinois Central survived the panic, but McClellan seemed more restless than ever, unsuccessfully seeking an army commission to join federal forces heading for the Utah Territory in the so-called Mormon War.[45]

As a railroad executive, McClellan enjoyed considerable success, but at times he seemed excessively cautious and often deferred to others. There was about him a puzzling inconsistency tied to a mercurial temperament that manifested itself in alternating periods of remarkable self-confidence and curious indecisiveness. Shortly after his marriage to Ellen in 1860, McClellan received a new job offer through the good offices of New York corporation lawyer and Democrat Samuel L. M. Barlow, with whom he had formed a professional friendship over the past several years. As a result of the Panic of 1857, the Ohio and Mississippi Railroad running between Cincinnati and Saint Louis had fallen into receivership. By becoming superintendent of this line (and eventually president of the railroad's eastern division), McClellan secured a princely salary of $10,000 and moved to Cincinnati. But because of the company's heavy indebtedness, this new job proved both challenging and, in some ways, unsatisfying.[46]

The bar of ambition remained high, and for McClellan, success with the railroad and his marriage to Ellen occurred just as the nation was plunging toward the abyss. Politically, he had undoubtedly absorbed a goodly amount of his father's Whiggish conservativism As the sectional crisis deepened, McClellan generally adopted moderate and strongly Unionist views, favoring the Compromise of 1850, expressing a decided contempt for abolitionist fanaticism, and in 1852 voting for Democrat Franklin Pierce. By the late 1850s, McClellan's family and friends had sided with Douglas in his break with President Buchanan over the administration's betrayal of popular sovereignty in Kansas. McClellan later described himself as a "strong Democrat of the Stephen A. Douglas school." For him, Douglas embodied the political moderation and avoidance of sectional extremism that suited both his views and temperament.[47] McClellan embraced the values of the professional soldier, and recent business success had in all probability only reinforced his general aversion to politics. With mounting sectional tensions and threats of secession, however, it would become increasingly hard for him to remain above the fray.

All these considerations posed quite different challenges for Abraham Lincoln, whose political fortunes were very much tied to the sectional crisis and his party's success. In 1860, even his Illinois friends likely failed to realize that his admission to having a little "taste" for the presidency masked a much deeper and more intense ambition. Lincoln often managed to appear diffident and unassuming even as he offered carefully crafted opinions about party questions and handicapped his main rivals. His strategy boiled down to having the united support of Illinois Republicans and being the second choice of many delegates who would attend the national convention in Chicago. Even after receiving word of his nomination, Lincoln pretended that Mary would be more interested than he was in the news. Lincoln could not campaign for himself but closely followed the canvass and tried to keep the various factions of the party in harness and pulling in the same direction. Yet he yearned to do more, appeared restless, and even considered a joint appearance with Seward. Late in the canvass, Lincoln claimed to prefer a term in the Senate, "where there was more chance to make [a] reputation, and less danger of losing it—than four years in the presidency." These comments, whether genuine or affected, nicely fit the era's expectations for candidates who tried not to be seen as lusting after office.[48]

Lincoln's election placed a man of seemingly limited and parochial qualifications in the presidency during what would prove to be the greatest crisis in the young nation's history. He had served but a single term in Congress and lacked administrative experience. Even before his inauguration, he would face an unprecedented political crisis. In only a little over a month after the election, the Deep South states began to secede, but it would not be until March 4, 1861, that Lincoln would hold the reins of power. He met with people after the election but had little to say about the all-consuming public questions. The president-elect could not blithely dismiss secession threats but still believed that most southerners opposed disunion. Lincoln even suggested that the current crisis would soon give the lie to southern fears about the dangers that a Republican administration might pose to southern peace and security. Demands for some reaction from him led Lincoln to draft a brief, and he presumed reassuring, statement to be inserted into a speech delivered in Springfield by Senator Trumbull a couple weeks after the election. Trumbull's remarks were interpreted as expressing Lincoln's views and so received wide publicity. It was time, Lincoln thought, that secessionists' warnings against the horrors that would follow a Republican victory be "brought to a practical test." He chided "disunionists" for being "in hot haste to get out of the Union" before the southern people realized there was no real peril to "their homes, and firesides, and lives." There then followed a remarkable statement from Lincoln that Trumbull discreetly left out of his speech: "I am rather glad of this military preparation in the South. It will enable the people the more easily to suppress any uprisings there, which their misrepresentations of purposes may have encouraged."[49]

If Lincoln's views on the dangers of disunion were ill-informed and at times naïve, his administrative inexperience cropped up in his cabinet selections. He had enough confidence in his own abilities to tap political rivals—Seward, Chase, and Edward Bates—but he had hardly created a well-functioning team of advisors, as the next four years would prove. In fact, like any nineteenth-century president, he faced a flood of importunate office seekers and their friends; patronage issues consumed precious time and energy.[50]

Lincoln faced a situation in which the national government appeared paralyzed. President Buchanan felt powerless to stop the tide of secession, Congress debated various compromise measures to no avail, and Lincoln refused to endorse any of them. In late January 1861, the *New York Herald,* citing a recent conversation, quoted the president-elect, "I will suffer death before I will consent or will advise my friends to consent to any concession or compromise which looks like buying the privilege of taking possession of this government to which we have a constitutional right." Lincoln would "regard any concession in the face of menace the destruction of the government itself." Such a betrayal of principle would bring "our system . . . down to a level with the existing disorganized state of affairs in Mexico." To Seward, who favored a more conciliatory approach, Lincoln stated his position in no uncertain terms: "I say now, however, as I have all the while said, that on the territorial question . . . I am inflexible. I am for no compromise which assists or permits the extension of the institution on soil owned by the nation. And any trick by which the nation is to acquire territory, and then allow some local authority to spread slavery over it, is as obnoxious as any other."[51] He could hardly repudiate the main plank of the Republican Party platform because "free soil" was the glue that held the disparate coalition together.[52] Indeed, not only the preservation of the Union but also the fulfillment of his own political ambitions depended on taking a stand and calling what many northerners considered to be the southerners' bluff.[53]

On his unhurried journey east from Springfield to Washington for the inauguration, Lincoln spoke at several stops along the way and always of the glorious Union. In Pittsburgh on February 15, he briefly claimed there was no crisis, only an "artificial one . . . as may be gotten up at any time by designing politicians." In various speeches and back-of-the-train remarks to crowds who gathered along the tracks, Lincoln assumed the mantle of a leader above partisanship even as his views on the crisis reflected a determination to keep Republicans unified. His tone remained that of the self-effacing servant of the people more interested in listening than talking. "It is true that while I hold myself without mock modesty, the humblest of all individuals that have ever been elevated to the Presidency," he told legislators in Albany, New York, "I have a more difficult task to perform than any one of them." Was Lincoln here thinking of the challenges faced by his hero George Washington? Perhaps his thoughts turned to those great Whigs, Daniel Webster and Henry Clay, whom he mentioned a day later at the Astor House in New York, ignoring their role as sectional compromisers as he incongruously defended his continuing reticence on public policy. In Trenton, New Jersey, Lincoln could mask ambition in providential terms: "I shall be most happy indeed if I shall be an humble instrument in the hands of the Almighty, and of this, his almost chosen people, for perpetuating the object of that great struggle." In Philadelphia, he again referred to an "artificial panic" that had aroused so much public anxiety, adding that there would be "no need of bloodshed and war . . . unless it be forced upon the Government."[54] The prospect of bloodshed had ironically become deeply personal, as a credible threat of assassination forced a reluctant Lincoln to travel incognito on a night train, arriving in Washington in the early morning hours of February 23, 1861.

Like Lincoln, George McClellan believed that this latest crisis of the Union was largely an artificial one that would blow over, though later claiming that, by the fall of 1860, he could see war coming. He recalled the mounting sectional tensions as "perhaps rendered inevitable by the violent course of a comparatively small number of men, on both sides of the line, during the thirty years preceding the war." Although in late December 1860 he believed that even northwestern Republicans would accept a compromise on the territorial question along with other adjustments, he remained wary of party politicians in Washington who failed to represent what he considered the true sentiments of most northerners. A little over a month later, he sounded even more hopeful that "the existing difficulties will be satisfactorily arranged." John M. Douglas, a director of the Illinois Central, however, wrote to McClellan about his fear of Seward's influence over Lincoln, who "is not a bold man" and "has not nerve enough to differ with his party and his leaders."[55]

In fact, Seward was more amenable to compromise than Lincoln, hoped that secession fever would be confined to the Lower South, and sought to keep the Upper South states quarantined from the contagion. On inauguration day, March 4, Lincoln acknowledged "apprehension" in the southern states but failed to plumb its depths, simply repeating that his party had no intention of interfering with slavery there. He added that the Constitution's fugitive-slave clause would be enforced, though three paragraphs of qualifiers only served to muddy the waters on that fractious issue. Entering office "under great and peculiar difficulty," Lincoln nevertheless claimed that the Constitution had made the Union "perpetual" and disunion impossible. Indeed, any rejection of majority rule in favor of secession would bring nothing but "anarchy." The territorial question remained the only "substantial dispute" between the sections, but he offered no solution while remaining mostly mum on any compromise aside from a lukewarm endorsement of a constitutional amendment guaranteeing the perpetuity of slavery in states where it already existed. For any further trouble, he placed the onus on southerners: "In *your* hands, my dissatisfied fellow countrymen, and not in *mine,* is the momentous issue of civil war." Lincoln had deleted a strong statement on retaking federal property in the seceding states from an earlier draft of the address and clearly adjured any use of force in delivering the mail or collecting customs duties.[56] But for all the care given to its preparation, he had not exactly laid out a clear policy. "A steel hand in a soft glove" was how one astute listener characterized the inaugural address.[57] But which carried more weight was anyone's guess.

As things turned out, the inauguration failed to calm the waters or offer the new president any respite from the crisis. News immediately arrived from Major Robert Anderson that the garrison at Fort Sumer would be starved out in six weeks, and General in Chief Scott recommended evacuation. Lincoln hoped to avoid bloodshed but had pledged not to surrender additional federal property. Should Sumter then be resupplied by force? The new cabinet was divided, and in any case, it was doubtful whether even abandoning the fort would guarantee that the Upper South states would spurn secession. There was growing concern that Lincoln and his advisers lacked any policy at all, and Seward's pacific assurances to Upper South Unionists and to Confederate commissioners were at best misleading. As was wise, given his lack of executive experience, the new president proceeded deliberately, still hoping that delay would somehow allow passions to cool. He considered holding on to Fort Pickens in Pensacola Bay, which would make vacating Sumter more palatable, but on March 28, Scott advised surrendering them both.

Seward played an increasingly desperate game, not only pressing Lincoln to let Sumter go but also boldly trying to take charge of administration policy, an effort that the president diplomatically but firmly rebuffed. In the meantime, Republican dissatisfaction mounted as the country appeared adrift without a compass. Confusion prevailed as separate plans for Sumter and Pickens proceeded haltingly and independently of each other. Lincoln may have at least hinted at giving up Sumter if the Virginia secession convention adjourned, yet that possibility also came to naught when he discovered that plans to reinforce Fort Pickens had gone awry. So instead, on the evening of April 6, Lincoln informed the governor of South Carolina that a naval expedition carrying relief supplies would soon be sailing for Charleston harbor. In the end, little of this mattered, as the impatient Confederates fired on Fort Sumter, in some ways taking Lincoln off the hook by assuming responsibility for starting the ensuing war.[58]

Although the president's call for troops prompted the secession of four more states, in the immediate aftermath of Sumter, northern opinion rallied to the administration. Lincoln had kept his party mostly unified, but this always-ambitious politician now faced a far greater challenge that would test his mettle and soon put him on the path toward collaboration and eventually collision with the equally ambitious George B. McClellan.

2

SAVIORS OF THE UNION

On April 15, 1861, President Lincoln called on the states for 75,000 volunteers for use against "combinations too powerful to be suppressed by the ordinary course of judicial proceedings." These troops were to "re-possess the forts, places, and property which have been seized from the Union." On April 19, he proclaimed a blockade of southern ports. A week later, while speaking to a group of Kansas volunteers, Lincoln still hoped that "our present difficulties might be settled without the shedding of blood," but responsibility for war would remain with the secessionists. The president dismissed talk of a short or easy conflict. "Man for man the soldier from the South will be a match for the soldier from the North," he warned his advisers, though presumably mobilizing the Union's superior resources and numbers should eventually bring the secessionists to heel.[1] In the short term, however, even Washington itself appeared to be in danger, and with the secession of Virginia, North Carolina, Arkansas, and Tennessee, the situation in the Border South—Maryland, Kentucky, and Missouri—greatly worried the president.

Congress would not be in session until July 4, and so Lincoln acted alone, stretching presidential authority to its limits if not beyond. Besides calling for troops and declaring a blockade, he expanded the regular army and suspended the writ of habeas corpus in various parts of the country. New problems kept cropping up, including the possibility that European nations might recognize the southern Confederacy, an especially alarming possibility after the British officially declared neutrality in the American conflict. Northerners eagerly volunteered to defend the flag against the southern traitors, but the government could not properly arm them. War Department inefficiency—under the feckless leadership of Simon Cameron—

and no small amount of corruption left state governors fuming and impatient northerners demanding the battle be taken to the enemy. And all the while Lincoln still had to deal with the problems of appointments, beset by a host of difficulties on everything from German Americans clamoring for their share of the patronage, to political bickering in Missouri, to incessant demands for bombproof jobs as military paymasters.[2]

On July 4, Lincoln's message to a special session of Congress cast the conflict in broader, well-nigh universal, terms. The larger question boiled down to a simple matter of whether "a constitutional republic, or a democracy—a government of the people, by the same people—can, or cannot, maintain its territorial integrity, against its own domestic foes." With so much at stake, Lincoln justified calling on "the war power of the Government" to resist "force . . . by force." Any measures taken before Congress had convened, "whether strictly legal or not," had resulted from "popular demand" and "public necessity."[3]

The new president received unified support from Republicans, but there were early signs of restlessness. Treasury Secretary Salmon Chase told a visitor that at this point, the administration had no plan or policy, adding, "I would have one if I were President!" Democrats—including the former attorney general Edwin M. Stanton—complained that too many military appointments had gone to undeserving Republicans. The president cordially greeted people, with one New Englander commenting that while Lincoln was "one of the ugliest men in the country," he had never met "a pleasanter or more kind-hearted" person. Lincoln's seemingly humble demeanor helped him fend off impatient politicians. "I don't know but that God has created some one man great enough to comprehend the whole of this stupendous crisis and transaction from beginning to end, and endowed him with sufficient wisdom to manage and direct it," he told a Maine senator. "I confess I do not fully understand, and foresee it all. But I am placed here where I am obliged to the best of my poor ability to deal with it. And that being the case I can only go just as fast as I can see how to go."[4]

A Pennsylvania soldier observed Lincoln greeting some hundred children at the White House one day and at the same time remarked that the new president was "showing a great deal of firmness and character." He had stood up to the Rebels and would be a forceful commander in chief. Soon after the firing on Fort Sumter, Lincoln had told a New York congressman, "I intend to give blows."[5] Yet it had been difficult enough to secure safe passage for arriving troops through secessionist Baltimore, and Washington appeared to be in danger until nearly the end of April. Less than a week after the firing on Fort Sumter, the Federals had evacuated Norfolk, Virginia, and the navy yard there. By May, troops were pouring into Washington, but by that time, perhaps a third of the regular army's officers had resigned, many to go with the Confederacy.[6]

The coming of war meant that George B. McClellan's frustrated ambition for martial distinction if not greatness might soon be gratified, and there was no shortage of people offering advice or seeking his talents. His old army colleague Fitz John Porter had recommended McClellan take some prominent position with either Pennsylvania or Ohio troops, and the governor of New York expressed interest as well. Rumor had it that Governor Andrew Curtin might appoint him to command the Pennsylvania Reserves. McClellan hoped that, based on their service together in Mexico, Winfield Scott would put in a word and asked Porter to tell the now nearly seventy-five-year-old commanding general of the U.S. Army, "I am ready as ever to serve under his command; I trust I need not assure him that he can count on my loyalty to him & the dear old flag he has so long upheld." In Columbus, Ohio, Scott conferred with Governor William Dennison, who had already sought his advice on defending Cincinnati. The general recommended enrolling militia (predictably disparaging a movement to raise "Home Guards" in the Buckeye State) and advised selecting locations for the erection of fieldworks across the Ohio River in Covington, Kentucky. For a man whose watchword would often be caution, he naturally warned Dennison: "It may well be that the necessity for all this will not occur, but there is only one safe rule in war—i.e. to decide what is the very worst thing that can happen to you, & prepare to meet it."[7]

Despite what Jacob Cox decades later recalled as a "quiet and modest" appearance, McClellan "showed no lack of confidence in himself," and so Dennison offered him command of Ohio's forces. William T. Sherman applauded the selection ("a better officer could not be found"), but McClellan inherited a chaotic situation in Columbus. He sat down immediately to work out detailed schedules of what he would need to equip 10,000 men. Ohio could supply up to 50,000 recruits, McClellan informed General Scott, duly noting that those already assembled were a "fine body of men" yet lacked both organization and discipline. Nor did these troops have much in the way of arms or ammunition—McClellan requested 10,000 stand of arms and enough camp equipment for 20,000 men.[8]

McClellan's dispatch to Scott (which had to be hand carried to Washington because the telegraph line through Maryland was down) had not quite captured how appalled he was at the condition of Ohio's defenses. "A fine stock of munitions on which to begin a great war!" he had remarked after seeing the pathetically small collection of rusted smoothbore muskets and altered flintlocks. Nevertheless, McClellan showed great energy, frequently visiting the newly named Camp Dennison near Cincinnati to check on everything from equipment to morale, and reports soon indicated not only his increased visibility but also his growing popularity with the troops. McClellan much preferred dealing with soldiers to "managing railroads and adding up columns of dollars and cents." He acknowledged the difficulties of handling raw recruits and quickly issued orders emphasizing the need for "discipline and instruction." After some lobbying of Lincoln by Illinois politicians (Governor Richard Yates, Senator Trumbull, and future general John A. McClernand) along with a warm endorsement from General Scott, McClellan was appointed a major general in the regular army.[9]

Sherman claimed that McClellan's "seniors" recognized the younger man's qualifications, given his record in Mexico and Europe, but difficulties with Scott began almost immediately. In Mexico, McClellan had learned to admire Scott's tactical sense and aversion to political interference in military affairs, but his attitude was hardly worshipful, and his customary problems with superiors soon reappeared. McClellan would not be given all the officers he had requested for his new command (the Department of the Ohio, encompassing Indiana, Illinois, and eventually parts of western Pennsylvania and western Virginia), and he received little guidance from Washington. After a fruitless visit seeking a staff position, Ulysses S. Grant later recalled that McClellan "had three times as many men with quills behind their ears" as would have been necessary even "in a much larger command."[10]

Only four days after receiving the appointment from Dennison, McClellan sent Scott plans to "bring the war to a speedy close." He viewed the western theater as key and favored a "strong diversion" to defend Washington and support military forces in the East. With the Northwest supposedly able to provide 80,000 men, he proposed entering western Virginia and moving up the Kanawha Valley for an advance on Richmond. The proposed plan dismissed any difficulty in crossing the mountains with a single sentence. Should Kentucky join the Confederacy, McClellan recommended advancing on Nashville. In either case, all the government had to do was supply the western troops with the necessary arms, ammunition, and other materiel.[11]

When this proposal reached his desk, Scott did not reply but instead scribbled a critical endorsement pointing to the impracticality of marching armies, horses, and supplies through the mountains and warning of a possible Rebel uprising in Virginia. He then briefly alluded to his own plan (the soon-to-be-dubbed Anaconda) of "enveloping" the seceding states by advancing down the Mississippi River and blockading southern ports. The general in chief admitted that an advance along the Mississippi would require over four months' instruction for the troops and could not get underway until November. In any case, as he awkwardly assured McClellan, it would "not [be] improbable [that] you may be invited to take an important part." Scott, however, pointed to a political obstacle: "the great danger now pressing upon us—the impatience of our patriotic and loyal Union friends." McClellan agreed with him that public pressure would likely be a serious impediment, appeared to favor Scott's plan without quite saying so, and in turn referred to his own "intimate knowledge of the country." He closed with a little flattery for the old man "under whom I had first learned the art of war." In a later dispatch, McClellan laid it on even more thickly: "Next to maintaining the honor of my country, general, the first aim of my life is to justify the good opinion you have expressed concerning me, and to prove that the great soldier of our country can not only command armies himself, but teach others to do so. I do not expect your mantle to fall on my shoulders, for no man is worthy to wear it; but I hope that it may be said hereafter that I was no unworthy disciple of your school."[12]

Writing to Governor Dennison, McClellan more candidly vented his frustrations. Given the "apathy" in Washington, the War Department's failure to communicate, and the refusal to grant many of his requests, he claimed to "almost regret having entered upon my present duty." By May 17, he had prepared—despite the absence of instructions from Scott—"to cross the Ohio River" with as many as 40,000 men rather than "see the loyal Union men of Kentucky crushed." He even believed that citizens of the Bluegrass State were ready to abandon "'armed neutrality' . . . to enter heart & soul into this contest on our side." Like Lincoln, McClellan recognized the vital importance of Kentucky and the delicate political situation there. Informing Scott that the Kentuckians "desire to remain in the Union, *without a revolution, under all the forms of law & by their own action,*" he recommended treading lightly until after the state elections. On June 7 in Cincinnati, McClellan met Major General Simon Bolivar Buckner, who commanded the Kentucky home guard, and a report soon circulated that McClellan had agreed to a tacit recognition of the state's neutrality, though Buckner's letter to Kentucky governor Beriah Magoffin (which soon appeared in the newspapers) was not entirely clear on this point. A brief flurry of charges and countercharges caused some embarrassment to McClellan, who described his two interviews with Buckner as "inconclusive and unsatisfactory." In explaining things to Scott, he threw in some more flattery: "My chief fear has been that you, whom I regard as my strongest friend in Washington, might have supposed me to be guilty of the extreme of folly." The detective Allan Pinkerton, whom McClellan had sent to gather information in Kentucky, warned of the political damage being done and even tried to intercede with Lincoln on his boss's behalf. Despite a flurry of alarmist newspaper accounts, neither official Washington nor eventually the press lent much credence to Buckner's claims. Later, of course, McClellan's critics would dredge up the Buckner episode to pad their bill of indictment.[13]

For now, McClellan eagerly accepted an expanded role in the war with officially stated modesty but occasional impatience. Scott tried to rein in his young subordinate by pointing out that commanding three-month volunteers in a large theater hardly called "for expeditions beyond its borders," apparently referring to the Kentucky scheme. In turn, McClellan complained to Dennison that Scott was "eminently sensitive, and does not at all times take suggestions from military subordinates especially when they conflict with his preconceived notions."[14]

After Virginia officially seceded in late May, and as Confederate troops advanced toward the railroad junction at Grafton, Scott warned of an effort to "overawe the friends of the Union." McClellan ordered his forces to proceed cautiously into western Virginia, mainly to protect bridges for the vitally important Baltimore and Ohio Railroad. Earlier he had concluded that Unionists there "lack courage," and even at this early stage in the war, his dispatches occasionally mixed in political observations with military advice.[15]

On May 30, McClellan's men reached Grafton, but the secessionists had already left. His dispatches to the War Department breathed energy and confidence. On July 3, Brigadier General Thomas A. Morris (who commanded a brigade of Indiana state troops) sent two attacking columns toward Philippi, where they surprised and routed some Virginia troops, though McClellan claimed many more prisoners would have been taken had he been given adequate cavalry.[16] From Parkersburg, Virginia, he wrote to the War Department expressing some uncertainty about enemy numbers, though this time he thought subordinates were overestimating them. In a typical mix of complaining and boasting, he told Nelly about his frustration with raw recruits but felt more than up to the task: "Everything here needs the hands of the master & is getting it fast."[17]

Shortages of transportation and rations caused some delay, but McClellan considered "the men in most excellent spirits," adding that they "require only careful handling." Interestingly enough, he reported this all to Treasury Secretary Chase, who naturally sought news about Ohio troops, but this letter reflected a not unusual practice among several Civil War generals who communicated with top officials outside the chain of command. In any case, McClellan would advance slowly, and as he again lamented to Nelly, "I am bothered half to death by delays in getting up supplies—unless where I am in person everything goes wrong."[18] Viewing himself as indispensable would not only lead McClellan to work far too long and hard but also prevent him from sharing his plans and problems with subordinates or even the War Department.

His moods often seemed volatile, sinking one moment, soaring the next. Assuming he could catch up to the enemy, McClellan expected to "thrash the infamous scamps before a week is over." On July 2, he reprimanded Brigadier General William S. Rosecrans (a "silly fussy goose') for advancing too quickly toward Buckhannon and possibly tipping off the Confederates. Still, McClellan wondered if the enemy would even fight and mused that perhaps "my successes will be due to maneuvers, & that I shall have no brilliant victories to record." With Confederates concentrating around Rich Mountain and Laurel Hill near Beverly, Virginia, McClellan was now in the field and, as would often be the case, working long hours. One night he alternately slept and froze after drowsily listening to a report from a loquacious Union colonel.[19]

With a hopefulness that expressed widely held northern views (including the president's), McClellan remarked: "It is wonderful to see how rapidly the minds of many of these people become enlightened when they find we can protect them! Fear & ignorance combined have made most of the converts to secession—the reverse process is now going on with great rapidity." As for his troops, he would not "throw these men . . . into the teeth of artillery & intrenchments." McClellan only hoped that Scott would realize both the wisdom and origin of this approach: "I am trying to follow a lesson long ago learned from him; i.e., not to move until I know that everything is ready, and then to move with the utmost rapidity and energy." It also had become clear that the increased responsibility, especially for his soldiers' lives, was beginning to weigh heavily. He nervously admitted to Nelly, "everything requires success in my first operations." She need not worry, however, because like so many other Americans, he affirmed that "God is on our side."[20]

Scott reported being "charmed' by the general's "energy, movements, and success," and this further lifted McClellan's spirits. Providing fresh details of his troop dispositions on July 6, McClellan informed the War Department that he soon expected to engage the enemy at Rich Mountain. Later dispatches reported the Confederates well entrenched in mountainous country that made military operations difficult. After skirmishing at Laurel Mountain on July 12, troops commanded by Rosecrans turned the Confederate position at Rich Mountain, taking a goodly number of prisoners and suffering only light casualties. McClellan had failed to support Rosecrans's attack and soon received undeserved credit for the victories in western Virginia. "Never was so complete success gained with smaller sacrifice of life," he wrote Nelly, at the same time declaring victory in western Virginia.[21]

By July 13, McClellan's troops reached Beverly, and for all practical purposes the campaign was over. So far McClellan had displayed caution, careful planning, an obsession with detail, and hesitation at the moment of crisis, but these qualities were not what contemporaries—including many Republicans—noticed. Not long after McClellan's promotion to major general, the *Chicago Tribune* had declared that "no fitter appointment could be made." Indeed, the paper attached to him nearly superhuman qualities: "He is now in the full vigor of his powers, both physical and mental. . . . [N]ature has endowed him with a close-knit frame which will enable him to endure any amount of fatigue. . . . With prudence and confidence in his strength, he will succeed where a bolder and rasher man would fail. *He will commit no mistakes*. When he advances, it will be with a strength that no ordinary force can oppose; if he recedes, ruin and disaster will not follow in his rear." As the western Virginia campaign unfolded, the *Washington National Republican*—already selected to publish "notices and advertisements" from the executive branch and which might be considered Lincoln's semiofficial organ—was almost equally effusive. An editorial praised McClellan's "unostentatious" manner, along with his "executive ability rarely equaled, and seldom or never excelled." Here was a leader who one day might assume the mantle of General Scott, "the greatest captain of the age."[22]

In commenting on the campaign in western Virginia, newspapers cast McClellan in a most favorable light; indeed "puffery," a term quite familiar to readers of the time, might not be too strong a word to describe the press reports. The *Chicago Tribune* even suggested that the young general was better off "being out of reach of Gen. Scott's telegraph." And newspaper readers would soon learn that it was McClellan—slighting Rosecrans—who had turned the Confederate position at Rich Mountain. Word of these victories had brought joy to Washington: "Citizens and soldiers sing his praise." McClellan does business with "quick dispatch," the *National Republican* announced. "No sooner does he come up with a rebel army, than he engages and defeats them." The general was becoming, according to a *New York Herald* headline, the "Napoleon of the Present War." In an article that ran for more than a column on the editorial page, the *Herald* favorably compared McClellan to the great commanders of history. After a long passage heaping praise on Scott, the editor went back to applauding McClellan's "Napoleonic despatches to the War Department" and the general's sheer "genius." Not satisfied with all this hyperbole, the editorial concluded: "The backbone of the rebellion is broken. It made Virginia its Waterloo, and it has been defeated; it resolved to test its strength there, and that strength has proved to be perfect weakness. The road to Richmond is open."[23]

A fawning letter from Treasury Secretary Chase claimed some credit for McClellan's appointment as major general and suggested his command be further expanded, envisioning McClellan leading armies through North Carolina, Georgia, Alabama, and all the way to Mobile and New Orleans. A flattering telegram from Scott, arriving on the heels of Rich Mountain, now reported not only himself but also the cabinet and the president "charmed with your activity, valor, and consequent successes." And even Michigan senator Zachariah Chandler, soon to be one of McClellan's harshest critics, exulted over the "good work in Western Virginia."[24]

If praise from the high and mighty were music to his ears, so were any signs of respect and affection from the troops. Despite his usual disparagement of volunteers, McClellan told Chase that he would put the enlisted men up against the best European troops. Morale "could not be better," he informed the War Department. From the beginning, McClellan showed an almost obsessive concern for the welfare of his men and certainly a great reluctance to place them in any unnecessary danger. Following the victory at Rich Mountain and ignoring Rosecrans's important role, McClellan's address to the troops, cast in the flowery and overblown rhetoric favored by several generals early in the war, recounted their accomplishments and praised them for having done all that had been demanded. The men had earned the thanks of not only their fellow citizens but also their commander: "Soldiers! I have confidence in you, and I trust you have learned to confide in me. Remember that discipline and subordination, are qualities of equal value with courage."[25]

McClellan closely connected good discipline with humane treatment of civilians. Reflecting the views of the Lincoln administration, Secretary of War Cameron had emphasized to McClellan that "the Union men in Western Virginia be aided and encouraged in every way possible." Weeks before, the general had already instructed his men to "respect" Virginians' "persons and property." The only real enemies were the "armed traitors," and even toward them, the troops should "show mercy . . . when they are in your power, for many of them are misguided." Such statements reflected several elements of McClellan's approach to the war and the Confederates. At West Point and during his earlier army service, he had enjoyed cordial relations with southerners. As a conservative Democrat, he had rejected secession but had maintained that the southern states had some legitimate grievances. To the Unionists of western Virginia, McClellan noted how "armed traitors" had attempted to bring on a "reign of terror" but declared that "your homes, your families & your property are safe under our protection." In addition, Federal forces should refrain from any "interference" with slaves. McClellan realized that his proclamations might be controversial and so wrote to Lincoln explaining how they were based on the president's "previous course and opinions." He felt "confident that I have not erred on this very important matter." Neither Lincoln nor Scott replied. After a company of Ohio troops robbed the house of a Virginia secessionist, McClellan court-martialed an officer and seven privates, explaining to Governor Dennison how his conciliatory policy had shown many Virginians that they had been badly misled by disunionists. The general seemed almost proud that the "Abolition papers" would criticize him on this score, but he would impose discipline on the troops even if some men had to be "shot or hung."[26]

Deeply affected by conversations with grateful Unionists, especially those who had been imprisoned, as well as the surprise expressed by captured Confederates over being treated humanely, McClellan felt fully vindicated in his conciliatory policy. He had waged a successful military campaign without oppressing or alienating the local population and even believed that some secessionists had been brought back into the Union fold. "I have tried to temper justice with mercy," he explained to Nelly. "I think these men [prisoners whom he had released] will do me no harm, but that some mothers and sisters and wives will bless the name of your husband." In a letter to a Confederate general discussing prisoners, McClellan spelled out a philosophy that would govern his conduct throughout the war. "While I am determined to play my part in this unhappy contest to the utmost of my energy & ability, permit me to assure you of my desire to do all in my power to alleviate its miseries, & to confine its effects to those who constitute the organized armies & meet in battle."[27]

McClellan would face little immediate criticism from the Lincoln administration or the northern public because the campaign in western Virginia had succeeded. Likewise, praise from the newspapers, plaudits from his superiors, affection from his soldiers, and apparent success with Virginia Unionists and Confederates alike confirmed McClellan in his most basic beliefs about the nature of the conflict and appropriate strategy. At a time when the war was not going well—there had recently been embarrassing defeats (albeit in relatively minor engagements) at Big Bethel, Virginia, and Carthage, Missouri—it is hardly surprising that many northerners, regardless of their politics, would not only welcome the news of Rich Mountain but also consider McClellan a budding military genius.[28]

On visiting Washington, McClellan's chief of staff (and father-in-law) Randolph Marcy met with Scott, who wondered (along with others) when the general's forces might resume their advance. Meanwhile, words of praise for the recent campaign continued, including a joint resolution of thanks from Congress. McClellan hoped to return soon to Cincinnati, where Nelly was in her seventh month of pregnancy, and anticipated hearing that Brigadier General Irvin McDowell's army had driven Confederate forces away from Manassas Junction, Virginia. On July 21, Scott wired him that within a few hours McDowell would turn the enemy flank, but instead of this resulting in Union victory, a reinforced Confederate army whipped the Yankees and sent them in headlong retreat toward Washington. The following day came a telegram from the adjutant general in Washington: "Circumstances make your presence here necessary. . . . [C]ome hither without delay."[29]

"Wanted—A Leader" had been the title of Henry J. Raymond's editorial in the *New York Times* that appeared less than two weeks after the firing on Fort Sumter. With Washington apparently still endangered, Raymond had described the cabinet as a collection of politicians who had outlived their usefulness. Lincoln's private secretary John Hay had taken this all as "a warning to the President that he will be superseded." While this had seemed more amusing than annoying to Lincoln, or at least that is the impression he conveyed, the press clamor for action was persistent. And for sure, Lincoln himself had pressed for an offensive and discounted General Scott's calls for more deliberate preparations.[30]

A series of delays had not augured well, but as McDowell's army was attacking at Bull Run, there had been great optimism in the capital. Anxious for news, Lincoln had spent much of the day at the War Department's telegraph office, but during the afternoon went over to see Scott, who was taking a nap. Even after the general awoke, he put little stock in the alarming reports drifting in from the battlefield. Denial followed by panic summed up the early reactions in Washington to the outcome at Bull Run. According to an Illinois congressman (and Douglas Democrat), Scott had admitted being too cowardly to resist administration pressure to fight the battle "against my judgment." Lincoln bristled at the implication "that I forced you to fight this battle." The general in chief then beat a hasty retreat, claiming that no president had treated him more kindly, which did not exactly address the question.[31]

Recriminations among the politicians and in the press continued, with both the president and his cabinet on the receiving end. After seven supposedly sleepless nights (perhaps because his newspaper had often led the "On to Richmond" drumbeat), Greeley wrote to Lincoln. "You are not considered a great man," he bluntly began, then suggested that much of the responsibility for the war's casualties would rest on the president. The editor was clearly beside himself when he drafted this peculiar letter, but he was right that so long as the war was going badly, the president would end up shouldering much of the blame. To former attorney general Stanton—a political chameleon who would change colors several times over the next eight years—the Bull Run disaster proved "the imbecility of this administration." Lincoln had been "running the machine," and Stanton now anticipated the Rebel "capture of Washington." As for Lincoln himself, he remained touchy about the Bull Run debacle. But the day after the battle, the president drafted a memorandum on military policy. He pushed forward the naval blockade and a few days later sketched out proposed offensives in Virginia and Tennessee. Not surprisingly, Scott's political stock was falling and McClellan's rising; the older and increasingly infirm general in chief presented a striking contract to his young, energetic protégé.[32]

For his part, Scott may have thought that McClellan was not yet ready for a larger command, though there is some evidence suggesting the opposite. One report had Lincoln pressing for McClellan's elevation over the objections of his cabinet. Newspapers of various stripes eagerly anticipated the general's arrival in Washington and even suggested that the salvation of the capital depended on him. Veterans of Bull Run, of McDowell's beaten army, would surely welcome a new commander; his mere presence was worth 10,000 men, according to the *Chicago Tribune*.[33]

On the morning of July 24, McClellan departed Beverly, Virginia, for the 153-mile ride to the nearest railroad station at Wheeling. From there he traveled to Pittsburgh to be welcomed by a large crowd at Union Station. In Philadelphia, McClellan spoke briefly from the balcony of his brother's home, and a waiting crowd shouted and cheered as the general rode through the streets in a carriage. He was accorded a private car for the ride to Baltimore, where he and two other officers walked the ten blocks between the President Street Station and the Camden Street Station—stepping briskly over the same streets where a mob had attacked Union troops barely three months before.[34]

The triumphant journey ended in Washington, where McClellan arrived in the afternoon of July 26 and immediately headed for Willard's Hotel.

That evening, he called on General Scott, and the next morning he reported at the War Department to Assistant Adjutant General E. D. Townsend, who sent him to the Executive Mansion. There McClellan met with Lincoln, and one can only speculate how much each man remembered about any of their fleeting contacts back in Illinois.[35]

At age thirty-four, McClellan struck most everyone as young looking, even "boyish," as one woman claimed. Around five feet, eight inches in height, with a forty-five-inch chest; broad, muscular shoulders; and short, thick neck, he exuded physical strength; his literary executor implausibly claimed to have seen McClellan bend a quarter over the end of his thumb and that the general could lift a 250-pound man into the air. Other observers described a well-formed head, face ruddy and healthy looking, dark mustache (some said reddish), and blue eyes (deep set and penetrating, according to a couple of European visitors). He impressed one Washington reporter as a "Napoleonic figure" with a quiet demeanor and dignified bearing. Others described McClellan as intelligent and pleasant; he could be a quite charming conversationalist, though at times he avoided looking people in the eye.[36]

In so many ways, not just physically, McClellan and Lincoln presented quite a contrast. For one thing, the president was very tall by the standards of the day—a towering six feet, four inches. At 180 pounds or so, he was certainly thin, perhaps reflecting a well-known indifference to food. At age fifty-two, Lincoln was not only considerably older than McClellan, but he looked it, having already been dubbed "old Abe." A British visitor described the president's face as "furrowed, wrinkled, and indented." It was a "strange, weird, and melancholy face," a young New York officer decided on seeing Lincoln for the first time. "Homely as a hedge fence," a much less tactful comrade remarked. There was sometimes a painfully awkward look about the man, and he walked with what Benjamin Brown French, the commissioner of public buildings in Washington, called a "peculiar swinging gait." Clothes hung loosely on Lincoln's lank frame, his pants were often too short, and his hair was unruly—the overall appearance unkempt. A kinder observer recalled the president's "unstudied ease" and "careless dignity." But these varied descriptions were not necessarily contradictory because Lincoln was a paradoxical figure. "He is a barbarian, Scythian, yahoo, or gorilla, in respect of outside polish," diarist George Templeton Strong wrote after a meeting with Lincoln. But Strong also thought him "a most sensible, straightforward, honest old codger," indeed, the best president since Andrew Jackson because "simplicity of purpose would compensate for worse grammar than his, and for even more intense provincialism." Even those who recoiled at Lincoln's appearance often commented on the man's finer qualities, including a courteous unpretentiousness and at times a deep sadness, regardless of his penchant for humor and ribald stories.[37]

McClellan often failed to see beneath the president's unprepossessing appearance and folksy talk, though at first he had no reason to try. After all, at this first meeting Lincoln made the young general commander of the Military Division of the Potomac, encompassing Washington and northeastern Virginia. This was heady stuff, and there followed a certain amount of preening and boasting. "I find myself in a new & strange position here," he wrote to Nelly. "Presdt, Cabinet, Genl Scott & all deferring to me—by some strange operation of magic I seem to have become *the* power of the land." McClellan surely made all this sound more mysterious and unexpected than it was because, in his own mind, he deserved the deference and the responsibility. Even "some small success" might now lead to calls for him to become "dictator," a possibility he treated with a light touch. But given his standing and obvious talent, McClellan felt he could diagnose the main causes of the "recent failure." He could then "remedy" any problems and "lead these armies of men to victory once more." Indeed, he would start doing so the very next morning. McClellan seemed inordinately proud of the fact that he was suddenly so busy that he would have to decline dinner invitations from Scott and no fewer than four cabinet members.[38]

For all their differences, however, as Lincoln biographer William Lee Miller has pointed out, both men "came rather suddenly into great power in 1861, and neither man had much preparation for the immense responsibility that fell to him." Now Lincoln and McClellan would have to work closely together—Stephen Sears counted some fifty-seven meetings they had in Washington during a six-month period. That the quite refined general might disdain the president's frontier background, rumpled appearance, and crude humor was perhaps unavoidable. Lincoln "was not a man of very strong character," McClellan later wrote. "He was destitute of refinement—certainly in no sense a gentleman—he was easily wrought upon by the coarse associations whose style of conversation agreed so well with his own."[39]

The arrival of McClellan meant that the president "will take no step backward," the leading Republican newspaper in Washington maintained, though a skeptical John Bigelow (a Seward ally who would soon receive a diplomatic appointment) groused that "there is no military genius whatever in the Prest. or his advisers." Despite the growing faith in McClellan, doubt remained that even he could remedy a situation beset by timidity and unimaginative leadership. Stanton feared the general being "thwarted by Scott's jealousy and cabinet intrigues at every step."[40]

Despite these early reservations, the McClellan appointment certainly seemed to lift spirits in Washington and perhaps elsewhere. Pictures of the young general appeared in shop windows and on dining-room tables; Matthew Brady offered a variety of McClellan photographs; newspapers printed laudatory biographical sketches. What press reports still called the "genius" of the western Virginia campaign stood in great contrast to the failure at Bull Run. "The gifted McClellan," declared one enthusiastic orator, "will wipe out the memory of the recent defeat and be crowned with complete victory." "Little Mac," the moniker soon picked up by newspapermen and soldiers alike, would be the savior of the Union. "There is a charm in this name [McClellan] which will yet work as a talisman upon the American heart," the *New York Herald* predicted. Here was the hero who appeared just at the moment of greatest need, and so comparisons to Napoleon Bonaparte began. "There will be no more Bull Runs," an ecstatic cashier in Indiana informed his bank's president, and he even viewed the general's appointment as an example of a special providence.[41]

To speak of great expectations for McClellan's success in some ways understates the case. Praising the general as a "young man, a soldier of the West," Michigan governor Austin Blair reportedly declared, "Our army cannot fail of victory." Two of Lincoln's private secretaries, Hay and William Stoddard, filed anonymous newspaper dispatches lauding McClellan. Hay described the general hard at work bringing order and efficiency to the army, rounding up absentees, and keeping soldiers away from the "rum-shop keepers." According to Stoddard, "Better one week of McClellan than a whole year of the red-tape officials who preceded him." With morale restored, soldiers were eager to meet the enemy once again.[42]

That was just the sort of report that enlisted men would soon enough deride; even discounting exaggerated accounts of chaos in the aftermath of Bull Run (some trumpeted by McClellan himself), the problems were all too real. If the capital was not in immediate danger of attack, the city's residents, politicians, and indeed military men remained on edge. Soldiers manned various fortifications on the Virginia side, but to the trained eye, local defenses appeared incomplete and inadequate. Enlistments for the three-month regiments would soon expire. "Imagine, if you can, fifty thousand men in an utterly demoralized condition—caring nothing for discipline, or anything else, with no restraint upon them, and you may then form some notion of our condition," Lieutenant Orlando Poe informed his wife. Desertions had risen, stragglers crowded the dusty, unpaved streets, and many officers were absent from their commands. Brazen thieves and drunken volunteers roamed the city.[43] Above all, the new man in charge—McClellan—would have to restore order and morale to the army, with press accounts feeding into a narrative of the brilliant young general salvaging a desperate situation. Word of McClellan meeting with Scott or various officers, inspecting fortifications, and visiting with the troops conveyed an impression of things being whipped into shape. His mere presence had infused a new spirit in the troops, who could rest assured he would lead them to victory.[44]

Not surprisingly, given his background and attitudes toward both volunteers and enlisted men, McClellan immediately turned to the matter of discipline. He appointed a provost marshal to roust soldiers lounging about in hotels and bars. Two keys to better order were restricting liquor sales and keeping men in their camps. These measures, along with more regular drills and picket duty, all reflected the commander's views on what it took to mold civilians into soldiers. Lax standards of behavior could no longer be tolerated, and incompetent officers would have to go.[45]

McClellan himself seemed omnipresent, riding about (sometimes in civilian garb), inspecting camps, conferring with subordinates, and checking reports of corrupt quartermasters. He at first accomplished much of this singlehandedly but quickly found officers to assist him. In articles planted in friendly newspapers, Lincoln's secretaries touted the army's rapid, indeed miraculous, transformation. Hay praised the "new vigor and spirit" in the soldiers, who performed their duties with determination and enthusiasm. Greeley's *New York Tribune* emphasized how McClellan cared for the troops in both mind and spirit, adding the increasingly common comparison to Napoleon. Only a week after taking charge, McClellan exulted to Nelly, "I have restored order very completely already."[46] Junior officers and enlisted men echoed press reports in praising him for instilling a greater ardor and determination in the recently demoralized regiments.

The general's youthful appearance as he rode though the camps reflected this sense of renewed energy.[47]

But there was more to it than dash and McClellan's flare for the dramatic. He looked after his men, including their material comfort, and they knew it. If he heard complaints about undrinkable coffee, inedible rations, or drunken quartermasters, he investigated and took action.[48] As the French theorist Adrant du Picq has argued, the formation and fighting of armies required an "understanding of its ultimate instrument, man, and his morale." Picq reminded his readers that the soldier "is flesh and blood; he is body and soul." To the troops, McClellan was not only a highly visible commander but also a very humane one, an approachable figure despite his dignified bearing and impressive appearance on horseback. A New Jersey quartermaster emphasized the general's "simple and unaffected" deportment. McClellan had a knack for drawing others, especially officers, into his orbit, and apparently the enlisted men never caught wind of his highly critical attitude toward volunteers. Their commander was visible, remembered names, and appeared the soul of confidence. After only a brief encounter, Brigadier General Oliver Otis Howard recalled, McClellan "won me, as he did junior commanders, by his cordial manner."[49]

A more cynical Hoosier thought that McClellan became popular by shamelessly flattering enlisted men and officers at every opportunity. At the other extreme, an articulate and conservative Massachusetts recruit claimed that virtually the entire army "learned to love McClellan." The general's evident concern for his soldiers was returned in kind, especially as they realized that he would not rush into battle or sacrifice lives needlessly; what many in the North might deem unreasonable delays impressed the men as sensible care and caution. "McClellan has got an army, not a mob," the *Chicago Tribune* reported. "He is a commander of great acuteness and fertility of resources and he is shaping his purposes for a victory."[50]

With Nelly still in Cincinnati awaiting the birth of their child, McClellan set up his headquarters only two blocks from the War Department at the corner of Pennsylvania Avenue and Nineteenth Street. This large three-story house, "without any gaudy pretensions," according to one newspaper correspondent, became both office and home. On the ground floor, staff filled the parlors, reading, smoking, writing; upstairs were the private quarters (three rooms at the front of the house). McClellan slept on a camp bed, and a large map hung on a nearby wall. It struck William Howard

Russell that the general might have been better off across the Potomac River with his troops and farther away from political busybodies. In any event, this headquarters was where McClellan both worked and lived even as he tried to steer clear of the capital's social whirl.[51]

He would have hardly enough energy in any case to cut much of a figure in Washington society. Each day usually began with breakfast just around the corner at Wormley's, a restaurant operated by a "colored gentleman." McClellan met with staff in the morning around ten and then again at nine in the evening. During the day, the general rode about the city and camps on horseback (on occasion for as long as twelve hours), sometimes skipping supper when he returned late. There were always documents to read, orders to issue, and aides to consult. One Sunday in August, McClellan received a "summons" from the president right after breakfast and "kept busy" until midnight, returning "from the long ride too tired to talk even." He felt compelled to spend so much time on horseback because, as he put it, "my army covers much space & unfortunately I have no one on my staff to whom I can entrust the safety of affairs." McClellan's inability to delegate often left him exhausted and may have brought back an old malarial complaint from his days in Mexico. In letters home, he recounted hectic and tiring days, but there was about as much boasting as complaining. Press reports presented a similar picture of a commander dashing about the camps at all hours managing details large and small.[52]

McClellan's young staff officers, including some recent West Point graduates, loyally served their commander, greatly admiring if not worshipping him. The sympathetic but not uncritical comte de Paris, a French prince who at age twenty-one served as a captain, later wrote at some length about McClellan's fine personal qualities but thought the general suffered from "inexperience" in managing men. All told, McClellan had three French princes and two Germans (one from a noble family) serving as aides or observers. After he added three German American officers to his staff, the *New York Tribune* lauded the general's statesmanship (and political acumen) in showing that "the adopted citizens . . . should share with the native born in the honors as well as the dangers of battling for the Republic." McClellan displayed fairly modern views about the role of army staff and made some more seasoned appointments as well, including Marcy and the quite capable engineer John G. Barnard.[53]

McClellan quickly restructured brigades and grouped them into divisions—over Scott's objections, a move that marked one of the first signs of tension between the two generals. He searched for capable officers (weeding out those who failed to properly care for their troops) and tried to shelve political appointees, though at this stage of the war, moderate Republicans and War Democrats made up the lion's share of general officers. McClellan won high marks for energy and efficiency and quickly issued detailed instructions to his generals, covering everything from officer training to guard duty, marches, and preparations for battle.[54]

Organizational changes raised expectations that McClellan would quickly revive his army's fighting spirit. His appointments favored West Pointers and regular army officers, though there were never enough of these men to fill all the most important positions. McClellan had to build up an army of enormous size, and precedents from the Mexican-American War, in which armies had been tiny by comparison, offered little guidance. A newspaper report about McClellan adding artillery batteries claimed that the deficiencies in that branch had led to the defeat at Bull Run, an opinion that certainly played to the general's views.[55]

For McClellan, troop reviews helped build esprit and, as he later recalled, "accustoming the troops to see[ing] me." He assumed that visibility was a key to leadership, and even though he claimed that impressing the public and the politicians was not his purpose, the larger affairs attracted considerable attention. On August 21, leading a party of dignitaries that included War Secretary Cameron, Treasury Secretary Chase, Navy Secretary Gideon Welles, and President Lincoln, McClellan spent nearly half a day inspecting Brigadier General George McCall's division.[56] But there was more here than flashy displays or McClellan's appearances with the enlisted men, their officers, and various politicians. Newspaper accounts—sometimes detailed descriptions of the larger reviews—kept the general's name in the public eye and gave the impression of a commander who appeared to be everywhere and seldom slept. Three days after inspecting McCall's division, McClellan rode alongside the president's carriage for yet another review. This time Lincoln climbed out of the carriage and mounted a dragoon horse, riding alongside the general for a quarter of a mile.[57]

McClellan's youthful appearance stood in great contrast to Old Abe's "honest face," but soldiers wildly cheered both men. When Lincoln was not on horseback, he stood up in his carriage, laughing and talking to the troops. At this point in the war, however, it was McClellan who attracted the most notice. A Wisconsin volunteer described the general as a "splendid looking man, just in the prime of life." His broad shoulders and chest exuded vigor, another young soldier recalled; here was McClellan "sitting [on] his frothing horse like a centaur," politely saluting the cheering troops with gloved hand. On one occasion, the general reportedly "smiled indulgently" at a stalwart but clearly inebriated Zouave before firmly shaking the man's hand. A more critical junior officer from Michigan conceded that McClellan "pleased the men remarkably" and "is taking a personal view of every Regt. in the army."[58]

McClellan basked in the attention. "I receive letter after letter—have conversation after conversation calling on me to save the nation," he exulted to his wife. There was now talk of the presidency, which the general claimed he would never take. "I am not spoiled by my unexpected and new position," he assured Nelly. Nevertheless, he felt that "God has placed a great work in my hands," and despite his own admitted weakness, in good Presbyterian fashion, he meant to "do right" because "God will help me & give me the wisdom I do not possess." McClellan's staff scrambled to keep up with a commander who appeared to never rest; one newspaper correspondent even reported the general staying in the saddle some fifteen hours one day and adopting "Bonaparte's idea, that six hours sleep is enough." Soldiers loved to see their increasingly admired Little Mac, who seldom failed to acknowledge them with a doff of his cap.[59]

From the outset, northern newspapers paid attention to the general's daily activities and portrayed him in a favorable light. On August 1, two omnibuses carried correspondents to McClellan's headquarters, where they were warmly greeted by the general and Colonel Marcy. McClellan had just come in dusty and sweaty from a ride but cheerfully expressed confidence in the press, including his faith that responsible newspapers would never publish anything that would help the enemy. Accounts of this meeting soon appeared in print, and newspapermen, evidently charmed by flattery from McClellan, seemed willing to abide by limits on what they could publish in exchange for detailed information on any military engagements. These early restrictions on press freedom proved temporary and largely ineffective; for their part, northern newspapers continued to run puff pieces on McClellan.[60]

By late summer, impressions of Lincoln were decidedly mixed, and critics complained that the president seemed weak and indecisive. New York diarist Strong credited a rumor that McClellan had threatened to resign over political pressure about certain military appointments but that Lincoln had quickly given way. Dissatisfaction with the administration had hardly reached any kind of crisis but was growing. "Lincoln has no element of dignity; not tact, not a spark of genius," Frederick Law Olmsted complained. "This is almost true of all his cabinet. He is an amiable, honest, good fellow. . . . There is the greatest conceivable dearth of administrative talent." To military men, the president lacked the proper bearing, appeared awkward on horseback, and did not quite know how to act when reviewing troops or meeting officers.[61]

Illinois senator Orville Hickman Browning, one of the president's few close friends, candidly warned Lincoln that matters in Washington "did not look hopeful" and recommended Cameron's dismissal. Calls for a cabinet reshuffling appeared even in papers friendly to the administration. Radical Republican senator Benjamin F. Wade of Ohio in August 1861 was already railing against the slowness and stupidity of the administration: "I do not wonder that people desert to Jeff. Davis, as he shows brains; I may desert myself." McClellan was clearly flattered at how people in the administration deferred to his judgment, though that hardly prevented him from disparaging Lincoln as an "idiot" and Scott as lost in his "dotage."[62]

The president was still trying to learn his own responsibilities as commander in chief, but McClellan had become the toast of the town (if not of the northern states more generally). The general certainly knew how to build up support in the army, and early on he courted the press. Here was that apparent success and fame he had long sought, and no one yet quite realized how formidable the suppression of the southern rebellion would prove to be. McClellan believed in organization, planning, and caution. The biggest test would come with the development of strategy and its execution on the battlefield, not to mention the ability to work with the president and others members of the administration. Grant, in an often quoted passage, would later describe McClellan "as one of the mysteries of the war." But what has been much less often noted was Grant's conviction that no commander was likely to succeed this early in the conflict:

> It has always seemed to me that the critics of McClellan do not consider this vast and cruel responsibility—the war, a new thing to all of us, the army new, everything to do from the outset, with a restless people and

Congress. McClellan was a young man when this devolved upon him, and if he did not succeed, it was because the conditions of success were so trying. If McClellan had gone into the war as Sherman, Thomas, or Meade, had fought his way along and up, I have no reason to suppose that he would not have won as high a distinction as any of us.[63]

3

STRATEGY AND POLITICS

On August 2, 1861—less than two weeks after being summoned to Washington—George B. McClellan presented to Abraham Lincoln a memorandum laying out not only a military strategy but also his thoughts on the nature of the war. Here, not for the first and certainly not for the last time, McClellan offered a combination of military and political recommendations, but of course the two cannot be so neatly separated (as the Prussian theorist Clausewitz and many others have observed).[1] During the American Civil War, distinctions between military and political advice were often ignored.

"In this contest it has become necessary to crush a population sufficiently numerous, intelligent, and warlike to constitute a nation," McClellan began. Terming the Rebels a "nation" may have alarmed Lincoln, but the general was simply acknowledging the fact that the United States faced more than a limited insurgency. Therefore, the task at hand was formidable: "We have not only to defeat their armed and organized forces in the field, but to display such an overwhelming strength as will convince all our antagonists, especially those of the governing, aristocratic class, of the utter impossibility of resistance." McClellan feared that the recent defeat at Bull Run "will enable the political leaders of the Rebels to convince the mass of their people that we are inferior to them in force and courage." The proper response was "overwhelming physical force" and a "rigidly protective policy" toward property and persons.

Virginia would likely become the main battleground, though McClellan also proposed movements in the West and along the Mississippi River. For what he called the "main Army of Operations," McClellan proposed raising a force of 273,000 men, which in cooperation with the navy would attack various points along the southern coastline—not only driving the Confederates out of Virginia but also eventually capturing Charleston, Savannah, Montgomery, Pensacola, Mobile, and New Orleans. Combined with offensives in the West, McClellan's great army would bring overwhelming pressure to bear on the Rebels. The object was to end the war in "the shortest possible time" by "crush[ing] the rebellion at one blow, terminate the war in one campaign."[2]

Defeating the Confederates with overwhelming force was and remained the crux of McClellan's approach to the war. To him, this one great military effort coupled with a conciliatory policy toward civilians formed the essence of a policy that might prove hard to sell. Lincoln never responded directly to the memorandum, but given the time required to assemble such large forces, McClellan's proposal, like Scott's Anaconda Plan, would not have relieved political pressure on the president. It is easy to critique the specific recommendations in McClellan's memorandum or even dismiss the entire scheme as unworkably grandiose, but the document also laid out a case for carefully marshalling the Union's superior resources and looking toward bringing the wayward southerners back into the constitutional fold.[3]

On matters large and small, the Union high command was hardly functioning as a team. Despite similar views on strategy and their service together in Mexico, George McClellan and Winfield Scott soon developed a toxic relationship. Once in Washington, McClellan had quickly decided that Scott was "becoming very slow and old." Admittedly, Scott, one of the commanding figures in American military history, second only to George Washington at the time, was long past his prime. His weight had ballooned to well over three hundred pounds, he could take but a few steps at a time, and he could no longer mount a horse. Whether his mental powers had also waned was unclear, but increasingly he dozed off in meetings. Some observers thought Scott was jealous of his young protégé's sudden ascendancy, and he certainly resented McClellan's withholding information while communicating directly with the War Department and cabinet members.[4]

On August 3, the contrast between the old and new was on display during a dinner at the Executive Mansion. It was a glittering occasion complete with the Marine Corps band, French military officers, diplomats, generals, and cabinet members. General Scott entered on McClellan's arm;

"I could see that many marked the contrast," the younger man later wrote. One was John Hay, who remarked: "Six-foot-four leaning upon five-foot-eight! Seventy-five upon thirty-five!"[5]

Less than a week later, McClellan was growing not only impatient with Scott but also worried that Confederate forces might be preparing to attack Washington. Shortly after arriving in the capital, he had summoned Allan Pinkerton, the famous detective, and told him to bring two or three of his "best men." Pinkerton, a Scot with an intense and fearless appearance along with a national reputation for working with railroads, had no background in military intelligence. As things turned out, it would be several weeks before he offered estimates of Confederates strength, yet that did not prevent McClellan from coming up with his own numbers based on amateur informants, a Confederate deserter, and assorted rumors. From such "various sources," he concluded that the Rebels had mustered a force of "100,000 men in front of" Washington, with more on the way. Confederate general P. G. T. Beauregard might attempt to envelop the capital because the Union's "present army is entirely insufficient for this emergency." McClellan urged Scott to call in reinforcements to match the estimated Rebel strength as well as to bring several other military departments under his command. He added that Washington itself was in "imminent danger" and sent an aide with a copy of this letter for the president. The result was a "row" with Scott. By the end of the day, McClellan had worked himself into a lather, complaining that general in chief was either "a *dotard* or a *traitor*" and in either case "entirely unequal to the emergency." The old general must go, McClellan wrote Nelly, or he would resign. He had not slept for three nights, he told her, and thought that only providence could prevent the Confederates from attacking.[6]

Quickly Scott bestirred himself and fired off an angry response—not to McClellan, but to Secretary of War Cameron. He could only wonder why the young general had not presented his views "in person" but then sharply observed that McClellan had often avoided meeting with him. Scott bristled at McClellan's opinion, "propagated in high quarters," that Washington stood in "imminent danger." Then, referring to his infirmities in detail, the general in chief asked to retire. McClellan thought his own letter had "thrown a bombshell that has created a perfect stampede in the cabinet," but Lincoln was in no mood for a stampede. Disheartened by the controversy, the president pressed him to withdraw his letter. With ill grace, McClellan defended it as a heartfelt assessment of a dangerous situation but was "willing to suffer whatever may be required" to "abstain from any word or act that could give offense to General Scott or embarrass the President." But instead of writing a separate note to Scott, McClellan simply sent along a copy of the letter he had written to Lincoln. "This slight was not without its influence on my mind," Scott huffily remarked. The general in chief welcomed a visit from the president, who tried to smooth things over, but Scott would not rescind his resignation. Instead, he complained that McClellan had been conspiring with the cabinet and had failed to consult him about important matters. Standing on his dignity and position as commanding general of the U.S. Army, Scott refused to resort to "filing daily complaints against an ambitious junior." The key word here was "ambitious," a quality that McClellan exhibited in spades, and one that was hardly absent in Scott or Lincoln.[7]

The president did not accept Scott's resignation, but this only left the old general in a kind of limbo. McClellan deemed Scott a "dangerous antagonist," which vastly overstated the case because Scott lacked both the energy and desire to truly thwart him. Scott could advance the career of Major General Henry W. Halleck (whom he preferred to be the next general in chief) but not much more. Then, too, by dealing so closely with the cabinet and eventually with members of Congress, McClellan left the impression that he had become the indispensable leader who would crush the rebellion. He was even quoted as saying that the war would prove "short, sharp, and decisive."[8]

Yet how this laudable goal would be achieved was anyone's guess. McClellan failed to share his plans with Scott or with anyone else. Even subordinates who expressed confidence in him noted how McClellan seemed always on the move but kept his own counsel. This very caution meant, as the sympathetic *New York Herald* reported, "that there is so much secrecy observed in all his movements that very little of the details is permitted to leak out." Yet surprisingly on August 17, Scott approved combining several military departments (as had been requested just nine days earlier) into a large Department of the Potomac under McClellan's command. Two days later there was a troop review with both Lincoln and Scott present. McClellan rode through the ranks as always, but Scott had to be helped out of his carriage by two officers. A young Massachusetts corporal noted the obvious contrast between Scott—"too old to command a large army composed of young men and officers"—and McClellan the dashing general.[9]

All these signs of activity fueled expectations that McClellan was preparing a campaign that would begin soon. "A few brief weeks must bring us to the opening of that much discussed 'fall campaign' which is to decide forever the destinies of the nation," one of Lincoln's secretaries wrote in another anonymous dispatch to a New York newspaper. "Stirring Events at Hand," a late August headline in the *New York Herald* proclaimed. McClellan, "that wonderful magician," had brought about "remarkable transformations and reforms." Twitting its great editorial rival, the *Herald* predicted that "Greeley will have no occasion to lose his patience and revive his war cry of 'On to Richmond' as an order to General McClellan." There was nothing very substantial on which to base such predictions, but newspapers paid attention to even the smallest signs of preparation or troop movements.[10]

Press snippets about reconnaissance missions in the Virginia countryside added to the anticipation of some forward movement. As is often the case, appearances were deceiving. "If Beauregard does not attack this week he is foolish," McClellan wrote the very day the *New York Herald* had raised expectations so high. Yet the general soon decided that the apparent delay by the Confederates now gave him more time to organize the cavalry and artillery; indeed, he thought that perhaps "the danger point is turned." Alternative moods of despair and confidence—often expressed in letters to Nelly—clearly belied the public image of the steady, hardworking commander. Yet for some time that image and the faith it inspired would persist. Reports soon appeared that both the officers and enlisted men had come to reflect the energy and confidence of their increasingly admired commander. The arrival of fresh regiments heartened McClellan, and newspaper dispatches described a force more than ready to meet the enemy. The gathering of such an army required time, the *Chicago Tribune* advised. "They [the antecedent here is indefinite] are making victories in advance."[11]

"The forests are being leveled, entrenchments thrown up and batteries erected," a New Yorker enthused. McClellan quickly decided to surround the capital with defensive works that would deter any attack from either the Virginia or Maryland side. Many years after the war, McClellan's chief engineer, John G. Barnard, recalled Lincoln commenting that fortifying Washington on the northern side was equivalent to God giving men breasts on the off chance they would one day have to nurse a baby, but at the time no one appears to have objected. Nearly fifty posts with over three hundred guns eventually ringed the city. Although this system would never really be tested, to contemporaries it appeared formidable.[12]

At this point, it seemed that McClellan's strategy, however ill-defined or understood, was winning the day. By September 1, the *New York Herald* reported, "within a few days General McClellan, in a single dash against the enemy, may do the work of a whole campaign." Should the Confederates now dare to attack, their forces would be utterly routed. By the middle of the month, a Vermont volunteer predicted that "the next general fight will settle the question and the war will be done." According to the recollections of a Wisconsin recruit, after a small skirmish near Lewinsville, Virginia, McClellan told some of the troops: "We've had our last retreat. We've met our last defeat."[13]

Yet the army would not be ready to advance before November, McClellan informed Nelly as his mood kept shifting. He ordered various commands to be in readiness to move, sent out the occasional scouting parties into northern Virginia, and even ascended in an observation balloon, but there was something schizophrenic about the seemingly frantic activity and continuous delays. A serenade at his headquarters one Friday evening prodded McClellan to finally show himself at a window and simply say, "I have my duty to do and cannot lose the time to acknowledge this compliment, if all the bands and all the people in Washington are in the street." Newspapers of various political stripes reported McClellan "organizing victory." Greeley's *Tribune* lauded the general's fine qualities and predicted that once McClellan struck his "one blow," this would "put an end forever to the struggle between Freedom and Slavery on this continent."[14]

Lincoln took note of all this activity, visiting regiments and joining McClellan for troop reviews. If the president himself could not attend, cabinet members often did. McClellan greeted soldiers warmly and adopted a common touch despite his reservations about the heavy reliance on volunteers. Both Frederick the Great and Napoleon had conducted such exercises, "A Waterloo Man" observed to a Washington newspaper. "You have no idea how the men brighten up now, when I go among them," McClellan exulted to his wife. "I can see every eye glisten." The men cheered wildly, and he thought Lincoln, too, enjoyed these affairs. For his part, the president made a decidedly mixed impression, cutting as he did a rather poor figure on horseback. Always dressed plainly, often in an ill-fitting and not entirely clean suit, he struck some observers as a very odd duck. But on a visit to Colonel Hiram Berdan's famous sharpshooters, Lincoln showed he knew how to handle a rifle—much to the soldiers' delight. His lack of pretension more than made up for any lack of military bearing. "There goes an honest man," one soldier remarked as Lincoln reviewed a Pennsylvania division.[15]

On such occasions, McClellan appeared in full uniform, riding his favorite mount, Dan Webster. A superb horseman, he presented quite a contrast to the comically awkward Lincoln, who appeared to be all arms and legs.[16] That the president and the general were such different men not only in appearance but also in personality deeply affected their dealings with each other—especially from the general's side. The enormous burden of being commander in chief with both his administration and the war in its infancy soon told on Lincoln's appearance and manner, not to mention his decisions. The president's mind was both logical and analytical, and while usually relying on his own judgment, early in the war he naturally enough deferred to the generals, including McClellan. Given his lack of executive and military experience, Lincoln was feeling his way away along and would have to learn some hard lessons in the process. The national crisis proved a great opportunity for leadership and the fulfillment of ambition, yet it threatened to overwhelm him.[17]

The gaps in understanding between presidents and generals are often considerable, but differences in temperament and McClellan's reticence as well as, to a lesser degree, Lincoln's own wariness made their relationship even more difficult. The president's sudden appearances at McClellan's headquarters annoyed the general. Lincoln himself seemed uncomfortable or distracted even among advisers he knew well, and despite all the storytelling and fits of laughter, there was always about the man an ineffable sadness as the bouts of melancholy never quite abated. Lincoln preferred listening to talking, and his unpretentious manner could be quite disarming, especially when he told homespun tales to avoid committing himself in difficult situations. Standing, the president could seem imposing but could never match the general for grace or dignity. Even Lincoln's censorious private secretaries granted that McClellan was personally attractive and could readily draw strangers into his orbit. There was about the general at this time, a careful observer noted, "an indescribable *air of success*" as if he were truly a man of destiny.[18]

But this apparent self-confidence proved deceiving. As historian Joseph Glatthaar has observed, McClellan struggled all his life with authority figures, from teachers to the president of the United States. Excessively sensitive and prone to detect slights in the most innocent comments, he had great difficulty seeing any situation from someone else's viewpoint. His personality showed occasional signs of paranoia, though any psychological analysis of a historical figure based on secondhand observations is at best a risky enterprise.[19] One problem, however, is that McClellan's words and actions certainly lent themselves not only to criticism but also to no end of speculation about his mental state.

On a broader level, civilian control of the military often leads to conflict between generals and politicians. In the fall of 1861, two obvious sources of friction were McClellan's secretiveness and the increasing public pressure for action. Even sympathetic newspapers began asking why the general had allowed the Confederates to linger so close to Washington. Estimates of enemy strength still gave him pause. On September 13, McClellan informed Cameron that the Confederates would soon take the offensive and claimed his army was outnumbered two to one. At the same time, the organization of his own forces would take more time, though he never said how much more, or explained all this to Lincoln. Yet at this point, any rumblings against the general were scattered and not especially serious, even among those who would soon become relentless critics.[20]

Reports of McClellan slowly gathering his forces indicated strength to some observers and fostered a belief that the army would soon vanquish the Rebels. Not at all concerned about the absence of any offensive movement, a Boston editor predicted that "when it shall become the policy of our leaders to advance, it [the Army of the Potomac] will be able to sweep all before it." According to William Howard Russell, an important sign of McClellan's "iron will" was that he would not move until his army had been fully equipped and well drilled, though whether this process would stretch northern patience to the breaking point remained an open question. Soldier confidence in Little Mac continued to grow, and even an order for Sabbath observance in the army and the general's attendance at church with several cabinet officers further increased public acclaim. For enlisted men, a McClellan order to supply hot coffee right after reveille (supposedly to guard against malaria) further showed that their commander cared about their welfare. Although some soldiers tired of the frequent troop reviews, a Minnesota chaplain compared the "enthusiasm" with which the men greeted McClellan to the French embrace of Napoleon. Scenes of McClellan gathering around the soldiers and offering encouragement further reinforced the image of an army and a commander cemented together with bonds of affection. A simple narrative now became embedded in the public imagination: McClellan had taken an army, demoralized by lax discipline and a stunning defeat, and had transformed it.[21]

At the same time, the general's organizational success raised expectations that he would soon take the field. By late September, several newspapers were predicting an "early advance" by the Army of the Potomac or even that a Confederate attack would produce a great Union victory, the crowning laurel of McClellan's career.[22]

The Civil War was a conflict rife with rumors; soldiers, civilians, and politicians often filled yawning gaps in reliable information with alarmist fears or wishful thinking. Given the scope of the conflict and issues involved, there was much impatience all around. Why did McClellan keep his headquarters in Washington rather than going into the field with his troops? As the general assembled a larger and larger force, why did it not move? Asked when the army was likely to advance, Lincoln could only deflect that question with a question: "Will you tell us the route to take to Richmond? We tried it at Manassas and found it like Jordan."[23]

Winfield Scott was not pushing McClellan into action and, in fact, clung to the wisdom of his Anaconda Plan. What the general in chief did worry about were continual breaches in the chain of command by McClellan and others. On September 16 Scott issued an order reinforcing proper procedures for junior officers communicating with superiors, up to and including the general in chief, the secretary of war, and the president. Rumor had it that McClellan failed to respect the old hero, though ironically newspapers quoted Scott as saying that McClellan would eventually become general in chief. On September 27, however, Scott "raised a row" with McClellan, who later congratulated himself on maintaining his "cool" but informed Nelly that if "war is declared—so be it. I do not fear him." Scott had naturally bristled over the fact that during a meeting with the president and several cabinet members, Seward had offered detailed information on the number of troops in and around Washington—information that had not been shared with the general in chief. The secretary and the Rebels, Scott remarked sarcastically, had been fully briefed; he had not. Cameron tried to defuse tensions by half-jokingly referring to Seward's meddlesome qualities. But Scott would not be calmed down so easily and, as the meeting was breaking up, remarked to McClellan: "You were called here by my advice. . . . When I proposed that you should come here to aid, not supersede, me, you had my friendship and confidence. You still have my confidence." This latest contretemps annoyed Lincoln, who said he "could not afford to let them [Scott and McClellan] disagree." But the two not only disagreed, they had become quite disagreeable.[24]

Little wonder Lincoln seemed testy. In early August, Confederates had seized Munson's and Upton's Hills southwest of Washington, and in late September there was occasional picket firing around Bailey's Crossroads. With his usual secrecy (though he apparently did inform Lincoln), McClellan planned to advance on the Confederate positions, but the Rebels left before he could do so. On September 28, the general and his staff crossed the Potomac and entered the abandoned works. Perhaps the enemy sought to lure McClellan into a trap, but expressions of confidence in the general persisted. "We believe Gen. McClellan is prepared for any emergency," Greeley's *Tribune* commented. "Every day adds strength to his columns."[25]

Preparation was of course McClellan' strong suit, but he was still not moving, and inaction eventually bred impatience. "The public spirit is beginning to quail," Attorney General Edward Bates feared. "Our people are weary of being kept always and every where upon the defensive." Still more pointedly, Postmaster General Montgomery Blair lamented to his father, "Lincoln himself begins to think he smells a rat." That two of the most conservative members of the cabinet sounded so exasperated suggested trouble ahead for McClellan. Newspapers might still talk of energetic planning by Scott, McClellan, various cabinet members, and the president, but there were precious few signs of any forward movement.[26]

Impatience ran in both directions. "I am becoming daily more and more disgusted with the administration," McClellan wrote Nelly in early October. He even mentioned resigning, but his main complaint was a lack of understanding from those in power: "No one seems able to comprehend my real feeling—that I have no ambitious feelings to gratify & only want to serve my country in its trouble, & when this weary war is over to return to my wife." He found planning for an advance against the Confederates "slow work" but blamed the Lincoln administration, for reasons never made clear. Countless hours in the saddle and an inability to delegate responsibility were wearing him down. Complaints about the administration filtered down to his staff, members of which reportedly engaged in their own jabs and jests aimed at the president.[27]

Much of this grousing, however, did not go beyond private conversations or capital gossip, and faith in McClellan remained strong in both the army and the press. By the beginning of October, expectations still ran high that the Army of the Potomac was about to rout the enemy. No defeat this time, one Vermonter declared, "McClellan will not run or allow the men to do so." The usual press reports about soldiers spoiling for a fight added to the sense of anticipation. The men understood that McClellan spent many hours riding about the camps and fortifications. Many had come to believe that they had a leader who would take care of them—uniforms, food, whatever was necessary to sustain body and soul.[28]

October proved to be a critical month for McClellan, not only with the army but also in dealing with the Lincoln administration, politicians in both parties, and the press. Reports of small movements or that the troops were about to drive in enemy pickets across the Potomac stirred speculation; perhaps the general just needed a few more regulars or a little more artillery. Yet the fine fall weather would surely not last much longer, and even as the government had seemingly given McClellan a free hand to organize an army and plan a campaign, anxiety and impatience increased.[29]

The seeds of doubt had not only been planted, they were beginning to sprout and would soon be growing. The thoughtful Massachusetts officer Wilder Dwight grounded his views in a philosophy about human nature: the great McClellan would likely prove fallible like anyone else. Dwight indeed worried that "the whole government" was "asleep." Some civilians meeting with McClellan marveled over the fact that a man who had accomplished so little had received so much adulation. A restiveness became apparent in the press, among the politicians, and even in the army, often expressed in astonishment that McClellan, with his ever growing divisions, had still not advanced against the enemy.[30]

Such critics, though as yet few in number, became convenient targets themselves. Had not the "On to Richmond" crowd caused the recent Bull Run defeat by hastening an ill-prepared army into combat? Some editors viewed signs of renewed impatience with McClellan as being cut from the same cloth. Sympathetic newspapers claimed that the general would resist political pressure and rescue the country from hasty and unwise counsels. Signs of energetic preparations in the army should satisfy the people that he knew his business and would advance only when he could win a decisive victory. If that argument was turning stale by this time, it nevertheless had staying power.[31]

Although the press had not yet gotten wind of the problem, conflict between Scott and McClellan had flared anew—and only a week after Lincoln had supposedly tamped it down. On October 4, the general in chief wrote to Cameron, referring to his earlier order about respecting the chain of command. Pointing out how he had welcomed McClellan's arrival in Washington, Scott again complained that his young subordinate had, from the beginning, communicated directly with the president and various cabinet members. Moreover, McClellan had ignored his order of September 16 and had communicated directly with Cameron at least twice and perhaps with Lincoln as well. At the same time, McClellan had failed to keep the general in chief informed about the numbers and positions of the troops in and about Washington. What recourse was there, Scott angrily inquired, when a "junior officer" showed such "persistent neglect and disobedience"? McClellan attributed any problems to Scott's jealousy and amazingly told Nelly that he had always treated the old general with respect.[32]

On the surface, matters appeared to go on as they had been for some time. Lincoln, McClellan, Seward, and on one occasion even Mary Lincoln continued to review troops and visit various headquarters. McClellan sounded impressed by both the size and condition of his forces. Even as the weather turned cooler, the cheering troops warmed the general's heart, though his long days made him increasingly tired.[33]

Part of his weariness may have stemmed from too frequent contact with the president of the United States. Lincoln liked to drop in on McClellan, sometimes at night. On occasion, an aide would tell the president that the exhausted general was lying down and could not be disturbed. Sometime in early October both William Howard Russell and Lincoln called on McClellan only to be told that the general had gone to bed. Lincoln had come wearing a "navvy's cap, and an ill-fitting shooting suit, from the pockets of which protruded paper and bundles." He had breezily asked one of McClellan's staff, "Is George in?" Such informality had irked the young McClellan at West Point, and the president's often careless appearance ran headlong into the general's strong sense of propriety. Occasional attendance at cabinet meetings proved equally trying. After many hours in the saddle on October 9, McClellan had to spend an evening with the cabinet. "Bored and annoyed," he dismissed Lincoln's counselors as "some of the greatest geese . . . I have ever seen—enough to tax the patience of Job." But McClellan's reactions could also swing in the opposite direction. The following evening Lincoln, Seward, and Hay descended on McClellan's headquarters. The general appeared greatly pleased with all that had occurred that day and seemed unusually voluble. The president, too, appeared relaxed and cheerful. As they were all leaving, McClellan said: "'I think we shall have our arrangements made for a strong reconnaissance about Monday to feel the strength of the enemy. I intend to be careful, and do as well as possible. Don't let them hurry me, is all I ask." Lincoln's reply was direct and sympathetic: "You may have your own way in the matter I assure you." For a time, McClellan appeared to at least tolerate if not always welcome seeing the president. On October 16, after a brief visit from Lincoln and Seward, he described how his callers had "nothing very particular to say" but instead told stories, "which were as usual pertinent & some very good." Still thinking the president a rather odd fellow, McClellan nevertheless appeared to be warming toward him: "I never in my life met anyone so full of anecdote as our friend Abraham—he is never at a loss for a story apropos of any known subject or incident."[34]

Lincoln's young secretaries Hay and Stoddard continued to write anonymous articles for the newspapers, chastising impatient on-to-Richmond editors while praising the energy and discipline of Little Mac's troops. Stoddard reported McClellan "full of confidence" and "eager, when the right time comes, to wipe out forever the disgrace of our one great battle." McClellan still kept any plans to himself, as generals, junior officers, and the newspapers remarked—albeit largely with approval. His caution received more praise than criticism. He would later claim that the army at this point lacked the "discipline, organization, and equipment" necessary for offensive operations; by mid-October, he reportedly had fewer than 50,000 men available for an advance against the enemy.[35]

McClellan apparently still thought the Confederates might attack. By this time, Pinkerton was presenting his first estimates of enemy numbers—nearly 100,000 opposing the Army of the Potomac a detailed October 4 report claimed. Pinkerton was honest in his assessments, offering some useful information on the composition of Confederate forces, but badly miscounted the number of regiments and troops. McClellan certainly believed these estimates (and at times further inflated them).[36]

The combination of careful preparation and secret planning reflected McClellan's ideas about what it meant to be a military professional. These views had long clashed with the nation's democratic ethos, and the tension would only grow during what Lincoln called this "people's contest." Even as a young soldier, McClellan had been wary of political meddling in military affairs, a feeling that intensified during his early months in Washington. Only days after a cordial meeting with Lincoln and Seward, the general again railed against Washington politicians, especially the cabinet. "I can't tell you how disgusted I am becoming with these wretched politicians," he informed Nelly.

> They are a most despicable set of men & I think Seward is the meanest of them all—a meddling, officious, incompetent little puppy—he has done more than any other one man to bring all this misery upon the country & is one of the least competent to get us out of the scrape. The Presdt is nothing more than a well meaning baboon. Welles is weaker than the most garrulous old woman you were ever annoyed by. Bates is a good inoffensive old man—so it goes—only keep these complimentary opinions to yourself, or you may get me into premature trouble.

In some ways, McClellan might have felt more at home in the Prussian army, whose officers during this time sought to steer clear of politics. Yet even if he shunned politicians as much as he claimed, after the campaign in western Virginia, he had become if not exactly a political figure, at least a person of great importance to Republicans and Democrats alike. By early October, the comte de Paris observed that Democrats hoped to impose a conservative stamp on Union war policy, while McClellan—a prewar Democrat—had already become suspect to some Republicans.[37]

McClellan's early visits to Congress and extensive press coverage inevitably dragged him into the political arena. From Washington to Illinois, politicians weighed not only the military merits but also the political prospects of McClellan (and the Radical Republican favorite, Major General John C. Frémont). The sharp-eyed (and sharper-tongued) Polish expatriate

Adam Gurowski feared that the general had fallen "under the fatal influence of rampant pro-slavery men" such as McClellan's old New York friend S. L. M. Barlow. Reports of politicians swarming around the general's headquarters (however overblown) hardly lacked foundation.[38]

This political speculation occurred just as McClellan was finally about to launch a cautious thrust against the enemy. His forces were advancing a couple miles a day into the northern Virginia countryside, and for once the general acted too precipitously. On October 19, McClellan sent McCall's brigade on a reconnaissance mission toward Dranesville, hoping that this would cause further Confederate withdrawals from the area around Leesburg. The following day, he ordered Brigadier General Charles P. Stone to scout out Leesburg and see how the Rebels responded, suggesting that a "slight demonstration on your part would have the effect to move them." Stone reported enemy pickets scrambling back to their entrenchments and claimed to have the "means of crossing 125 men once in ten minutes at each of two points [along the Potomac]." Meanwhile, McCall was leaving Dranesville, though Stone apparently thought that the Pennsylvanian's brigade remained nearby in support, and McClellan never informed him otherwise. Further reconnaissance on October 20 led Stone to conclude that few Confederates remained at Leesburg. He sent Colonel Edward D. Baker, an Oregon senator and old Illinois friend of Lincoln's, to Harrison's Island; his troops then crossed the river at Ball's Bluff but quickly came under attack, and Baker was killed.[39]

Word of Baker's death hit Lincoln hard. He received the news at the War Department telegraph office and later emerged with hands clasped on his chest and his head down as if carrying an enormous weight. Sleep would not come, and Lincoln walked the floor during much of the night. The next day McClellan broached the subject of Baker's death in an odd way. He advised Lincoln: "There is many a good fellow that wears the shoulder-straps going under the sod before this thing is over. There is no loss too great to be repaired. If I should get knocked on the head Mr. President you will put another man immediately in my shoes." These awkwardly phrased sentiments hardly struck the right note and, in fact, put the focus on McClellan. Lincoln responded by simply telling him to "take care of yourself." McClellan did not attend Baker's funeral, where the still disconsolate Lincoln openly wept.[40]

More than a week later, McClellan presented his version of the Ball's Bluff encounter to Cameron, briefly outlining how he had never authorized Stone or Baker to attack the enemy or cross the river. Yet McClellan had given Stone discretionary instructions, and his own flawed understanding of the geography and the distribution of various forces contributed to this small but stunning defeat. Ball's Bluff likely reinforced his cautious tendencies and made him more resistant to political pressure for offensive operations. He blamed the "disaster" on Baker and exonerated Stone. "Well," McClellan sarcastically commented about this time, "so far we seem to have applied a new maxim of war, always to meet the enemy with an inferior force at the point of attack."[41]

"The Result Satisfactory to McClellan" read the headline in the *Chicago Tribune,* which claimed that Confederate casualties far exceeded Union losses (the reverse was true). McClellan himself sounded weary and irritated. To Nelly, he bemoaned the "terrible butchery" while denying any responsibility: "the whole thing took place forty miles from here without my orders or knowledge." Friendly newspaper correspondents even reported that Scott had ordered Stone to cross the river. But doubts about McClellan's leadership began to grow. Major Rutherford B. Hayes of the 23rd Ohio Infantry sneered that perhaps "West Pointers are no better leaders than volunteers." A Pennsylvania volunteer considered McClellan the "author" of the "blunder" at Ball's Bluff but also blamed Lincoln for being "either too blind to see them [the mistakes of his generals] or too weak to remove those who make them." Carrying such critiques a step further, abolitionist orator Anna Elizabeth Dickinson charged McClellan with "treason."[42]

Few would go that far, but Lincoln's personal secretary Hay acidly remarked that McClellan "had no plan or the slightest idea of what Stone was about." Whether "the Tycoon" (as Hay often referred to Lincoln) shared his young protégé's views is not clear, but certainly from this period on, Hay would have little good to say about McClellan. A reconnaissance toward Fairfax Court House, vague reports of Confederate movements, and rumors that the Rebels had been tipped off about the Army of the Potomac's recent operations all clouded the strategic picture—as did several days of bad weather. Perhaps the enemy was stronger than had been thought, a notion that surfaced in the press and likely in McClellan's mind as well. Yet predictions of a rapid advance and great victory still circulated; the *New*

York Herald forecast, "a Waterloo defeat awaits the arms of the Southern confederacy."[43]

McClellan's approach to the war (and to the enemy) remained conservative. His troops would not advance, the general said repeatedly, until they were disciplined enough to respect civilian property. The army would not degenerate into a band of marauders and brigands. On October 1, he had cited "depredations of an atrocious character" but claimed that such "outrages" against civilians and their property never received "the sanction of the mass of the army" and promised that any future plundering would be severely punished.[44] Even at this early stage, however, a goodly number of the men likely believed that protecting Rebel property was, in soldier parlance, "all played out." Whether McClellan's orders deterred foraging or even outright theft is difficult to say, though many of the volunteers probably did shy away from wanton destruction.[45] Even so, reports of McClellan's supposedly tender approach toward the Rebels and their property (along with various delays and the fallout from Ball's Bluff) were exacting a political cost.

Like many northern politicians and the public more generally, the Radical faction of the Republican Party had at first welcomed McClellan's rise to command. In August, Senator Charles Sumner of Massachusetts had dubbed him "a greater soldier than any, on this Continent, and as a strategist unsurpassed." By October, however, the Radicals' displeasure was palpable, and McClellan's entire approach to the war had become a source of considerable frustration if not anger. Senator Wade, one of the more volatile and opinionated members of what Hay termed the "Jacobin club," had come to doubt that the Lincoln administration ("blundering, cowardly, and inefficient") was up to the task of putting down the rebellion. "You could not inspire Old Abe, Seward, Chase, or Bates with courage, decision, and enterprise with a galvanic battery," the Ohioan fumed. Lincoln seemingly had no plan to win the war, and traitors supposedly "lurked" in several government departments. Giving way to unbridled frustration, Wade even suggested it might be best if the Rebels captured Washington along with the president and cabinet. As for McClellan, he seemed to "have adopted the maxim of the old woman who laid it down that 'all boys should learn to swim well before they went into the water,' so the General is determined his troops shall all be veterans before he permits them to come under fire."

Senator Chandler of Michigan, agreed, adding that McClellan "seems to be devoting himself to parades and military shows instead of clearing the country of Rebels."[46]

Matters came to a stormy head only days after the Ball's Bluff fiasco on October 25, when Wade, Chandler, and Senator Trumbull of Illinois met with McClellan at Postmaster General Blair's house. The senators pressed for a move against the Confederates, but after a three-hour discussion that dragged on past midnight, the only conclusion reached was that Scott had to go and McClellan should take his place. Wade dismissed the president as a "fool" controlled by Seward, "a coward and a sneak," and feared that the cabinet favored the army going into winter quarters. McClellan responded (rather disingenuously) that he could accomplish nothing so long as Scott remained in place and that he now faced a Confederate force of over 200,000 men, a claim repeated in subsequent meetings with other senators, including Andrew Johnson of Tennessee. The following day McClellan told the president that Wade had said he preferred a defeat to inaction and had even coldly stated that any losses would be readily replaced with "swarming recruits." Lincoln recommended taking the political pressure into account but told McClellan not to "fight until you are ready." With his usual penchant for melodrama, the general replied: "I have everything at stake. If I fail I will not see you again or anybody."[47] Such histrionics reflected his ambition and insecurity, in the process revealing no little self-absorption.

That same day, Wade, Chandler, and Trumbull called on Lincoln, who defended McClellan as the three senators wildly threatened to cut off both money and men if the army did not advance soon. The confab did not break up until around midnight. The government was wasting its superior resources, Chandler feared, and northern men now stood before all the world as "deficient in courage." He later told a political friend back in Michigan that Lincoln was "timid and weak" and that, even more remarkably, if the Army of the Potomac would simply take the offensive, the war "could end in a day." On Sunday, the twenty-sixth, Hay and the president dropped in on Seward. Chandler and Wade were there, haranguing the secretary of state on the need for a battle; Hay thought they talked a good deal of "trash."[48] The administration seemed increasingly on the defensive, the public increasingly impatient, and McClellan increasingly under pressure to take the field.

Then, too, some objections to McClellan extended well beyond disagreements over military strategy. The Radicals clearly preferred Frémont, whose military prowess was questionable but whose antislavery credentials were impeccable. According to the comte de Paris, it was supporters of Frémont (and those, like Scott, who were jealous of McClellan's rapid rise) who "kept up the party rancor against the general." By McClellan's account—details are sketchy and the date uncertain—he had bluntly informed Sumner (and apparently other Republican senators) that despite viewing slavery as a great evil (especially for white southerners), he objected to any general emancipation "unless accompanied by arrangements providing for the new relations between employers and employed." This apparent lack of concern for the enslaved must have alarmed the Massachusetts Radical, who in any case had no desire to discuss the future of free labor. McClellan favored some gradual form of emancipation. Yet even though his troops were no longer returning fugitive slaves, the general hardly seemed a friend of freedom. With a singular lack of finesse, McClellan said he had no interest in fighting for emancipation or the Republican Party and claimed the Radicals failed to understand the cost of carrying out schemes that rested largely on sentimentality and partisanship.[49]

Such impolitic statements could only harm McClellan's standing with Republicans and perhaps the Lincoln administration because, on military matters, opinion had not yet turned against him. Many newspapers, including Republican ones, disparaged McClellan's impatient detractors. Armchair critics knew little about the condition of the army, several editors remarked, and appeared to be following the script that had led to the Bull Run debacle. Some accounts echoed accusations of a conspiracy against McClellan that circulated among the general's staff.[50] Whatever doubts they were starting to have, neither the president nor his advisers had turned against McClellan. One of Lincoln's secretaries wrote an anonymous newspaper piece reporting "the most perfect *entente cordial* between McClellan and the Administration." Lincoln himself asked McClellan to join him in reviewing some new "repeating guns, on wheels," but the general begged off. Reports appeared that on military strategy and more specifically the timing of any offensive action in Virginia, the president and his general remained on the same page.[51]

McClellan would have disagreed. In his mind at least, Lincoln sometimes seemed as impatient as Wade or Chandler. The general later claimed to have shared his thinking and plans in frequent conferences, though at the time he had grown tired of the president dropping in at his headquarters and now confided few details to Lincoln or anyone else in the administration. At the end of October, the president asked for a report on the condition of the Army of the Potomac (and at least by implication on the timing of any forward movement). McClellan obliged with a lengthy letter to the secretary of war. He began by pointing out that on several occasions he had "stated the force I regarded as necessary to enable this Army to advance with a reasonable certainty of success." The choice had now become either to go into winter quarters or to advance against the enemy "with forces greatly inferior in numbers"—that is, compared to those McClellan considered "desirable and necessary." Presenting the alternatives in this way stacked the deck by justifying further caution, if not inaction. However that might be, with a glancing blow aimed at Scott, McClellan deplored the lack of unity in command and the failure to concentrate forces on the war's primary theater in Virginia. In contrast, the general claimed that Confederates had deployed some 150,000 men against him, and it would be necessary to match these numbers in the field while safeguarding the Potomac line and Washington. More precisely, he would require some 208,000 men, estimating that presently he had no more than half the force necessary for an offensive in Virginia. The goal all along had been to "enable the Army of the Potomac to assume successfully this season . . . offensive operations." This would involve overpowering the Confederate forces around Manassas, a plan that fit in with his overall strategy of defeating the enemy with overwhelming strength in one great effort to bring the war to a successful and speedy end.

Then, in an odd change of tone and subject, McClellan boasted of having sacrificed his financial interests to fight in the country's cause. Perhaps wishing to allay any worries about possible political aspirations, he promised—once the rebellion had been defeated, of course—to "return to the obscurity from which events have drawn me."[52] These personal references along with their self-pitying tenor if anything drew attention to McClellan's ambitions and perhaps had just the opposite of the effect intended. He still tried, albeit inconsistently, to divorce strategic questions from political ones, but that ill prepared him to deal with the complexity, delicacy, and messiness of civilian-military relations in this or any modern war.

McClellan had spent much of October 31 working on this lengthy document, holed up in Stanton's house on K Street, "concealed" there to "dodge all enemies in the shape of a 'browsing' Presdt, etc." Fed up with the frequent tête-à-têtes with Lincoln, he groused about the "set of scamps" who demanded so much attention and worried that the administration intended to "throw whatever blame there is on my shoulders." Having grown sick of such dealings, he could not resist firing off a broadside against Lincoln and the cabinet: "It is terrible to stand by & see the cowardice of the Presdt, the vileness of Seward, & the rascality of Cameron—Welles is an old woman—Bates is an old fool. The only man of courage & sense in the Cabinet is Blair, & I do not altogether fancy him." As was often the case when writing to Nelly, his frustration had boiled over. McClellan felt "thwarted & deceived by these incapables at every turn." He had done everything in his power "to get ready to move before winter sets in—but it now begins to look as if we are condemned to a winter of inactivity." In any case, the fault "will not be mine—there will be that consolation for my conscience, even if the world at large never knows it."[53]

At least Scott would no longer stand in his way. The dispute between McClellan and the general in chief had never entirely abated and finally came to a head. In mid-October, McClellan had "determined to force the issue" because Scott leaned toward "inaction & the defensive." Old Fuss and Feathers appeared to "cripple me in every way" while the newspapers "begin to accuse me of want of energy." Scott reportedly complained about McClellan and Seward scheming privately and ignoring him altogether. Lincoln's frustration with the inability of his two generals to work together became increasingly apparent, and Hay thought the president even showed signs of unusual petulance on the very day he read to the cabinet a draft letter acceding to Scott's wish to retire. By October 19, McClellan had received word that he would become general in chief, news that inevitably leaked to the press. Several newspapers reported a supposed plot by Scott and his allies (jealous of all the public praise heaped on McClellan) to make Halleck the new general in chief. Hay denied such speculation in a dispatch to the *Saint Louis Republican,* writing that McClellan looked upon Scott with "filial love and respect," even claiming that Little Mac favored bringing Halleck east for some large command.[54]

Seward's alter ego and political henchman Thurlow Weed feared that all the stories of conflict between Scott and McClellan had become "damaging," and he largely blamed the younger general. As for McClellan, he detected a great popular uprising against Scott in which both officers and enlisted men "declare that they will fight under no one but me." He wanted to be loved by the troops and reveled in any displays of affection. "I ought to take good care of these men, for I believe they love me from the bottom of their hearts," he informed Nelly. "I can see it in their faces when I pass among them." He plainly anticipated taking on greater responsibility. On November 1, the cabinet met in the morning, and Lincoln presented the order retiring Scott. In the afternoon, the officials visited Scott's quarters, and the president made what Attorney General Bates termed a "neat and feeling address." Lincoln was somewhat confused about whether there was even such a position as general in chief, but Bates assured him that the general in chief was "only your lieutenant." According to the attorney general's diary, "it was agreed that Genl. McClellan should succeed Scott," but there was no mention of how the matter was discussed or the decision made.[55]

McClellan had finally gotten rid of his nemesis but still saw "difficulties in my path." He deplored "the impatience of the people, the venality & bad faith of the politicians, the gross neglect that has occurred in obtaining arms, clothing, etc." To Nelly, however, he also sounded a note of humility leavened with a Presbyterian view of providence: "I feel in my innermost soul how small is my ability in comparison with the gigantic dimensions of the task, & that, even if I had the greatest intellect that was ever given to man, the result remains in the hands of God. I do not feel that I am an instrument worthy of the task, but I *do* feel that I did not seek it—it was thrust upon me." He nevertheless believed, "my previous life seems to have been unwittingly directed to this great end." Later McClellan remarked that he could not "discover in my own heart one symptom of gratified vanity or ambition."[56] The lack of self-awareness or at least forthrightness was stunning.

If McClellan remained at this point reticent about his plans, Lincoln remained mostly reticent about his general. Each was coming to view the other warily. On the night of November 1, the president, accompanied as was often the case by his secretary Hay, paid McClellan a visit. The general had drafted an order announcing Scott's retirement and his own assumption of command. Lincoln thanked him but then added, "I should be perfectly satisfied if I thought that this vast increase of responsibility would not embarrass you." McClellan expressed "relief" that the change had been made. The president hoped the general would "draw on me for all the sense I have, and all the information. In addition to your present command, the supreme command of the army will entail a vast labor upon you." McClellan responded in a low voice, "I can do it all." Whether this reassured Lincoln seems doubtful. After taking his leave, the president strolled over to Seward's house for a long discussion. Hay thought Lincoln had given "a grave and fatherly lecture" to McClellan that "was taken in good part, advising him to enlarge the sphere of his thoughts and feel the weight of the occasion."[57] Had Lincoln and McClellan really understood each other, or had they instead sown more seeds for future confusion and conflict?

4

THE GENERAL IN CHIEF AND THE COMMANDER IN CHIEF

AT LAST THERE was resolution, or at least the appearance of one. On November 1, 1861, President Lincoln announced the retirement of Winfield Scott and directed that "Maj. Gen. George B. McClellan assume the command of the army of the United States." In his own general order, McClellan struck the proper notes of patriotism, duty, humility, and confidence: "In the midst of the difficulties which encompass and divide the nation, hesitation and self-distrust may well accompany the assumption of so vast a responsibility; but confiding as I do in the loyalty, discipline, and courage of our troops, and believing as I do that Providence will favor ours as the just cause, I cannot doubt that success will crown our efforts and sacrifices." With a diplomatic touch, he added two paragraphs lauding Scott's military service and praising the Virginia-born general's unswerving loyalty to the Union.[1]

On November 2, McClellan rose at four in the morning and, in the middle of a downpour, mounted up with a cavalry squadron to escort Scott to the train depot. The two men exchanged generous compliments, McClellan once again gave the old general his arm (as he had weeks earlier during the party at the White House), and he accompanied Old Fuss and Feathers to the cars. McClellan found the departure for New York a touching scene, but his description turned the focus on himself: "It may be at some distant day I too shall totter away from Washn," he told Nelly. "The sight of this morning was a lesson to me which I hope not soon to forget. I saw there the end of a long, active & ambitious life . . . & it was a feeble old man scarce able to walk—hardly any one there to see him off. . . . Should I ever become vainglorious & ambitious remind me of that spectacle." Of course, McClellan could be both vainglorious and ambitions, and his wife hardly discouraged those qualities. He could afford to sound a note of grace toward Scott, whom he had long treated with condescension, flattery, or contempt. Much of this was hidden from public view, and press accounts emphasized the more moving and emotional elements of the occasion. Newspapers quoted Scott as advising his young protégé to resist undue pressure and act according to his own best judgment. For his part, McClellan responded with deep gratitude and appeared convinced that Scott thought him to be "the best man & the best General that ever existed!" He apparently believed that once again the old man had succumbed to his winning charm and insincere praise.[2]

McClellan now had a much greater burden of responsibility with one less excuse for delay or inaction. Even the friendly *New York Herald* observed that it was now up to "General McClellan to show himself worthy to wear the mantle which has fallen on his shoulders." He remained in the eyes of skeptics an untested general. Wishful thinkers read their own assumptions and preferences into his words and actions: some thought the Army of the Potomac was sure to advance, others saw winter quarters in the offing. Opinion among the officers and enlisted men appeared divided, and there was evident jealousy and tension between the regulars and the volunteers.[3]

Hopefulness still held sway in many quarters. Perhaps McClellan's taking the reins would discourage importunate editors and politicians from pressing too hard for a premature offensive. With McClellan in charge, divided counsels would presumably no longer be a problem. Seward (despite his own apparent skepticism about McClellan's ascension) hosted a cabinet dinner honoring the new general in chief. Little Mac now seemingly had a free hand, and John Hay even penned a newspaper piece not only claiming that the Lincoln administration and McClellan were in perfect agreement on policy but also emphasizing that the president and cabinet would not force the general in chief into advancing before the army was ready. Another of Lincoln's secretaries, William Stoddard, wrote that McClellan's youth provided the "strength necessary for the work before him."[4]

According to McClellan's old New York friend Sam Barlow, a member of the general's staff had said that an offensive would begin before the end of November. Some observers—including Republican senator Trumbull of Illinois—appeared to have more confidence in McClellan than in the president or the cabinet. There would now be no more delays, one editor predicted. "The war cannot be long. It may be desperate," was a McClellan statement repeatedly quoted in the camps and in the press. When a crowd gathered around the secretary of war's house one evening, Cameron proclaimed that the government had plenty of guns, money, and men. As for McClellan, "he has settled matters for future victory."[5]

The general's career and reputation had reached its apogee. On November 3, a delegation representing the city council of Philadelphia presented him with a ceremonial sword, the hilt of which was set with pearls and diamonds. In brief remarks, McClellan requested "forbearance, patience, and confidence." This would not be the last time he would ask the northern people to exhibit such qualities. But for the moment, he remained the toast of the capital, whom many still hoped would become the war's great hero by decisively defeating the Confederates and bringing the rebellion to a speedy close. A little over a week after the sword presentation, Brigadier General Louis Blenker's largely German brigade held a torchlight procession to honor the new general in chief. Other soldiers and civilians joined the festivities, which included fireworks along with red, white, and blue lights. After parading past Willard's Hotel and the White House (where Lincoln briefly appeared), the marchers stopped at McClellan's headquarters. Blenker, an immigrant Forty-Eighter, jokingly told the crowd he would surely fight the enemy more readily than he spoke their language. William Seward also appeared, praising the volunteers and telling the throng that they now had the general they had so long desired. Despite loud calls for a speech, McClellan would do no more than bow politely.[6]

Certainly, all seemed to be going well for the young general. On October 12, Nelly had given birth to a daughter, Mary, and McClellan acquired a spacious house for them all on the corner of H and Fifteenth Streets—a residence once owned by presidential widow Dolley Madison. William Howard Russell remarked that the McClellans "were awfully in love with each other." The general's brother Arthur and his father-in-law, Randolph Marcy (recently appointed McClellan's chief of staff), soon moved in. Nelly's recovery from childbirth had been painfully slow, and McClellan impatiently awaited his wife and baby's arrival. It was not until early December that McClellan left Washington by train to bring Nelly, little Mary, and his mother-in-law to Washington.[7]

As was his wont, the general threw himself into his new duties. On the day of his appointment, McClellan toiled away for eighteen hours and was still writing to Nelly at one the following morning. He now frequently ate at his desk. McClellan continued to ride about inspecting his forces and examining everything from artillery pieces to pontoon bridges. One evening the general took his staff on a ride that lasted some eight hours, until four the next morning—a feat widely reported in the press.[8]

Simply put, McClellan had become the military power in the land. Cameron reportedly remarked that the administration had had no choice because neither he nor the president knew much about military matters. Whether McClellan could serve as general in chief *and* command the Army of the Potomac remained uncertain; despite assuring Lincoln, "I can do it all," it soon became clear that he could not. Lincoln had promised not to hurry McClellan, but this did not prevent leading Republicans from hurrying Lincoln. Congress would "not allow the Army of the Potomac to winter" in Washington, Ben Wade warned. "Something, Mr. President, must be done. War must be made on the secessionists, or we will make war on the Administration."[9]

The task of simultaneously readying the Army of the Potomac and coordinating military operations elsewhere proved daunting and at times overwhelming. "I find the 'Army' just about as much disorganized as was the Army of the Potomac when I assumed command," McClellan complained. "Everything at sixes & sevens—no system, no order, perfect chaos." Not to worry, he promised Nelly, "I *can & will* reduce it to order—I *will* soon have it working smoothly." Perhaps so, but he quickly discovered that the general in chief's duties were ill defined. Even under the best circumstances, the relations between the general in chief and secretary of war were awkward, and Cameron failed to inspire confidence in anyone. Presumably, McClellan would plan strategy, and Cameron would supply the wherewithal. The War Department structure itself was antiquated and cumbersome, with seven bureau heads reporting to the secretary of war, each of whom McClellan had to cultivate to see that the armies' needs were met. So, he would have to bypass Cameron just as he had once bypassed Scott.[10]

Lincoln continued to visit McClellan almost daily, often at night and sometimes accompanied by Seward. Publicly the president remained patient and supportive even as he was anxious to learn about the general's plans. On one occasion, McClellan returned late from a daylong ride, felt unwell, and so begged off seeing Lincoln that evening. Typically, during such visits, the general listened quietly as Lincoln talked about the day's events or told stories. One time McClellan invited his staff and the president for a performance from a "great magician," who asked Lincoln for his handkerchief. "You got me now, I ain't got any" was the president's surprising response. One can only speculate whether the bad grammar or the absence of a handkerchief appalled the punctilious general more. Once, after the president had left at the end of a visit, McClellan remarked, "Isn't he a rare bird?" Lincoln was clearly sizing up his new general in chief, but McClellan came to see the constant scrutiny as pointless and annoying. His epithets directed against the president—some borrowed from Stanton—grew increasingly harsh. After one especially frustrating day in mid-November, he wrote to Nelly about conferring with the "original gorilla" at the White House and later that evening at Seward's home. "What a specimen to be at the head of our affairs now," he sniffed.[11]

Lincoln faced his own problems, including public impatience over the lack of military progress. Journalist Noah Brooks remarked on the president's alarming appearance: "His hair is grizzled, his gait more stooping, his countenance sallow, and there is a sunken, deathly look about the large, cavernous eyes, which is saddening to those who see there the marks of care and anxiety, such as no President of the United States has ever before known." Some Republicans showed fresh signs of irritation with the administration. "Lincoln means well but he has no force of character," Zach Chandler feared. "He is surrounded by Old Fogy Army officers more than half of whom are downright traitors and the other half sympathize with the South." The Michigan Radical and several other Republican senators had "raised an awful commotion" with McClellan and the president. Even Lincoln's old law partner Billy Herndon had grown frustrated, blurting out in his usual fashion, "Does he [Lincoln] suppose he can crush—squelch out this huge rebellion by pop guns filled with rose water?" For their part, McClellan's conservative supporters hoped the general could crush the insurgency and settle the whole matter in a broad and generous way that quickly brought repentant southerners back into the Union.[12]

All depended on carrying out a successful military strategy. That in turn rested on McClellan's ability to coordinate operations in various theaters, all the while commanding his own growing army at Washington. The new general in chief initially sounded as if he had worked out all the difficulties.

McClellan fancied himself a superb strategist and now occupied a stage suitable to his talents, though this may have provided more reasons for delaying the Army of the Potomac's advance against the Confederates.[13]

McClellan had reportedly said in October that by late November he would be advancing against Confederate forces around Manassas Junction. Yet Lincoln was also concerned about the Shenandoah Valley and even more adamant about the suffering Unionists of East Tennessee. Frank Blair Jr., brother of the postmaster general and member of the influential Blair clan, pressed for operations along the Mississippi River line, claiming this would be the best way to gain the most advantage at the least cost. So, McClellan hardly suffered from a shortage of advice. Sympathetic observers noted that a remarkably young man now occupied a position where competing expectations limited his options. Despite the importance of planning and logistics, Civil War generals won their reputations, for better or for worse, as battle captains, so for McClellan, the real test must come on the battlefield—and quickly.[14]

Historian Joseph Harsh once observed that students of the Civil War should pay more attention to McClellan's strategy and less attention to his personality, but the general's conservative politics and limited war objectives, however sound they might have appeared, were less than inspiring and increasingly less attuned to the public mood. The assignments of Major General Halleck and Brigadier General Don Carlos Buell to command in Missouri and in Kentucky, respectively, were consistent with such an approach and, for the time being, in line with Lincoln's own policy. Operating in the shadow of the Ball's Bluff debacle, unwilling to risk another stunning defeat with a more direct advance against Confederates in Virginia, and wary of a prolonged stalemate, McClellan favored a war of maneuver that included combined operations with the navy.[15]

After all, in McClellan's mind, his forces were still badly outnumbered. In late October, Allan Pinkerton had reported 80,000 Confederate troops around Centreville, Virginia, and McClellan pegged enemy strength in the entire state at 140,000. He would simply have to convince the administration and Congress of the need for more troops. But even cautious generals such as Nathaniel P. Banks wondered if some of these estimates were exaggerated. Returns on November 12 showed the Army of the Potomac at nearly 170,000 men, but of course a good number of these troops would have to remain in and around the Washington defenses. As historian Allan

Nevins has pointed out, McClellan still faced a shortage of good officers and in some cases arms and ammunition, yet the continuing Confederate presence along the Potomac proved harder to explain by the day. With regiments steadily arriving in the capital, it appeared that the time for a forward movement had come.[16]

"I am more anxious to advance than any other person in this country," McClellan informed his friend Sam Barlow. But he expected the war "to be decided by the next great battle" and so would not move until "I have reasonable chances in my favor." The Army of the Potomac—the strength of which "has been vastly overrated in public opinion"—could certainly defend the capital. But given the forces to be left in Washington, around Baltimore, and elsewhere, he could not yet match enemy numbers. Regardless of public pressure, he would continue to build up his army so that when "the blow is struck it will be heavy, rapid, & decisive." What would then follow, McClellan did not say, but Barlow expected this success would lead to peace negotiations, though he harbored doubts about the Lincoln administration being able to "profit from such a victory."[17]

McClellan and his staff—including the French princes—continued to ride about reviewing troops; on occasion Lincoln joined them. Even during a drenching rain on November 9, McClellan doffed his hat to greet the soldiers, and the men followed suit. A perceptive Michigan volunteer thought Little Mac realized how such a gesture caught the men's attention; a Massachusetts artillerist was impressed that McClellan looked him right in the eye.[18]

Inspections and drills still took up much of the men's duty hours, and discipline steadily improved. "Intemperance has been checked by vigorous measures," the *Chicago Tribune* reported approvingly. To the soldiers, McClellan very much looked the part of a commanding general; his ease on horseback and sheer stamina made a lasting impression. With the officers, his easy manner and facility for remembering names helped cement bonds of loyalty. The general's life-size portrait painted on the side of one of Thaddeus S. C. Lowe's gas-filled balloons symbolized McClellan watching over his army and paying attention to the smallest details.[19]

Even junior officers recognized their young commander's splendid opportunity to achieve great success and even greater renown. One captain figured that McClellan would hardly "risk his reputation" by going into winter quarters. Indeed, the continuance of good weather and dry roads through November and into December—as reported by McClellan's chief engineer, Barnard—made it ever harder to explain why the Army of the Potomac did not advance. The always suspicious Count Gurowski detected Scott's lingering influence, but McClellan also had to devote attention to the war's western commands, deciding that his army was not yet in "fit condition" for offensive operations.[20]

Prudence exacted a price. McClellan may have been correct in delaying an advance until spring, but he should have explained this to his generals and to the president. Public impatience (especially among Republican politicians) was both understandable and unavoidable. McClellan's changing views on strategy in Virginia and early consideration of transferring troops by water rather than moving overland against the Confederates around Centreville again may have made perfect sense, but he developed them largely without consultation. Secretary of the Navy Welles fretted that McClellan had no plan at all. A New York colonel and old political friend explained to Attorney General Bates that McClellan hoped to fight against a much smaller force in the spring, when many Confederate enlistments would have expired.[21]

McClellan ignored political pressure at his peril. He always claimed to be operating on the basis of purely military considerations, but this was not entirely true. Most of his critics (and likely some of his friends) were skeptical. First of all, despite the wishes of McClellan and many other conservatives, the slavery question would not go away. Both McClellan and Marcy are "strong proslavery men," an outraged New Yorker complained to Senator Chandler. Reports of him ordering the return of fugitive slaves not only incensed abolitionists but also worried many Republicans. As slaves flocked toward Federal lines, McClellan felt some sympathy for their plight:

> There is something inexpressibly mournful to me in that—those poor helpless ignorant beings—with the wide world & its uncertainties before them—the poor serf with his little bundle ready to launch his boat on the wide ocean of life he knows so little of. When I think of some of the features of slavery I cannot help shuddering. Just think for one moment & try to realize that at the will of the brutal master you & I might be separated for ever! It is horrible, & when the day of adjustment comes I will, if successful, throw my sword into the scale to force an improvement in the condition of these poor blacks.

He told Nelly that African Americans ought to have "some of the rights of humanity," yet he despised abolitionists, in part blaming them for the outbreak of war. Moreover, he asked his friend Barlow to help him "dodge the n——." To achieve a Union victory, "we cannot afford to raise up the negro question—it must be incidental & subsidiary. The Presdt is perfectly honest & is really sound on the n—— question—I will answer for it now that things go right with him."[22]

Barlow agreed that Lincoln's "sensible views" heartened northern conservatives, and he hoped that Radical Republican criticism would drive a wedge between the president and his party. But this question of partisanship, the fact that McClellan was increasingly seen as a Democrat, further weakened the general's position not only with the administration but also with a healthy section of the northern public. That his loudest supporters were also hostile to Lincoln and the Republicans inevitably thrust McClellan into the roiling politics of war. Some Democrats viewed him as a prospective presidential candidate, and their increasingly open support did him little good. Prominent Democrats reportedly gathered at his Washington headquarters to plot against the Lincoln administration. After spending a week with the general in Washington, Barlow informed one leading Democrat that McClellan was perfectly safe on the "great questions of the day" and that Stanton's views, too, remained "eminently sound & conservative."[23]

McClellan may have spoken to Barlow more openly and fully than was his custom, a quiet reticence being one of his most often observed traits. After being introduced by Lincoln, historian and Jacksonian Democrat George Bancroft found the general "silent, uncommunicative, [and] reserved." "He is one," Bancroft surmised, "who if he thinks deeply keeps his thoughts to himself." McClellan did much the same with his generals, who sometimes complained that their commander seldom discussed plans and strategy. He apparently stayed mum in part for fear of leaks, and he complained about sensitive information appearing in the newspapers.[24]

McClellan's reticence along with his shifting moods of exultation and exasperation became most apparent in his dealings with Lincoln. On one occasion, when Little Mac had kept him waiting, Lincoln simply said, "Never mind; I will hold McClellan's horse if he will only bring us success." On the evening of Blenker's torchlight procession, the president had walked over to see McClellan and suggested this might be a good time to probe the enemy. "I have not been unmindful of that," the general replied calmly. "We will feel them tomorrow." Hay noted how both men seemed "very jolly over the news."[25]

Two days later, however, on November 13, there occurred the notorious snubbing incident as told by Hay and recounted by many historians since. One problem with this is that Hay's diary is the only contemporary source, and Hay became decidedly hostile to McClellan. After the war while working with John Nicolay on their massive Lincoln biography, Hay wrote: "I think I have left the impression of [McClellan's] mutinous infidelity, and I have done it in a perfectly courteous manner. . . . It is of the utmost importance that we should seem fair to him, while we are destroying him." So his account may have been colored by his own views of McClellan, but the incident nevertheless deserves careful attention.

Lincoln, accompanied by Seward and Hay, had stopped by McClellan's house in the evening. A servant said that McClellan was attending a wedding; the visitors waited for an hour before his return. The general "without paying any particular attention to the porter who told him the president was waiting to see him, went up stairs." After waiting another half hour, they sent the poor servant to tell McClellan they were still there, but word came down that the general had gone to bed. Hay claimed that he had recorded this incident "without comment," but he did in fact describe it as an act of "unparalleled insolence" and a "portent of evil to come." He spoke about the incident to Lincoln, who "seemed not to have noticed it specially, saying it was better at the time not to be making points of etiquette & personal dignity." Some historians have suggested that McClellan had drunk a little too much that evening and did not feel up to speaking with the president, though there is no direct evidence on that score.[26] He was likely tired and perhaps annoyed by yet another unscheduled presidential visit. However that might be, the incident reveals McClellan's obliviousness to the demands of his new position and his relationship with the commander in chief. In his dealings with Lincoln, the general often did blow hot and cold, with his reactions ranging from bemused to angry. McClellan's mood swings from overweening self-confidence to deep despair likely contributed to the difficult relations with a president who suffered mood swings of his own.

Lincoln and McClellan continued to appear together on public occasions. On November 20, at Bailey's Crossroads, Virginia (eight miles from

Washington) an impressive review of troops (perhaps as many as 70,000 men) lasted for some five hours. An estimated 30,000 people had commandeered carriages, omnibuses, wagons, buggies, and horses to witness the spectacle. Bursts of cannon fire, the long lines of troops, and the appearance of dignitaries (including cabinet members and foreign ministers) made for an imposing display.[27]

McClellan, Lincoln, Seward, and Cameron, all on horseback and followed by a cavalry escort, passed rapidly along a semicircular line of troops stretching for some four miles; participants, spectators, and reporters alike described thunderous cheering, especially for Little Mac. Observers on Munson's Hill remarked on the strength of this mighty army, though this certainly proved to be a long, tiring day for the troops.[28]

McClellan was in full dress uniform and mounted on a fine horse, a Michigan lieutenant observed, "sitting up straight as an arrow, with hat in hand at a full gallop bowing & waving his hat." Lincoln on the other hand looked anything but comfortable: "one hand hold of the bridle, the other convulsively clutched in the mane of his horse which never relaxed its hold except for a moment to crowd his hat further down over his eyes. His long legs were well clasped around the body of the horse, his hair & coat tails horizontal. He looked as though he was determined to go through if it killed him but would be most almighty glad when it was over." A less critical Massachusetts artillerist simply thought the president seemed "careworn," a word soldiers incessantly used to describe him during the war. Lincoln, like McClellan, wanted to be seen, and certainly many a soldier wrote home about catching a glimpse of the president, whatever they might have thought of his horsemanship. McClellan's ease and grace presented quite a contrast: a Philadelphia reporter deemed him "one of the best horsemen in the country," while several soldiers described Lincoln as an awkward rider, one Pennsylvanian thought him a "miserable one." Much more charitably, Nicolay claimed the president "was more graceful in the saddle than anywhere else I have seen him," though perhaps that was a left-handed compliment.[29]

The whole affair "went off splendidly," McClellan thought, adding that he had never seen a military review in Europe done so well. He felt "delighted beyond expression," and no doubt the soldiers' cheers added greatly to his satisfaction. But then that might prove to be a liability because such a display of affection for McClellan could naturally provoke misgivings among the attending politicians, who decided to ride past the troops themselves and "not let the General get all the day's honors." Anyone reading the account in the *New York Times* would have concluded that McClellan was not only a man of formidable strength (the correspondent repeated the old story about Little Mac bending a coin double) but also a general whose tireless attention to detail and prudent wisdom inspired confidence.[30]

To some observers, too, the grand review at Bailey's Crossroads promised an imminent advance by the Army of the Potomac. There would presumably be no reason for such an elaborate review except as preparation for a forward movement. Speculation about the tight-lipped McClellan's plans might be just that, sheer speculation, a *New York Times* correspondent admitted, but that hardly stopped the exercise. Another correspondent predicted that within ten days there would be "an engagement along the whole line." Reports of this general or that naval officer conferring with McClellan fueled anticipation. But to fix an actual date when the Army of the Potomac was likely to take the field seemed beyond the knowledge of even the boldest editor.[31]

Impatient to learn of McClellan's plans and determined to prod him into action, Lincoln asked how long it would take to "make a forward movement of the Army of the Potomac, without awaiting further increase of numbers, or better drill & discipline." This carefully worded question presumably disposed of standard excuses for delay, and the president in fact offered a plan of his own. He proposed sending 50,000 troops forward to "menace the enemy at Centreville." Then two additional columns of troops (of unspecified strength) would cross the Occoquan River and sweep into the rear of the Confederate forces. This was the outline of a plan at least, though it said nothing about logistics or the difficulty of coordinating three separate forces. In the meantime, Lincoln praised McClellan in his annual message to Congress, even claiming that Scott had favored his elevation to general in chief. Remarkably enough, when asked by Commissioner of Public Buildings Benjamin Brown French why the Army of the Potomac did not move, Lincoln replied in words that could have easily come from McClellan's mouth: "If I were *sure* of victory we would have one at once, but we cannot stand a defeat, & we must be certain of victory before we strike."[32]

McClellan continued organizing his army and gathering information on the enemy. The superintendent of the census prepared a map of states that would likely see fighting, complete with statistics on the military-age population in each county and the number of slaves along with the locations of railroads, canals, and roads. Pinkerton offered intelligence on Confederate artillery positions; Chief Engineer Barnard reported good progress on the fortifications around Washington. McClellan pored over the scattered reports of Confederate troop strength, and the comte de Paris decided that Ball's Bluff had convinced the new general in chief to make even more meticulous preparations before launching a campaign.[33]

Where and when remained the key questions. For some weeks, McClellan had been considering a water route for an advance on the Confederate capital. Brigadier General Samuel Peter Heintzelman—certainly no fan of McClellan—favored a movement along the York and James Rivers that "would carry off a large portion of the Rebel army now at Centreville & Manassas." Belatedly responding to Lincoln's proposed Occoquan plan, McClellan remained vague about his own intentions: "I have now my mind actively turned towards another plan of campaign that I do not think at all anticipated by the enemy nor by many of our own people." He had apparently broached the idea of shifting his operations to a line along the Rappahannock, York, or James Rivers, but Barnard had doubts about carrying out the required preparations in secrecy and warned that Confederates might seize the opportunity to threaten Washington. One newspaper correspondent reported hopefully that McClellan would adopt a Scott-like strategy, which would "quell the rebellion by a mighty pressure, and not by a mighty slaughter."[34]

That would mean avoiding any direct attack on a numerically superior force, and McClellan remained convinced that he was outnumbered. Since October, Pinkerton had been sending agents into Virginia, including trips to Richmond, though their trustworthiness and even their loyalty came into question. There is also the possibility that Pinkerton inflated the numbers because he knew that would confirm McClellan's assumptions. Some operatives reported reasonably accurate estimates for Confederates forces around Manassas and Centreville, but others offered much higher totals.[35]

For McClellan, security made for additional worries. When the *New York Times* published a map showing federal fortifications and troop dispositions around Washington, the general exploded in anger and told Cameron that "this treasonable sheet" must be suppressed. The *Times* editor, moderate Republican Henry J. Raymond, claimed that the map had been copied from one widely available in Washington bookstores and denied that it revealed much about the Army of the Potomac. McClellan and Pinkerton remained anxious about newspapers gaining access to their telegrams or in other ways compromising necessary secrecy.[36]

At this point, skeptics might have asked if McClellan had any plans that required secrecy? Although the general still appeared to be hard at work, the army seemed likely to go into winter quarters. On an especially cold and windy day in early December, a Wisconsin surgeon pointed to the men freezing in open tents and wondered how long McClellan needed "for getting ready." Doubts about the general had begun to spread in the upper ranks. Cautious men such as Brigadier General George Gordon Meade were asking if Little Mac was up to the task, or even lacked "moral courage." Much less judiciously, Brigadier General Philip Kearny—who quickly became one of Little Mac's most vocal and voluble critics—might not yet think it was time for McClellan to go, but he harbored grave doubts about his military abilities and expressed even less faith in his political judgment. On the other hand, McClellan's friend Brigadier General Ambrose E. Burnside asked an importunate newspaperman if he could stomach the ten thousand casualties the Army of the Potomac would suffer if it tried to seize Manassas and advance on Richmond.[37]

The pressure on the general in chief was undeniable, and public discussion heated up even as the Union war effort appeared stalled. "Wise men," a Massachusetts artillerist noted with a strong note of sarcasm, had given up on McClellan. But the army's rank and file still thought "he is just the man to lead us to victory WHEN HE GETS READY AND NOT WHEN Horace Greely [*sic*] says go or any other n—— lover." Of course, Greeley was nothing if not erratic (in mid-December the *New York Tribune* still offered the general in chief some support), but McClellan partisans complained both publicly and privately that newspapers (and abolitionists) kept unfairly criticizing as well as spreading false reports about their hero. Barlow warned Stanton of a cabal in Washington including Secretary of War Cameron and several generals who had grown "very abusive." McClellan himself realized—at least after the fact—that Democrats rallying to his defense did no good, even a fair amount of harm.[38]

It was hard to say whether it was McClellan's dilatory strategy or his unsavory political associations that angered Republicans more. Rumor had it that the Blair family had swung over to the general's side, a sure sign of trouble for party stalwarts. As Congress came back into session at the beginning of December, a Republican caucus met to consider the war's progress and, perhaps more importantly, to vent grievances against the Lincoln administration and the more conservative elements in the party. Firebrand Representative Thaddeus Stevens of Pennsylvania wildly accused McClellan of trying to control both the executive and legislative branches of government.[39]

On December 10, in part as a reaction to the Ball's Bluff fiasco, Congress created the Joint Committee on the Conduct of the War, chaired by Ben Wade, one of McClellan's most relentless critics. Wade knew little about military affairs, nor did any of the other committee members, and most were suspicious of West Pointers and professional soldiers. Zach Chandler was just as strong a Radical as Wade and just as disparaging of McClellan. Representative John Covode of Pennsylvania proved to be an equally solid Radical and roughhewn. House member George Washington Julian of Indiana was a virtual abolitionist skeptical about Lincoln's performance. Not as partisan as his Republican colleagues, Representative Daniel W. Gooch of Massachusetts would prove to be a strong defender of the committee's work. Senator Johnson of Tennessee was a prototypical Jacksonian Democrat who had bravely resisted secession in his home state, thereby winning national acclaim. Compared to these more prominent and strong-willed members, Democratic New York representative Moses Fowler Odell seemed like a political cipher but did his work conscientiously and even got along with the Republicans. As the committee was being established, Senator Henry Wilson of Massachusetts pled with his colleagues to "remember that we have no men in America of military experience on anything like the scale on which they are now required to act," a sound assessment that would never carry much weight. If members of Congress seemed ill equipped to judge generals and strategy, that would hardly prevent them from doing so.[40]

Just as the committee was beginning to investigate military operations (and especially the Army of the Potomac), there landed on the desk of every member a pamphlet whose title well summed up its contents: *The Army of the Potomac, and Its Mismanagement.* Written by civil engineer Charles Ellet Jr., who would eventually command a ram fleet on the Mississippi River, the work started off by blaming McClellan for Ball's Bluff and for allowing Washington to be threatened by numerically inferior Confederate forces. According to Ellet, the general was in over his head and missing opportunities "for annihilating the rebellion in Virginia at a blow." Ironically, he suggested, the army had become too large for McClellan to handle. He proposed confining the general in chief to the Washington defenses and sending a more competent and energetic commander into the field. Until that happened, precious time and good weather were going to waste. While it would be easy to dismiss Ellet as a crank or to point out the dangers of goading the army into an offensive campaign, the pamphlet for all its eccentricities echoed steadily mounting criticism of McClellan.[41]

"Young Napoleon is going down as fast as he went up," one Hoosier scoffed. The dissatisfaction with McClellan "finds universal utterance," a Massachusetts congressman wrote. Even discounting such exaggerations, doubts about the general in chief were all too real. Before any testimony had been taken, some members of the joint committee were meeting privately with generals to share misgivings about McClellan.[42]

Repeating a well-worn caution, a *New York Times* correspondent worried about Congress forcing McClellan into an ill-advised offensive and even praised him for following a "line of policy fully approved by Gen. Scott before his retirement." How solid such support would be remained in doubt because Republican members of Congress had lost patience with the administration and with Lincoln. The president's fine personal qualities could not make up for an apparent lack of direction and backbone in managing the war. Bankers had reportedly threatened to stop lending money to the government.[43]

McClellan had repeatedly promised speedy action, but so far there had been barely any action at all, which made it hard for Lincoln to remain patient. The president appeared sympathetic to McClellan but puckishly suggested to one New York Republican that Congress should perhaps take a recess, and by the time the lawmakers reassembled, winter rains would have ended all talk of an early movement by the Army of the Potomac. It seemed that the administration would receive little help from either McClellan or congressional Republicans. Lincoln's old friend Joshua Speed feared that "a large and powerful party of the ultra men" would "make war upon the President and his conservative policy." Speed, who had become extremely conservative, harbored his own doubts about Lincoln's competence and energy. All the while, McClellan remained in the Washington limelight, cutting a dashing figure (along with the charming Nelly) during a mid-December levee at the White House. A *New York Herald* correspondent noticed the Lincolns and the McClellans in cordial and animated conversation, but for critics, action on the social scene only highlighted inaction on the military front. Uncertain how to deal with McClellan, Lincoln asked another conservative Illinois friend, Orville Hickman Browning, to call on the general in chief. In his diary, Browning lauded the good sense and pleasant manners of both McClellans, but that was not exactly what the president was looking for.[44]

McClellan's social visibility stood in marked contrast to the secrecy shrouding his military plans, which he still had not shared with the president. At this point, he was sketching out broad outlines for a movement of the Army of the Potomac by water for an advance on Richmond. Although reports by Barnard and the prince de Joinville offered little encouragement, McClellan remarkably enough had informed Secretary of the Treasury Chase that he wished to send 50,000 troops to Urbanna on the Rappahannock River. He would then advance on the Confederate capital before the Rebel forces around Manassas and Centreville could move to block his way. Rather than make a costly direct attack on the Confederate forces in his front, McClellan hoped his plan could end the war quickly with far fewer casualties. Nor did he intend to subjugate the Rebels, he confided to a War Department official, but rather to avoid "harshness and violence" by conducting the war along the conciliatory lines that he had favored ever since the campaign in western Virginia.[45]

William Howard Russell concluded—with his usual hyperbole—that only the president and the cabinet retained faith in McClellan, who now must "fight or resign." But in McClellan's mind there was still no great hurry, and despite all the political rumblings, obstacles remained. Pinkerton reported some 80,000 Confederate troops around Centreville (nearly double the actual number of "effectives"); a Philadelphia newspaper correspondent agreed with this estimate. Though administration sources still expressed confidence in McClellan (at least for public consumption), they did not sound entirely convincing.[46]

The army was clearly going into winter quarters, leaving both the president and his top general in a precarious position. Matters only worsened when, after a review of Fitz John Porter's division on December 21 (followed by a heavy rain), McClellan fell ill. Unable to go into the office, he conducted some business through subordinates, issuing several general orders, though the comte de Paris later wrote that his illness "paralyzed work at headquarters." Newspapers reported the general suffering from a severe cold (in fact both McClellan and his father-in-law had contracted typhoid fever). McClellan later wrote that he had been "very weak and ill" but that a "strong constitution enabled me to retain a clear intellect" and conduct necessary business. He met with Lincoln to discuss General Burnside's expedition to North Carolina but on another occasion was asleep when the president called.[47]

One thing the general did not do was appear before the Joint Committee on the Conduct of the War. On the very day McClellan had been scheduled to testify (December 23), General Heintzelman received a subpoena, and on the following day the committee grilled him about the "present conduct of the war at some length." Significantly, Heintzelman told the members that enemy numbers have been greatly overestimated. He admitted knowing little about McClellan's plans but did not favor flanking the Confederates near Manassas or directly attacking them at Centreville. The day after Christmas, Brigadier General William B. Franklin testified that McClellan had consulted with him a dozen times or so, but Franklin refused to disclose any plans before first checking with the general in chief. Yet without saying that this was McClellan's preference, he recommended an advance on Richmond by a water route. That same day, General McDowell told the committee that he did not favor that approach, adding only that the army could not afford to remain idle all winter. As the parade of generals continued, it became painfully clear that the committee would learn little about McClellan's plans or much of anything that would assuage their doubts.[48]

With the general in chief indisposed, Lincoln sought to assess the military situation himself. He began reading books on strategy, studying reports, and meeting with generals. At a New Year's Eve cabinet meeting, the main topic was the apparent military stalemate. Attorney General Bates deplored the "lack of system and concentrated intelligence," urging Lincoln to assert himself as commander in chief by appointing additional staff to write and execute his orders. That evening, the president met with members of the joint committee and received a tongue lashing from Wade: "Mr. President, you are murdering your country by inches in consequence of the inactivity of the military and the want of a distinct policy in regard to slavery." Lincoln said nothing, but the next day he informed McClellan of hearing talk that the "doings of an Investigating Committee, give you some uneasiness." Trying to sound reassuring, the president vaguely and misleadingly reported that he had met with the members for an hour and a half and "found them in a perfectly good mood." At the same time, he began communicating directly with Generals Halleck and Buell about operations in the western theater.[49]

As 1862 began, according to a report in the *New York Tribune*, McClellan's condition had worsened. The diagnosis of typhoid was confirmed, and there was a wildly implausible rumor that Senator Wade might succeed the ailing McClellan as general in chief along with a more believable report that Halleck might assume command of the Army of the Potomac. Two homeopathic doctors arrived to treat McClellan and Marcy (now a brigadier general); aside from the novelty of such unorthodox care, given McClellan's family background, word of their visit perhaps further undermined faith in McClellan's professional judgment. By January 2, the general's condition had begun to improve, and he was able to handle some paperwork. Lincoln, who had reported McClellan "dangerously ill" just the day before, now found him "very much better." A Washington newspaper cheerfully predicted that McClellan would be out and about as soon as the weather moderated.[50]

Because he had not testified before the joint committee, McClellan had not been able to defend his course of action or outline his plans in front of his chief critics. Amid this dearth of information, politicians, newspapers, and common soldiers stepped in to debate military policy and the general in chief's capabilities. One sympathetic editor complained that McClellan's illness had encouraged his enemies to look for a replacement. Indeed, a hostile newspaper excoriated the bedridden general for failing to appear before the joint committee. A Wisconsin recruit serving in the western theater dismissed McClellan as a "great puffed up toad."[51]

Those who were still optimistic even speculated that the barely convalescent McClellan (with continued comparisons to Napoleon) was about to launch a winter campaign. That was perhaps not the best historical reference, given the fate of the French army before Moscow, but by January 6, newspapers reported McClellan able to ride about in a carriage. This in turn fueled hopes that demoralized Confederates would presumably evacuate their lines around Manassas and in any case could never hold their own against the Army of the Potomac. Word of his continued recovery only increased speculation about a forward movement beginning soon.[52]

Lincoln appeared depressed, one observer thought, to the point of even conceding that a dissolution of the Union was unavoidable. That surely overstated the case, though the cabinet had grown restive. Bates kept urging the president to take charge of military policy, though he feared this "excellent man" still lacked "will and purpose." Chase, who had once been a strong ally, decided he had been mistaken about McClellan. In an anonymous newspaper piece, John Hay suggested that if the general's illness lingered, the president might have to take over the war's strategic direction and appoint a new commander for the Army of the Potomac. For his part, Lincoln tried to prod Halleck and Buell into acting "in concert" in the West. McClellan on January 3 managed to send a message to Halleck, reiterating the need to cooperate with Buell, and three days later he sent a dispatch to Buell, emphasizing the importance Lincoln placed on a campaign to relieve East Tennessee Unionists.[53]

All the while, McClellan's congressional critics conferred with generals and cabinet members. Heintzelman, a senior general who never shied away from offering strategic advice and did not think much of his young superior, continued to consult with Chandler, who in turn talked with Chase about the possibility of turning over command of the Army of the Potomac to McDowell. The Chief Engineer Barnard told Senator John Sherman of Ohio that McClellan was a "stupendous failure" who had brought the country to the "verge of ruin." Another senior Republican reportedly said of McClellan, "This young man's wings must be clipped." The usual Washington gossip took on a sharper tone, with rumors of plots against McClellan and even plans to supplant him with a member of what one newspaper correspondent termed the Senate's "Jacobin Club." Congressional testimony—especially if hostile to McClellan—managed to leak out, further poisoning the political atmosphere.[54]

On the evening of January 6, members of the joint committee met with the president and the cabinet. They recommended appointing McDowell general in chief. They were shocked to learn the administration had no inkling of McClellan's plans, as both the president and Secretary of War Cameron appeared very much in the dark. Seward expressed some confidence in Little Mac, while Chase sounded equivocal, both sharing the committee's anxieties and sympathizing with the recuperating McClellan for being overworked. After a lengthy back and forth, Lincoln promised only to ask the general in chief what he thought about dividing command responsibilities. On January 9, the president urged McClellan to meet with the joint committee and complained that neither Buell nor Halleck could "name the day when they can be ready to move." McClellan offered him no assurance on either count. He claimed to have "completely overtaxed" his strength the previous day. A physician had directed him to see no one aside from a couple of aides, so he could not testify before the joint committee for at least another two or three days.[55]

January 10 proved to be an especially long and miserable day for Abraham Lincoln. Bates once again pressed him to take charge as commander in chief; the attorney general doubted whether McClellan had any plans at all and hoped to bring all these questions before the cabinet. Lincoln and Cameron feared this would anger McClellan. Receiving a letter from Halleck that seemed to offer more excuses for inaction, the president forwarded it to Cameron, scrawling a quick note at the end: "It is extremely discouraging. As everywhere else, nothing can be done." Likely seeking information on whether the Army of the Potomac was properly equipped to advance, Lincoln paid a visit to Montgomery Meigs, the very able quartermaster general. Meigs observed that with typhoid, McClellan could remain *hors de combat* for some time, then pointed out the danger of allowing the Confederates to gain strength and possibly threaten the capital. As Lincoln sat in Meigs's office in front of a fire, he let loose a litany of woe: "General, what shall I do? The people are impatient; Chase has no money and he tells me he can raise no more; the General of the Army has typhoid fever. The bottom is out of the tub. What shall I do?"[56]

That evening, Lincoln summoned Generals McDowell and Franklin to the White House, where they were joined by Seward, Chase, and Assistant Secretary of War Thomas A. Scott. The president quickly reviewed the sorry state of affairs on several fronts: foreign relations, finance, congressional sniping, disappointing reports from Buell and Halleck, and then of course McClellan's illness. Because he simply had to talk to somebody, Lincoln had decided to consult the two generals—interestingly enough one of McClellan's closest confidants and one who clearly was not. If McClellan did not want to take the army into the field, the president wryly, though no doubt sadly, suggested he would like to "borrow it." Based on doubtful sources of information, Seward reported that Confederates could quickly muster over 100,000 men in Virginia. For once, Chase said little. When Lincoln asked what might be done with the army, McDowell, eager to restore his reputation post Bull Run, offered something that McClellan had not yet presented: a plan. He recommended organizing the army into four corps, establishing a supply route along the Orange and Alexandria Railroad, and luring the Confederates out of their works for a decisive battle—a proposal that largely followed Lincoln's early December plan. Obviously reflecting McClellan's thinking, Franklin favored an advance along the York River toward Richmond, but Assistant Secretary Scott doubted there was adequate transportation to launch such a campaign any time soon.[57]

So indeed, the bottom did appear to be out of the tub. A rumor spread among confident Confederates that McClellan did not really want to advance, that he had even feigned illness to avoid taking the field. Northern critics complained of spinelessness, and even the more generous minded decided that McClellan had already squandered opportunities to drive the Rebels away from the Potomac and advance on Richmond. On the other hand, the general's supporters—there was still a goodly number of those—worried that the political wolves were gathering to destroy him. What many people failed to realize was that the initiative was passing to the president, and Lincoln was increasingly taking Bates's advice to act as commander in chief. He seemingly had little choice. Congressman Owen Lovejoy, who had been a staunch Lincoln supporter back in Illinois, thought the American people had a right to demand results from a war costing them some two million dollars a day. He heaped scorn on a policy that seemed to rest on the vain hope of luring the Rebels back into the Union by not hurting them. Privately, he sneered, "Winter Quarter[s]—winter quarters," suggesting that there would be no fighting because of sheer cowardice.[58]

The timing for McClellan's bout with typhoid could not have been worse. The president simply believed that he had to act; in many ways, McClellan had lost control of the situation. Lincoln would not yet accede to the demands coming from Wade and the joint committee, but his own frustration combined with political pressure was fundamentally altering the relationship between the commander in chief and the general in chief.

5

WINTER OF DISCONTENT

"EVERYBODY GROWLS DREADFULLY . . . and the President is trying to put life and motion into an inert army," Secretary of the Treasury Chase confided to his beloved daughter Kate. "The truth is McClellan's sickness has cost the country more than can be estimated." He added that everyone remained in the dark about McClellan's plans. The treasury secretary had joined the clamor for McDowell's promotion to major general, presumably to become the new general in chief, but at this point, military planning had a large number of moving parts, and Lincoln was trying to operate the machine.[1]

On January 11, 1862, McDowell and Brigadier General Franklin had gathered from the Ordnance, Quartermaster, and Commissary Departments the information Lincoln had requested at the end of their meeting the previous evening. The first priority, McDowell argued, must be to "overcome" the Confederate forces "in our front" before pursuing a line of operations along the York River. The two generals conferred with Chase, who revealed (despite what he just told his daughter) that McClellan had shared with him the general outlines of a plan to move the army to Urbanna on the Rappahannock River for a campaign against Richmond. Franklin suggested briefing McClellan on what they were doing, but McDowell demurred (supported by Chase) and maintained it was up to the president to decide if and when to bring the general in chief into the picture.[2] As described by both Franklin and McDowell, this entire discussion appeared decidedly awkward, with none of the participants exactly laying their cards on the table.

That evening, they met with Lincoln at the White House, where McDowell read a memorandum calling for an overland offensive by the Army of the Potomac. This document laid out objections for any advance along a water route, including the time required to assemble transportation and impassable roads once the troops had landed. A reference to siege trains hinted at a prolonged campaign against Richmond. Franklin later claimed that he had opposed an immediate overland advance against the Confederates, but whether he said so in this meeting is not clear. Chase, Seward, and Assistant Secretary of War Scott once again joined the discussion, but this time Postmaster General Blair joined as well. Blair strongly objected to McDowell's recommendations and instead favored a campaign either along the York River or from Fort Monroe. McDowell's proposal, he warned, might only reprise the Bull Run disaster. Seward avoided committing himself, and Chase indirectly went along with McDowell. Lincoln wanted to hear from Meigs about water transportation, so he asked McDowell and Franklin to confer with the quartermaster general in the morning and return to the White House in the afternoon.[3]

The same group, plus Meigs, reassembled for further discussion at the Executive Mansion. Meigs had told McDowell and Franklin that another six weeks would be required to gather transportation if the army was to move by water, and so he favored an overland campaign. Lincoln said that he had heard that McClellan's health had improved dramatically, and Franklin later recalled an announcement by Seward that McClellan was a "well man." With this news it became clear that no decision would be reached that day, though there followed desultory discussion about general strategy and even about whether Brigadier General Burnside's expedition to North Carolina should be canceled. Lincoln thought that operation should continue, but decided they should all meet the following day with the now presumably recovered general in chief.[4]

McClellan—still not feeling very well—caught wind of all this from Edwin Stanton, who warned that the general's enemies (presumably the Radical Republicans along with McDowell and Chase) "are counting on your death, and are already dividing among themselves your military goods and chattels." At the same time, however, the wily and opportunistic former attorney general was conferring with Chase about the general. An alerted and alarmed McClellan had come to the White House on the morning of January 12 and later claimed that he had told the president "in a general and casual way what my intensions were."[5] Yet he apparently had not gone into any detail and so hardly relieved Lincoln's mind.

The following afternoon there occurred one of the most peculiar councils of war in American history. With the previous day's group now joined by McClellan, Lincoln was still feeling his way toward asserting himself as commander in chief. As historian Ethan Rafuse has pointed out, the president had allowed McClellan to regularly violate the chain of command when Scott was general in chief, and now McClellan was being treated in a similar fashion. Franklin and McDowell were dealing with the president directly, and whether intentionally or not, they were undermining McClellan's authority.[6] So in several respects this highly important and unusual meeting began under inauspicious circumstances.

Lincoln briefly reviewed the earlier meetings for McClellan's benefit and, pointing to a map, asked McDowell to go over his proposal. McDowell reviewed how he and Franklin had investigated various options and summarized the findings that had been presented to the president two days earlier. Perhaps recognizing the awkwardness of having explored campaign plans without consulting the general in chief, McDowell offered some sort of apology, but McClellan curtly replied, "You are entitled to have any opinion you please!" Franklin added that he had mentioned the York River because that was consistent with what he knew of McClellan's thinking. Obviously annoyed by McClellan's reticence and seeming rebuff, McDowell then said he had "acted entirely in the dark." Meigs later noted that the general in chief sat "with his head hanging down and mute." The quartermaster general moved his chair over to McClellan's side and quietly suggested that he promise some movement toward Manassas, adding that his army was strong enough to do so. One of the stranger features of the meeting, at least as McClellan recalled it, was that various participants kept whispering to those near them—something that undoubtedly fed the general's suspicions.

Lincoln tried to steer the discussion back to the key question: what could be done and when? According to McDowell, McClellan claimed to not know how large a force he could count on for carrying out an offensive and wondered out loud if Burnside should be recalled or whether Major General Benjamin F. Butler should be allowed to depart for Ship Island off the Mississippi coast. As McClellan appeared to dither, Chase bluntly asked what he intended to do with the Army of the Potomac. For some moments, the general in chief said nothing—likely both collecting his thoughts and reining in his anger. He then talked of forcing Buell to make a move in Kentucky. Pausing again, he expressed great reluctance to share his plans because the fewer people who knew about them the better, given previous leaks. If he told the group what he intended to do—McClellan at one point whispered to Meigs—the information would appear in the *New York Herald* the next day because Lincoln could not keep a secret and might even blab to his young son Tad. McClellan then announced that he would not reveal his plans "unless ordered to do so"—presumably by the president. With Chase, McDowell, and Franklin off to one side of the room, the secretary of the treasury quietly remarked that if McClellan refused to address the question at hand, "he is a ruined man." Lincoln calmly asked if the general had a time fixed for beginning a campaign. McClellan said he had but left it at that, and the president abruptly adjourned the meeting. Meigs summed matters up: "Much discussion not much accomplished."[7]

On the heels of this remarkable confab, Edwin Stanton—about to become the new secretary of war—arranged for McClellan to meet Malcolm Ives, a reporter for the *New York Herald*. After Stanton left the general's study, McClellan locked the door and began to tell Ives all about Monday's council of war. Information on future strategy that he had refused to disclose the day before the general would share with Ives and his boss, James Gordon Bennett. McClellan appreciated how Bennett and the *Herald* had stood by him while he was being abused by other newspapers. Remarkably enough, he stressed Confederate weaknesses even as he noted how the same worries cited by Lincoln—finances, foreign relations, and public pressure—made success on the battlefield ever more imperative. Where McClellan chose to deploy his forces, however, would depend on how the Burnside expedition fared and on the timing of Buell's campaign in the West. He spoke of a crushing Confederate defeat—a "Waterloo" fought somewhere between Lynchburg and Richmond that would quickly bring peace and a restored Union. For once sounding pleased with Lincoln, a suddenly more understanding McClellan now thought the president's penchant for storytelling and light conversation mostly harmless. He added the hope that Bennett would continue to "preach patience, forbearance, and confidence."[8] Yet for all his volubility and seeming candor, McClellan in this three-hour discussion with Ives had painted with a very broad brush and had not exactly revealed important details about any upcoming campaign—at least not one by the Army of the Potomac.

Despite McClellan's peculiar behavior during both the recent council of war and the meeting with Ives, perhaps caused by weakened stamina and will stemming from the bout with typhoid, he attempted to coordinate army movements and at least acknowledge the demands for action. He pressed Halleck about sending troops to assist Buell in Kentucky. "You have no idea of the pressure brought to bear here upon the Government for a forward movement," he advised Buell. McClellan believed that a campaign into East Tennessee would yield both strategic and political benefits. At the same time, as part of the planning for an advance by the Army of the Potomac, he began to give some attention to the defense of Washington. Not surprisingly, McClellan let Lincoln know how he had labored until midnight on January 13 and put in a good deal of work the following morning. But all this toil had "fatigued" him so much that on January 14 he could not come to see the president.[9] Thus he tried to show Lincoln signs of increased activity while appealing for understanding and perhaps wishing to avoid another meeting.

Lincoln weighed strategic possibilities himself, and told his friend Browning (who had been appointed to fill Stephan A. Douglas's Senate seat) that he considered taking the field himself. This no doubt reflected more frustration than intention, but on the same day as the dramatic meeting with McClellan, Lincoln sent a long dispatch to Buell (copied to Halleck) that revealed a growing assertiveness, if not exactly confidence, in his role as commander in chief. First there came a bit of self-deprecation: "For my own views, I have not offered, and do not now offer them as orders; and while I am glad to have them respectfully considered, I would blame you to follow them contrary to your own clear judgment—unless I should put them in the form of orders. As to Gen. McClellan's views, you understand your duty in regard to them better than I do." After this uncertain and confusing prelude, Lincoln laid out clearly his views on strategy: "We have the greater numbers, and the enemy has the greater facility of concentrating forces upon points of collision; that we must fail, unless we can find some way of making our advantage an over-match for his; and that this can only be done by menacing him with superior forces at different points, at the same time; so that we can safely attack, one, or both, if he makes no change; and if he weakens one to strengthen the other, forbear to attack the strengthened one, but seize, and hold the weakened one, gaining so much." Lincoln made specific suggestions to both generals: "Applying the principle to your [Buell's] case, my idea is that Halleck shall menace Columbus, and 'down river' generally; while you menace Bowling-Green, and East Tennessee."[10] The president would favor this "cordon offensive" strategy for the rest of the war, though implementing it was long a sticking point. In any case, the "suggestions" to Buell and Halleck showed that Lincoln was starting to act more forcefully as commander in chief, absent a meeting of minds with his general in chief.

The president might retain faith in McClellan as some administration officials claimed, but these same sources acknowledged the public impatience. A correspondent for the once-sympathetic *Chicago Tribune* accused the general of being in league with northern Breckinridge Democrats—conservatives who had supported the southern Democrat John C. Breckinridge in 1860—and perhaps not having his heart in the war. The administration still had no war plan, Ben Wade complained; if only "the President had his wife's *will*," Senator William Pitt Fessenden of Maine lamented. There is at least some evidence that even Mary Lincoln hectored her husband about McClellan's inaction, dismissing the general as a "humbug."[11]

The absence of the secretary of war from the recent flurry of meetings may seem striking, but the explanation is simple: Simon Cameron was on his way out. Cameron might have been an adequate secretary of war in peacetime, but not during the greatest military crisis in American history. In fact, his political skills, especially in dispensing jobs and contracts to his friends, became liabilities. Lincoln had reluctantly agreed to him entering the cabinet in the first place, and the two had never developed a working relationship. McClellan rightly considered the secretary to be of little help but likely appreciated the fact that Cameron largely left him alone and posed no obstacle in his communicating directly with the president or other cabinet members. Beginning in September 1861, complaints about Cameron had mounted, with much talk of cronyism and corruption in the War Department. Matters came to a head when, without consulting Lincoln, Cameron inserted a paragraph in his annual report recommending the enrollment of African American troops. The president ordered the passage deleted. Rumor had it that Thaddeus Stevens told the House Republican caucus that McClellan had threatened to resign if the report was not changed. In an anonymous newspaper article, John Hay refuted that story but described McClellan as a "young man who has never won a battle," who had received ceremonial swords from "servile corporations," and who had somehow been invested "with mysterious attributes of heroism." He added, however, that the general had always left political questions to the president and the cabinet. Hay clearly sought to deflate McClellan's reputation by questioning the basis of his standing in the country, but his piece also showed that the administration was not yet ready to jettison a still-popular commander.[12]

Without consulting the cabinet—apparently at Chase's urging and with Seward's approval—Lincoln on January 11 had accepted Cameron's resignation and two days later had appointed Edwin Stanton the new secretary of war.[13] Based on previous contacts and conversations, McClellan considered fellow Democrat Stanton to be an ally who shared his views about the war, the administration, and above all the Radical Republicans. Stanton had expressed confidence in McClellan to Sam Barlow and had reinforced the general's own doubts about Lincoln. McClellan proved himself vulnerable to the sort of flattery that Stanton dished out liberally when it served his purposes, though Little Mac should have wondered why Lincoln was now adding a man to his cabinet who for the past several months had been such an acerbic critic. McClellan later recalled how Stanton had asked whether he should accept the appointment and had claimed that his only desire was to assist the general in the great work ahead. When McClellan urged him to take the post, Stanton agreed and added, "Now we two will save the country."[14]

On January 14, the president visited McClellan at his house to apologize for not having consulted him on Stanton's appointment. Lincoln knew that the two were on friendly terms and so assumed McClellan would approve. According to the general in chief's recollection, the president had hoped to avoid any suspicion that McClellan had used his influence to have a fellow Democrat chosen for the post. Adding to this initial good feeling, a Massachusetts newspaper soon quoted Stanton as declaring McClellan to be the "greatest military genius upon the continent," and other journalists reported McClellan to be quite pleased by the appointment. The general's friend and political adviser Barlow tried his own brand of blandishment on Stanton, predicting that he and McClellan would now work together to keep the war moving along conservative lines.[15]

The Stanton appointment, the comte de Paris agreed, meant the government would be pursuing a conciliatory war policy. After all, Cameron had been courting abolitionists, and Stanton had served in Buchanan's cabinet. The ex-president, however, sounded distinctly ambivalent about his former attorney general's qualifications, offering his niece a mixed assessment while adding that Stanton had "flattered me ad nauseum." Speculation about the new secretary of war's views began almost immediately, with most everyone seeing what they wanted to see. The more conservative members of the Supreme Court approved the selection, and a Philadelphian rejoiced because he was sure Stanton would favor "enforcing the constitutional obligations and not for the fanatical object of abolitionizing the South." Yet because Stanton's political stripes appeared to change according to time, place, and audience, Charles Sumner drew exactly the opposite conclusion, that Stanton "goes as far as I do in directing the war against Slavery." Such widely divergent assessments occasionally put people on their guard. An influential banker friend of Seward warned that Stanton could be a "dangerous foe—a sleuthhound sort of man who never lost his scent or slacked in his purpose."[16]

For his part, Stanton told a *New York Herald* reporter that "the policy of the War Department would fully accord" with McClellan's views and those of the president. He gossiped about possible cabinet changes and offered pointed, often critical opinions of his new colleagues. At the same time (and just as the Senate was considering his nomination), Stanton met with Senator Fessenden to assure him of their complete harmony on the conduct of the war and the slavery question.[17]

On Monday morning, January 20, Stanton strode into the War Department. At first glance, the new secretary's most striking feature was a flowing, black beard streaked with gray, but many noticed intense eyes that could flash with anger at any moment. Catching sight of Stanton during an opera performance one evening, an artillery colonel saw only a "long-haired, fat, oily, politician-looking man." Stanton's demeanor—as changeable as his political principles—was a bundle of contradictions. Fanny Seward remarked on his "cheery look, & a merry twinkle of the eye," though few other contemporaries offered a similar description. Stanton seemingly trusted no one; his temper was short and often volcanic. Standing behind a writing desk, he appeared irritable and ever ready to dismiss most any request with an abrupt "no." A leading Republican recalled how Stanton sometimes spoke with a "withering sneer." Utterly serious, like McClellan, he grew noticeably impatient while listening to Lincoln's droll stories. Often imperious and always hard driving, Stanton could not brook obstacles in his path. He was given to berating and bullying but could also be unctuous, sycophantic, and on occasion even charming. His bulldog tenacity, hard work, and dedication to the task at hand impressed Lincoln, though other members of the cabinet were often suspicious and wary of their new colleague. Indeed, he was a master of intrigue who soon came to be a dominant figure among the president's advisers.[18]

Stanton decided that Cameron had run the War Department far too haphazardly. Attempting to bring order (and always a sense of personal control), he sharply curtailed admission to the offices, hoping to reduce the flood of private citizens and politicians seeking favors of one kind or another. He tried to funnel military dispatches by creating a central telegraph office. He took over the matter of civilian arrests from Seward and scrutinized the loyalty of department employees. That Stanton had earlier shared his views on military policy with friendly members of Congress and newspaper correspondents became apparent as reports appeared that the new secretary would invigorate Union war strategy and get the armies moving.[19]

Stanton's impatience reflected that of the northern public and accorded with Lincoln's reading of the military and political situation. The president's often slipshod administrative practices contrasted with yet complemented the war secretary's insistence on rules and order. Stanton had no trouble turning down the importunate petitions from soldier families or approving stern disciplinary measures. including executions; Lincoln could then decide when to soften official policy, make exceptions, and take into account the human element. Prone to browbeating subordinates, Stanton seldom acted so imperiously with Lincoln. The Philadelphia department-store king Alexander T. Stewart had even anticipated that Stanton's appointment would bring harmony to the cabinet.[20]

That doubtful prediction contained at least a kernel of truth—there had not been much harmony in the administration so far, and Lincoln's risky selection of former (and in the case of Chase, future) political rivals had yielded mixed results. Despite speculation about further changes, Stanton decided his most immediate problem was to deal with the general in chief and the Army of the Potomac. Relations between Stanton, McClellan, and Lincoln took center stage. To one observant officer, McClellan still looked pale and much reduced from the bout with typhoid; the general himself admitted to being "still weak." Despite frustrations with Lincoln, McClellan later claimed they had always gotten along well until illness had allowed his enemies (now including Stanton) to gain the president's ear. Information to this effect appearing in the press may have come from the general himself. Yet in a long discussion with Browning, Lincoln still expressed "great confidence" in McClellan.[21]

"A most unexpected piece of good fortune" was how the general in chief had first described Stanton entering the cabinet. On January 20 at noon, McClellan and his staff along with scores of army officers, all in full uniform, arrived at the War Department to pay their respects to the new secretary. For a time, he and his allies remained convinced that Stanton would work with them. The secretary did nothing at first to disillusion them, even as he was courting congressional Radicals. No longer passing on information to the *New York Herald* through correspondent Ives (whom he now had arrested after an exchange of heated words at the War Department), Stanton sent a fawning note to Charles Dana of the *New York Tribune* in which he promised action (implicitly abandoning his one-time friend McClellan): "As soon as I can get the machinery of the office working, the rats cleared out, and the rat hole stopped, we shall *move*. This army has got to fight or run away; and while men are striving nobly in the West, the champagne and oysters on the Potomac must be stopped."[22]

This would be music to the ears of ardent Republicans, and Stanton had clearly been telling them what they wanted to hear. He cultivated members of the Joint Committee on the Conduct of the War—especially Chandler and Wade—feeding their already serious doubts about McClellan. On the evening of January 20, at his request, Stanton met with the committee for several hours. What was discussed was never revealed, but the following day Wade sent a note to him asking whether there was really such a position as general in chief—an obvious effort to knock McClellan down a notch or two. For their part, committee members continued to discuss the military situation with generals such as Heintzelman, whom they already knew had little confidence in McClellan.[23]

On January 15, the same day the Senate had confirmed Stanton's appointment as secretary of war, McClellan finally met with the joint committee. "If I escape alive I will report when I get through," he jocularly wrote to Lincoln. Yet this was not simply McClellan appearing before a congressional committee. For one thing, the committee did not have the testimony recorded (though McClellan was reportedly with them for six hours), and so what was said remains uncertain, as does the exact purpose for the session. The two primary accounts of the proceeding could hardly be in greater disagreement. McClellan informed journalist Ives that he had been treated with "marked courtesy." Wade supposedly said the committee was "exceedingly anxious to sustain him," and the general replied that he realized why the members might be impatient with delays. This description of a cordial conversation stood in marked contrast to Chandler's later account. The Michigan Radical asked the general in chief why he did not attack the Confederates. McClellan complained there were only two bridges across the Potomac and talked about the need for lines of retreat. Chandler sounded incredulous: "General McClellan, if I understand you correctly, before you strike at the Rebels you want to be sure of plenty of room so that you can run in case they strike back!" "Or in case you get scared,"' Wade interjected. An indignant McClellan then lectured the committee at some length on the art of war; after he left the room, Chandler dismissed the entire performance as "infernal, unmitigated cowardice." Likely influenced by McClellan's account to Ives, the *New York Herald* and other newspapers claimed that the general had made a quite favorable impression on the committee, adding that public sentiment had turned in his favor and restored faith in his strategy. Other press accounts reported McClellan eager to meet the enemy in the field.[24]

McClellan's political friends at times did as much damage as his Radical detractors. Strong support from Democratic newspapers (including some of the most extreme editors) hardly helped the general avoid the political shoals. The *New York Herald* assailed McClellan's critics (especially Bennett's archrival Greeley) as "abolition bloodhounds" who would lead the nation into another Bull Run disaster. Rumors continued to fly about McClellan regularly entertaining key Democrats at his headquarters. Yet even some Democrats—Sam Barlow among them—hoped that McClellan would recognize that his army could not remain idle long and that he should be more forthcoming about his plans with members of Congress. At the same time, they still assumed that the presence of Democrat Stanton in the cabinet would only help matters.[25]

McClellan would not be hurried and bristled when Brigadier General Frederick W. Lander recommended crossing the Potomac to attack Confederates who were threatening the Baltimore and Ohio Railroad. To McClellan, who had grown weary of suggestions for offensives from military men and civilians alike, such a proposal seemed sheer "folly." For one thing, the weather during January—alternating periods of freezing and thawing, of snow and rain—made any advance on Virginia's muddy roads out of the question. At the same time, McClellan was slowly developing his Urbanna plan to force a Confederate retreat from Manassas and Centreville. The availability of water transportation remained a problem, though a staff officer reported that there were no heavily fortified enemy positions along the Urbanna route. Word leaked out that McClellan was finally planning to move.[26]

Pinkerton sent a series of reports offering estimates of enemy strength around Manassas and Centreville. He had twenty-four operatives in the field; collected information from prisoners, deserters, slaves, and refugees; but never properly sorted out the fragmentary and often contradictory assessments. One source, a man of "very limited education," claimed there were 70,000–80,000 troops at Centreville; a compilation of reports on January 7 placed the number at 50,000. A Confederate deserter claimed there were only 45,000 men at that town, but by January 22, Pinkerton had raised the estimate to over 80,000, though five days later another source claimed there were only 60,000. McClellan had two of his French aides digest these intelligence reports. While they set the numbers lower than many of Pinkerton's estimates, the general then did some inflating of his own.[27]

Even as the Army of the Potomac showed few signs of movement, McClellan had not yet exhausted public support. Friendly newspapers still pointed out how the Confederate press assailed President Jefferson Davis and General Beauregard for not attacking Washington just as some northern sheets relentlessly criticized McClellan. To the general's defenders, armchair critics failed to understand the risks of frontal assaults against fortified positions, and so they hardly merited much consideration. Patience, faith, and avoiding head-on attacks remained the watchwords, though a Massachusetts volunteer, while explaining to his family back home why people should still have confidence in McClellan, conceded that the Army of the Potomac must do something soon.[28]

Predictions that people would recognize the wisdom of McClellan's plans to crush the rebellion did not sound all that convincing when there was little prospect of such a glorious result anytime soon. Reports that McClellan strongly favored offensive operations, that furloughs had been suspended, or that the Confederates were about to abandon Manassas had worn thin. Recent visitors from Washington assured diarist George Templeton Strong of good prospects for some movement by March 1, though Strong sounded skeptical. Criticism at times gave way to sarcastic humor, including a joke that circulated in Washington hotels: "McClellan is waiting for the Chinese population of California to increase to such a vast number that they will be able to cross the Rocky Mountains and bring up his right wing by which time the Russian Possessions and Greenland will have a redundant population, which can be drafted down to the support of the grand left wing of the Union army—and that when these great events take place, the war will commence in earnest!"[29]

Yet how much longer could the country be satisfied with word of an *impending* movement, and indeed one anticipated ever since the Bull Run defeat? Editor Joseph Medill and his *Chicago Tribune* now looked to Stanton rather than McClellan to prod the armies into action. In London, Henry Adams decided that "McClellan must do something within six weeks or we are done." There even appeared a long poem entitled "Tardy George" that plaintively asked, "what are you waiting for, George, I pray?" The author ran through a litany of excuses for inaction and then suggested that McClellan did not want to harm his "southern friends."[30]

Lincoln did not buy suspicions of treasonous intent, but he complained to one visitor that McClellan is "never ready to move." Given his recent illness, it is hardly surprising that word came out of Washington that McClellan was simply overwhelmed by his dual roles as general in chief and commander of the Army of the Potomac. By January 27, the president's impatience (and perhaps his reading in books on military strategy) led him to issue General War Order No. 1, calling for simultaneous movements by U.S. land and naval forces on Washington's birthday. Lincoln had drafted this document on his own, read it to the cabinet, but did not ask for advice. However politically necessary this order may have been, it struck many people at the time and later historians as amateurish. But one thing was certain, Lincoln (and his new secretary of war) had now seized the reins of military policy. In light of the president's order, Stanton sent a "most confidential" note to Senator Wade claiming that what was now required was for the government to take control of the railroad and telegraph. The secretary of war railed against the New York papers for publishing advance information about military and naval operations.[31]

Visiting Washington, diarist Strong thought McClellan had not quite recovered from his illness and looked "careworn"—the word so often used to describe Lincoln. Stanton seemed to impress everyone, claimed Strong, who praised the secretary of war's clearheaded intelligence and earnest demeanor. McClellan was in frequent contact with the new war secretary and still thought that "Stanton's appointment has helped me infinitely thus far, & will still more in the future." At the same time, as Senator Trumbull informed another influential Illinois Republican, the "earnest men" who had talked with Stanton "say he is fully up to all you could ask." The *Chicago Tribune* reported the secretary of war taking charge and the administration no longer meekly deferring to McClellan. Indeed, the general in chief finally shared the outlines of his Urbanna plan with Stanton for presentation to Lincoln.[32]

But on the last day of January, Lincoln rejected McClellan's proposal and instead ordered that by February 22, the Army of the Potomac should launch an "expedition" for the purpose of "occupying a point upon the Rail Road South Westward of what is known of [*sic*] Manassas Junction." The president had also prepared a memorandum comparing their respective proposals, focusing on resources, timing, the likelihood and value of any resulting victory, and even routes of retreat. The general in chief asked if he could submit his objections to the president's plan and his reasons for preferring the Urbanna route in writing. Lincoln agreed. That evening, McClellan attended a soiree for the diplomatic corps at Seward's house, but amid what one reporter termed a "large array of fashionable beauty," he must have been churning over in his mind what the president's new executive assertiveness and strategic independence meant.[33]

McClellan had drafted a twenty-two-page document reviewing events going back to July 1861 and served as much to defend his generalship as to lay out his strategic thinking. He emphasized how much had been accomplished since the summer—especially given his enormous responsibilities. The greatest mistake, by his lights, had been to underestimate the poor condition of the various armies. As for the Army of the Potomac, the relative strength of the Union and Confederate forces did not warrant a "direct attack" on the enemy at Manassas and Centreville. Thus, there were serious disadvantages to the president's proposal for operating along the Occoquan River. McClellan described these in some detail and highlighted probable obstacles, including roads and weather, along with the tactical difficulties that would work to the enemy's advantage. In his view, Lincoln's plan would at best force the Confederates to retreat and escape into the Richmond defenses. In contrast, an advance from the "Lower Chesapeake Bay" offered "the shortest land route to Richmond," and McClellan added the remarkable claim that "the roads in that region are passable at all seasons of the year." He fully expected the Confederates to retreat from the Manassas entrenchments to defend Richmond and Norfolk, and soon after Federal forces would control the entire state of Virginia. McClellan suggested possible offensives by other Federal forces from eastern Virginia to western Tennessee, including the eventual capture of southern seaports and control of the Mississippi River. He pressed for a landing of troops at Urbanna but mentioned other routes as well. By bringing additional regiments into Washington, he hoped to take the field with between 110,000 and 140,000 men. Better to delay another thirty days, he advised, to gain a "decisive victory." While admitting the uncertainties of war, the general in chief sounded supremely confident that his plan was not just preferable, it would achieve great results.[34]

McClellan later claimed his memorandum must have "produced some effect upon the mind of the President" since Lincoln did not insist that his earlier order be executed. One of Lincoln's secretaries anonymously wrote in a newspaper piece that plans for the army and the navy were moving along well. The president was not going to force McClellan to adopt his Occoquan plan, nor was he ready to remove McClellan from command, given the absence of an obvious successor and the general's popularity with the troops.[35]

McClellan still had good reason to be anxious. In looking for a scapegoat for the Ball's Bluff defeat, the Joint Committee settled on General Stone, though his conservative views on slavery and rumors of disloyalty likely weighed more with the committee than military performance. Stone appeared before his inquisitors twice but was never allowed to see the evidence against him. There was suspicion that their real target was McClellan. "They want a victim," the general remarked to one of his aides, who then ominously added, "Yes—and when they have once tasted blood . . . no one can tell who will be the next victim." McClellan proved reluctant to follow Stanton's order to arrest Stone but did not really come to his defense either, instead keeping his distance from the situation lest the committee turn their fire on him next. One newspaper correspondent claimed that the Stone case had "greatly affected McClellan both in mind and spirit." The general had reportedly taken to his bed and a physician summoned.[36]

Critics thought that Lincoln still treated McClellan too delicately and detected Seward's malign influence. Discontent in Congress had broken out in heated exchanges on the House floor during debate over an army appropriations bill. Unfortunately for McClellan, his chief congressional champion became Samuel Sullivan Cox of Ohio, an ardent Democrat who accused the general's detractors of really aiming their fire at Lincoln. Cox lauded McClellan for supporting a war "for the Union and the Constitution, for the salvation of the white man's free government in America." Impatient attacks on the general simply reflected military ignorance. There is no question that support from men such as Cox and Barlow thrust the general in chief deeper into partisan politics. "McClellan has almost ruined your administration and the country," *Chicago Tribune* editor Medill warned Lincoln. "He is thinking of the Presidency in '64" by "placating the Rebels." One rumor circulating in New York blamed the general's wife for pushing her husband into the political fray. *New York Times* editor Henry J. Raymond had given up on McClellan, claiming the general had fooled the public long enough.[37]

Military policy had become a partisan issue, as had the whole question of command. Rumors spread that the president planned to promote some general (presumably Halleck) and place him over McClellan (perhaps as general in chief); or maybe Stanton would take charge of military operations. Vice President Hannibal Hamlin flatly recommended McClellan's dismissal and, when asked by Lincoln to name a replacement, suggested veteran Brigadier General Charles F. Smith, who then commanded a division in the western theater. "The Abolition War on General McClellan," screamed the *New York Herald,* even as it dismissed reports of the general's impending demotion and pointedly added that Lincoln and Stanton knew little about military affairs.[38]

Yet the president (and as would soon be apparent, the secretary of war) was asserting himself more and more in military matters. Lincoln "at last seems to be waking up to the fact . . . that responsibility is upon *him* . . . and seems inclined to take a personal supervision" to "see that Generals & subordinate officers do their duty," Trumbull wrote approvingly to Illinois governor Richard Yates. The president kept pressing McClellan for information about operations in various theaters. Had too much been expected of the young general in chief, the increasingly critical *Chicago Tribune* asked. With patience running low, the president even talked (though largely in exasperation and jest) of taking command of the Army of the Potomac himself. Noticing how quiet McClellan seemed during one meeting with Lincoln, Senator Browning decided that the general "does not seem to me big enough for his position."[39]

Lincoln anxiously awaited military news from the West even as he pressed McClellan on possible operations in Maryland and Virginia. McClellan advised Halleck on advancing against Nashville and urged him to "throw all available force on Fort Henry & Fort Donelson." On February 6, Fort Henry, on the Tennessee River, was captured by Federal forces; ten days later Brigadier General Ulysses S. Grant accepted the "unconditional surrender" of Fort Donelson on the Cumberland River. Coupled with General Burnside's success on Roanoke Island, the war appeared to turn in the Union's favor. According to a *New York Times* correspondent, "the avalanche of good news" meant that "McClellan's star is in the ascendant." Nelly declared her husband "the happiest man in Washington." Recent victories emboldened his defenders, and a Boston editor pointed to the wisdom of having a general in chief. Yet renewed expressions of confidence in McClellan's leadership could not erase the fact that the Army of the Potomac had not ventured far from the Washington defenses.[40]

Administration sources reported that McClellan would no longer be general in chief once he had taken the field with the Army of the Potomac, though no official announcement would come right away. An anonymous newspaper piece by William Stoddard reported Stanton winning "golden opinions by his energy, efficiency, and conscientiousness." The secretary of war appeared "terribly in earnest" and had become the "strong right hand of the President."[41]

With ostentatious modesty, Stanton complained to the *New York Tribune* of the "undue merit for recent victories" that had come his way. Instead, people should credit "the gallant soldiers and officers" and the "spirit of the Lord." In his view, talk of "military combinations and organizing victory" (which might suggest offering praise for McClellan) smacked more of "infidel France" than Christian America. This statement signaled a conflict between the general in chief and the secretary of war that finally burst into public view over a seemingly minor but acrimonious newspaper brouhaha. On February 20, Stanton addressed a railroad convention in Washington, and the Associated Press reported him paying "a high compliment to the young and gallant friend at his side, Major-General McClellan, in whom he had the utmost confidence and the results of whose military schemes, gigantic and well matured, were now exhibited to a rejoicing country." The general's editorial allies had already been accusing certain newspapers of trying to stir up trouble between McClellan and Stanton, and soon they were quoting with approval the secretary of war's supposed praise for their hero. Stanton heatedly denied making any such statement, dismissing it as a "ridiculous and impertinent effort to puff the General." John Hay tried to smooth things over in yet another anonymous newspaper piece claiming that McClellan and Stanton remained on perfectly cordial terms, but after Charles Dana had Stanton's version published in the *New York Tribune,* it was clear that relations had soured.[42]

The *New York Times* discounted stories about a rift between McClellan and Stanton but now seemed more intent on defending the latter than the former. Some Democrats and other conservatives had a hard time believing reports that Stanton had sold out to Greeley or was aligning himself with congressional Radicals, but gradually they decided that was exactly what was happening. Greeley's *Tribune* kept up the editorial drumfire, claiming that every Rebel-sympathizing editor in New York had become "a noisy and intolerant eulogist of Gen. McClellan." In addition, a cabal of army officers—all warm supporters of the general—were reportedly determined to preserve slavery. "If anyone is in possession of evidence that Gen. McClellan is—as we know Secretary Stanton to be—in favor of thoroughly crushing out the rebellion in the shortest practicable time and by the most readily effective means, we will thank him for that evidence," Greeley remarked with dripping sarcasm. More criticism cropped up in the army. General McDowell decided that McClellan lacked sincerity; General Kearny complained that most generals seldom saw Little Mac and sneered at his engineering approach to war. A company officer in a Pennsylvania regiment thought that the general in chief had flat-out failed, and a New Jersey volunteer felt "inexpressibly tired and disgusted with McClellan's do-nothing policy."[43]

In the Army of the Potomac, however, McClellan had defenders who remained convinced that he was just the man to whip the Rebels. The general's appearance still elicited enthusiasm in the ranks, and the troops reportedly scorned newspapers that disparaged their commander. McClellan's critics, General Meade believed, remained a distinct minority whose noisy attacks made them seem more formidable than their actual numbers. In middle to late February, much of this back and forth, while politically ominous, had little to do with the military situation because, as several observers noted, Virginia mud had become the major obstacle to a forward movement.[44]

Military inactivity seemed to breed political activity. On February 19, the joint committee turned its attention to the "blockade of the Potomac." Confederate batteries along the lower Potomac and Confederate troops along the Baltimore and Ohio Railroad had proven embarrassing, eliciting protests from merchants and the Ohio legislature. Chairman Wade and Andrew Johnson walked over to the War Department to meet with Stanton, who melodramatically informed them that "he did not go to his bed at night without his cheek burning with shame at this disgrace upon the nation." Stanton then summoned McClellan, who vaguely spoke of resolving the problem in "a matter of days." Again careful to leave open lines of retreat, he planned to throw a temporary bridge over the river. Wade scoffed at this and wondered why the Army of the Potomac, now numbering 150,000 men, could not easily handle the Confederate forces, adding that any Union troops coming back across the river should do so "in their coffins." Even the usually matter-of-fact committee journal noted the Ohioan's "pretty strong and emphatic language." Stanton went along with Wade and "indorsed every sentiment he uttered." McClellan did not reply. The next day the committee itself met at Stanton's home to discuss raising the blockade of the Potomac. The secretary agreed with their views entirely, stood ready to work with the committee in every possible way, and offered to consult with them at least once a week.[45]

All this maneuvering occurred at the worst possible time for Lincoln, who not only felt the ever-heavier burdens of the presidency but also faced a family crisis. The two young Lincoln sons were always a handful, but the president was an indulgent father, and their youthful hijinks made the White House a happier place. In early February, both Willie and Tad fell ill (likely of typhoid fever), and by February 18 Attorney General Bates described the president as "nearly worn out with grief and watching." Two days later Willie died. "My boy is gone—he is actually gone!" Lincoln cried out to his secretary John Nicolay. McClellan dispatched a warm sympathy note to the president, a "kind true friend" whose "confidence has upheld me when I should otherwise have felt weak." At the funeral, with tears in his eyes, the general bowed in prayer. As for Lincoln, the burdens of war, the deaths of friends, the loss of his dear son, fears for his wife's sanity, and the growing volume of criticism not only added to his natural melancholy but also called forth physical, intellectual, and emotional reserves.[46]

On the day Willie Lincoln died, McClellan was gathering troops at Point of Rocks, Maryland, in preparation for crossing the Potomac River to Harpers Ferry to reopen the Baltimore and Ohio Railroad. For at least a month, the general had been working on a plan for constructing a bridge of canal boats and had apparently spoken about it to Chase and Lincoln. He later claimed that if the bridge of canal boats did not work, he would see to the rebuilding of the railroad bridge. According to one source (admittedly one hostile to McClellan), the general had told the president: "If this move fails, I will have nobody to blame but myself." This sounded like McClellan in one of his self-confident mood swings.[47] It was therefore doubly ironic that this seemingly straightforward plan failed because of an engineering error.

On February 26, McClellan, still looking thin after his recent illness, traveled to Sandy Hook, Maryland; after a pontoon bridge was quickly laid, infantry, artillery, and cavalry crossed and held the Virginia side, presumably in enough strength to hold off any Confederate attack until a sturdier and more permanent bridge was completed. Canal boats were transported from Washington on the Chesapeake and Ohio Canal and were to enter the Potomac through a river-access lock. But the boats were four to six inches too wide for the lock, a problem no one had apparently anticipated.[48]

McClellan had reported to Stanton on that day's success, then on the following day had to inform him that the problems with the canal boats and river lock would mean another delay. The best alternative now seemed to rebuild the railroad bridge across the Potomac, which would take several weeks. In one of the few quips ever attributed to the humorless secretary of the treasury, Chase remarked that the whole endeavor had "died of lockjaw." Unfortunately for McClellan, the president found nothing amusing about the matter. Early in the evening of February 27, Stanton brought the general's dispatches to the White House. Likely for dramatic effect, he first read the one about the pontoons being laid, which pleased Lincoln, and then read the one about the lock being too narrow, which seemed to suggest indefinite delay if not abandonment of any campaign in the

Shenandoah Valley. "What does this mean?" asked the anxious president. "It means that [it] is a damned fizzle," Stanton immediately answered. "It means that he doesn't intend to do anything." Lincoln quietly wondered why no one had bothered to measure the lock beforehand. When McClellan's chief of staff, General Marcy, arrived later, Lincoln repeated the question, only with greater emphasis and considerable anger. "Everything seems to fail," he lamented, fearing the impression was growing that McClellan "does not intend to do anything." In no mood for excuses, Lincoln cut off a reply from poor Marcy and dismissed him. Unlike many politicians of the era, Lincoln seldom cursed, but on this occasion, according to a *Chicago Tribune* reporter, he "swore like a Philistine." He might have shown a bit more patience or have been wary of Stanton's apparent eagerness to share bad news, for McClellan managed to have the railroad bridge rebuilt quickly. Major General Banks then pushed into the lower Shenandoah Valley and captured Winchester.[49]

Sometime after his return from Harpers Ferry on March 1, McClellan drafted a long memorandum outlining what had taken place, including the problem with the canal boats. He claimed that "military railroad employees" had incorrectly informed the engineers that the lock was wide enough. Nevertheless, he had been able to send out various bodies of troops on reconnaissance missions and so came back to Washington "well satisfied with what had been accomplished." He had heard that the president was "dissatisfied with the state of affairs," but Stanton told him that all had been acceptably explained to Lincoln. McClellan did not immediately meet with the president and later claimed that Stanton had "deceived" him. According to Senator Sumner, Lincoln was still upset and "expressed himself quite angrily" in discussing the Harpers Ferry fiasco but had now resolved to "talk plainly" with McClellan.[50]

Whether McClellan would talk plainly in return remained uncertain. "I expect to fight a desperate battle somewhere near Richmond, the most desperate of the war," he informed Halleck, who by then was commanding the Department of the Missouri. "I have but few friends in Congress," he confessed. "The Abolitionists are doing their best to displace me, and I shall be content if I can keep my head above water until I am ready to strike the final blow." McClellan did not mention Stanton as a potential enemy, though Halleck had for some time been wary of him. Congressional criticism grew more insistent as Senators Wade and Johnson told

Lincoln that McClellan was both "incompetent" and "treacherous." Stanton evidently agreed and increasingly sought to keep McClellan from meeting with the president. When two congressmen complained about Confederate forces still threatening the capital, an exasperated Lincoln replied that if Washington, Napoleon, or Andrew Jackson commanded the Army of the Potomac, "they would be obliged to move or resign his position." The army would advance soon, he promised, "either under General McClellan or some other man."[51]

General Meade, who regretted hearing of attempts "to sew discord" among the various generals, nevertheless adopted a realistic view of the situation. "From all I learn," he informed his wife, "McClellan's star is rapidly setting, and nothing but a victory will save him from ruin." In a conversation with Chief of Staff Marcy, an inspector general of New York volunteers learned that McClellan was well aware of "the plots against him" and that something would happen soon "to bring matters to a head." The question became, his friend Barlow worried, whether McClellan would be given enough time to achieve military success (and hurt the Republican Party) before his enemies in Congress and the cabinet could displace him.[52]

By this time, the division commanders had some inkling of the Urbanna plan and discussed the problem of Confederate batteries on the lower Potomac. The recent victories in the western theater brought rejoicing in the Army of the Potomac and a bit more patience with McClellan, so long as he was intent on avoiding another Bull Run, the hangover from which lingered. Then, too, some officers became aware of the gathering political clouds (including Stanton's recent volte-face) and speculated on who might succeed McClellan.[53]

March 7 proved to be another turning point in the Lincoln-McClellan relationship. The president summoned the general for an early morning meeting. Lincoln still wanted to discuss the Harpers Ferry debacle, and McClellan discovered that Stanton had never shown his memorandum to the president. McClellan later stated (and unfortunately his memoir and report are the only accounts of the meeting) that his explanations seemed to satisfy Lincoln. But then the president turned to an "ugly matter." He had apparently been told that the Urbanna plan would leave Washington vulnerable to Confederate assault, and some people thought McClellan's intentions "traitorous." The general could hardly believe that the president could swallow such nonsense, but apparently he did. McClellan then stood up and demanded that Lincoln "should retract the expression" because he would permit no one to call him a traitor. According to McClellan's later recollection, the president was "much agitated, and at once disclaimed any idea of considering me a traitor, and said that he merely repeated what others had said, and that he did not believe a word of it." McClellan again hotly denied such a charge, and Lincoln apologized a second time.[54] There is much that is curious in the exchange. If Lincoln did not believe the rumors about McClellan, why bring them up? Was he trying to prod the general into action by showing how far the critics would go? Historian Stephen Sears doubts that enough was yet known about McClellan's Urbanna plan to induce such fears about the safety of Washington.[55] Yet some details could have leaked out through Chase, Stanton, or perhaps from a general such as Heintzelman.

McClellan told Lincoln that he had called a meeting of division commanders that very morning at his headquarters on Jackson Square to consider what to do about the Confederate batteries and present the Urbanna proposal. He and Marcy arrived at 10 a.m., the general in chief spread a large map on the table, and the chief of staff briefed everyone on the planned offensive. The details were largely new to those present, with a few exceptions, and before leaving them to discuss it, Marcy asked for the consideration of two questions: whether the base of operations should be shifted, and what to do about the enemy batteries along the Potomac. Marcy took Heintzelman (and perhaps others) aside and spoke of an effort underway to "supersede" the general in chief. According to Heintzelman, both Halleck and General Frémont had been mentioned as replacements.

This so-called council of war lasted for at least three hours as the generals hashed out both these matters. McDowell later complained that "the question was to be determined on personal grounds, not on the merits of the case." What he meant was that the more independent-minded senior generals, including himself, Heintzelman, Brigadier General Edwin V. Sumner, and Brigadier General (and Chief Engineer) Barnard, recognized the flaws in the Urbanna plan, but those generals either close to McClellan or dependent on his favor (Blenker, Franklin, Brigadier General Erasmus D. Keyes, McCall, Brigadier General Henry M. Naglee, Brigadier General Andrew Porter, Fitz John Porter, and Brigadier General William F. "Baldy" Smith) voted in favor. Barnard outlined objections that he had earlier raised with McClellan, but to no avail. A proposal to make the generals' recommendation unanimous, Heintzelman and McDowell noted, "excited considerable feeling."[56]

That evening, the generals reassembled at the White House to report on their deliberations. Marcy explained the plan for transferring troops to Annapolis and then to Urbanna (bypassing those pesky Confederate batteries along the Potomac). According to McDowell, Lincoln then remarked: "Napoleon could not stand still with such an army. I don't care, gentlemen, what plan you have, but just pitch in." This was not exactly true because once the Urbanna proposal was presented, Lincoln raised objections focusing on the safety of Washington; he still favored a direct advance by the shortest possible route that would keep the capital well covered. Naglee reported on how the generals had voted, and Stanton questioned those supporting the Urbanna plan quite intently, especially on the issue of how long it would take to execute such a change of base. Barnard later claimed that in all the discussion he had not heard a good reason to move the army to Urbanna. Lincoln may have indicated that he would go along with the majority or even that he had decided not to relieve McClellan of his command, but in any case, the president would meet with the generals again the following morning. He closed the session with one final question: should the army be divided into corps? To this, the generals readily agreed. Stanton later remarked to Hay, "We saw ten generals afraid to fight."[57]

At ten o'clock the next morning, the same group called at the White House to confer with Lincoln and Stanton. According to one participant, Lincoln said he had slept better than he had for the past two weeks because he had made some decisions. The president agreed to send 50,000 troops to the Chesapeake and to double that number if the batteries along the Potomac were neutralized or the Confederates withdrew from Manassas. He told them all, Heintzelman wrote in his diary, to "go in heartily for this plan." Seemingly, McClellan and the other generals had persuaded the president, though in fact Lincoln was going along with a plan he did not really approve. He had taken charge in one sense but had also decided that he could not remove McClellan. "We can do nothing else than adopt this plan, and discard all others," he told Stanton. "With eight out of twelve division commanders approving it, we can't reject it and adopt another." To insist on the overland route would mean "assuming all responsibility in case of the failure of the one we adopt." Lincoln and Stanton might "understand nothing of military affairs," as the comte de Paris complained, but they had decided that McClellan had assembled an immense army and would have to use it. "The enemies of McClellan are at his heels," Barlow wrote, but he optimistically predicted that the general would "soon be out of their way."[58]

Having broached the question of army corps the night before, Lincoln acted the following day by appointing corps commanders. Talk about organizing the Army of the Potomac into corps had been going on for months, and there had been reports not only that it was imminent but also that McClellan was strongly in favor. By the end of 1861, word spread that the general in chief was now resisting the idea, but soon pressure would come from the Joint Committee on the Conduct of the War, whose members insisted the president organize the divisions into corps, supposedly to increase military efficiency. Lincoln noted McClellan's opposition, and there were rumors that the general might resign if the matter were pressed. By February, Stanton was urging Heintzelman to talk with Lincoln about the idea. On February 25, and again on March 5, the committee met with the president to raise the question, with the added impetus that Stanton wanted it done.[59]

Lincoln's order of March 8 divided the Army of the Potomac into four corps, along with a fifth corps commanded by General Banks. As corps commanders, Lincoln selected the most senior generals—McDowell, Sumner, Heintzelman, and Keyes—only one of whom (Keyes) had favored the Urbanna plan. The president had not consulted with McClellan on the selection; the general in chief thought his division commanders should be tested in a campaign beforehand, and in any case, he would have preferred appointing younger generals who were more energetic and more in his orbit.[60] So, McClellan would be launching a campaign with corps commanders he had not selected and who knew he would not have chosen them—not exactly a formula for success.

In finally preparing to move the army, McClellan asked for a delay in the formation of the various corps, but Stanton's frosty reply was brief and unequivocal: "I think it is the duty of every officer to obey the President's orders, nor can I see any reason why you should not obey them in present instance." Yet after further explanation from McClellan, Stanton reluctantly agreed to suspend the president's order while the general was shifting divisions into the field. Word about this leaked out; Heintzelman even heard that Stanton had resigned. But on March 13 McClellan carried out the president's order, though he asked that no changes be made in the organization of the divisions.[61]

With a third general war order on March 8 authorizing the Urbanna movement, Lincoln had further reined in McClellan's strategic authority. The directive included the president's previously expressed restrictions on the number of troops to be moved and the requirements for the defense of Washington. With the proviso that the Confederate batteries along the Potomac had to be cleared, it also specified that the movement of troops to the Chesapeake would begin as early as March 18. Perhaps this reflected Stanton's influence because a Washington newspaper reported that the new secretary "has but two words since he took charge of the War Department, 'Advance!' and 'Fight!'" As McClellan well knew, Lincoln had only reluctantly agreed to a change of base, and he later complained about the president's obliviousness to questions of weather, roads, and transportation.[62]

March 8 in many ways was a pivotal day—on the water as well as on land. In Hampton Roads, Virginia, the Confederate ram *Virginia* (formerly the U.S. frigate *Merrimack*) inaugurated the era of ironclad warfare by destroying two Federal frigates. Word reached Washington on Sunday morning, March 9; one observer thought Lincoln looked "thin and wasted." At the White House, there was much anxious talk, with Stanton, Seward, and Welles joining Assistant Secretary of War Peter H. Watson, Nicolay, and McClellan. Nicolay described how "a very much excited" Stanton "walked up and down the room like a caged lion." Welles too noted how the "frightened" secretary of war worried about the Confederate ironclad destroying every vessel in Federal service. Stanton apparently thought Boston and New York might be in danger. As the secretary of war "scolded and raved," Welles prided himself on remaining self-possessed. Stanton and Lincoln gazed out a window, apparently expecting the *Virginia* to come steaming up the Potomac. That same day, the secretary of war told Lincoln's friend Browning about his lack of faith in McClellan. But then news arrived that the Union's own ironclad, the *Monitor*, had won its titanic battle with the *Virginia* (though in fact the engagement had largely ended in a draw). With equal drama came reports that Confederates had abandoned their batteries along the Potomac and were withdrawing from Manassas.[63]

McClellan later claimed he had already decided to advance his forces against General Joseph E. Johnston's army at Manassas and Centreville, though the Confederate withdrawal had been rumored for several days. However that might be, McClellan's horse and staff were ready to move by noon on March 9, a Sunday. With Nelly and the baby watching from an upper-story window, McClellan left that evening. As the commander and his army crept forward, they received word that the Confederates had in fact evacuated Centreville and the batteries along the Potomac. Given the hasty departure, lack of orders, and a scattered staff, the movement of McClellan's forces was at times halting, especially at first over very muddy roads. The comte de Paris speculated that McClellan had sent Fitz John Porter and Franklin ahead, hoping they might garner some laurels chasing the retreating enemy. The departure from Washington with flags flying and bands playing presented a fine picture—one McClellan likely intended—but perhaps that made the empty enemy entrenchments all the more disappointing and the entire affair largely anticlimactic. Describing for Nelly the abandoned works at Centreville, a worn-out McClellan complained that the rascals in Washington "are after me again." Yet he hoped the march to Manassas, however devoid of results, had prepared the troops for future campaigning. Chief of Staff Marcy urged him to return immediately to brief Lincoln and Stanton on what he now proposed to do, but the general pleaded exhaustion.[64]

McClellan had promised the president and secretary of war "to push the retreat of the Rebels as far as possible." That was now beside the point, and so the old question recurred what to do next with his large, well-equipped army. On March 13, at Fairfax Court House, Virginia, McClellan convened another council of war. This time the newly appointed corps commanders agreed to transfer operations to somewhere between the York and James Rivers, Johnston's retreat from Manassas having scotched the Urbanna plan. They assumed that the *Virginia* would no longer be a threat, that transportation from Washington and Alexandria would be adequate to carry the troops down the Potomac, and that Washington would be left well protected with a force of 40,000 men. That same day, Stanton wired McClellan that Lincoln had approved this plan.[65]

Suddenly in a more forthcoming mood, McClellan wired Stanton about various troop movements and sketched out his immediate intentions. Marcy sent assurances from Lincoln that McClellan "need have no fears about being molested," though that all was a matter of perspective, as discontent seethed in the cabinet. In approaching Manassas, Bates remarked, recalling a phrase from Oliver Goldsmith, McClellan had "advanced cautiously 'with fainting steps and slow' from one deserted entrenchment to another." Rumor had it that there had been an angry discussion among Lincoln's advisers and talk of replacing McClellan with McDowell, who had reportedly wept while revisiting scenes of his July defeat. Barlow was finally growing suspicious of Stanton, though at the same time the secretary of war promised McClellan that "nothing you can ask of me or this Department will be spared to aid you in every particular."[66]

As it turned out, McClellan's advance to Manassas only produced more controversy. The general and his allies described formidable Rebel fortifications and masked batteries. But soon there appeared accounts, including testimony before the joint committee, of logs painted to look like cannon ("Quaker guns") in the Confederate works, not to mention signs that enemy numbers had been greatly exaggerated for weeks if not months. "They [the Confederates] have deceived us," a Pennsylvania colonel informed his wife. At Manassas, he found few batteries, and the entrenchments were little more "than heaps of dirt." He did note that fortifications at Centreville were much more extensive.[67]

That McClellan had been fooled by the enemy turned out to be one of the milder criticisms. Contrasting the sight of wooden guns (soldiers had "fairly cried for shame," said one newspaper correspondent) with the inflated estimates of enemy strength stirred yet another round of outcries. Anyone with the "brain of a woodchuck," a Massachusetts journalist fumed, would come back from Manassas convinced that the winter delay had been a "gigantic blunder." Rather than pursue the retreating foe, General Kearny railed, "this ass McClellan . . . has brought us all back." Even the conservative and sympathetic Nathaniel Hawthorne claimed that McClellan's advance on Manassas bordered on the "ludicrous."[68]

The simple fact was, as one of Fitz John Porter's staff officers confided to his father, McClellan "is a failure." One-time admirers had clearly had their faith shaken; those who had been critical all along grew only more so. Senator William Pitt Fessenden of Maine dismissed McClellan "as utterly unfit for his position" and could only wonder why Lincoln kept him in command. In reviewing the general's career, it now seemed he had never been qualified for such a lofty post in the first place. A so-so stint as a railroad executive, an inflated reputation in the prewar army, and undue credit for the victories in western Virginia added up to what now seemed an unimpressive record. To make "a great military chieftain out of McClellan," one correspondent commented dismissively, was a great "humbug." Ignoring early accounts of how hard the general worked, critics now pointed to a decided lack of energy compounded by an absence of anything approaching audacity. McClellan the great engineer had proven to be no great general.[69]

People had waited more than long enough for this budding military genius to accomplish something. Greeley's *Tribune* led the chorus of criticism with four and a half densely packed columns of newsprint decrying McClellan's every imaginable shortcoming. It seemed apparent that hostile officers were feeding information to the *Tribune*'s Washington correspondent. Some attacks dripped with sarcasm; abolitionist audiences hissed at the mention of McClellan's name. Of course, the ultimate charge against the general—at least some Radicals in Congress accepted it—was that he was simply a traitor whose heart was not in the fight and who was hell-bent on preserving slavery.[70]

Public opinion about such a noted figure as McClellan could be quite changeable or even "whimsical," as the sympathetic General Meade observed. Barlow found evidence of Little Mac's genius in the supposedly forced Confederate evacuation of Manassas and still expected him to take Richmond. Yet as Barlow acknowledged, McClellan "is fearfully beset by open enemies as well as by pretended friends [perhaps referring to Stanton]." He considered Seward surprisingly supportive but had come to doubt whether McClellan could "keep a sufficient hold upon the president to enable him to weather the storm."[71]

The general's most ardent editorial supporters, most notably the *New York Herald*'s Bennett still called him a master strategist. Instead of throwing his men up against formidable entrenchments at Manassas and Centreville, McClellan had compelled the Rebels to retreat without shedding blood. Considering the recent victories in the West, some optimists believed that the backbone of the rebellion had been broken and the road to Richmond lay open, albeit by way of the Potomac and Chesapeake. Reports of cheering troops who idolized McClellan persisted.[72]

Once the real facts about McClellan's recent movement came to light, or so the general's friends hoped, then he would stand on more solid footing with the country. As it was, too many generals, including McDowell, made up an anti-McClellan faction that, along with certain cabinet members, were bound and determined to undermine his plans. McClellan's enemies in the press, in Congress, and elsewhere had gathered their forces. Critics would use the Confederate "escape" from Manassas to bludgeon McClellan, and the superintendent of the census urged Lincoln to "withstand the clamors of prejudice" against the general in chief.[73]

McClellan's supporters had reason to worry. On March 11 what had for some time been rumored finally came to pass: McClellan would no longer be general in chief. Lincoln's stated reason for the change was that McClellan had "personally taken the field as the head of the Army of the Potomac." Stanton had insisted in a cabinet meeting "that something must be done to relieve the other armies and the country of the Potomac incubus." Seward strongly supported the president's decision, referring to the "imbecility" of recent operations on the upper Potomac. The secretary of state agreed with Lincoln that they were doing McClellan a "great kindness" by leaving him in command of the Army of the Potomac. Tired of McClellan's secretiveness and adopting Stanton's increasingly hostile attitude, Bates feared that the general was "fumbling and plunging in confusion and darkness." Lincoln conveniently issued the order while McClellan was still at Fairfax Court House; the general only learned of the change when he read about it in the *National Intelligencer*.[74]

Ohio governor William Denison would formally deliver the news to McClellan and try to soften the blow. Word spread among some high-ranking officers that the president had succumbed to pressure from the Radical Republicans. By all appearances, McClellan seemed to accept the demotion with remarkable calm. He immediately wrote Nelly not to worry and to tell no one what had happened. "God will not desert me," he added. Assuring Lincoln that Dennison had explained matters fully, he vowed to "work just as cheerfully as ever before, & that no consideration of self will in any manner interfere with the discharge of my public duties."[75]

At times, McClellan had been his own worst enemy, but Lincoln had hardly shown great wisdom or decisiveness. The president was allowing a general in whom he had lost confidence to launch an ambitious campaign about which he had serious reservations. He might have been well advised to have relieved McClellan entirely, though he clearly could not yet see an alternative to Little Mac. The general had failed to confide in the president or even share his strategic thinking and plans in a timely or detailed way. Lincoln, goaded by Stanton and Bates, was asserting himself as commander in chief but still had much to learn. In temporarily taking over McClellan's old job, the president and secretary of war appeared ill equipped to devise military policy. Lincoln might have left McClellan to formulate military strategy and placed someone else in command of the Army of the Potomac. Yet desk generals, no matter how skillful, do not win the sort of lasting fame that McClellan sought. He had supposedly shunned the capital's vicious politics and now bade fair to escape to the Virginia Peninsula. But McClellan had not been as politically innocent as he pretended, and his would-be political allies and promoters had done him no favors.

6

HALTING PLANS

IT WAS ONE of those grandiloquent statements that some Civil War generals made on the eve of battle. From Fairfax Court House, on March 14, 1862, George McClellan announced that the time for action had arrived. Preparing to launch what would become known as the Peninsula Campaign, McClellan issued an order to the Army of the Potomac that summarized several points in his strategic thinking and indirectly revisited the controversies of recent months. "For a long time I have kept you inactive, but not without a purpose," he began, deflecting one of the chief criticisms of his generalship. The men had been "disciplined, armed and instructed," which of course was the general's strong suit. But to what end? The army was now prepared to "give the deathblow to the rebellion that has distracted our once happy country." Here was the heart of McClellan's approach to the war: defeat the Rebels with overwhelming force in a single, decisive campaign. He lauded the troops' "patience" and claimed to see "victory" in their faces. At the same time, he sounded a paternalistic note: "I am to watch over you as a parent over his children; and you know that your General loves you from the depths of his heart." As if responding to newspaper editors and other amateur tacticians who favored gallant, headlong charges on entrenched positions, he promised the men "to gain success with the least possible loss," adding that "my fate is linked with yours."[1] Surely his army's success would not only restore the Union but also fulfill McClellan's ambitions for glory.

Soldiers in the Army of the Potomac shared this order with their homefolks, and soon it was printed in the newspapers. Friendly journalists deemed it "stirring" and spoke of rekindled hopes for a short war. The general's most fervent defenders viewed the address as a vindication of his steady course amid mounting and baseless criticism (especially from "abolitionists," though use of that term was rather elastic). Such praise appeared just as the first troops were embarking for the Peninsula. But the increasingly hostile *Chicago Tribune* more pointedly remarked how "undisciplined western boys" who had "shown the road to victory" in Missouri and Tennessee had little faith in the more cautious "strategy" favored in the Army of the Potomac.[2]

With McClellan's recent demotion, both the strategic and political grounds had shifted. Secretary of War Stanton now acted as de facto general in chief and soon convened a "War Board," which included the adjutant general along with various bureau heads. At the board's first meeting, Stanton predicted that the Army of the Potomac would "require very little attention" because it would not long remain in the camps around Washington. He hoped the War Board (convening daily for an hour) would become "an informal organization for his own instruction" and thereby "bring to bear the whole power of the government upon the operations of the present war." Indeed, it appeared that the secretary of war—McClellan slowly came to realize he was no friend—was rapidly gaining ascendancy in administration councils. Stanton had reportedly complained of McClellan having been too busy reconstructing the Democratic Party to fight the Rebels.[3] The secretary had summoned sixty-three-year-old Ethan Allen Hitchcock to Washington, ostensibly as an advisor, but then pressed him as a replacement for McClellan as commander of the Army of the Potomac. Hitchcock at this time had been retired after a long military career, was in poor health, and was happiest pursuing a panoply of esoteric subjects in his study. "I was amazed," the old general later wrote about Stanton's importunities. "[I] told him at once that I could not [take command of the Army of the Potomac]." That hardly deterred the secretary of war, who spoke of mounting calls for McClellan's removal and later regaled Hitchcock with details of the younger general's incompetence. Such talk upset Hitchcock, so he did agree to chair the War Board.[4] That position proved to be a nominal one because from this point on, Lincoln and Stanton were directing military strategy.

Persistent rumors of McClellan's impending removal hardly boded well for his imminent move to the Virginia Peninsula. Even those in Washington who had long given him the benefit of the doubt began to waver. According to press accounts, a congressional resolution calling for the general's removal had been withdrawn only at the last minute. McClellan could hardly ignore such reports, though he remained hopeful of launching his campaign before the naysayers could strike. Some soldiers refused to believe that their commander was in any danger, but doubters such as General Kearny could not understand why McClellan was sticking with his plan to move by water after the enemy had abandoned Manassas. Trying to sort out the various bits of Washington and army gossip, General Meade deplored Lincoln's "timid and vacillating" course. He worried that McClellan had failed to build relationships with veteran generals—he mentioned Heintzelman, Sumner, McDowell, and Keyes—and at the same time had shown favoritism toward younger and more pliable subordinates.[5]

The problem remained that the Lincoln administration had gone along with McClellan's change of base to the lower Chesapeake but without really approving it, indeed having imposed restrictions—some reasonable, some not—on the disposition of forces and the army's movements. McClellan's reluctance to share information with subordinates and superiors further hampered operations. The general came increasingly to see the administration, and especially Stanton, as both unhelpful and unfriendly. As for Lincoln, the president showed a limited understanding of military affairs, plotting strategy on a map without paying much attention to geographical barriers (such as the mountains of East Tennessee) or logistical considerations.[6]

McClellan matched Lincoln's military naïveté with a remarkable and often willful obliviousness to political realities. Admittedly, he could have done little to assuage the hostility of the Radical Republicans, yet he also ignored advice to court moderates. Attorney General Bates still hoped that McClellan could be sustained against the "scheming ultras of the north" unless further damaged by "his imprudent political friends." The general thought carping critics deserved little notice. "*The President is all right*," he informed Sam Barlow. "He is my strongest friend." The general still received considerable newspaper backing, but a *New York World* reporter recognized that the country demanded "action" and advised Fitz John Porter that McClellan should hurry off his "flotilla" toward the Peninsula before the president succumbed to rising political pressure.[7]

The hopes of the nation, McClellan's supporters claimed, were about to be fulfilled. "Our army is ample to whip anybody in rebeldom, and we would march to victory," Porter informed his newspaper friend Manton Marble.

The general's only worry was that "treason is at work and the abolition element is working with Southern Rebels to produce dissensions and break up our army." Even without political headwinds, the undertaking was formidable. Simply transferring an army of over 100,000 men (with little more than a month's real preparation) to Fort Monroe proved challenging, and this made McClellan especially sensitive to any Washington interference. For some three weeks, the streets of Alexandria and its wharf were crowded and noisy; steamboats, schooners, barges, and other craft carried away the soldiers, along with the mountain of supplies (not to mention the artillery, horses, and wagons) that the army required.[8]

On March 17, McClellan bade farewell to his family, and Nelly held the general's hand for some time. There was occasional confusion about the capacity of the vessels, so the boarding and departures proceeded in fits and starts; there were apparently no naval officers present. McClellan, who took a spill when his horse stumbled on the wharf, admitted to Stanton that there was at first a "want of system" but that he had taken charge of the arrangements. By March 19, he declared the embarkations "well systematized" and the soldiers in "splendid spirits." Reports of cheering troops and McClellan's dashing appearance further suggested there were great things in the offing, though one observer thought the young general looked "old and care-worn."[9]

That same day, McClellan sent detailed campaign plans to Stanton. Fort Monroe would be the initial base of operations before an advance on Richmond by way of Yorktown and West Point. "We shall fight a decisive battle between West Point and Richmond," he predicted. McClellan maintained that a combined operation with the navy against Yorktown would yield "the most rapid and decisive results." Without full naval cooperation, he warned, the campaign could drag on for "many weeks." When the secretary of war made no immediate response, McClellan urged him to see Lincoln at once. "Nothing decisive at the President's," Stanton reported. "The plan seemed to find favor with all who spoke," but he could offer no tangible assurance of naval support. General McDowell had earlier discussed the movement with Assistant Secretary of the Navy Gustavus Fox, who had promised to make all the resources of his department available, though given the recent panic over the Confederate ironclad *Virginia,* McClellan might have recognized that there could be serious limits to how much help the navy could or would provide. Lincoln, accompanied by John A.

Dahlgren, commander of the Washington Navy Yard, came to Alexandria on March 21 to meet with McClellan and McDowell. In the early evening, McDowell and Dahlgren joined Lincoln at the White House along with Stanton, Welles, and Fox. Significantly, the latter two "threw cold water" on a proposal for the navy to attack Yorktown.[10] This council of war, like so many others, ended with no resolution.

According to one newspaper, the president "adheres firmly to the plans of Gen. McClellan," and some Radical Republicans feared that was all too true. "I am rejoiced you are getting along so well," Stanton wired McClellan as the troops were leaving Alexandria (and he was spreading tales of the general's incompetence). Lincoln had "gone back to his first love as to General McClellan," Stanton complained to members of the Joint Committee on the Conduct of the War. Besides cataloging McClellan's faults, the secretary charged there were "traitors in his command." The anonymous journalism of Lincoln's secretaries also began tilting in Stanton's favor at this time. So powerful were McClellan's foes, General Meade feared, "The slightest check or disaster will ruin him at once." Shortly before leaving for the Peninsula, McClellan smoked a friendly cigar with Seward but surely had an inkling that he was on thin ice with much of official Washington.[11]

The departure of troops for the Peninsula hardly quelled military and political speculation about McClellan's future. Whether the ambitious McDowell could be trusted as a loyal subordinate remained to be seen, one officer commented. The soldiers heard plenty about intrigue in Washington (including discussions of McClellan's views about slavery and prospects as a presidential candidate), and it is fair to say that both the general's enemies and friends kept the pot stirred.[12] A conservative Boston editor might accuse abolitionists and their allies of praying for McClellan's defeat and the Union's destruction, and predictably enough a rival Boston editor would reply that northern "secession newspapers" (including "Bennett's Satanic Herald") flattered the general and abused his critics because they wanted slavery preserved and the southern rebellion to succeed. Predictions that McClellan was about to win a major victory elicited ridicule and sarcasm from some Republicans.[13]

On March 31, even before he had left Alexandria, McClellan learned that his force would be reduced because Lincoln had agreed to transfer Brigadier General Blenker's division to the newly created Mountain Department, commanded by Republican favorite Major General Frémont.

The president assured McClellan that he had felt "constrained" (presumably by political pressure) and had made the decision "with great pain, understanding that you would wish otherwise." McClellan said that he could ill afford to lose these men but would accede to Lincoln's judgment. On this occasion, John Hay found the general "more pleasant and cordial in manner" than was his usual mien. In a note to the president, McClellan even claimed to appreciate the "circumstances of the case" and considered "the tone of your note as in the highest degree complimentary to me, & adding one to the many proofs of personal regard you have so often honored me with."[14] This laid it on thick, but then McClellan's mood obviously brightened as he was finally escaping the capital.

Aboard the flagship *Commodore* on the afternoon of April 1, McClellan sailed down the Potomac. He had feared being called back to Washington and so rejoiced at breaking free from "that sink of iniquity." He sent a confusingly worded dispatch to the War Department, laying out how he had met Lincoln's requirement that the capital be left well defended. His total of over 70,000 men included troops not yet arrived in the Washington garrisons and regiments serving with Banks in the Shenandoah Valley. From a military standpoint, McClellan had left behind adequate forces, but he had not carefully explained this (or his arithmetic) to Lincoln. Nor had he bothered to meet with the president before leaving, and a belated dispatch did not help much. A meeting of the War Board on March 27 had seemingly declared the capital secure, but on April 2, with McClellan in the field, Brigadier General James S. Wadsworth (recently appointed military governor of the District of Columbia) complained to Stanton that the fewer than 20,000 troops in his command were hardly sufficient. The secretary of war immediately ordered Adjutant General Lorenzo Thomas and Hitchcock to investigate. The two generals questioned whether Banks's troops "should be regarded as part of the force available for the protection of the immediate front of Washington" but then declined to offer an answer. They nevertheless concluded that "the requirement of the President that this city shall be entirely secure . . . has not been fully complied with."[15]

McClellan's math had been slippery, including the double counting of some units, though his biggest mistake had been not explaining clearly how Washington remained perfectly safe from Rebel attack. His professional arrogance, persistent reticence, and occasional contempt for civilian superiors again proved to be a key weakness. As always there was politics.

Wadsworth was a strong Republican without military experience, and McClellan had objected to his appointment. He later described Wadsworth as being as two-faced as Stanton. It was true that Wadsworth had for some time been privately grumbling that McClellan had done little with his large army. Shortly before McClellan left for the Peninsula, there appeared a rumor—hotly denied—about Wadsworth having sent to *New York Times* editor Henry J. Raymond a letter "so abusive" of McClellan that Raymond had declined to publish it. The comte de Paris considered Republican support for Wadsworth (and Frémont) as part of an abolitionist scheme to weaken McClellan and dismember the Army of the Potomac.[16]

McClellan's faith in military professionalism and a brotherhood of arms going back to his service in Mexico made him impatient not only with volunteer officers but also with civilians who seemed hopelessly ignorant about military affairs. Campaigns should be planned and conducted on a scientific basis by those who understood such matters, he strongly believed. As the general told the troops, he hoped to win a great victory on the Peninsula without resorting to unnecessary sacrifice of life.[17] Yet even before McClellan departed Alexandria, the Confederates in the Shenandoah Valley complicated matters. On March 11, Major General Thomas J. "Stonewall" Jackson's small army had left Winchester, moving up the Valley with Federal forces in close pursuit. On March 23, Jackson attacked Brigadier General James Shields's division at Kernstown. This tactical Union victory proved to be a strategic defeat because Jackson, having taken the offensive, made Lincoln and others more anxious about the safety of Washington and forced Banks to remain in the Valley. This also meant sending troops that would have been stationed about Manassas to Banks, and that, too, worried Stanton and the president. McClellan doubted that Jackson would be reinforced and certainly believed Banks could handle the situation, but he should have anticipated that all this might force some adjustment to his plans.[18]

Even as McClellan arrived at Fort Monroe, another obstacle loomed: John E. Wool, the oldest general to command troops on either side. On March 13, Stanton had assured McClellan that Wool "could be relieved of command" whenever he chose. The problem was that Wool retained control of the troops at Fort Monroe, and not surprisingly McClellan recommended that the old general be assigned to a different post. Stanton asked Wool to "waive the exercise of your authority temporarily in his [McClellan's] favor." Wool quickly promised full cooperation. Diplomatically trying to please both men, Lincoln stated that McClellan "must not be interfered with by Gen. Wool" but then added, "Yet I do not wish Gen. Wool's feelings hurt and I am ready to make him a Major Genl. if it will do any good." Stanton commended both generals for their cooperative spirit and clearly hoped the matter had been settled, though Wool bristled over McClellan's plan to place the troops at Fort Monroe into a division under Brigadier General Joseph K. F. Mansfield, apparently even speaking of having McClellan arrested. By March 26, Stanton's recommendations to Wool had become a presidential order. Yet only a week later, apparently after some lobbying by Wool's Republican allies and reflecting continued worries for the safety of Washington, a new order was issued leaving the command situation at Fort Monroe in a muddle and appearing to reduce McClellan's authority.[19]

Word was that when McClellan disembarked at Fort Monroe on April 2, he would order an immediate advance, and the general's dispatches exuded energy and determination. In a quick note to Nelly, he promised, "The grass will not grow under my feet." McClellan, Heintzelman, Fitz John Porter, and Baldy Smith stayed up that night until after 2 a.m. discussing the next day's operations. A confident McClellan dismissed a shortage of wagons as a temporary impediment and believed that "the éclat of taking Yorktown will cover a delay of the few days necessary to get everything in hand & ready for action." At first, he appeared not to have considered the heavy rains that had fallen recently or the muddy roads over which his men would have to march. On April 3, McClellan reported having 53,000 men at his disposal, and with Wool and the naval officers appearing cooperative, he anticipated making great progress the next day.[20]

On the morning of April 4, the troops moved forward in columns and met little resistance. The men wildly cheered McClellan—"Soldiers don't share the hatred which politicians feel towards him," a Massachusetts lieutenant remarked—though one skeptic thought Little Mac "looked too young for his position." The general continued to sound exuberant. "Everything has worked well today—I have gained strong positions without fighting & shall try some more maneuvering tomorrow." Indeed, it had been a day that fit perfectly into his view of how the war should be fought. "I shall try to invest Yorktown & may have a fight," the daily note to Nelly promised.[21]

Others echoed McClellan's optimism, and expectations for a short and winning campaign proved contagious. Surely his vast army would triumph, though the desperate Rebels would no doubt fight hard. Even the hypercritical Kearny conceded that the Union's superior resources and the slowness of Joe Johnston meant that "McClellan will no doubt pass down in history as a great General" despite having "stupidly blundered in carrying out his own plans." Minus his superior's sarcasm, a colonel commanding a regiment in Kearny's brigade agreed that McClellan was "destined to be one of the great men of the age." After noting how people were offering bets that "McClellan will dine in Richmond next Sunday," George Templeton Strong remarked, "Maybe so, maybe not."[22]

That McClellan had moved at last heartened the Lincoln administration, but worries about Confederates in the Shenandoah and the defense of Washington led to an important decision. On April 3, the president instructed Stanton to retain McDowell's corps "in front of Washington." As for McClellan, he should "commence his forward movement from his new base at once." Despite suspicions that Stanton was behind this move (General Franklin informed McClellan of the secretary of war's complaints about McClellan favoring strategy over combat and harboring political aspirations), Lincoln insisted that the decision had been his. On April 5, McClellan received word from the War Department that "McDowell's army corps should be detached from the forces operating under your immediate direction." By midafternoon, he learned that Banks's troops had been organized into a new Department of the Shenandoah and that McDowell now commanded a new Department of the Rappahannock. Thus, within a short period of time, McClellan had lost Blenker's division and McDowell's corps; the creation of new military departments in Virginia and Maryland along with the independent commands of Wadsworth and Wool had reduced the scope of his authority.[23]

Stanton sought to cushion these blows by praising the advance on Yorktown, denying that the creation of new departments would "in any degree affect your control over all the supplies, transportation, and materials that has been left behind or that you may at any time require" and promising that "the whole force and material of the Government" remained "fully and speedily under your command." McClellan was not to be so easily mollified. With stunning hyperbole, he blasted the order detaching McDowell from his command as "the most infamous thing that history has recorded. . . . The idea of depriving a General of 35,000 troops when actually under fire!" General Meade fumed over the matter, too, and while he feared that McClellan might resign, predicted his commander still had a large enough force to "accomplish much" and "silence his enemies." Though no fan of McClellan, Heintzelman deemed the withholding of McDowell "a great outrage." McClellan later claimed that Lincoln's decision had paralyzed his plans, though McDowell's corps had been scheduled to arrive last, so whether it was vital for the early capture of Yorktown, as McClellan maintained, is doubtful.[24]

Then there is the question of McDowell's role in this. Upon taking command of the Army of the Potomac, McClellan recalled feeling sorry for McDowell and therefore had kept him in "nominal command" of troops on the Virginia side of the Potomac. He later felt "deceived" when the general joined in the Washington backbiting. According to Brigadier General Marsena Patrick, McDowell's wife served as a "rallying point for all the Abolitionists & anti-McClellan men." Even before the Peninsula Campaign had begun, among McClellan's staff there was wariness about McDowell as a gossiper and intriguer. On April 1, McDowell had testified before the joint committee that McClellan had miscalculated the logistical requirements for his offensive. That same day, he talked with Lincoln, who "seemed to be a little disturbed about the state of affairs in front of Washington," yet publicly the general denied playing any role in the detachment of his corps from McClellan's command.[25]

The campaign would proceed regardless of the shifting organizational and command arrangements. On April 5, the day he received word about the loss of McDowell, McClellan continued the advance toward Yorktown. Heavy rains, sweltering heat, and muddy roads further delayed the march, as did thick woods. The Confederate defenses proved more formidable than expected, and the Warwick River, rather than paralleling the James as some maps showed, actually flowed across the Peninsula and formed a barrier in its own right. Behind the Warwick, thanks to the efforts of Confederate major general John Bankhead Magruder, stood redoubts, rifle pits, and other fortifications. Inadequate information about the road network further hampered operations and revealed a lack of adequate preparation—remarkable given McClellan's engineering background. Smarting over the loss of McDowell's corps, the general begged Lincoln to at least send him Franklin's division because his reduced ranks made an immediate assault on Yorktown impractical.[26]

McClellan would in fact lay siege to Yorktown, a decision that fit with his engineer's approach to war and indeed anticipated in a memorandum to Marcy some two weeks earlier that listed siege guns as required for the

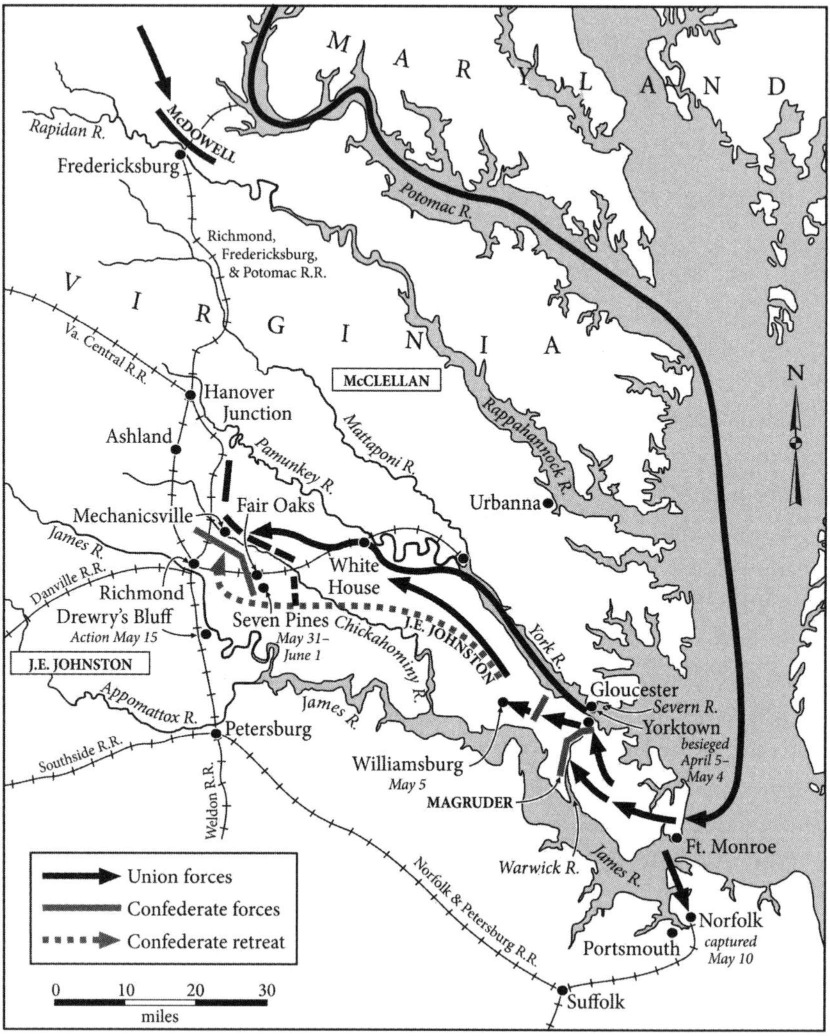

PENINSULA CAMPAIGN

campaign. McClellan already harbored doubts about how much naval cooperation he would receive after a timid foray of four underpowered gunboats, the commander of which quickly decided that the forts at Gloucester and the water batteries at Yorktown were too formidable to handle.[27]

On April 6, the advance toward Yorktown proceeded despite the mud, rain, and heat. Artillery fire could be heard at various times, and twice

McClellan ascended in one of Thaddeus S. C. Lowe's balloons to survey the landscape. He maintained old habits, working long into the night—Marcy in a corner loudly snoring on one occasion—and often failing to consult his subordinate commanders. From the outset there had been problems with staff officers, both their numbers and how McClellan chose to use them, and ironically the comte de Paris later claimed that there simply were not enough engineers on the Peninsula. Combine this with McClellan's desire to have all preparations completed to perfection under his direction, and the pace of the campaign became frustratingly slow.[28]

"You now have over one hundred thousand troops," Lincoln curtly wired McClellan. "I think you better break the enemies' lines from Yorktown to Warwick River, at once. They will probably use *time,* as advantageously as you can." Annoyed with the general's complaints about withholding McDowell, and likely spurred by Stanton's "slighting remarks" (as noted by Dahlgren), the president was running low on patience. Hay, among others, could not understand how the paltry Confederate forces at Yorktown had stalled such a mighty army, though one of his anonymous newspaper pieces still predicted that McClellan's troops "will make clean work of it." Lincoln had earlier told his friend Browning of having taken McClellan's measure and concluded that the general excelled at organization and preparation but felt too heavily the weight of responsibility, growing too nervous to act when the time for action arrived. As might have been expected, the general did not respond well to presidential prodding and believed that he had scared the folks in Washington by raising such a stink about McDowell. As for Lincoln's advice to break the Confederate lines, McClellan commented to Nelly, "I was much tempted to reply that he had better come & do it himself."[29] Rather than hashing out their differences on strategy, McClellan and Lincoln now could do no better than exchange telegrams—testy in Lincoln's case, whiny in McClellan's. The general could have acceded to the president's wishes or Lincoln could have made a change. Lincoln was starting to act like the commander in chief, but he could still not bring himself to remove McClellan. The general had grown increasingly suspicious of the administration and would neither try to sooth the president's fears nor recognize political realities.

McClellan's friends still claimed that Lincoln not only trusted Little Mac but also had given him a golden opportunity for success. Much of this was wishful thinking because opinion in the administration had shifted. During one meeting, Stanton handed Lincoln a letter claiming that McClellan had joined the notorious Knights of the Golden Circle at the behest of Alabama fire-eater William Lowndes Yancey (or in another version at the urging of Jefferson Davis). A member of the influential Ewing clan from Ohio wrote to Lincoln repeating similar rumors. Other correspondents suggested that McClellan was simply a coward and, again raising questions about Little Mac's loyalty, hinted that somehow Confederates had received advance word on any Federal movements. Stanton did nothing to discourage such talk.[30]

Attacks on McClellan's generalship continued. "How can the country afford to worship this do-nothing, this moral coward, if not, as some think, traitor?" the chief Washington correspondent of the *New York Tribune* asked one of the leaders of the U.S. Sanitary Commission. Others remarked that McClellan's forte remained inspecting troops. For sheer sarcasm, the *Chicago Tribune* won the prize with the comment that Little Mac "has rented a summer house at Fortress Monroe . . . in anticipation of a lengthened stay at what is not inaptly termed 'Point Comfort.'" The editor predicted more troop reviews, more serenades, and more speeches from the "Young Napoleon." Ultimately it would be the soldiers who paid the price for the ill-conceived move to the Peninsula and all the delays that would follow.[31]

None of this deterred the general's most loyal supporters from praising the cautious advance on the Peninsula, what one correspondent even dubbed the "Anaconda Policy." Francis Preston Blair Sr. advised McClellan not to worry about moving slowly, pointing to the example of the British who "had filled the trenches of Gen. Jackson at New Orleans with their bodies & their blood." Editors likewise praised McClellan for bearing relentless criticism with supposedly stoic indifference. The general had not exactly been phlegmatic but at least publicly had appeared coolly confident. His political allies still expected great things of him—including overwhelming success in the current campaign. McClellan did not care about politics, they asserted, but this, too, was only partly true because politics was a large part of the problem. In one of the letters likely passed on to Lincoln by Stanton, an Ohioan advised Senator Wade that McClellan's friends wanted to make him president to "break down the administration and Republican party."[32]

In any case, prospects for a triumphal march into Richmond appeared fading. McClellan reported the line of the Warwick River strongly defended and that Confederate reinforcements were arriving. For the first time, on April 7 he mentioned getting up his siege train against Yorktown; with little subtlety Stanton informed McClellan about the capture of Island No. 10 in the Mississippi River and the "brilliant victory" at Shiloh. Heavy rains continued, as did the usual newspaper reports of soldiers eager for a fight.[33]

Opinions in the army now ran the gamut. One enlisted man standing picket along the Warwick still believed that despite the formidable Rebel entrenchments, Little Mac was about ready, "and when the Ball does open, it will be of short duration." An even more enthusiastic Massachusetts private gave three cheers for McClellan and Lincoln, adding that he wished a regiment of "n—— worshipers" would come out to "sleep under a poncho in wet clothes and wet blankets." These soldiers heaped scorn on a hypercritical press and Washington politicians; camp gossip had one of McClellan staff officers boasting that the army was about to fight the last battle in Virginia (or even the last battle of the war). Yet some soldiers wondered why it was taking so long to prepare for that contest. As a New York officer pointed out, McClellan had still not commanded men in combat, and other volunteers reported faith in their commander waning, even that he had become "all played out."[34]

"Poor McClellan! I really fear he will fizzle into acknowledged impotence," Attorney General Bates worried. Lincoln seemed to agree. "Your despatches complaining that you are not properly sustained, while they do not offend me, do pain me very much," the president wrote to McClellan on April 9. Somewhat defensively, Lincoln explained everything from the detachment of Blenker's division to the establishment of new commands in Virginia. He laid out his concerns about Washington being left inadequately defended and bluntly stated that his orders on the matter had been "neglected." Therefore, his only option had been to withhold McDowell because "this is a question which the country will not allow me to evade." Repeating an earlier admonition, Lincoln again pressed for action: "It is indispensable to you that you strike a blow. I am powerless to help this." He then went back over his earlier objections to the Peninsula strategy: "You will do me the justice to remember I always insisted, that going down the Bay in search of a field, instead of fighting at or near Manassas, was only shifting, and not surmounting, a difficulty—that we would find the same enemy, and the same, or equal, intrenchments, at either place. The country will not fail to note—is now noting—that the present hesitation to move upon an intrenched enemy, is but the story of Manassas repeated." Lincoln had surely tried to deal with too many issues in one dispatch, and several points were bound to rankle McClellan. The president added a few encouraging words, though even those closed with a demand for action: "I beg to assure you that I have never written you, or spoken to you, in greater kindness of feeling than now, nor with a fuller purpose to sustain you, so far as in my most anxious judgment, I consistently can. But you must act." Postmaster General Blair, the cabinet member who retained the most faith in McClellan, advised the general to "make no complaints" and attack the enemy as soon as possible, noting that "the President thinks you are not sufficiently confident and that disturbs him." Lincoln himself was not feeling well—he took to his bed the following day—and later shared with his friend Browning the dispatch to McClellan, perhaps seeking reassurance that he was pursuing the right course with his troublesome general. Rumors flew of a "rupture" between McClellan and the president. Hay sarcastically remarked how "the little Napoleon sits trembling before the handful of men at Yorktown afraid either to run or fight."[35]

Soldiers (including all of Sumner's corps) were still arriving on the Peninsula, and the whole question of troop dispositions and numbers remained in flux. When Lincoln finally agreed to send Franklin's division from McDowell's corps to the Peninsula, one Maryland Unionist gossiped that Stanton had refused to sign the order and had even threatened to resign. Franklin feared his division had been punished for being so closely associated with McClellan and indiscreetly wrote to his wife about Stanton and Lincoln's "imbecility and folly," all the while feeding McClellan information about the machinations of Stanton and McDowell. Once the decision to send Franklin had been made, McClellan thanked the secretary of war and declared, "I am confident as to results now."[36]

By his reckoning, however, McClellan would never have enough men for the campaign, and numbers became a major source of contention. He had at first reported Confederate forces of around 15,000 men opposing his advance toward Yorktown, but soon those figures climbed. One of Pinkerton's sources counted 40,000 Confederates reaching Yorktown since the first units of the Army of the Potomac had landed at Fort Monroe; a Union colonel had heard that Joe Johnston was there and commanded 80,000 men. All these estimates overstated the size of Magruder's forces at Yorktown, but that was not the only problem. There was not even agreement on the number of troops in McClellan's command. Administration officials tallied over 100,000 men, but McClellan set the number at under 70,000; part of the difference rested on which totals, aggregate or effectives, were used. "There is a curious mystery about the number of the troops now with you," Lincoln had written McClellan on April 9. "When I telegraphed you on the 6th. saying you had over a hundred thousand with you, I had just obtained from the Secretary of War, a statement, taken as he said, from your own returns, making 108,000 then with you, and en route to you. You now say you will have but 85,000, when all en route to you shall have reached you. How can the discrepancy of 23,000 be accounted for?"[37] How indeed, and such disputes over numbers would plague the Lincoln-McClellan relationship for its duration.

The promise of Franklin's division briefly pleased McClellan, who even claimed to understand Lincoln's viewpoint, and there was talk of siege operations yielding quick results. The arrival of the artillery, including siege guns, surely meant that the Federals would soon be bombarding the Yorktown entrenchments. "Franklin is delighted. McDowell is chagrined," a Washington reporter informed editor James Gordon Bennett. Yorktown will prove to be the "Waterloo" of the war, an enthusiastic Pennsylvanian wrote from the newly established Camp Winfield Scott. Riding among the troops, McClellan cheerfully shouted, "Good night my lads; we will find what is in front of us and then go at them."[38]

Even that summons to action suggested a cautious, if not painfully slow advance, and for the general's critics inside and outside the army, that was the problem. Heintzelman, Barnard, and Kearny, among others, believed (at least in hindsight) that Yorktown could have been seized easily had McClellan pushed his troops forward immediately.[39] Whether such a rapid movement could have been launched so quickly after the first troops had arrived is questionable, especially given the lack of accurate information about geography and inadequate preparation more generally.[40]

In any case, McClellan and his men settled down to a siege. There were streams to be bridged, roads to be improved, artillery to be landed, and batteries to be placed. "I cannot exaggerate the difficulties of reconnaissances here," McClellan informed Stanton. "But we are surmounting them." Meanwhile, the Confederates had been strengthening their defenses, though the Federals managed to silence some of the batteries along the Warwick River. McClellan's dispatches to the War Department described steady progress.[41]

Careful execution suited the general's temperament. He had studied the famous siege of Sevastopol during the Crimean War, and though he placed his friend Porter in charge of siege operations, he paid close attention to each day's progress. McClellan undertook reconnaissance missions on his own—supposedly he lacked enough staff officers—and declared he would methodically press on regardless of any clamor in Washington or elsewhere. On April 13, War Board chairman Hitchcock visited the army, and McClellan explained his plans with apparent confidence. Yet he was showing signs of overwork once again, and one soldier felt the general looked not only "care worn" but also much older than he had appeared at the beginning of the war.[42]

McClellan thought he still needed at least another division (in addition to Franklin's) but nevertheless reported everything going along "admirably" with the artillery and other siege preparations. As historian Ethan Rafuse has observed, McClellan was willing to "sacrifice time in order to preserve lives." This wariness of futile assaults against entrenched troops shaped his thinking and won favor with many officers and enlisted men. In McClellan's view, advancing his fieldworks constituted an offensive operation and epitomized military science. He would let his artillery do the work and "avoid much loss of life." A goodly number of soldiers applauded this strategy.[43]

Newspaper accounts of a forward movement on the Peninsula and soldiers eager for a big fight failed to mollify skeptics or reassure the northern public, but McClellan appeared increasingly indifferent to criticism. On April 23, he told Nelly, "I am getting along splendidly with my *slow* preparation." He thanked Lincoln for the "firm friendship and confidence you have evinced for me." In one of his upbeat moods, McClellan even recognized that he should explain the situation more fully to the president: "Do not misunderstand the apparent inaction here—not a day, not an hour has been lost, works have been constructed that may almost be called gigantic—roads built through swamps & difficult ravines, material brought up, batteries built." He went into detail about the construction of parallels and redoubts. A Massachusetts corporal ruefully wished that Little Mac would order an attack because he was tired of chopping and digging. A Pennsylvania volunteer feared that "rain and mud had outgeneraled" McClellan, but he noted the enormous difficulty of bringing up artillery "through swamp, and morass, swollen into turgid lakes and inland seas." The general praised his men's hard work and believed that the "morale is on our side."

Among his subordinates, however, there were complaints that he planned to push aside the corps commanders in favor of Porter and Franklin.[44]

To the troops, McClellan remained both highly visible and approachable. The general readily shared a drink of water with a Massachusetts enlisted man whose blackened cup, which had been used for boiling coffee, was then saved as a "relic of the war." Many men continued to praise or at least show patience with their commander's strategy. They in turn hoped people at home would understand why great victories could not be won overnight. Others grumbled about politicians scheming against McClellan or newspapers carping over the army's slow advance.[45]

For the general's critics, here were the usual excuses for delay—muddy roads, powerful entrenchments, enemy batteries—and one editor sardonically suggested that there would soon be more troop reviews. Aside from reading comments in the newspapers, McClellan received continuous warnings about enemies in Washington anticipating, if not hoping for, a humiliating defeat. Such men allegedly feared McClellan's success, his growing popularity, and losing the next presidential election.[46] The Army of the Potomac itself had become politicized, with McClellan allies such as Porter convinced of a growing conspiracy against their commander. Condemnations of abolitionists and political demagogues enlivened campfire conversations. "I see McClellan has got some Enemies yet," a Massachusetts private ranted. "I wish they were all the other side of Hell." The politicians should leave McClellan alone, pled one Michigan volunteer, who railed against the drunken Zach Chandler and his clique.[47]

But it was hardly Chandler or Wade or any other congressional Radicals who most clearly stood in McClellan's way. The general's allies increasingly turned their fire on the secretary of war. Stanton proved to be a vulnerable target because few of the leading generals had much good to say about him; if truth be told, neither did many of his cabinet colleagues. Stanton had come to despise McClellan, especially after receiving importunate requests for more troops. The secretary of war had assumed control of military telegraph operations and determined which messages should be shown to the president and which should not. Yet at the same time, he sent encouraging wires to McClellan, never once revealing his deep reservations about the Peninsula operation and its commander.[48]

Some newspapers reported McClellan and Stanton working well together, but that sounded doubtful. Differences between McClellan and the

War Department over troop numbers along with complaints about Stanton interfering in the campaign received an airing in the press. Reports of the secretary of war hamstringing McClellan spread through the army's ranks. Editors might downplay rumors of Stanton's impending resignation or wild tales about plots to injure McClellan, but such reports inevitably raised questions about Lincoln's role. One of the president's political allies in Illinois noted the press's increasingly critical treatment of McClellan and how the general's friends complained that Stanton had gone over to the abolitionists. The war secretary's defenders countered that the fault lay with the commander of the Army of the Potomac. After all, Stanton and several members of the joint committee had recommended McClellan's removal, but Lincoln had decided otherwise.[49]

By mid-April, the Army of the Potomac appeared stalled before Yorktown. Whether the president would stand by Little Mac remained an open question, especially as the general's defenders blamed the administration for meddling in the campaign. In their anonymous newspaper correspondence, Lincoln's secretaries had not yet turned against the general, but their earlier enthusiasm had cooled. Acknowledging McClellan's popularity, they nevertheless thought he had been badly served by friends in Congress, especially the more extreme Democrats; McClellan could not be held responsible for idle barroom threats against Republicans, but Hay thought it hardly surprising that people would criticize a man whose champions were "contractors, parasites, and semi-traitors." Indiscreet staff officers and other McClellan allies had begun to attack Lincoln. Ironically, the general's editorial boosters adopted a similar line of argument to separate Lincoln from administration skeptics, especially Stanton, and the congressional partisans who assailed their hero. The general's friends and detractors alike kept insisting that Lincoln shared *their* views. Still, talk of McClellan turning traitor persisted. Senator Sumner insisted that Lincoln had lost confidence in McClellan and feared that the Yorktown siege would drag on for several weeks. The Massachusetts Radical thought that even Montgomery Blair's support for McClellan had waned.[50]

When McClellan wrote asking for Parrott guns that had supposedly been delayed, Lincoln shot back that the request "alarms me—chiefly because it argues indefinite procrastination. Is anything to be done?" Many others were posing the same question, but faith in McClellan died hard. The moderate *New York Times* kept predicting that the decisive battle would begin at any moment and continued to berate the rival *Tribune* for refusing to give McClellan credit for "planning the great series of victories" that had driven the Confederates from one fortified position after another. On a visit to the Army of the Potomac, diarist George Templeton Strong found McClellan's staff "in the best of spirits, confident of success." Noting how the poor condition of the roads and steady rains hampered bringing up the heavy artillery, McClellan nevertheless sent Stanton optimistic dispatches, even as he complained to Nelly about "enemies . . . abolitionists & other scoundrels" and wondered if his friends were all that helpful. The most recent report from Pinkerton pegged Confederate forces at Yorktown at just under 120,000 (roughly double the actual numbers), which likely created more uncertainty. McClellan still planned to open on the Rebel defenses any day but was feeling the strain. "I need rest," he plaintively told his wife. "My brain is taxed to the extreme—I feel that the fate of a nation depends upon me, & I feel I have not one single friend at the seat of Govt." Both the general and the comte de Paris feared he might be relieved of command at any time.[51]

There remained staunch McClellan defenders in the army, and some thought that the president's withholding McDowell had thwarted the campaign from the outset. Even so, a great victory by Little Mac, a Maine recruit predicted, would "put to shame the miserable politicians who have been trying so long to oust him and kill him from any political celebrity he might gain by success." With equal acerbity, Massachusetts private Roland Bowen recommended that if Horace Greeley "thinks we are slow, why in the name of God don't he come down and try the shovel a few nights himself." That McClellan knew his business and would spare the army unnecessary casualties were recurrent themes in soldier remarks. With the Army of the Potomac facing the enemy and surely about to advance on Richmond, this was no time for fire in the rear.[52]

McClellan later claimed that he had planned to have artillery open on the Confederate works on May 6, but on the morning of the fourth, his men discovered that the Rebel defenses were emptied out. This no doubt saved many lives, a Union artillery officer conceded, but he wondered if McClellan's enemies would now blame him for letting the enemy escape. Controversy erupted over the strength of Confederate positions at Yorktown and whether McClellan should have moved on them much earlier—and more aggressively. "Their works here were very formidable," McClellan informed

Winfield Scott. The Confederates "must have been badly scared to have abandoned them in such a hurry," he wrote hopefully. McClellan was justifiably pleased by all the Rebel artillery and ammunition left behind and from this considered the enemy greatly demoralized. Stanton quickly congratulated him and "rejoiced to hear that your forces are in active pursuit."[53]

The siege had ended, but the question immediately arose whether the results had been disappointing, given the fact that the enemy had managed to safely withdraw. Had the Confederates gained valuable time to strengthen Richmond's defenses? Fooled by the traitors was how the arch-critic Adam Gurowski assessed the situation. Other observers, however, favorably compared McClellan's siege of Yorktown to George Washington's siege of Yorktown over eighty years earlier. If the enemy had not suffered much, neither had the Army of the Potomac, so soldiers naturally emphasized the victory's bloodless character. The most wildly optimistic voices anticipated the war wrapping up by the end of the month. Even Chief Engineer Barnard, who had been critical of McClellan's generalship and would later become even more so, conceded that "the forcing of such a line with so little loss . . . is an exploit less brilliant, perhaps, but more worthy of study, than would have been a murderous assault, even if it had proved successful."[54]

If McClellan's defenders now felt vindicated, the Yorktown victory hardly silenced the detractors. Washington remained a hotbed of charge and countercharge, fostering deep divisions and intense partisanship. Radical Republicans had not been won over and would not keep quiet, though even the general's friends recognized that the value of the Yorktown triumph depended on if and when the Army of the Potomac marched into Richmond. Might Lincoln still seek a change in command? General Howard, then leading a brigade in Sumner's Second Corps, believed that the Confederates had fooled McClellan in retreating from Yorktown and decided that Little Mac "lacks the genius for his profession," in part because "he inclines too much to *engineering*." That was a harsh judgment, but for the time being, Jessie Benton Frémont, the general's ambitious wife and no mean political force in her own right, offered the best rough assessment of the political situation in the aftermath of Yorktown: "McClellan has another victory by default and one side cry shame and the other side shout glory. You can make your choice. The war is not ended."[55]

7

RECRIMINATIONS

DESPITE VICTORIES IN the West, Lincoln knew the war was far from over, and the slow progress of McClellan on the Peninsula only made him more impatient and restless. The day after receiving news of the Confederate abandonment of Yorktown, the president boarded a revenue cutter headed for Fort Monroe, accompanied by Chase and Stanton. After conferring with General Wool and Flag Officer Louis M. Goldsborough, Lincoln sailed around Hampton Roads and discussed sending Federal forces against Norfolk. "Why not take Norfolk?" he implored, and upon learning that there were few Confederates there, kept pressing the matter. Along with Stanton, the president boarded a tugboat to check out possible landing spots. He followed the entire operation with great interest. By May 10, Norfolk was in Union hands, and the Confederates had been forced to destroy the unseaworthy *Virginia*. Still in high spirits over this military adventure, the president returned to Washington the following day.[1]

Lincoln, Stanton, and Chase may have exaggerated the importance of seizing Norfolk, but their success contrasted with the problems McClellan confronted. On May 4, the general had wired Stanton that he would "push the enemy to the wall," though one report claimed that McClellan was so surprised when the Confederates evacuated Yorktown that he hardly knew "what to make of it." Indeed, the general remained at Yorktown as Franklin's troops arrived because he planned to send them toward West Point on the Richmond and York River Railroad. He had placed General Sumner in charge of the troops moving toward Williamsburg, with little expectation of their facing much opposition. No one questioned Sumner's bravery, but many doubted his capacity to direct soldiers in battle. One of McClellan's French staff officers who witnessed Federal forces coming under fire early at Williamsburg complained of "three old women [presumably Sumner, Keyes, and Heintzelman] in the advance" and urged his commander to leave Yorktown at once. McClellan seemed unaware that Williamsburg was becoming much more than a rearguard action.[2]

The fight at Williamsburg produced both command conflict and needless casualties. Artillerist Charles Wainwright believed that "jealousy among our leading generals" added to the army's woes that day. McClellan finally arrived on the battlefield late in the afternoon, and as usual the troops cheered wildly; one soldier recalled that "even the wounded and dying joined in the shouts." McClellan found Brigadier General Winfield Scott Hancock's brigade (Keyes's corps) heavily engaged with the enemy; otherwise, there appeared to be much confusion (Sumner had been a "complete fool"). McClellan nevertheless reported a "complete" victory even while claiming that his own army, in terms of numbers, was "considerably inferior to that of the Rebels."[3]

In recounting to Nelly the "brilliant victory" at Williamsburg, McClellan added that "Hancock was superb." All the praise for Hancock that soon appeared in the press rankled Brigadier General Joseph Hooker, who commanded a division in Heintzelman's corps. McClellan had inflated Hancock's role and slighted his own, Hooker groused. At one point, he vented his spleen (albeit with a double negative) to an Oregon senator: "He [McClellan] is not only not a soldier, but he does not know what soldiership is. . . . He is no more of a man than McDowell." Kearny, who had for some time questioned McClellan's ability, charged that "all the chief officers blundered grossly." More than a week after the battle, he was still railing against his commander's incompetence and mendacity. This discontent seeped into the ranks, and Kearny's denunciations of McClellan were forwarded to Lincoln.[4]

Whether such dissension in the army was significant depended on one's political perspective. McClellan's staunchest editorial supporters emphasized the soldiers' continued faith in Little Mac and the politicians' dishonesty. The Radicals in Congress would complain when the Confederates failed to fight at Yorktown and were equally dissatisfied when the Army of the Potomac had to fight at Williamsburg. After disparaging McClellan's relatively bloodless victories, one Republican paper predicted, "Bullets and bayonets must be resorted to at last." It was just such snide commentary that irked McClellan's supporters, who in turn praised the general's supposedly stoic silence in the face of unfair attacks. The real problem lay with the government. Indeed, McClellan's victories would have been even greater, the *New York Herald* sharply commented, had the War and Navy Departments lent him proper support.[5]

Lincoln reportedly deplored criticism of McClellan, and his secretary John Nicolay thought the general was "making good headway toward Richmond." The Rebel capital "is practically held in siege by General McClellan," Seward wrote home. Chase favored sending 5,000 more troops to the Peninsula, but such praise and support were misleading. Chase, for example, apparently favored reinforcements so that *McDowell* could advance on Richmond, and he scorned McClellan's "staff of letter-writers." John Hay's anonymous newspaper correspondence took a decidedly critical turn. Remarking on a great "run of luck," he believed the victories on the Peninsula had been won "in spite of ourselves." Yorktown had been gained "without an effort on our part." At Williamsburg, the enemy had both deceived and escaped McClellan. The general had created a "superb army," Hay conceded, but he "will only tarnish his laurels by seeking to add to them the praise of a great thinker and military genius." Surrounded by "flatterers and sycophants," Little Mac too readily exaggerated enemy numbers and too quickly complained about a lack of support.[6]

Defenders of the Lincoln administration rebuked McClellan's friends for reviling Stanton, as one editor put it, "at every hotel and upon every street corner." In their view, McClellan had received all the necessary troops, and the government had to make sure that Washington was properly defended. The general's allies hardly served his interests by relentlessly assailing the administration, particularly the secretary of war.[7]

McClellan had seemed unprepared for the Confederates' retreat and scrambled to follow up after Yorktown and Williamsburg. He praised his army's performance, made short speeches to a couple of regiments, and then began explaining why his army could not pursue the enemy more vigorously. Heavy rains caused more delays. Transporting artillery, caissons, ammunition, and supply wagons over the resulting execrable roads brought no end of frustration. In addition, many of the troops had gone without food. Keyes, Hooker, and Barnard all insisted that McClellan should have advanced immediately, and his failure to do so elicited more grumbling in the army and in Washington. Yet as temperatures climbed, so did the toll from disease.[8]

"Am very tired; had but little sleep last night," McClellan wrote to Nelly on May 6 at midnight. His clothes had gotten soaked in the rain, he did not even have a toothbrush, and he faced new dilemmas along with new opportunities. By the following day, Franklin's troops held West Point, the terminus of the Richmond and York River Railroad. McClellan had hoped to shift his base of operations to the James River, but when Union gunboats came under attack at Drewry's Bluff on May 15, that idea was abandoned, at least for the time being. Then, too, McClellan still estimated Johnston's forces as numbering between 80,000 and 120,000 men. A friendly newspaper correspondent claimed that the size of the Army of the Potomac had been greatly exaggerated by members of Congress and other critics.[9]

Whether one called these "justifications" or "excuses," McClellan always seemed to have a ready supply, soon adding one more. On May 8, he asked Stanton for permission to reorganize the army corps, having found the "present arrangement . . . very bad" and claiming that it had "nearly resulted in a most disastrous defeat." To Nelly, he railed about "the utter stupidity & worthlessness of the Corps Comdrs" and added, "Heaven alone can help a General with such commanders under him." With his usual penchant for exaggeration, McClellan claimed that "at least a thousand lives were really sacrificed" because he had been forced to organize the army into corps. In a self-pitying tone, the general remarked how he would have won more praise had the casualties at Yorktown and Williamsburg been higher.[10]

Fearing further rancor in the army yet unwilling to simply deny McClellan's request, Lincoln refused to have "the Army corps organization broken up" but would allow a "suspension" given the likelihood of impending battle. The president reviewed the reasons for its establishment and pointed out how McClellan's "struggle against it is received in quarters which we cannot entirely disregard." Here the politics of command took hold because McClellan's opposition to the corps arrangement "is looked upon as merely an effort to pamper one or two pets, and to persecute and degrade their supposed rivals." With this passive construction, Lincoln did not reveal how or from whom he had learned this, though criticism of McClellan among the army's upper echelons had become increasingly evident. The president mentioned discontent in Congress along with reports that McClellan communicated with no one but Generals Fitz John Porter and Franklin. He then pointedly asked: "Are you strong enough, even with my help—to set your foot upon the necks of Sumner, Heintzelman, and

Keyes all at once?" McClellan seemingly accepted this counsel and, rather than moving against the three corps commanders, created two new corps, the Fifth commanded by Porter, and the Sixth commanded by Franklin. This action appeared both compliant and defiant: McClellan had not moved against the senior corps commanders but instead had turned to younger generals—both Democrats.[11]

Some soldiers worried that McClellan might soon be removed from command. Such action would fatally demoralize the army, one Pennsylvania captain (and strong Democrat) warned. Would scores of officers then resign, as some predicted? For the time being, recent successes had allayed skepticism and even rekindled hopes about the war's speedy termination. Congressional critics received little consideration from the soldiers. "The hounds who pursued you so bitterly," Sam Barlow assured McClellan, "are now repaid and they know it. The most noisy abolitionists now fear to say anything openly & the politicians among them are trying to get on your side." Perhaps now Stanton, Greeley, and others would finally concede that Little Mac was no traitor.[12]

To prove this point, one seemingly had to look no further than Representative Owen Lovejoy, a fervid abolitionist, who on May 9 introduced a resolution in the House thanking McClellan for recent victories and "for the display of those high military qualities which secure important results with but little sacrifice of human life." McClellan could not have put it better himself, and the incongruity of Lovejoy and his resolution appeared striking. Regardless of his strong antislavery sentiments, however, the Illinois congressman was a friend of Lincoln who had seldom found fault with the administration. As the *New York Times* observed after this resolution received unanimous approval, here were men who had been among the general's harshest critics bowing to political reality. Massachusetts senator Henry Wilson, who chaired the Military Affairs Committee, flatly denied that he, Sumner, and Stanton had sought to interfere with McClellan's plans. Perhaps the tide of opinion was turning, though conservatives doubted that their political opponents were truly rallying to McClellan's side. Lovejoy was the first to make an "open somersault, for which he is simply laughed at," Barlow sharply observed to one of McClellan's staff officers.[13]

As was his wont, McClellan could operate methodically, with the political pressure for immediate results seemingly dissipated. Troop movements toward the Chickahominy River—this narrow stream prone to flooding would play an outsize role in the rest of the campaign—proceeded slowly. The men gained no more than two miles a day, according to one estimate. To both his wife and to Stanton, McClellan reported steady progress and high troop morale. He expected the Confederates to concentrate their forces (always reported as larger than his own) for a "life and death contest." As usual, he called for reinforcements.[14]

The troops cheered whenever their commander appeared; caps flew into the air as expectations mounted that they would soon be in Richmond. On some days, McClellan admitted that the advance was slow, but he blamed substantial enemy forces ahead, bad roads, or the weather. Receiving no response from Stanton about the Confederates concentrating "all their available force" to defend Richmond, McClellan appealed to Lincoln. Noting how his own numbers had been reduced by illness and other factors, he wildly reported facing an enemy army twice the size of the Army of the Potomac. If properly supported, however, he promised a decisive victory.[15]

Reportedly, McDowell had sought to join McClellan, and there were rumors of grumbling among McDowell's division commanders. By late April, he was near Fredericksburg and—rather like McClellan—felt relieved to be away from Washington. Lincoln and Stanton were keeping their eye on the Shenandoah Valley, especially on any movements by Stonewall Jackson. For his part, McDowell claimed that Lincoln's orders, along with supply problems, had prevented him from crossing the Rappahannock River and advancing against the enemy. By mid-May, Seward advised Lincoln to send McDowell up the York River to join McClellan. Even so, McClellan appeared diffident about even sympathetic cabinet members and found a visit from Seward, Welles, and Bates nothing but a "nuisance." He wrote of being tired of "public life" and sounded anxious to return home, which seemed more like venting for Nelly's benefit. Lincoln assured the general that he had "done and shall do, all I could and can to sustain you," but Stanton (and the War Board), watching Confederate movements in the Shenandoah, worried about a rumored enemy thrust toward Washington. To McClellan's way of thinking, as he complained to Seward, there were simply too many "independent columns" moving against the Confederates. At Fort Monroe, an equally dissatisfied General Wool warned that he did not have enough troops to defend Norfolk should McClellan be defeated, and he remained prickly about his command authority.[16]

On May 17, Stanton informed McClellan that Lincoln would not be sending McDowell to him by water, in part for fear of uncovering Washington. Instead, his corps would advance overland toward Richmond, cooperating with McClellan but still not under his command. McClellan later maintained that this forced him to abandon any thought of shifting his base of operations to the James River, but at this point, he seemed to still favor the York River line. Although Stanton had sent the new orders to McClellan by telegraph, he drove the point home by having an assistant deliver them in person. In the Army of the Potomac, some officers continued to see McDowell as an intriguer jealous of McClellan. Even Heintzelman doubted that Washington was in any great danger and believed that with McDowell's corps, the army could enter Richmond within forty-eight hours.[17]

Finally, having given up on his erstwhile friend, McClellan now considered Stanton "without exception the vilest man I ever knew or heard of." Fitz John Porter, who disparaged the secretary of war generally and downplayed fears for the safety of Washington, undoubtedly reinforced his commander's views. Writing to a former college classmate who was eager to fend off attacks by McClellan's friends, Stanton took the gloves off. The secretary of war dismissed critics as either "scheming politicians" or "plunderers" he had driven out of the War Department. Claiming to have been a sincere friend of McClellan upon entering the cabinet, Stanton oddly referred to presidential interference with the army and wrote at length about the need to defend Washington but did not mention his suspension of recruiting. Stanton cast himself as a patriot without political motives, working tirelessly to save the Union. He denied having done anything to interfere with McClellan's current campaign, despite his lack of faith in the strategy. In a fifteen-page letter, Stanton sought most of all to defend his record. While he could be accused of protesting too much, there seems little doubt that he had assumed a larger and larger role in military operations.[18]

Had Stanton at this point decided that McClellan would have to go? Likely enough, and that feeling was growing in Washington and beyond. Leading Republicans came to the secretary's defense whenever McClellan's newspaper apologists attacked. Stanton had for some time sown seeds of doubt about the general in the administration, and those seeds were not just germinating but flowering. Chase told Greeley that he now considered McClellan a "dear luxury," one presumably no longer affordable. Even amid word that the Army of the Potomac was moving toward the Chickahominy, Nicolay anticipated more delay and was starting to think it was time for a change.[19]

McClellan reported an advance along several routes, was anxious to learn about McDowell's position, and also inquired about Banks, Frémont, and Wool. On May 20, despite rain and muddy roads, the first troops had reached the Chickahominy at Bottom's Bridge. McClellan discovered weak defenses there and predicted that the Confederates would seek to fight a decisive battle in front of Richmond, though one of his staff officers wrote, "We may get Richmond without a fight." Wool passed along a report from two fugitive slaves, recently in the Confederate capital, that Richmond was about to be evacuated. Newspapers sounded equally optimistic. According to the returns filed that day, the Army of the Potomac now exceeded 100,000 men present for duty, though its slow forward movement also meant more soldiers falling ill in the muggy climate.[20]

At this point, McClellan's careful preparations appeared to be paying off, whether the Confederates decided to flee or fight. Some soldiers naturally wondered why the army had not advanced any faster, but confidence in their commander remained high. McClellan trumpeted his own military skill at Yorktown and thought he had barely saved the day at Williamsburg, but he continued to explain how poor maps and worse roads hampered his columns and of course how the Rebels badly outnumbered him. "The enemy are in force on every road leading to Richmond" west of the Chickahominy, he informed Lincoln. A "desperate battle between the opposing armies" loomed. McClellan kept pressing the president to send McDowell by water and admitted that his forces were being weakened by disease. By May 23, the army commander himself had fallen ill and appeared unsure about what the apparent lack of enemy resistance along the Chickahominy meant. For once agreeing with McClellan, Heintzelman recommended to the chairman of the Senate Military Affairs Committee that Wool and McDowell's troops, along with several thousand more from the Washington defenses, should be sent to the army.[21]

Unfortunately for McClellan, Stonewall Jackson had been stirring in the Shenandoah Valley. Banks and Frémont could presumably handle this new danger, but on May 23 Jackson routed a small Federal force at Front Royal and threatened to cut off Banks. As planned by General Robert E. Lee, Confederates in the Valley were trying to prevent McClellan from being reinforced. These events grabbed the attention of official Washington, if not throwing the Lincoln administration, and especially Stanton, into a panic. On May 22, Lincoln had decided to visit McDowell, and the following day he and Stanton arrived in Fredericksburg. They returned to Washington that evening, and early the next morning the president promised McClellan that McDowell would start marching toward him in three days. Yet by five that afternoon, Lincoln wired McDowell that this movement was suspended and that instead he would be cooperating with Frémont to bag Jackson. Stanton then sent Chase to explain Lincoln's order to McDowell. "This is a crushing blow to us," McDowell complained even as he proceeded to obey the order, and he soon wrote at greater length to point out how (with a "heavy heart") he could do little for Banks because even on a map it looked doubtful that he could help Frémont cut off Jackson's retreat. He later expressed doubts that Banks had ever been in any real danger, though regrettably the alarm in Washington was all too predictable.[22]

Lincoln explained to McClellan how Federal forces in the Valley had become "thinned," and so Banks was now in "some peril." The president asked him to help cut off supply lines for Confederates opposing McDowell but promised that McClellan would "have command of Gen. McDowell after he joins you." There soon followed, however, a brief telegram to McClellan announcing that McDowell, rather than linking up with Army of the Potomac's right wing, would be thrown in the rear of Confederate forces in the Valley. "I will make my calculations accordingly," McClellan replied that evening. The general seized on Lincoln's comment about moving "cautiously and safely," which suited both his strategy and temperament. In any case, he proceeded to have bridges rebuilt across the rain-swollen Chickahominy.[23] At this point, decisions made in Washington, the dicey political situation, the weather, as well as McClellan's ill health and excessive caution all worked together to further hamper the campaign. As was often the case, McClellan underestimated his own army's strength and considered the Confederates twice again as strong, though even one of Stanton's assistants passed along reports of more than 200,000 Rebel troops in the vicinity of Richmond.[24]

Both the president and McClellan had grown frustrated; neither seemed much inclined to consider the other's view of the situation. On May 25, Lincoln informed the general of Confederates driving Banks before them in a "general and concerted" movement. "I think the time is near when you must either attack Richmond or give up the job and come to the defense of Washington," he advised, without going into any detail. "Let me hear from you instantly." The note of alarm was unmistakable. McClellan received the dispatch midafternoon and quickly wrote Nelly that the president was "terribly scared about Washington"; he thought that he might soon be summoned to save the capital. Convinced that Jackson's movements were diversions, he could hardly contain his ire, "Heaven save a country governed by such counsels." Finishing up a reply to Lincoln, McClellan added a further note to his wife in which his anger and insecurities overflowed: "It is perfectly sickening to deal with such people & you may rest assured that I will lose as little time as possible in breaking off all connection with them—I get more sick of them every day—for every day brings with it only additional proofs of their hypocrisy, knavery & folly—well, well, I ought not to write in this way, for they may be right & I entirely wrong." To the president, McClellan offered assurance that he would attack Richmond soon and maintained that the Confederates were simply trying to prevent reinforcements from being sent to the Army of the Potomac—which was certainly true. That evening, Lincoln replied with more detail on the military situation in the Valley, closing with a brief justification for recent decisions: "If McDowell's force was now beyond our reach, we should be utterly helpless. Apprehension of something like this, and no unwillingness to sustain you, has always been my reason for withholding McDowell[']s force from you. Please understand this, and do the best you can with the force you have."[25]

There was a subtle note of resignation here, and nerves in Washington remained on edge. Banks had been "stampeded in the Valley," Nicolay told his fiancée. There were rumors of rioting in Baltimore, and one woman at Willard's Hotel asked him if she had better leave Washington, presumably before the Confederates arrived. A perfectly frantic Stanton alerted northern governors that "the enemy in great force are advancing on Washington" and asked them to forward all available troops. Chase doubted that McClellan needed more men to break the Confederate lines in front of Richmond. "There is a storm brewing in Congress," an influential senator informed his family, and Republicans should no longer hesitate to "censure our friends . . . for we are drifting upon the rocks." The president seemed "nervous," and for good reason.[26]

Lincoln was losing sleep and, on May 26 shortly after midnight, wired McClellan. At least Banks had saved his army, the president reported with some relief. McClellan's forces were still at work along the Chickahominy, and the general expected his army soon to be within "shelling distance" of Richmond. That no doubt raised false hopes in Washington (Lincoln soon asked if the army could "get near enough to throw shells into the city?"), but then McClellan's mood appeared to be on the uptick once again, despite recent clashes with the administration and the return of his "old Mexican complaint." Then just as suddenly, confident predictions gave way to doubts and hesitation. McClellan had lost some three thousand men "by sickness and casualties" in about ten days, and for once he worried about his troops remaining idle. Did this mean he intended to advance against the enemy soon? He in fact wrote to Lincoln suggesting just the opposite: "Situated as I am, I feel forced to take every possible precaution against disaster and to secure my flanks against the probably superior force in front of me."[27]

His moods remained mercurial, and McClellan suddenly sounded more self-assured—at least to Nelly. Morale among the troops remained high, and he expected to defeat the Rebels and end the war. In his view, Virginians had tired of fighting and were ready to come back into the Union. He mentioned "the shame of Banks' stampede" and claimed he had been right all along about McDowell's forces and the coming fight for Richmond. As always, he vacillated from overconfidence, to despair, to self-pity. His attitude toward Lincoln remained equally changeable, and he condescendingly termed some of the president's dispatches over the past two days "amazing in the extreme."[28]

What the public should make of the rapidly shifting military situation and the varying signs of tension between McClellan and the administration was anyone's guess. One newspaper claimed that balloon reconnaissance showed Confederates evacuating their capital. McClellan's political supporters continued to praise his careful and methodical advance on the Peninsula, but the *Chicago Tribune* refused to give any credit for "bloodless victories" and ridiculed the notion of McClellan becoming a military hero, having "never fought a great battle." In turn, a Pennsylvania volunteer disparaged such criticism because only the "purely ignorant" measured the worth of victories with casualties. Defenders still praised McClellan's "scientific" approach to warfare that avoided needless sacrifice of life.[29]

Had McClellan's "success" on the Peninsula silenced congressional detractors, as one newspaper claimed? Perhaps temporarily, but Charles Sumner thought all the recent military trouble "directly traceable" to McClellan, who had left Washington "defenseless." Much of the senator's information apparently came from conversations with Lincoln and Stanton, another ominous development for McClellan. To the more staunch Republicans, his politics remained as worrisome as his lethargic campaigning, and indeed the latter had supposedly grown out of the general's Democratic loyalties and commitment to preserving slavery. The political stakes were high because if McClellan emerged victorious on the battlefield, Democrats had likely found their presidential candidate. On the other hand, should the general fail on the Peninsula, his friends would surely blame the Lincoln administration. Even sympathetic men in the ranks worried that questionable political associations, along with praise from newspapers such as the *New York Herald,* might well ruin McClellan's standing in the country.[30]

Having reached the Chickahominy, McClellan moved to deal with any threat to his right flank, presumably to prepare for eventual reinforcement by McDowell. He sent Porter with a division and two brigades toward Hanover Court House. On May 27, Porter routed the badly outnumbered Confederates and proclaimed (as did McClellan and Franklin) a magnificent victory, but the rejoicing among both generals and the troops was short lived as campaigning in the Valley would still hold up McDowell. McClellan, however, touted Porter's success to Stanton and to his wife. "It is a fair presage of the great victory which awaits us at Richmond," he wired Nelly, even claiming his greatest fear to be that Johnston might not stand and fight.[31]

Another problem, as McClellan saw it, was that Lincoln did not properly appreciate the victory at Hanover Court House, especially when the president pointed out the failure to seize the Richmond, Fredericksburg, and Potomac Railroad, and questioned whether the Confederates were in fact concentrating their forces for the defense of Richmond. It was painfully clear by this time that, on even relatively minor matters, the president and the general would be at loggerheads, with mounting suspicion and distrust in both quarters.[32]

Heavy storms on May 26 and 27 churned up more mud, and the swollen Chickahominy left McClellan's army dangerously divided. The land around the river was swampy, with approaches treacherous, the vegetation variegated and dense, and mosquitoes and snakes a constant irritant. Given the uncooperative weather, difficult terrain, poor communications, and inadequate intelligence, any immediate attack on Richmond seemed out of the question. Rumors circulated that General Beauregard had arrived in Richmond with Rebel reinforcements. To cap it all off, a frustrated McClellan could see no reason why at least some of McDowell's men were not arriving.[33]

On May 28, McClellan had ridden some forty miles, returning soaking wet and having had nothing to eat. The next morning the malarial fevers returned, and on May 30 he took to his bed. And just as illness struck, so did Joe Johnston. The following day the Confederates advanced against the two corps of the Army of the Potomac that remained south of the Chickahominy, near Fair Oaks Station and the intersection of Williamsburg and Nine Mile Roads called Seven Pines. But the attacks were delayed and poorly coordinated, giving McClellan time to send Sumner's corps to the rescue, though a torrential rain the previous evening left the crossings hazardous. At midnight, Heintzelman met with McClellan, whose washed-out face revealed his greatly weakened condition. The army commander gave some general instructions and managed to cross the Chickahominy himself the next day. By that time the fighting had stopped, and the Confederates had retired. McClellan appeared deeply moved by what one army surgeon termed "the shattered regiments" that had finally driven off the enemy.[34]

In a wire to Stanton, McClellan praised Sumner, along with Kearny and Heintzelman, but of course there would always be grumbling over newspaper accounts and whether various generals received their proper due. Kearny thought he had saved McClellan from "irretrievable disgrace" without that fact being acknowledged. Heintzelman sought promotion, perhaps even aspired to command the Army of the Potomac, and would soon become convinced that McClellan had to go. But the immediate question became whether McClellan would take advantage of the Confederate repulse to go on the offensive. Could the army then have marched into Richmond, as some generals and politicians claimed? Sumner, Hooker, Heintzelman, and Barnard among others believed so, and eventually each said as much in congressional testimony. At the time, many inside and outside the army expected an immediate advance on the Confederate capital.[35]

The Confederates had hastily abandoned wagons, caissons, and supplies, but according to McClellan, the "state of the roads and impossibility of maneuvering artillery prevented further pursuit." The bridges over the Chickahominy remained an unreliable link between the wings of the army. On June 1, McClellan learned that Wool's department would finally come under his control, and the following day Stanton promised reinforcements. Doubts about the secretary of war's good faith spread in the army. For the moment, even some Republican newspapers appeared to at least tolerate the slow progress on the Peninsula and continued to accept inflated estimates of Confederate strength.[36]

McClellan issued an address to the army on June 2 announcing that the "final and decisive battle is at hand." Victory was certain because the troops had already proven their "superiority." Soldiers could rest assured that their commander would be with them in the coming battle and "share its dangers." One of Porter's staff officers sent the address home as a keepsake and reported the men cheering when it was read at dress parade. McClellan hoped that the Chickahominy would recede soon, and he had his men working hard on the bridges. Once Stonewall Jackson was "disposed of," Stanton promised, help from McDowell could be expected. In short notes to Nelly, McClellan sounded more buoyant as he raised the possibility of the road to Richmond being open "without further fighting." That was his decided preference because of the mangled corpses he had seen at Fair Oaks: "Victory has no charms for me when purchased at such cost."[37] McClellan's reluctance to fight bloody battles, however questionable that might have appeared to some contemporaries and later historians, was one reason he had so many supporters in the Army of the Potomac.

Heavy rains made it impossible to conduct any fighting at all, which in turn caused Lincoln to worry about the Chickahominy and the army's lines of communication. McClellan sounded irritated that the president might think he was overlooking an obvious problem such as the "confounded Chickahominy." Perhaps Lincoln had taken to heart the more sanguine predictions in some of the general's dispatches, and one newspaper correspondent reported the president remarking on Fair Oaks as a last desperate effort by the Confederates before their final defeat loomed.[38]

The army would keep advancing, but not right away. McClellan noted the weather uncertainties and other problems in messages to Lincoln and the War Department. "You must make your calculations on supposition," he advised the president, "that I have been correct from the beginning in asserting that the serious opposition is to be made here." This naturally meant that the speedy arrival of reinforcements remained vital. One can detect in all this, along with Lincoln's dispatches to McClellan, small irritants, each of which might seem relatively minor but with a cumulative effect that would only further distance the general from the president. McClellan sensed the prevalence of "selfishness and petty feeling" in Washington (and perhaps among some of his generals), but not of course in himself.[39]

The atmosphere in the capital hovered between worried and uncertain. Lincoln anxiously read the latest dispatches at the War Department, hungry for good news or any sign of progress. The fate of McClellan's campaign weighed heavily. Nicolay complained of McClellan's "extreme caution, or tardiness" and found himself "very nervous at the long delay before Richmond." One evening at Willard's Hotel, a drunken Zach Chandler loudly denounced the general as a "liar and coward." As early reports of the hard fight at Fair Oaks came in, a War Department official wrote that McClellan was "utterly unfit for the position he holds."[40]

At least the promised reinforcements were on their way, beginning on June 6, when Brigadier General McCall's division from McDowell's corps was ordered down by water. This briefly lightened McClellan's mood, though he was still not recovered from the recent bout of illness. In the meantime, McDowell's other two divisions had failed to bag Jackson in the Valley. Stanton asked when the Army of the Potomac might be ready to undertake its "final movement." McClellan promised, "I shall be in perfect readiness to move forward and take Richmond once McCall reaches here and the ground will admit the passage of artillery." That last qualifier was significant because the countryside was a "perfect bog" largely impassable for artillery, and the narrow roads there meant that any "general movement" must await "favorable weather."[41]

McDowell assured a skeptical McClellan of his eagerness to link up with the Army of the Potomac. Suggesting that the corps commander was opportunistically changing his tune as opinion seemed to be shifting in Washington, a suddenly confident-sounding McClellan told Nelly that the president and Stanton were "becoming quite amiable of late." But then he added, "How glad I will be to get rid of the whole lot." The rains kept coming, however, and McClellan fatalistically referred to divine providence. He still credited reports of Beauregard reinforcing the Confederates at Richmond and continued to accept highly inflated estimates of enemy strength.[42]

In early June, McClellan received considerable credit for the recent victories at Yorktown, Williamsburg, and Fair Oaks. His systematic conduct of the campaign appeared wise to many of his troops, who increasingly scorned the general's critics back home. By June 11, McClellan was finally able to ride his horse and certainly thought it important that the troops see their commander moving about and doffing his cap. Unassuming in his dress, McClellan's youthful appearance likely reinforced the soldiers' belief that he understood them and cared about their welfare.[43]

The army would soon be close enough to shell Richmond, an enthusiastic New York volunteer hoped. On June 12, however, McClellan again protested—this time to both Stanton and Lincoln—against McDowell being sent to the Army of the Potomac overland and warned of "serious hazard" if he had to extend his army's right wing to link up with him. One Washington official assured McClellan that Lincoln stood by him and deplored captious critics. Stanton himself expressed unswerving support and friendship in a dispatch on June 11, but on that very day, a newly appointed assistant secretary of war (who happened to be Stanton's brother-in-law) complained that McClellan kept making excuses and that the disastrous first day of battle at Fair Oaks was being covered up.[44]

Did the army retain confidence in McClellan despite signs of waning enthusiasm, as a recent recruit surmised? Was Little Mac afraid to fight, as one young officer wondered? Of course, General Kearny had gone well beyond mild doubts and had concluded that McClellan was not smart enough to conduct a campaign and would never believe he had enough troops. The civilian critics agreed, and even sympathetic observers now questioned whether McClellan was up to the job.[45]

Despite signs of eroding support, McClellan's defenders inside the army and out readily attributed delays or other problems to the Lincoln administration. The president and Stanton had taken matters out of McClellan's hands, Brigadier General John F. Reynolds, serving under McCall in Porter's corps, complained. If McClellan received enough troops, he would take Richmond. Brigadier General John Sedgwick, who commanded a division in Sumner's corps, feared that "persons entirely ignorant of military matters" were directing operations. Men in the ranks agreed that political interference was hamstringing the army.[46]

By June 14, McClellan reported the weather improving (despite temperatures in the nineties), bridges across the Chickahominy nearing completion, and the ground drying out, but the question of McDowell's troops still hung fire. Reports of Confederates rapidly entrenching suggested to McClellan that the enemy would fight desperately to save Richmond. The next day he wired that another hard rain had caused the ground to become "soft and boggy," making it impossible to move artillery. By reporting such details so often, the general created more uncertainty about if and when he would advance, and he highlighted conditions on any particular day rather than presenting a clearer picture of his plans. Little wonder, then, that Stanton and eventually Lincoln came to see his dispatches as a litany of excuses when that was not necessarily their intent. McClellan complained to General Heintzelman that Lincoln either had written "insulting letters" or had not responded at all.[47]

Word of Republican politicians turning their fire on McClellan, along with rival newspapers either attacking the general or lambasting his critics, cast other shadows over the campaign. Some correspondents echoed McClellan's dissatisfaction with slow-arriving reinforcements and accused Republican editors of refusing to give conservative generals proper credit for military victories. Complaints about the War Department censoring correspondents' dispatches aroused further suspicion about the administration's treatment of McClellan.[48]

There had been earlier grumbling about the prolonged (and presumably unnecessary) siege of Yorktown, and it appeared to some observers that McClellan would proceed against the Confederate capital in similar fashion. General Meade thought it reasonable for McClellan to await reinforcements before "pushing his lines any further forward" and believed he was proceeding confidently. At this point, the slow unfolding of his plans did not much bother the rank and file, who continued to believe that their commander's patient, methodical approach would save many lives. One junior officer favorably compared McClellan to the Roman general Fabius—he did not say who was to play the role of Hannibal.[49]

Amid the continuing delays, McClellan had entered dangerous political waters. On June 15, his aide Thomas M. Key met with the veteran Georgia politico and Confederate brigadier general Howell Cobb to work out details for a prisoner exchange. The discussion lasted several hours and meandered far afield, as McClellan later reported to Stanton. Neither Key nor Cobb apparently claimed to have any authority to discuss the larger issues of the war except in a purely personal way. The Georgian insisted that any reunion could only be achieved by "subjugation and permanent military occupation," that even the fall of Richmond would not end the war. The two men disagreed over how much Unionist sentiment remained in the seceding states, but Key tried to reassure Cobb that loyal northerners had no desire to subjugate the South and denied that Lincoln wished to go beyond excluding slavery from the national territories or the recent abolition measure in the District of Columbia. Key significantly reported that the Confederates would fight hard for Richmond, and McClellan passed on this assessment to the secretary of war.[50]

Had Republican members of Congress gotten wind of this meeting, it would only have reinforced their distrust of McClellan. Ever since the campaign in western Virginia, there had been criticism about his kid-glove treatment of Confederate property and conservative views on slavery. Shortly after the Battle of Fair Oaks, a brief but sharp controversy arose over the status of a small house owned by Robert E. Lee's oldest son that stood amid the Union supply base at White House Landing. After McClellan placed guards over this property, once owned by George Washington, trouble began. Complaints soon arose—passed along to McClellan by Stanton—claiming that the building should have been used as a hospital. The secretary of war forwarded a preposterous story about wounded soldiers having to pay for glasses of water. Such charges caused McClellan "great pain." He pointed out that the building in question was too small to serve as a hospital and that there was simply no foundation for the wild accusations contained in Stanton's dispatch. The secretary of war hastily accepted this explanation and claimed that he would correct "the misrepresentation." He later declined a congressional request for the relevant correspondence, though newspaper reports of the discussion in the House made reference to the Washington connection to the property. McClellan soon realized that Stanton had once again played him false.[51]

Yet he was facing a much larger problem without realizing it. Following the wounding of Johnston at Fair Oaks, General Lee had taken over command of the Confederate forces defending Richmond. Under Lee's aggressive leadership, the initiative in the campaign was shifting to the Confederates. Following his request for a reconnaissance of the Union right, on June 12 Brigadier General Jeb Stuart's cavalry ended up not only gathering the desired intelligence but also riding completely around the Army of the Potomac. This bold stroke sharply and unfavorably contrasted with

McClellan's evident lack of progress, as diarist George Templeton Strong remarked.[52]

Questions about reinforcements hung in the air. McDowell asked Lincoln to send every available soldier, but the president told McClellan that he doubted McDowell's men could arrive in time whether they came by land or water. There was still talk that McDowell was hostile to McClellan and very much under Chase's influence, though the corps commander wrote at some length to his wife about the foolishness of dispatching his forces to the Valley and his desire to assist on the Peninsula. On June 18, McDowell suffered a fall from a horse that left him "delirious," and the following day Lincoln and Stanton arrived in Fredericksburg for consultations. Sending word that Jackson was being reinforced in the Valley, the president claimed he could be of much greater assistance if he knew when McClellan planned to attack Richmond. A "general engagement may take place any hour," the general responded, but only "as soon as Providence will permit," given uncertainties about the weather. On June 24, Lincoln met with the retired General Scott at West Point to ask his views on troop dispositions. The old general considered the number of troops in the Valley and around Washington adequate but strongly recommended that McDowell's forces at Fredericksburg be immediately sent by water to McClellan. The defeat of the Confederates at Richmond, he predicted, would virtually end the rebellion.[53]

This was not the advice that Lincoln either expected or desired, and he sought to squelch rumors about an impending removal of McClellan, denying that the purpose of the West Point visit had been to "make or unmake generals." One of the president's secretaries wrote an anonymous newspaper piece claiming that the tide of opinion had turned in McClellan's favor. Stanton's friends were gathering damaging information about McClellan's generalship for the press, and the secretary of war scoffed at Little Mac's weather reports. Joseph Holt pointed to the Army of the Potomac being decimated, thought that Washington could well be in danger, and had little use for McDowell or McClellan. Sam Barlow assured McClellan that Postmaster General Blair stood with him and hoped that the arrival of Seward's political crony Thurlow Weed in Washington would do some good. In a letter to Nelly, McClellan sounded perplexed: Stanton and Chase had reportedly "fallen out," Seward and Blair were favorably disposed, Chase perhaps was becoming friendlier, and Lincoln "has again fallen into the hands of my enemies & and is no longer a cordial friend." At the same time, new suspicions about the general's loyalty arose, including a report about a meeting with arch-Copperhead Fernando Wood. McClellan's more perceptive friends recognized that any talk of their hero as a Democratic presidential candidate hurt, and in any case they maintained that the "abolition" faction in Congress sought to keep the war going until the country was forced to emancipate the slaves.[54]

In some quarters, calls for McClellan's removal grew louder. A historically minded New Yorker warned Lincoln against becoming the Lord North of the current war, with McClellan and Stanton playing the role of the Howe brothers. With no fear of hyperbole, the governor of Maine deemed the removal of McClellan worth 100,000 men to the Union side. The prominent Philadelphia merchant Alexander T. Stewart recommended replacing McClellan with Major General John Pope, who had captured Island No. 10. The fear of McClellan's growing political prominence was obvious, and the ambitious General Keyes told the easily influenced Chase that McClellan and his clique would never treat Republican officers fairly. Few editorial voices had yet openly called for a command change in the Army of the Potomac, but they would soon enough.[55]

McClellan faced rising expectations for a decisive battle as newspapers reported the army inching ever closer to the Confederate capital. One widely circulated story had the general climbing high up a tree to get a better view of the city's defenses. Had he received McDowell's corps, McClellan told a group of generals, he would long since have been in Richmond. No longer did he imagine the Rebels giving up their capital without a fight and would now have to proceed carefully against superior numbers. On June 20, returns from the Army of the Potomac reported over 127,000 men present for duty, though by this time Confederate authorities were desperately gathering troops to save Richmond. Porter wondered if Lincoln, who had supposedly fallen under Stanton's control, might wish McClellan defeated so that he could bring back McDowell to command the Army of the Potomac. On the other hand, should McClellan take Richmond, the victorious volunteers would hardly favor turning the conflict into an "abolition war."[56]

"No man in this army is so anxious as its General to finish the campaign," McClellan wrote home, but he added that "every poor fellow that is killed or wounded haunts me!" On June 24 McClellan ordered Heintzelman to advance his pickets and plan to seize ground for Federal artillery.

He also received word that Jackson had left the Valley to join in a Confederate attack against him. McClellan's most immediate problem was the potentially precarious position of his divided army, with McCall's troops and Porter's corps north of the Chickahominy, so he asked Stanton for information about Jackson's position and movements. In a detailed dispatch, the secretary provided little beyond sketchy reports and rumors. An advance of two divisions from Heintzelman's corps on June 25 toward Old Tavern, south of the Chickahominy, was stopped by a Confederate division near Oak Grove. More information provided by fugitive slaves (along with a dispatch from Porter and a report from Pinkerton) convinced McClellan that he was facing an army of 200,000 men with an assault on Porter north of the Chickahominy imminent. Shortly after 6 p.m., McClellan conveyed this alarming news to Stanton and complained yet again about not being adequately reinforced. With equal portions of melodrama, self-pity, and vainglory, he added, "I will do all that a General can with this splendid Army I have the honor to command & if it is destroyed by overwhelming numbers can at least die with it & share its fate." In such a circumstance, "the responsibility cannot be thrown on my shoulders—it must rest where it belongs." He prepared for an attack north of the Chickahominy and late that night even wired the secretary of war, claiming that with just one additional division he "could laugh at Jackson."[57]

As McClellan anticipated, on June 26 the Confederate attack north of the Chickahominy began. In the middle of the night, McClellan had ridden over to check on Porter; the responsibility for any defeat, he observed in discussions with several generals, would rest in Washington. He advised both his wife and Stanton that they might not hear from him for several days. At noon, McClellan reported quiet along the Chickahominy, though he would have preferred "more noise." He told Porter to hold his position and asked if a movement south of the river toward Old Tavern would help relieve the pressure of the gathering Confederate forces. Without waiting for Jackson (or orders from Lee), Major General A. P. Hill launched attacks east of Mechanicsville; by evening, McClellan was praising his troops for holding their own. He would be "ready for anything tomorrow," he promised Stanton. That sounded ominously as though he would simply wait for the Rebels to strike again.[58]

As suggested by his question to Porter and other comments, McClellan apparently considered having his forces south of the Chickahominy advance against the Confederates—exactly what Lee feared most. This would have been a bold stroke—out of character for McClellan—but one that held immense promise. Alternatively, he could have concentrated more of his forces north of the Chickahominy, though that would have been a riskier move, endangering his communications and cutting off a line of retreat. Instead, McClellan would eventually decide to withdraw his forces to the south bank of the Chickahominy and shift his base of operations to the James River. Lee's recent moves suggested superior numbers, and so this strategy seemed both advantageous and prudent. After all, McClellan could still point out that the government had not properly supported him, though this was the very point that most annoyed Lincoln. Having read the general's complaining dispatch to Stanton sent the previous day, the president remarked how it "pains me very much." He had obviously heard enough from McClellan about needing more troops and was running short of his legendary patience: "I give you all I can, and act on the presumption that you will do the best you can with what you have, while you continue, ungenerously I think, to assume that I could give you more if I would. I . . . shall omit no opportunity to send you reinforcements whenever I possibly can."[59]

In the process of deciding on the change of base on June 26 and 27—if that is in fact when it had been decided but more likely claimed in hindsight—McClellan had appeared hesitant and uncertain, weighing alternatives without always reaching a conclusion. This was especially troubling to his chief engineer, Barnard, who had to worry about the bridges across the Chickahominy. McClellan had left Porter's headquarters at one in the morning on June 27, but no decision had seemingly been reached on where the troops north of the Chickahominy should take their stand. By midmorning, McClellan deemed everything ready on either side of that stream to "take advantage of the first mistake made by the enemy." But by early afternoon, after finally getting a bit of rest, he vaguely talked of being "forced to concentrate between the Chickahominy and James." He offered yet another plea for unity of command, a problem that had proved frustrating ever since the campaign's beginning. Reports of enemy troop movements orchestrated by Major General Magruder led to fears that the Federals south of the Chickahominy would soon come under attack. Marcy informed Stanton that the army had been fighting all day "against greatly superior numbers." By evening, McClellan repeated that phrase but reported his men holding their own. He did not describe how Porter's lines had been pushed back at Gaines's Mill with heavy losses but admitted the possibility of being "forced to give up my position during the night." Should he receive "20,000 fresh and good troops we would be sure of a splendid victory to-morrow." Despite the afternoon nap, McClellan was still exhausted, having slept little for two nights. By eleven that evening, Heintzelman found McClellan's headquarters packed up and ready for a change of base to the James River. There was lingering talk of attacking Confederate forces south of the Chickahominy, but nothing came of it.[60]

Whether this was a missed opportunity or not, McClellan was in no mood to think calmly about alternatives. Shortly after midnight, he sent a long telegram to Stanton recounting the events of the day, including the repulse of "several very strong attacks" north of the Chickahominy, where his troops were eventually "overwhelmed by vastly superior numbers." He predicted that this engagement at Gaines's Mill would prove to be "the most desperate battle of the war." McClellan again claimed that with "20,000 or even 10,000 fresh troops to use to-morrow 1 could take Richmond." The Army of the Potomac had lost a battle "yet preserved our honor."

Even as he denied any responsibility for what had transpired, McClellan sounded almost unhinged, and he would yield not an inch in his demands on the government. Lincoln had described a previous dispatch as "ungenerous"; but had it not spoken an obvious truth about the need for reinforcements? McClellan's mind kept looping back to points already made. In the final two paragraphs of a telegram to Stanton, pent-up grievances, resentments, and feelings of betrayal came pouring forth:

> I feel too earnestly tonight—I have seen too many dead & wounded comrades to feel otherwise than that the Govt has not sustained this Army. If you do not do so now the game is lost.
>
> If I save this army now, I tell you plainly that I owe no thanks to you or to any other persons in Washington—you have done your best to sacrifice this army.[61]

McClellan essentially declared that he had been right all along about the unfolding campaign on the Peninsula, and only the failure to receive proper support had prevented him from winning a great victory.

Sent by an exhausted general who appeared to be at the end of his emotional tether, the telegram reached Washington amid great tensions and deep anxiety about what might be happening to the Army of the Potomac. To Lincoln, it may well have confirmed what he already suspected and feared about McClellan, but it likely also reinforced the president's faith in his own judgment. During a breakfast meeting with Browning and several others at the Soldiers' Home more than a week earlier, Lincoln had laid out his version of recent events. He had firmly believed that the great battle should take place at Manassas. McClellan, however, had favored the Peninsula route, as had a majority of the twelve generals called to offer their counsel. Lincoln had yielded to their vote in favor of McClellan's plan, but what followed convinced him that his original assessment had been correct.[62] So both Lincoln and McClellan remained dug in (and the Army of the Potomac would soon be literally so). The commander in chief's judgment would ultimately prevail, but where McClellan now fit into the picture became a vitally important question to the administration, to the army, and to the country.

George B. McClellan and Mary Ellen McClellan

The Lincoln family (*left to right*):
Mary, Robert, Abraham, and Tad (image of Willie on the wall)

George B. McClellan and Abraham Lincoln at Antietam

The Gunboat Candidate

Little Mac, in His Great Two-Horse Act, in the Presidential Canvass of 1864

8

THE BATTLE IS JOINED

"SAVE YOUR ARMY at all events," Lincoln instructed McClellan as the Army of the Potomac came under a series of attacks from Lee's Army of Northern Virginia. The president promised reinforcements but then justified previous decisions about safeguarding Washington, and he explained to Seward why sending more soldiers to McClellan might still endanger the capital. Lincoln acknowledged a need for 100,000 more men, though he feared another call for troops might cause a panic, and then sounded a McClellanesque note: "I expect to maintain this contest until successful, or till I die, or am conquered, or my term expires, or Congress or the country forsakes me." John Nicolay found Washington "wild with rumors and suspense" and worried that the public was not prepared to hear bad news. In seeking reinforcements from the western theater, Stanton informed Halleck that McClellan had met a "serious reverse."[1]

In writing to McClellan, Lincoln had added what was likely an unwelcome postscript: "Gen. Pope thinks if you fall back, it would be much better towards York River than towards the James." Like McClellan, Major General John Pope could exude self-confidence, but he was an antislavery Republican who favored a much tougher policy toward Confederates and their property. Related by marriage to Mary Todd Lincoln's family, Pope had graduated from West Point, fought in Mexico, enjoyed some success in the western theater, and in May 1862 was serving under Halleck. He was a shameless self-promoter but an aggressive general who had attracted Lincoln's attention, and on June 19 Stanton had summoned him to Washington. Arriving five days later, Pope learned that Stanton and Lincoln planned to consolidate the Federal forces in the Valley with McDowell's

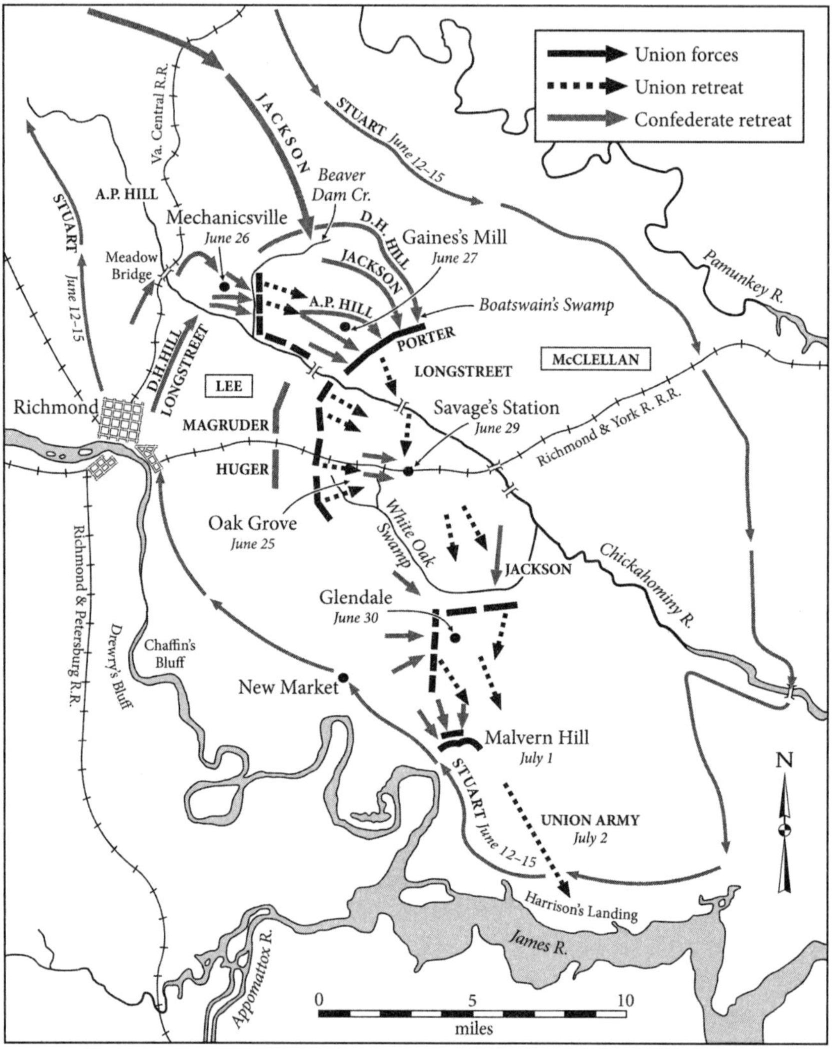

SEVEN DAYS' BATTLES

corps to form what became known as the Army of Virginia. McClellan had undoubtedly inflated Confederate numbers, Pope told members of Congress, expressing contempt for Little Mac and his conservative views on the war. He told Lincoln that McClellan's change of base was all wrong and that the Army of the Potomac should instead gather its forces on the north side of the Chickahominy. Playing into already existing fears, he pointed to the continuing danger of a Confederate strike toward Washington.[2]

Transferring the army to the James River was no mean task, but McClellan thought he might gain time if the Confederates did not immediately discern his intentions. On the night of June 27, he issued orders to the corps commanders and on the following day remained at Savage's Station. To Nelly he tartly noted, "I thank my friends in Washn for our repulse." The most immediate challenge was to move the wagon trains and artillery through White Oak Swamp. A newspaper correspondent informed Lincoln that the army's losses of both men and materiel had been heavy. Communication with McClellan had been cut off by the fighting, so Lincoln had little to go on but rumors.[3]

Whether McClellan had ordered the destruction of baggage, equipment, and supplies would later become a bone of contention in congressional testimony, but moving immense trains along a single road was slow work. In addition, there was fierce fighting north of White Oak Swamp, with Confederates reportedly advancing in great force toward Savage's Station. On June 29, McClellan gave brief instructions to the corps commanders but left them to work out the details. In the searing heat, aides became exhausted, and orders miscarried. McClellan did manage to fire off a message to Major General John A. Dix, who had replaced General Wool at Fort Monroe. McClellan requested assistance in protecting Yorktown, but most of the dispatch repeated familiar complaints. He railed against the government and the "selfish men who have caused the lives of so many gallant men to be sacrificed." Dix should keep this confidential unless McClellan himself was killed, then he could "make such use of it as you deem best."[4]

By the morning of June 30, Lee threatened to cut off the retreating Federals. McClellan instructed Sumner, Heintzelman, and Franklin on troop deployments to safeguard the crossroads at Glendale but otherwise stayed away from the battlefield. By four in the afternoon, he was miles away at Haxall's Landing on the James River. Less than an hour later, he had boarded the gunboat *Galena*. McClellan's absence from the fighting, and especially his appearing to take refuge on the *Galena*, made him an easy target for criticism. Here was a commanding general who no longer seemed to be in command; instead he chose to perform tasks that could have been safely assigned to a subordinate. To Stanton, McClellan admitted having to abandon a good amount of supplies and insisted that reinforcements be sent to Fort Monroe and soon. "If none of us escape," he concluded, "we shall at least have done honor to the country." Simply "worn out," he confessed to Nelly, "no sleep for many days."[5]

With no word from McClellan and with dark rumors swirling, the president had lost sleep, too, as Mary Lincoln confided to a naval officer. A Washington bureaucrat observed his "peculiar look of pain, anxiety and discouragement." The absence of news only increased doubts about McClellan, and Lincoln could only hope that some great failure had not followed the reports of heavy fighting. Perhaps the retreat to the James was being carried out with some success, but a call for another 300,000 troops would be issued the following day.[6]

On that first day in July, the Army of the Potomac was finally ready to absorb whatever Lee's army could dish out. McClellan had drafted a late-night dispatch to the War Department (this time sent to Adjutant General Lorenzo Thomas rather than to Stanton) reporting on the position of his forces and asking for 50,000 more men, though claiming that even a few thousand could make a difference. He then returned to Haxall's Landing and again boarded the *Galena*. For the next three hours or so, he traveled to Harrison's Landing on the north bank of the James River to check out a more secure location for his army. By midafternoon, he was back at Malvern Hill and remained on the right of the Union line. Under Porter's direction, Union forces repulsed the attacking Confederates and inflicted heavy casualties. At 9:30 that evening, an hour or so after the firing had died down, Porter informed McClellan that if provided with fresh troops and replenished ammunition, "we will hold our own and advance if you wish." McClellan, however, had already ordered a withdrawal to Harrison's Landing. He described the army as "worn out & war worn," though as always he relished the soldiers' cheers and claimed that he and his men retained great confidence in each other. A note to Nelly spoke volumes: "I am completely exhausted—no sleep for days—my mind almost worn out—yet I *must* go through it. I still trust that God will give me success & I cheerfully entrust to his will."[7]

Lincoln, too, sounded beleaguered, and had long since tired of McClellan's pleas for more men. For the time being, there were no troops to send, so he simply told the general that his army must be saved even it had to "fall back to Fortress Monroe." On July 2, Lincoln elaborated on these points with even less patience. He dismissed McClellan's request for

50,000 men as "absurd." All his talk of who bore responsibility for the army's retreat (likely referring to the infamous dispatch to Stanton) clearly angered the president, who warned McClellan to "not ask impossibilities of me." Lincoln did promise to eventually strengthen the Army of the Potomac from among the 300,000 volunteers just requested from the governors.[8]

Having succeeded in getting his army (albeit in what turned out to be a mad scramble) through a driving rain to Harrison's Landing, McClellan emphasized the success of that movement and the good spirits of his troops. The roads were a mess, and he asked for "enough breathing space to reorganize and rest the men and get them into position before the enemy can attack again." This still sounded like leaving the initiative with Lee, but at the same time, Little Mac upped the ante for reinforcements to 100,000 men. Lincoln had promised some additional troops, and Stanton was scouring various commands. What had threatened to become a sharper conflict between the president and McClellan abated briefly, as both men adopted a more cooperative and seemingly understanding tone, at least when communicating directly. McClellan admitted heavy losses and could only hope that the Confederates were as "worn-out" as the Army of the Potomac. He sent Marcy to brief Lincoln on what had occurred during the past few weeks. The chief of staff reported back that somewhere between twenty thousand and thirty thousand reinforcements were on their way and briefly added, "The President and Secretary speak very kindly of you and find no fault."[9]

Lincoln wired McClellan about the promised reinforcements, though these would probably not be enough for the army to resume the offensive for a month or more. Not to worry, he wrote reassuringly, McClellan should remain on the defensive and simply save his army. Lincoln thought that with the additional regiments on the way, the Army of the Potomac could hold its "present position." He added that whenever the general felt ready to 'take the offensive, you are not restrained from doing so." McClellan, however, bristled at the president's failure to appreciate "the glorious achievements of this Army." After all, Lee's army had been badly bloodied, and his casualties roughly exceeded Federal losses by some four thousand men. He would save the army, McClellan told Marcy, "in spite of all enemies in all directions." Letters to his wife more clearly revealed McClellan's troubled mind. His brave soldiers would stand with him to the last man, but he still needed rest and found "no peace except when in front of my men." Then, as if to rationalize his absence from Glendale and his presence on the *Galena,* he explained how "the duties of my position are such as often to make it necessary for me to remain in the rear—it is an awful thing." In further justification of his conduct, the general sent a long dispatch to Lincoln praising the army's performance during the recent battles and explaining the movement to a strongly held position at Harrison's Landing. The Army of the Potomac had been horribly weakened by recent casualties, he might have added by disease. As for the change of base to the James, here was a movement "unparalleled in the annals of war."[10]

At noon on July 4, McClellan reviewed the troops and offered an inspiring address. The army's recent achievements "illustrated the valor and endurance of the American Soldier!" These noble men had been assailed by "vastly superior forces and without hope of reinforcements"—always McClellan's refrain when it came to summing up the Peninsula Campaign. The Army of the Potomac nevertheless had taken its place "among the celebrated armies of history." It should prepare anew to "enter the capital" of the "so-called Confederacy" and thus preserve the sacred Union. Amid artillery salutes and band music in celebration of the nation's birthday, McClellan rode through the camps. "We were a good deal amused at this Napoleonic and spread eagle address," one skeptical volunteer sharply commented. Yet he admitted that many soldiers welcomed and cheered it.[11]

In the immediate aftermath of the campaign, confidence in McClellan persisted. One engineer bought the change-of-base argument and deemed the result "not a defeat, but a retreat." Many soldiers accepted the fact that their commander could do little until he received fresh troops. Even wounded junior officers remained enthusiastic McClellan supporters, praising the withdrawal to the James—in words that would have greatly pleased their commander—as a masterstroke. Such success had admittedly been costly, but the bloody engagements had strengthened the army by showing the soldiers what would be needed for victory.[12]

Yet army opinion had become decidedly mixed. In campfire discussions, men debated the merits of both the strategy and the strategist. Uncertainty about the Army of the Potomac's future fed skepticism about Little Mac's plans. Some simply dismissed the recent campaign as a disaster. McClellan "has been completely outwitted," claimed one Massachusetts colonel. The supposed brilliancy of the retreat to the James appeared hard for one New York captain to grasp. Others dismissed the general's July 4 appeal as bombast and greeted it with derisive laughter. Besides the heavy casualties, perhaps McClellan's political ambitions had also died on the Peninsula, claimed one Hoosier volunteer.[13]

Even so, soldiers who increasingly criticized their commanding general might still blame the government for not sending more troops. An Indiana lieutenant even suggested that McClellan could march his army to Washington and "prorogue that miserable abortion of a congress." Suspicion surfaced that a resentful McDowell had undermined McClellan and prevented the sending of reinforcements. "My patriotism is about played out," a weary Massachusetts artillerist confessed. The "damn Politicians are willing the country and army may go to the devil if they can only carry out there party schemes."[14]

McClellan's political backers agreed. Complaints about the government's failure to supply enough men became standard editorial fare and readily eclipsed any consideration of the general's responsibility for delays and mistakes. The Union's "exhausted heroes" deserved better from a government that had failed to strengthen the Army of the Potomac for a drive against Richmond, Frederick Law Olmsted concluded. Once the army recuperated and fresh troops arrived, McClellan could advance on the Rebel capital again, a hope shared by his men.[15] Each of these points rested on the belief that the army had been and remained outnumbered by the Confederates, an assumption that even found support in the pages of newspapers that often doubted McClellan's generalship.[16]

Skeptics might ridicule this "change of base," but to the general's supporters, it showed military genius. Newspaper reports anticipated McClellan's later claims that he had carefully planned to shift his army to the James: In doing so, he had saved both Washington and the nation, the *New York Herald* rejoiced; a Kentucky editor waxed even more enthusiastically, "The glorious star of McClellan culminates, and will soon reach its zenith"; the *New York Times* declared him "in all respects the master of the situation." To the general's defenders, the only thing that stood in the way of the Army of the Potomac's ultimate triumph was uncertain support from the administration and continued opposition from Radical Republicans and abolitionists, who could not see beyond their obsession with slavery.[17]

Even as political debate heated up, the country struggled to understand what the latest news from the Peninsula meant. "Defeat of McClellan," New York newsboys had shouted shortly before Gaines's Mill, and it had become clear soon after that the Army of the Potomac was in retreat. "The darkest day we have seen since Bull Run," George Templeton Strong remarked on June 30. By July 2, the *New York Times* was reporting heavy losses despite official denials. Wild speculation, including the usual rumors that England and France were about to grant the Confederacy diplomatic recognition, followed on the heels of incomplete reports as crowds gathered on street corners to pool their ignorance about the great battles being fought. Now people bandied about the word "disaster," though moods still swung wildly with each sensational dispatch posted outside a newspaper office. The strategic withdrawal to the James, however well executed, failed in many quarters to allay the despair, and "gloomy" best described the mood in Washington. Would McClellan have to surrender his army, as some panicky civilians feared? Greeley privately dismissed him as "a fool, probably a traitor."[18]

Calls for ditching McClellan intensified. Senator Fessenden of Maine accused the general of being a coward "morally and physically," his military career nothing but a "series of blunders." With the army reportedly cowering at Harrison's Landing, McClellan's conservative views on slavery and Confederate property seemed even more unacceptable and suggested a fatal weakness. The political pressure on the Lincoln administration intensified, and the recently arrived Pope fed the president's fears of further losses of men and supplies if the Army of the Potomac remained at Harrison's Landing.[19]

As usual, Lincoln walked over to the War Department to read the latest dispatches. He grew ever more anxious, though the mixed news from the army could both raise hopes and plunge the capital into despair. Whether McClellan's army remained in danger of Confederate attack aroused new fears. To visitors, Lincoln at times appeared inconsolable and even described himself as the "loneliest man in America." Should the president decide to relieve McClellan, who would take his place? Ben Wade had once impatiently told Lincoln that "anybody" would do, but the president had sharply retorted that "'anybody' will do for you, but not for me, I must have somebody."[20]

There was fresh talk of a cabinet overhaul, though who should go—speculation centered around Seward, Chase, or Stanton—became a point of some dispute. Cabinet councils remained divided on McClellan and other matters, and Chase's political ambitions hardly helped matters. The secretary of the treasury favored withdrawing the army from the Peninsula and, having fallen under Pope's spell, was convinced that McClellan would never enter Richmond. Seward's position was much less clear. His frequent meetings with Lincoln aroused suspicion and envy, but he was the soul of discretion, seldom criticized generals directly, and in public sounded his usual cheerful self. Yet the secretary of state realized that some influential Republicans favored McClellan's removal, and his own position in the cabinet would seem increasingly tenuous for several months. "Seward's vanity and folly" along with Lincoln's "weakness and obstinacy," Fessenden worried, might soon ruin the country. One especially strident critic blamed McClellan sympathizers in the cabinet more than the general himself for recent military debacles.[21]

Concerned that the Army of the Potomac might still be in danger from a Confederate attack, Lincoln decided to see for himself. Early on July 7, the president, along with Assistant Secretary of War Watson and Missouri congressman Frank Blair, left Washington on the *Ariel,* steaming toward Fort Monroe and arriving at Harrison's Landing late in the afternoon on the following day. After conferring with McClellan for nearly two hours, evidently poring over maps, Lincoln in his signature stovepipe hat set off with Little Mac on a "hot and dusty" ride to review the troops. According to General Heintzelman, soldier "enthusiasm was not very great," and some colonels in Franklin's division "forgot to have their men cheer." Elsewhere the response was more spirited as Lincoln rode through the ranks in the moonlight. His awkwardness on horseback and his tall, thin frame contrasting with Little Mac's short, stout one greatly amused a New York chaplain.[22]

After Lincoln asked about the size and condition of his army, McClellan reported a force of 80,000 men whose health was "better than in any encampment since landing at Fort Monroe," though given the already heavy toll from disease, that was not saying much. The president pointedly inquired whether the army could be safely withdrawn from Harrison's Landing, and McClellan replied that would "be a delicate & very difficult matter." The following day Lincoln posed similar questions to the corps commanders. Sumner, Heintzelman, and Porter strongly objected to removing the Army of the Potomac from its current position. Keyes disagreed and recommended that the army be brought back to Washington. Franklin thought the army should take a position along the Rappahannock River.[23]

"You need not be ashamed of your husband or his army," McClellan had assured his wife the day before Lincoln's visit. The president had found the army in "excellent spirits," but the general doubted that Lincoln understood what he had seen. "He really seems quite incapable of rising to the height of the merits of the question & the magnitude of the crisis." The president might well have said the same of him. As it was, McClellan remained suspicious and thought Lincoln acted like "a man about to do something of which he was much ashamed." Again striking the martyr pose, McClellan appeared obsessed with his own reputation, a burning desire for martial glory at times eclipsing his attention to immediate strategic problems.[24]

The meeting with Lincoln had partially revealed McClellan's ambitions—perhaps political as well as martial. In a June 20 dispatch to the president that included the usual explanations for the army's slowness and laments about facing superior enemy numbers, McClellan had asked "permission to lay before your Excellency by letter or telegram my views as to the present state of military affairs throughout the whole country." Lincoln would be "glad" to receive McClellan's thoughts but cited security concerns about discussing troop dispositions and numbers by telegraph. Perhaps recognizing that this was not quite the right time, McClellan would "defer for the present the communication I desired to make."[25]

When Lincoln arrived at Harrison's Landing, McClellan handed him a three-page document that he had probably been working on for some time. He readily admitted that his views on military policy were not directly related to matters at hand but offered them anyway. To McClellan as to Lincoln, the fight for the Union was a sacred one—"the cause of free institutions and self-government." He urged the president to "determine upon a civil and military policy covering the whole ground of our national trouble." Because the war "should be conducted upon the highest principles known to Christian civilization," McClellan rejected the idea of subjugating the rebellious states or warring against the southern people and was emphatic about what should *not* take place: "Neither confiscation of property, political executions of persons, territorial organization of States, or forcible abolition of slavery should be contemplated for a moment."

As he had since the war's beginning, McClellan emphasized protecting civilian property and deplored military arrests and oaths. Even as Congress was debating a stronger confiscation bill, McClellan would continue to deal with slaves as "contraband" of war under the provisions of the First Confiscation Act. Like Lincoln, he favored compensated emancipation, emphasizing both the Christian and constitutional character of such a measure.

A more radical policy, he warned, "especially upon slavery, will rapidly disintegrate our present armies." McClellan briefly mentioned the need to deploy concentrated military force against Confederate armies and, though denying that he sought such a post, recommended the appointment of a "Commander-in-chief of the Army" to carry out the president's policies.[26]

"I have written a strong frank letter to the President," McClellan told Nelly. "If he acts upon it the country will be saved." Yet even here, the general sounded more concerned with his own conscience and reputation. According to McClellan, Lincoln read the famous Harrison's Landing letter when it was handed to him, thanked the general for it, but offered no comment then or later. McClellan apparently assumed that his views largely accorded with the president's, and there was some truth in that. What he did not recognize was that the course of the war itself, not to mention political pressure from Republicans and others, was leading Lincoln toward a policy of general emancipation. The president's views were evolving, but McClellan's were not. Little Mac remained locked into a military strategy (with an accompanying set of political principles) that would place him at loggerheads with Lincoln, the cabinet, and an important swath of the northern public. Here was an army commander offering military advice fraught with political implications, though this was not that unusual during the Civil War. Then, too, McClellan did not publish the letter and did not deploy it for partisan purposes, nor did it become public knowledge for some time.[27]

Relations with the president and the administration had clearly soured. "In this weary world," McClellan claimed to have enjoyed "little happiness" aside from his wife and infant daughter. Although Lincoln had found the Army of the Potomac in better condition than expected (likewise confirmed by several press reports), he too was enjoying little happiness. To his old friend Senator Orville Hickman Browning, the president appeared weighed down by a host of troubles and, rather like McClellan, was starting to think about his own mortality. Take care of your health, Browning advised, but there was deep sadness in Lincoln's voice and tears in his eyes. To the frustrated president, it seemed that once again McClellan's numbers did not add up. The government had presumably sent some 160,000 men to the Peninsula, but only half that number remained; on July 13 Lincoln pressed McClellan to explain the large number of absentees.[28]

The response would hardly lighten the president's mood. McClellan patiently explained how all generals "find the actual strength less than the strength represented on paper." Remarkably, he claimed not to have his own returns at hand but doubted that he had in fact received 160,000 men. He reported over 80,000 "present for duty," with nearly 40,000 absent, both authorized and unauthorized. This last figure was admittedly excessive, and he seemed to place the blame on the War Department.[29]

There began a period of mutual recrimination that dragged on through the summer. Back on July 4, Marcy had been in Washington briefing the administration on McClellan's change of base and, according to Stanton, had suggested that the Army of the Potomac might have to "capitulate." In something of a panic, the secretary of war had immediately gone to Lincoln. Called on the carpet by the president, poor Marcy had stumbled through "some kind of explanation, excuse or apology." This apparently had calmed things down, and Stanton had perhaps then advised Lincoln to pay his visit to Harrison's Landing.[30]

The secretary of war, in his usual oleaginous style, now tried to smooth things over with McClellan. "There is no cause in my heart or conduct for the claim that wicked men have raised between us for their own selfish purposes," Stanton wrote reassuringly, even as newspapers and other sources were detailing worsening tensions. "No man had ever a truer friend than I have been to you and shall continue to be. You are seldom absent from my thoughts and I am ready to make any sacrifice to aid you." Even by the secretary of war's standards, this was a stunningly misleading and hypocritical statement. McClellan at first seemed to welcome those soothing words, though he quickly set the record of their relationship straight. At the time of Stanton's appointment, the general wrote, "I considered you my intimate friend and confidential adviser." McClellan had thought Stanton the best man for the job, but once in office, "your official conduct towards me . . . was marked by repeated acts done in such manner as to be deeply offensive to my feelings and calculated to affect me injuriously in public estimation." The withholding of troops during the Peninsula Campaign, McClellan thought, had meant that Stanton's mind "had been warped by a bitter personal prejudice against me." If the general had been mistaken on these points, as the secretary of war's note suggested, he would happily "resume on my part the same cordial confidence which once characterized our intercourse." Together they could still save the Union, and he urged Stanton to read the letter he had handed Lincoln at Harrison's Landing.[31]

Even while trying to worm his way back into McClellan's good graces,

Stanton was abandoning any pretense of support for his erstwhile friend. It would not have been a surprise if McClellan had in fact "capitulated with all his forces to the rebels," he informed his sister. "Every one here almost except the President says he [McClellan] ought to be removed." Apparently, Stanton's own strong views on the subject were becoming well known in Washington political circles. Chase and Stanton evidently recommended sending Pope to Harrison's Landing to replace McClellan.[32]

Amid a raging press battle, rumor had it that both McClellan and Stanton might soon have to resign. Perhaps General Banks would become the new secretary of war, as one newspaper suggested. Some editors blamed the administration—especially Stanton—for failing to sustain McClellan. The governor of Ohio begged Stanton to "stop the wrangling between the friends of McClellan and yourself in Congress." On the other hand, was the secretary of war, as one New Yorker speculated, being criticized for mistakes made by Lincoln? One of the president's friends deplored the "wicked newspapers" that sowed distrust in the country's political and military leaders by condemning Stanton and McClellan as "political tricksters, trying to get undue advantages of each other, at the sacrifice of the Country and its interests."[33]

Besides a reported contempt for strategy, doubts about Stanton's military acumen led to calls for his dismissal. According to McClellan's aides, the secretary of war had withheld reinforcements from the Army of the Potomac because Little Mac was becoming too popular. Through his work with the Sanitary Commission, Frederick Law Olmsted had come to view Stanton as a "canting imposter . . . liar, hypocrite, and knave." There was political animus in such criticism. Many people regarded Stanton as a "tool of the abolitionists," as the *New York Herald* declared in a piece entitled "The Mismanagement and Mismanagers of the War Dept." A young Iowa storekeeper, believing that politicians who wished to prolong the war had gotten in McClellan's way, offered a salty assessment: "this Abolition Congress is not worth a Shit."[34]

Still expressing confidence in McClellan, Brigadier General John Gibbon hoped that Stanton would be replaced by Halleck, another general with a reputation for conservatism. Instead, on July 11, just a few days after meeting with McClellan, Lincoln assigned Halleck "to command the whole land forces of the United States, as General in chief" and summoned him to Washington. Halleck's reputation as a military intellectual did not necessarily make him suitable for solving practical strategic problems or managing difficult generals. Able subordinates such as Grant deserved much of the credit for Halleck's achievements in the western theater, and contemporaries had remarkably little positive to say about a general once dubbed "Old Brains." Slow in both speech and movement, Halleck often appeared reticent if not diffident, and John Hay would later term the general "little more than a first rate clerk."[35] That harsh judgment went too far, but Halleck would certainly prove a disappointment to Lincoln, especially in dealing with McClellan and future Army of the Potomac commanders.

The new general in chief feared clashing with McClellan's Washington allies or, for that matter, dealing with Stanton. Little Mac perhaps had expected a return to his old post as general in chief, so hardly welcomed the news. He resented not having been consulted about the appointment and only learned about it through the press. To McClellan's way of thinking, calling Halleck to Washington was just the first step toward removing him from command. Sam Barlow considered it "a direct slap in the face to McClellan" and again warned his friend against being taken in by Stanton, "the greatest hypocrite alive." McClellan had already decided that there was no chance for a genuine détente with the secretary of war, and he had told Nelly shortly after receiving Stanton's fawning letter (and learning of Halleck's new post) that the secretary of war was the "most unmitigated scoundrel." Indeed, "had he [Stanton] lived in the time of the Saviour, Judas Iscariot would have remained a respected member of the fraternity of the Apostles."[36]

If the military and political situation were not already tumultuous enough, there was John Pope and his Army of Virginia. Shortly after taking command, Pope had promised full cooperation with the Army of the Potomac, and McClellan had approved Pope's plans to concentrate his forces. McClellan pledged to "move upon Richmond" should the Confederates attempt to strike his newly formed army. Yet despite these cordial assurances, Pope was preparing to testify before the joint committee that McClellan should have moved overland rather than taking the Peninsula route, and he would not promise to coordinate with the Army of the Potomac. A cynical newspaper correspondent suggested that Pope might be able to rescue the overrated Young Napoleon, though Pope told Lincoln that any move by his army to the Peninsula would risk its destruction. He reportedly advised the president to relieve McClellan before Halleck arrived in Washington. Hostility to Little Mac soon spread among Pope's troops.[37]

In the Army of the Potomac, antagonism to Pope followed a similar, poisonous trajectory. Pope's notorious braggadocio, best embodied in the famous address to his troops about showing no concern for "lines of retreat," as well as his orders about foraging, holding local civilians responsible for guerrilla attacks, and arresting men who refused to take an oath of allegiance outraged McClellan and his conservative subordinates. Fitz John Porter thought Pope had always been "an ass." By July 22, McClellan was predicting that Stonewall Jackson would soon be after Pope, and "a paltry young man who wanted to teach me the art of war will in less than a week either be in full retreat or badly whipped."[38]

All the while, for the Army of the Potomac at Harrison's Landing, a deadly enemy lurked. Olmsted worried about the effects of crowded camps, idleness, homesickness, and especially disease; indeed, he thought it best to withdraw the troops. McClellan reported the health of his men "improving somewhat," though the army had many absentees on sick leave. "McClellan has lost thousands already from sickness," an Ohio volunteer later lamented. "We hear the guns firing every night over the Graves of Dozens of poor victims to his strategic views." According to General Keyes, the men were growing steadily weaker through the sickly summer months. Malaria, diarrhea, and various fevers had already ravaged McClellan's army and would continue to do so as rain, heat, humidity, and supply holdups added to the misery.[39]

To Kearny and other critics, the Army of the Potomac appeared "boxed in" along the James, stuck in a vulnerable and unhealthy location. Taking the offensive might be the best solution, and McClellan seemed to agree—provided reinforcements arrived. With the men supposedly eager for another go at the Rebels, the general promised to advance on Richmond "if we have little more than half a chance." He worried that his available manpower was much smaller than the president and the War Department realized and continued to bemoan "the stupidity & wickedness at Washington." He suspected Lincoln would "avail himself of the first opportunity to cut my head off." With the usual references to God's will, he had learned "to despise earthly honors & popular favor as vanities." It would be "grating to have to serve under the orders of a man [Halleck] whom I know by experience to be my inferior." McClellan thought his days in the army were numbered and had decided that "no position in the gift of the country can ever tempt me into public life again."[40]

Such dark thoughts and resentments appeared to subside whenever McClellan rode about the camps. He enjoyed speaking with the troops, and they appreciated his unpretentious and frequent appearances. Their cheers pleased him, and despite the retreat and the casualties, some continued to idolize their commander.[41] Like McClellan, these men cited the difficult conditions on the Peninsula and the need for reinforcements. Again like McClellan, many believed that success depended on the War Department and the president supplying the necessary forces without meddling in army operations. The people back home should stop complaining and criticizing, even as the soldiers roundly cursed the politicians (most notably the Radical Republicans and abolitionists) who needlessly sowed division.[42]

What McClellan failed to acknowledge were the divisions and demoralization in his own ranks—including disparagement of both his generalship and his politics. Disillusioned by a retreat, heavy casualties, and unhealthy camps, some soldiers even sounded more receptive to emancipation. Faith in McClellan was gone and not likely to return, one volunteer remarked. Some officers clearly favored the general's removal, and there were growing doubts about whether, even with reinforcements, McClellan could accomplish anything on the Peninsula.[43]

Such sentiments reverberated in Washington. The chance to take Richmond, Zach Chandler told his wife, had been lost through McClellan's "imbecility . . . if nothing worse." The general had proven to be an "*awfull* humbug and deserves to be shot." Admittedly Chandler had given up on McClellan months ago and tended to spout off, especially when in his cups, but his position on the Joint Committee on the Conduct of the War and frequent confabs with Stanton made him a dangerous foe. On July 7, Chandler introduced a Senate resolution requesting orders and correspondence between Lincoln and McClellan related to the Peninsula Campaign. In a short but pointed speech, he began with the march on the abandoned Confederate works at Centreville and Manassas but then quickly turned to the question of who was responsible for the Army of the Potomac languishing in the fever swamps of Virginia. There is "criminality" here, Chandler thundered. Men who had long sympathized with treason, the senator cried, were now trying to foist the blame on Edwin M. Stanton. On July 10, Chandler brought a slightly modified resolution to the floor for a vote, but Indiana senator Joseph A. Wright warned that such a measure not only would divide the friends of the Union but also was designed to bring "contempt and dishonor" upon McClellan. In reply, Chandler accused the general of having left Washington nearly defenseless, then further showed his hand by defending Lincoln and Stanton. It soon became clear that even some Republicans did not wish to embrace their colleague's broadside attacks on McClellan. Largely supporting Chandler, Lyman Trumbull of Illinois ridiculed McClellan's passion for entrenching. In response, Democrats accused Republicans of questioning the general's loyalty, and one senator tried to shift the debate to a discussion of Stanton's performance. Chandler's resolution passed easily—both McClellan's critics and defenders sensed an advantage in seeing the orders and correspondence.[44]

Pleased with his short speech, Chandler would tenaciously pursue McClellan while praising his friend Stanton. To the senator's way of thinking, the general's precious earthworks had cost valuable lives even as he had refused to use the labor of confiscated slaves. In the conservative press, Chandler proved to be a convenient whipping boy, while the most ardent Republicans and abolitionists welcomed any blows struck against McClellan.[45]

On July 16, at the end of the congressional session, Chandler delivered a much longer address, lambasting McClellan for almost every imaginable sin. The day before, Chandler had pushed a motion through the joint committee authorizing "any member" to use its testimony in congressional debate. To McClellan's disadvantage, the Michigan firebrand quoted several witnesses at length. Paying no attention to the general's role in organizing and training the Army of the Potomac, he kept asking why it had remained idle for so long. The country had expected a "Napoleonic stroke" from its supposedly brilliant young general, Chandler sneered. What happened instead was "wholesale murder" at Ball's Bluff. The president and cabinet (as well as the joint committee) had eagerly awaited the army's advance during the winter, and the troops had suffered greatly in harsh conditions. But when McClellan was at last forced to move toward Centreville and Manassas, he had not continued overland toward Richmond. By Chandler's reckoning, the Army of the Potomac could have entered the Confederate capital by the first of May. He dismissed any criticism of Stanton for interfering with McClellan, noting how "the whole treasonable press of the country has been howling after the Secretary of War." What had McClellan done? He had left his troops on the Peninsula, suffering horrendous losses from disease, all the while having his men perform "menial labor" that could have been handled by freed slaves. Having bravely presented these facts to the country, Chandler declared that anyone who objected must be "traitors" or "fools."[46]

Rumor had it that Stanton had written the speech, but regardless, the secretary of war endorsed its contents. McClellan supporters could hardly contain their outrage. In editorial comments later appearing as a pamphlet, the *New York World* charged that Chandler's speech had provided important intelligence to the Rebels. Defending McClellan on all points, the editor also claimed that both Lincoln and Halleck still had great faith in Little Mac. Barlow thought it unwise for McClellan to answer Chandler directly, though information might be provided to a sympathetic senator who would rise to his defense. The general deemed Chandler "beneath notice" and, in any event, expected to be "relieved from command." His old friend Burnside offered the best advice: "I do know my dear Mac that you have lots of enemies, but you must keep cool, don't allow them to provoke you into a quarrel."[47]

The quarreling would proceed regardless. A Republican editor cited Chandler's speech as vindication of both Stanton and the administration amid all the clamor from conservative newspapers. McClellan's "caution" had ruined the country, a New York hospital volunteer feared. The Army of the Potomac's retreat on the Peninsula would only lengthen the war; at Harrison's Landing McClellan might be safe enough, but so was Richmond. Even moderate editors complained about the Army of the Potomac being defeated and demoralized by wielding picks and spades, and Chandler's lengthy critique of McClellan's generalship reverberated in the press. In London, the cautious American minister Charles Francis Adams thought it probably best for the Army of the Potomac to retreat to Fort Monroe under the protection of gunboats. The phrase "change of base" became a term of derision, and even the word "strategy" met with ridicule.[48]

Labeling McClellan a failure became a staple of Republican rhetoric, especially for those favoring Frémont and attacking "red tape" West Point generals. Given the heavy losses from both disease and battle, even some conservatives wondered if fresh regiments could be raised quickly enough for McClellan to launch a new campaign. The *New York Times*, which had long granted McClellan the benefit of the doubt, conceded that faith in the general had been "shaken to its foundations." Growing doubts about McClellan not only carried a partisan tinge but also reflected misgivings about the general's views on slavery. The army should no longer be a "slavery saving machine," one of Chandler's constituents asserted.[49]

In response, McClellan's friends in journalism and politics took up the cudgel for their hero. If McClellan had been given all the necessary troops, Olmsted admonished a *New York Tribune* reporter, he would "almost certainly have been successful, comprehensively and completely so." The *Tribune* had been guilty of "special pleading" in its attacks on McClellan, and Olmsted deemed Stanton capable of "deliberately plotting the destruction of the republic with a view of his personal elevation upon its ruins." Some newspapers continued to tout Little Mac's military genius and praise his Peninsula strategy. Accepting the view that the Army of the Potomac had faced overwhelming numbers, politicians and editors alike called for funneling reinforcements to the Peninsula.[50]

Did Lincoln retain faith in McClellan, as some press accounts maintained? Was Chandler's speech really an attack on the administration? This all became a subject of no little speculation. One Republican paper accused McClellan's supporters of trying to shift the blame for the Peninsula fiasco onto Lincoln and Stanton. On July 14, some visiting New Yorkers pressed Lincoln to remove McClellan and dismissed Halleck as a "proslavery General in chief." Lincoln reportedly referred to McClellan as a superb defensive general who never seemed ready to fight; the president and others increasingly cited the general's engineering background as making him ill suited for offensive operations. "What a wretched conclusion," John Hay fumed, to McClellan's "boasting addresses and orders we have seen on the bloody banks of the Chickahominy." After failure on the Peninsula, Chase believed, McClellan "should at once have been dismissed [from] the service in disgrace." Even in the conservative Blair family, support for McClellan waned, but the general's status as a future Democratic presidential candidate, and his supporters' attacks on Stanton (and the administration more broadly), made McClellan's standing with Lincoln and his advisers yet more precarious.[51]

"I have commenced receiving letters from the North urging me to march on Washington & assume the Govt!" McClellan had told Nelly shortly after Lincoln's visit to Harrison's Landing. Whether he was flattered by this talk or simply wanted to impress his wife, McClellan increasingly expected a showdown with the administration. There was grumbling among the officers about the question of reinforcements, and Heintzelman feared some "secret designs" in Washington to weaken the Army of the Potomac. Rumors that Lincoln no longer supported McClellan and that the general might soon resign gained currency. Expecting to be sacrificed at any moment on the altar of political intrigue, McClellan referred to Lincoln as "an old stick" and "of pretty poor timber at that." The young general had lost respect for the entire administration and felt increasingly beleaguered.[52]

Lincoln had become convinced that McClellan would not fight, but he was not yet prepared to bring down the hammer. On July 22, Halleck at last arrived in Washington to become general in chief. One staff officer described him as "a thoughtful, soldierly-looking man" whose advent meant that "the small fry of generals and politicians who have heretofore managed our military affairs to our ruin are superseded"; McClellan might even be freed "from the persecutions, criticisms and thwartings." Some newspapers reported McClellan delighted with Halleck's appointment or even claimed he had recommended it. Others maintained—correctly—that this could hardly be the case. But what did Halleck think of McClellan? One New Yorker offered an implausible secondhand report of a conversation in which Halleck had lauded McClellan as the "ablest military man in the world."[53]

The ability of Halleck and McClellan to work together would be tested soon enough. On July 24, the new general in chief left Washington to visit McClellan at Harrison's Landing. At the top of the agenda was whether the Army of the Potomac should advance on Richmond or join Pope's Army of Virginia. Lincoln had given him discretion to decide if McClellan should be relieved from command, but Halleck seemed no more anxious than the president to take that step. On the afternoon of July 25, the two generals conferred on strategy as well as reinforcements. McClellan proposed advancing on Petersburg rather than on Richmond—the objective being to sever Rebel communications with the capital. Instead, Halleck recommended that he join forces with Pope and move against Richmond. McClellan countered that with 30,000 more men, the Army of the Potomac could attack the Confederate capital with "a good chance of success." Pressed by Halleck, he admitted that he could safely withdraw his army from the Peninsula but that it would demoralize the troops. Based on information from Lincoln and Stanton, Halleck could send him no more than 20,000 additional soldiers. By the next morning, McClellan agreed that he could carry out his plan with the reinforcements Halleck had offered. Burnside had accompanied Halleck to Harrison's Landing, and the two conferred with the corps commanders and several other generals. Most apparently favored withdrawing the army from the Peninsula, though the meeting was informal, and no vote was taken.[54]

Halleck found himself in a tough spot. He had been at his new post only a short time, Lincoln had left some critical decisions in his hand, and he disagreed with the most powerful general in the Union army. Halleck may have taken some comfort in what Burnside had learned from his conversations with several generals. Indeed, General Keyes soon emphasized to Quartermaster General Meigs the impossibility of the Army of the Potomac taking the offensive (in part because Keyes, like McClellan, believed the army faced some 200,000 Confederates). Yet when meeting with McClellan after Halleck left, the corps commanders sounded much more sanguine about an advance on Richmond. On an ominous note, Meigs had heard some officers one night wildly discussing a march on Washington to "clear out those fellows." With a withering dismissal of these words as "flat treason," Burnside had managed to disperse this cabal, though it is hard to tell how seriously to take such camp talk.[55]

For several days, any final decision hung in the air. Halleck doubted McClellan's claims of enemy strength, and Meigs provided a more detailed and accurate estimate. "General McClellan is in many respects a most excellent and valuable man," Halleck conceded. "But he does not understand strategy and should never plan a campaign." Lincoln himself had grown in strategic sophistication and confidence when dealing with various generals, and perhaps he was at last waking up to McClellan's serious deficiencies, as one Washington correspondent suggested. Other press reports claimed either that Halleck and McClellan were working well together or that Little Mac's political allies had already turned their guns on the new general in chief.[56]

McClellan had discussed with Halleck the idea of crossing the James, making a quick dash toward Petersburg, and from there moving against Richmond. After Halleck's return to Washington, McClellan continued to press for reinforcements but did not explain in any detail what he planned to do with them. Did he still believe that he faced an enemy numbering some 200,000 men? He appeared to backtrack on that figure while seeking to avoid having his army withdrawn from the Peninsula. On July 24, he had held another troop review, riding along and chatting with the men. As usual, McClellan thought his veterans looked "tough, brown & fearless." Visiting the sick and wounded aboard a steamer that had just arrived from

Richmond, the general talked to patients, listened to their stories, and believed he had brightened their day. He regarded all this as a duty, at times unpleasant, but one that other generals should emulate.[57] The reviews and visits in turn reinforced McClellan's faith in his own rectitude and ability to command loyalty.

While McClellan waited for word about reinforcements or about his future in command, debates over leadership, strategy, and politics continued, often with considerable acrimony. One disgruntled soldier, convinced that with enough reinforcements McClellan could have taken Richmond, spouted off to his uncle back in Pennsylvania: "If they would hang about one half of the political office hunters about Washington they would do the country a great service." One seemingly genteel woman recommended a similar fate for the cabinet. Politicians versus Little Mac was how many people framed the issue, with Greeley, Henry Ward Beecher, and the abolitionists as favorite targets of execration.[58]

Full-throated defenses of McClellan in the *New York Herald* and other newspapers only aroused more skepticism among the general's growing body of critics. As a not unsympathetic surgeon wrote with considerable truth: "I think McClellan's friends have injured him by claiming too much for him." Disputes over the merits of various generals, including McClellan, grew out of differences over both policy and politics. The real divisions in the army, claimed one abolitionist editor, stemmed from "opposing ideas" on the intertwined questions of strategy and slavery. The more radical voices continued to question McClellan's loyalty. What the Army of the Potomac could accomplish if it remained in its current position seemed highly doubtful. "General McClellan's forte is digging and not fighting," Ben Wade complained with his customary sarcasm. "Place him before an enemy . . . he will burrow like a woodchuck." All the while, as the *New York Times* reported, the Army of the Potomac remained in a precarious position on the Peninsula, with camp conditions deteriorating and sick lists growing.[59]

Republican dissatisfaction with the Army of the Potomac could easily give way to doubts about the administration. Diarist Strong feared that people were losing faith in Lincoln, though whether the president had yet lost all faith in McClellan remained uncertain. The president "has been from the first McClellan-mad," Senator William Pitt Fessenden lamented, "and to some degree remains so." Less prominent Republicans called for

McClellan's removal and often extended their critique to other conservative generals such as Halleck and Buell.[60]

Chase was especially eager to settle McClellan's fate. Pope apparently thought that Little Mac might be retained in command, but the secretary of the treasury feared that even a successful move toward Richmond "would only restore undeserved confidence and prepare future calamities." Even as Halleck was returning from the Peninsula, Chase cited the "financial importance" of removing McClellan. Newspaper attacks on Stanton further lowered the general's stock in the cabinet, though Seward remained noncommittal as Chase pressed for getting rid of both McClellan and Buell. When asked what he would do if he were president, the treasury secretary simply recommended consulting Halleck on the question. Yet the new general in chief was not yet ready to move against McClellan.[61]

On July 29, McClellan still had heard nothing from Washington. Perhaps the government "intend & hope that I & my army may melt away under the hot sun." This bit of self-pity quickly gave way to false bravado; McClellan claimed to feel "like taking my rather large military family to Washn to seek an explanation." Perhaps Halleck and Lincoln were trying to force his resignation. If the Army of the Potomac was withdrawn from the Peninsula, a troubled Heintzelman wrote in his diary, "The country is ruined." He favored an advance on Petersburg and feared that Pope "will meet with some disaster." McClellan learned that command of the Army of the Potomac had been offered to Burnside, who promptly turned it down; he suspected that the "rascals" simply hesitated to risk public wrath and army morale. McClellan even doubted he would carry out the recently passed Second Confiscation Act, though that would lead to a "serious row." What he thought, however, now mattered little. By steadily increasing demands for reinforcements after Halleck returned to Washington, McClellan had already weakened his position and likely helped the hesitant general in chief reach a decision. On the evening of July 30, the briefest of telegrams arrived informing McClellan that arrangements were being made to evacuate the sick from the Army of the Potomac.[62]

That same day, Halleck wrote a letter to McClellan that was almost worthy of Stanton. Citing great reluctance to hold such a responsible position, he claimed he had done "everything in my power to avoid coming to Washington." Having long avoided being sucked into "politico-military affairs," Halleck nevertheless feared he would still "receive more abuse than thanks" because the newspapers would "cry down" anyone who was not a partisan. This sounded McClellan-like, and perhaps that was intentional. The final paragraph heaped flattery on McClellan and then struck a patriotic note: "The country demands of us that we act together and with cordiality." But there was also a question of individual ambition: "If we permit personal jealousies to interfere for a single moment with our operations we shall not only injure the cause but ruin ourselves." Halleck claimed to have written to McClellan "frankly" and in the spirit of "friendship," but the letter concealed far more than it revealed, and it hardly achieved its purpose of softening up McClellan for what would be a most unpalatable decision by the administration.[63]

McClellan's reply, too, lacked sincerity. Denying any ill feelings and claiming he had welcomed the selection of Halleck as general in chief, McClellan pledged to work with him "cordially and honestly." Together they could save the country, if only the "selfish politicians" stayed out of the way. Objecting to Pope's recent orders, he still believed that "this contest should be conducted by us as a war, and as a war between civilized nations; that our efforts should be directed toward crushing the armed masses of the rebels, not against the people." Although the government should "prevent the rebels from making use of their slaves, we should avoid any proclamations of general emancipation" and continue to protect civilian property. Finally, McClellan observed that he hardly need repeat his strong objections to withdrawing the Army of the Potomac from the Peninsula.[64] This dispatch to Halleck must have further convinced Lincoln of his vast differences with McClellan, both military and political.

McClellan realized "there can be little mutual confidence between the Govt & myself." Anticipating removal from command at the "earliest opportunity," he vaguely wrote, "There are *some* things to which I cannot submit & to which nothing can induce me to yield." Nelly only reinforced these feelings of persecution and isolation. She hoped her husband would eventually enjoy "revenge" on his enemies: "I almost wish you *would* march up to Washington & frighten these people a little." Once again, Burnside offered more tempered counsel, hoping the two old friends could "give our undivided support to the cause" and remember that "we can't expect to have it all as we wish."[65]

To McClellan, that last thought must have seemed a great understatement. Even sending off the sick was no simple matter until he knew whether he was expected to restart offensive operations or begin the "disastrous measures of a retreat." He worried that "Halleck has begun to show the cloven foot already." Early in the evening of August 3, the general in chief wired McClellan of the decision to "withdraw your army from the Peninsula to Aquia Creek." Halleck made no effort to explain the decision or to soften the blow. This telegram, McClellan wrote at midnight, "has caused me the greatest pain I ever experienced," and the withdrawal could only "prove disastrous to our cause." From its current position, the Army of the Potomac could advance to within ten miles of Richmond before having to fight a battle. But should Halleck's order be carried out, both the army and the country would be demoralized. Still pleading for reinforcements, he had stated his views forthrightly and had done "the best in my power to avert disaster from my country."[66]

The widening gulf between McClellan and the Lincoln administration over military policy, campaign strategy, and the nature of the war itself had made Halleck's withdrawal order nearly inevitable. Whether the president should have left McClellan on the Peninsula to launch another thrust at Richmond is a question without easy answers, but it would be another two years before a Federal army would be that close to the Confederate capital. Once the Army of the Potomac prepared to leave the Peninsula, General Lee had what he wanted—an opportunity to strike at Pope's Army of Virginia. McClellan's distrust of Lincoln and the cabinet, along with his own uncertainties about how to proceed, had weakened the case for leaving his army in place. He not only multiplied enemy forces but also multiplied his own problems by complaining, repeatedly asking for reinforcements, and giving way at times to crippling insecurity. But others bore responsibility as well. McClellan suffered from the backbiting and political hostility in Washington—especially from Stanton. He and Halleck were ill suited for working together. All too many of the actors involved—Lincoln, McClellan, Halleck, Stanton, and others—sought to avoid direct confrontations, often put off decisions, and allowed others to sow seeds of discord. At this point, aside from the obvious costs of military stalemate, the politics of war was exacting a heavy price.

9

SHELVED AND RETURNED

"You cannot regret the order of the withdrawal more than I did the necessity of giving it," Halleck wrote in response to McClellan's protest. Yet he made it clear that the order would not be rescinded, and this seemingly placed McClellan in command limbo. Much would depend upon Pope's operations and how they might be supported by the Army of the Potomac. Then, too, there was the question of how Pope and McClellan could cooperate despite their strategic, political, and personal differences. Whether Halleck, Stanton, and Lincoln had a clear idea of how they expected all this to work out is uncertain, and the war in the eastern theater had entered a new phase of command conflict.

On August 6, Halleck sent a long dispatch to McClellan that began with an almost word-for-word repetition of his previously expressed regret for the withdrawal order and then offered a fuller explanation. Citing McClellan's high estimate of enemy strength after Quartermaster General Meigs had provided a much lower number was certainly disingenuous but helped make the case for McClellan joining forces with Pope. Halleck wanted the Army of the Potomac and the Army of Virginia to unite somewhere in the Fredericksburg vicinity. He dismissed McClellan's fear of demoralization among the troops by pointing out that no such problems had occurred when the army had changed positions, indeed retreated, before. The impossibility of sending the reinforcements that he kept requesting, along with the approaching fever season, further justified the withdrawal order. The following day, Halleck wrote reassuringly about agreeing with McClellan on how the war should be conducted and reporting that Lincoln's "present policy" was "conservative." As the general in chief had advised the president, some of Pope's orders had been "injudicious" but would not be withdrawn.[1] Halleck was walking a tightrope in the hope of compelling McClellan to make a timely withdrawal from the Peninsula and aid Pope.

McClellan had briefly considered an offensive thrust on the Peninsula with Hooker's division, though he still reported large Confederate forces in his front and decided to abandon the idea, given the impending withdrawal of the army. His grumbling to Halleck persisted: "No human power could have moved the sick in the time you say you expected them to be moved." He passed along details about troop departures and pointed to shortages of transportation and other logistical problems. Halleck had run out of patience and grumbled to his wife, "I cannot get General McClellan to do what I wish."[2]

McClellan might well have said the same about the new general in chief. "Halleck is turning out just like the rest of the herd," he told Nelly, more convinced than ever of a plot to force his resignation. On August 10, McClellan predicted that Pope will be "thrashed during the coming week—& very badly whipped he will be & ought to be—such a villain as he is ought to bring defeat upon any cause that employs him." Porter railed against Pope and McDowell, adding that Halleck was in over his head and doomed to fail. He even fantasized about the Army of the Potomac descending on Washington to "rid us of incumbents ruining our country." In Heintzelman's view, the army was being "broken up to get rid of McClellan" because no one in Washington had enough "moral courage" to "act openly." Some junior officers wondered if Halleck would do any better, and McClellan's most ardent supporters in the ranks worried that the people back home were being fed lies about the Army of the Potomac and its young commander.[3]

They might have worried more about what was going on in Washington and with the Army of Virginia. Chase and Stanton clearly wanted to shelve McClellan and hoped to use Pope for that purpose; the general's openly expressed sympathy with the Republican Party made that prospect even more appealing. Unfortunately for Pope, he had to forge three corps under weak leadership into a field army that would soon face Stonewall Jackson.[4]

Given all the uncertainties arising from the newly created Army of Virginia and the slow withdrawal of the Army of the Potomac from the Peninsula, rumors flew, command confusion reigned, and resentments born of frustrated ambitions festered. There was already speculation that Pope might be replaced by Burnside, and a clumsily fought battle at Cedar Mountain on August 9 would reveal further disarray in the Army of Virginia.[5] All along there had been predictions—especially from McClellan loyalists—that Pope was likely to be whipped. After being ordered to Aquia Creek, Porter had groused that this all seemed designed to prevent the Army of the Potomac from "being of any use." Once Pope had advanced toward Culpeper and Burnside had reached Falmouth, across the Rappahannock River from Fredericksburg, Porter was convinced that such a deployment "deserves defeat." To Halleck, however, all this meant that there must be no further delay in the Army of the Potomac's withdrawal from the Peninsula. After yet another reference to transportation bottlenecks, McClellan closed one dispatch to the general in chief with a complaint about "the harsh and unjust tone of your telegrams of late." Suspicious as always, he feared the government "will try to throw upon me the blame of their own delays and blunders." While everyone sought to shift responsibility, Lee took advantage of the confusion and delays to move against Pope.[6]

As what would become the Second Bull Run Campaign began to unfold, the Federals' infighting continued. One day when it was too hot even to take a nap, a restless McClellan smoked heavily and enjoyed reading a defense of his actions in the *New York World*. He planned to counter Pope's "infamous orders" and "take the highest Christian ground for the conduct of the war." Denouncing Radical Republicans and abolitionists, Porter expected Pope's prospects to wane, wondered if Halleck might he removed, or alternatively speculated that the general might succeed in "overthrowing Stanton." Stanton reportedly assured one visitor that he remained McClellan's friend, certainly expecting that news to be passed on, as it was eventually by Sam Barlow. Pained by attacks from the more conservative newspapers, the war secretary claimed that he alone had prevented Lincoln from removing McClellan. Despite doubting whether McClellan should believe any of this, Barlow recommended making up with Stanton to foil the "jealousy of your own Generals." As for Lincoln, he was "weak, vacillating and at times obstinate," while Stanton at least had "courage."[7] The information in Barlow's letter was misleading and inaccurate, but it stood as one more sign of the confusion and uncertainty that hampered military operations and poisoned the political atmosphere.

Chase regretted having held out such high hopes for McClellan, but now he strongly favored the general's removal, disagreed with Halleck about strategy, and would soon be disappointed with Pope. Seward deplored the clamor for action from an ill-informed public yet acknowledged that the government had not raised enough men. Criticism of cabinet members from McClellan's press supporters only added to suspicions about the general's political ambitions. Worse still, in speeches at the Ohio Democratic convention and later in Dayton, the notorious Clement L. Vallandigham blasted the abolitionists for stymying McClellan, lauded the general along with other conservative commanders, and claimed that three-quarters of the enlisted men were Democrats. Such statements attracted Republican notice and added to unease about McClellan's ambitions.[8]

Lincoln faced a dicey situation—strategically and politically—but was not ready to force a resolution. Addressing a Union meeting in front of the U.S. Capitol, he sought to tamp down or at least minimize the clashes between McClellan and Stanton. "These two gentlemen are not nearly so deep in the quarrel as some pretending to be their friends," the president declared in words carefully chosen but subject to various interpretations. He then made the odd argument that, simply based on "selfishness," both the commander of the Army of the Potomac and the secretary of war would wish to be successful. Lincoln chalked up disputes over the size of McClellan's army or the number of reinforcements to mere differences over how the totals were tabulated. He would not blame McClellan for asking for men or Stanton for not providing them when there were "none to give." Seeking to take responsibility without quite doing so, the president said that any criticism aimed at Stanton should instead be directed at him. The crowd appeared enthusiastic, and Lincoln's brief comments played well in various circles; Chase praised the supposedly impromptu remarks. The more conservative newspapers appeared to take the president at his word and even displayed a more conciliatory, or at least tolerant, attitude toward Stanton, with Bennett's *New York Herald* blaming recent military failures on the "Jacobins" in Congress. The hope remained that Halleck would sort out any command problems.[9]

That proved delusional. Ignoring the chain of command (a practice that Lincoln had all too often tolerated or even fostered), Heintzelman sent his wife, Margaret, to give the president a letter pleading for reinforcements. To the ambitious Heintzelman, the situation appeared critical: the Army of the Potomac could force the Rebels "to abandon Petersburg without a battle," but if it failed to advance, "the country is ruined." To drive home the point, he added a sobering estimate of the number of men likely to desert. A couple days later, McClellan promised to drive the Confederates "into the works around Richmond" and then enter the Rebel capital. In doing so, the Army of the Potomac could ease the pressure on Pope and "relieve Washington from all danger." Hooker had reportedly advised him to ignore orders and press forward. This appeared to be a golden opportunity, as a correspondent for the *New York World* reported the Confederates short of rations and likely to suffer severely from disease.[10]

All these suggestions came to naught, as the Army of the Potomac's withdrawal from the Peninsula was proceeding and Halleck was growing testy about delays while stoutly denying McClellan's charge of having been "harsh" or "unjust." McClellan naturally reported moving as quickly as the available transportation allowed and, with great understatement, told Halleck of his fear that they "have been lately working at cross purposes." He blamed Halleck's advisers (among them presumably Stanton), who ought to realize how difficult it was to conduct such a massive logistical operation. In words that must have alarmed the War Department and the White House, McClellan concluded: "It is not possible for any one to place this army where you wish it, ready to move, in less than a month."[11]

With the Army of the Potomac at last leaving the Peninsula, however slowly, officers and enlisted men speculated about McClellan's future. Porter acknowledged that Halleck's order had to be carried out, though he still hoped McClellan would command all the Union forces in Virginia. One junior officer thought the withdrawal was a "pretty severe blow" to the general's reputation." Even the sympathetic George Gordon Meade decided that McClellan "is irretrievably gone, and has lost the greatest chance any man ever had on this continent."[12]

An increasingly uneasy McClellan sought news of Pope's movements and once more complained about Halleck being uncommunicative. He stressed the safety of the Army of the Potomac over a speedy linkup with the endangered Army of Virginia and emphasized the challenge of withdrawing his army in the face of the enemy, even though the Confederates were already heading off to battle with Pope and had no intention of threatening McClellan's forces. Proud of his men's performance, he nevertheless deemed the retreat "a terrible blow to me." McClellan wired Halleck asking for information on "the condition of affairs in the army" and later groused to Nelly that the increasingly beleaguered general in chief "did not even behave with common politeness." In a dispatch that must have annoyed Stanton, Army Adjutant General Thomas reported from Fort Monroe that the withdrawal of the Potomac units was going smoothly and morale remained high, adding that "no one could have made the movement more skillfully or in less time." Several newspapers followed suit in commending McClellan for carrying out such a difficult operation.[13]

Even as the transfer of the Army of the Potomac to northern Virginia was being completed, McClellan grumbled that Halleck "was not disposed to treat me in a candid or friendly manner." Burnside continued to mediate between Little Mac and the general in chief, though with apparently little effect on either man. McClellan perhaps sensed weakness in Old Brains and thought he might still end up "master of the situation." By August 16, the last soldiers had departed from Harrison's Landing, and the following day, four of the five corps had crossed the Chickahominy. Exhausted from supervising the withdrawal, McClellan believed that the troops knew he was not responsible for such a wrongheaded movement. In requesting that Halleck issue an order praising the Army of the Potomac, he claimed to need no kind words for himself. He appeared eager to match up his troops against Pope's men, which was hardly a basis for cordial cooperation.[14]

By this time, the Army of Virginia was being pressed hard by the Army of Northern Virginia, so Halleck pushed McClellan to send troops forward as "rapidly as possible," even if supply trains had to be left behind. "No time will be lost," he promised as he reported the positions of various corps. An increasingly panicky Halleck implored Little Mac, "You can scarcely imagine the pressure on me for the last two weeks and the anxiety I have had in regard to your movements." Then he offered some condescending advice that would not sit well: "My dear general, we must not let little things annoy us, but push right ahead to the great end in view." Unless McClellan could join with Burnside to aid Pope, Halleck feared that Washington stood in "great danger."[15]

On the one hand, McClellan grumbled about not receiving enough information from Halleck, but on the other hand, he decided that the general in chief's pleading telegrams boded well. After being ridiculed as a "'procrastinator,' the 'coward' & the 'traitor,'" McClellan reveled in Washington's apparently desperate need for his help and decided he had finally "triumphed." Again, he pledged to be with his men once they were engaged with the enemy, though he believed that some of his generals—among them Franklin and Baldy Smith—were not showing much energy or efficiency. Yet whatever sense of vindication McClellan felt was short lived, and he was soon predicting that any summons to Washington would simply allow the administration to cast him aside.[16]

On August 23, McClellan sailed with his staff for Aquia Creek, still largely in the dark about his own status or what was happening with Pope. Halleck offered some direction on how McClellan should attempt to join forces with the Army of Virginia but did little to deal with transportation issues. He hoped that Pope's troops could hold the Rappahannock River fords until reinforcements arrived, but neither he nor McClellan had much definite information about the location of the various corps. On August 26, Halleck still believed that the Confederates were moving a "large force into the Shenandoah Valley."[17]

The following day, McClellan reached Alexandria and prepared to funnel troops to Pope, but he soon heard that Halleck's staff had reported a failure to prevent a Confederate "raid" on Manassas and by implication had blamed McClellan. Although neither Halleck nor Pope yet realized it, the Army of Virginia stood in serious peril. Confederates had captured a vast quantity of supplies at Manassas, and Jackson was advancing rapidly in a flanking maneuver. Equally in the dark, on the afternoon of August 27, Lincoln wired McClellan, "What news from the front?" A flurry of dispatches between Halleck and McClellan that day only slowly brought matters into focus. Marching toward Warrenton, Porter reported "a general battle imminent." Halleck instructed McClellan to take charge and send troops out from Alexandria but still did not know the disposition of Pope's forces. McClellan requested maps and sought information on bridges over Bull Run. "Our affairs here much tangled up," he told Nelly. "In a day or two your old husband will be called upon to unsnarl them." By early afternoon, Halleck at last decided that the Confederates were attempting to "turn Pope's right." Supposedly swamped by dealing with the western theater, Halleck had "no time for details" about operations in Virginia and told McClellan "as ranking general in the field, direct as you deem best; but at present orders for Pope's army should go through me." McClellan might have seen this as promising but sought instructions on how to dispose of his troops, explained why certain corps could not advance more rapidly, and seemed to anticipate that Pope's campaign would prove disastrous.[18]

As early as mid-August, if not sooner, McClellan's hostility to Pope had spread to his staff, to his generals, and down into the ranks. An artillery officer who had served with distinction on the Peninsula pointedly wrote home: "When that ass Pope shall have lost his Army and when Washington shall again be menaced . . . then & only then they will find out that our little General [McClellan] is not in his right place & then they will call loudly for aid." To General Heintzelman and others, it appeared that the retreat from the Peninsula would likely bring ruin to Pope as well as to the country. McClellan seemed depressed over his apparent loss of power and command, though his hostility to Pope and McDowell was palpable. After one of Pope's brigades had been badly cut up by A. P. Hill near Manassas, railroad man Herman Haupt asked for a strong force to protect his trains, but McClellan proved as risk averse as ever.[19]

Late on August 27, McClellan arrived in Washington to consult with Halleck, and their discussions dragged on into the early morning hours. Acknowledging that the general in chief had a great deal on his plate, McClellan suddenly considered him "well disposed" but planned to steer clear of the cabinet and the president. Halleck sounded quite anxious as bad news from the Army of Virginia trickled in. McClellan feared there was a large concentration of the enemy between his forces and Pope; he even sounded concerned about the safety of Washington. There followed excuses for why his troops were not racing to Pope's aid. By the afternoon, Halleck was imploring him to rescue Pope, but McClellan said that neither Franklin's nor Sumner's corps were in any condition to fight, so sending them forward would be calamitous. By the end of the day, Halleck had heard enough and told McClellan that his men must advance even if they had to carry their own provisions.[20]

On August 29, McClellan still dragged his feet, telling Halleck that Franklin's corps lacked reserve ammunition and transportation. Those troops did finally move out, though a dispatch to Halleck mentioned manning the Washington forts—almost as if McClellan assumed that Pope's men would inevitably have to scurry back into the capital's defenses. In the middle of the afternoon, he sent what proved to be a fateful dispatch to Lincoln that offered the president two choices: either "concentrate all our available forces to open communications with Pope" or "leave Pope to get out of his own scrape, and at once to use all our means to make the capital perfectly safe." The president quickly responded in favor of the first option, then added: "I wish not to control. That I now leave to Gen. Halleck, aided by your counsels." The harried general in chief simply told him to "dispose all troops as you deem best" and seemed most concerned about a potential Rebel cavalry raid on Washington. This created a vacuum of authority and seemed to give the discretion that McClellan sought, but he sounded increasingly unhinged. After a sleepless night, he felt the burden of "a terrible task on my hands" but without the authority or means to remedy the situation. "I find the soldiers clinging to me," he noted plaintively. "Yet I am not permitted to go to the post of danger!" These laments were all too familiar, and as usual he was unburdening himself to Nelly: "I am heart sick with the folly & ignorance I see around me."[21]

Even to Halleck, McClellan appeared equivocal about carrying out Lincoln's instructions as Sumner's corps approached Washington. A report that Franklin's corps had stopped before reaching Pope infuriated Halleck. Once again asking for instructions, McClellan bristled at the suggestion that he was "disregarding orders when I have simply exercised the discretion you committed to me." He anticipated a "row" and, with another abrupt shift in tone from comments just the day before, deemed Halleck "not a refined person at all & probably says rough things when he don't meant them." Remarkably, he downplayed any danger toward the Army of Virginia.[22]

Ironically, Pope seemed equally in the dark about his deepening peril, though he complained to Halleck that McClellan demanded a cavalry escort for troops coming to his aid. On the morning of August 30, as McClellan still worried about the garrisons on the north side of the Potomac being too small, Halleck expressed great dissatisfaction with Franklin's halting progress and could not believe that there was any shortage of transportation. McClellan finally ordered Sumner to advance toward the Army of Virginia, and Halleck pressed for sending artillery ammunition quickly. "No one in Washington appears to know the condition of matters," McClellan told Nelly. He had been left "without a command" and felt "too blue and disgusted to write any more now, so I will smoke a cigar & try to get into a better humor. . . . I never felt worse in my life." McClellan often exaggerated his discomfiture, but he was being increasingly pushed by Halleck, and his uncertain authority rankled, though it hardly should have prevented him from sending more reinforcements to Pope with fewer excuses. By evening, he was pleading with Halleck for permission to leave Alexandria the next day and "go to the scene of the battle."[23]

There was speculation that Halleck might take command in the field, but as it happened, neither he nor McClellan got anywhere near the fighting. The general in chief appeared to be at a complete loss. Navy Secretary

Welles had once noticed how Halleck would rub his elbows nervously when he did not quite know what to say, but Lincoln had assigned a good deal of responsibility and placed a good deal of confidence in his new general in chief. An anonymous newspaper piece penned by John Hay had reported Halleck steadily working to extricate the Army of the Potomac from a most dangerous position. Some editors praised Halleck along similar lines, and rumor had it that the general in chief favored McClellan's removal from command. Yet neither he nor Lincoln had been able to talk the self-effacing Burnside into taking McClellan's place. There were even reports that McClellan was eager to retire from active service.[24]

This all assumed that Halleck would take charge and that Pope would be able to handle Lee, but neither would be the case. After Stonewall Jackson's raid against Union supplies at Manassas, Pope believed that he could whip Jackson before the rest of Lee's army arrived, then turn on Major General James Longstreet's divisions. But Pope had trouble locating Jackson's forces, initially assuming they were withdrawing, and his subsequent attacks on them once located were piecemeal. He lost track of Longstreet as well, and the result of his own errors and Lee's aggressiveness was a striking Confederate victory. By the early morning of August 31, McClellan reported the Army of Virginia "badly beaten." Losses had been heavy, and some "corps entirely broken up into stragglers." Halleck could offer no instructions without first seeing Lincoln, so McClellan remained adrift. "I feel like a fool here—sucking my thumbs & doing nothing but what ought to be done by junior officers," he told Nelly. By evening, he reported 20,000 stragglers from Pope's army between Centreville and Alexandria but could do little in his "undefined position" and urgently asked to meet with the general in chief. Without answering McClellan's inquiries, Halleck pleaded for help: "I beg of you to assist me in this crisis with your ability and experience. I am utterly tired out." McClellan feared the "total destruction" of Pope's army, and the only solution seemed to be falling back toward the Washington defenses.[25]

McClellan's position remained anomalous; neither Lincoln nor Halleck had been willing to decide on command arrangements. The general clearly believed that Stanton had become his enemy, and Nelly only reinforced his suspicions of both the secretary of war and the president. Even fellow cabinet member Welles thought that "Stanton is so absorbed in his scheme to get rid of McClellan that other and more important matters are neglected."

On August 22, Stanton had flatly told General Heintzelman that he had given up on McClellan. According to Washington talk overheard by Frederick Law Olmsted, the "great scoundrels" Frémont and Pope were "just fit to plan with Stanton."[26]

On August 28, Stanton had sent a note to Halleck showing his hand. He asked four questions dealing with the withdrawal of the Army of the Potomac from the Peninsula and the movement of Franklin's corps toward Pope. The withdrawal orders, Halleck reported two days later, were "not obeyed with the promptness I expected and the national safety . . . required." Unfortunately, Pope's operations had grown out of and depended upon the orders to McClellan being carried out. McClellan had offered several excuses for Franklin's slow advance toward Pope, as Halleck noted in some detail. Even before Halleck replied to Stanton's inquiries, however, the secretary of war had called on Chase to discuss getting rid of McClellan. They readily agreed this had to be done and then visited Halleck to press him on whether the general had disobeyed orders.[27]

"McClellan must be a good military man," Lincoln had reportedly remarked to a group of visitors. "Everybody says he is." The tone was both ironic and skeptical, and the president went on to draw his own conclusion: "He never embraces his opportunities. That's where the trouble is. He always puts off the hours for embracing his opportunities." Lincoln, however, evidently still found some merit in him as a general, though questions about his loyalty persisted among Republicans.[28]

Chase had for some time favored McClellan's removal, but since Halleck's ascension, no one had apparently listened to him. Both the treasury secretary and Pope blamed McClellan for not rescuing the Army of Virginia and held him responsible for the debacle of Second Bull Run.[29] Then, too, Chase had an aggressive ally in Stanton, who drafted a strongly worded document for the president denouncing McClellan for wasting much blood and treasure while proving "incompetent for any important military command." He had disobeyed orders, Stanton insisted, "twice imperiled the army commanded by General Pope," and would endanger not only "our armies" but also "our national existence." Attorney General Bates insisted on softening the language, but the revised draft still drove home the main point: "it is not safe to entrust to Major General McClellan the command of any Army of the United States." Secretary of the Navy Welles agreed that McClellan should go but refused to sign because it was "discourteous and disrespectful to the President." According to him, Stanton declared that he "could not and would not submit to a continuance of this state of things." Chase and Stanton apparently did not bother to consult Postmaster General Blair or Seward. On August 30, Lincoln pondered McClellan's fate but decided for the moment to leave him at Alexandria. That morning, the president had ridden with Hay from the Soldiers' Home back into Washington, taking the opportunity to bemoan McClellan's conduct. Had Little Mac wanted to see Pope whipped? Was he perhaps a "little crazy"? Lincoln of course cited the "leave Pope get out of his scrape" dispatch as evidence. Hay no doubt reinforced these fears and now considered McClellan the "chief alarmist and grand marplot of the Army." At a dinner that evening, Stanton continued to harp on the general's many sins and even favored a court-martial.[30]

On Sunday morning, word came that Pope was retreating, though Welles thought there was no need for panic despite Halleck's apparent alarm for Washington's safety. Walking into Hay's bedroom early in the morning, Lincoln announced, "Well John, we are whipped again, I am afraid." Yet apparently holding out some hope, a few hours later, Lincoln remarked, "We must hurt this enemy before it gets away."[31]

News reaching Washington suggested that Pope was "all right," and so Halleck still would not order a retreat. Pope was now wiring him about "demoralization" among the officers in the Army of the Potomac. These "tools and parasites" would produce "disastrous results," he warned, yet Pope himself recommended that the Army of Virginia be withdrawn back into the capital's defenses. Halleck issued the order and anxiously summoned McClellan to Washington. A warm reception from the various regiments greeted the general on his way into the city, and one observer noted his "attractive and winning deportment which adapted itself to all sorts and ranks of men." During their meeting, Halleck verbally placed McClellan in charge of the Washington defenses and later told him to meet with the president. According to McClellan, the general in chief had begged "to help him out of the scrape."[32]

Pope's comments about demoralization in the Army of the Potomac had reached Lincoln, who pressed McClellan to order his senior officers to cooperate. Believing that the president had been "misinformed," McClellan nevertheless wired Porter. His instructions sounded emphatic and sincere—" I ask of you for my sake, that of the country, and the old Army of the Potomac, that you and all my friends will lend the fullest and most cordial cooperation to General Pope in all the operations now going on"—but these words came too late to do any good. At the same time, McClellan may have considered insisting on the removal of Halleck and Stanton before taking charge of the troops in Washington.[33]

Discontent in the cabinet had not abated. Chase presented Welles the toned-down version of the cabinet protest, already signed by Stanton, Chase, Smith, and Bates. Welles still objected to this method of proceeding. Seward was conveniently out of town, perhaps to avoid entanglement in Stanton's plotting against McClellan. To Chase, the choice seemed simple: either get rid of McClellan or "break up" the administration. Welles even reported him spouting that McClellan should be shot, but that seems doubtful. All the while, newspapers speculated about whether Lincoln shared his advisers' disenchantment with McClellan.[34]

However that might be, Lincoln made a decision without consulting the cabinet. Before the sun was even up on September 2, he and Halleck called on McClellan and formally asked him to take command of the forces in and around Washington. By McClellan's later account, he assured the president and the general in chief that he would save the capital. At the time, he summed up the situation to Nelly: "A terrible and thankless task—yet I will do my best with God's blessing to perform it." At a cabinet meeting that day, Lincoln seemed especially distraught after being presented the cabinet remonstrance—according to Bates almost ready to "hang himself" after enduring Stanton's fury—and after hearing another harangue by Chase. Lincoln said he did not know of anyone more capable of defending the capital than McClellan. The general's engineering skills and organizational abilities were impressive, he added, but readily agreed about McClellan's incapacity for offensive operations while also tellingly observing that the general retained the army's confidence. Chase insisted that Hooker, Sumner, or Burnside "could do the work better." Stanton sharply noted that both Halleck and McClellan could now dodge any responsibility for the consequences of the ill-conceived command assignment; indeed, Halleck was worn out for lack of sleep but took credit for bringing the Army of the Potomac back toward Washington in the nick of time. In his diary, Welles put his finger on one important problem: "Personal jealousies and professional rivalries, the bane and curse of all armies, have entered deeply into ours." Blair still supported McClellan but said little aside from calling Pope "a braggart and a liar." Chase kept insisting that restoring McClellan to command would prove disastrous and became increasingly critical of Lincoln.[35]

During the withdrawal from the Peninsula, Radical Republican congressman Thaddeus Stevens of Pennsylvania had assumed McClellan would control only a "residue" of his command. But that hope was soon dashed as Pope ran into difficulties, and speculation soon began that McClellan was coming back. Rumors reported as fact on newspaper bulletin boards compounded the problem. That McClellan had failed to properly support Pope grew into an article of faith even before the retreat from Bull Run. Delays by the general's subordinates confirmed cabinet suspicions and perhaps led the president to suspect treachery. According to the *New York Times,* McClellan had simply "lost the confidence and high consideration which he once enjoyed at the hands of the American people."[36] This made talk of Little Mac's return to command all the more perplexing. Financier Jay Cooke's brother Henry could not understand why so many officers and enlisted men kept calling for McClellan. There would be no more offensive operations, he feared, once McClellan was restored to command. Echoing Chase, the *Chicago Tribune* foresaw "nothing but disappointment and disaster for the future." In New York, stockbrokers had soured on McClellan. Blame fell on Lincoln (and Seward) for sticking with him, though the president reportedly again deflected such criticism by claiming that military matters rested in Halleck's hands.[37]

Like Lincoln, however, others asked if any general was better than McClellan for organizing a defense of the capital—and that was not the half of it. The defeat of Pope intensified demands for restoring McClellan to full command. Even his army critics conceded that many officers and enlisted men viewed Little Mac as their true leader, and the contrast with Pope helped him. Loss of faith in Pope and other generals only boosted McClellan's standing in the Army of the Potomac and elsewhere.[38]

"Confidence" became the watchword for those longing for McClellan's restoration. Even soldiers who harbored doubts admitted that many of their comrades thought there was no better general. Had McClellan been in command, one New Hampshire volunteer believed, the Army of Virginia's recent campaign would have had a much different outcome; even the usually critical Joe Hooker agreed with that assessment. When McClellan's return became known, one Massachusetts soldier recalled, "joy beyond measure was carried to the hearts of all the soldiers." Seemingly demoralized troops threw their caps into the air. As McClellan rode through the ranks on September 2, the cheering that he so valued greeted him all along the lines.[39]

Such enthusiasm carried political overtones. Only secessionist sympathizers and abolitionists would try to get rid of McClellan, a Pennsylvania private told his skeptical father. Denunciations of both Pope and McDowell intensified, and the recent losses made a more cautious strategy seem more appealing. Now the Army of the Potomac was in roughly the same position it had occupied last March, one of Porter's staff officers lamented, but he took some comfort in Lincoln and Halleck desperately turning to McClellan. General Meade agreed and then noted: "McClellan's star is again in the ascendant, and Pope's has faded away."[40]

Back in his old Washington headquarters, McClellan was in his element. Preparing for the arrival of Pope's battered brigades in the city, he had guards placed on various roads, sent out cavalry to escort the wagon trains, and sought Pope's assistance in coordinating troop movements. To Lincoln, he expressed some anxiety about bridges and railroad connections to Baltimore, but his dispatches on September 2 exuded both activity and confidence. As the bedraggled Pope and McDowell entered the Washington defenses, it was clear that McClellan commanded the situation, and he seemed exultant.[41]

Lincoln ordered Halleck "to organize an army for active operations," but the disheartened general in chief—at times bedridden with hemorrhoids—was hardly up to the task. Lee's army was reportedly on the move, having disappeared from the Washington area, and that only intensified discussion of McClellan's new role. The general was working hard reorganizing the Army of the Potomac, though whether his authority extended much outside the Washington defenses remained up in the air. "Again I have been called upon to save the country," he wrote grandiloquently. Hooker noted how many of the troops from the badly whipped Army of Virginia were hardly up to marching, and McClellan remarked with a mixture of sympathy and satisfaction how soldiers kept calling out, begging him not to leave them again.[42]

The settling of John Pope's fate at least cleared up some of the confusion. On September 3, he met with Lincoln, who, according to Chase, had expressed satisfaction with the general's performance and said that McClellan's post would be "temporary." But on September 5, Halleck informed him that he had been relieved of command. Pope would not go quietly. He had already drafted a report on the recent campaign when Halleck sent an oddly worded dispatch (obviously trying to deflect responsibility from himself) noting that Pope "cannot serve under him [McClellan] willingly." Halleck added the flimsy pretext that Pope would have to testify at courts of inquiry for Franklin and Porter, who had been suspended pending an investigation of their recent conduct, but that hardly softened the blow. To make matters worse, Lincoln and the cabinet had agreed that his report on the recent campaign should not be published. "Is it that I am to be deprived of my command because of the treachery of McClellan & his tools?" Pope angrily inquired of Stanton. An exhausted Halleck feared that Pope's wrath might soon fall on him and observed that "differences and ill-feeling among the generals are very embarrassing to the administration, and unless checked will ruin the country." Even after being sent off to the northern plains to deal with a Sioux Indian uprising, Pope fired off letters to Illinois governor Richard Yates and to Halleck denouncing McClellan and the clique of traitors who ultimately sought to displace Lincoln. McClellan would not only fail to be a true friend, Pope warned, but also maneuver to destroy Halleck, whom he at the same time accused of bad faith. Halleck naturally bristled at this, but his reply to Pope only elicited another letter complaining that the government was willing for him to be "sacrificed."[43]

Getting rid of Pope did little to calm the political waters. On September 5, Lincoln talked through recent events with John Hay. At the War Department, he had learned that "McClellan is working like a beaver" but then added that "this public feeling against him will make it expedient to take important command from him." Again noting the cabinet uproar and how everyone (except Blair) was ready to denounce him for restoring McClellan, Lincoln, if not exactly second-guessing his decision, could see their point. McClellan had "acted badly" and had "wanted him [Pope] to fail," yet "we must use what tools we have." Then referring to McClellan's undisputed organizing ability, he pithily added, "If he can't fight himself, he excels in making others ready to fight." Earlier, Welles and other cabinet members had reached similar conclusions about McClellan's weaknesses; at the same time, the secretary of the navy feared "factiousness" in the army and worried that Stanton's relentless hostility to McClellan had "aggrieved other officers." New York financier and Democrat August Belmont told Lincoln that people had lost faith in the War Department. At home in Auburn, New York, Seward retained confidence in Halleck, reacted to McClellan's reinstatement with his customary equanimity, and remained sanguine about military matters more generally.[44]

One of McClellan's more hopeful editorial supporters praised Lincoln for taking control and overruling his more radical counselors. Perhaps there would even be a "reconstruction" of the cabinet along more conservative lines. Yet to Republicans, including many moderates, Lincoln had shown weakness by reinstating McClellan; the administration appeared to be adrift, and the president's stock was falling. Agreeing that McClellan was fine for defending fortified positions, the *New York Times* did not think him suited for "active command of a force destined for offensive operations" and defined winning victories as the only real measure of a general's worth.[45]

By September 6, Lee's Confederates were reportedly marching toward Rockville, Maryland. McClellan was still working out command arrangements (while claiming that even Stanton cordially supported his plans), but Lincoln deferred questions to Halleck. Likely driven by his growing hostility to Stanton, Welles complained that the War Department "is bewildered, knows but little, does nothing, proposes nothing." Rather than march by the White House to pay their respects to the president, Welles noted, departing troops passed by McClellan's headquarters and lustily cheered their commander. McClellan might not be the equal of Lee or Jackson, one solder commented, but "he is infinitely the best we have." A Rhode Island volunteer agreed that Little Mac is "the only General that has the entire confidence of the army."[46]

As McClellan took the field again (though no authorization orders were apparently ever issued), he would have some 60,000 men, with an additional 73,000 left, for the time being, in the Washington defenses until Confederate intentions became clearer. Problems ranging from transportation to disease, morale, and absenteeism arose immediately; straggling ate away at effective strength. Reinforcements eventually gave McClellan an army of roughly 87,000 men. On September 7, he headed toward Rockville, hoping with "God's blessing to gain a decisive victory." Once again in a triumphant mood, he reveled in the "entire confidence of the Govt & love of the army—my enemies are crushed, silent & disarmed." Should the Rebels be defeated, he would be "master of the situation." But what was the Confederate objective? Did the enemy intend to threaten Washington, perhaps Baltimore, or would they move into Pennsylvania? In any case, McClellan's burst of activity impressed even some skeptics in the ranks, though whether this hastily assembled army would move quickly enough to stop the Army of Northern Virginia seemed doubtful.[47]

With the Army of the Potomac leaving Washington, Chase buttonholed Welles to repeat familiar laments. The secretary of the treasury feared that things were going terribly wrong, McClellan was having his own way, and the country was ruined. He harangued the navy secretary about not signing the cabinet remonstrance, but Welles replied that whatever McClellan's faults, dismissing him would have been "impolitic." Despite agreeing that McClellan had sought to ruin Pope, Lincoln thought nothing could be done for the present. On the evening of September 7, Welles had met McClellan on his way out of Washington and had bluntly remarked, "the country will expect you to go forward." By September 8, Lincoln (who according to Chase said he "felt badly all day") had received word about straggling in the Army of the Potomac—hardly surprising given the infusion of new regiments filled with greenhorn soldiers whose feet quickly blistered on the challenging marches. Only three days before, Lincoln had remarked sadly, "we had the enemy in the hollow of our hands," but quarreling generals had let the Rebels escape. He still spoke favorably of Pope, who had supposedly been undone by the prejudice against him in the Army of the Potomac. One visitor assured him that McClellan was not angling for the presidency, but that offered little comfort. Even Blair wondered whether the general would be successful but placed much of the blame for the army's condition on Pope. Senator John Sherman of Ohio had given up on both McClellan and the president, and other Republicans thought it was high time Lincoln listened to his true friends. All these reactions were mild compared to the outrage of Zach Chandler, who claimed that the reinstatement of McClellan marked the triumph of "imbecility" and "treason." Lincoln, he feared, had been bullied by the "traitor generals" and was "as unstable as water." The Michigan firebrand favored having the "loyal governors" demand the president change policy and generals.[48]

Lincoln's counselors remained divided. Welles may have been right in deeming Henry Wilson an alarmist, but the Massachusetts senator was convinced that there was a plot afoot by several generals to set up a provisional government. Secretary of the Interior Caleb Smith had heard similar rumors and blamed Seward—seemingly always having Lincoln's ear—for getting the administration into such a bind. Welles thought Stanton and Chase had become so obsessed about McClellan that they had foisted Pope and Halleck on the country. Reports of divisions in the government only added to the fears about what McClellan's return might bring. The country demanded, the *Chicago Tribune* thundered, "that poltroons, imbeciles, and traitors shall not command its armies—shall not willfully and with impunity jeopardy [*sic*] its life, and the precious interest of humanity bound up with it." Despite recognizing that McClellan retained the army's confidence, George Templeton Strong sarcastically remarked about "masterly fieldworks" soon to be erected from the "Potomac to the Susquehanna."[49]

The whole McClellan question increasingly disturbed not only Republicans but also their opponents. In a Rhode Island speech, August Belmont portrayed McClellan as the country's savior, thwarted by "political meddlers and ambitious demagogues [who] step in and arrest our victorious progress." Belmont derided the "abolition press" but praised Lincoln as a man of conservative instincts. Although McClellan's more fervent supporters wondered if even friendly newspapers had been laggards in trumpeting their hero's virtues, conservative editors and politicians welcomed the general's return to command and rejoiced over Pope's comeuppance. The *New York Herald* recommended McClellan insist on a reconstruction of the cabinet, a sentiment that could only have made the general appear to be an even more dangerous to the Lincoln administration.[50]

Whether the Army of the Potomac itself had become heavily politicized, some soldiers weighed in on McClellan's troubles with the government. "Are the enemies of Little Mac satisfied?" snarled one Pennsylvania officer, who wished such critics could see how the troops loved their commander. Others thought that politicians and folks back home should stop trying to second-guess and interfere with McClellan's plans. Some went further, declaring that McClellan's defensive tactics seemed much more acceptable after Pope's reckless campaign. The men in the ranks could rest easy, as Brigadier General Hiram Berry (a Democrat) remarked, because with McClellan back in command, "no great blunder will be committed."[51]

With uncertain information about the location of Confederate forces, Halleck remained wary of sending too many regiments away from the Washington defenses. Toward evening on September 8, Lincoln anxiously wired McClellan: "How does it look now?" It looked like the Confederates had indeed crossed into Maryland, but McClellan had to tell the president that his forces had not discovered much. To Halleck, he described both the knowns and unknowns but promised, "As soon as I find out where to strike, I will be after them without an hour's delay." By this time, there was alarm in Maryland and Pennsylvania about reports of advancing Rebels.

McClellan doubted Lee intended entering the Keystone State, but Governor Curtin believed otherwise and was not that convinced by reassurances to the contrary. Even before leaving Washington, McClellan along with Seward had warned about the vulnerability of the Federal forces at Harpers Ferry should the Confederates cross the Potomac, but the general in chief treated the matter "lightly." To his wife, Halleck sounded increasingly distraught, complaining of "too many cooks" meddling in military strategy, but felt even more "tired and disgusted with this great political machine."[52]

To one newly appointed staff officer, McClellan talked of an early advance and even thought his cavalry would prove more than a match for Jeb Stuart. In camp near Rockville on the morning of September 9, he once again emphasized to Nelly how he simply had to "do the best I could with broken & discouraged fragments of two armies defeated by no fault of mine." By afternoon, he informed Halleck that Confederates had appeared in "large force" near Frederick, Maryland, and Rebel prisoners talked of heading into Pennsylvania. There was much contradictory information, and McClellan seemed to hold conflicting (and at times illogical) views of the situation. He appeared to discount cavalry reports of over 100,000 Confederates having already crossed the Potomac and at the same time hoped to "catch them in some mistake." To Fitz John Porter, he sounded confident that his troops were well positioned to prevent Lee's army from escaping, though he still worried about a possible second Confederate force south of the Potomac. To Halleck, he suddenly sounded no longer uncertain about Confederate intentions: "almost the entire rebel army in Virginia, amounting to not less than 120,000 men, is in the vicinity of Frederick City." He requested one or two additional corps be sent to his army and recommended the evacuation of Harpers Ferry, then held by a mere 14,000 largely inexperienced troops commanded by Colonel Dixon S. Miles, an officer who had been drunk during the first battle at Bull Run. McClellan then added what instantly set off alarm bells in the capital: "But even if Washington should be taken while these armies are confronting each other, this would not, in my judgment, bear comparison with the ruin and disasters which would follow a signal defeat of this Army." As the midnight hour approached, McClellan wired Halleck: "I have ordered a general advance tomorrow. Send me all the troops you can spare."[53]

Bombarded by panicky telegrams from Governor Curtin and chary about sending more reinforcements, Lincoln believed that McClellan

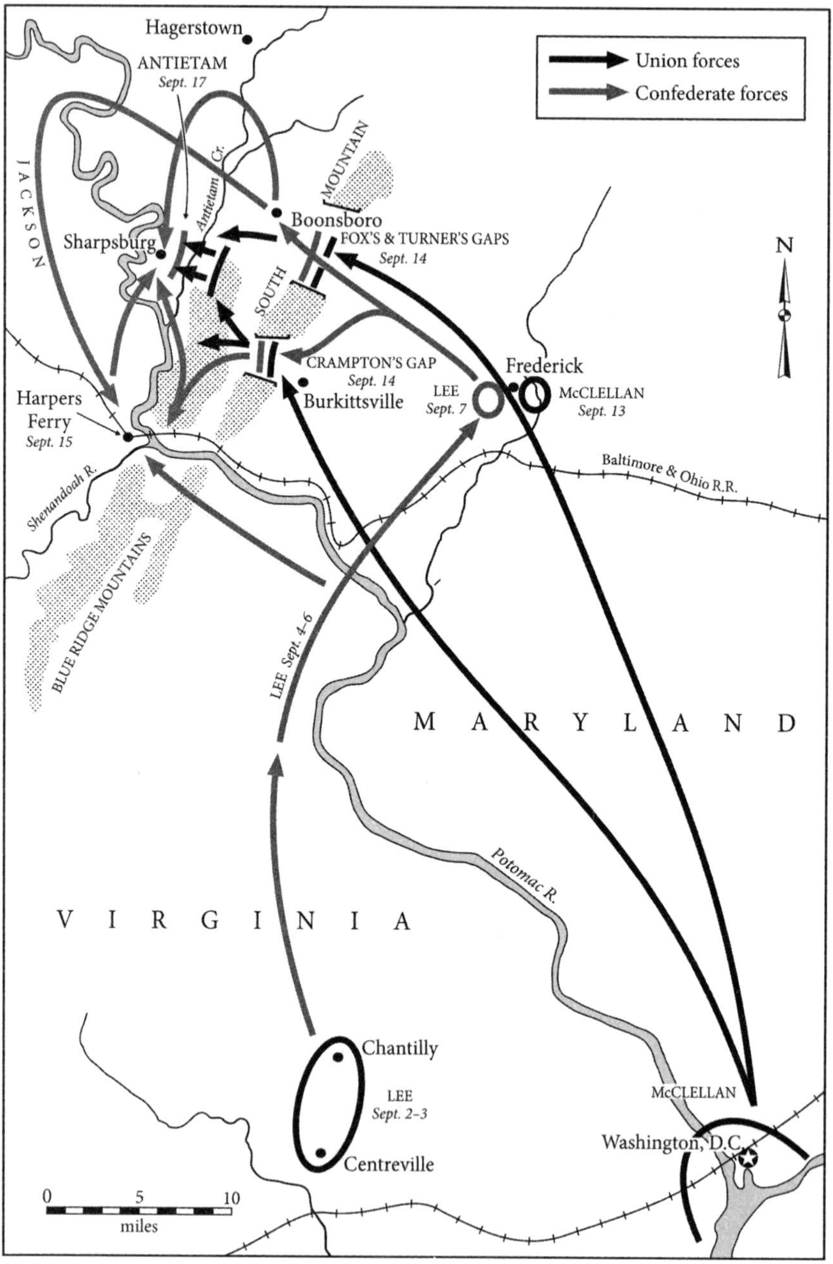

ANTIETAM CAMPAIGN

would soon have over 100,000 men. On September 11, the general sounded exhausted and pressed Halleck to send him the troops from Harpers Ferry along with three other corps. Should the Confederates head into Pennsylvania, he promised a rapid pursuit.[54]

On September 12, McClellan dispatched Burnside toward Frederick and was beginning to move most of his army in that direction. To this point the advance had been slow—one might say "McClellan-like"—but the general's information on enemy numbers and location was uncertain, the reorganization of his army continued, and logistics remained a headache. A 4 a.m. wire from Lincoln again asked, "How does it look now?" The president apparently considered visiting McClellan at Frederick, but General Banks advised against it. McClellan discovered that the Confederates had largely abandoned that town, and a midmorning dispatch to Halleck sounded upbeat without stating any specific objective for the forward movement of his army. "From all I can gather secesh is skedadelling," he told Nelly. "I don't think I can catch him unless he is really moving into Penna. . . . He evidently don't want to fight me." Yet McClellan himself hardly seemed eager to engage the foe, likely hoping to simply maneuver the enemy out of Maryland. Lincoln also suspected the Confederates were recrossing the Potomac and feared just the type of bloodless outcome that McClellan preferred: "Please do not let him [the Confederates] get off without being hurt." McClellan planned to relieve the pressure on Harpers Ferry and that evening, while promising to pursue the main body of the enemy, feared they would cross the Potomac "before I can catch them."[55]

Around midmorning on a fateful September 13, McClellan rode into Frederick. Union flags fluttered in the breeze, and citizens leaned out of windows and balconies waving handkerchiefs. Joyful and relieved Unionists cheered the arriving troops; people came out to shake McClellan's hand and festooned his horse with bouquets and flags, some even throwing their arms around the animal's neck. There were the inevitable babies to be kissed. But the hour of decision had come. McClellan learned that the garrison at Harpers Ferry was seriously threatened. About 9 a.m. some Indiana troops who had just crossed the Monocacy River stumbled across a copy of General Lee's Special Orders No. 191 wrapped around three cigars. By midafternoon, this document had wound its way to McClellan, who sought to verify its authenticity, to see if it comported with already observed enemy movements, and to determine how to proceed against Lee's divided legions. Because it did not reflect the most up-to-date information on troop dispositions, the "Lost Order" led McClellan to conclude that the Confederates were much closer to the gaps on South Mountain than they actually were, and that would shape his orders for the following day.[56]

Just as McClellan was planning his advance against Lee's divided army, a dispatch arrived from Halleck, still worried about "uncovering the capital" and chastising him for taking a cavalier attitude toward defending Washington. "No more troops can be sent from here till we have fresh arrivals from the North," the general in chief pointedly noted.[57]

By early evening, McClellan informed General Franklin that he had "full information as to the movements & intentions of the enemy." He ordered Franklin to cross South Mountain through Crampton's Gap, cut off any retreating Confederates, and hasten to the relief of Harpers Ferry. The other wing of McClellan's army was to cross South Mountain at Turner's Gap and head toward the Confederates at Boonsboro. Late in the evening, McClellan shared with Halleck the contents of the Lost Order, summed up the day's activities, and briefly sketched his plans for the following day, again emphasizing that there was little danger of an enemy thrust toward Washington. He expected a "severe general engagement to-morrow." At midnight, McClellan sent an exuberant note to Lincoln claiming that Lee had made "a gross mistake, and that he will be severely punished for it." He mentioned being "received most enthusiastically by the ladies" in Frederick and promised to "send you trophies."[58]

McClellan probably felt a certain relief at being away from Washington, where the fallout from recent military failures continued to breed suspicion and division. Accusations of disloyalty against the general, along with talk of a proslavery clique in the army, refused to die down. Hostility to West Point generals, compounded by worry that McClellan was simply not up to the mark, reflected waning public confidence as the Army of the Potomac was about to be tested as it had never been tested before. By the same token, McClellan's defenders and Stanton's critics continued to have their say, even slyly praising Lincoln for rising above the backbiting among his generals. One-time champions of Little Mac appeared to be wavering. The general's well-documented caution now threatened the very life of the republic, though Lincoln had to shoulder some of the blame. The president "is unequal to his place," diarist Strong lamented. "His only special gift is fertility of smutty stories." If McClellan did not win a great victory—and that seemed doubtful—the whole administration might collapse. On the very day that McClellan received the Lost Order, the governor of Ohio wired Stanton about a hastily organized meeting of northern governors that might soon spell trouble for both the general and the Lincoln administration.[59]

With reports of McClellan loyalists in the army ready to mutiny on their hero's behalf or push for a military dictatorship, the atmosphere had grown rancorous. However much Lincoln might discount such rumors, Senator Chandler and others gave them credence. Stanton railed against Lincoln's "humiliating submissiveness" to McClellan, and Chase deplored the president's kowtowing "to Border States and negrophobic counsels" that could only further alienate most Republicans. Bringing back McClellan had been Halleck's call, Lincoln still maintained. Claiming that he had only intended to place him in charge of the Washington defenses, Lincoln again praised the general's organizational abilities but then said, "He can't go ahead—he can't strike a blow." Commenting on the snail-like advance toward Rockville, the president rehashed what he saw as McClellan's even more dilatory movements on the Peninsula. Welles along with Blair attributed the slowness to West Point training and noted that General Scott had been similarly cautious. Blair allowed that McClellan was probably the best of the major generals at the time and scoffed at the idea of putting Banks in his place. Walking away from the White House after a meeting, he told Welles that he had wanted to let Lincoln know that the country needed a secretary of war capable of something besides "intrigue" and likewise grumbled about Seward's machinations. Should McClellan succeed in Maryland, Welles speculated, "he may overthrow Stanton." At the same time, Lincoln's counselors conceded that the general retained much support in the army.[60]

There was part of the rub. His generals and many of the troops believed in Little Mac, and he was advancing into Maryland despite the Lincoln administration's loss of faith in his capabilities. Regardless of doubts and reservations, the president had restored McClellan to command. For his part, McClellan had given up on Halleck, saw Stanton as an enemy, and as always blew hot and cold on Lincoln. The cabinet had lost confidence in McClellan, and some members doubted that Lincoln was tough enough to remove a popular general. None of this boded well as the Army of the Potomac prepared to meet the foe.

10

VICTORY, DELAY, AND DANGER

MARCHING THROUGH MARYLAND to intercept an advancing enemy in mid-September could be a hot and dusty (sometimes even muddy) slog, as a Vermont captain ruefully wrote home. He admitted to feeling discouraged about ever putting down the rebellion. But with McClellan in charge again, "everything looked brighter" because, regardless of what people at home might think, there is "but one opinion in the Army . . . that he is the man to lead us." This soldier exaggerated, but while others chaffed at delays, and some veterans of the Peninsula Campaign had lost faith in Little Mac, his standing with the troops overall remained solid.[1] The Lincoln administration had turned to him again seemingly out of desperation, and McClellan himself—even taking into account the usual mood swings—appeared to be confidently (albeit slowly) leading his army forward to engage Robert E. Lee's dispersed forces. The stakes were high—militarily, diplomatically, and politically—for the Union, for McClellan, and for Lincoln.

Early in the morning of September 14, Brigadier General Alfred Pleasonton's cavalry conducted a reconnaissance along the National Road toward South Mountain. With heavily wooded ravines and poor roads (aside from the National Road), South Mountain proved formidable and confusing to both attackers and defenders. Eventually, two columns of Union infantry advanced against Fox's Gap and Turner's Gap, where sharp fighting soon erupted as the Federal forces confronted more opposition than McClellan and his generals had expected. That same morning, McClellan had received word that the garrison at Harpers Ferry was surrounded and likely unable to hold out for more than two days. Despite his claiming to be "reasonably confident of success" and making vague references to a "general battle" that day or the next, any plans still seemed tentative. With the attacks at South Mountain proceeding in the late morning and early afternoon and encouraged by apparent progress, McClellan promised an all-out effort to relieve Harpers Ferry. Halleck still worried about Confederates forces south of the Potomac threatening the army's flank, but McClellan was most concerned about pushing Franklin's corps toward Burkittsville as a preliminary to rescuing Colonel Miles's command. Franklin slowly deployed two divisions to seize Crampton's Gap, faced far less resistance than other Union forces that day, but did not advance rapidly enough to rescue the Harpers Ferry garrison.

The Federals initially planned nothing more than a reconnaissance, but as the day advanced, the fighting at Fox's Gap and Turner's Gap grew more intense. Confederate major general D. H. Hill had deployed over 5,000 troops along a two-mile front to defend the passes. Pleasonton's cavalry advanced on the National Road and was later supported by infantry from Brigadier General Jacob Cox's Kanawha Division (Ninth Corps). By nine in the morning, Cox's Ohio regiments were engaged with the Confederates at Fox's Gap and by midday had shattered a Confederate brigade. Brigadier General Orlando Willcox's division arrived in the early afternoon and soon came under heavy fire from Confederate artillery and infantry reinforcements. By 4:30, two more Ninth Corps divisions had appeared. Confederate counterattacks did little but amass casualties; the Federals eventually controlled the area around Fox's Gap but had failed to fully exploit Cox's early success.

On the Union right, Hooker's First Corps proceeded much more slowly; the two lead divisions, commanded by Meade and Brigadier General John P. Hatch, did not reach Turner's Gap until late afternoon. By 4:30 or so, there was heavy fighting and a good deal of confusion along with missed opportunities on both sides. The bluecoats ultimately prevailed, but the delayed advance prevented McClellan's men from defeating Lee in detail before he could reunite his scattered forces.

What became known as the Battle of South Mountain resulted in more than 2,000 Federal casualties out of approximately 28,000 troops engaged. That evening, McClellan informed Halleck: "Thus far all goes well. . . . I have the troops in hand. They are confident, and hope to have full possession of the passes by dark." He commended the work done by Hooker and Franklin's men, along with those commanded by Major General Jesse Reno, who was mortally wounded at Fox's Gap. "It has been a glorious victory," McClellan concluded. "I am hurrying up everything from the rear, to be prepared for any eventuality."[2]

Early the next morning, Hooker reported the enemy in full retreat, as did local civilians. At 8 a.m., McClellan wired Halleck about these successes and praised the troops, who once again cheered their commander. "The morale of our men is now restored," he exulted. A half hour later, he informed Halleck that "the enemy is making for Shepherdstown in a perfect panic." McClellan promised to harry the enemy in what appeared to be a headlong retreat. To Nelly. he termed the victory "complete" and added, "God has seldom given an army a greater victory than this." McClellan appeared to be driving his men forward with unusual speed, but there was also a contretemps between him, Hooker, and Burnside (with perhaps some involvement from Porter) that left Burnside with a reduced command by detaching Hooker's corps from his wing. Still, all seemed to be going well. McClellan paused to have a word with the wounded at a house near Turner's Gap, and reports of such incidents further endeared soldiers to their commander.[3]

Unsure about what was happening at Harpers Ferry, by early afternoon, McClellan was cautioning Franklin not to advance before determining the strength of the opposing forces in his front. "Thus far our success is complete, but let us follow it up closely, but warily. Attack whenever you see a fair chance of success." His orders may have been clear, but he failed to see about their execution, and so the progress on September 15 proved uneven as the troops emerged from the South Mountain gaps to face Lee's hastily reassembling legions and catch their first glimpse of Sharpsburg and Antietam Creek. By afternoon, McClellan told Burnside that the Confederates had gathered in force behind Antietam Creek. Reconnoitering a position along a ridge near Keedysville, McClellan himself came under Rebel artillery fire and decided it was too late in the day to launch an attack.[4]

Whatever the military calculations involved, delay at this point would be politically costly. Talk of the country losing faith in the president and the administration grew as the war dragged along inconclusively, with the Confederates on the offensive in Maryland as well as a Rebel advance in the western theater. Fall elections were rapidly approaching. Little wonder that each dispatch from McClellan received minute attention in Washington, and the precarious situation of the Harpers Ferry garrison only compounded the anxiety. After a long talk with Seward ally Thurlow Weed,

Chase observed that the secretary of state "had adhered too tenaciously to men who proved themselves unworthy and dangerous such as McClellan." He later walked over to the War Department and saw the wire declaring that Lee had been whipped. Seward sent home a brief report of this success, but a more skeptical Welles doubted that the results were as decisive as reported. Yet Lincoln sent along news of a "great victory" to an Illinois political ally, which in turn produced a response from Governor Yates that told of people being "filled with the wildest joy" and firing off salutes. "God bless you, and all with you," the president wired McClellan. He clearly hoped and perhaps expected greater success, telling his young commander, "Destroy the rebel army, if possible."[5]

To McClellan's political supporters, the news from South Mountain appeared to stymy the "abolition faction's" designs. The *New York Herald* deemed Washington "safe from the rebels" and "equally safe from the radicals." One editorial absurdly claimed that the cabinet stood united behind McClellan, so all that was required was that the government let the Young Napoleon proceed with his plans. This same newspaper decried the "revolutionary radical press" opening fire on McClellan "from their masked batteries" and threatening to demoralize and disorganize the army. In reply, one Republican sheet charged the *Herald* with seeking to make McClellan a dictator.[6] With little solid information on the unfolding contest in Maryland, rumors and alarms left Washington in a political haze.

Likewise, heavy fog on the morning of September 16 prevented McClellan from ascertaining Confederate positions and numbers, but he would use the day to quickly bring up supplies because "many of our men are suffering." Lee's army in fact was not retreating and instead held some advantageous ground behind Antietam Creek near the village of Sharpsburg, a community of shopkeepers and farmers located three miles north of the Potomac River. There were four stone bridges that spanned the creek. The road from Keedysville crossed the Upper Bridge, which seemed to offer the best crossing point for troops to position themselves to attack Lee's left flank, a task assigned to Hooker's First Corps. There the terrain seemed more inviting, but cornfields and woods along with rocky and uneven ground posed sometimes unforeseen obstacles.[7]

An aide to Governor Curtin who had visited McClellan's headquarters reported that Hooker would launch an attack by noon; McClellan also informed Franklin, "if the enemy is in force here, I shall attack him this morning." That he actually intended to do so is doubtful; indeed, at the same time he told Nelly that Pennsylvania and Maryland had been "delivered." McClellan might well have been satisfied if Lee's men had simply scampered back across the Potomac. As the fog burned off, the day grew beastly hot. During an early morning reconnaissance south of the Boonsboro Pike, McClellan again came under artillery fire. He discovered that the Confederates had moved their batteries into strong positions, with infantry well concealed. The general spent time checking out the ground and hurrying along the supply trains, but it was not until afternoon that he began moving troops into position for an attack. Halleck still worried about Lee's forces slipping across the Potomac and cutting off the Army of the Potomac from Washington; indeed, a signal station set up on Red Hill at first reported that Confederate trains were crossing the river and heading toward Shepherdstown. McClellan appeared not to have a developed a detailed battle plan but had decided to use Hooker to attack the Confederate left, while his old friend Burnside would assume a supporting role against the Confederate right. In the early afternoon, McClellan ordered Hooker to cross Antietam Creek and perhaps attack the Rebel flank but left the question of reinforcements and Hooker's exact mission up in the air.[8]

On September 16, McClellan had belatedly ordered Major General Joseph K. F. Mansfield's Twelfth Corps to cross Antietam Creek in support of Hooker but denied Sumner's request to have his corps join them as well. With predictable caution, he kept Franklin's Sixth Corps—it would march toward the battlefield only the following morning—protecting the army's rear. These dispositions were far from ideal, presenting a problem of coordination that would plague the army throughout the battle. Burnside was to cross Antietam Creek and assault the Confederate right, but the Ninth Corps (now commanded by Cox) had not been properly deployed; on the morning of September 17, its timing quickly became confused. Relations between McClellan and Burnside now grew testy. McClellan had not shared his thinking on the coming engagement with his subordinates, so they hardly knew how their movements would fit into an overall battle plan. The result was delays and piecemeal attacks.[9]

The engagement started off well enough, with Hooker advancing at daybreak and pushing back the Confederates. Early morning dispatches brightened McClellan's mood, and he remarked to a group of officers, "All goes well; Hooker is driving them." But the First Corps faced hard and

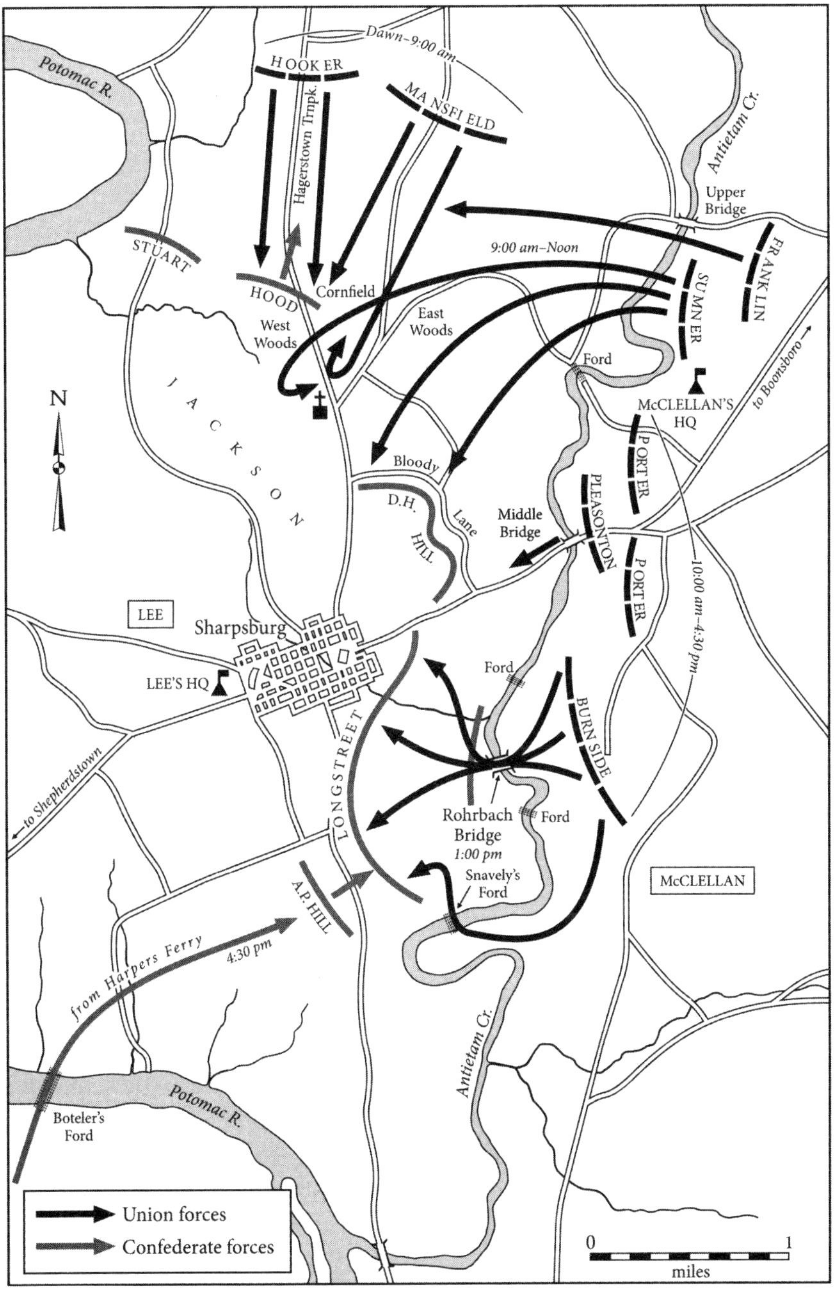

BATTLE OF ANTIETAM

bloody going in the Cornfield and East Woods, uncertainty about whether Hooker could order Mansfield's corps into battle, and soon enough both commanders were wounded, Mansfield mortally. Mansfield's men had reached the Dunker Church (where Smoketown Road ended at the Hagerstown Turnpike) and forced Rebel infantry back into the West Woods. McClellan eventually sent Sumner's corps into this fight but urged caution because of a supposed Confederate threat to the army's right flank. Shortly after 9 a.m., McClellan ordered Burnside to "open your attack" against the Confederate right. Once Major General John Sedgwick's division of Sumner's corps was mauled in the West Woods, McClellan became even more tentative; Stephen Sears and other historians have argued that he was fighting now to stave off defeat rather than win a victory. Assaults by two Second Corps divisions (commanded by Brigadier General William H. French and Major General Israel B. Richardson) produced yet more casualties along a sunken road soon-to-be-dubbed "Bloody Lane," though by early afternoon, Richardson's men had driven off the Confederates.[10]

During the morning, McClellan had moved his headquarters from the Pry House (where he had watched the contest unfold for about two hours) to Porter's headquarters, three-quarters of a mile closer to Burnside's front. He could see much of the field but remained rather far removed from the battle, and communications with subordinate commanders on the Union left came through aides carrying dispatches because no signal station had been set up on that part of the field. Porter used a telescope resting on a rail fence to observe the fighting and convey information to his commander. Upon realizing that the attacks against the Confederate center had brought some success, McClellan exclaimed, "By George, this is a magnificent field, and if we win this fight it will cover our errors and misfortunes forever." He may have been referring to Bull Run, at least according to one aide. Yet atoning for one defeat with a victory would hardly seem adequate. In any case, Confederate resistance was inflicting heavy casualties, and the uncoordinated attacks were not producing the desired results.[11]

On the Union left, with direct orders from McClellan, Burnside moved to cross Antietam Creek on the narrow Rohrbach Bridge, but the creek itself and Confederate positions on the other side proved to be serious impediments, with three assaults repulsed. With Union attacks on the right now stalled, McClellan became ever more insistent that Burnside get across the creek. By 1 p.m., Brigadier General Isaac P. Rodman's division had crossed downstream at Snavely's Ford, and around that same time, one New York and one Pennsylvania regiment from Brigadier General Samuel D. Sturgis's division managed to charge and cross the Rohrbach Bridge (soon to be called the "Burnside Bridge").[12] Even after Burnside had crossed Antietam Creek and advanced (albeit slowly) against the Confederates, McClellan seemed content with having the rest of his forces hold their own, and Porter glumly reinforced this passivity. Some of the hesitation stemmed from a pessimistic assessment from Sumner, despite Franklin's advice to send in the Sixth Corps against the enemy positions west of the Hagerstown Turnpike. The old general appeared demoralized, and McClellan ordered two brigades from Porter's corps to reinforce the troops holding Bloody Lane. Early in the afternoon, he wired Halleck that his army was "in the midst of the most terrible battle of the war—perhaps of history." There were great odds against him—as usual he greatly overestimated Confederate strength—and while he could certainly use reinforcements reported that Porter's Fifth Corps might soon attack the Confederate center. For a moment, McClellan offered a revealing comment about his own mental state but, before sending the dispatch, decided to cross it out: "It [the result of the battle] will be either a great defeat or a most glorious victory. I think & hope that God will give us the latter." Indeed by 3 p.m., Burnside's men were advancing toward Sharpsburg, but the arrival of A. P. Hill's division from Harpers Ferry changed the tide of battle once again and drove many of the bluecoats back across Antietam Creek on the same bridge that had so stymied them only a few hours earlier.[13]

By evening, word spread that McClellan would renew his attacks the following day; that was certainly General Franklin's understanding and Burnside's recommendation. Fresh troops would arrive, though McClellan still overestimated Lee's numbers and underestimated how much damage had been inflicted on the Army of Northern Virginia. The following morning, he emphasized to Halleck how long the battle had lasted but said it would "probably be resumed today."[14]

In writing to Nelly, McClellan struck different notes: "I hope that God has given us a great success. It is all in his hands, where I am content to leave it. The spectacle yesterday was the grandest I could conceive of—nothing could be more sublime. Those in whose judgment I rely tell me that I fought the battle splendidly & that it was a masterpiece of art. I am well nigh tired out by anxiety & want of sleep." He appeared to acknowledge that the victory was incomplete, but then he decided that the prospects for success were not great enough to risk continuing the fight. Despite the presence of fresh troops who had not been engaged on September 17, his men were exhausted, and the casualties had been heavy. Porter and McClellan would later claim that the Army of the Potomac did not have enough ammunition left to advance against the Confederates. Franklin still wanted to attack, but Sumner remained opposed. McClellan met with Franklin, Baldy Smith, and Major General Henry W. Slocum, a division commander in the Sixth Corps. Before them was the spot where Mansfield had died, with festering bodies strewn about the Cornfield, and these sights no doubt reinforced McClellan's belief that his army was simply in no condition to attack. He did not realize that the Army of Northern Virginia was in even worse shape and extremely vulnerable. At the same time, he had been warned often enough to make sure that Washington not be left open to a Rebel offensive.[15]

By September 18, McClellan was ill (apparently with his old malarial complaint from Mexico) and riding in an ambulance. He wired Halleck that the victory at Antietam was "complete," a word choice that would haunt the rest of his tenure with the Army of the Potomac. After all, Lee had abandoned the field and slipped back across the river. "Escaped," McClellan's detractors would have said. With Washington safe and the Rebels driven from Maryland, McClellan appeared satisfied with what had been accomplished. Despite his earlier recommendation for an attack on the defeated Confederates, Franklin had decided that the army was "too tired & too much diminished in numbers . . . to do a great deal of work."[16]

Success at Antietam briefly sent McClellan's mood soaring, in part because his critics had seemingly been silenced; it was a victory not only over the Rebels but also "over your own enemies," as a conservative Republican senator informed him. "My military reputation is cleared," McClellan exulted. "I have shown that I can fight battles & *win* them! I think my enemies are pretty effectively killed by this time!" He took pride in having "defeated Lee so utterly" and having saved the northern states from invasion. He could now replace Halleck as general in chief and insist on Stanton's removal, noting that even the great Napoleon had not been so adored by his troops. Yet McClellan also talked of retiring with his career vindicated. A telegram from Halleck (whose own health remained shaky) disturbed these reveries with a complaint about being "left entirely in the dark in regard to your [McClellan's] own movements and those of the enemy." McClellan countered with his own lament about Halleck finding it "necessary to couch every dispatch I have the honor to receive from you in a spirt of fault-finding." The general in chief had offered no word of praise for his great victory at Antietam, nor had Stanton or the president.[17]

Stanton had no intention of doing so, and along with Chase assured Senator Chandler that they had been "powerless" to prevent McClellan's reinstatement. Lincoln's counselors remained divided. Stanton had to go, Blair thought, and he not only congratulated McClellan on his victory but also confided that after the close of a cabinet meeting, Lincoln had spoken very kindly about the general. Welles, too, had much to say against Stanton, even as he expressed disappointment about the incomplete victory at Antietam, adding that the general's dispatches were "seldom full, clear, or satisfactory." In the cabinet, there was no real discussion of army management beyond the "occasional sneering remark" by Stanton and Chase. The president, Chase told Senator Sherman, did not seriously consult the cabinet, whose members hardly functioned as a unit; the secretary of the treasury visited the wounded Hooker, who proclaimed his own superior strategic wisdom, which would have produced decisive victories on the Peninsula and at Antietam. Even Seward deemed the results of Antietam "not entirely satisfactory," though perhaps people expected too much, but he thought that the dark cloud of public despondency was at least lifting. As for Halleck, Chase believed, as did Stanton, that the general in chief had simply surrendered to Little Mac.[18]

McClellan's allies rejoiced at reports of grudging respect for the general, accusing Radical Republican editors of tying themselves in knots to avoid praising their bête noire. Having disparaged McClellan and weakened soldier morale, the *New York Tribune* (at least according to its chief editorial rival) now denied ever having done so. With that approach played out, the *Tribune* would now simply ignore the general's role in the victories at South Mountain and Antietam. For its part, the *Tribune* reminded readers of earlier talk of McClellan as a dictator, and other Republican papers emphasized the incompleteness of the victory at Antietam, along with McClellan's failure to pursue the enemy.[19]

Nor would rumors of a conspiracy by an Army of the Potomac "clique" to install McClellan as a dictator go away. After all, he, Porter, and perhaps other general officers were nothing but traitors; the destruction of the republic and a military despotism loomed on the horizon. Then, too, Antietam failed to convince McClellan critics of the general's ability to defeat the Confederates. Brigadier General James A. Garfield, then in Washington convalescing from chronic diarrhea and an ankle sprain, fumed over McClellan's refusal to pursue Lee. "There is great bitterness here," he wrote from Willard's Hotel. "If this nation dies, it will die in consequence of the timidity of its rulers."[20]

McClellan's supporters doubled down on their praise, blaming Halleck along with Stanton for the failure to destroy Lee's army. McClellan alone, some editors claimed, retained the troops' confidence, and such comments set off political alarms. In an anonymous newspaper piece, one of Lincoln's secretaries praised McClellan's organizational abilities but hoped that his ambitions did not stretch beyond the battlefield. An Interior Department clerk and friend of Caleb Smith predicted that the general would soon "have a party," that "a new and conservative era has commenced." Rumor and speculation flourished in an increasingly chaotic political atmosphere. McClellan had his limitations, Frederick Law Olmsted allowed, but was an "infinitely better General than Lincoln is President."[21]

Events outraced such political calculations. On September 24, a group of "loyal" governors met in Altoona, Pennsylvania. Two days earlier, Lincoln had issued a military and political bombshell: the preliminary Emancipation Proclamation. The governors endorsed the president's decision, but on military matters they failed to reach a consensus. Governors John A. Andrew of Massachusetts and William Sprague of Rhode Island favored McClellan's removal, but Curtin of Pennsylvania and Richard Tod of Ohio objected, pointing to the recent victory at Antietam; the discussion dragged on into the evening without resolution. Two days later, a delegation of governors visited Lincoln. After some conversation about emancipation, Samuel J. Kirkwood of Iowa pointed to McClellan's unfitness to command an army. The president tried to deflect this with a joke, but Kirkwood then wondered if the administration was afraid to remove McClellan. Lincoln apparently reddened, and the governor explained how people feared that the general and "his toadies" had infected the army with their conservative views. Collecting himself, Lincoln coolly remarked that he was not yet ready to shelve McClellan but when the time came, he would do so. When Kirkwood asked for assurances of McClellan's loyalty, Lincoln bristled, stood up, and declared McClellan to be as loyal as anyone in the room.

He readily conceded that the general did not know how to follow up a victory but would hear no more about removing him. According to one wild rumor, some of the governors wished to cast aside Lincoln and make Frémont dictator.[22]

Word of the governors' attack on McClellan outraged a sergeant in the regulars, who thought the northern people should be wary lest the "army turn against you, or at best *stack arms*." Other soldiers cursed the proceedings of the "Abolition Governors in convention." The troops "believe with all their hearts in McClellan," a New York volunteer wrote home. They "are unwilling to be slaughtered in the experiment of muddle headed political generals." Some men made increasingly dismissive comments about politicians and editors, such as Greeley, who styled themselves military strategists. With occasional swipes at Stanton and Halleck, they deplored Washington interference with the Army of the Potomac and emphasized how McClellan had performed so much better than Pope.[23]

Despite the horrors of Antietam, some soldiers remained convinced that McClellan knew his business, and they cheered his every appearance. According to a Massachusetts volunteer, admirers outnumbered detractors by ratio of ten to one. A Minnesota clergyman who visited a hospital in Frederick, Maryland, marveled at how the sick and wounded implored God's blessings upon McClellan. If the government would allow the general to direct operations as he saw fit, so the argument ran, more victories would quickly follow.[24]

Yet in the aftermath of Antietam, the bond between McClellan and the Army of the Potomac showed signs of strain. Opinion grew more mixed: his obvious organizational ability did not mean that he had enough energy or dash to lead an army into battle. Some men asked why McClellan had not put in more of his troops for one last assault across Antietam Creek. Others criticized their commander for letting Lee's army escape. Could the Army of the Potomac win a decisive victory under McClellan's leadership? That seemed increasingly doubtful because he appeared incapable of waging an offensive campaign.[25]

It was exactly such anxieties that disturbed official Washington. Both Chase and Stanton worried about Lincoln letting matters drift. Whatever his doubts about McClellan, Welles considered Stanton a wily intriguer, a rude colleague, and an indifferent administrator. He even wondered if the secretary of war was truly loyal to the president. According to the gossipy navy secretary, the wily Stanton was growing increasingly close with Seward. All the while, the slowly recovering Hooker kept feeding Chase dirt on McClellan. Caleb Smith disparaged McClellan's "slow trench digging defensive tactics" and considered the so-called victory at Antietam "fruitless except of slaughter to our troops."[26]

As for Lincoln, he remarked that Antietam had perhaps vindicated turning to McClellan again. The prince de Joinville, who had closely observed McClellan and the Army of the Potomac, assured the administration that even if he was not quite a "complete general," McClellan was not prone "to abuse of his power." Yet the Frenchman's suggestion that sometimes a republic in times of danger might require a "temporary military dictator" hardly seemed reassuring. Lincoln had to weigh what McClellan had accomplished in Maryland. In his view, the general should have both committed more troops to the fight and then pursued Lee's retreating army. At one point the president told an apt tale about "Bap's red rooster," who was "great on dress parade, but not worth a damn in a fight." To make matters worse, Lincoln had learned of a conversation in which Major John Key (a War Department staff officer and brother to McClellan's aide Colonel Thomas M. Key) said that capturing Lee's army had never been part of the plan because that would have thwarted both a compromise settlement and the preservation of slavery. Major Key was swiftly dismissed from the service, but this incident was soon reported in the *New York Times*. In an anonymous newspaper piece, John Hay later asserted that McClellan's "most bitter partisans" shared Key's views. At the same time, Hay told Lincoln of his worries about a "McClellan conspiracy."[27]

Doubts about the general's competence and his loyalty might have abated had the Army of the Potomac advanced against the badly weakened Army of Northern Virginia, but there were no signs of that happening. On September 20, a sharp engagement at Shepherdstown, Virginia, bloodied a detachment from Porter's corps and discouraged further pursuit. In any case, McClellan hardly believed that his exhausted troops could mount offensive operations. His inadequately supplied forces would have great difficulty crossing the Potomac, so for the time being, he would have to reorganize the army and carefully guard the river. As usual, he asked for reinforcements—twenty new regiments.[28]

McClellan requested wagon bridges across the Potomac and Shenandoah Rivers, proposing to advance from Harpers Ferry "in force" and even offering engineering specifications. Halleck wanted to know much more about his plans before granting "such large sums of money." Nor would he commit to sending more troops. Doubting whether he would be given a free hand by the administration, McClellan simply told Halleck that the Army of the Potomac was "not now in condition to undertake another campaign nor to bring on another battle." He cited an officer shortage, skeleton regiments, and supply problems. Significantly enough, conservative newspapers were already reporting his assessment of the situation.[29]

At 6 a.m. on October 1, Lincoln, accompanied by a few western politicians and army officers, boarded a special train for Harpers Ferry. The party arrived six hours later, and the president met with McClellan in the afternoon. "I don't know where we are drifting but do not like the looks of things," the general had written to his wife earlier in the day. "I do not yet know what are the military plans of the gigantic intellects at the head of the Govt." The two men reviewed Sumner's troops on Bolivar Heights, a twenty-one-gun salute and repeated cheers rang out along the lines, and Lincoln regaled the troops with "humorous anecdotes." McClellan looked somber as he passed by depleted regiments. Lincoln accompanied General Sumner the following morning, inspecting troops on Loudon Heights and Maryland Heights. The president's real purpose, McClellan feared, was "to push me into a premature advance into Virginia." The general knew that his troops were "not fit to advance," but "these people don't know what an army requires & therefore act stupidly."[30]

The next day, Lincoln rode to McClellan's headquarters and briefly surveyed the Antietam battlefield; to one observer, the president seemed little interested, though another claimed he listened to McClellan with "marked attention" during the tour. Music filled the air that evening along with laughter, as Lincoln entertained his dinner companions with several wry stories.[31]

The following morning, October 3, McClellan and Lincoln rode out again, this time reviewing Burnside's corps. As before, assessments of Lincoln on horseback varied but tended toward the humorous or the condescending. One account, however, had the president on a spirited steed, dashing across the field with ease, one hand in the air and the other holding the bridle. Soldiers before had found Lincoln a decidedly odd-looking character on a horse, the signature stovepipe hat only adding to his lean and lanky look. Some commented on the obvious contrast with the dashing McClellan while expressing a certain affection for "Old Abe." One man thought the president looked rather like a preacher with "his big mouth ajar, after the manner of a sick oyster," but nevertheless deemed him the nation's "amiable magistrate."[32]

To some soldiers, Lincoln looked "homely," but those who were either more sensitive or got a better look at the president as usual chose the word "careworn." Despite a kindly countenance, his face seemingly revealed his sorrows. A Hoosier private decided that Lincoln's "rough camp look" was just the thing to please the enlisted men. Perhaps, as one of McClellan's aides concluded, Lincoln embodied both the strengths and weaknesses of a rough-hewn republic. Seeing him being carried along in an army ambulance, an artillerist drew a ludicrous picture of the president doubled up, with knees almost to his chin, and "grinning out of the windows like a baboon." To Charles Wainwright, he appeared to be "uncouth and gawky."[33]

During the afternoon, Lincoln and McClellan reviewed troops from Porter's, Reynolds's, and Franklin's corps. To Rufus Dawes of the 6th Wisconsin, the weary president "seemed touched at the worn appearance of our men." After spending a couple days with Lincoln, Little Mac looked "cross," at least according to a Maine private. Some evidence suggests that the troops responded to McClellan more enthusiastically than to the president, perhaps in part because of displeasure with the recently announced emancipation policy.[34]

On October 4, Lincoln and McClellan visited the wounded, surveyed the South Mountain battlefield, and then parted, the president going on to Frederick before returning to Washington. McClellan was no doubt glad to see him go, though the evidence for what had passed between the two men is sketchy. McClellan had described the army's condition and explained his reasons for not immediately pursing the enemy. He told Nelly that Lincoln "was very kind personally, . . . was convinced I was the best general in the country." McClellan later admitted that Lincoln thought he "was perhaps too prone to be sure everything was ready before acting." A New York journalist reported the president admonishing the general for always stopping "just short on this side of results." According to his old Illinois friend David Davis, Lincoln had advised McClellan that he would be a "ruined man if he did not move forward rapidly and effectually."[35]

Lincoln had also come to check on the Army of the Potomac, though as he reportedly remarked with great sarcasm, that army was merely "General

McClellan's body guard." At the close of his visit, he asked McClellan why regiments of new recruits remained at Frederick but received no satisfactory answer. Lincoln wrote down an estimate of the army's total strength during the Battle of Antietam but had expected it to be much larger. He sadly remarked some time afterward that "sending men to that army is like shoveling fleas across a barnyard, not half of them get there."[36]

Lincoln saw his visit as a way to reassure the army that he had rectified a mistake by transferring Pope and bringing back McClellan. The soldiers should understand that the administration had given McClellan all necessary support but that the general had thrown away a golden opportunity for a decisive victory. To the cabinet, it seemed doubtful that much had been accomplished by Lincoln's trip. Chase seized on a rumor that McClellan wished to retire but still sought to open a channel of communication with the general. An old Illinois friend posed a question to the president that had likely crossed his mind more than once: "Why cannot Buel[l] or McClellan fight like Grant does?" Tired of McClellan's "pompous" statements about safeguarding Maryland and Pennsylvania, Caleb Smith saw "darkness and doubts" looming on the horizon "while the best blood of the country has been poured out like water." Hearing rumors of Stanton threatening to resign, Welles dismissed them out of hand, but he had predicted all along that conflict between the secretary of war and various generals "must inevitably work disastrously." Fresh talk of "cabals" in Washington and the impending departure of Stanton and Halleck, along with a rumor that the convalescent Hooker would soon be given an important command (presumably McClellan's), only added to Lincoln's worries about what to do with the Army of the Potomac.[37]

Did the president's visit to McClellan portend "the grandest military movements and Union victories," as the *New York Herald* predicted? With troops presumably reinvigorated and fine weather cooperating, surely the army would soon take the field. Halleck had already pressed McClellan to cross the Potomac while the river was low, and fresh regiments had been sent to bolster the ranks. But Franklin thought that McClellan "loses influence every day," and Meade feared that Washington underestimated the losses sustained in the recent battle. On October 6, Halleck wired McClellan: "The President directs that you cross the Potomac and give battle to the enemy or drive him South. Your army must move while the roads are good." Lincoln had been reading up on military strategy and recommended that the Army of the Potomac adopt "the interior line between Washington and the enemy." At first, McClellan thought he would advance through the Shenandoah Valley but later decided to operate east of the Blue Ridge Mountains. Halleck said that it might take a while to fill up old regiments through either volunteering or a draft. In any case, the Army of the Potomac should advance with hard marches and limited rest periods, thus matching the standards set by both the Rebels and European armies. He added that stragglers should be shot. McClellan briefly replied that no time would be lost in carrying out the orders but went on at some length about the need for shoes, clothing, and tents, along with more troops. Deeply frustrated with him and still not feeling well, Halleck told his wife, "I cannot persuade him [McClellan] to advance an inch."[38]

The supply problems in the Army of the Potomac were real enough and local resources scanty. As McClellan's numbers increased, so did the length of the baggage and supply trains, and despite the efforts of Quartermaster General Meigs and others, the logistical situation delayed offensive movements. Although McClellan may have exaggerated and made excuses, some pause in campaigning was unavoidable but nevertheless frustrating and disheartening. Then, too, a newspaper report that McClellan had made a requisition for five thousand spades surely reaffirmed the views of those who dismissed him as an entrenching rather than a fighting general.[39]

In certain quarters, patience was exhausted. Some Republicans hoped that Lincoln's visit to the Army of the Potomac would spell McClellan's doom. In wordy fashion and without even mentioning the general by name, Governor Oliver P. Morton of Indiana made that point to Lincoln: "I would rely with infinitely more confidence upon the man of strong intellect, whose head is inspired by his heart, who believes that our cause is sacred and that he is fighting for all that is dear to him and his country, although he be unlearned in military science, than upon the cold and polished professional soldier whose sympathies, if he has any, are most likely on the other side." New York philanthropist and reformer Charles Loring Brace spoke for critics who thought McClellan had been too cautious and too slow ever since the Confederate blockade of the Potomac and the Peninsula Campaign; despite the supposed victory at Antietam, he would never conquer the Rebels. Why, the *New York Times* asked, had no one seen any battle reports from McClellan? Perhaps the general mainly sought to advance his political prospects.[40]

Republicans had long been wary of anyone who loudly praised McClellan. One of Lincoln's secretaries wrote an anonymous newspaper article claiming that the general's friends were doing him great harm with wild charges about Washington conspiracies and talk of striking back at enemies. Jealousies and rivalries, including the widely reported conflict between McClellan and Halleck, undermined public confidence. Attacks on McClellan in turn generated furious rebuttals. Responding to his friend Brace's critique, Olmsted defended McClellan's record point by point, derided the "liar" Stanton, deplored Washington interference in various campaigns, and considered any talk of McClellan staging a coup to be the empty frothing of abolition newspapers. Anyone who believed the general should have accomplished more at Antietam not only was ungrateful and ignorant but also served the interests of scheming partisans. Friendly editors warned of plots against McClellan, and as the fall election campaign moved into full swing, conservative politicians trumpeted their support for Little Mac.[41]

The crosscurrents of opinion seemed to reinforce soldier support for McClellan. If only Washington would stop interfering, all would be well and the Union saved. A New York lieutenant dismissed those calling for McClellan's removal as "mean contemptible politicians." Shove aside such marplots along with the selfish contractors, and success would follow. One artillery officer who had initially wondered why McClellan did not cross the Potomac right after Antietam decided that the condition of the army—in part because of unfilled supply requisitions—prevented an immediate advance. With memories of Pope and McDowell still fresh, expressions of confidence in McClellan persisted. A skeptic might say that the general was popular with his men because he kept them out of harm's way, yet the bloody field at Antietam seemingly gave the lie to that canard. As an Ohio major observed, Union troops were hardly better fighters than the Rebels, so success for any offensive operation required superior numbers.[42]

Amid the back and forth between the administration and McClellan about the army's plans, the politics of slavery added a serious complication. Worries about political support for McClellan from conservative Democrats doing more harm than good only grew as the general faced pressure to say something about Lincoln's preliminary Emancipation Proclamation. One old friend from his railroad days recommended denouncing the measure as unconstitutional. But Montgomery Blair, still the general's strongest supporter in the cabinet, referred to the recent dismissal of Major Key and warned that the government's new emancipation policy would surely "incite" the general's enemies "to new efforts to secure your removal." He urged McClellan to publicly reaffirm the primary goal of preserving the Union, which would bring about the eventual demise of slavery. Blair added a warning that no large segment of northern opinion would favor the continuation of slavery after the war. His father, the old Jacksonian Francis P. Blair Sr., agreed and told McClellan to "baffle" his enemies by sustaining Lincoln's proclamation; in this way, the general could hew to a moderate course that would jibe with public sentiment. A few sympathetic Republicans offered similar advice.[43]

Soldiers in the Army of the Potomac greeted news of the preliminary Emancipation Proclamation with skepticism and ambivalence, though some men firmly opposed the change in policy and a minority welcomed it. In a long letter to editor Manton Marble, Porter noted how McClellan appreciated support from the *New York World* and then waded into a political minefield: "The [Emancipation] proclamation was ridiculed in the army—caused disgust, discontent, and expressions of disloyalty to the views of the administration, and amounting I have heard, to insubordination." Lincoln's new policy would only prolong the war by enraging the South and exposing him as a "political coward." Porter clearly favored a conservative war policy, with McClellan returning as general in chief, and called for the voters to punish the politicians who had thwarted the army. A *New York Herald* reporter in Washington privately described the reaction to Lincoln's proclamation: "The army is dissatisfied and the air is thick with revolution. It has been not only thought of but talked of and the question now is where the man can be found." He quickly added that despite being "idolized" by his men, McClellan seemed to "have no political ambition." His letter closed with an ominous prediction about a "change in the Government and in the form of Government within a very few days." Yet some soldiers impatient with McClellan's slow movements welcomed emancipation as a sign of energy from the administration, although a Pennsylvania private who applauded Lincoln's proclamation nevertheless doubted it would bring the war to a rapid close. Dismissing the idea of McClellan as a defender of slavery, he predicted that the general would continue to do his duty.[44]

Some Republicans for nearly a year had lamented McClellan's conservative views on slavery, but according to the general's political allies, the bulk of the army did not share their reservations. Indeed, until the summer if not later, it was commonly believed that on the slavery question, Lincoln and McClellan were on the same page. McClellan told a small group of general officers that he still thought that manumission should be gradual, that slaves escaping into Union lines should be free, but that Lincoln's proclamation was "premature." The change in policy, he worried, might incite "servile insurrection." To his old friend William Aspinwall, he inquired about the reaction among conservative men in New York. According to Baldy Smith (whose account was later passed on to Hay), McClellan had drafted a letter to Lincoln condemning the proclamation but was persuaded to tear it up. Smith is not the most reliable witness, but there is little doubt that McClellan disagreed with the new policy, one that only added to his frustration in dealing with Lincoln and the War Department. Some officers apparently urged him to defy the administration, but others, including Burnside, counseled against such a course. After some reflection, McClellan decided to "submit to the Presdt's proclamation & quietly continue to do my duty as a soldier."[45]

On October 7, McClellan forwarded to Lincoln a statement he had issued to the army. The document expounded on the well-established principle that the civilian administration set policy and the armed forces "sustain the Civil Authorities and are to be held in strict subordination . . . in all respects." This certainly threw cold water on any loose talk about defying the proclamation, much less setting up a military dictatorship. Should officers and enlisted men go beyond mere discussion of "public measures," this would "tend greatly to impair & destroy the discipline and efficiency of troops by substituting the spirit of political faction for that firm steady & earnest support of the Authority of the Government which is the highest duty of the American soldier." In these words, one could hear echoes of the founders and classic republicanism. Yet McClellan added what amounted to a warning: "The remedy for political error if any are committed is to be found only in the action of the people at the polls." This statement seemed gratuitous, but it scotched any talk of mutiny or marching on Washington. At the same time, it undoubtedly made folks in Washington more wary of McClellan's presidential ambitions and his political associates.[46]

McClellan won plaudits for a statesmanlike defense of civil authority. This gave conservatives an opportunity to ridicule Radical fears about a would-be dictatorship and laud the general's selfless patriotism. Normally critical editors offered at least measured praise for his wise and prudent stand, and a Philadelphia paper reported that McClellan would no longer conciliate proslavery politicians. None of this of course cooled speculation about him angling for the presidency.[47]

Lincoln may or may not have worried about McClellan's political aspirations, but considering the army's continued inactivity, he certainly felt the political pressure. Editor Joseph Medill even suggested that stragglers and deserters from the Army of the Potomac were trying to escape "McClellanism." Fine weather was being wasted as the troops remained idle, and the fall political campaign was going badly. "Drive McClellan to his work or kick him out of the army," Medill advised the president. Tired of hearing the general's excuses, Lincoln reportedly said he would remove McClellan immediately were it not for the approaching elections.[48]

In Connecticut, Nelly had told a reporter that her husband had "accomplished such a triumph [that is, Antietam], after all that had been done to degrade him," and had remained silent in the face of unjust criticism. As McClellan worked to get the Army of the Potomac back into shape, he arranged for a family visit. Lincoln even suggested Washington as a possibility, but instead McClellan met Nelly and the baby in Philadelphia. Along with his mother-in-law, they all took up residence at a farmhouse in the Pleasant Valley near Harpers Ferry, where McClellan reported to Sam Barlow, "We are having a very quiet & pleasant time all by ourselves."[49]

That word "quiet" cut to the heart of the problem. To Lincoln and the cabinet, not to mention McClellan's more relentless critics, "quiet" summed up what with wrong with the Army of the Potomac post-Antietam. McClellan is "going into housekeeping," George Templeton Strong sniffed, and with gold prices soaring, the Army of the Potomac seemed "immovable as the pyramids." The "do-nothing policy of last fall is to be repeated," the *Chicago Tribune* feared. Even if the public retained faith in McClellan, the demand for action would obviously grow, regardless of any talk about supply problems, transportation difficulties, or disease outbreaks. Little Mac would likely dither until the fall rains turned the roads into mud, one cynic suggested. A Washington correspondent expected the Army of the Potomac to go into winter quarters and not advance until spring.[50]

In the meantime, another raid by Jeb Stuart's cavalry around the Army of the Potomac proved embarrassing, though it also gave McClellan an opening for pushing Halleck to strengthen the cavalry arm. Of limited strategic importance, Stuart's latest exploit nevertheless infuriated Lincoln. A "disgraceful" affair, Welles thought, with the humiliation compounded by McClellan's absence as Rebel horsemen circled his army.[51]

In a sharply worded letter, Lincoln reminded the general how he had been warned against his "over-cautiousness." The president pointedly asked, "Are you not over-cautious when you assume that you can not do what the enemy is constantly doing?" He noted that McClellan's army stood closer to Richmond than did Lee's army in the Valley and so should strike at the enemy's communications. The president sketched out various routes of advance and concluded with a sentence bound to provoke McClellan: "It is all easy if our troops march as well as the enemy; and it is unmanly to say they can not do it." Claiming to be "not wedded to any particular plan of operations," the general promised to "advance the moment my men are properly shod and my cavalry sufficiently renovated to be available." Yet by this time, Lincoln openly complained about McClellan having "the slows," and Welles sadly noted the waning of public confidence. News of Lincoln's letter soon leaked, fueling fresh speculation about the general's plans and his falling stock with the president and cabinet.[52]

McClellan continued to badger Halleck about "filling up the old regiments at the earliest possible moment." The thinned ranks had done hard service, so some time would be required to reorganize, drill, and gather supplies. Reports of various movements fueled speculation that the army was about to advance while also prompting demands that it do so. To McClellan, however, the logistical situation remained unsatisfactory. On October 11, he wired Halleck about serious shortages of clothing and shoes. Quartermaster General Meigs reported supplies (except for blankets) going forward but noted some interruptions on the rail lines and canal. Corps commanders complained of shortages, and a New York artillerist told his sister that the folks at home needed to understand how delays in sending supplies and reinforcements "render it impossible for him [McClellan] to advance." Several newspapers echoed that assessment. Of course, the sheer size of McClellan's army inevitably led to bottlenecks, but by October 18, supplies were arriving.[53]

Doubts about McClellan's generalship and his capacity to conduct an offensive campaign remained the talk of Washington. "I can discover no sign of life in the Army of the Potomac," John Nicolay groused. Lincoln seemed impatient and stood prepared to order McClellan forward. Hard-pressed himself, Halleck bluntly advised the general: "The President does not expect impossibilities, but he is very anxious that all this good weather should not be wasted in inactivity." Lincoln's secretary William Stoddard penned an anonymous newspaper piece warning McClellan not to "lose this last opportunity for placing his fame and popularity upon a more enduring basis." It was high time that he proceed with vigor and trap Lee's army. A more sympathetic George Meade agreed that if McClellan did not move soon, he might well be removed.[54]

Rumors flew about McClellan's impending removal. Perhaps Little Mac would supersede Halleck as general in chief, but in any event, his tenure with the Army of the Potomac seemed precarious. That McClellan either had to advance against the enemy or give way became an all-too-common sentiment. Hooker seemed the odds-on favorite to command the Army of the Potomac, though the press both trumpeted and discounted that possibility; some sources suggested that Hooker had not yet sufficiently recovered from his Antietam wound. Hooker was reportedly a Democrat opposed to abolition, but Meade tartly remarked that the general might well change his stripes because he "is open to temptation and liable to be seduced by flattery."[55]

The mood in both Washington and in the Army of the Potomac had soured after Antietam. The question of the hour had become: when would McClellan move? Or perhaps more pointedly: why hasn't McClellan moved? After a visit home, John Gibbon bluntly told one of McClellan's staff officers that unless the army advanced soon, the general's removal was inevitable. Even some of his political friends acknowledged that fact, and his enemies were hard at work to make it so. "But I may not have command of the army much longer," McClellan confided to one of his generals. "Lincoln is down on me."[56]

11

THE LAST CAMPAIGN, THE POLITICS OF REMOVAL, AND THE NOT-SO-FINAL FAREWELL

EVEN IN LONDON, the reported "slowness" of McClellan had set diplomats' nerves on edge, while at home, political pressure on Lincoln continued, with the fall election season underway. The war appeared stalemated, and doubts about McClellan had grown into doubts about the Lincoln administration's ability, or even its determination, to defeat the rebellion. Aside from critical newspaper commentary, editors spelled out their worries in notes to the president, explicitly tying the Army of the Potomac's inactivity to potential Republican losses across the northern states. McClellan's lethargy was depressing sales of government bonds, financier Jay Cooke warned the president. On October 24, the equally sluggish and conservative Don Carlos Buell was relieved of command in the western theater, and Stanton favored the same fate for McClellan, denying that it would hurt the administration in the approaching elections. Lincoln disagreed and was not quite ready to dispose of Little Mac.[1]

Whether McClellan was ready to move was the more pressing question. On October 22, he informed Halleck that he would be following Lincoln's advice and operating east of the Blue Ridge, perhaps hoping to gain more reinforcements by going along with the president's recommendation. As with Lincoln, the pressure on McClellan had increased, and there remained the possibility—by now likelihood—that he would be removed from command. At least Halleck promised 20,000 more troops, and by October 26, McClellan had begun crossing the Potomac.[2]

All along, McClellan had claimed to need more time while his army was being resupplied, and even at this late date, his newspaper supporters parroted that argument. Stanton inquired of Montgomery Meigs whether there had been any undue supply delays, and the quartermaster general replied that "every requisition had been promptly met." Yet the requisitions had been "large," there had been problems with rail transportation, and bottlenecks occurred once the supplies reached the Army of the Potomac. "I have frequently remarked that an army will never move if it waits until all the different commanders report they are ready and want no more supplies," McClellan's chief quartermaster conceded. He added that McClellan had sent no complaints his way. There were, however, real supply problems, and Meigs acknowledged the difficulties in filling requests for another 13,000 horses.[3]

Those horses were a sticking point in McClellan's campaign plans and became a flash point with Lincoln. Confederate raids over the past several months justified strengthening the cavalry arm, and McClellan claimed that deploying his troopers against Jeb Stuart "completely broke down nearly all of our cavalry horses." He and Meigs sharply disagreed over the number of mounts that had been supplied to the Army of the Potomac. Halleck sent him reassuring telegrams, but McClellan responded that he did not even have enough horses to patrol the Potomac River line properly. The short-tempered Meade had to buy horseshoes in Frederick, Maryland, and with some exaggeration noted that the animals were nearly starving for lack of fodder. Even as McClellan prepared to carry out Lincoln's order to move and reported his supply situation otherwise improved, he asked for more cavalry and artillery horses.[4]

On October 25, in a note to Halleck, McClellan quoted the commander of the 1st Massachusetts Cavalry bemoaning "sore-tongue" horses and other equine maladies. Unfortunately for him, Lincoln saw the message and fired off a barbed response: "I have just read your dispatch about sore-tongued and fatigued horses. Will you pardon me for asking what the horses of your army have done since the battle of Antietam that fatigues anything?" McClellan replied by detailing recent cavalry operations, then closed with a barb of his own: "If any instance can be found where overworked cavalry has performed more labor than mine since the battle of Antietam, I am not conscious of it." The president would not let the matter drop and replied with a short dispatch unfavorably comparing McClellan's cavalry with Stuart's horsemen. Continuing the tit for tat, the general outlined his cavalry's accomplishments and claimed that Stuart's most recent raid had only succeeded because the Rebel general had received fresh horses and had stolen additional ones in Pennsylvania. Lincoln partially apologized for his sharp tone but, pointing to the Army of the Potomac's "more than five weeks total inaction," wondered whether McClellan's cavalry horses would ever be properly rested.[5]

Amid these squabbles, reports of an impending change in command or an even larger Washington shakeup circulated. Both the general's doubters and defenders believed that his days with the Army of the Potomac were numbered. McClellan might soon displace Halleck, the *New York Herald* reported, and speculated that Hooker would take over the Army of the Potomac. Rumors about fallout from the recent conference of northern governors pointed to pressure on the Lincoln administration to make even more far-reaching, though unspecified changes. After reading press accounts, one officer in the regular army decided that the government "intend to take McClellan away from us again." Just as quickly as such stories cropped up, they were refuted in later accounts.[6]

A remarkably accurate piece in the *Boston Herald* reported that McClellan still had a couple of "lukewarm" friends in the cabinet, but that Chase, Stanton, and Bates were insistent that he be forced to fight. Everyone appeared to have an opinion about what might be needed to end the military impasse. Horace Greeley, Henry Ward Beecher, and some leading New Yorkers agreed that McClellan and Halleck would have to go, lest the war drag on and the rebellion gather strength. After a visit to Washington, a Massachusetts officer feared that too many people had swallowed Hooker's criticism of McClellan and worried that "Fighting Joe" would "do us a mischief if he ever gets a large command." McClellan's removal would hearten the more earnest Republicans, and perhaps Lincoln had already stood by him so long that the political damage had been done. On a trip to Illinois, John Hay warned that sending the general west would "demoralize the army," and he sounded especially anxious about the remaining elections.[7]

Hay's concern mirrored the views of other Republicans. For some time, Democrats and some conservative Republicans had warmly supported McClellan, and even the general's friends worried about him being dragged into the partisan arena. Lusty cheers for McClellan rang out in Democratic meetings during October, most notably during the heated New York gubernatorial canvass. At a conservative meeting in Boston, one speaker dubbed him "the glorious young Christian hero who, under God, has saved the country." Ohio congressmen Samuel Sullivan Cox defended the war record of Democratic generals, officers, and enlisted men who had volunteered to save the Union rather than fight an abolition war. The slanders of Greeley and his ilk, Cox predicted, would eventually make McClellan president. When arch-Copperhead Vallandigham's newspaper organ trumpeted McClellan's military achievements, Republicans could express alarm and point to new evidence of his traitorous friends. Many of the Union volunteers who closely followed politics back home recognized the connection between the fall elections and the possible removal of McClellan from command. Privately, McClellan welcomed Democratic victories but worried about the "ultra tone" of some campaign speeches. Having heard more than enough from partisans trying to make generals into presidential candidates, one newspaper correspondent blasted both parties: "The scarcity of great men is painfully manifest, when one has to erect McClellan as a political name and leader, and the other can find no one but that most wretched and selfish humbug, Frémont."[8]

High-minded disdain for party wirepullers was a luxury that Lincoln could ill afford. The president had to decide what to do about McClellan as his own political stock and that of his party was plummeting. Reports circulated that he feared to remove McClellan until the fall elections were over, and indeed the elections largely explain the timing. The president's big mistake, Chase had come to believe, was that he had "committed the management of the war almost exclusively to his political opponents" and in return had received little save excuses for delays. Lincoln had supposedly told a reporter that there was no reason to turn McClellan into a martyr, though as John Nicolay observed, "The President keeps poking sharp sticks under little Mac's ribs," and this had forced the laggard into action.[9]

The Army of the Potomac was at last moving, but with no guidance from Halleck, who seemed to take pride in the fact he had issued no orders to McClellan. It would take several days for troops to cross the Potomac, given the poor condition of the cavalry, and McClellan was "mad as a 'march hare'" over Lincoln's sharp dispatch, "one of those dirty little flings that I can't get used to when they are not merited." Men in the ranks sensed that McClellan had been forced into a new campaign by Washington. Rain almost immediately slowed progress. The general again asked

Lincoln about filling up "skeleton" regiments but promised not to postpone his advance. He provided a few details about the routes of various corps, and the president replied that he "was much pleased with the movement of the army." Lincoln wanted to know what the enemy was up to, and McClellan responded with bits of information on the disposition of Lee's forces.[10]

But McClellan remained as wary of official Washington as ever. He deplored the "tone" of Halleck's and Lincoln's dispatches and worried that the president viewed any delays as intentional. As far as McClellan could tell, newly recruited soldiers were not being used to fill up the old regiments, and the much-needed cavalry horses were being sent elsewhere. He reverted to calling Lincoln the "Gorilla."[11]

As the Army of the Potomac advanced slowly, McClellan was met by cheering soldiers, but many of these men had no doubt heard rumors that their commander was in trouble. The president was directing the campaigns rather than his generals, Fitz John Porter grumbled. By November 2, McClellan informed Lincoln that the last troops were crossing the Potomac and promised that "the entire army will advance rapidly." Some of the men sounded confident, but there was underlying skepticism, sometimes expressed in biting sarcasm. For the time being, with the army at last moving forward, a few newspaper dispatches sounded more optimistic. Some editors condemned "On to Richmond" cries, while others worried about the Army of the Potomac going into winter quarters. There was talk of going back to the old Peninsula route, and even McClellan's friends in the press hardly sounded sanguine.[12]

The real problem, a New Jersey Republican ranted, was that McClellan's "blind worshipers & secession supporters" would do anything to achieve their "political or traitorous purposes at the expense . . . of the very life of the Nation." In his view, "paid Reports, & subsidized correspondents" would convert "defeats & repulses" into "successes and victories for the 'Young Napoleon's' peculiar benefit" and throw any blame on the cabinet and Lincoln. Why then did the president not act? On October 28, Stanton appeared determined to force the issue and asked Halleck a series of pointed questions about supply problems and orders to advance. This inquiry served as a predicate for removing McClellan from command. That same day, Halleck outlined in detail how army requisitions had been filled as quickly as possible; "no armies in the world while in campaign have been more promptly or better supplied than ours." McClellan had not only dithered in pushing the army forward but also delayed making his needs known, and so many of his complaints were groundless. Reporters caught wind of this report and wrote off supply problems as mere excuses for McClellan's halting movements.[13]

In poor health and greatly discouraged, Halleck seemed powerless. He confessed to being "sick, tired, and disgusted with the condition of military affairs in the East" and thought he might better serve in the western theater. In Washington, he could "get nothing done." Halleck hardly knew what do with McClellan. "There is an immobility here that exceeds all that any man can conceive of," he informed Missouri governor Hamilton R. Gamble. "It requires the lever of Archimedes to move this inert mass." Yet the general in chief was often passive himself, appearing cowed by McClellan and his vocal supporters. McClellan dismissed Halleck as a "stupid idiot" with his mind perhaps addled by drink. He hoped for a successful military campaign to drive Stanton out of the War Department.[14]

During a trip to New York and Boston, Mary Todd Lincoln heard people say her husband should "put a fighting General, in the place of McClellan." She herself had come to view McClellan's removal as absolutely necessary. On November 2, the general informed Lincoln that he could hear the sound of artillery fire and might soon face "serious resistance." Such encouraging dispatches had been sent before, and doubts that he would engage the enemy persisted. Eager for his boss to get rid of McClellan, Nicolay summed up the general's problem: "He won't fight offensively." Lincoln readily agreed.[15]

On November 4, Lincoln read to the cabinet an earlier letter to McClellan ordering an advance. Stanton offered caustic comments about Halleck and McClellan. Attorney General Bates suggested Halleck should command the Army of the Potomac, but the president and his advisers quickly scotched that idea, in large part because Halleck shunned responsibility. While the administration was deliberating McClellan's fate, the Army of the Potomac had actually gained some momentum in what had been a slow and tentative movement, but the general's own reticence, his frequent requests for more men and supplies, and news of Republican election losses (especially in New York) all combined to push Lincoln toward acting. Some soldiers still cheered their commander and sounded exuberant about their march into Virginia, but in the aftermath of the recent elections, a Vermont volunteer claimed the army did not "idolize" McClellan or have much faith in him, likely due as much to the general's political associations as his military deficiencies. A case in point: in New York City, the crowds waiting for election returns interpreted votes for the Democratic gubernatorial candidate Horatio Seymour as endorsements of McClellan.[16]

So why did Lincoln still hesitate to let the axe fall, the usually moderate *New York Times* implored. A striking editorial entitled "Lessons of the Day" urged the president to take control of military affairs and make sure that the generals recognized the need for an energetic strategy. Democratic gains should convince the president to act, even though one bloody battle might have to follow on the heels of another. Ironically, a few Republicans thought the retention of McClellan helped deflect blame for the military stalemate from the Lincoln administration. The *Chicago Tribune* spoke for many disappointed Republicans: "The President has McClellan mainly to thank for the results of the October and November elections. . . . Why has he not been displaced long ago?" That question became all the more painful when victorious Democrats in New York began trumpeting McClellan for the presidency. Dismayed over the elections in Illinois and elsewhere, Senator Lyman Trumbull feared a "humiliating compromise" and could only hope the purblind Rebels would reject such a bargain.[17]

On November 5, Lincoln finally ordered Halleck to relieve McClellan and appoint Burnside to command the Army of the Potomac.[18] The president offered no detailed explanation, and he did not need to, but he soon made comments that pithily summed up his thinking and showed how he had simply run out of patience. On the evening of November 6, Frank Blair Sr. came to the White House on a mission: to talk Lincoln out of removing McClellan. He cited the army's devotion to Little Mac and the difficulty any successor would have in handling "so complicated a machine." Lincoln's down-to-earth response was that he "had tried long enough to bore with an augur too dull to take hold." Yet Blair persisted, warning the president against yielding to the Radical Republicans and even claiming that a successful campaign by McClellan would divide Democrats and turn the general into a political ally. Lincoln simply told him that the general had the "slows" and would have to go. Of course, Lincoln had been slow enough himself, according to those who had given up on McClellan some time ago. The president had retained a general who had hoped the war would end somehow with a compromise. McClellan's "sympathies . . . had always been with the South," the *New York Times* editorialized. Like other commentators, this newspaper observed that "political partisans" for many months had been grooming McClellan as a presidential candidate to challenge Lincoln. In turn, the general had often ignored or defied the orders of his own government and had greatly endangered the Union cause.[19]

Suitably enough on the fateful evening of November 7, a snowstorm blanketed the troops around the general's headquarters at Rectortown, Virginia. Earlier in the day, McClellan had sent a dispatch to Lincoln reporting a concentration of his forces near Warrenton. In the early afternoon, he had started writing to Nelly about the army's movements but kept getting interrupted. At 11:30 that evening came another interruption, as Brigadier General Catharinus Buckingham (Stanton's envoy) along with Burnside and two aides appeared with the removal order. Herman Haupt thought that the order came as a great surprise to McClellan, and that may have been true at the moment, but for some time he had speculated about his possible dismissal. Resuming the letter, he told Nelly of sympathizing with his old friend ("Poor Burn") who "feels dreadfully, almost crazy." But McClellan would show no emotion in front of Buckingham and the others: "not a muscle quivered nor was the slightest expression of feeling visible on my face." He believed the president and his advisers had "made a great mistake—alas for my poor country." Despite admitting to mistakes of his own, McClellan believed he had done his duty and could not discern "any great blunders."[20]

Burnside had twice before turned down the appointment but now, and most reluctantly, thought he must accept it, at least if the alternative was Hooker, as Buckingham informed him. The modest Burnside considered himself unworthy to command such a large army. McClellan simply said, "I am sorry for him."[21]

In a farewell address to the troops, McClellan expressed deep pride in the Army of the Potomac, which had "grown under my care." Aside from battles won and glory obtained, he rejoiced over having never detected "doubt or coldness" among the men—an implied contrast to the plotters in Washington who had engineered his removal. McClellan pointed to sacrifice and suffering but, more importantly, to "the strongest associations that can exist among men, unite us still by an indissoluble tie." One might speculate whether persistent loyalty and affection for their deposed commander would influence the Army of the Potomac's future operations and add weight to whatever political ambitions McClellan chose to pursue, yet for the moment nothing loomed but a painful departure. McClellan later told a staff officer that he would "rather die than leave it [the Army of the Potomac]."[22]

On hearing the news, McClellan's generals ruminated over the army's future and their own. Franklin and Baldy Smith welcomed the change, though the conservative Franklin applauded the Democratic victories in New York and was not entirely sure whether a better commander could be found. Some generals focused on their own chances for advancement or feared the consequences of having a new commander. Meade speculated that Lincoln's decision would backfire politically, "making a martyr of McClellan and putting him in the White House." Skeptics acknowledged McClellan's hold on many generals. Brigadier General Andrew Atkinson Humphreys fumed over the injustice of McClellan's departure and reportedly "wished the Confederates would get into Washington and drive the whole d—d abolition posse into the Potomac." Just as with the preliminary Emancipation Proclamation, the removal of McClellan highlighted political divisions in the army. Denunciations of abolitionist influences became shorthand for support of McClellan and political conservatism more broadly. The general's most ardent admirer, Fitz John Porter, thought the politicians feared that McClellan would bring the war to a successful conclusion. How else to explain the removal of a general amid a campaign that promised great success?[23]

The shock and confusion over the news quickly filtered into the ranks. Some men agreed with Porter about the folly of removing a general on the eve of a great victory. "Our favorite Genl is disgraced and insulted to satisfy the *Black Republicans* of the north," a New York volunteer wrote home. "If McClellan should take Richmond it would make him the next president." Other soldiers saw the removal as a sign of wavering and uncertainty in the government. A Massachusetts captain who had a decidedly mixed opinion of the general's abilities nevertheless agreed that McClellan should have been allowed to carry out the current campaign without Washington meddling.[24]

With McClellan preparing to bid his beloved army farewell, the word "despair" captured the reactions of some men. "I am willing to give up," one New York volunteer scrawled in his diary. "The removal of McClellan has cast a gloom over our army such as I have never seen before," a Pennsylvania captain lamented. Let the stay-at-homes or armchair generals such as Greeley come fight was certainly a sentiment that had been expressed before, but now more than ever, it reflected a disgust with McClellan's enemies. A Vermont captain well summed up the anguished reaction of many others: "I believe that it was the darkest day we have seen when McClellan was suspended for it is a dangerous thing to take from the Army one whom they love and worship almost, just because he cannot be driven or moved against the decisions of his own judgment."[25]

Recrimination usually follows in the wake of any controversial decision, and the question became who was to blame for McClellan's departure. What a New York sergeant termed "blockheaded abolitionists" remained favorite whipping boys. Other soldiers cursed politicians more generally, or homed in on "political generals" and the northern press, though one Pennsylvanian who greatly admired McClellan added that the northern public "could not understand the difficulties of his position and chafed at his delays."[26]

However reluctant soldiers might have been to criticize "Father Abraham," several blamed the president and the cabinet for demoralizing the Army of the Potomac or zeroed in on the War Department and Stanton as the main culprits. One volunteer thought Halleck and Lincoln together had schemed against McClellan. An officer in one of the regular infantry regiments believed that McClellan was sacrificed to an irrational bloodlust: "The Administration puts me in mind of the famous dragon, which was never satisfied, except with a feast of 'humans.'" According to a New York lieutenant, Lincoln was determined to "take off his [McClellan's] head in revenge" for being a Democrat and opposing the new emancipation policy.[27]

The soldiers' dedication to McClellan heightened indignation over his removal. A New York colonel credited the general with having "trained us from our first condition as an 'armed mob.'" The general's most passionate admirers were sure that the army would never have a commander who inspired more devotion, and some swore they would never go into battle again. A few even hoped Burnside would fail, and occasionally the sentiments bordered on the treasonous.[28]

The word "mutiny" cropped up as officers and enlisted men denounced Lincoln's order. In the heat of the moment, scores of officers threatened to resign, loudly declaring they would no longer serve in the Army of the Potomac. Some sent in their resignations, and a New Yorker guarding the

Army of the Potomac's headquarters claimed that two hundred officers had resigned, though senior officers often talked their subordinates out of doing it. The anger engendered by the president's decision produced a good deal of brave (and often empty) talk, and cynics might well observe that some of the officers had just been looking for an excuse to go home. Enlisted men in any case had to stick it out. Speaking for countless others who deplored what was happening, Private Elisha Hunt Rhodes observed: "Like loyal soldiers we submit."[29]

That is precisely what happened. Rumors of mutiny proved to be just that—rumors. Despite countless expressions of dismay around the campfires, there was no real trouble, and the men would surely fight under Burnside as they had under McClellan. However much the recent turn of events had jolted the army, Brigadier General John F. Reynolds observed to his sister, "it created less feeling than I feared." Acquiescence and obedience characterized the soldiers' response once tempers had cooled. "The feelings which newly pledged soldiers experience at the removal of their favorite general are very much like those which an ardent young man experiences when he finds himself compelled to give up the idol of his affections," a Pennsylvania volunteer recalled. "He dreads the pain of separation and dies a thousand deaths at the bare reflection; but, when the thing is once over, he consoles himself with the idea that there are as good fish in the sea as there are out of it, and that, after all, he may find another and perhaps a better one in the end." All in all, the army had calmed down quickly. A Pennsylvania captain who had lost confidence in McClellan some time ago even predicted that the general's name would soon be hardly mentioned in camp.[30]

That overstated the case by a long shot and ignored evidence of continuing faith in Little Mac, but there were a fair number of soldiers whose reactions to his removal were ambivalent. A member of the signal corps, who worried that recent Democratic victories had dampened the soldiers' spirits, simply concluded that the inexperienced Young Napoleon had done his best—not exactly a ringing endorsement. A Massachusetts captain admired McClellan but thought "he lacked some important qualities that go to make up the perfect general." A young lieutenant, who deplored the Democratic political resurgence, noted that his comrades' worshipful attitude hardly made the general a military genius.[31]

Some men shared the impatience of the politicians and the northern public. If McClellan had failed to move aggressively, it was time to find a general who would. Perhaps he simply lacked force of character, claimed one staff officer, who railed against the sycophants and martinets reinforcing the general's natural passivity. After all, McClellan had faltered on the Peninsula, and a New York artillerist considered Antietam a "three-quarters success." In sum, Little Mac's service with the Army of the Potomac had been a series of wasted opportunities. Had he really been the answer, the Confederate capital would already be in Union hands; therefore, his removal might open the way for future victories.[32]

Echoing the laments of Lincoln and others, frustrated soldiers criticized the Army of the Potomac for being inactive and McClellan for being slow. A Pennsylvania volunteer who loved McClellan nevertheless decided that the general had to go because he "*refused* to move." One Pennsylvania colonel decided that Lincoln had perfectly good reasons for shelving McClellan; an especially disillusioned volunteer hoped that Little Mac would never receive another command. In some cases, the politics seemed clear cut, with a *New York Times* correspondent noting how Pope's veterans were far more satisfied with the change than men who had served with McClellan on the Peninsula. Nor was there any doubt that his removal gave the Democrats an opportunity to howl in protest and make him a tool of their partisan ambitions.[33]

In the evening of Sunday, November 9, McClellan met with the headquarters staff and other officers for a glass of wine and a fond farewell. The men crowded into and outside his tent; McClellan shook hands with each one and offered a few words of appreciation. He claimed to have known little about the removal order except that it had been made right after the results of some key state elections had been announced. Seeking to tamp down the more strident expressions of outrage by younger staff members, McClellan reminded them of their duty to obey orders. Among those present, according to Marsena Patrick, there was "a feeling as deep as I have ever seen." Reynolds made a few remarks about how everyone regretted his departure. Much affected and close to tears, McClellan spoke of the great blow that had fallen on him. He toasted the Army of the Potomac and added, "God bless the hour when I shall be with you again."[34]

A final parting with the army the next day was followed by one more gathering of officers, many from Porter's Fifth Corps, where feelings ran high and tears flowed, especially since their own commander had also gotten the axe. As men doffed their hats and bowed, some "expressed strong opinions" and even suggested resistance, but McClellan offered no encouragement and urged them to serve Burnside faithfully. At times, he appeared too overwrought to speak. As before, he shook each man's hand and extended a parting word or two. McClellan noted that he might have been made dictator had he wished, adding, "I shall look to history to do me justice."[35]

It had been quite a day for George McClellan and the Army of the Potomac. Earlier in the morning, the general (mounted on his favorite horse, Dan Webster) had ridden along with his staff and Burnside through the lines of assembled troops near Warrenton, Virginia. "It was more like a triumph than a dismissal," one Massachusetts officer recalled. The scowls on some men's faces reflected their indignation toward Washington politicians, claimed a Bay State artilleryman. Cannons fired and the troops cheered—thunderously, according to several accounts, which described a great outpouring of affection for the departing commander. The whole affair had an orchestrated quality, but one staff officer was convinced that these demonstrations were "spontaneous and sincere."[36]

To some, McClellan appeared sober and unsmiling amid the enthusiastic reception. Riding along bareheaded, the general politely bowed to each brigade. According to other onlookers, McClellan seemed deeply affected and barely able to say much as he passed through the ranks for the final time. A Pennsylvanian noticed tears in the general's eyes. "I did not know before how dear they [the troops] were to me," McClellan wrote to Nelly. "I never before had to exercise so much self-control. The scenes of today repay me for all that I have endured."[37] He had long cherished and cultivated the solders' good will, reveling in any signs of admiration.

McClellan described how veterans had swarmed around him with "tears streaming down their cheeks." Officers and enlisted men alike tossed caps into the air. Even those who had only served under McClellan a short time appeared deeply moved. Men broke ranks to greet their beloved commander, with some even declaring that they would advance on Washington should he give the word. Others compared his ride through the lines to a funeral procession for a man whose career had been sacrificed to unprincipled politicians. According to a friendly newspaper correspondent, some even chased after McClellan's party, begging the general to come back.[38]

To one critical observer, the past several days had all seemed well staged for McClellan to enjoy one last—and hardly spontaneous—outburst of adulation. As was standard practice, officers had prompted the men to shout and cheer. Whether such scenes were contrived and evanescent remained to be seen, as were the military and political consequences of Lincoln's decision. Even men who resented standing in formation and showed little interest in McClellan's final sendoff might be equally skeptical about those in Washington who sought to make political capital out of the war and advance a Radical Republican agenda. Some diehards predicted that the government would eventually have to restore McClellan to command; surely their hopes had been father to that thought.[39]

Late in the morning on November 11, McClellan and his staff left Warrenton Junction for Washington. Cannons fired salutes as the train rolled along. There was a brief protest over the departure, and McClellan again reminded the troops of their duty. He informed Nelly that he would only tarry in the capital until the next train departed, would certainly not see anyone, and hoped to proceed with "as little fuss as possible." Nevertheless, at the Washington depot, McClellan shook hands and exchanged a few words with a crowd before leaving on a late-afternoon train. In Philadelphia, people gathered at the station to catch a glimpse of the famed general and local hero. When the train arrived late in the evening, a band struck up "Hail to the Chief" amid loud cheering. McClellan appeared on the train's rear platform and shook hands for fifteen minutes, then thanked everyone for their kindness but noted his sad parting from the Army of the Potomac and declared it was no time for a speech. The Philadelphia Common Council later adopted resolutions praising McClellan, who "having triumphed over the enemies of his country, . . . has also triumphed over himself, thus giving a fresh proof that he is worthy of the confidence which his countrymen have reposed in him."[40]

At four in the morning on November 12, McClellan and his staff finally reached Trenton, New Jersey (where he had been ordered to report to await further orders). Foul weather delayed any public reception, but on the following day, a crowd gathered at the hotel where the general was staying. Acknowledging the cheering, McClellan urged people "to see that the war is prosecuted for the preservation of the Union and Constitution." The streets filled with well-wishers, and a cornet band played a new composition, the "McClellan Polka."[41]

Generals removed from command were seldom accorded such treatment, but McClellan's prominence and his political connections explain the detailed press coverage. "The country breaths freer," the *New York Times* editorialized, because the president "by one bold stroke laid low the charmed myrtle." Loyal northerners had waited patiently for so long, but now the Army of the Potomac must move. For the more insistent Republicans, and especially abolitionists, the question remained why Lincoln had stuck by McClellan so long. Was the president too magnanimous and cautious? Unfortunately, Lincoln had not acted before the Democrats had taken advantage of the government's dilatoriness to prevail in the recent elections. Even now, this belated act of justice, Adam Gurowski growled, would hardly absolve Lincoln, Seward, and Blair of responsibility for a series of military disasters. Lincoln should have taken Stanton's advice, the *Chicago Tribune* maintained, and dismissed McClellan the day after the Battle of Antietam. Defending the War Department, the *Tribune* and other Republican newspapers recommended the release of correspondence that would highlight the general's many failures, including the most recent waste of fine campaigning weather, allowing Lee's weakened army to recoup its strength.[42]

That delays and excuses had ultimately spelled McClellan's doom became the standard Republican line. The dire consequences predicted to follow Lincoln's decision had failed to materialize, the financial markets had readily absorbed the news, and there had been no panic. Recently elected congressman James Garfield deemed the general's removal not only better than "a decisive victory over the enemy" but also "in itself a decisive victory over the rebels at home." From some statehouses and the halls of Congress came rejoicing that Lincoln had finally acted. One Illinois Republican recommended the press still "pitch into" McClellan because if Burnside faltered, there might be pressure for McClellan to take command again, or become the next president, or even assume the mantle of "military dictator." Political considerations at times overshadowed military ones. Lincoln had waited too long to get rid of McClellan, Maine senator William Pitt Fessenden feared, and had been far too conciliatory toward Democrats.[43]

By the same token, criticism of the president and defenses of McClellan remained politically potent. History would vindicate Little Mac, the *New York Herald* predicted, favorably comparing him to Napoleon, Cincinnatus, and Washington in a single editorial. The country should never forget how

McClellan had retrieved Union fortunes after First Bull Run or how he had restored the Army of the Potomac's morale and led it to victory at South Mountain and Antietam. Like Washington during the Revolution, McClellan had been unfairly maligned. Eventually the country would wake up, the *Herald* hoped, and he would either again be appointed general in chief or become president. Other voices continued to laud his superb organizing ability, rehashed the Army of the Potomac's supply problems, or blamed petty jealousy and political scheming for hampering military operations.[44]

Whether McClellan's removal had come about primarily because of political differences with the administration remained a bone of contention. The general's defenders interpreted the recent elections as votes in his favor and continued to hammer away at the idea that abolition radicals had forced the Lincoln administration's hand. Political intriguers who despised McClellan because of his refusal to elevate emancipation over Union had prevailed. Was there a "secret history" behind all this, as the *New York Herald* reported? The paper's Washington correspondent blamed "a formidable cabal organized by the radical politicians . . . in and out of the Cabinet." Chase had supposedly taken charge, and now Seward, Caleb Smith, and Blair might be on their way out. All this then explained the president's decision and likely comported with the thinking of McClellan and many of his supporters, who derided Lincoln for being under the Radicals' thumbs. It was high time for a cabinet shakeup, the *New York World* declared.[45]

Some Republicans worried that McClellan and his supporters might yet stage a coup, or at the very least ally themselves with Copperhead Democrats. The Lincoln administration's newspaper organ in Washington vehemently denied that politics had played a role in McClellan's removal and ridiculed those who claimed that the general had been about to achieve some stunning success. A leading Black clergyman, Henry McNeal Turner, charged that McClellan had been "Napoleonized through the papers, and crowned by the negro chattel-makers, monarch of America." The general's sympathies had always been with the Rebels, the *Chicago Tribune* agreed. Indeed, his loudest defenders were often men of the most doubtful loyalty. McClellan himself may not have been disloyal, but doubts about whether his heart had been in the fight lingered, suspicions only compounded by some of the general's political supporters. On the heels of Democratic election victories and McClellan's removal, New Yorker John Van Buren (son of the president and often sarcastically referred to as "Prince John") sang the general's praises and predicted that Democrats would support him for president. One of the most reactionary publications applauded McClellan for opposing the preliminary Emancipation Proclamation and fighting for the rights of white men.[46]

Republicans, too, spoke of McClellan as a likely Democratic presidential candidate while bravely declaring that his military record would surely sink his political ambitions. But they also had to face rumors of a serious cabinet disruption, with Seward and Blair coming under increasing pressure from their more radical colleagues. Nor had the removal of McClellan weakened the political storm swirling around the president, with speculation that the Republicans might have to replace Lincoln on their ticket with a fighting general. Looking on the bright side, Nicolay was pleased that there had not been more excitement and that McClellan had arrived in Trenton without saying much along the way. "Whether he will continue to behave himself properly or not, is of course yet a question." He expected McClellan to stay quiet in light of his military failures, but neither the Lincoln administration nor the American people had heard the last of the Young Napoleon.[47]

12

WAITING GAME

On November 20, 1862, McClellan left Trenton, New Jersey, for New York. Taking up temporary residence at the Fifth Avenue Hotel, he was serenaded the following evening by the Young Men's Democratic Union Club. A large crowd gathered with cheers for McClellan and "groans" for Greeley and Frémont. In brief remarks, the general referred to his service with the Army of the Potomac and the great contribution New Yorkers had made to the Union cause. He then withdrew to the drawing room, where he was warmly greeted by a large crowd of women. Local officials hoped to stage a public reception, but McClellan thought such an affair inappropriate when "so many of my former comrades are enduring the privations of war."[1]

No one expected McClellan to retire quietly, and there would be persistent speculation about his military and political future. Might he become general in chief again, or perhaps return to the Army of the Potomac, or be given another command? Would the still-popular general become a candidate in the next presidential election? Newspapers, both friendly and unfriendly, kept his name before the public, and everyone from army privates to high-ranking officers and politicians consumed the latest rumors and offered their own predictions. This all seemed to make his every move worth recording. The *New York Herald* even reported McClellan and his wife going out for an evening to some unknown destination.[2]

One day, McClellan visited a grammar school, where the students cheered him; on another occasion, the general reviewed a company from a boys' school with the unfortunate name "McClellan Greys." Visitors to the city caught wind of the general and Nelly unobtrusively attending church each Sunday. Once, accompanied by her mother, the couple was warmly received on a visit to sick and wounded soldiers in Bellevue Hospital. Whenever the McClellans returned to New York from a trip, crowds hailed them at the train station. Even word that McClellan *might* be attending some social gala received newspaper notice.[3]

As the press kept McClellan in the public eye, New York politicians courted the general. An aldermen proposed the city spend $1,000 for a portrait, which was quickly approved. McClellan had received permission from the War Department to leave Trenton for New York, and by mid-January 1863, the McClellans' household goods were in transit. A group of wealthy and influential New Yorkers presented Mrs. McClellan with a four-story, expensively furnished, and fully stocked house at 22 West Thirty-First Street. Reportedly, Sam Barlow had paid for the property. McClellan later described their new residence as a "bright cheerful house . . . in one of the most pleasant portions of the City."[4]

Just as McClellan had been warmly welcomed in New York, leading Bostonians of a conservative bent (including some Republicans) staged a series of dinners, balls, and receptions during a nine-day visit in late January and early February. A sizable crowd greeted the McClellans at the train depot, stores closed, and a levee was held at Faneuil Hall. On February 2, an overflow crowd of 10,000 gathered at Tremont House to shake the general's hand. Some Republican newspapers made light of such outpourings, but his visit received wide notice. McClellan enjoyed the attention but said little other than observing that the "conservatism" he discovered in New England boded well for the nation. Whether such fanfare portended his future restoration to command or his potential strength as a presidential candidate were questions widely bruited about. That McClellan was not about to disappear from the public stage was clear enough.[5]

Even in New York, however, the general could not escape army politics or the fallout from his removal from command. A late November 1862 report by Halleck on military operations covering the period from late July through mid-September sparked more debate between McClellan's defenders and critics. The general in chief outlined the reasons for ordering the Army of the Potomac to withdraw from Harrison's Landing, pointedly mentioned McClellan's delay in carrying out the order, and deemed the failure of several corps to promptly aid Pope's beleaguered Army of Virginia to be "neither creditable nor excusable." According to one Republican newspaper, McClellan's friends steered clear of Halleck's report because they cannot "meet its facts nor its logic." That document "has put the last clod of earth upon McClellan's coffin lid," Zach Chandler exulted. Predictably enough, the *New York Herald* reached the opposite conclusion, defending McClellan point by point, and claiming that Halleck "has demolished himself." Soon an anonymous pamphlet appeared, written by McClellan's friend, newspaperman, and future literary executor, William C. Prime, that slammed Halleck for his own slow movements in the western theater and dismissed the report as nothing but a mediocre lawyer's self-serving brief.[6]

The poisonous fallout from the Second Bull Run Campaign dragged McClellan back to Washington. In September, McDowell had asked Lincoln for a court of inquiry to clear his name after charges of "treachery" had been leveled by a mortally wounded officer, though this investigation soon expanded to include much of McDowell's wartime service. Early in December, McClellan appeared as a witness, and people cheered as he proceeded across Pennsylvania Avenue from Willard's Hotel to a building on South Fourteenth Street where the inquiry was being held. One member of the court even hosted a dinner for the general. In testimony on December 10, McClellan answered questions about both the retention of McDowell's corps in Alexandria at the start of the Peninsula Campaign and the later retention of his forces at Fredericksburg in May 1862. McClellan told the court that the latter decision had prevented the capture of Richmond, but he did not think that McDowell bore any responsibility for the blunder. McClellan dragged his feet on discussing the Washington defenses but finally stated that the capital had been left adequately protected. Likewise, he could see no good reason for McDowell's corps remaining in Alexandria at the outset of the campaign or failing to join the Army of the Potomac once Porter's corps had reached Hanover Court House. In sum, his testimony reinforced McDowell's statements while vindicating his own conduct of the Peninsula Campaign. The press parsed McClellan's words according to their own previously expressed opinions about who bore responsibility for the state of the Washington defenses and the subsequent failures on the Peninsula.[7]

McClellan was later called back to the capital to give evidence at the court-martial of Fitz John Porter, who was accused of disobeying Pope's orders and "misbehavior in front of the enemy" during the Second Bull Run Campaign. By prosecuting Porter, Stanton and his allies were indirectly going after his friend McClellan. On January 2, 1863, McClellan testified briefly that Porter had carried out orders promptly and had done everything possible to aid Pope. His testimony made little impression on a court-martial stacked with compliant officers ready to swallow dubious testimony and magnify Porter's own indiscreet statements. Porter was found guilty and cashiered; he would spend the next sixteen years seeking exoneration.[8]

These investigations, along with rumors about McClellan's military and political future, all occurred as the Lincoln administration tried to recover from the recent election losses and as pressure mounted on Burnside, now commanding the Army of the Potomac, to take the offensive. Hooker, who shared his own ideas for a campaign with Stanton, hoped that the delays that had been so commonplace under McClellan had come to an end. But, writing to his mother from the suitably named "Camp Misery," a Massachusetts lieutenant wished the "On to Richmond" crowd could share some of the suffering before blithely demanding a winter campaign. "I am not A McClellan man, A Burnside man, A Hooker man," one Wisconsin volunteer informed his father, but he was tired of reading the "damned infernal lies" in Republican newspapers. Whatever his other shortcomings, McClellan deserved praise for his organizing abilities, and the Republicans had gone after him for largely partisan reasons. Yet in this soldier's view, the Democratic editors were almost as bad when they raised so much hell over their idol's departure.[9]

Those soldiers who remained faithful to McClellan continued to criticize his removal as a great mistake that had prevented the Army of the Potomac from advancing toward Fredericksburg and eventually taking Richmond. Increasingly, the more conservative men in the ranks denounced the government for turning the conflict into what a Rhode Islander called a "Negro war." A Missouri lieutenant faced a court-martial for saying that McClellan should have "driven Old Abe and those damned Abolitionists out of Washington and taken the reins of Government in his own hands." Others simply wished for and expected McClellan's return to command.[10]

Such openly expressed sentiments fueled Republican worries that the Army of the Potomac remained a nest of disloyal Democrats who not only would oppose the Emancipation Proclamation but also seemed indifferent to putting down the rebellion. Amid the continuing lamentations about McClellan's removal, the *New York Times* suggested that the public was ill equipped to assess generalship, that popularity was hardly a sound basis for keeping anyone in command. The *Chicago Tribune* wondered if the

Democrats intended to incite a mutiny in Army of the Potomac to force Lincoln to bring back their hero. Since his removal from command, several editors complained, the general had largely associated with notorious Copperheads. Even sympathetic observers worried that McClellan had fallen under the spell of partisan intriguers.[11]

That conservative northerners (including some Republicans) would continue to favor McClellan (and call for his return to command) remained an article of faith in Democratic circles. Recent elections had shown the strength of conservatism in key states—a conservatism that had made McClellan the special object of Radical wrath. One speaker at a Democratic ratification meeting in New York elicited great cheering when he predicted that the government would again have to summon McClellan to the helm. In Congress and out, vindication of McClellan became part and parcel of Democratic assaults on the Lincoln administration. To Republicans, it seemed that their opponents expected or even hoped that Burnside would falter so that McClellan would return.[12]

"I think I can see through the policy of some of the press who . . . are constantly speaking in such unqualified praise of McClellan," one of Burnside's staff officers had remarked just as the Fredericksburg Campaign was being launched. "Should any mishap take place in the Army of the Potomac, Burnside will get it right & left, let the reasons be what they may." Should the campaign succeed, those same papers would undoubtedly say that McClellan's organizing and training of the army deserved the credit. By the same token, General Marcy thought it fortunate that his son-in-law would not have to conduct a winter campaign.[13]

Much of this proved prescient. On December 11 and 12, Burnside's army finally crossed the Rappahannock River to confront Lee's Army of Northern Virginia at Fredericksburg. On December 13, a series of poorly coordinated attacks, many against strongly entrenched positions, led to one of the worst Union defeats of the entire war. Only days after the Battle of Fredericksburg, rumor had it that McClellan had returned to command the Army of the Potomac. There was cheering in the camps around Falmouth, across the river from Fredericksburg, and soldiers eagerly told of sighting a familiar figure on horseback. Of course, they were mistaken, and the reports of McClellan's restoration to command proved false, but that did not prevent some of the troops from wishing it were so. In Washington, soldiers lustily sang a new song, "McClellan Again at the Head of His Men."[14]

The stunning Union defeat produced a chorus of indignation from those who had (or claimed they had) predicted just such a disaster. Even before the Army of the Potomac had been withdrawn from Fredericksburg, newspapers railed against Lincoln's great "blunder" in removing Little Mac. "Jeff Davis still laughs at the follies of our military directors," the *New York Herald* insisted. One volunteer in the Army of the Potomac blamed the politicians: "I do wish our statesmen . . . would stop this infernal meddling with the war and leave everything to our beloved McClellan." McClellan got closer to Richmond than any of the other generals, a New York private commented pointedly, adding that "our greatest disasters occur when we try somebody else."[15]

Deriding civilian authorities for hamstringing generals was hardly unusual; in both the North and South, and regardless of party, ordinary citizens, newspapers editors, and politicians regularly complained about the president or War Department not properly supporting or unnecessarily interfering with the supposedly brilliant operations of their favorite commanders. "The politicians have ruined the country," a New York cavalryman wrote home. "If Gen. McClellan could appear here today, with unrestricted authority—the air would be rent with shouting, the army doubled in strength." Even members of the Young Ladies' Aid Society in Canandaigua, New York, wrote to McClellan expressing their support as he battled "traitorous politicians and fanatical defamers." Whether it was scheming congressmen or ignorant civilians, the general's enemies were clearly ruining the country. Soldiers still talked of McClellan's genius or his ability to match wits with Robert E. Lee. Even before the news of Fredericksburg, speculation grew that, just as in the aftermath of Second Bull Run, Lincoln would be forced once again to call on their favorite general to save the country.[16]

Put simply, there remained a deep well of affection for McClellan. As one Hoosier volunteer who had seen some of the worst of the fighting put it only days after Fredericksburg, the camp now rang with the cry, "McClellan is the man." Soon the troops were reportedly singing, "McClellan is our leader, so march along." Another new tune, Septimus Winner's "Give Us Back Our Old Commander," enjoyed brisk sales and even elicited a charge of treason from Stanton as it became popular in the Army of the Potomac. For diehards, faith in Little Mac remained as strong as ever. Had McClellan been in command, the army would have been on its way to Richmond or would have already seized the Rebel capital, some soldiers avowed. Others speculated that he could have seized Marye's Heights without launching disastrous frontal assaults. Perhaps the Army of the Potomac was just "Mac's old army," in the words of a Massachusetts soldier. Critics who had second-guessed McClellan's slow movements would now have to reckon with the Fredericksburg carnage, and the reality that the Lincoln administration's decisions had produced the inevitable disaster.[17]

One point was made repeatedly: unlike the hapless Burnside, McClellan had known when to fight and when not to fight. Significantly, given his well-deserved reputation for caution, the emphasis was all too often on what he would *not* have done. Commenting on the slaughter in front of the stone wall beneath Marye's Heights, some of the Fredericksburg wounded came right to the point: "McClellan would not have led us there—he knew better." Survivors let their families know that their former commander would never have attacked such strong positions. Cursing Burnside and calling for McClellan's return enlivened many a campfire conversation. Even soldiers who did not entirely share such sentiments recognized that McClellan and his allies were riding high on a wave of despondency in the army and at home. About the Battle of Fredericksburg, a Republican congressman from Ohio dourly observed, "McClellan's friends chuckle and secretly rejoice over the result."[18]

Surely, there must be some place for a man of McClellan's talents. Herman Haupt, who supervised the military railroads, advised Lincoln to appoint a military council, including McClellan, to plan campaigns. That veteran advisor to presidents Francis Preston Blair simply recommended bringing him back to the Army of the Potomac. The general's strongest supporters apparently expected his imminent summons to Washington, perhaps to replace Halleck as general in chief. Blair approved of that suggestion, while recommending that both Halleck and Stanton be sacked.[19]

Everyone from privates to corps commanders had an opinion, and the enlisted men and junior officers seemed to believe that if they wanted McClellan back, that should settle the matter. In defending what amounted to citizen-soldier democracy, they fondly recalled how McClellan had cared for his men, and their affection appeared both genuine and deep. Some soldiers reported sentiment in the general's favor as nearly unanimous. Such conviction readily produced a strong expectation that he would soon be with them.[20]

And why not? According to this line of reasoning, McClellan was the "only" man who could do the job; no one else could come close to restoring the army's confidence. Such sentiments reflected conservative views in the army and the opinions of many Democrats and some Republicans back home, accompanied by pointed criticism of Lincoln, Stanton, Halleck, and Burnside. Let McClellan have a free hand, and the military situation would surely improve, his most loyal supporters maintained. In this view, he was *the* general who could lead the army to victory.[21]

That the demoralized troops would rally around McClellan seemed obvious to the general's most fervent defenders inside and outside the army. Upon his return to command, McClellan would instantly revive spirits and reestablish discipline. "When George was commander-in-chief," a Massachusetts volunteer enthused, "everything went as merry as we could wish to have it." For those who might point to Little Mac's lack of aggressiveness, a plainspoken soldier in faraway Arkansas noted: "It is now nearly four months since McClellan was laid on the shelf. Richmond aint taken."[22]

Yet the renewed calls for McClellan highlighted divisions in the Army of the Potomac. Skeptics worried about a "McClellan clique" trumpeting their hero's supposed virtues, conspiring against potential rivals, and in the aftermath of Fredericksburg working to undermine Burnside. "Idolism," meaning the cult of "McClellanism," complained a Massachusetts officer, had deeply infected the army. "Rule or ruin has been the motto of many of his [McClellan's] friends," a Wisconsin surgeon grumbled. Another surgeon believed that Democrats would be more than willing to see the Army of the Potomac defeated so long as that would bring back their "darling little Mac." Or perhaps they preferred prolonging the war so they could make McClellan president. Naïve folks at home (especially those who freely criticized but refused to enter the ranks themselves) appeared blind to the general's record of failure. Increasingly open Democratic support for McClellan in turn made some soldiers wary. One veteran of the regular army thought that there was about the general "too much of the traitor."[23]

There were several explanations for McClellan's popularity with the Army of the Potomac, but critics pointed to a coterie of his friends ensconced in brigade, division, and corps commands who continued to exert a malign influence. The always loyal Major General Franklin—whose own performance at Fredericksburg could be generously described as lackluster—thought McClellan's stock was "rising" and that Burnside taking responsibility for the defeat unfortunately let Lincoln and the cabinet off the hook. From Memphis, William T. Sherman—who took a backseat to no one in detesting politicians—predicted that "McClellan will be recalled sooner or later." Admiral Andrew Foote claimed that McClellan was the only general capable of commanding a large army. Perhaps if he were given free rein, the war could be brought to a speedy conclusion. "We must have McClellan back with unlimited and unfettered powers," Brigadier General Gouverneur Kemble Warren wrote from Falmouth, Virginia. "His name is a tower of strength to every one here."[24]

Other reactions to the idea of bringing back McClellan ranged from skeptical to apoplectic. Stationed in western Virginia, Colonel Rutherford B. Hayes coolly assessed McClellan as a general with serious weaknesses but acknowledged that he would not have made the same mistakes as Burnside. With considerable exaggeration and animus, John G. Barnard, who had once been chief engineer in the Army of the Potomac, claimed that most officers whose opinions might be worth heeding viewed their former commander as a "stupendous failure." Political intrigue in the army, however, along with the maneuvers of leading Democrats, would mean that dedicated partisans and gullible civilians would continue to puff McClellan's military prowess.[25]

McClellan followed the reports from Fredericksburg closely, expressed sympathy for his old friend Burnside, deplored the "useless" sacrifice, and somewhat cryptically remarked that "a change *must* come ere long—the *present* state of affairs *cannot* last." Whether he expected a new command or not, he continued to rail against Lincoln and the cabinet. Partisan defenses of his record, along with the usual complaints about Radical Republicans hampering military operations, grew ever louder and dovetailed with conservative critiques of the Emancipation Proclamation. According to Congressman Samuel S. Cox of Ohio, McClellan had been sacrificed to the Republicans' "ebony fetish." A New York Republican congressman could only hope that defenses of McClellan by supposed Copperheads would widen the gulf between the president and the general, making "his recall to the command of the army impossible."[26]

Besides Democratic politicians with their eye on the 1864 presidential election, McClellan received considerable support among conservative northerners. Repeated claims that his removal had been a capital error, along with more general disillusionment with Lincoln's war policies, echoed from the business ranks of New England to influential clergymen to the diplomatic corps. Even some Republicans favored a rapprochement with McClellan. The army was a "great political, as well as war machine," Francis Preston Blair told Lincoln, and McClellan "will bring them to the Support of the Country and to you." During a mid-December trip to Washington to testify before the Joint Committee on the Conduct of the War, McClellan met with Montgomery Blair and several conservative Republican officials who expressed warm support for him privately, if not publicly. The inauguration of Democrat Horatio Seymour as governor of New York caused great consternation in Republican circles, perhaps making some party leaders more amenable to working with McClellan.[27]

The *New York Herald* suggested that the return of McClellan—"with the exception of the President, the only honest man in and around Washington"—would actually help the Lincoln administration. Conservative editors continued to describe him as a superior strategist and blamed the war's mismanagement on Halleck, Stanton, and Radical Republican interference with the army. Letters from officers and enlisted men published in Democratic newspapers echoed these sentiments.[28] In some quarters, no praise for McClellan could be too lavish, especially after Fredericksburg. Comparisons to George Washington now complemented previous tributes to the Young Napoleon. Even the great commanders of history had never organized and fought such large armies. After Sherman's failed assault near Vicksburg in December 1862, there were calls for McClellan to displace Stanton, with Halleck's position as general in chief abolished. The idol of the people—another encomium tossed the general's way—would yet receive a suitable post; the public would demand it.[29]

With Union morale sagging at the end of 1862 and the beginning of 1863, Republicans talked wildly of a Democratic plot to bring back McClellan, possibly as the first stage in a military coup. The general's friends "chuckled & secretly rejoice" over the Fredericksburg disaster, an Ohio Republican congressman lamented; for their part, defenders of the administration countered by disparaging McClellan's military record and political associates. A case in point: McClellan attended the opera one evening in New York and, after sitting in a box with Sam Barlow and August Belmont, was brought forward to take a bow by John Van Buren. By the end of 1862, the politics of the McClellan question became more deeply entwined with disparagement of his military performance. One of Lincoln's private secretaries wrote an anonymous newspaper piece reminding people that Fredericksburg had been far less costly than the Peninsula Campaign, a point seconded by Zach Chandler. Republicans worried that McClellan's continuing influence had caused disaffection in the Army of the Potomac. The always blunt Thaddeus Stevens summed up the thinking of the Radical faction: "He [McClellan] must be broken down before he breaks us down."[30]

Fredericksburg had established a pattern, with each major battle or change in commanders leading to new calls for McClellan. He became a cat's paw for critics of the Lincoln administration, for Democratic partisans, and for disheartened northerners more generally. His name still evoked warm support and righteous anger, and it was often impossible to separate army politics from civilian politics.

If McClellan's stock appeared to be on the rise, Lincoln's seemed headed in the opposite direction. The president had eagerly read the dispatches coming in from Fredericksburg only to have his hopes dashed, as early promising reports gave way to word of yet another crushing defeat. Lincoln seemed utterly downcast and at one point remarked, "if there is a worse place than hell I am in it." A correspondent for the staunchly Republican *Chicago Tribune* considered the defeat worse than McClellan's retreat from the Peninsula. On the heels of this bad news, Lincoln faced a political firestorm in Washington as angry senators pressed for getting rid of Seward. Radical Republicans had for some time deplored the secretary of state's conservative, secretive, and allegedly malign influence on the administration. Growing yet more despondent, Lincoln remarked to his friend Browning, "we are now on the brink of destruction." Seemingly the political mastermind, he managed to keep the cabinet intact but found little comfort in that achievement. To journalist Noah Brooks, the president looked terrible: "his hair is grizzled, his gait more stooping, his countenance sallow, and there is a sunken deathly look about the large cavernous, eyes."[31]

Republican critics appeared almost ready to give up on Lincoln. In any case, he had to contend with signs of both demoralization and disaffection in the army, as several generals sought to undermine Burnside. The disastrous Mud March of late January 1863 cast more gloom over the country and the president. Burnside proposed sacking Hooker and three other generals, then brought Lincoln a note resigning his own commission. On Sunday morning, January 25, the president—without consulting the cabinet—appointed Joseph Hooker the new commander of the Army of the Potomac. Lincoln had acted decisively, but not without misgivings.[32]

The replacement of Burnside with Hooker only intensified the discussion and spawned fresh rumors. Whatever their opinion of Hooker, who had long schemed to take command, many soldiers' comments reflected respect if not longing for McClellan. A Pennsylvania captain noted how the troops sang "McClellan's our leader, he is gallant and strong." Bring him back and Richmond would be taken, declared a Vermont lieutenant, who added, "if the politicians would let us alone."[33] McClellan's removal had unleashed rivalries among the generals, and his return would presumably unify the army, restore discipline, and stop the recent wave of desertions. It was high time, a New York private advised, for the "chuckle heads" in Washington (including President Lincoln) to realize that "the recall of McClellan will be an indispensable necessity."[34]

"Indispensable" was exactly the right word, the general's most ardent friends avowed. No one else could effectively command the Army of the Potomac, much less get it to fight successfully, they claimed, sentiments often coupled with disgust for the Lincoln administration. Such judgments regularly cropped up in remarks made to camp visitors and in letters home. For sure, the men would fight under Hooker or any other commander, just not with as much élan or confidence. The army would remain loyal to Lincoln, a Massachusetts officer informed his mother, but its affection for McClellan might eventually make him president. Indeed, remove all the McClellan supporters and "croakers," a Michigan enlisted man warned his skeptical father, and "they will send the whole army home." Even troop reviews proved unenthusiastic affairs because the soldiers might respect Hooker, but they still loved Little Mac.[35]

Perhaps just as disturbing to many Republicans were reports that began circulating not long after Hooker assumed command of the Army of the Potomac. Rumor had it that Lincoln had considered bringing back McClellan, but the cabinet had been opposed. However that might be, the president had done nothing to purge the McClellan faction from the army, Senator Chandler, feared. Greeley's *Tribune* ridiculed the idea of turning again to McClellan, but the rival *New York Times* suggested that some command should be found for the general, albeit not one that required "dash and vigor." Enemies of Seward still tried to link his name with McClellan and other failed generals in the aftermath of the recent cabinet crisis. Continuing support for McClellan especially mystified the Radical faction, but Republicans had good reason to worry about the military situation in the eastern theater and the political fallout from continued stalemate.[36]

Radical Republicans took to the floor of Congress, denouncing McClellan and decrying reports of his possible reinstatement. In the House, George W. Julian of Indiana offered a detailed review of the general's failures and concluded that his "unflinching champions . . . would sooner see the Republic in ruin than the slaves set free." Such statements reflected fears that Lincoln might succumb to political pressure and appoint McClellan to some command, even in the Army of the Potomac. Yet would this not be a way, more conservative Republicans countered, to win the support of the so-called War Democrats for the administration? Orville Hickman Browning informed Lincoln that some officers swore they would never fight under Hooker because McClellan "possessed their confidence to a greater extent than any other man." The president responded that McClellan would not fight, though he conceded that the general was highly regarded by professional military men.[37]

To Republican critics, it became all that more imperative to damage McClellan's public reputation and paint his most vocal supporters as disloyal. This made McClellan's March 1863 appearance before the Joint Committee on the Conduct of the War of great importance. The general thought he was treated politely, though his enemies were using the hearings to mount a "last grand attack." Some observers described him as nervously evasive, and rumors about the content of the testimony by both the general and his critics appeared in the newspapers. A jubilant Chandler predicted that the committee's report would kill McClellan "deader than the prophets." Charges that the general had never intended to fight the Rebels, even sympathized with the Copperheads, followed on the heels of the committee report's publication in early April.[38] This document may have hurt McClellan's standing in the army and more broadly in the country but not nearly as much as Chandler, Wade, or the other Radicals had expected or hoped. Democrats readily dismissed the document as a partisan attempt to malign certain generals and protect others.[39]

Union forces had failed to crush the rebellion, Thad Stevens charged, because "Breckinridge Democrats" had commanded the armies. Indeed, McClellan from the outset of the war had attempted to undermine General Scott's authority. Charges of disloyalty against him still cropped up in congressional speeches. In response, conservative senator William A. Richardson of Illinois, who strongly opposed the Lincoln administration, claimed that Chandler had preferred thousands of men dying in front of Richmond to Little Mac capturing the Rebel capital.[40]

In the wake of their election victories and the continuing Union military failures in the East, Democrats moved to press their advantage and viewed McClellan as a valuable asset. A meeting at the Young Men's Union Democratic Headquarters in New York offered enthusiastic shouts for both McClellan and Porter. Even at a meeting to raise money for the poor in Ireland, someone gave three cheers for "President George B. McClellan." In mid-February, the New York legislature considered resolutions lauding McClellan and inviting him to visit Albany. When a Republican objected, Democrats praised the general for saving Washington three times, but the resolutions had to be watered down to a simple invitation, and even then they were tabled in the state senate amid reports of Republican divisions over the matter. One Democrat offered a resolution calling on the Lincoln administration to bring back McClellan as general in chief. At Rhinebeck, New York, McClellan met with Governor Seymour in a confab that would set off alarm bells by bringing together two men widely mentioned for the 1864 Democratic presidential nomination. McClellan praised the governor as a "conservative as well as an able man." In New York City, Democratic politicians kept McClellan's name before the public. On May 19, editor Manton Marble hosted a dinner for him attended by conservative politicians and journalists, including Sam Barlow, Samuel J. Tilden, and W. H. Hurlbert. The multicourse French feast no doubt served as a fine prelude for discussing national affairs in general and McClellan's future in particular.[41]

However much congressional committee reports or Democratic maneuvering might affect McClellan's future (and Lincoln's calculations), military developments mattered most. Hooker, both self-confident and aggressive, planned to cross the Rappahannock and force Lee to come out in the open and fight for his supply lines. Yet having successfully carried out the first part of this complicated plan in early May, Hooker faltered and handed the initiative to a most dangerous opponent. Lee boldly divided his army and attacked. Hooker's once promising campaign unraveled, with horrific casualties on both sides.

For Lincoln and the country, the defeat of Hooker at Chancellorsville loomed large. "Had a thunderbolt fallen upon the President he could not have been more overwhelmed," observed one friendly journalist. On May 6, upon seeing a dispatch reporting yet another crushing loss, Lincoln appeared shattered and cried out: "My God! my God! What will the country say! What will the country say!" Once again, criticism fell heavily on the administration and the president. "I wish Lincoln was out of the way," John Sherman stated bluntly. "He is subject to the deepest depression of spirits amounting to Monomania. He looked upon Hooker as his 'last card.'"[42]

Here was a new low in Union morale, and Little Mac's standing improved accordingly. Criticism of Hooker became strongly linked to calls for McClellan; the loss of faith in the former helped rekindle confidence in the latter. One editor tartly suggested that perhaps Hooker was going into "summer quarters," then claimed that the only way for Lincoln to restore public confidence was to bring back McClellan. "The universal cry" arose once again, "Give us McClellan," wrote Captain George Armstrong Custer, who assumed that the Lincoln administration would have to agree. "I think the whole nation would cry out for McClellan," one Massachusetts officer concluded. Toasting Little Mac remained commonplace, especially among the regulars. Claims that the Army of the Potomac was virtually unanimous in such sentiments were wildly overblown, but after Chancellorsville, just as after Fredericksburg, disheartened soldiers declared that McClellan would never have led them into such a disaster and, indeed, could still save the country and crush the rebellion.[43]

While calls for McClellan's return to the Army of the Potomac or even his appointment as general in chief echoed from the ranks, general officers certainly lent their support and in some cases their voices. John Gibbon explained to McClellan at some length how Hooker had bungled. He even recounted how one general at Chancellorsville had been mistaken for McClellan; supposing that Little Mac was with the army again, "every man sprung to his feet to look but dejectedly sat down again when they discovered their mistake." At various headquarters, other generals spoke openly about getting McClellan back. Should this occur, perhaps this time he would receive the necessary backing from the administration and from the people.[44]

So, the familiar cycle recurred. Reports about continued support in the army, along with added comments and speculation in the Democratic press, provoked the expected reaction. Indeed, the seriousness of the calls for McClellan's return appeared, ironically, in the very vehemence of Republican objections. "The government has not lost its memory, nor the people their senses," a *New York Times* editorial asserted, with perhaps more hope than conviction. To replace Hooker with McClellan, given his record of failure, would be the height of folly. To many Republicans, it seemed there were fiendish plots afoot. The general's supporters would attempt to dragoon Lincoln into giving in and returning McClellan to the army, and the Democrats (and the Confederates) could then hold out until the end of Lincoln's term and make their champion president. Perhaps the taint of Copperhead support would foil such a scheme, but Radicals fumed over the possibility that Seward might be among the conspirators. Whether the secretary of state was involved, once again the Blairs appeared in the thick of things. After presenting Lincoln with a detailed critique of Hooker's performance at Chancellorsville, Francis Preston Blair delicately raised the McClellan question. He blamed Stanton for having misled the president about army opposition to Little Mac, adding that the secretary of war had become a tool of the Radical faction and was no true friend of the administration. The clear implication was that McClellan should supplant Stanton or Halleck. One press report had McClellan leaving New York on a train bound for Washington.[45]

At the same time, there was speculation—Republican newspapers, mostly—that McClellan would resign his commission since he was no longer in active service. He denied this, but often contradictory rumors about his future kept appearing. And it was not only the defeat at Chancellorsville or the continued support for McClellan in the army that fueled the speculation. Once he had settled in New York with apparent financial assistance from local Democrats, the general inevitably became even more of a political lightning rod. Democrats (and some reporters), perhaps with encouragement from the Blair clan, courted him and sought to elicit his views on the war. Seward's longtime ally Thurlow Weed recommended that McClellan call for a vigorous prosecution of the war and disavow the Copperheads. At the same time, crowds in both New York and Philadelphia cheered the names of McClellan and Vallandigham simultaneously. The general remained wary of publicly addressing political issues and rebuffed overtures to run for governor in Ohio on the Democratic ticket. With Lee's Army of Northern Virginia heading north, word leaked out about McClellan meeting with Governor Seymour again. So, it appeared that regardless of his public reticence, the general had become increasingly entangled in politics.[46]

By mid-June, Lee's army was crossing the Potomac into Maryland. What the *New York Herald* termed the "Rebel Raid" only intensified discussion of the McClellan question. Restoring him to command became the surest way to stop the invasion, the general's advocates predictably argued. Soldiers would show a renewed fighting spirit, communities would offer generous enlistment bounties, and civilian morale would soar. Even Republicans, they claimed, and no few officials in Washington would rejoice to have the general leading his troops in the field once more. Of course, there was precedent: had not the administration called on McClellan to save the army (if not the country) during Lee's first foray into Maryland? Even some local officials, and especially the Democratic press, kept up a drumbeat for McClellan aimed at putting added pressure on Lincoln and his advisers.[47]

Petitions and letters reached the White House from a variety of sources, including some conservative Republicans. Pennsylvania senator Edgar Cowan reported general despondency and bitter opposition to abolitionists in his state, adding that the "better sort of Republicans" favored bringing McClellan back to the Army of the Potomac. After both the Fredericksburg and Chancellorsville debacles, surely the general's well-known prudence and caution appeared in a much more favorable light. One report reached McClellan that even Lincoln now conceded that Little Mac was "not selfish" and "whatever he did, was to the best of his ability and for the good of the country." Longtime Whig (and future Gettysburg orator) Edward Everett claimed that the general's return would be worth 50,000 additional troops; he added that the public still had great confidence in "our ablest commander" and that all Democrats, along with a good many Republicans, retained faith in him. Some correspondents suggested that McClellan raise troops in Pennsylvania to counter the invading Confederates. Recommendations ran the gamut: the general might recruit in his home state, he might again command the Army of the Potomac, or he might again become general in chief.[48]

At the end of June, as the two armies were about to clash at the crossroads town of Gettysburg, Pennsylvania, importunate pleas arose to at least send McClellan to the Keystone State. Even the moderate Republican and former governor of New York Edwin D. Morgan hoped the president could find some post for McClellan. On the eve of the fight at Gettysburg, Lincoln ally and influential journalist Alexander K. McClure downplayed McClellan as a political threat to the administration and agreed with many Democrats that the general was just the man to rally the troops as Confederates moved deeper into Pennsylvania.[49]

The president's reply to McClure was truly Lincolnian: "Do we gain anything by opening one leak to stop another?" In an equally terse response to a similar plea from New Jersey's Democratic governor, Joel Parker, Lincoln stated in no uncertain terms that only he understood the difficulties and complexities that had been involved in removing McClellan. The cabinet remained largely opposed to bringing the general back, but there was also division and intrigue. Did former secretary of war and notorious spoilsman Simon Cameron now favor McClellan's return, as several newspapers claimed? Were Rebel sympathizers plotting to use McClellan in some sort of coup? Lincoln himself must have felt besieged and perhaps a little bemused by all the conflicting advice that poured in from prominent Pennsylvanians.[50]

Many officers and no few enlisted men followed the crosscurrents of news with more than passing interest. Familiar arguments echoed in letters home and camp discussions: Richmond would have been liberated by this time had Lincoln not removed McClellan; the general's wide popularity and singular ability meant that he must again save the army and the nation. One Pennsylvania officer went right to the point: "Six months since McClellan was removed, six months of blunder, disaster, and defeat." Out west, Sherman reportedly stated that only McClellan could cope with Lee. Doubts about McClellan's loyalty to the Union cause were dismissed out of hand.[51]

Talk of McClellan's return, which had persisted ever since his removal and spiked after Fredericksburg and Chancellorsville, grew even more intense right before and even during the Battle of Gettysburg. Despite the complaints against Hooker from several generals, Lincoln had been reluctant to remove him. Yet he and the president had trouble agreeing on how to respond to Lee's movements, and Hooker clashed with Halleck over whether troops at Harpers Ferry should be sent to the Army of the Potomac. Here were echoes of the troubles with McClellan, and so Lincoln accepted Hooker's resignation.[52]

When Meade replaced Hooker, some speculated that this was but a temporary move before McClellan was called back. The Washington rumor mill again had McClellan replacing Halleck, but the more common report, especially among troops in the Army of the Potomac, was that he was about to become their commander again.[53]

And indeed he had—at least according to reports that began circulating on the last two days of June and continuing even as the Army of the Potomac and the Army of Northern Virginia headed for a confrontation in the Pennsylvania countryside. Passing through one small Pennsylvania town, a Vermont corporal "saw a little boy sitting on a fence holding a picture of McClellan up for us. Some of the boys tried to buy it but he didn't want to sell it." As Union forces moved toward Gettysburg, word came that McClellan was arriving with 60,000 men or that he was already back in charge; as this news spread through the marching columns, cheers erupted. Should Meade be whipped by Lee, claimed the secretary of the U.S. Sanitary Commission, Frederick Law Olmsted, Lincoln would have to swallow his pride and turn to McClellan. On July 3, a wounded soldier told a reporter that McClellan had arrived with 30,000 troops, so the war might end in a couple hours. As it was, Meade had managed to hang on to the high ground around Gettysburg for three days, and in the bloodiest battle of the war, the Army of the Potomac had held off repeated attacks from the Army of Northern Virginia. For the time being, the performance of Meade and his army put a quietus on the rumors and speculation. McClellan conceded that Gettysburg would enable the administration to "keep me in retirement."[54]

McClellan promptly congratulated Meade on the great victory; Meade in turn noted how reluctant he had been to accept the command and recognized that any expressions of appreciation would be fleeting. Some soldiers believed that Little Mac could have managed the battle better, but at the same time, Meade's success should presumably end talk that the Army of the Potomac could only win victories under McClellan. On July 4, Governor Seymour had been compelled to forego "a fierce attack upon the war management of the Government" as well as any "eulogy of McClellan," one War Department official exulted. "The glorious news from the army fills the Copperheads with dismay."[55]

Perhaps Gettysburg would stifle noisy Democrats who had taken advantage of military defeats to hail McClellan and keep the Lincoln administration on the defensive. Of course, a few people would continue to hope or even expect that McClellan would yet take the field or supplant Halleck. In New York, McClellan remained the toast of Democrats, but the New

York City draft riots and his consultations with Governor Seymour brought renewed charges of disloyalty. There had been rumors, Everett noted, that the general intended to raise an army, march on Washington, and "expel the present administration." He denied ever hearing about, much less countenancing, such a scheme, but the general's Democratic friends often hurt him nearly as much as his Radical Republican enemies. And so in July, the McClellans suddenly left their house in New York and moved back to New Jersey.[56] Lincoln might have welcomed this news, but neither he nor the general would find much of an escape from the partisan sniping or the politics of war that had long plagued their relationship and shaped the military conflict.

13

A DIFFERENT ARENA OF CONFLICT

THE UNION TRIUMPH at Gettysburg and the surrender of Vicksburg on July 4, 1863, eclipsed speculation about McClellan's military future and took pressure off Lincoln to find a new appointment for Little Mac. Once the Confederate garrison at Port Hudson, Louisiana, surrendered on July 9, the Federals at last had control of the Mississippi River.

Yet when the Army of the Potomac cautiously pursued the retreating Army of Northern Virginia, there was an obvious comparison to be made. Meade appeared satisfied with sending Lee back across the Potomac, and the Rebel army's escape both frustrated and angered Lincoln. Was not Meade acting just as McClellan had after Antietam? So why should Republican newspapers go easy on Meade when they had relentlessly criticized McClellan? Predictably enough, the *New York Herald* claimed that in both cases, the War Department had been responsible for the Rebel forces eluding capture. On the other hand, some critics dismissed Meade as both a Democrat and a McClellan man. As for Vicksburg, a Boston editor pointed out the importance of entrenchments during that campaign and noted how it had "taken two years to convince the country, what General McClellan learned long ago, that spades are trumps." Referring to Lincoln's letter to Grant admitting that he had been wrong about Vicksburg and Grant had been right, the *New York Herald* recommended the president draft a similar letter to McClellan admitting mistakes in withholding McDowell's corps from the Army of the Potomac and in removing McClellan from command after Antietam.[1]

Early in August, the McClellans arrived at Sag Harbor, Long Island, on their way to East Hampton for a family vacation. Friendly newspapers reported enthusiastic crowds welcoming the couple, including some local Republicans eager to shake hands with the general. While taking a dip in the ocean, McClellan was caught in a powerful undertow but was a good enough swimmer to escape.[2] As summer ended, however, he would find the political undertow to be stronger and almost as hazardous.

Once again, the Army of the Potomac came under suspicion as a hotbed of political intrigue. In the fall of 1863, Major General John Sedgwick launched a campaign to raise money for a McClellan testimonial. Although there had recently been similar subscriptions for other generals, including Meade, Secretary of the Treasury Chase as well as Secretary of War Stanton believed the purpose was to insult the president. In point of fact, neither man could abide the idea of any such effort on McClellan's behalf and likely saw it as an attempt to boost his presidential prospects. Lincoln left Stanton to handle the matter, and so a regulation forbidding anyone in the army from "conveying praise, or censure, or any mark of approbation toward their superiors or others in the military service" was invoked to quash the project.[3]

This episode, however, showed how the McClellan faction remained potent even as Republicans in the Army of the Potomac were starting to push back. Aside from Franklin and Fitz John Porter (neither any longer with the army), Meade and Sedgwick were considered strong McClellan men. Sedgwick's efforts had raised money from all ranks, with contributions ranging from ten cents from privates to twenty dollars from major generals. Although one New York private viewed the scheme as an attempt to "destroy the prestige of the government in the minds of the soldiers," and some detected a nefarious partisan plot by the general's Democratic coterie, others believed the chicanery was all on the other side. "Some damn fools got troubled and began to cry out Politics," a Massachusetts corporal complained. "*Great Big Men* said it [the testimonial] was in violation of the articles of *War*. . . . So you see the Black Hell Hounds have not left off scenting anything that smells of McClellan and he is the Ghost that troubles there slumbers." Amid great "indignation" in the army over the War Department order, artillerist Charles Wainwright nevertheless admitted "getting accustomed to the tyranny of the ruling party, and learning to obey the curb and whip without kicking over the traces." Rumor had it that Stanton had prepared orders sacking several generals and other officers who had been most active in soliciting contributions but had been talked out of doing so by a leading Republican. Some officers speculated that the Army of the Potomac might soon be "broken up" to get rid of the McClellan influence. Editorial comment from a variety of perspectives, despite sharp disagreements over who was responsible for the controversy, all pointed to its political nature and implications.[4]

When McClellan commanded the Army of the Potomac, a Massachusetts officer avowed, "few of us knew what his politics were except that he was making every exertion in his power to suppress the rebellion by force of arms." In his view, the army had little use for abolitionists or Copperheads, and he refused to believe that McClellan fell into the latter category. In Washington on September 9, the recently displaced Hooker (soon to be sent west) dined with John Hay and talked at great length about McClellan's shortcomings, especially missed opportunities on the Peninsula. Hooker sourly dismissed McClellan as a "baby" who had turned the Army of the Potomac "into a mass of languid inertness destitute of either dash or cohesion." This may have been an indirect swipe at Meade, but at this point, the Lincoln administration (and especially the ambitious Chase) surely viewed McClellan mostly as a potential political rival. In fact, that same day, Sam Barlow wrote to McClellan about a dinner with August Belmont in which they discussed the timing and location of the 1864 Democratic convention—and of course the good general as a possible presidential nominee.[5]

For Democrats, however, the most immediate concern was the fall 1863 elections. By the end of September, Barlow asked to consult with McClellan on a variety of matters. He was especially worried about Pennsylvania and the Democratic gubernatorial candidate, George Woodward, a jurist whom Republicans sought to tar with the Copperhead brush. Barlow pressed McClellan to appear in Philadelphia and lend at least tacit support to the Democratic ticket. When a rumor circulated that he might endorse instead the conservative Republican incumbent, Andrew Curtin, in the governor's race, the general had to deny it and then drafted an ill-advised letter (published in a Philadelphia newspaper on Election Day) stating he had recently enjoyed a "'full conversation" with Woodward. According to McClellan, Woodward favored "prosecution of the war with all the means at the command of the loyal states until the military power of the rebellion is destroyed." The two agreed that the war should be waged consistently "with the principles of humanity and civilization" and that "the *sole* great objects of this war are the restoration of the unity of the nation." Both the more radical *Chicago Tribune* and the more conservative Gideon Welles doubted that McClellan's supportive letter would do Woodward much good. It astounded the secretary of the navy that a man "so cautious and intelligent" as McClellan "should have been so indiscreet and unwise" but chalked up the blunder to the general's "injudicious partisan friends." In Welles's view, the letter had "effectually killed McClellan." Or in the words of diarist George Templeton Strong, "the McClellan pipe is nearly smoked out."[6]

A sarcastic editorial in the *New York Times* noted that for once in his life, McClellan had moved quickly. Yet his letter proved to be nothing but a vain attempt not only to rescue a floundering candidate but also to repudiate an administration and its policies under which he had long served. McClellan had come under considerable Democratic pressure to come out for Woodward—with an explicit warning from Manton Marble that failing to do so might alienate leading Democrats and scotch any future political prospects. Marble himself, however, later admitted that McClellan had faced a choice of "two evils." There was little chance that an earlier endorsement (much less one made on Election Day) could have pulled out the contest for the Democrats. In the end, Woodward lost, as did McClellan. His ham-handed intervention in the Pennsylvania election outraged Republicans and administration supporters, and distressed friends in the Army of the Potomac. According to one dismayed loyalist, McClellan "in the purity of his own mind . . . has met some of the greatest scoundrels in that [Democratic] party without knowing them to be such, and has doubtless been led on to this." Another volunteer who still admired McClellan's "military genius" detested his "politics and meddling." Questions about his loyalty resurfaced, and one New York cavalry officer hoped there would be "too much good sense" in the country to make McClellan president. Was he trying to take revenge on the Lincoln administration for suppressing the testimonial, a Republican editor asked. One editorial blasting the general for touring Copperhead "watering holes" and consorting with traitors carried the headline, "The Suicide of McClellan."[7]

Ohio Democratic congressman Samuel S. Cox admitted to Hay that McClellan might have "lost some prestige" with the Woodward letter but added that the general is "our best ticket." At the same time, Republican victories in the fall elections surely pleased Hay and his boss, though Senator Chandler warned Lincoln against the danger of allowing conservatives such as Weed, Seward, or the Blairs to steer him in a more moderate direction.[8] These men all remained favorably disposed to McClellan, yet in light of the Woodward letter, the election results, and all the talk of Little Mac as a presidential candidate, it was hardly likely that Lincoln would appoint him to any command.

McClellan himself probably recognized that his military service had reached a dead end, and he drafted a letter resigning his commission. He thanked Lincoln "for the confidence and kind feeling you once entertained for me, and which I am unconscious of having justly forfeited." As it was, he would have to be satisfied with the fact that no general could ever exceed his love for the Army of the Potomac. McClellan apparently expected to take a job as president of the New Jersey Railroad and Transportation Company, but that never happened, so the resignation letter was never sent. Indeed, his friends in the army as well as his political supporters continued to lament the Lincoln administration's failure to find a new place for a man of such ability.[9]

Even with Democrats putting his name forward as a presidential nominee, McClellan, in a letter to his mother, hardly sounded enthusiastic: "I feel very indifferent about the White House—for very many reasons I do not wish it—I shall do nothing to get it & trust that Providence will decide the matter." Yet his recent actions hardly suggested he was leaving it up to the Almighty. After all, and very much like Lincoln himself, McClellan was deeply ambitious and still longed to be the savior of the Union. The *New York Herald* sharply contrasted the politicians in power at Washington with "scientific and practical" men, such as McClellan, Banks, or Grant, who might be just the sort of presidential candidate who could redeem the country. The editor added that perhaps Grant would be protected from becoming another victim of the "radical Juggernaut." Meade again appeared to be a general of sound judgment right out of the McClellan mold when in early December he refused to attack Lee's strong positions at Mine Run in the Wilderness area of Virginia.[10]

McClellan's political allies and defenders consistently praised his military record, and the general himself drafted a voluminous report on his service with the Army of the Potomac. As word spread about the document's length, the *Chicago Tribune* contrasted it to Grant's much shorter accounts of more significant victories. At the same time, however, McClellan's editorial allies darkly suggested that the War Department had withheld the report until after the fall elections. Not surprisingly, however, his extended work of self-justification—finally printed early in 1864—changed few minds.[11]

Skeptics remained unconvinced and accused McClellan of omitting embarrassing documents. Who would ever read such a lengthy apologia in any case, the *New York Times* asked. This "unexampled self-display" was "all political" and only served to promote McClellan's "aspirations as a presidential candidate." He continued to see himself as a "peculiar victim" relentlessly persecuted by the Lincoln administration. Early on, James Russell Lowell charged, the general had become entangled in politics, had tried to set policy, and through a cautious defensive strategy had only succeeded in lengthening the war. And now, what amounted to a campaign document was being printed at government expense. What McClellan's report had done, the *Chicago Tribune* scoffed, was "build up an immense verbal structure, with cracks carefully puttied, to conceal his failure. It reminds one of the interminable lines of heavy shoveling that kept the Army of the Potomac too busy to trouble the enemy."[12] In late February 1864, newspaper correspondent William Swinton, who would later publish a valuable book on the Army of the Potomac, wrote the first of twelve substantial articles critiquing McClellan's report point by point. He began by rejecting excuses for delays and estimates of enemy numbers as "baseless." Many of McClellan's claims were inconsistent, misleading, or delusional. By early 1862, Swinton maintained, Lincoln had discerned McClellan's fatal flaws but remained too patient and deferential to the general. Not only had McClellan left Washington inadequately defended during the Peninsula Campaign, but he also had proceeded to heap complaints and recriminations on the government, persistently blaming others for his blunders. Like other McClellan critics, Swinton pointed to the general's preference for digging over fighting and his absences when any fighting did take place. Swinton even raised doubts about his loyalty. By October 1864, Swinton's articles—condensed and revised—became an anti-McClellan campaign pamphlet with the subtitle, *His Military Career Reviewed and Exposed.*[13]

Democrats acknowledged the political nature of McClellan's report, but they viewed it as a vindication of the general's record and made plans for its sale, distribution, and even public readings. McClellan had set the historical record straight and shown how, at least according to the patriarch of the Blair family, Lincoln had been misled into relieving him from command. To a Massachusetts officer, McClellan's report proved the general's "sagacity

& foresight, both political & military." A New York artillerist noted how the accompanying dispatches alone revealed "the obstinate conceit of the President in his own ideas of military matters, the petty spite of Halleck, or the rancorous hate of Stanton." Had Lincoln simply allowed Little Mac to proceed with his plan, another New York volunteer told his sister in early March, the rebellion might already have been snuffed out. Marsena Patrick hoped the report was changing minds and believed that "there is a strong feeling in his [McClellan's] favor, all through the Country."[14]

Although a Pennsylvania sergeant feared that McClellan had been treated so badly by the Lincoln administration that he had no political future, beginning in December 1863, several local meetings and state conventions (including newly formed "McClellan Clubs" in New York) trumpeted the general as a presidential candidate. A March gathering at Cooper Institute in New York featured a large portrait of the general with the slogan "McClellan and Liberty." A speech by that old Jacksonian Amos Kendall extolled his "conservative" principles, and a resolution was adopted lauding the general as "the deliverer and savior of our country."[15]

Perhaps, as the *New York Times* remarked, the Democrats had been so desperate for leadership, they had turned to McClellan too early in the war and had vainly tried to transform a failed general into a military hero. The *Chicago Tribune* reported that at the time McClellan was a West Point cadet, his father had literally had his head examined. According to this tale, a phrenologist had offered a reading that showed "an inordinate development of the organ of caution," with "combativeness and destructiveness small."[16] But beneath the ridicule lay worry about McClellan's potential as a presidential candidate, and as always, much would still depend on the military situation.

In early 1864, the stalemate in Virginia stood in striking contrast to the successful campaigns in the western theater, even as Grant was soon to become the new general in chief. In January, the usually friendly *New York Herald* had begun to change its tune about McClellan. While denying any loss of confidence in Little Mac's military ability, James Gordon Bennett nevertheless promoted Grant as a presidential candidate, in part because partisan divisions would only grow wider should McClellan become the Democracy's standard bearer. Indeed, the Radical plotting so long deplored by the *Herald* had fatally damaged McClellan's political prospects. But never a slave to consistency, Bennett later decided that because of their supposed disinterest in both politics and the presidency, either Grant or McClellan would be preferable to Lincoln.[17]

Whatever one's presidential preference, it was clear that Democrats and other opponents of the Lincoln administration would turn their guns on the commander in chief. McClellan's report, at least according to the *New York Herald,* revealed Lincoln's direct responsibility for various disasters. From overruling General Scott's advice and pushing General McDowell into the Bull Run debacle to the disappointing results of the Gettysburg Campaign, the president had proven incapable of managing the Union war effort. "Lincoln is a tolerable politician and a fluent joker," Bennett allowed. "Let the war be left to the generals, and we shall have peace by the Fourth of July." Lincoln's real mistake, Republicans countered, was showing too much patience with incompetent generals such as McClellan. After all, the Copperheads, despite having little heart for the Union cause, would naturally blame any military setback on the president. In defending Lincoln against a possible McClellan candidacy, Republicans harped on the general's Woodward letter to bind him hand and foot to the Peace Democrats.[18]

Defenses of McClellan in turn bled over into charges that Republicans sought partisan advantage in prolonging the war. The Radical faction had been especially bloodthirsty, consequences be damned, in pushing their abolition agenda. Consequently, McClellan had been shelved largely because of his skepticism about both emancipation and hard-war policies. In a series of newspaper articles for conservative New York newspapers, old-line Whig Hiram Ketchum revived the charge that Republicans had not wanted McClellan to capture Richmond, leading Lincoln and Stanton to make decisions that hamstrung the general. He added that the defeats at Fredericksburg and Chancellorsville had stemmed directly from the administration's foolhardy shelving of McClellan.[19]

The general himself would obviously have agreed, and during the spring of 1864, he presented his own ideas on strategy in two articles. These anonymously written pieces expressed deep reservations about the government's likely course. According to McClellan, the Lincoln administration had determined that military success in the spring and summer would improve Republican political prospects in the fall. Once again, the Army of the Potomac would move overland rather than along McClellan's favored James River route; the inevitable result would be "another fruitless attempt to reach Richmond." For him, the war's objective remained what it had always been: restoration of the Union. This in turn still dictated a conciliatory approach (since the fall of 1862, McClellan had remained mum on the emancipation question) to the enemy: "It must be in accordance with the enlightened maxims of the New Testament, not with the bloody and barbarous code of the nations of old time, who fought solely to destroy and enslave. We must in this, as in all other matters, serve our own merciful God, not Moloch and Baal." The best approach, then, was to defeat the main Confederate armies, sever lines of communication, occupy the most important points, and immediately offer amnesty to the erring brethren. One of the more perceptive critiques of McClellan's recent report, appearing in the newly established *Army and Navy Journal,* noted how, early in the war, McClellan had called for the concentration of forces for one great blow against the enemy. Yet this strategy required public patience and demanded a great deal of a government feeling its way forward, though the author might have noted that many of Lincoln's expectations were and remained just as unrealistic. At the same time, this not unsympathetic critic conceded that despite McClellan's lack of dash and at critical times lack of self-confidence, he had shown signs of growth, especially in his conduct of the Antietam Campaign.[20]

Now the standard of comparison would be McClellan to Grant. Even before the spring campaign season began, a friendly competition between the two reflected how they both remained front and center in any evaluation of generals—and not coincidentally of presidential prospects. On April 4, a Metropolitan Fair opened in New York to raise money for the Sanitary Commission. Tiffany & Company donated two swords to be given to the army officer and naval officer who received the most votes (in dollars) from the visitors. Each day, the New York press sought to drum up excitement and contributions by reporting the latest tallies. From the outset, the contest for the army sword became a two-man race between McClellan and Grant. Supporters of Little Mac gave their hero an early lead, and deep-pocketed citizens prepared to make large donations to push their favorite over the finish line. Day after day, McClellan held to a slender lead (aided by "Copperheads and secessionists" according to the *Chicago Tribune*), but a final push by Grant supporters gave him twice as many votes as McClellan in the final count.[21]

This served as a suitable prelude to the spring campaigning season, when General in Chief Grant, traveling with the Army of the Potomac and making all the key strategic decisions, would eclipse McClellan in public attention and acclaim. For some of the most crucial campaigns of the Civil War to be unfolding in Virginia and Georgia during a presidential election year further highlighted the inextricable links between military and political affairs. Lincoln had removed McClellan from command, but with Democrats talking up the general's political prospects, Republicans could hardly ignore him. "All who hate the union, and desire its destruction, are enthusiastic in his [McClellan's] favor," the *New York Times* declared, adding, with a nativist twist, that many of the general's loudest supporters were foreign born. An unholy alliance of "domestic traitors" and "alien enemies" revealed the disreputable basis of McClellan's appeal.[22] In the coming presidential campaign, Republicans would pound away at the question of "loyalty." After all, if many of McClellan's followers were Peace Democrats or worse, the general's own devotion to the Union remained doubtful. Did he not associate with the likes of Seymour and Vallandigham? Had he not shown tenderheartedness toward slaveholders and their property? Had he not wished all along to prolong the war until some shameful compromise with the Rebels could be arranged?[23] In March, one wildly implausible tale circulated about McClellan meeting with General Lee for several hours right after Antietam, a story that soon appeared in several versions but gained little credence.[24]

For soldiers and civilians alike, McClellan's military and political futures remained a subject for heated debate. At the end of 1863, a report came from Saint Louis that Grant not only denied any interest in the presidency but also wished that McClellan still commanded the Army of the Potomac. Calls for his return to command had diminished greatly after Gettysburg but had hardly disappeared. Adding a new twist, Bennett recommended that Lincoln find some place for both McClellan and Frémont, thereby inducing both generals to leave politics alone. In mid-April, the *New York Herald* claimed that Grant wanted McClellan for an important command but that the Lincoln administration would not hear of it, a story that was quickly denied. How much support McClellan retained in the Army of the Potomac generated a fair amount of discussion; some soldiers still maintained that his return would breathe new life into the army, but others were not so sure. Even a sympathetic Massachusetts officer predicted that in a presidential contest, Little Mac would receive no more than half the army vote and that Lincoln would garner the other half.[25]

Even as the military and political campaign seasons began, rumors of McClellan being recalled to some important post persisted. In late April, Montgomery Blair tried to bring that into being, sending a note to Sam Barlow advising that if "McClellan could have kept himself out of politics I am sure he would have been at the Head of his army." In reply, Barlow assured him that "every officer in the Army of the Potomac will admit that the reappointment of McClellan . . . would nearly double the effective force of the army." His response to the thrust of Blair's letter was disingenuous if not simply misleading: McClellan "is in no sense a politician" and was "disgusted" about his name being bandied about as a presidential candidate. Whether Blair believed this is uncertain, but in any case, he warned Barlow (and McClellan) against attempting to "supplant a president who is as associated with the Union as Davis is with the Rebellion, and throwing himself in with a party hostile to its administration." Responding to this advice in a letter to Barlow, McClellan denied conducting any military campaigns with an eye to political advantage or to defeating Lincoln. In his view, success in the war could only come with a "change of Administration & policy," though he hotly denied ever seeking to "conciliate the peace party." Nor, on the other hand, could he possibly "come out in favor of Mr. Lincoln & his policy." McClellan closed the letter on a note of indignant self-righteousness: "I will not sacrifice my friends my country & my reputation for a command." Nor would he even discuss the matter with Lincoln.[26]

That was just as well because the president would hardly have been receptive. To Barlow, Lincoln appeared "willing to hazard everything rather than incur the displeasure of the Radicals." Nor was there much appetite left in the administration for dealing with McClellan. Even the conservative Welles was appalled that Blair was parleying with Barlow ("a Copperhead leader"). "Poor George," Lincoln supposedly remarked about McClellan. "I did all I could for him, but he could do nothing for himself." Then, too, Lincoln's own ambition for a second term would dictate keeping the general at arm's length to avoid strengthening his political hand.[27]

After coming east and being appointed general in chief, Grant determined to fight the Confederates on an overland route, a strategy that Lincoln had long favored. On May 5–6, 1864, the Army of the Potomac and the Army of Northern Virginia faced off in the Battle of the Wilderness, and though Grant's forces suffered over 17,000 casualties, he refused to retreat. The Army of the Potomac then attempted to turn Lee's right flank, and the result was an extended slugfest around Spotsylvania Court House (May 9–21) that piled up another 18,000 Union casualties.

As Grant's Overland Campaign proceeded along its bloody path, McClellan eagerly scanned the latest reports from the fighting. When the first news came in from the Battle of the Wilderness, he feared another sanguinary stalemate but knew whom to blame: "It makes my heart sick when I think of the thousands of brave men who have been sacrificed by the blunders of our rulers." He sensed people steeling themselves for "disaster." Comparisons between Grant and McClellan enlivened editorial pages and campfire arguments. The *New York Times* noted how Little Mac had often telegraphed if not announced his plans, while Grant simply went about his work quietly and with "impenetrable reserve." Yet the horrible toll of combat in the Wilderness and around Spotsylvania Court House produced more sobering and at the same time politically charged comparisons. The *New York World* contrasted McClellan's losses during the Peninsula Campaign to the staggering figures for the Army of the Potomac under Meade and Grant. Of course, Grant had kept advancing while also inflicting heavy losses on Lee, and the rival *New York Times* praised both Grant and Lincoln for their perseverance and "magnificent successes" while wryly commenting that "McClellan fever has addled the brains" of leading Copperheads. McClellan had always exercised great "caution," and Grant now displayed welcome "vigor." Gone were the old excuses, including talk of the enemy's overwhelming numbers.[28]

But what had Grant accomplished? Although denying that he had ever been "daft" about him, Theodore Lyman, one of Meade's staff officers, believed that McClellan was "the greatest general this war has produced." Traveling with the Army of the Potomac over horrible roads and finding that Grant and Meade had conducted the current campaign "with admirable skill," Lyman nevertheless noted how the Army of Northern Virginia had only been weakened and remained a formidable foe. According to him, Grant had better troops under his command than McClellan had two years earlier and did not have to worry about the War Department withholding reinforcements. Suddenly it seemed that digging had become all the rage, with Grant entrenching as eagerly as McClellan. Indeed, for some soldiers, the current campaign proved that McClellan had been right all along. "They [McClellan's 1862 campaign and Grant's recent campaign] both had the same objective—Richmond," artillerist Charles Wainwright wrote at the beginning of a long diary passage. "Both ended in the same way, failure and the James River." Serving as Sherman's chief engineer, Orlando M. Poe considered "Grant's recent campaign as a complete vindication of McClellan's two years ago."[29]

Republicans grew sensitive to charges that Grant's offensive had piled up unprecedented casualties. With the tables now reversed, the usually importunate *New York Tribune* suddenly counseled patience. For McClellan's most loyal supporters, a series of bloody but futile engagements showed Grant's lack of generalship. "What would be the cry against our old commander, Little Mac, if he had lost so many men in such a short time," a Michigan sergeant grumbled. A Pennsylvania editor drew an equally sharp and partisan contrast: "Grant is to-day, after a loss of not less than 50,000 since the beginning of the campaign, where McClellan was, with comparatively no loss, when he began the first siege of Richmond." As the Army of the Potomac advanced toward Petersburg, a Massachusetts artilleryman laid out the case in especially forceful language: "I fail to see what damn great things Grant has done more than George B. done before and he was cursed and reviled by the very men that now pretend to say that Grant is working wonders." Grant's movements had been no more rapid than those of the oft-criticized McClellan, but if the government had properly supplied Little Mac with troops two years ago, the war would have long been over.[30] The argument had come full circle. Lincoln's removal of McClellan had been a great blunder, the administration had ignored pleas for his return to command, and the nation was now reaping the results of this folly.

McClellan offered no critique of Grant's generalship—at least publicly—but did travel to West Point on June 16 for an address at the laying of a cornerstone for a monument to those members of the regular army who had died in the war. The affair was a suitably solemn occasion but not lacking in political overtones. McClellan larded his remarks with references to ancient and biblical history. He described the regulars as "few in number, a small band of comrades, united by peculiar and very binding ties." War itself had become a "science" that required both strategic and theoretical knowledge: "To count upon success when the plans or executions of campaigns are intrusted to men who have no knowledge of war, is as idle as to expect the legal wisdom of a Story or Kent from a skillful physician." Aside from stating his longstanding preference for professional over volunteer soldiers, McClellan reiterated his views about the war as "just and righteous, so long as its purpose is to crush rebellion, and to save our nation from the infinite evils of dismemberment." Like many northern Democrats and some conservative Republicans, he denounced "extremists" in both sections and called on patriots to rise above partisanship.[31]

"A dull speech," declared George Templeton Strong, who "detected the symptoms of a latent Copperhead . . . under a pile of commonplace flowers of rhetoric." He deemed cadets serenading McClellan as "our next president" particularly offensive. According to Sam Barlow, however, the address might advance McClellan's standing particularly with the legal community; eventually, it would be published along with the general's Harrison's Landing letter as a campaign document. One friendly newspaper compared him to the Greek general and orator Pericles, though McClellan's boilerplate defense of the Union war effort as "just and righteous" apparently alarmed some already leery Peace Democrats.[32]

The divide between their War and Peace factions would hamper the Democrats even as they worked to challenge an increasingly vulnerable Republican president. In January 1864, New York financier August Belmont had convened a meeting of the Democratic National Committee that decided to delay the party convention until July 4 and hold it in Chicago. In February, Belmont pressed New York Democrats for an early endorsement of McClellan's candidacy, but the effort fizzled. All the same, talk of McClellan as a presidential prospect had begun almost as soon as the general gained national prominence and intensified after his removal from command. By early 1864, however, Democrats were worried about both selecting a candidate and somehow mending or at least papering over their differences on the war question. Mentioning McClellan and Seymour as possible nominees, editor Marble predicted that "any man who runs for the Presidency on an open Peace Platform . . . is doomed to an utter rout at the polls." On the other hand, leaders of the peace faction wondered whether McClellan would receive much support outside the officeholder class, much less inspire voters who had given up on the war. And all the while Republicans took undisguised delight in the disarray among their opponents despite facing divisions of their own.[33]

With Grant and Sherman stalled on the roads to Richmond and Atlanta respectively, Democratic leaders considered further postponing their convention until August—presumably to allow public disenchantment with the Lincoln administration to fester. McClellan discussed the matter with

Seymour but refused to commit himself and suspected that a later date might strengthen the New York governor's claim to the nomination. Barlow worried about Vallandigham gaining influence and hoped to have some plan in place before the convention. Shortly after his trip to West Point and once the Democrats had decided to reschedule their convention for late August, McClellan sounded his own note of uncertainty: "I probably don't know enough of the state of affairs to judge, but my instinct is against the movement, & I feel now perfectly free from any obligation to allow myself to be used as a candidate. It is very doubtful whether anything could now induce me to consent to have my name used."[34]

Even amid discussion of a presidential candidacy, talk of a new command for McClellan refused to die. After Grant became general in chief in March 1864, there was again newspaper speculation about a McClellan appointment. With a predictable swipe at Stanton, the *New York Herald* favored making him secretary of war. Former New York governor (and moderate Republican) Edwin D. Morgan suggested that McClellan be authorized to raise 50,000 troops to be stationed at Elmira, New York, as a reserve force.[35]

Yet at this point, it seemed more likely that McClellan would become the Democrats' presidential nominee. To head off this possibility, Francis Preston Blair and his son Montgomery hoped McClellan would disavow a White House run in exchange for a new military command—presumably the Washington defenses. Around July 20, the elder Blair visited several editors in New York looking to heal breaches in the Union Party coalition. Meeting with McClellan at the Astor House, Blair admitted that he had not come at Lincoln's behest or with any authority to make an "overture" from the administration. He had little doubt that McClellan would be nominated by the Democrats but was equally certain that the general would lose the election. Blair strongly recommended that McClellan forego any political ambitions, which would then open up the opportunity for a new military appointment. If no command were then offered, Lincoln would have to live with the consequences, and McClellan could then show his enemies that political calculations had never shaped his military conduct. Disclaiming any desire for the presidency, McClellan thanked him for the suggestions but did not say how he planned to proceed. Blair told Lincoln of this exchange and predicted that McClellan would soon be writing to him, but the president, while courteous to the old Jacksonian warhorse, "neither expressed approval nor disapprobation of what I [Blair] had done." Indeed, both McClellan and Lincoln seemed to approach the whole matter skeptically, so Blair's effort died aborning.[36]

With Grant's campaign grinding on and casualties mounting during the summer of 1864, the *New York Herald* and several other newspapers (reportedly with some Republican support) recommended that Grant summon McClellan to Washington. Some claimed his name alone would raise an army of 100,000 to operate in conjunction with the Army of the Potomac. When Lieutenant General Jubal Early's Rebel forces threatened the capital, speculation grew that McClellan would take over the defenses. Public confidence would supposedly soar, and gold prices would fall back to a more reasonable level. The Confederate advance on Washington, Stanton's special agent Charles Dana feared, would make McClellan president. A flurry of discussion occurred in the army, with both military and political considerations duly weighed. Rumors flew once more. Lincoln naturally heard from both sides and perhaps briefly considered finding a place for McClellan.[37]

Word of Blair's mission leaked to the press; here was another item for partisans to bat back and forth. Democrats cited the episode as an example of McClellan's patient and principled patriotism, while Republicans emphasized Lincoln's and Grant's lack of interest in pursuing such a chimerical project. McClellan himself claimed that he had never sought a presidential nomination, nor would he attempt to influence any party convention, but of course could not turn down a nomination "spontaneously conferred." This statement followed the classic pattern of the available candidate claiming not to seek the office. McClellan further denied that political considerations had ever shaped his relations with Lincoln. Admitting to serious differences with the president over policy, however, he believed that the administration's course "unnecessarily embitters the inimical feeling between the two sections" and hampered efforts to bring the war to an end.[38]

Whether policy differences merely signified or fed McClellan's political ambition is another question. Political friends in New York had long touted his potential as a presidential candidate, and though not as politically innocent as he claimed to be, McClellan had done little to encourage them.[39] He had sought military glory rather than public office yet did not rule himself out of the presidential sweepstakes. He continued to receive warnings about Stanton's machinations, including the hiring of detectives to gather dirt on McClellan and other potential nominees and perhaps even to arrest some of the general's political sponsors.[40]

With the convention delayed until late August, New Yorkers trumpeted McClellan's candidacy. On July 4, with Andrew Jackson's immortal words about preserving the Union emblazoned on a streamer, the Tammany Society honored various generals (of the Democratic persuasion), including McClellan. Public meetings called for McClellan to become the party standard bearer, and during the summer, both the crowds and the enthusiasm had grown. In early August, despite a heavy rain, voters in Hempstead on Long Island rallied for Little Mac, who briefly appeared in order to shake hands and offer what the *New York Herald* termed "anodyne remarks." In various wards of the city, "McClellan Associations" gathered to sing their hero's praises and denounce Lincoln's policies. A mass meeting in Union Square drew a crowd of 100,000 (as claimed by the Democrats, 30,000 according to Republicans), but however vehement the attacks on Republicans, the speakers said little about any policies or principles that McClellan might endorse. Republican papers derided the "small fry" speakers and ridiculed the Democrats for failing to define their positions for the coming campaign.[41]

McClellan commented in only the most general terms on Democratic plans and sounded ambivalent about the postponement of the party convention. His reticence remained striking, and how interested he was in the nomination appeared uncertain. In a note to Sam Barlow shortly before the large meeting in Union Square, McClellan reported that he would not be coming to New York before the Democratic convention met in Chicago, adding, "don't send to me any d—d politicians."[42]

Little wonder Republicans ridiculed the idea of McClellan in politics but at the same time warned that he was becoming a pawn for a Democratic cabal, which (to mix the metaphor) was determined to pull the proverbial wool over the electorate's eyes. Despite some ominous signs for the Lincoln administration, the *New York Tribune* questioned McClellan's potential as a presidential candidate. Although Chase's effort to challenge Lincoln for the nomination had fizzled early in the year, a convention of the "Radical Democracy" nominated Frémont, a strident critic of the president but the hapless choice of a hapless gathering of abolitionists, reformers, and German American politicians. Republicans viewed this whole affair as a futile effort to drain away votes from Lincoln and strengthen McClellan.[43]

Whatever help the Democrats and McClellan might receive from the quixotic Frémont movement, the party's peace faction was determined to exert pressure on, if not control, any presidential nomination. A letter from Saint Louis demanded assurances that McClellan was not part of the "radical war party." Members of the peace faction in Philadelphia floated the idea of turning to ex-presidents Millard Fillmore or Franklin Pierce as the party's nominee. An Ohioan urged McClellan to call for an armistice, leading the general to complain to his friend William C. Prime, "If these fools will ruin the country I won't help them." Then, too, one editor sympathetic to the peace faction deemed it "delusional" to think that nominating McClellan would take away soldier votes from Lincoln. Yet some soldiers were sick of the war and remained opposed to emancipation. Whether Republicans believed that such opinions were widespread, they worried about McClellan's residual influence in the Army of the Potomac and the willingness of officers to criticize their own government and meddle in politics.[44]

Both Republicans and Peace Democrats attributed support for McClellan to a coterie of New York wirepullers who hardly spoke for the party's rank and file, especially in the Old Northwest. Somewhere around half the delegates, Samuel S. Cox warned, could well oppose a McClellan candidacy. Of course, he might still receive the nomination, but Republicans predicted that Democratic leaders would kowtow to Copperheads and Rebels. A *New York Times* correspondent predicted that the Democrats would go with McClellan but adopt a peace platform—a tradeoff the peace faction stood ready to make.[45]

With the Army of the Potomac making little headway around Petersburg, any speculation about Grant's political future had abated; as some soldiers pointedly remarked, he was having as much trouble on the road to Richmond as his predecessors, including McClellan. There were some outright calls for peace, even signs of Copperhead sentiment. Indeed, the campaign's staggering butcher's bill made soldiers fondly recall their old commander. McClellan should not say anything derogatory about Grant, General Marcy and others advised, but rather throw any blame for the ill-advised line of advance in Virginia on Lincoln.[46]

At least according to the more hopeful observers, McClellan could beat the president—provided he steered clear of the Copperheads. Some advised pushing for a "war" platform or at least avoiding surrender to the peace faction. Then, too, a military candidate, one Wisconsin officer hoped, might ease partisan strife. McClellan's strongest backers held that Lincoln was losing ground in the army. Neither Marble nor Barlow would help advance McClellan's interest at the convention because they would not be attending. Barlow rightly worried about the strength of the peace faction, was wary of Seymour's intentions, but nevertheless expected McClellan to win many soldier votes and attract some Republican support. Barlow and others firmly believed that the Democrats' only chance lay with the general.[47]

When the Democrats convened in Chicago on August 29, party chair August Belmont opened the proceedings with a plea for harmony by reminding delegates of the disastrous breakup four years earlier. That same day, Alexander Long, an Ohio congressman and outspoken Copperhead, introduced a resolution calling on Lincoln to suspend the draft until after the election. On August 30, Seymour, as president of the convention, spoke at some length, largely blasting the Lincoln administration while calling for unity without addressing the question of where the party should stand in the coming campaign. Despite such pleas and a seeming willingness of all factions to make concessions, there was an immediate delay in presenting a party platform.[48]

By late afternoon, the committee on resolutions submitted their report. The vociferous peace faction, led by Vallandigham, gained what they most wanted: a resolution that described the war as "four years of failure" and called for a "cessation of hostilities" to be followed by a "convention of the states" so that "at the earliest practicable moment, peace may be restored on the basis of the Federal Union of the States." There were resolutions criticizing the government for interfering in elections and violating civil liberties, but this brief document said nothing about emancipation, finances, or foreign relations.[49]

With the peace faction having won the concessions they most desired, the convention proceeded to the nominations. A New Jersey delegate placed McClellan's name before the convention. Amid considerable hubbub, a Marylander denounced the general as a "tyrant" for his role in arresting secessionist members of the Maryland legislature in 1861. With points of order being raised, McClellan supporters in the galleries attempted to drown out the discussion. The Maryland delegate asserted that McClellan had been just as guilty as Lincoln of violating civil liberties and went on to disparage the general's military record. Other nominations were made and sometimes withdrawn, but sharp debate over McClellan's record on civil liberties ensued, with Copperhead thrusts and vigorous defenses.[50]

After considerable wrangling, the convention adjourned in the late afternoon, then the following morning proceeded to nominate McClellan, with only a scattering of votes for other candidates. Seymour tried to smooth over any hard feelings as the galleries erupted in wild cheering, women waved handkerchiefs, and some men stood on chairs swinging their hats. McClellan supporters from New York marched into the hall with a large portrait of Little Mac, "Our Country's Hope and Pride." After Vallandigham called for making the selection unanimous, another discordant note was struck. Belmont had hoped to see James Guthrie of Kentucky nominated for vice president, but even the New York delegation would not follow his lead. Instead, the delegates selected George H. Pendleton of Indiana, a Peace Democrat in the Vallandigham mold.[51]

Republicans pointed to the obvious tensions between the Democrats' calls for defense of the Union and a peace platform, including the dilemma this presented to the party's nominee. One wing of the party would tout the platform and the other the candidate. As for McClellan, Republicans charged, he lacked sufficient backbone to defy the Copperheads. One editor charged that people wishing to see the Union dissolved—among them New York politicians with money from "foreign capitalists"—were behind the McClellan movement. "The Chicago party," the *Boston Advertiser* declared, "has set the alternative before us—the war for the Union under Mr. Lincoln, or an armistice, a disgraceful peace and almost certain disunion under General McClellan." Editors warned that McClellan would be the "Copperhead President" and that Jefferson Davis would cheer the results of the Chicago convention.[52]

Should he secure the nomination, McClellan had told Barlow, "we win everything and are free as air." He disdained making any "bargains," but the platform would in fact saddle him with an inescapable burden. At first, Democrats struck a hopeful note. "Peace and Union," the *New York World* headlined. "The campaign to be short, sharp, and decisive." The general's closest New York friends and political allies sounded optimistic. In Orange, New Jersey, his neighbors greeted the nomination with sporadic gunfire, band music, and wild cheering. The general appeared briefly and simply said he would not make a speech.[53]

Nor should he have, for now the question became on what terms he would accept the nomination. "Do not listen to any of your Eastern friends who in an evil hour may advise to insinuate a little war into your letter of acceptance," Vallandigham warned. Other Democrats, however, feared that the platform had put a damper on the nomination. So, McClellan was quickly caught in the Democratic infighting that continued despite the supposed show of unity in Chicago.[54]

Even as Republicans at first aimed criticism more at the platform than the candidate, some Democrats deemed the war-failure plank disastrous. It had lost the ticket 50,000 votes in three days, the no longer sanguine Barlow feared. Calls for an armistice and a convention of the states, with seemingly no preconditions, would neither rally Democrats nor attract disaffected Republicans. A greatly alarmed New York banker warned McClellan of the platform becoming a "political scaffold."[55]

During the first week in September, each day's mail brought reams of advice for McClellan. He should simply decline the nomination, urged a New Hampshire correspondent, rather than risk "going down to posterity with a bad name." Perhaps he should just "ignore" the platform, as a New York Presbyterian editor suggested; after all, the peace plank was nothing but a "sop to the 'copperheads,' who secretly hate you with a perfect hatred." To this way of thinking, McClellan's true friends were moderate Republicans and War Democrats. Given widespread disillusionment with political parties, perhaps he should draft his own platform.[56]

Much of the proffered counsel centered on two closely related themes. First, McClellan should make it clear that he upheld the twin pillars of the Union and the Constitution. Here were echoes of Jackson. A broad defense of "Union" would lift McClellan above "narrow" partisanship, but the Chicago platform had not declared the Union to be inviolable. Indeed, both Barlow and Belmont urged McClellan to make it clear that surrendering any territory to the Rebels was unacceptable and that peace could only be established on the basis of the seceded states returning to the Union.[57]

Proclaiming seemingly indisputable general principles, however, said nothing about future policy and could not quite either paper over Democratic divisions or deal directly with the problems posed by the platform, so a second strand of advice looked to McClellan's previous statements. Several correspondents recommended the general simply run on his Harrison's Landing letter and his 1864 West Point speech. This would attract voters who could not stomach the Democrats' peace plank but who had no great love for Lincoln either. Such gains might more than offset any Copperhead defections.[58] The logic seemed clear cut even if the promised groundswell of support was likely to prove illusory.

According to Boston attorney and old-line Whig George T. Curtis, the very "incongruity" between the platform and the candidate made McClellan "master of the situation" who could lay down his own principles, then "the people will compel the politicians to *toe* the mark, and you will be elected." His old friend William Aspinwall agreed that if McClellan would simply speak his mind, he could "put to rest" claims that he had become "a tool in the hands of trading politicians." By declaring political independence, presenting himself as a true patriot, and avoiding narrow partisanship, McClellan would draw support from the many citizens—most notably the soldiers—who agreed that the war must continue until the Rebels laid down their arms.[59]

But where the platform declared the war a "failure" became the crux of the problem. To overcome this difficulty, a Boston cotton broker advised McClellan to make it clear that should reasonable peace efforts fail, the war should be prosecuted "until the Rebels beg for mercy." Peace could only come once the Union had been preserved. He should not only repudiate the platform, New Yorker William J. Danes recommended, but also "should appear before the country as a war candidate pure and simple."[60]

This was all easily enough advised, but there was little here that was pure and simple. Barlow agreed that McClellan could ill afford to make any concessions on the question of Union but thought he should avoid even using the word "war" when he drafted a letter accepting the nomination. The general took several days to work on this document, which went through six drafts, though the various revisions were largely matters of emphasis or minor editing, with few significant emendations.

After modestly stating that the nomination had come to him unsought, McClellan expressed deep reverence for the Union, the Constitution, and the flag; at the same time, he appealed to a spirit of compromise. He would welcome peace negotiations with the Rebels, though only on the basis of reunion. As for the war itself, "I could not look in the face of my gallant comrades of the Army and Navy, who have survived so many bloody battles, and tell them that their labors, and the sacrifices of so many of our slain and wounded brethren have been in vain." If all attempts at peace negotiations on the basis of reunion failed, he had little doubt that his patriotic fellow citizens "would without a murmur make the further sacrifices necessary to maintain their honor and secure permanent reunion of the States," though he removed this passage from the final version. Working on the letter, McClellan assured Nelly that it would plainly express his convictions. He had considered various suggestions, adding a reference to the Harrison's Landing letter along with some general criticisms of the Lincoln administration, but all was in "my style." In the end, his message was most succinct: "The Union is the one condition of peace. We ask no more."[61] The letter reflected views that McClellan had long held. The Chicago platform had neglected the soldiers' sacrifices altogether and had failed to uphold the indivisibility of the American Union. McClellan could hardly let those omissions stand, much less lend support to an immediate armistice or a convention of the states.

To his warmest supporters, the acceptance letter masterfully handled the Janus-faced nature of the Democratic coalition. It had presumably undone the mischief done in Chicago and offered hope for winning over anyone disenchanted with the Lincoln administration as well as conservative northerners more generally. The most optimistic assessments anticipated many Republican converts. The letter "will do much to retrieve the follies of Chicago and give a less questionable tone to many organs of the Democratic party," Amos Kendall hoped. In what was for him a rare effort at political analysis, McClellan informed Ohio congressman Samuel S. Cox (whose sympathies lay with the peace faction) that running on the platform adopted at the convention would mean losing Pennsylvania and New York.[62]

Cox had recommended simply accepting the platform as written, but he later praised McClellan's letter and wrote reassuringly that the "friends of peace" were on board. At the same time, however, newspapers reported that leading peace men might repudiate McClellan. Although the Democratic press largely fell into line, Democratic leaders worried that Pendleton would prove a drag on the ticket, and the vice-presidential candidate's reticence during the campaign made him an easy target. A war-weary Pennsylvanian who deemed conscription unconstitutional claimed that McClellan's letter "has fallen like a wet blanket" upon the leading peace men. An even more plainspoken Ohioan told him that the peace faction had been in control of the Chicago convention and "you were nominated because they could not help it." McClellan dared not declare that the war's sacrifices and suffering had been in vain, but the *New York Freeman's Journal and Catholic Register* asked how he could tell the widows and orphans that the fighting must continue to uphold the "Lincoln despotism."[63]

Reports persisted of a possible "bolt" by the peace faction in New York or in the western states. Some Copperhead organs continued to criticize

McClellan for his arrest of the Maryland legislators, and there were even calls for another convention to nominate a different candidate. Vallandigham publicly challenged several key points in McClellan's acceptance letter, though Barlow wrote reassuringly that there was "nothing to fear from the peace men." Some Republicans offered faint praise for McClellan's letter because it had apparently thrown a bombshell into the Democratic camp. "The Copperheads seem to be in a great snarl," Republican Elihu Washburne exulted. "Little Mac don't seem to go down very well with the real rebels, but they will have to swallow him." Or, as one Pennsylvanian speculated, not vote at all.[64]

Yet the general's greatest opportunity (and peril) came with more moderate voters. That McClellan had never been a politician and occupied "a middle ground of reason and law" became important selling points in a late September campaign speech by George Curtis. Likewise, a Catholic editor praised the candidate for being neither a partisan nor a peace fanatic. But the breadth of the general's centrist appeal remained questionable. McClellan might be "a gentleman, a Christian, and a man of superior ability," the prominent Presbyterian theologian Charles Hodge admitted, yet he could not vote for Little Mac on the Democratic ticket—"a first-rate Captain in a very bad ship, and with a horribly bad crew." That prototypical moderate Edward Everett personally admired McClellan but feared that a "change of Administration would paralyze military operations" and ultimately bring about the "dissolution of the Union." The former Whig soon agreed to serve as a Republican elector. As a Boston textile manufacturer informed McClellan, the Everett defection might not make all that much difference, but it did show "how strongly the Republican tide is running."[65]

For Republicans, the Democratic platform remained a political godsend. A few wondered how anyone could think that McClellan's letter could be squared with the party's platform. But the more common line of attack emphasized how that letter had not really scuttled the party's peace plank. For one thing, the general had been evasive. George Templeton Strong dismissed his letter as "platitudes floating in mucilage, without a single plain word against treason and rebellion." Conceding that the document was "artfully drawn," Strong feared that it "may do its work," especially if followed by untimely battlefield setbacks. "An ingenious wriggle and twist," Charles Sumner conceded, but one that would hardly help the candidate. "A dishonest document, intended to obtain votes on false pretenses," claimed the *New York Times*. "It was an attempt to ride two horses; to carry water on both shoulders."[66]

In reality, Republicans asserted, McClellan was stuck fast to the odious Democratic platform. He had neither condemned the rebellion nor called for crushing it by military force; the general remained what he had always been—far too tenderhearted toward traitors. Quoting Copperhead papers coming around to McClellan's support further drove home the point. The general might stand uncompromisingly for the Union, but did that mean he would return slaves to their masters, compensate Rebels for their lost property, or even pay off the Confederate war debt? Based on false reports in Democratic newspapers, Republicans claimed that in early July, McClellan had preapproved the peace plank in his party's platform.[67]

However much he might try, McClellan could not escape the decisions Democrats had made in Chicago. The normally humorless Sumner jested that McClellan might have to heed the railroad conductor's cry, "It is dangerous to stand on the platform." The Massachusetts senator added: "Siamese twins are united together, so that the two cannot be separated. As well cut apart Chang and Eng as cut apart McClellan and Chicago."[68] Republicans were determined never to let him escape the platform's clutches.

Because the timid McClellan had refused to abandon the Democratic platform outright, he must surely embrace its principles. Whatever skills the general displayed as a horseman, *Harper's Weekly* sneered, he could hardly "ride two horses going different ways." In October, a cartoonist offered a similar take by picturing Little Mac attempting to sit upon two stools, one labeled "letter of acceptance" and the other "Chicago platform." McClellan had been as slow in releasing his acceptance letter as he had been in advancing against Richmond, and this belated attempt to "dupe" one group of voters or another would surely fail, Greeley's *Tribune* predicted.[69]

The 1864 election was hardly a normal presidential contest. That it would be held at all amid a terrible civil war was itself extraordinary, though postponement had never received much consideration. McClellan hardly displayed burning political ambition, but Lincoln greatly wanted to be reelected; neither candidate could easily assess his own prospects. The summer's massive bloodletting, the shifting tides of opinion, the uncertain military situation, and varying predictions about the soldier vote made the usual handicapping of parties and candidates much more difficult. Political confidence appeared to be in short supply.

14

THE FINAL BATTLE

On August 23, 1864, Lincoln offered a bleak assessment of the political situation. He had drafted a document for his cabinet to sign without reading. This "blind memorandum" marked another low point in his presidency: "This morning, as for some days past, it seems exceedingly probable that this Administration will not be re-elected. Then it will be my duty to so co-operate with the President elect, as to save the Union between the election and the inauguration; as he will have secured his election on such ground that he can not possibly save it afterwards."[1] Lincoln's pain was palpable in both his wizened face and in his dark thoughts. The military stalemate and political sniping from many directions threatened to thwart his desire for reelection, along with his drive to save the American Union during its greatest political crisis and carve out his own place in history. The ambition that his old law partner William Herndon had noticed back in Illinois still burned brightly, but since the beginning of the war, if not before, it had become tied to the Union's future.

The summer had brought grim news from the battlefields, and as Lincoln weighed the prospects, his preternatural melancholy had reappeared. In July, the Radical Republican faction, fed up with the president's cautious approach to reconstruction, had gone on the offensive with the Wade-Davis bill, which imposed more stringent requirements on the seceding states. With Congress adjourning, Lincoln had refused to sign it (thus using a pocket veto), and he even issued an unnecessary and testy message that defended his own policy. He pointed out problems in the congressional measure, but then said that any state could choose to follow that blueprint. Ben Wade and Henry Winter Davis angrily responded with a scorching "manifesto" blasting Lincoln for issuing his own "political manifesto against the friends of the Government." They not only critiqued his reconstruction plans but also questioned whether the president was acting in good faith on emancipation. Further excoriating Lincoln for unbridled political ambition and "dictatorial usurpation," the two ardent Radicals concluded on an ominous note: "let them [the supporters of the government] consider the remedy of these usurpations, and having found it, fearlessly execute it."[2]

For much of the summer, Lincoln had heard reports of Republican discontent. In a late July conversation with important German American general and politician Carl Schurz, an unusually voluble Lincoln lashed out at those calling for him to withdraw from the campaign in favor of a "better man"—as if such a person could necessarily unite the factious Republicans and broader Union coalition. The president bristled at charges of having been "seduced" by a lust for power. In early August, with both sadness and irritation, he remarked to a White House visitor: "You think I don't know I am going to be beat, but I do and unless some great change takes place badly beaten." He especially resented people blaming him for Grant's failure to capture Richmond when he had "promised them no such thing." Lincoln still claimed to be carrying on the war for the "sole purpose of restoring the Union" but could hardly abandon the use of Black soldiers or retreat on emancipation. Shortly before the Democrats met in Chicago, he told the journalist Noah Brooks: "They must nominate a Peace Democrat on a war platform, or a War Democrat on a peace platform; and I personally can't say that I care much which they do."[3]

But of course, Lincoln did care, cared terribly, however frustrated and despondent he might appear and however much he might try to disavow personal ambition. He could not help paying attention to those who disparaged the administration and discounted his chances for reelection. Shortly after the National Union Convention had met in Baltimore in early June and renominated the president, even many Radicals might have conceded that most Republicans preferred Lincoln.[4] The Frémont candidacy was going nowhere, though Henry Winter Davis held out hope that somehow the general might be persuaded to withdraw and Lincoln be forced to step aside; exactly how that political trick was to be pulled off, he could not say. Amid mounting signs of Republican anxiety, the president recognized that much still depended on military developments. Had the election been held in June, he told one visitor, he would have won easily, but by mid-August, "I hardly feel certain of what state I should carry." Surely all the talk of the war as a failure would demoralize both the soldiers and the people at home. By mid-August, Ohio congressman James Ashley, one of the most inveterate Lincoln critics, was advancing a scheme for a new convention to nominate Major General Benjamin F. Butler, supposedly to attract the votes of War Democrats. According to one report, all the "leading men" in New York already considered Lincoln beaten. Horace Greeley agreed and favored finding another candidate with or without another convention. Days before the Democrats met in Chicago, both Thurlow Weed and Republican National Committee chairman Henry J. Raymond sounded panicky and worried about insistent calls for peace negotiations.[5]

Republicans could hardly change candidates at this late date, the antislavery railroad magnate and philanthropist John Murray Forbes pointed out. But Forbes nevertheless feared that if the Democrats did not blunder in Chicago, reelecting Lincoln appeared doubtful. For those Republicans willing to try another candidate, the timing never seemed quite right. Perhaps holding the party convention back in June had been a mistake, but to call another one might simply compound the error. Wade thought it best to wait and see what the Democrats did, but Winter Davis saw precious time being lost. Fed up with the "diseased restlessness" that had infected "growling Republicans," John Hay dreaded a replay of the discord that had destroyed the Whigs.[6]

Maybe the Republicans should have postponed their convention until fall, with hopes for success on the battlefield in the meantime, but complaints about everything from the influence of "shoddy" contractors and corrupt officeholders to the staggering human and financial costs of the war and general cries for "change" hardly offered a way forward. Conservative Republicans deplored the influence of Radicals, who for their part, at times felt equally powerless to influence the president or the campaign. Talk of Lincoln's possible withdrawal in favor of another candidate (some suggested Grant or even the old conservative general John A. Dix) persisted even as the Democrats were meeting in Chicago. Perhaps the McClellan nomination might help unite the Republicans. The mercurial Greeley assured John Nicolay: "I will fight like a savage in this campaign. I hate McClellan."[7]

However much some Republicans might distrust Lincoln and Seward, as one Delaware politician observed, "They fear McClellan more." And so, Greeley evidently backed off from seeking another candidate, but one of

Lincoln's old Illinois friends visiting New York heard that Sumner, Wade, Winter Davis, Chase, Frémont, and Henry Wilson were planning some sort of meeting in Buffalo, New York. A group of New Yorkers proposed summoning a national convention to meet in Cincinnati at the end of September, in part because of fear that McClellan might prove wildly popular even as Lincoln's standing with the public fell. Support from Boston and New York reformers and a few Radical Republicans failed to advance that plan very far, in part because it depended on getting Frémont to withdraw his candidacy. By September 1, Sumner had decided that whatever Lincoln's weakness as a candidate, it was time to "unite in opposition to the common enemy." Attempts to enlist northern governors in a dump-Lincoln effort received only lukewarm support, and it quickly died.[8]

Neither party sounded confident, and given the unprecedented circumstances of the election, even the wiliest professionals must often have been scratching their heads and wondering what might occur to upset their political calculations. Some Republicans saw McClellan as a formidable opponent who could unite the Democrats' warring factions and win over conservative Republicans. However belatedly or reluctantly, some staunch Radicals were working to assure Lincoln's reelection. Zach Chandler claimed to "prefer the traitor Jeff Davis to the equal traitor" McClellan. "The one has brains, the other has none," the Michigander sneered. "But give me a smart villain before a fool one."[9]

In the end, the McClellan nomination, combined with the Democrats' war-failure plank, seemed to light a way forward for Republicans. Gideon Welles deplored the sway of timid men such as Raymond or the unpredictable Greeley, but he believed the Democratic convention had been an "almost traitorous proceeding," thus making the contest a choice between continuing the war with Lincoln or accepting a humiliating peace with Jefferson Davis brokered by McClellan. By way of contract, Radical editor Theodore Tilton considered the Republican platform "the best in American history," so the party could live with a "second-rate candidate." Although he believed that any number of other Republicans would have been a better choice than the current president, Sumner assured an English friend that the Chicago convention had guaranteed Lincoln's reelection. Ohio senator John Sherman would have preferred Chase as the party nominee and offered only lukewarm praise for Lincoln, who was at least "better than so timid & unworthy a man as McClellan."[10]

No doubt buoyed by the capture of Atlanta in early September and other promising war news, Lincoln began to sound more hopeful. Speaking with a Wisconsin judge, the president reportedly denied being driven by "personal vanity or ambition" and maintained that a Democratic triumph "must result in the permanent destruction of the Union." He dismissed any talk of McClellan and strategy from a party that would shun the services of the 200,000 Black men who were vital to bringing the war to a successful conclusion. Had the Democrats nominated McClellan on a platform calling for a "vigorous prosecution of the war," Lincoln later remarked, his own prospects for reelection might have become very doubtful. Instead, the Democracy had put forward the notorious peace plank, and he believed that, considering the sacrifices already made, the voters would not deem the war a failure. When McClellan briefly delayed accepting the nomination, Lincoln, with a twinkle in his eye, said, "He must be intrenching." That remark was clever, and it reflected the president's belief that McClellan could never act decisively or quickly. But by the summer and fall of 1864, it was rather off the mark, as use of the spade had become commonplace in both Grant's and Sherman's armies.[11]

Lincoln would disparage McClellan's generalship (and his political judgment as well), while the Democrats had chosen to nominate a military candidate whom many Americans admired. If much still depended on what happened on the battlefield, the soldiers' response to the parties, and especially to the McClellan nomination, seemed vitally important.

Reporting from the Chicago convention, the journalist Brooks claimed that many of the delegates had not been all that enthusiastic about McClellan but had nominated him to attract soldier votes. "If the Army of the Potomac goes against you, we are defeated," Senator Wilson warned Lincoln, and he recommended pushing various generals, including Grant, "to come out for you." Letters from the army reported continued affection for Little Mac. "The President is not popular," a Pennsylvania officer declared. "Nothing can save him, but the idea that his election is necessary to prevent the South dictating their own terms." Yet there was the rub. With the outcome of the war still uncertain, events on the battlefield could well tip the balance regardless of voters' reservations about the candidates.[12]

Nor was it clear that soldiers would neatly fall on one side or the other, especially given their dim views of parties and politicians. Some were trying to decide whether to cast a ballot at all. A New York volunteer asserted that there was "little or no Political sentiment manifested in the Army," even as many of his comrades reacted to McClellan's nomination and began weighing their choices. The lesser of evils became the default position for those who found little to praise in either candidate. Though he thought both Lincoln and McClellan to be "sound, and almost identical in their personal views," artillerist Charles Wainwright dismissed the two parties as "equally corrupt, and equally far from my views in their extreme doctrines."[13]

Wainwright had long admired McClellan but did not want the general "to have anything to do with politics." For other soldiers, it was not political involvement itself but McClellan's involvement with the Copperhead-tainted Democratic Party that was the problem. Soldiers who still lauded the general's ability and character worried that, as many put it, he had fallen in with "bad company." For this very reason, a Michigan infantryman expressed both "pity and contempt" for a man who would "allow ambition to ruin him." As this soldier noted sadly, "There is no more magic in his name." Admiration for McClellan's military service would not necessarily translate into votes.[14]

A sizable corps of staunch supporters, however, rejoiced over news of McClellan's nomination, at least initially. According to a Massachusetts private, the mere sight of McClellan would inspire the men, who had never lost confidence in their old commander. From his most enthusiastic backers came predictions for a great harvest of army votes. This reflected much wishful thinking, though perhaps not entirely so, given the political volatility of the past several months. Denying that Copperheads would welcome the Democrats' choice, a Vermont volunteer avowed that McClellan favored "a vigorous prosecution of the war . . . to the bitter end." Recalling the general's concern for their welfare, some soldiers even thought a McClellan victory would bring better food, lower sutler prices, and more regular visits from the paymaster.[15]

Indecision and ambivalence persisted, however, as officers and men in the ranks began to weigh their options, sometimes in surprising or contradictory ways. A Michigan hospital steward doubted that McClellan was gaining support in the army, did not in any case think he would capitulate to either the Copperheads or Jefferson Davis, but still hoped to see him "gloriously beaten." Unable to make up his mind about the election, another Michigander declared himself "for the man that makes peace the

Soonest." He was willing to fight a "while longer," hoped McClellan could obtain a "compromise on honorable terms," and thought that with Lincoln, "there is compromise only to free the nigers." McClellan would not necessarily stop the fighting right away but would not prolong the bloodshed for the sake of emancipation, claimed men who had soured on Lincoln.[16]

For most soldiers, to declare the war a failure was intolerable, and that very plank in the Democratic platform did more damage to McClellan's standing in the army than anything else. "Dissatisfaction with the platform is almost universal," commented one officer from the Army of the Potomac's Second Corps headquarters. Enthusiasm for Little Mac had reportedly evaporated once soldiers learned about the Democrats' official stance on the war. Word that the arch-Copperhead Vallandigham had moved in the convention to make the nomination unanimous further alarmed some soldiers, including lifelong Democrats.[17]

McClellan's letter accepting the nomination failed to stir either much interest or much support in the army. That he had accepted the nomination from a Copperhead-tainted party was enough to alienate a goodly number of citizen-soldiers. McClellan had written an adequate letter that "don't whine about peace" and "talks war," wrote a major in Sherman's army. Yet at the same time, the general had become a "man of straw," supported by the worst elements in the Democratic Party, and hardly deserved a loyal man's vote. Accepting the nomination while seeming to repudiate the key plank in the platform appeared weak and unlikely to win much support. Even a sympathetic soldier in the Second Corps decided that both the platform and the letter would hurt McClellan's chances, while "political matters are more mixed up than ever." On the most basic level, disgusted men in the ranks declared themselves done with McClellan and even accused him of betraying his comrades. Memories of those fallen in battle meant never voting for a candidate nominated by a party ready to give up on suppressing the rebellion.[18]

As the summer of 1864 neared its end, however, war weariness was palpable, and some McClellan supporters in the ranks made the simple point that reelecting Lincoln would mean another four years of war. Other soldiers, equally tired of war, favored only such a peace as would come when the last Rebel had given up the fight. And if McClellan would agree to a settlement in which the Confederates kept their slaves, might the contest eventually have to be resumed all over again? Better to stick with Lincoln than allow the Democrats to make humiliating concessions to Jefferson Davis. According to Brigadier General Lysander Cutler, formerly commander of the renowned Iron Brigade, the men in uniform would never "vote for the cowardly policy of any temporary expedients which shall shift the trouble from us to another generation."[19]

Word spread that McClellan had little chance of winning the soldier vote, or the election for that matter—about as likely as being struck by lightning, a Maine volunteer thought. Even staunch Democrats were reportedly defecting, and a Connecticut captain was willing to bet a hundred dollars that Little Mac would lose. There might be a few McClellan supporters in his regiment, an Illinois sergeant allowed, but "they are weak-kneed cowards who want him elected merely to stop the fighting so they may not have to endanger their worthless necks anymore."[20]

The tide appeared to be running in Lincoln's favor, at least in some parts of the army. "The McClellan men here are not so boisterous as they were a few weeks since," a New York engineer stationed along the James River remarked in mid-September. Employing imagery that surely resonated back in Pennsylvania, a cavalryman declared that Lincoln had "driven the team so that he ought to drive it through. If McClellan undertakes to drive, the team will run away and break the wagon." A conservative New York private who despised abolitionists but could not support the Democratic candidate conceded, "I don't like Lincoln at all, but I have to go with him or none, as he is the most available."[21] Political turmoil, military uncertainty, and sometimes muddled political thinking set the stage for a heated if generally unenlightening fall canvass.

By early September, both parties were campaigning in earnest. Democratic "ratification meetings" either attracted excited crowds or failed to arouse much enthusiasm, depending on which partisan press accounts one chose to credit. All that was needed was some "gunpowder, music and rum" to bring out a crowd in New York, one observer decided. Speakers such as August Belmont lauded McClellan's service to the nation (including saving Washington) and largely ignored the party platform. Veteran Massachusetts Whig Robert C. Winthrop declared McClellan's Harrison's Landing letter and West Point speech the "true platforms of the hour."[22]

Democrats projected confidence even as they tried to steer away from issues of peace and loyalty by excoriating the Lincoln administration's record. The war's human and economic cost had grown beyond anyone's anticipation; a bungling military policy threatened the country with financial ruin. Vast public debt piled up as the war dragged on. In a mid-September campaign speech, an Albany, New York, judge warned that another term for Lincoln simply spelled "draft after draft," more taxes, "starvation prices and finally bankruptcy and dissolution." Other campaigners appealed for constitutional liberty or railed against official corruption. As for Lincoln, Democratic editors dismissed the president as a weak "buffoon," or worse.[23]

The peace faction in the Democratic Party had not been entirely mollified by the platform and remained leery of McClellan. When state elections in October went Republican, it seemed that Democrats had gained little from nominating a general ostensibly to secure the soldier vote. A convention in Cincinnati that sought to organize a party resting upon states' rights, Jeffersonian principles, and peace blasted the Chicago convention, sharply criticized McClellan's record, but adjourned without selecting a presidential candidate. As for Vallandigham, the most notorious Copperhead of all, his support for the Democratic ticket hardly helped McClellan.[24]

Although the *New York Herald* recommended McClellan issue another letter to clarify his political views, this was not going to happen. A return of his old "Mexican complaint" laid him low for a time, though he appeared to believe the campaign was going reasonably well. He tired of writing letters to old army associates but seemed pleased to receive encouraging notes from "privates & ex-soldiers." McClellan said little publicly and, for the most part, remained out of sight in Orange, New Jersey. When asked to meet with some one hundred leading New York Democrats, he asked his friend William C. Prime to "invent *some* way of getting me out of the scrape." He sounded like a man who simply wanted to be left alone, and the newspapers were hard pressed to find much worth reporting.[25]

A mid-October address in Connecticut by Robert C. Winthrop perhaps embodied the kind of campaign speech that McClellan would have delivered. Claiming that good citizens might well differ on the issues of the day, Winthrop sought to defuse partisan rhetoric and urged his audience to rise above "arrogant assumptions of superior patriotism and loyalty." He lauded McClellan, "whose quiet endurance of injustice and calumny has been one of the most beautiful illustrations of his character, and has won for him a respect which will outlive the ephemeral notoriety of his revilers." Winthrop welcomed battlefield victories in Georgia and the Shenandoah Valley, and he duly noted how the military situation had greatly improved since the Democratic convention. Claims that this had dimmed McClellan's electoral prospects he dismissed as unworthy of consideration. Winthrop slyly referred to unverified reports that Lincoln had recently offered McClellan a new command in exchange for his declining to be a candidate for president.[26] Refusing to attack Lincoln personally, Winthrop noted that the president had received "harder blows" from Wade and Winter Davis than from Democrats. Unfortunately, Lincoln had abandoned the Whig precedent of a single-term presidency in the interests of patronage and power that could only delay a restoration of the old Union. The Republicans had "so fattened on this rebellion" with "contracts and spoils" that "they are in danger of forgetting that their country is bleeding and dying on their hands."[27]

Like McClellan, Winthrop declared "Union" to be the singular war aim. In contrast, the Republicans would seek "the total abandonment of slavery," which in turn would mean "wading through seas of blood in order to reorganize the whole social structure of the South." Arguing that the Constitution forbade the pursuit of emancipation once the Rebels laid down their arms, Winthrop shied away from dealing with the future of slavery while maintaining the impracticality of abolition. As one conservative editor pointed out, McClellan and his supporters doubted the "expediency" of the Emancipation Proclamation and feared that pressing for liberating slaves in areas still under Confederate control would only complicate the restoration of the Union.[28]

As he had throughout the war, McClellan shied away from dealing with slavery and race, even though northern opinion had shifted significantly over the past four years. As historian Mark Neely has observed, very few letters written to McClellan during the campaign season had much to say about the subject.[29] The Episcopal bishop of Rhode Island urged him to declare that he would return no person freed by the war to slavery and that he supported gradual emancipation carried out by the states. From a conservative Vermont Republican came the suggestion that McClellan endorse the use of Black soldiers while steering clear of compromises with proslavery interests or with abolitionists. For their part, Democratic leaders were coming to see any defense of slavery as a losing proposition. Although ostensibly opposed to the Lincoln administration's policies on emancipation, they realized that an antislavery constitutional amendment would likely make it through Congress—attracting some Democratic votes.[30]

The politics of slavery had proven hazardous for the nation as well as the politicians, and a growing acceptance of wartime emancipation hardly spelled the end of complications. In a speech at Auburn, New York, on September 3, Seward pointed out how, once the guns had fallen silent, the "war measures . . . which affect slavery, will cease also." In that event, "questions affecting slavery . . . will by force of the Constitution, pass over to the arbitrament of courts of law, and to the councils of legislation." Appealing for unity and less partisanship, Seward criticized both Radical Republicans and Democrats who reacted diffidently to Union victories because of dissatisfaction with the government's current policies. Was Seward saying, as moderates such as Edwin Morgan and Henry J. Raymond had suggested during the summer, that the administration should compromise on the slavery question to achieve peace? Ironically, despite the political uncertainty it appeared to embody, Seward's speech was largely a celebration of Sherman's capturing of Atlanta and Admiral David Farragut's success at Mobile Bay, victories that changed the calculus of the fall election campaigns.[31]

Seward's remarks might have garnered more attention and worried Republicans, but the dramatic news from Atlanta, the Gulf, and later from Major General Philip Sheridan in the Shenandoah Valley made it easier to tamp down party infighting. Between September 19 and October 19, victories at Winchester, Fisher's Hill, and most dramatically at Cedar Creek capped off more than a month of Union triumphs. Even soldiers with decidedly conservative leanings noted how news from the battlefields had quieted Little Mac's supporters. McClellan himself remained mum on these Union victories even when delivering brief remarks after a torchlight procession in Trenton, New Jersey. His silence in turn only provided fresh ammunition for Republican newspaper editors like Greeley.[32]

For Republicans, the success of Sherman, Farragut, and Sheridan offered a perfect contrast to McClellan's military record. Little Mac would receive a "*final* blow . . . through exposure of his generalship," Winter Davis had earlier exulted to Chandler, whose position on the Joint Committee on the Conduct of the War offered access to much presumably damaging information. Toward the end of the fall campaign, fellow committee member Wade delivered a lengthy address at Cincinnati excoriating his generalship. Even as the Democrats were preparing to nominate McClellan, the Union Congressional Committee had already prepared a pamphlet entitled

McClellan's Military Career Reviewed and Exposed, which did just what its title promised in thirty-two densely packed pages. Not to be outdone, William Lloyd Garrison's *Liberator* listed no fewer than twenty-two of Little Mac's blunders. According to the *New York Times,* both American and European military thinkers had written off McClellan as a failure. The man "falls far below mediocrity," especially given Sherman's accomplishments, vice-presidential nominee Andrew Johnson told a Louisville audience.[33]

Republicans eagerly dredged up McClellan's slowness and reluctance to attack. "Like a genuine Christian gentleman," Adam Gurowski scoffed, "McClellan avoided fighting." Soldiers who served under Grant, Rosecrans, or Sherman, journalist William Swinton asserted, "are not the men to fall in love with McClellan's feeble and fruitless style of warfare." Pointing to Sheridan's victories in the Shenandoah Valley, the *Chicago Tribune* noted how McClellan had been "absent" during the heaviest fighting on the Virginia Peninsula. There the timid Little Mac had been consistently fooled and outfought, and the whole campaign had ended in a humiliating retreat, along with heavy losses from combat and disease.[34] As an especially pointed feature of these wide-ranging critiques, McClellan was portrayed in both words and images as the "Gunboat candidate," sitting on a saddle astride the bowsprit of the *Galena* while his troops were fighting gallantly at Malvern Hill.[35]

Democrats stood ready to defend McClellan the general. After all, their champion had been right about the war from the beginning, but all too often, his advice had been rejected by Lincoln and others. Just as Swinton back in the spring had slammed McClellan's report on military operations, so now the general's advocates quoted from official documents to make their case. Given the summer's heavy losses, it was hardly surprising that the *New York World* and others offered full-throated defenses of McClellan's preference for entrenchments and, more broadly, his penchant for "strategy." To explain the outcome of the Peninsula Campaign, one need look no further than Lincoln and the cabinet, especially Secretary of War Stanton. The president had tried foolishly to direct military campaigns and had failed miserably.[36]

For Democrats, debating past campaigns might be preferable because rapidly brightening Union prospects further highlighted problems with the war-failure plank. Republicans charged that good news such as the fall of Atlanta dismayed Copperheads. Had not the Chicago convention been merely a gathering of the disloyal, ready to forge a humiliating peace with the Rebels? Of course, it was scandalous that General McClellan should associate with such men; for good measure, the *New York Times* threw in references to Judas Iscariot and Benedict Arnold. According to a Hoosier lieutenant, "every copperhead, peace snake, and outspoken rebel of the North will sustain and vote for the democratic candidate for the presidency." Should McClellan lose, the Copperheads were threatening violence, at least according to vague reports in Republican newspapers.[37]

Should McClellan be elected, the peace faction would be in control and thereafter push for the promised armistice and convention of the states. Highlighting speeches from the notorious Fernando Wood, Republican editors stated plainly that a McClellan administration would be a Copperhead administration. Shortly before the election, General Wool even accused McClellan of representing the subversive Knights of the Golden Circle and Sons of Liberty.[38]

That the Rebels preferred McClellan became a Republican certitude. Was not McClellan adviser Sam Barlow a confidant of Confederates John Slidell and Judah Benjamin? Did not the southern press (along with British Tory and French monarchist sheets) trumpet the Democratic candidates? According to a *New York Times* correspondent, the Rebel general Sterling Price was urging Missourians to vote for Little Mac. On the front lines, northern soldiers heard Confederates cheering for both Jefferson Davis and McClellan. Likewise, Confederate prisoners favored McClellan because Democrats winning the election offered the best opportunity for dissolving the Union once and for all.[39]

In the more perfervid campaign rhetoric, the syllogism was straightforward: northern traitors support McClellan, southern traitors support McClellan, therefore, McClellan himself must be a traitor. In a stump speech right before the election, Andrew Johnson declared that there were "but two parties in the country traitors and patriots. Traitors with Jeff. Davis at their head and McClellan as their candidate, seek to destroy the Government." A letter to the *Chicago Tribune* claimed that McClellan had been ready to surrender his army to General Lee at Malvern Hill; Lincoln received supposedly fresh information, too, about the old tale of McClellan secretly meeting with Lee on the Antietam battlefield. Wild charges about Confederate connections to McClellan circulated privately and publicly.[40]

Seeing pamphlets that labeled McClellan a traitor, Attorney General

Bates—he would leave the cabinet after the election—worried that such baseless accusations might end up "discrediting the best-founded objections against him, and exciting a popular sympathy for him, as a persecuted man." Democratic leaders could only hope that was the case, but Barlow had heard that Lincoln held a damaging letter from McClellan advising the president to assume "dictatorial powers" and even arrest members of Congress. Reports that the general had early on recommended a draft would not sit well with libertarian Democrats.[41]

No matter who won the election, the *New York Herald* maintained, the war would continue along its current course, but such a calm assessment sounded out of place amid a heated campaign in which questions of loyalty took center stage. Dire predictions about the possible consequences of a McClellan victory became a stock part of Republican appeals. Should he win the presidency, the most traitorous elements of the Democratic Party would control the new administration; surely, Confederate independence would follow. An armistice, a phony peace, and national ruin seemed entirely predictable. The great republic would die, arch-Radical Thaddeus Stevens warned, and "on its ruins will spring up numerous petty empires, whose future condition will be one of perpetual wars and of grinding slavery."[42]

Only "traitors, thieves and cut throats," are for McClellan, a Connecticut soldier declared as the state elections in October were being held. The citizen-soldier was a thinking voter who could see that McClellan had been "bewitched by politicians." Worse still, electing him president threatened to undo all that had been accomplished in over three years of fighting. The future of republican government itself was at stake, and as an engineering officer put it, "the welfare of millions yet unborn is dependent upon us."[43]

By mid-October, speculation about how the men in uniform would cast their ballots filled many a newspaper column. The October state elections, which went Republican with the aid of soldier votes, seemed to show that McClellan's appeal to the rank and file had waned. Although the Army of the Potomac might retain pockets of support for their old commander, the *New York Times* reported, the western troops had never felt such affection, and the Chicago platform along with McClellan's Copperhead associates had alienated a goodly number of the eastern troops. According to an Illinois sergeant, the "Grave Digger of the Chickahominy is playing out every day." Only the new recruits appeared to prefer McClellan, claimed a New York battery captain.[44]

The Democratic press marshaled its own evidence showing continued soldier devotion to McClellan. To counter stories about Confederate soldiers cheering for Democrats, there appeared stories of Rebel pickets telling their Union counterparts about being ready to kick out Jefferson Davis and come back into the Union once McClellan became president. Reportedly, the general could still count on significant support in the Army of the Potomac, especially in the Second, Fifth, and Sixth Corps. With his customary histrionics, McClellan wrote that he would "doubly savor success and be quite reconciled to defeat if I felt that my old comrades still clung to the commander whom they never failed in battle."[45]

Shortly after the Chicago convention, Manton Marble had urged him to "keep up a diligent *friendly* correspondence with all your old friends in the army," hoping to counter the damage done by the party platform. Perhaps McClellan could convince some prominent generals to endorse his candidacy, though there is no evidence that he attempted to do so. In mid-September, however, Edwin Morgan advised Stanton of plans afoot "to get the principal officers in the Army committed to McClellan with expectation of getting the soldier vote."[46]

If that was true, such efforts failed. Halleck agreed with Sherman in steering clear of politics but nevertheless believed that McClellan would "lose the respect of all honest, high-minded patriots" by associating with "traitors and copperheads." Hooker, too, repudiated the Chicago platform, and despite contradictory reports, he along with Burnside favored Lincoln. Although Meade decided not to vote, he considered McClellan's chances poor, having been "very unfortunate in his friends and associates." Sherman could recognize both Little Mac's strengths and weaknesses, but there was no foundation to newspaper reports that he supported the Democratic ticket.[47] Less well-known generals and regimental officers expressed similar sentiments. The platform, along with the Copperhead connections, were enough to get even lifelong Democrats voting for Lincoln, however much they might still admire McClellan personally and professionally. Some high-ranking officers still favored Little Mac, a few with great reluctance, and others simply because they could not stomach reelecting Lincoln.[48]

Despite the war, the usual campaign hoopla proceeded. In Boston and New York, the "McClellan Legion" brought together officers, mostly veterans from the Army of the Potomac, to march and shout for their hero. Street rallies, including torchlight processions with flags and banners flying, were "enthusiastic beyond precedent," Horatio Seymour assured McClellan. "A great political revolution is going on." Much of this was in the eyes of partisan beholders, especially the tendency to dismiss the opponents' meetings for lacking both numbers and fervor, with New York always an important battleground. Discharged soldiers, whether War Democrats or Republicans, worked with the Union League or various campaign clubs, and in cities, the formation of paramilitary groups sparked a few armed confrontations.[49]

Republicans flooded the armies with campaign literature and tried to prevent the circulation of Democratic newspapers. Stanton's War Department worked hard for Lincoln's reelection, dismissing employees accused of "McClellanism" and charging army officers who had endorsed the Democratic ticket with disloyalty. For his part, Lincoln told a group of Pennsylvania election commissioners to "leave the soldiers entirely free to vote as they think best" and then sent the men off to the see the secretary of war. Viewing Indiana as a vitally important election, the president urged Sherman to send as many Hoosiers home to vote as could be done safely.[50]

An order issued by Stanton on the first day of October allowed governors or the political parties to appoint one agent for each army corps to take charge of distributing tickets to the soldiers. Civilian inspectors from each party would be present on Election Day. This order forbade "political speeches, harangues, or canvassing among the troops" and enjoined commanding officers to see that voting was conducted with "due regard to good order and military discipline."[51]

Stanton's order left details up in the air, and a patchwork of state laws added to the confusion. New York election commissioners appointed by Seymour were accused of "fraudulently signing and forging names of officers and soldiers." For his part, the New York governor hoped McClellan might persuade Grant and Sherman to issue orders preventing "undue influence or menace" to would-be voters. Stanton said that convalescent men could be sent home from hospitals to cast their ballots; also, he urged Major General George H. Thomas to provide "passes and safeguards" for election agents and commissioners to visit headquarters between Nashville and Atlanta.[52]

Those men trying to supervise the army voting ran into a host of difficulties, everything from soldier indifference, to countless questions from the illiterate and ignorant, repetitive paperwork, and defects in state election laws. Complaints of highly partisan officers and fraudulent voting rounded out the list of problems. Yet despite frustration and grousing, in many camps, the election passed off quietly and without incident.[53]

Republicans highlighted any signs of Democratic opposition to soldier voting. One widely circulated pamphlet simply asked why Democrats feared the men in uniform casting ballots? The answer was that such votes would not run in McClellan's favor. Seymour and other Democratic leaders had supposedly conspired to prevent soldier voting but then had dispatched agents who substituted McClellan ballots for Lincoln ones and committed other frauds.[54]

Democrats in turn accused everyone from Stanton down to company officers of suppressing McClellan voters. Soldiers who favored Lincoln were more likely to receive furloughs to vote, and a few outspoken Democrats were court-martialed. A Michigan private serving in Virginia wrote to McClellan about enlisted men being offered promotions if they voted for Lincoln; those voting for the Democrat might face a reduction in rank. In some places, Democrats found it hard to receive ballots, faced physical threats, or might be conned into not voting. At one camp in front of Petersburg, soldiers burned McClellan tickets and drove away two Democratic agents.[55]

Whether any of these irregularities had much effect on the soldier vote is hard to determine. By the last week in October, newspapers began publishing regimental election returns that ran strongly in Lincoln's favor. At the same time, the soldiers themselves were sending home news of the balloting. In some regiments and companies, the margins seemed suspiciously lopsided and in a few others surprisingly close. To a New York lieutenant, it appeared that "Old Abe is good for another four years . . . without any armistice or convention of the states or any such thing." In sending the vote totals for his regiment to a Philadelphia newspaper, a Pennsylvania volunteer derided McClellan for having "fallen among thieves" and become a "traitor." A New Yorker who was no fan of abolitionists nevertheless defined the choice as being "Lincoln and the universal rights of man" or McClellan and "another compromise with the Devil."[56]

The army vote revealed persistent pockets of Democratic strength, occasionally reported with embarrassment by Lincoln supporters appalled that Little Mac should poll anything resembling a respectable total.[57] Despite leaning toward McClellan, some discouraged soldiers did not vote at all. Others went for Little Mac on the assumption that reelecting Lincoln simply meant continuing the war.[58]

Regardless of difficulties in estimating how the soldiers voted because of varying state laws and incomplete returns, Lincoln carried around 80 percent of the regiments and over half of those with more than 75 percent of the vote. Even the Army of the Potomac failed to rally for McClellan.[59] The soldiers undoubtedly voted for the "Union," but as historian Jonathan W. White has observed, this did not necessarily translate into support for Republican policies such as emancipation. Given the Democratic platform and its Copperhead taint, many soldiers cast negative votes that did not reflect much enthusiasm for Lincoln, a calculation that influenced civilian voters as well.[60] The soldier vote did not prove decisive in and of itself, but newspaper reports of sentiment in the ranks along with the thousands of soldier letters sent home during the campaign undoubtedly helped swell the Lincoln vote.

Whatever the difficulties in both measuring and interpreting the soldier vote, Lincoln won reelection with over 55 percent of the popular vote and an Electoral College landslide of 212 to 21. To the president, the support of the soldiers must have been quite gratifying. In brief remarks to a New York regiment less than two weeks before the election, Lincoln had praised the troops for upholding both him and the Union cause: "To you who render the hardest work in its support should be given the greatest credit. Others who are connected with it, and who occupy higher positions, their duties can be dispensed with, but we cannot get along without your aid. While others differ with the Administration, and, perhaps, honestly, the soldiers generally have sustained it; they have not only fought right, but, so far as could be judged from their actions, they have voted right, and I for one thank you for it."[61] Earlier, the president had been encouraged when favorable results in New England elections coincided with Union victories on the battlefield. In mid-September, Lincoln had handicapped the electoral vote as 172 to 66 in his favor, but by October 13, state-by-state estimates had narrowed his advantage to a mere 6 votes.[62]

Political prognostication by either party appeared difficult. Lincoln himself had tried to tamp down rumors that should the reelection bid be lost, he would seek to "ruin the government" or that a victorious McClellan would attempt to seize the reins of power before Inauguration Day. "Whoever may be constitutionally elected . . . in November," Lincoln assured some Washington serenaders, "shall be duly installed as President on the fourth of March."[63]

Even on Election Day, November 8, the president had nervously awaited the returns and seemed to think the outcome might be in doubt. In remarks to John Hay, Lincoln suggested that his own disposition hardly fit the politics of the times: "It is a little singular that I who am not a vindictive man, should have always been before the people for election in canvasses marked for their bitterness." He scrutinized every bit of information that came in, later requesting detailed election returns and repeatedly pressing laggard state officials for the numbers.[64]

On November 11, the president finally revealed the contents of the "blind memorandum" to the cabinet. Lincoln explained how, in the event of a Democratic victory, he had planned to meet with McClellan so they could jointly "raise more troops" and "save the country." Seward commented sharply that McClellan would likely have appeared receptive to such a proposition but then would have done nothing. The day before, Lincoln had defined the stakes in the election more philosophically:

> It has long been a grave question whether any government, not too strong for the liberties of its people, can be strong enough to maintain its own existence, in great emergencies. On this point the present rebellion brought our republic to a severe test; and a presidential election occurring in regular course during the rebellion added not a little to the strain. . . . But the election was a necessity. We can not have free government without elections; and if the rebellion could force us to forego, or postpone a national election, it might fairly claim to have already conquered and ruined us.

Lincoln rejoiced in what had been gained by refusing to postpone the voting: "But the election, along with its incidental, and undesirable strife, has done good too. It has demonstrated that a people's government can sustain a national election, in the midst of a great civil war."[65]

Here was Lincoln the statesman assessing what was in fact an extraordinary achievement—conducting a presidential election during a bloody civil war. In his December 6 annual message to Congress, Lincoln again emphasized "the calmness and good order" of the canvass and observed what the most ardent Republicans would have been loath to admit: that candidates of various stripes had all sustained the Union cause whatever their differences on the "means" of doing so. In the end, it had not really been a contest between loyalty and treason, all the campaign rhetoric to the contrary notwithstanding. Ego and pride had also been involved. In a conversation with journalist Noah Brooks the day after the election, Lincoln had conceded this point. "Being only mortal after all," he allowed, "I should have been a little mortified if I had been beaten in this canvass before the people."[66] This was true enough, though the adjective "little" was certainly misleading.

All along, Lincoln's ambition for reelection and vindication had been a driving force. In some ways, it was hardly surprising that an incumbent president would eagerly seek reelection, but no president since Jackson had been elected to a second term. Lincoln had long been a member of the Whig Party, a party that rose in response to what its members considered Jackson's executive tyranny and overweening ambition. For most Whigs, a single-term presidency appeared ideal.[67] During the emergency of civil war, Lincoln had wielded powers that violated Whig beliefs in limited executive authority and ran contrary to the views of his Lyceum Address of many years before. Yet he early on acknowledged that suppressing the rebellion required extraordinary measures. His political success had become closely linked to the preservation of the Union, which in turn would guarantee his place in history. The summer of 1864 had been a dark one, and critics across the political spectrum (including many in the Republican Party) had been relentless, but what Herndon later termed Lincoln's "little engine that knew no rest" had kept churning.

For McClellan, as he approached his thirty-eighth birthday, there was little left to do but resign from the army and think about the future. Even during the campaign, Republicans had sniped at him for retaining his commission and collecting his pay when, since the fall of 1862, he had been performing no military duties. On Election Day, McClellan did resign his commission, and Lincoln accepted it two days later without comment, even though a few of the general's diehard supporters had held out hope that after the election, the president might finally offer Little Mac another command.[68]

McClellan's political confidants extended words of consolation for what must been a painful loss for all involved. At least McClellan would avoid the "fearful responsibility" of taking the reins of power as the rebellion continued and the country faced a host of other problems, Sam Barlow wrote. Nor would he have to deal with all the patronage headaches that would have followed his election, Manton Marble observed, though the editor gloomily thought the voters had not been ready to face the reality of "calamities" to come. "I was fully prepared for the loss and not in the slightest degree overcome by it," McClellan assured Barlow. This may have been partly true, but his political allies had certainly offered promising assessments up to the very eve of the election. In a dramatic turn of phrase typical of the man, he then added that as a result of "cool judgment," he had "abandoned public life forever." He was already thinking about a family trip to Europe. To his mother, McClellan spoke of the election reflecting the "will of God" and claimed to be glad that the presidency's "dreadful responsibility" had not fallen on his shoulders. Still believing that his political principles would eventually be vindicated, he had not lost faith in the republic. There was more than a touch of the old vainglory when he told Marble that "some yet unborn Homer or Milton" might yet celebrate "a struggle of honor patriotism & truth against deceit selfishness & fanaticism."[69]

In the election postmortems, Democratic leaders who had managed both the timing of the convention and the nominations took their lumps. Party chairman Belmont and others wanted McClellan to remain at least the titular leader of the party until the next presidential election, so the general's proposed trip to Europe appeared to them an abdication of responsibility. Talk of him as a possible senator from New Jersey only produced more ridicule from one Republican, who snidely remarked that McClellan in Congress would likely be just as dilatory as McClellan in the field. A *New York Tribune* correspondent celebrated "the political death of McClellan." Republicans continued to hammer away at his character and described Democratic voters in most unflattering ways. Chase even proposed a thorough investigation of McClellan's entire military service, with the implication that his loyalty remained an open question.[70]

The general seemed eager to escape further political entanglements. In early January 1865, as the McClellans prepared to leave for Europe, diarist Mary Lydig Daly thought the women in the family still felt the sting of the election but that "the General himself looked as serene, amiable, thoughtful and self-contained as though he [had] never been out of his library all these four eventful years." McClellan reportedly declined friends' offer of a private vessel and instead, on January 25, departed for Liverpool on the Cunard steamer *China.*[71]

The American press episodically tracked the family's European itinerary. McClellan was pleased with his reception on the continent. "All treat me as a gentleman & seem disposed to exaggerate very much the importance of my part in the war, & to give me a much higher position than I merit," he informed Barlow from Rome. "Here we are the equals of the best—at home there is always the wretched feeling of partisan[ship] to be encountered." He planned to "remain abroad until the expiration of Uncle Abraham's term of service."[72]

While in Rome, McClellan met with Pope Pius IX (a "pleasant old gentleman") but, finding little to admire in the trappings and ceremonies of Roman Catholicism, declared himself thankful to be "born & bred in a Protestant country." On April 14, the Good Friday of Lincoln's assassination, McClellan enjoyed a full day of sightseeing; on Easter Sunday, he attended High Mass conducted by the Pope at Saint Peter's. In the tragedy at Ford's Theater, McClellan noted the same irony that hit home with so many others Americans: "How strange it is that the military death of the rebellion should have been followed with such tragic quickness by the atrocious murder of Mr. Lincoln!" Thinking back on their relationship, McClellan remarked, "Now I cannot but forget all that had been unpleasant between us & remember only the brighter parts of our intercourse."[73] Unfortunately for McClellan, history would later focus mostly on the "unpleasant" aspects of the relationship. In a sermon preached a little over a week after Lincoln's death, a leading Presbyterian minister observed that the nation had attempted to make McClellan into an idol after the Union disaster at Bull Run, but God had refused to allow it. Instead, Lincoln became the martyr president and McClellan his foil, a simple story later baked into the standard Civil War narrative, and one that to this day often resists even the mildest revisions.[74]

NOTES

ABBREVIATIONS

AHEC	U.S. Army Heritage and Education Center, Carlisle, PA
AL	Abraham Lincoln
ALPLC	Abraham Lincoln Papers, Library of Congress
BPHL	Samuel L. M. Barlow Papers, Henry E. Huntington Library, San Marino, CA
CCW	*Report of the Joint Committee on the Conduct of the War*
CWL	Lincoln, *Collected Works*
FSNMP	Fredericksburg and Spotsylvania National Military Park
GBM	George B. McClellan
MCWP	McClellan, *Civil War Papers*
MOS	McClellan, *McClellan's Own Story*
MPLC	George B. McClellan Papers, Library of Congress
NYMMVRC	New York Museum and Veterans Research Center, Saratoga Springs
LC	Manuscript Division, Library of Congress
OR	*War of the Rebellion* (all citations to ser. 1 unless otherwise noted)
OR: Supplement	*Supplement to the Official Records of the Union and Confederate Armies* (all citations to part 1 unless otherwise noted)
SPHJ	Samuel Peter Heintzelman Journal, Heintzelman Papers, Library of Congress

INTRODUCTION

1. Grimsley, "Lincoln and Little Mac," 26–27, 72; Grimsley, "Little Mac Fauntleroy," 26–27, 74. For information about McClellan's reputation online at the time of the Civil War sesquicentennial that reinforces these points, see Kenneth W. Noe, "'I Am Completely Checked by the Weather': George B. McClellan, Weather, and the Peninsula Campaign," in Bledsoe and Lang, *Upon the Fields of Battle*, 45–46.

2. For an excellent account of the production of McClellan's memoirs, see Sears, "Curious Case of General McClellan's Memoirs," 101–14. For a provocative and close reading of *McClellan's Own Story* that offers suitable warnings about facile assessment of its weaknesses,

see Cushman, *Generals' Civil War,* 103–33. Cushman is especially perceptive about the importance of religion and sentiment in understanding McClellan's approach both to the war and to his troops.

3. See also Richard Slotkin's well-received and certainly well-written popular account of the Antietam (Maryland) Campaign, which emphasizes political context and not only follows the standard line but also paints McClellan as a relentless conspirator, coming close at several points to labeling him a traitor. Slotkin, *Long Road to Antietam,* xiv, xvii, 27–30, 405–6.

4. See, for example, Murray and Hsieh, *Savage War,* 541–42. For a contemporary comparison (both implicit and explicit) of William T. Sherman and McClellan on campaign strategy, see Hitchcock, *Marching with Sherman,* 147, 287.

5. Palfrey, *Antietam and Fredericksburg,* 134–35.

6. On this point, see Cohen, *Supreme Command,* 8–9. For a recent work that emphasizes political interference with military operations and political hostility to McClellan, see Stotelmyer, *Too Useful to Sacrifice,* 146ff.

7. See the point-by-point defense of McClellan, from a historian often critical of Lincoln administration policies, in Randall, *Lincoln the President,* 2:68–70.

8. For such an assessment of the Peninsula Campaign that takes into account both the enormity of the task and the political factors involved, see Rowland, "'Heaven Save a Country,'" 15–17. For a concise account that summarizes the standard critique of McClellan in the spring and summer of 1862, see Stephen W. Sears, "Lincoln and McClellan," in Boritt, *Lincoln's Generals,* 33–35.

9. For not entirely convincing defenses of McClellan on these counts, see Harsh, "McClellan and the Forgotten Alternative," 30–31; and Rowland, *McClellan and Civil War History,* 150–64.

10. Adams, *Living Hell,* 122.

11. Miller, *President Lincoln,* 191–92.

12. Rafuse, *McClellan's War,* 384–90.

13. For the links between iconography, songs, and McClellan's popularity in the army, see Fry, *Republic in the Ranks,* 24–26.

14. Miller, *President Lincoln,* 168; Cohen, *Supreme Command,* 21–22. A useful corrective to the standard narrative on Lincoln's relationship with his generals is Rafuse, "'Spirit Which You Have Aided,'" 1–39.

15. For two short books on McClellan and Lincoln that follow the standard narrative line about the relationship between the two men, see Waugh, *Lincoln and McClellan,* and Hearn, *Lincoln and McClellan at War.*

16. Craig, *Politics of the Prussian Army,* xvi; Fry, *Republic in the Ranks,* 1–5.

17. For the tension between liberal democracy and military values, see Huntington, *Soldier and the State,* 99–100.

18. For a pointed analysis of McClellan's repeated disdain for politicians, the general's own political ambitions, and his vain attempts to separate the conduct of war from politics, see Holden Reid, "McClellan and the Politicians," 101–12. Risa Brooks has pointed out how an emphasis on military professionalism can foster disdain for politicians and more broadly speaking a kind of contempt for democratic society. Brooks, "The Paradoxes of Huntingtonian

Professionalism," in Beehner, Brooks, and Mauer, *Reconsidering American Civil-Military Relations*, 27–28.

19. On Lincoln's at-times indecisive and contradictory dealings with generals, see Pryor, "Conflict, Chaos, and Confidence," 24–28.

20. Melville, *Battle-Pieces*, 248.

1. TWO MEN OF AMBITION

1. George B. McClellan, "Valedictory Address as President of the Dialectic Society," [June 1846], MPLC.

2. *CWL*, 1:109, 112, 114.

3. Burlingame, *Inner World of Abraham Lincoln*, 365–67; Donald, *Lincoln*, 80–83; White, *A. Lincoln*, 86–88. For a useful warning about reading too much into a fairly conventional piece of oratory, see Wilson, *Honor's Voice*, 195–98. For the connection between ambition and Lincoln's love for Shakespearian tragedies and histories, see Pryor, *Six Encounters with Lincoln*, 333–36.

4. Wilson, *Honor's Voice*, 54–58; Burlingame, *Lincoln*, 1:15–17; *CWL*, 4:60–63; Robert H. Weibe, "Lincoln's Fraternal Democracy," in Thomas, *Abraham Lincoln and the American Political Tradition*, 18.

5. Herndon and Weik, *Herndon's Lincoln*, 15; *CWL*, 4:60–61; Burlingame, *Lincoln*, 1:3–11, 42–48; Burlingame, *Inner World of Abraham Lincoln*, 37–42; Shenk, *Lincoln's Melancholy*, 14–16.

6. Burlingame, *Lincoln*, 1:11–15, 27–29; Herndon and Weik, *Herndon's Lincoln*, 31.

7. Nicolay, *Personal Traits of Abraham Lincoln*, 213–16; *CWL*, 1:229; Shenk, *Lincoln's Melancholy*, 4–23, 27–65, 69–80, 84–96; Wilson, *Honor's Voice*, 124–29; Burlingame, *Inner World of Abraham Lincoln*, 92–113.

8. Michie, *General McClellan*, 1, 4–7; Myers, *Study in Personality*, 1–6; Rafuse, *McClellan's War*, 13–26. Sears, *McClellan*, 2–3.

9. Michie, *General McClellan*, 7; Rafuse, *McClellan's War*, 27–29; George B. McClellan, "Notes on Childhood," MPLC; Sears, *McClellan*, 3–4.

10. Sears, *McClellan*, 1, 5; Myers, *Study in Personality*, 7–19; Michie, *General McClellan*, 11–12; McClellan, "Jomini," 875; *MOS*, 18–19; Harsh, "McClellan and the Forgotten Alternative," 107–8.

11. Hagerman, "Professionalization of George B. McClellan," 113–16; Rafuse, *McClellan's War*, 30–39; Sears, *McClellan*, 6–10; Willcox, *Forgotten Valor*, 55; Keyes, *Fifty Years' Observation*, 440; GBM to John H. B. McClellan, January 21, 1843, MPLC.

12. *CWL*, 3:511, 4:60–62; Herndon and Weik, *Herndon's Lincoln*, 41, 64–65; Wilson, *Honor's Voice*, 58–67; Burlingame, *Lincoln*, 1:30–41, 62–67, 87–92; *Wall Street Journal*, May 22, 2021.

13. Nicolay, *Oral History of Abraham Lincoln*, 8–9; *CWL*, 3:512; 4:64; Burlingame, *Lincoln*, 1:67–71.

14. Donald, *Lincoln*, 70–74, 96–106, 142–52, 154–58; Burlingame, *Lincoln*, 1:131–37; 309–56; *CWL*, 2:81–82; Dirck, *Lincoln the Lawyer*. Dirck's fine study offers many perceptive insights on Lincoln as an attorney.

15. McClellan, *Mexican War Diary and Correspondence,* 18, 21–22, 24–25, 34, 38, 42, 44; Rafuse, *McClellan's War,* 43–47; Sears, *McClellan,* 13–15.

16. Sears, *McClellan,* 16; McClellan, *Mexican War Diary and Correspondence,* 17, 38–39, 49, 72.

17. Sears, *McClellan,* 17–25; Rafuse, *McClellan's War,* 45–47; McClellan, *Mexican War Diary and Correspondence,* 56. 63–67, 131. For a later collection of stories about McClellan's physical courage in both the Mexican and Civil Wars, see Z, "Anecdotes of McClellan's Bravery," *Century Magazine* 31 (February 1886): 515–17.

18. McClellan, *Mexican War Diary and Correspondence,* 48–49, 65, 97–98, 133, 145; Sears, *McClellan,* 26; Rafuse, *McClellan's War,* 42–49.

19. McClellan, *Mexican War Diary and Correspondence,* 134–37, 154–55, 171–77; Myers, *Study in Personality,* 55–69; Sears, *McClellan,* 28–32; Rafuse, *McClellan's War,* 50–51. For a consideration of the military officer as professional, see the classic description in Huntington, *Soldier and the State,* 11–18.

20. Sherman, *Sherman's Civil War,* 452; Howard, *Autobiography,* 1:166.

21. Rafuse, *McClellan's War,* 51–52, 59–61; Sears, *McClellan,* 32–41; Ecelbarger, *Frederick W. Lander,* 20–21; Michie, *General McClellan,* 33–34.

22. Myers, *Study in Personality,* 83; Rafuse, *McClellan's War,* 61–64; Sears, *McClellan,* 42–49; Weigley, *Towards an American Army,* 68–74; McClellan, *Armies of Europe,* 5, 10–14, 28, 34–35.

23. Hooper, *Lincoln's Generals' Wives,* 82–83; Sears, *McClellan,* 41–42; *MCWP,* 540; Myers, *Study in Personality,* 123–32.

24. Robertson, *A. P. Hill,* 27–29; Sears, *McClellan,* 60–63; A. P. Hill to GBM, June 18, 1859, MPLC; Hooper, *Lincoln's Generals' Wives,* 84–88; Strother, *Virginia Yankee in the Civil War,* 137.

25. Extracts from letters from GBM to Mary Ellen Marcy, 1859–60, MPLC. For a provocative treatment of both the advantages and disadvantages of the marriage, see Hooper, *Lincoln's Generals' Wives,* 89–96. For a largely positive assessment of the marriage, see Michie, *General McClellan,* 50–51.

26. Burlingame, *Lincoln,* 1:26–27, 97–101, 123–39, 168–84; Wilson and Davis, *Herndon's Informants,* 13, 21, 25, 73, 155–56, 387, 440, 443; Wilson, *Honor's Voice,* 109–24; *CWL,* 1:78.

27. Turner and Turner, *Mary Todd Lincoln,* 588; Wilson and Davis, *Herndon's Informants,* 443. I have found Jean Baker's *Mary Todd Lincoln* along with her spirited essay, *The Lincoln Marriage,* to be invaluable. Another helpful and sympathetic account appears in Clinton, *Mrs. Lincoln.*

28. Herndon and Weik, *Herndon's Lincoln,* 145 To balance the more positive treatments of the marriage by Mary Lincoln biographers, see the very useful and more critical accounts in Burlingame, *Lincoln,* 1:173–84; and Wilson, *Honor's Voice,* 215–59, 288–92.

29. *CWL,* 1:305.

30. Baker, *Mary Todd Lincoln,* 94; Herndon and Weik, *Herndon's Lincoln,* 258; Wilson and Davis, *Herndon's Informants,* 357, 449, 453, 465–67, 512, 597, 646, 692, 722, 729; Burlingame, *Lincoln,* 1:201–24.

31. Herndon and Weik, *Herndon's Lincoln*, 80–81; Herndon, *Brief Analysis of Lincoln's Character*, 1–2; Donald, *"We Are Lincoln Men,"* 29–107; Burlingame, *Inner World of Abraham Lincoln*, 38, 73–85.

32. Herndon and Weik, *Herndon's Lincoln*, 231; Herndon, *Herndon on Lincoln*, 130; Nicolay, *Personal Traits of Abraham Lincoln*, 64; McClure, *Lincoln and Men of War-Times*, 75; Nicolay, *Oral History of Abraham Lincoln*, 7. Writing to his collaborator Jesse Weik in 1886, Herndon even more candidly connected Lincoln's driving ambition to other character traits: "I have often said to you that Lincoln was terribly ambitious and to that extent he was egoistic—selfish-cold." Herndon, *Herndon on Lincoln*, 190.

33. *CWL*, 1:8–9; Wilson and Davis, *Herndon's Informants*, 42; McClure, *Anecdotes and Stories of Abraham Lincoln*, 50; Burlingame, *Inner World of Abraham Lincoln*, 236–57.

34. Burlingame, *Lincoln*, 1:82–85, 112–21; Burlingame, *Inner World of Abraham Lincoln*, 147–208; Wilson, *Honor's Voice*, 142–64, 293–317; Shenk, *Lincoln's Melancholy*, 112–25.

35. Burlingame, *Lincoln*, 1:261–73; *CWL*, 4:65–67.

36. The major provisions of the Compromise of 1850 included the admission of California as a free state; the organization of the Utah and New Mexico Territories, with the slavery question to be decided by each future state's constitution; the enactment of a tougher fugitive slave law; the abolition of the slave trade in the District of Columbia; and the adjustment of the western boundary of Texas.

37. Burlingame, *Lincoln*, 1:122–27, 294–308, 357–90, 403–35; Burlingame, *Inner World of Abraham Lincoln*, 20–37; *CWL*, 2:316, 318, 320, 4:67.

38. Herndon and Weik, *Herndon's Lincoln*, 239–40; Wilson, *Honor's Voice*, 198–201; *CWL*, 2:136.

39. Herndon and Weik, *Herndon's Lincoln*, 230; Nicolay, *Personal Traits of Abraham Lincoln*, 117–18; *CWL*, 2:461–62.

40. Burlingame, *Lincoln*, 1:550–51; *CWL*, 3:336, 339, 340, 346. Popular sovereignty was the idea that it was up to the people of a territory or later state (not the federal government) to decide on the status of slavery within its boundaries.

41. *CWL*, 2:382–83.

42. In the Cooper Union address in New York on February 27, 1860, Lincoln argued that a majority of the founding fathers believed that Congress could prohibit slavery in the national territories. At the same time, he pledged that the Republicans did not intend to interfere with slavery where it already existed, though northerners must stand firm against any further expansion of the institution.

43. Oldroyd, *Lincoln Memorial Album*, 476; Villard, *Lincoln on the Eve of '61*, 6–7; *CWL*, 3:365–66, 394–95, 4:45; Donald, *Lincoln*, 233–41. On Lincoln's continuing obsession with Douglas, see Burlingame, *Lincoln*, 1:560–62. On Mary Lincoln and ambition, see Herndon, *Herndon on Lincoln*, 287.

44. *MOS*, 36; "McClellan's Own Story," manuscript, MPLC, 16; Wilson and Davis, *Herndon's Informants*, 406; Sears, *McClellan*, 58–59; Burlingame, *Lincoln*, 1:435–38; Rafuse, *McClellan's War*, 74–75. McClellan later claimed a cordial acquaintance with Lincoln during this period. *MOS*, 162.

45. GBM to Randolph B. Marcy, February 15, 1857; and Marcy to GBM, April 24, 1857, MPLC; Illinois Central Railroad Company, *Annual Report* (1857), 2; Rafuse, *McClellan's War*, 68–69; Michie, *General McClellan*, 47–48; Sears, *McClellan*, 50–57.

46. Biddle, "Recollections of McClellan," 461; Beatie, *Army of the Potomac*, 1:403; Sears, *McClellan*, 63–65; Rafuse, *McClellan's War*, 81–82.

47. Rafuse, *McClellan's War*, 56, 58–59, 71, 83–91; *MOS*, 30–39. Unfortunately, much of what we know about McClellan's political views during the 1850s comes from his later autobiographical writings, and the amount of direct contemporary evidence is disappointingly slim.

48. Donald, *Lincoln*, 241–56; *CWL*, 4:34; Burlingame, *Lincoln*, 1:558–59; Nicolay, *With Lincoln in the White House*, 7.

49. Donald, *Lincoln*, 256–61; *CWL*, 4:141–42; Potter, *Lincoln and His Party*, 9–19. Lincoln quickly decided that saying anything had been a mistake and declared that "party malice" would lead people to misinterpret any statement he would make. *CWL*, 4:146.

50. For a highly critical account of Lincoln's administrative shortcomings, see Pryor, "Conflict, Chaos, and Confidence," 14–21.

51. *CWL*, 4:175–76, 183; Nicolay and Hay, *Lincoln*, 3:280; Villard, *Lincoln on the Eve of '61*, 58–59.

52. On Lincoln as a partisan leader and his recognition of the centrality of slavery restriction to the Republican Party's appeal, see Potter, *Lincoln and His Party*, 200; Burlingame, *Lincoln*, 1:708–12; and McClintock, *Lincoln and the Decision for War*, 94–95. For an account that adds Lincoln's lack of understanding of southern concerns and his own antislavery convictions to partisan considerations, see Cooper, *We Have the War upon Us*, 73–81.

53. For an astute analysis of Republican pressures on Lincoln to reject any compromise on the territorial question, see Cooper, *We Have the War upon Us*, 97–112.

54. *CWL*, 4:211, 226, 230, 235–36, 240–41. For a spirited defense of the quality of Lincoln speeches on his inaugural journey, see Holzer, *Lincoln President-Elect*, 341–43. For sharp critiques, see McClintock, *Lincoln and the Decision for War*, 181–83; and Cooper, *We Have the War upon Us*, 194–97.

55. *MOS*, 30; *MCWP*, 3–4; John M. Douglas to GBM, January 26, 1861, MPLC. Ethan Rafuse has pointed out that McClellan's more extensive contacts with southerners perhaps led him to take threats of secession more seriously than Lincoln did. Rafuse, *McClellan's War*, 88.

56. *CWL*, 4:262–71. See the analyses of Lincoln's first inaugural in Potter, *Lincoln and His Party*, 318–29; and Cooper, *We Have the War upon Us*, 210–15.

57. SPHJ, March 4, 1861, LC, reel 7.

58. *CWL*, 4:316–17; Donald, *Lincoln*, 285–94; Burlingame, *Lincoln*, 2:98–130; McClintock, *Lincoln and the Decision for War*, 202–53; Cooper, *We Have the War upon Us*, 219–68.

2. SAVIORS OF THE UNION

1. *CWL*, 4:331–32, 338–39, 345; Nicolay and Hay, *Lincoln*, 4:79.

2. Burlingame, *Lincoln*, 2:149–66. For the problems with appointments, see *CWL*, 4:333–420.

3. *CWL*, 4:421.

4. Burlingame, *Lincoln,* 2:167, 173–76; Perry, "Chapter in Interstate Diplomacy," 354; Dix, *Memoirs of John Adams Dix,* 2:20; Shaw, *Blue-Eyed Child of Fortune,* 91; Nicolay, *Oral History of Abraham Lincoln,* 54–55.

5. James Cornell Biddle to Gertrude Biddle, May 13, 1861, Biddle Letters, Historical Society of Pennsylvania; Hamilton, *Reminiscences of James A. Hamilton,* 477.

6. For various estimates, see Pryor, *Six Encounters with Lincoln,* 30; and Hsieh, *West Pointers and the Civil War,* 91–92.

7. Sears, *McClellan,* 68–69; *MCWP,* 4–7; George B. McClellan to Fitz John Porter, [April 18, 1861], Porter Papers, LC, reel 1; *OR,* ser. 3, 1:121–22.

8. Rafuse, *McClellan's War,* 93–94; Cox, *Military Reminiscences,* 1:8–10, 12; Sherman, *Sherman's Civil War,* 74; Jacob D. Cox, "War Preparations in the North," in Johnson and Buel, *Battles and Leaders,* 1:90–91; *MCWP,* 7–10.

9. Cox, *Military Reminiscences,* 1:10; Cox, "War Preparations in the North," 1:90; *MCWP,* 8, 11; Sears, *McClellan,* 71; Harsh, "McClellan and the Forgotten Alternative," 161–62; Rafuse, *McClellan's War,* 95–96; Richard Yates, Lyman Trumbull, John A. McClernand, and others to AL, April 19, 1861, copy from the National Archives, Papers of Abraham Lincoln Project, Springfield, IL.

10. Sherman, *Sherman's Civil War,* 88; Sears, *McClellan, 26; OR,* 51(1):342–43; *MOS,* 44–47; William S. Rosecrans to GBM, June 5, 1861, MPLC; Young, *Around the World with General Grant,* 2:215n.

11. *MCWP,* 12–14.

12. *MCWP,* 13–14n, 16–18; *OR,* 51(1):369–70. For differing assessments of McClellan's proposal, see Sears, *McClellan,* 75–76; and Rafuse, *McClellan's War,* 96.

13. *MCWP,* 19–20, 30–31, 38–40; Sears, *McClellan,* 81–83; Rafuse, *McClellan's War,* 107–8; Moore, *Rebellion Record,* 2 (Documents):163; Allan Pinkerton to GBM, June 26, 1861, MPLC; Pinkerton to AL, June 27, 1861, ALPLC; Chase, *Papers,* 3:71–73; *Chicago Tribune,* June 27, 1861; *Washington National Republican,* June 28, 1861; *New York Daily Tribune,* June 27, 1861; *Washington Daily National Intelligencer,* June 28, 1861; *Washington Evening Star,* June 27, 1861.

14. *MCWP,* 24–25; *OR,* 51(1):386–87.

15. *OR,* 2:44–50, 648, 652–53; *MCWP,* 19–20, 23.

16. *MCWP,* 27; *OR,* 2:66–68, 655–56.

17. *MCWP,* 33–34; *OR,* 2:195.

18. *MCWP,* 36–37, 40.

19. *MCWP,* 40–41, 43–44.

20. *MCWP,* 45–46.

21. *OR,* 2:200–208; *MCWP,* 54; Sears, *McClellan,* 85–91; Rafuse, *McClellan's War,* 113–15. For two sharp critiques of McClellan's conduct in the western Virginia campaign and specifically at Rich Mountain, see Cox, *Military Reminiscences,* 1:50–58; and Beatty, *Citizen-Soldier,* 25.

22. *Chicago Tribune,* May 14, 1861; *Springfield (MA) Republican,* n.d., in *Louisville (KY) Daily Journal,* July 10, 1861; *CWL,* 4:328; *Washington National Republican,* June 13, 1861.

23. *Chicago Tribune,* June 25, 28, July 12, 13, 15, 16, 1861; *New York Daily Tribune,* July 18, 1861; Rafuse, *McClellan's War,* 116; *Washington National Republican,* July 16, 1861;

Washington Daily National Intelligencer, July 24, 1861; *Washington Evening Star,* extra, July 14, 1861; *New York Herald,* July 16, 1861. For one correspondent's dissenting view that emphasized the incompleteness of McClellan's victories, see Reid, *Radical View,* 1:38–39. McClellan blamed the failure to bag all the Confederates on the inability of Cox and other subordinates to carry out his orders. *MCWP,* 58, 61, 65.

24. *MCWP,* 60–61; Schuckers, *Life and Public Services of Salmon Portland Chase,* 427; *OR,* 2:204; Zachariah Chandler to his wife, July 16, 1861, Chandler Papers, LC.

25. *MCWP,* 36, 37, 45, 59; Hassler, *McClellan,* 13–14.

26. *OR,* 2:46, 705; *MCWP,* 25–26, 28, 35–36, 47, 49–50; Styple, *McClellan's Other Story,* 23–24, 46–47; Rowland, *McClellan and Civil War History,* 76–85; Harsh, "McClellan and the Forgotten Alternative," 50–63; *MOS,* 52; Sears, *McClellan,* 85; General Orders No. 18, July 3, 1861, William S. Rosecrans to Major S. Williams, July 6, 1861, MPLC.

27. *MOS,* 62; *MCWP,* 53, 56–57.

28. McClure, *Lincoln and Men of War-Times,* 212–13; Cox, *Military Reminiscences,* 1:57; Nevins, *War for the Union,* 1:224–25; Nicolay and Hay, *Lincoln,* 4:339–40.

29. R. B. Marcy to GBM, July 19, 1861, Thomas M. Edwards to GBM, July 24, 1861, MPLC; *MCWP,* 60–61; *OR,* 2:746, 753, 755. For criticism and defense of the Marcy appointment, see Gurowski, *Diary,* 1:94; *Chicago Tribune,* October 24, 1861.

30. *New York Times,* April 25, 1861; Hay, *Inside Lincoln's White House,* 15–16; *Burlingame, Lincoln,* 2:178–81.

31. Bates, *Lincoln in the Telegraph Office,* 88–91; Nicolay, *With Lincoln in the White House,* 51–52; *Congressional Globe,* 37th Cong., 1st sess., 246.

32. Burlingame, *Lincoln,* 2:184–87; Horace Greeley to AL, July 29, 1861, ALPLC; Buchanan, *Works,* 11:213–14; Herndon and Weik, *Herndon's Lincoln,* 326; *CWL,* 4:457–58; *New York Herald,* July 23, 1861; Butler, *Private and Official Correspondence,* 1:179.

33. Sears, *McClellan,* 96; Kelley, *Lincoln and Stanton,* 2–3; Rice, *Reminiscences of Abraham Lincoln,* 588; *Chicago Tribune,* July 23, 25, August 2, 1861; *New York Herald,* July 23, 25, 1861.

34. *OR,* 2:759; *MCWP,* 67; *MOS,* 55; Rafuse, *McClellan's War,* 119; *Under the Maltese Cross,* 19; *Washington Evening Star,* July 27, 1861; Beale, "Education of an Artist," 502; *Chicago Tribune,* July 26, 1861; Edge, *McClellan and the Campaign on the Yorktown Peninsula,* 6.

35. *Washington Daily National Intelligencer,* July 27, 1861; Horatio Nelson Taft Diary, July 27, 1861, LC; Rafuse, *McClellan's War,* 118; *MOS,* 66.

36. Bacon and Howland, *Letters of a Family,* 1:171; *MOS,* 20; Leech, *Reveille in Washington,* 108; Howard, *Autobiography,* 1:167; *New York Daily Tribune,* June 19, 1861; Wainwright, *Diary of Battle,* 109; *Washington Evening Star,* August 5, 1861; comte de Paris, *Voyage en Amérique,* 90n; Russell, "Recollections of the Civil War," 745; Rusling, *Men and Things I Saw in Civil War Days,* 25; Pisani, *Prince Napoleon in America,* 107–9; Prim, *General McClellan and the Army of the Potomac,* 14; Francis Brooks Diary, February 3, 1863, Massachusetts Historical Society.

37. *CWL,* 3:512; Pisani, *Prince Napoleon in America,* 97–101; Dicey, *Spectator of America,* 91–92; Favill, *Diary of a Young Officer,* 25; Davis, *Lincoln's Men,* 47; Burlingame, *Lincoln,* 1:41–42; French, *Witness to the Young Republic,* 365, 373, 381; Herndon and Weik, *Herndon's Lincoln,* 215–16; Olmsted, *Papers,* 4:126; Gilmore, *Personal Recollections,* 14; Strong, *Diary,* 3:204; Du Pont, *Samuel Francis Du Pont,* 1:94.

38. *OR*, 2:763, 51(1):428; *MOS*, 66; *MCWP*, 70.

39. Miller, *President Lincoln*, 170; Stephen W. Sears, "Lincoln and McClellan," in Boritt, *Lincoln's Generals*, 11; McClellan memoirs draft, MPLC.

40. *Washington National Republican*, July 30, 1861; Clapp, *Forgotten First Citizen*, 148; Gurowski, *Diary*, 1:72–73; Gorham, *Life and Public Services of Edwin M. Stanton*, 1:222.

41. Holland, *Life of Abraham Lincoln*, 323; *Boston Post*, n.d., in *Chicago Tribune*, July 29, 1861; *Columbus (OH) Gazette*, August 2, 1861; *Philadelphia Press*, n.d., in *Chicago Tribune*, August 3, 1861; *Cincinnati Commercial*, n.d., in *Washington National Republican*, July 27, 1861; *Washington National Republican*, August 6, 10, 1861; "A Military Man" to GBM, July 26, 1861, MPLC; Prentiss, *Free Christian State and the Present Struggle*, 36–37; *New York Herald*, July 28, 1861; McCulloch, *Men and Measures*, 298. There soon appeared a newspaper story that, while in Cincinnati, McClellan had visited a prominent local pastor and asked him to pray for both himself and the country. *Washington Daily National Intelligencer*, August 3, 1861; *Washington National Republican*, September 12, 1861.

42. Engle, *Gathering to Save a Nation*, 94; Hay, *Lincoln's Journalist*, 81; Stoddard, *Dispatches from Lincoln's White House*, 16.

43. *OR*, 5:11; *CCW*, 1:420; *MOS*, 66–69; Poe, *My Dear Nelly*, 53; Swinton, *Army of the Potomac*, 62–63; Averell, *Ten Years in the Saddle*, 305.

44. *Chicago Tribune*, July 29–30, 1861; *New York Herald*, July 29, 31, 1861.

45. *OR*, 2:770, 5:564–65; *Chicago Tribune*, July 31, August 1, 1861; *Boston Herald*, July 30, 1861; Regan, *Lost Civil War Diaries*, 20; *Boston Daily Advertiser*, July 30, August 3, 1861; *Washington Evening Star*, August 2, 1861; *Washington National Republican*, August 5, 1861.

46. *Boston Herald*, August 29. 1861; comte de Paris, *Civil War in America*, 1:397–98; Stoddard, *Dispatches from Lincoln's White House*, 17; Hay, *Lincoln's Journalist*, 82–83; Du Pont, *Samuel Francis Du Pont*, 1:125; *New York Daily Tribune*, August 1, 1861; *MCWP*, 75.

47. Dwight, *Life and Letters*, 85; Haydon, *For Country, Cause, & Leader*, 70; Hoadley, *Memorial of Henry Sanford Gansevoort*, 95.

48. *Chicago Tribune*, August 30, 1861.

49. Picq, *Battle Studies*, 3; Rafuse, *McClellan's War*, 130–31; Harsh, "McClellan and the Forgotten Alternative," 115–18; *Boston Daily Advertiser*, August 6, 1861; Sears, *McClellan*, 110–11; Howard, *Autobiography*, 1:167–68.

50. Pickrell, *Third Indiana Cavalry*, 33–34; Mann, *Fighting with the Eighteenth Massachusetts*, 38; Ford, *Cycle of Adams Letters*, 1:38; McClure, *Lincoln and Men of War-Times*, 218–19; Shaw, *Blue-Eyed Child of Fortune*, 132; *Boston Daily Advertiser*, July 25, 1861; *Chicago Tribune*, August 31, 1861.

51. Sears, *McClellan*, 100; *Philadelphia Inquirer*, n.d., in *Chicago Tribune*, August 9, 1861; Russell, *My Diary North and South* (1988), 193; *MCWP*, 84; Horatio Nelson Taft Diary, October 28, 1861, LC; Russell, "Recollections of the Civil War," 746–47; Harsh, "McClellan and the Forgotten Alternative," 118–20.

52. *MCWP*, 84–85, 89; *Philadelphia Inquirer*, n.d., in *Chicago Tribune*, August 9, 1861; Williams, *Lincoln and His Generals*, 29; *Washington Evening Star*, August 19, 1861; *MOS*, 84–85; GBM to AL, n.d., 1861, ALPLC; Sears, *McClellan*, 110; *Chicago Tribune*, August 13–14, 1861.

53. *MCWP,* 71; comte de Paris, "McClellan Organizing the Grand Army," in Johnson and Buel, *Battles and Leaders,* 2:112–13; Michie, *General McClellan,* 102; Sears, *McClellan,* 115–16; *Chicago Tribune,* July 31, September 4, 1861; Beatie, *Army of the Potomac,* 1:496–511. After he rode through the camp of Brigadier General Louis Blenker, McClellan remarked, "When I am among you Germans, I always feel as if I had got among soldiers." *New York Daily Tribune,* September 7, 1861.

54. Rusling, *Men and Things I Saw in Civil War Days,* 24–25; Beatie, *Army of the Potomac,* 1:422–27; *OR,* 5:12; Paludan, *Presidency of Abraham Lincoln,* 100–101; Polsky, "Mr. Lincoln's Army Revisited," 192; *Boston Daily Advertiser,* August 5, 1861; *New York Daily Tribune,* August 10, 20, 23, 1861; *MCWP,* 76–78; *New York Herald,* July 31, 1861. For a useful account of the departures and appointments through October 1861, see Sears, *Lincoln's Lieutenants,* 85–104.

55. GBM, "The Peninsular Campaign," in Johnson and Buel, *Battles and Leaders,* 2:161–62; Sears, *McClellan,* 112–14; Du Pont, *Samuel Francis Du Pont,* 1:109–10; Pisani, *Prince Napoleon in America,* 110–14; Joinville, *Army of the Potomac,* 18; *Washington National Republican,* August 5, 1861; *Chicago Tribune,* August 3, 1861.

56. *MOS,* 97–98; *Chicago Tribune,* August 22, 1861; *New York Herald,* August 22, 1861; *Washington Daily National Intelligencer,* August 23, 1861. For McClellan's approach to training, including target practice and bayonet exercises, see Hsieh, *West Pointers and the Civil War,* 146–47.

57. *New York Herald,* August 25, 1861; Schurz, *Reminiscences,* 2:333.

58. Heffelfinger, "Dear Sister Jennie," 118–19; Faller and Faller, *Dear Folks at Home,* 26–27; Dawes, *Service with the Sixth Wisconsin,* 21; King, "Boy's Recollection of our Great Generals," 130.

59. *MCWP,* 82; Russell, *My Diary North and South* (1988), 301; *Chicago Tribune,* September 3, 1861; Sears, *McClellan,* 97–98.

60. Andrews, *North Reports the Civil War,* 149–50; U.S. House, *Telegraph Censorship, H. Rpt.* 64, 37th Cong., 2nd sess., 2; Russell, *My Diary North and South* (1988), 291–92; *Chicago Tribune,* August 6, 12, 1861; Moore, *Rebellion Record,* 3 (Rumors and Incidents):11; *Washington National Republican,* August 14, 1861; *Washington Evening Star,* September 16, 1861; Ford, *Cycle of Adams Letters,* 1:38; *Boston Post,* n.d., in *Washington Daily National Intelligencer,* August 28, 1861.

61. Strong, *Diary,* 3:177; Olmsted, *Papers,* 4:138; Dwight, *Life and Letters,* 70–71; Richard Colby to AL, May 18, 1861, ALPLC. On Lincoln and military officers, see Pryor, *Six Encounters with Lincoln,* 11–62.

62. Orville Hickman Browning to AL, August 19, 1861, ALPLC; *Boston Herald,* August 12, 1861; Gurowski, *Diary,* 1:90; *MCWP,* 85–86.

63. Young, *Around the World with General Grant,* 2:216–17.

3. STRATEGY AND POLITICS

1. For an excellent introduction to McClellan's approach to strategy, see Rafuse, *McClellan's War,* 1–7.

2. *MCWP,* 71–75.

3. For standard critiques of McClellan's memorandum, see Williams, *Lincoln and His Generals,* 30–31; and McPherson, *Tried by War,* 45–46. For more sympathetic analyses, see Harsh, "McClellan and the Forgotten Alternative," 185–89, 193–208; and Grimsley, *Hard Hand of War,* 32–34. Note also the observation by historian John Hennessy that McClellan (and his ally Fitz John Porter) "represented a conservative philosophy and vision of war shared by a significant percentage of the northern population." Hennessy, "Conservatism's Dying Ember: Fitz John Porter and the Union War, 1862," in Rafuse, *Corps Commanders in Blue,* 15.

4. *MCWP,* 75–76; *MOS,* 136–47; Dennis Hart Mahan to AL, n.d., 1861, ALPLC; Townsend, *Anecdotes of the Civil War,* 62; Harsh, "McClellan and the Forgotten Alternative," 189–93. For an excellent analysis that notes how similarities in temperament were bound to bring Scott and McClellan into conflict, see Johnson, *Winfield Scott,* 228–30.

5. *MCWP,* 78–79; Seward, *Reminiscences,* 182–83; Hay, *Lincoln's Journalist,* 89–90.

6. *MCWP,* 70, 79–81; Averell, *Ten Years in the Saddle,* 307–8; Fishel, *Secret War for the Union,* 53–55, 102–3; *OR,* 5:553; Sears, *McClellan,* 102; Sears, *Lincoln's Lieutenants,* 83–84. For the problems that arose in McClellan's relations with Scott, see Grimsley, "Overthrown," 20–29. For a less favorable view of McClellan's role, an examination of the failure to use "combined operations," and a provocative defense of the Anaconda strategy, see Canfield, "Opportunity Lost," 685–90.

7. *OR,* 11:3–6; *MCWP,* 81–83; Nicolay and Hay, *Lincoln,* 4:463; Russell, *William Howard Russell's Civil War,* 114. On the often difficult relations between secretaries of war and generals in chief, see Huntington, *Soldier and the State,* 208–11.

8. *MCWP,* 84–85; Nevins, *War for the Union,* 1:298; Smith, *Francis Preston Blair Family in Politics,* 2:126; Swinton, *Army of the Potomac,* 68–69.

9. Gould, *Hiram G. Berry,* 70; *New York Herald,* August 5, 1861; *OR,* 5:567, 575; GBM to Mary Ellen McClellan, August 19, 1862, MPLC; Regan, *Lost Civil War Diaries,* 23–24.

10. Stoddard, *Dispatches from Lincoln's White House,* 19; *New York Herald,* August 28, 1861; French, *Witness to the Young Republic,* 373.

11. *OR,* 5:557–58; *New York Herald,* August 20, 23, 1861; *MCWP,* 87, 89, 90–92; *Washington Evening Star,* August 28, 1861; *Chicago Tribune,* August 28, 1861.

12. Applegate, *Reminiscences and Letters of George Arrowsmith,* 68; *OR,* 11(1):106; *New York Tribune,* October 21, 1885; Nevins, *War for the Union,* 1:291–92; Swinton, *Army of the Potomac,* 65–66; Cooling, *Symbol, Sword, and Shield,* 57–67.

13. *New York Herald,* September 1, 6, 1861; *Chicago Tribune,* September 9, 1861; *MOS,* 95; Priest, *Shouts and Whispers,* 47; King, "Boy's Recollections of Our Great Generals," 130; *Louisville (KY) Daily Journal,* September 13, 1861.

14. *MCWP,* 95, 98–99; *OR,* 5:167–69, 584; GBM to brigade and division commanders, September 7, 1861, MPLC; Johnson, "Sensitivity and Civil War," 358; *Washington Evening Star,* September 9, 1861; Guarneri, *Lincoln's Informer,* 67; *New York Daily Tribune,* September 6, 9, 1861.

15. Moore, *Rebellion Record,* 3 (Diary of Events):22; *Washington Evening Star,* September 18, 1861; SPHJ, September 10, 1861, reel 7; *Washington Daily National Intelligencer,* September 11, 1861; *Washington National Republican,* September 11, 1861; Campbell and

Campbell, *"Him on One Side and Me on the Other,"* 45–46; *MCWP,* 98; Doster, *Lincoln and Episodes of the War,* 15; Bradley, *Leverett Bradley,* 14; Dicey, *Spectator of America,* 91–92; Stephens, *Berdan's United States Sharpshooters,* 9–10; Leonard, "Letters of a Fifth Wisconsin Volunteer," 57; *New York Daily Tribune,* September 11, 1861.

16. *Washington Evening Star,* September 25, 1861; *New York Daily Tribune,* September 25, 1861; McClure, *Recollections of Half a Century,* 473–74.

17. McClure, *Lincoln and Men of War-Times,* 78; Cohen, *Supreme Command,* 2. Lincoln preferred dealing with people face to face, so he took to stopping by McClellan's headquarters. The president often walked from the Executive Mansion to the War Department telegraph office to read the latest dispatches, sometimes remaining there late into the night. *Chicago Tribune,* September 21, 1861; Bates, *Lincoln in the Telegraph Office,* 7–9, 26, 40–42.

18. Dicey, *Spectator of America,* 91–92; Doster, *Lincoln and Episodes of the War,* 15; Nicolay and Hay, *Lincoln,* 4:443–45; Randall, *Lincoln the President,* 2:71–72.

19. Glatthaar, *Partners in Command,* 92; Rowland, *McClellan and Civil War History,* 16–37.

20. Cohen, *Supreme Command,* 10; *Washington Evening Star,* September 21, 1861; *Chicago Tribune,* September 11, 1861; Russell, *My Diary North and South* (1988), 313; *MCWP,* 95–96, 100. For sympathetic assessments from later critics, see *Chicago Tribune,* September 17, 1861; and Zachariah Chandler to his wife, September 17, 1861, Chandler Papers, LC.

21. *Boston Daily Advertiser,* September 13, 1861; *Philadelphia Press,* September 21, 1861, in *New York Daily Tribune,* September 23, 1861; Russell, *William Howard Russell's Civil War,* 129; Leonard, "Letters of a Fifth Wisconsin Volunteer," 56; *Providence (RI) Journal,* n.d., in *Washington Daily National Intelligencer,* September 14, 1861; *New York Daily Tribune,* September 16, 1861; SPHJ, September 24, 1861, reel 7; *Washington National Republican,* September 17, 1861; Sears, *McClellan,* 111; Stoddard, *Dispatches from Lincoln's White House,* 27; Olmsted, *Papers,* 4:172, 178.

22. *New York Times,* September 23, 1861; *Boston Daily Advertiser,* September 23, 1861; *Chicago Tribune,* September 26, 1861.

23. Gurowski, *Diary,* 1:99–100; Burlingame, *Lincoln,* 2:190.

24. *OR,* 51(1):492; Gurowski, *Diary,* 1:103; *Boston Daily Advertiser,* September 19, 1861; *MCWP,* 103–4; Welles, *Diary,* 1:241–42; Burlingame, *Lincoln,* 2:194. One historian has remarked that, given McClellan's background, his persistent ignoring of military protocol was striking. Green, *McClellan and the Union High Command,* 55–65.

25. Beatie, *Army of the Potomac,* 2:1–22; comte de Paris, *Voyage en Amérique,* 108; Jonas D. Richardson to "Dear Parents and Brother," September 30, 1861, Richardson Correspondence, Bentley Library, University of Michigan; *Washington Evening Star,* September 30, 1861; *Louisville (KY) Daily Journal,* October 1, 1861; *New York Daily Tribune,* September 30, 1861.

26. Bates, *Diary,* 193; Nevins, *War for the Union,* 1:300; *New York World,* n.d., in *Boston Daily Advertiser,* October 2, 1861. For cabinet dissatisfaction, see also Gideon Welles to Montgomery Blair, November 23, 1873, Blair Family Papers, LC.

27. *MCWP,* 105; *MOS,* 167–69; Styple, *McClellan's Other Story,* 66.

28. Strathern, *Civil War Letters,* 20; Priest, *Shouts and Whispers,* 54; *Washington National Republican,* October 3, 1861. One writer has argued that McClellan's supposed care

for his men was more "sentimental" than "authentic" and centered on the general's "self-love." Slotkin, *Long Road to Antietam*, 46–47.

29. *Boston Daily Advertiser*, October 4, 1861; *Chicago Tribune*, October 4, 1861; *Washington National Republican*, October 4, 1861; Dwight, *Life and Letters*, 111–12, 115.

30. Dwight, *Life and Letters*, 109–10; Gurowski, *Diary*, 1:104–9; Russell, *My Diary North and South* (1988), 324; Styple, *McClellan's Other Story*, 68–69; *National Antislavery Standard (New York)*, October 12, 1861; Engle, *Gathering to Save a Nation*, 116; Duff, *To Petersburg*, 22–23.

31. *Washington National Republican*, October 18, 1861; *New York Daily Tribune*, October 19, 1861; *Boston Herald*, October 19, 1861.

32. *OR*, 51(1):491–92; *MCWP*, 105–6. See also Dahlgren, *Memoir of John A. Dahlgren*, 345.

33. SPHJ, October 8, 1861, reel 7; *Washington Evening Star*, October 7, 1861; *Chicago Tribune*, October 9, 1861; *New York Daily Tribune*, October 9, 1861; *Washington Daily National Intelligencer*, October 9, 1861; *MOS*, 169. For glowing praise of these affairs, see *New York Herald*, October 13, 1861.

34. Burlingame, *Lincoln*, 2:196; *New York Herald*, September 29, 1861; Russell, *My Diary North and South* (1988), 317; *MCWP*, 106–7; Hay, *Inside Lincoln's White House*, 24–25. For a good analysis of visits to McClellan and of Lincoln sizing up the general, see White, *A. Lincoln*, 445–47. At this time McClellan was also relieved to learn that his wife had delivered their first child, a daughter named Mary. Ethan Rafuse has suggested that this may have put him in a better frame of mind to tolerate Lincoln's storytelling. *MCWP*, 107; Rafuse, *McClellan's War*, 138–39.

35. Hay, *Lincoln's Journalist*, 105–6; Stoddard, *Dispatches from Lincoln's White House*, 34–36; Mason, *Until Antietam*, 116; Dwight, *Life and Letters*, 115; *Chicago Tribune*, October 14, 17, 1861; *New York Herald*, October 17–18, 1861; *OR*, 5:35; *MOS*, 75–79; Ropes, *Story of the Civil War*, 1:258–59; S. Hanscom to James Gordon Bennett, October 6, 1861, Bennett Papers, LC.

36. Fishel, *Secret War for the Union*, 104–7; E. J. Allen [Allan Pinkerton] to GBM, October 4, 1861, MPLC.

37. Rafuse, *McClellan's War*, 390–92; *MCWP*, 106–7; Craig, *Politics of the Prussian Army*, 217, 277, 280; Harsh, "McClellan and the Forgotten Alternative," 122–40; Cohen, *Supreme Command*, 9; *Chicago Tribune*, September 6, 1861; S. L. M. Barlow to George B. McClellan, October 10, 1861, Barlow Letterbook 7, BPHL, reel 6; comte de Paris, *Voyage en Amérique*, 115. Many of the early volunteers also hoped to keep politics out of the war and shared McClellan's disdain for politicians. Fry, *Republic in the Ranks*, 17–18.

38. *New York Herald*, July 31, 1861; *Chicago Tribune*, August 2, October 7, 1861; William B. Franklin, "The Great Crime of the War," in *Annals of the War*, 73; Richard Yates to Gustave Koerner, September 23, 1861, Yates Family Papers, Abraham Lincoln Presidential Library; Gurowski, *Diary*, 1:94–95; *Boston Daily Advertiser*, October 10, 1861.

39. Hay, *Lincoln's Journalist*, 121; *MCWP*. 109; *OR*, 5:290–91.

40. Coffin, *Boys of '61*, 57; Hay, *Inside Lincoln's White House*, 27; Hay, *Lincoln's Journalist*, 122; Burlingame, *Lincoln*, 2:200; *Washington Evening Star*, October 26, 1861.

41. *OR,* 5:32–34, 290, 626; comte de Paris, "McClellan's Organizing the Grand Army," in Johnson and Buel, *Battles and Leaders,* 2:114; Hattaway and Jones, *How the North Won,* 82; *Washington Evening Star,* October 23, 1861; Dwight, *Life and Letters,* 122. For useful accounts of McClellan's role—all critical to one degree or another—see Sears, *McClellan,* 120–22; Rafuse, *McClellan's War,* 139–41; and Beatie, *Army of the Potomac,* 2:61–111.

42. *Chicago Tribune,* October 24, 1861; Dahlgren, *Memoir of John A. Dahlgren,* 348; *MCWP,* 110–11; *MOS,* 171; *Boston Herald,* October 29, 1861; Hayes, *Diary and Letters,* 2:127; Russell, *My Diary North and South* (1988), 321; Duff, *To Petersburg,* 25; Gallman, *America's Joan of Arc,* 19.

43. Hay, *Inside Lincoln's White House,* 28; *Boston Daily Advertiser,* October 21–23, 1861; Fitz John Porter to Randolph B. Marcy, October 22, 23, 1861, MPLC; Noe, *Howling Storm,* 61–62; *New York Herald,* October 23, 26, 1861.

44. *OR,* 5:611–12; *Chicago Tribune,* October 3, 1861; *Boston Daily Advertiser,* October 16, 1861.

45. For later complaints about troops plundering civilians while on the march, see John F. Reynolds to his sisters, October 22, 1861, Reynolds Family Papers, Franklin and Marshall College.

46. Donald, *Sumner and the Rights of Man,* 25; Benjamin F. Wade to Zachariah Chandler, October 8, 1861; and Chandler to his wife, October 12, 1861, Chandler Papers, LC.

47. Benjamin F. Wade to Caroline Wade, October 25, 1861, Wade Papers, LC; Montgomery Blair to Zachariah Chandler, October 25, 1861, Chandler to his wife, October 27, 1861, Chandler Papers, LC; *MCWP,* 112; Hay, *Inside the White House,* 28–29.

48. Zachariah Chandler to his wife, October 27, 1861, Chandler Papers, LC; George, *Zachariah Chandler,* 56–57; Hay, *Inside Lincoln's White House,* 29. For a somewhat different account of these meetings, see Wade's later campaign document, *Facts for the People,* 1–2.

49. L. V. Brieux[?] to Benjamin F. Wade, November 1, 1861, Wade Papers, LC; comte de Paris, *Voyage en Amérique,* 115; *MOS,* 33; "McClellan's Own Story," manuscript, MPLC.

50. *Washington Daily National Intelligencer,* October 24, 1861; *Boston Daily Advertiser,* October 30, 1861; *New York Daily Tribune,* October 28, 1861; Dahlgren, *Memoir of John A. Dahlgren,* 347; *Chicago Tribune,* October 25, 26, 1861.

51. Hay, *Lincoln's Journalist,* 126; *CWL,* 5:4–5; *New York Herald,* November 1, 1861.

52. *OR,* 5:8–9; *MCWP,* 114–18; Cohen, *Supreme Command,* 8. For a more realistic assessment of enemy numbers, see Williams, *Lincoln Finds a General,* 1:127–30.

53. *MCWP,* 113–14. For discussion of Stanton's relationship with McClellan at this time, see Marvel, *Lincoln's Autocrat,* 146.

54. *MCWP,* 107, 109; Hamilton, *Reminiscences of James A. Hamilton,* 532; *Boston Daily Advertiser,* October 29, 1861; Hay, *Inside Lincoln's White House,* 27; Bates, *Diary,* 196–97; comte de Paris, *Voyage en Amérique,* 141; Strong, *Diary,* 3:188; Marszalek, *Commander of All Lincoln's Armies,* 106; *Chicago Tribune,* October 31, 1862; *New York Herald,* October 19, 23 26, 1861; *Washington Evening Star,* October 23–24, 1861; Hay, *Lincoln's Journalist,* 125–26.

55. Thurlow Weed to William H. Seward, October 27, 1861, ALPLC; *MCWP,* 112; Bates, *Diary,* 199–200. Chase later wrote that the cabinet was unanimous on the need for a change. Schuckers, *Life and Public Services of Salmon Portland Chase,* 445.

56. *MCWP,* 112–14. Yet Seward apparently admired both Scott and the Anaconda Plan, appeared wary of McClellan's rapid rise to power, and may have worried about the young general's political ambitions. Comte de Paris, *Voyage en Amérique,* 154.

57. Hay, *Inside Lincoln's White House,* 30.

4. THE GENERAL IN CHIEF AND THE COMMANDER IN CHIEF

1. *OR,* 5:639; *CWL,* 5:9–10; *MCWP,* 122. McClellan later confessed that he wrote the passages praising Scott for a "particular market." Ibid., 126.

2. *MCWP,* 123, 126; Stewart, *Camp, March, and Battlefield,* 54–55; *New York Herald,* November 4, 1861; *Washington National Republican,* November 6, 1861. At this time McClellan disavowed any presidential ambitions. Dahlgren, *Memoir of John A. Dahlgren,* 348.

3. *New York Herald,* November 2, 1861; Duff, *To Petersburg,* 26; *Boston Daily Advertiser,* November 6, 1861; Beatie, *Army of the Potomac,* 2:261; Cleaver, *Your Affectionate Son,* 54; *New York Times,* November 2, 1861; *New York Daily Tribune,* November 6, 1861.

4. Catton, *Terrible Swift Sword,* 92; *Chicago Tribune,* November 4, 8, 1861; Dwight, *Life and Letters,* 137; French, *Witness to the Young Republic,* 379; Hay, *Lincoln's Journalist,* 128–29; Stoddard, *Dispatches from Lincoln's White House,* 41.

5. Samuel L. M. Barlow to August Belmont, November 5, 1861, Barlow Letterbook 7, BPHL, reel 6; *New York Times,* November 4–6, 1861; White, *Life of Lyman Trumbull,* 171–72; *New York Herald,* November 4, 6, 1861; *Boston Daily Advertiser,* November 7, 1861; Dwight, *Life and Letters,* 138.

6. Moore, *Rebellion Record,* 3 (Diary of Events):64; *New York Times,* November 4, 12, 1861; Horatio Nelson Taft Diary, November 12, 1861, LC; Griner, "Civil War of a Pennsylvania Trooper," 42; Bacon and Howland, *Letters of a Family,* 1:204; *Washington Evening Star,* October 14, November 12, 1861; Leech, *Reveille in Washington,* 118.

7. *MCWP,* 124, 128–29; Russell, *William Howard Russell's Civil War,* 170; *Washington National Republican,* November 11, 1861; *New York Times,* December 5, 1861.

8. *MCWP,* 123; Beatie, *Army of the Potomac,* 2:268; Gurowski, *Diary,* 1:127–28; *Washington Daily National Intelligencer,* November 28, 1861; *Washington National Republican,* November 25, 1861; *Chicago Tribune,* November 25, 1861.

9. Gurowski, *Diary,* 1:117; Dwight, *Life and Letters,* 137; *New York Times,* November 1, 1861; comte de Paris, "McClellan Organizing the Grand Army," in Johnson and Buel, *Battles and the Leaders,* 2:116; Burlingame, *Lincoln,* 2:195–96.

10. *MCWP,* 123; comte de Paris, *Voyage en Amérique,* 159; Paludan, *Presidency of Abraham Lincoln,* 85, 102; Beatie, *Army of the Potomac,* 2:268–69.

11. Hay, *Lincoln's Journalist,* 130–31; Nicolay and Hay, *Lincoln,* 4:468, 5:155; Randolph B. Marcy to AL, November 9, 1861, ALPLC; *MCWP,* 135–36, 137; SPHJ, November 11, 1861, reel 7. For more on magician Herrmann, see Hay, *Lincoln's Journalist,* 149; and *MOS,* 152. As journalist Alexander McClure later observed, McClellan paid a very high price for misunderstanding and distrusting Lincoln. Alexander McClure to Mary Ellen McClellan, January 13, 1892, MPLC; McClure, *Lincoln and Men of War-Times,* 225.

12. Brooks, *Lincoln Observed,* 13; Trefousse, *Radical Republicans,* 180–81; Herndon, *Herndon on Lincoln,* 19; Samuel L. M. Barlow to Henry D. Bacon, November 18, 23, Barlow Letterbook 7, BPHL, reel 6.

13. Meigs, "General M. C. Meigs on the Conduct of the War," 291; *New York Times,* November 6, 1861; Michie, *General McClellan,* 461–62.

14. Ethan Allen Hitchcock, "Notes upon the Report of Major General George B. McClellan," n.d., Hitchcock Papers, LC, 7; Beatie, *Army of the Potomac,* 2:349–51; Francis P. Blair Jr. to GBM, November 4, 1861, ALPLC; comte de Paris, *Voyage en Amérique,* 153–54; Murray and Hsieh, *Savage War,* 102.

15. Joseph L. Harsh, "Lincoln's Tarnished Brass and the Attempt to Fight the Early Civil War as a Limited War," in Heleniak and Hewitt, *Confederate High Command and Related Topics,* 124–41; Weigley, *Great Civil War,* 92; Rafuse, *McClellan's War,* 148–50; Reed, *Combined Operations in the Civil War,* 32–39.

16. Comte de Paris, *Voyage en Amérique,* 52; *OR,* 5:650–51; E. J. Allen [Allan Pinkerton] to GBM, October 28, November 15, 26, 1861, MPLC; Nevins, *War for the Union,* 1:302–3; *New York Times,* November 11, 1861; *New York Herald,* November 14, 1861; Castleman, *Army of the Potomac,* 50.

17. *MCWP,* 127–28; Samuel L. M. Barlow to P. W. Withers, November 8, 1861; and Barlow to Henry D. Bacon, November 9, 1861, Barlow Letterbook 7, BPHL, reel 6.

18. SPHJ, November 11, 1861, reel 7; Horatio Nelson Taft Diary, November 8, 1861, LC; Regan, *Lost Civil War Diaries,* 29; comte de Paris, *Voyage en Amérique,* 171; *Washington Evening Star,* November 9, 11, 1861; *New York Herald,* November 10, 1861; *MOS,* 174; Jonas D. Richardson to his parents and brother, November 10, 1861, Richardson Correspondence, Bentley Library, University of Michigan; Chase, *Yours for the Union,* 13, 15.

19. Beatie, *Army of the Potomac,* 2:282–83, 292–93; *Chicago Tribune,* November 18, 1861; Glatthaar, *Partners in Command,* 59; Macnamara, *Ninth Regiment Massachusetts Volunteer Infantry,* 60; Rowland, *McClellan and Civil War History,* 53–55; Jonas D. Richardson to his parents and brother, November 7, 1861, Richardson Correspondence, Bentley Library, University of Michigan.

20. Favill, *Diary of a Young Officer,* 52–53; Haydon, *For Country, Cause, & Leader,* 133–34; *CCW,* 1:389, 422; Gurowski, *Diary,* 1:115.

21. Swinton, *Army of the Potomac,* 70–71, 74; Welles, *Diary,* 1:103; Bates, *Diary,* 202.

22. William Doubleday to Zachariah Chandler, December 6, 1861, Chandler Papers, LC; *National Antislavery Standard (New York),* November 2, 1861; Boutwell, *Emancipation,* 2; Brewster, *When This Cruel War Is Over,* 69; *Chicago Tribune,* December 10, 1861; *MCWP,* 128, 132.

23. Samuel L. M. Barlow to George B. McClellan, December 14, 1861; Barlow to McClellan, November 11, 1861; Barlow to Randolph Marcy, November 20, 1861; Barlow to Edwin M. Stanton, November 21, 1861; and Barlow to James A. Bayard, December 2, 1861, Barlow Letterbook 7, BPHL, reel 6; Michie, *General McClellan,* 156; Barnard, *Peninsular Campaign,* 4–5; comte de Paris, *Civil War in America,* 1:572; Kelley, *Lincoln and Stanton,* 6–7; *MCWP,* 128.

24. Howe, *Life and Letters of George Bancroft,* 2:147; Michie, *General McClellan,* 151; SPHJ, November 13, December 8, 1861, reel 7; *CCW,* 1:117; Rafuse, *McClellan's War,* 162.

25. Burlingame, *Lincoln,* 2:197; King, *Turning on the Light,* 241–42; Gurowski, *Diary,* 1:123; Hay, *Inside Lincoln's White House,* 32.

26. Hay, *Inside Lincoln's White House,* 32; Taliaferro, *All the Great Prizes,* 238; Randall, *Lincoln the President,* 2:72; Hassler, *McClellan,* 41; Beatie, *Army of the Potomac,* 2:338–40; Sears, *McClellan,* 425–26n10. Ethan Rafuse has suggested that the wedding might have distressed McClellan because of his continued separation from Nelly. Rafuse, *McClellan's War,* 439n47. For a partial defense of McClellan, see Rowland, *McClellan and Civil War History,* 47–48.

27. Jonas D. Richardson to his parents and brother, November 23, 1861, Richardson Correspondence, Bentley Library, University of Michigan; Horatio Nelson Taft Diary, November 20, 1861, LC; Nash, *Forty-Fourth New York,* 55; Shortell, *Civil War Letters,* 16, 18; Dawes, *Service with the Sixth Wisconsin,* 30; *New York Times,* November 21, 1861; *Boston Daily Advertiser,* November 21, 1861; *New York Herald,* November 21, 1861.

28. *New York Times,* November 21, 23, 1861; *New York Herald,* November 21, 1861; *Washington Evening Star,* November 20, 1861; Bennett, *Musket and Sword,* 38.

29. Haydon, *For Country, Cause, & Leader,* 129–30; Chase, *Yours for the Union,* 19; Davis, *Lincoln's Men,* 31–32, 41–43 56–57; *New York Herald,* November 21, 1861; *Boston Daily Advertiser,* November 25, 1861; Nicolay, *With Lincoln in the White House,* 61–62.

30. *MCWP,* 137; Beatie, *Army of the Potomac,* 2:287; *New York Times,* November 23, 1861.

31. *New York Times,* November 23, 25, 28, 1861; *New York Daily Tribune,* November 24, 1861.

32. *CWL,* 5:34–35, 50–51; Burlingame, *Lincoln,* 2:190.

33. *Chicago Tribune,* December 6, 1861; E. J. Allen [Allan Pinkerton] to GBM, December 2, 8, 1861, MPLC; *OR,* 5:676, 678–85; Beatie, *Army of the Potomac,* 2:116.

34. SPHJ, November 25, 1861, reel 7; *MCWP,* 143; *OR,* 5:671–72; *Boston Daily Advertiser,* December 9, 1861.

35. Fishel, *Secret War for the Union,* 84–111; E. J. Allen [Allan Pinkerton] GBM, December 4, 14, 16, 23, 1861, MPLC; *OR,* 51(2):403. Stephen Sears has argued that moving against the numerically inferior forces of General Joseph Johnston at Manassas would have been one of McClellan's best opportunities "to crush or cripple his foe." Sears, *Lincoln's Lieutenants,* 129.

36. *MCWP,* 142; Simon Cameron to Proprietors, *New York Times,* December 11, 1861; Henry J. Raymond to Cameron, December 13, 1861, Raymond Papers, New York Public Library; Fitz John Porter to Randolph Marcy, December 12, 1861; and E. J. Allen [Allan Pinkerton] to Andrew Porter, December 13, 1861, MPLC.

37. *New York Times,* December 2, 1861; Castleman, *Army of the Potomac,* 58; Meade, *Life and Letters,* 1:232; De Peyster, *Personal and Military History of Philip Kearny,* 221–22; McClure, *Lincoln and Men of War-Times,* 70–71.

38. Meade, *Life and Letters,* 1:239; Chase, *Yours for the Union,* 40; *Washington Evening Star,* December 24, 1861; Williams, *Lincoln and the Radicals,* 57; *New York Daily Tribune,* December 18, 1861; Samuel L. M. Barlow to Edwin M. Stanton, November 27, December 10, 1861, Barlow Letterbook 7, BPHL, reel 6; *MOS,* 35.

39. Gurowski, *Diary,* 1:134; *New York Times,* December 10, 1861; Stevens, *Selected Papers,* 1:230.

40. Tap, *Over Lincoln's Shoulder,* 24–32, 44–48; *Congressional Globe,* 37th Cong., 2nd sess., 32; *Washington Daily National Intelligencer,* December 7, 1861. On politicians' suspicion of professionally trained soldiers, see Huntington, *Soldier and the State,* 153–55.

41. *Chicago Tribune,* December 13, 1861; *New York Daily Tribune,* December 18, 1861; Ellet, *Army of the Potomac,* 3–16; Hay, *Lincoln's Journalist,* 177; *Boston Daily Advertiser,* December 16, 1861.

42. A. Denny to Benjamin F. Wade, December 16, 1861, Wade Papers, LC; Burlingame, *Lincoln,* 2:214; *Chicago Tribune,* December 14, 1861; SPHJ, December 16, 1861, reel 7.

43. *Boston Daily Advertiser,* December 21, 1861; *New York Times,* December 17, 1861; Burlingame, *Lincoln,* 2:214–16.

44. Kelley, *Lincoln and Stanton,* 10; Rice, *Reminiscences of Abraham Lincoln,* 74; J. F. Speed to Joseph Holt, December 8, 1861, Holt Papers, LC; Hay, *Lincoln's Journalist,* 176; *New York Herald,* December 18, 1861; Horatio Nelson Taft Diary, December 17, 1861, LC; Browning, *Diary,* 1:515, 517. On Nelly McClellan as a great hit in Washington society, see Sears, *McClellan,* 135.

45. Rafuse, *McClellan's War,* 160–62; Schuckers, *Life and Public Services of Salmon Portland Chase,* 445; Chase, *Papers,* 1:317; *MOS,* 157–58, 203.

46. Russell, *William Howard Russell's Civil War,* 208; E. J. Allen [Allan Pinkerton] to GBM, December 25, 1861, MPLC; *OR,* 5:974; *New York Times,* December 15, 23, 1861; Stoddard, *Dispatches from Lincoln White House,* 48–50.

47. Rafuse, "Typhoid and Tumult," 5–6; George Monteith to "numerous relatives & friends," December 21, 1861, Monteith Papers, Bentley Library, University of Michigan; comte de Paris, "McClellan Organizing the Grand Army," in Johnson and Buel, *Battles and the Leaders,* 2:120; *Washington Evening Star,* December 23, 1861; *New York Times,* December 24, 30, 1861; Johnson, "Sensitivity and Civil War," 369, *MOS,* 155.

48. SPHJ, December 23–24, 1861, reel 7; *CCW,* 1:68–69, 117–45; Julian, *Political Recollections,* 202; Williams, *Lincoln and the Radicals,* 77. Brigadier Generals Fitz John Porter and George A. McCall confirmed the high estimates of Confederate strength around Centreville and Manassas. Like Franklin, Porter declined to testify about McClellan's plans. *CCW,* 1:163–78.

49. Nicolay and Hay, *Lincoln,* 5:155–56; Bates, *Diary,* 217–19; Trefousse, *Radical Republicans,* 184; *CWL,* 5:84, 86–88.

50. *New York Daily Tribune,* January 1, 1862; *Chicago Tribune,* January 1, 3, 1862; *Boston Daily Advertiser,* January 2, 1863; Rafuse, "Typhoid and Tumult," 6–9; Meade, *Life and Letters,* 1:242; *New York Times,* January 3, 1862; *Washington Evening Star,* January 3, 1862; *CWL,* 5:87–88.

51. *Boston Daily Advertiser,* January 2, 1862; *Cincinnati Gazette,* n.d., in *Chicago Tribune,* January 3, 1862; A. H. Hood to Thaddeus Stevens, January 8, 1862, Stevens Papers, LC; Greene, *Letters to My Wife,* 8–9. On the importance of McClellan's inability to testify, see the insightful analysis in Sears, *McClellan,* 136.

52. *New York Herald,* January 4, 6, 1862; *Washington Evening Star,* January 6, 1862; *New York Times,* January 6, 1862; Rafuse, "Typhoid and Tumult," 10; *Boston Herald,* January 8, 1862; *Chicago Tribune,* January 8, 1862; Samuel L. M. Barlow to "Withers," January 7, 1861, Barlow Letterbook 7, BPHL reel 6.

53. Dahlgren, *Memoir of John A. Dahlgren,* 354; Bates, *Diary,* 220; Warden, *Life and Public Services of Salmon Portland Chase,* 397; Hay, *Lincoln's Journalist,* 187; *CWL,* 5:86–87; *MCWP,* 146–48.

54. SPHJ, January 6, 9, 1862, reel 7; Chase, *Papers,* 1:321; Cooling, *Symbol, Sword, and Shield,* 100; Averell, *Ten Years in the Saddle,* 381; *New York Times,* January 7, 1862; *New York Herald,* January 9, 1862; Gurowski, *Diary,* 1:147–48.

55. Julian, *Political Recollections,* 201–2; Chase, *Papers,* 1:321–22; *CWL,* 5:94; GBM to AL, January 9, 1862, ALPLC.

56. Bates, *Diary,* 223–26; *CWL,* 5:95; Meigs, "General M. C. Meigs on the Conduct of the War," 292.

57. William B. Franklin to Thomas A. Scott, January 10, 1862; and Irvin McDowell to Thomas A. Scott, January 10, 1862, ALPLC; Raymond, *Lincoln,* 773–74; William B. Franklin, "The Great Crime of the War," in *Annals of the War,* 76–77.

58. Griffin, *Gentleman and Officer,* 136–37; *Boston Daily Advertiser,* January 10, 1862; Dwight, *life and Letters,* 186; Pearson, *James S. Wadsworth,* 102–3; *Congressional Globe,* 37th Cong., 2nd sess., pt. 2, 194; French, *Witness to the Young Republic,* 384.

5. WINTER OF DISCONTENT

1. McClure, Lamphier, and Kregar, *"Spur Up Your Pegasus,"* 193; Chase, *Papers,* 1:324.

2. William B. Franklin, "The Great Crime of the War," in *Annals of the War,* 77; Raymond, *Lincoln,* 774–75.

3. Raymond, *Lincoln,* 775, 777–78; Franklin, "Great Crime of the War," 78.

4. Meigs, "General M. C. Meigs on the Conduct of the War," 292, 302; Franklin, "Great Crime of the War," 78; Raymond, *Lincoln,* 776; Chase, *Papers,* 1:324–25. Oddly enough, Seward wrote home that same day: "McClellan remains sick. The Army is idle, and incapable of movement, for want of direction." Seward, *Seward at Washington,* 46. It seems that either Seward received contradictory reports about McClellan's health or that Franklin misremembered his words.

5. Rafuse, "Typhoid and Tumult," 13; *MOS,* 155–56; Chase, *Papers,* 1:324; Sears, *McClellan,* 140.

6. Rafuse, "'Spirit Which You Have Aided,'" 6–14.

7. Raymond, *Lincoln,* 776–77; Franklin, "Great Crime of the War," 78–79; Meigs, "General M. C. Meigs on the Conduct of the War," 292–93, 303; *MOS,* 157–59. McClellan later claimed that he begged the president not to succumb to "improper influences" and instead trust McClellan's judgment, promising to take responsibility and bring everything to a successful conclusion. No other source confirms this, though it does sound like McClellan. Interestingly, Chase made no diary entry for this critically important meeting.

8. "Federal Generals and a Good Press," 285–90. Ives worried that McClellan had perhaps been too forthcoming and told Bennett: "I cannot say that I advise the publication of the above [specific details about the western theater], and I would rather deprecate it; but General McClellan permitted the use of the facts, and so I tell you. He is as guileless and innocent as a child, and we must be careful not to injure him, even to promote Herald interests." Ibid., 291.

9. *OR,* 7:547–48, 5:703–5; *MCWP,* 151–53.

10. *CWL*, 5:98–99.

11. Browning, *Diary*, 1:523; Stoddard, *Dispatches from Lincoln's White House*, 50–51; *Chicago Tribune*, January 16, 1862; Fessenden, *Life and Public Services of William Pitt Fessenden*, 1:259–60; Keckley, *Behind the Scenes*, 132–33.

12. Burlingame, *Lincoln*, 2:239; Williams, *Lincoln and the Radicals*, 59–60; Trumbull, "Statesman's Letters," 49; *Boston Daily Advertiser*, December 12, 16, 1861; *New York Times*, December 12, 1861; Hay, *Lincoln's Journalist*, 161–63. See the full and useful account in Marvel, *Lincoln's Autocrat*, 148–50.

13. Bates, *Diary*, 226; Chase, *Papers*, 1:325; McClure, *Lincoln and Men of War-Times*, 165–66; Welles, *Diary*, 1:57–59.

14. Marvel, *Lincoln's Autocrat*, 146; Thomas and Hyman, *Stanton*, 128–32; *MCWP*, 135; Flower, *Edwin McMasters Stanton*, 122–24; Welles, *Diary*, 1:54–57; Styple, *McClellan's Other Story*, 69; Gorham, *Life and Public Services of Edwin M. Stanton*, 1:234; GBM, "The Peninsular Campaign," in Johnson and Buel, *Battles and Leaders*, 2:163.

15. *MOS*, 161; Burlingame, *Lincoln*, 2:245; *New York Times*, January 14, 1862; Samuel L. Barlow to Edwin M. Stanton, January 14, 1862, Barlow Letterbook 7, BPHL, reel 6.

16. Comte de Paris, *Voyage en Amérique*, 250; Buchanan, *Works*, 11:247; Robert Grier to Edwin M. Stanton, January 13, 1862, Stanton Papers, LC; Sumner, *Selected Letters*, 2:98; Samuel Ward to William Henry Seward, January 14, 1862, Seward Papers, Special Collections, University of Rochester, Rochester, NY, reel 68.

17. "Federal Generals and a Good Press," 285–86; Fessenden, *Life and Public Services of William Pitt Fessenden*, 1:230–31.

18. Marvel, *Lincoln's Autocrat*, 153; Wainwright, *Diary of Battle*, 9–10; Johnson, "Sensitivity and Civil War," 545; McClure, *Lincoln and Men of War-Times*, 170–71; Doster, *Lincoln and Episodes of the Civil War*, 114–16; Arnold, *Life of Abraham Lincoln*, 241–42; Wilson, "Edwin M. Stanton," 240; Welles, *Diary*, 1:67–69.

19. Flower, *Edwin McMasters Stanton*, 119; Johnson, "Reminiscences of Hon. Edwin M. Stanton," 72–73; Marvel, *Lincoln's Autocrat*, 155–56; Smith, *Francis Preston Blair Family in Politics*, 2:141; *New York Times*, January 22, 1862.

20. Nicolay and Hay, *Lincoln*, 5:141–42; Browne, *Every-Day Life of Abraham Lincoln*, 480–81; Alexander T. Stewart to Edwin M. Stanton, January 20, 1862, Stanton Papers, LC.

21. Patrick, *Inside Lincoln's Army*, 32; *MCWP*, 154; *MOS*, 160–62; *New York Herald*, January 20, 1862; Browning, *Diary*, 1:525.

22. *MCWP*, 154; *Boston Daily Advertiser*, January 21, 23, 1862; Patrick, *Inside Lincoln's Army*, 32; Samuel L. M. Barlow to Henry D. Bacon, January 17, 1862; and Barlow to August Belmont, January 17, 1862, Barlow Letterbook 7, BPHL, reel 6; Marvel, *Lincoln's Autocrat*, 155; *New York Times*, February 11, 1862; James H. Todd to Edwin M. Stanton, February 12, 1862, Stanton Papers, LC; Andrews, *North Reports the Civil War*, 57–58; Dana, *Recollections of the Civil War*, 5.

23. Detroit Post and Tribune, *Zachariah Chandler*, 218–19; Julian, *Political Recollections*, 203–4; Cochrane, *War for the Union*, 19; *CCW*, 1:75–76; SPHJ, January 20, 1862, reel 7.

24. *MCWP*, 144; *CCW*, 1:74–75; Malcolm Ives to James Gordon Bennett, January 16, 1862, Bennett Papers, LC, reel 1; Detroit Post and Tribune, *Zachariah Chandler*, 224–26; *New York*

Herald, January 16, 19, 1862; *New York Times,* January 16, February 3, 1862; *Boston Daily Advertiser,* January 20, 1862.

25. Weisberger, *Reporters for the Union,* 258–60; *New York Herald,* January 16, 1862; Flower, *Edwin McMasters Stanton,* 126, 131; Henry Douglas Bacon to Samuel L. M. Barlow, January 15, 1862, BPHL; Barlow to Bacon, January 22, 1862; and Barlow to Jesse D. Bright, January 16, 1862, Barlow Letterbook 7, ibid., reel 6.

26. *MCWP,* 150; *CCW,* 1:424–26; GBM, "Peninsular Campaign," 165; Barnard, *Peninsula Campaign,* 55–57; Noe, *Howling Storm,* 75–77; Beatie, *Army of the Potomac,* 2:393–98; SPHJ, January 13, 1862, reel 7. For assessments of McClellan's Urbanna proposal recognizing both strengths and weaknesses, see Hattaway and Jones, *How the North Won,* 87–89; Glatthaar, *Partners in Command,* 69–70; Sears, *To the Gates of Richmond,* 9; and Stoker, *Grand Design,* 81–91.

27. Fishel, *Secret War for the Union,* 113–26; E. J. Allen [Allan Pinkerton] to GBM, January 6, 7, 8, 10, 14, 22, 27, 1862; and Louis Phillipe d'Orleans to GBM, January 21, 1862, MPLC.

28. *New York Times,* January 12, 15, 20, 1862; *Boston Daily Advertiser,* January 13, 16, 1862; Dwight, *Life and Letters,* 189.

29. *Boston Herald,* January 16, 1862; *New York Times,* January 30, 1862; Castleman, *Army of the Potomac,* 76; Strong, *Diary,* 3:202; *Chicago Tribune,* January 29, 1862. Malcolm Ives told James Gordon Bennett that McClellan had promised to move by March 1 and that the general would let them know when he was about to advance. "Federal Generals and a Good Press," 291–92.

30. *Chicago Tribune,* January 17, 1862; Joseph Medill to Edwin M. Stanton, January 21, 1862, Stanton Papers, LC; Ford, *Cycle of Adams Letters,* 1:104; Harwell, *Union Reader,* 97–99.

31. Burlingame, *Lincoln,* 2:290; *Chicago Tribune,* January 23, 1862; *CWL,* 5:111–12; Hay, *Inside Lincoln's White House,* 35; Nevins, *War for the Union,* 1:408; Ropes, "McClellan's Plans for the Campaign of 1862," 77; Gorham, *Life and Public Services of Edwin M. Stanton,* 1:333–34; Edwin Stanton to Benjamin F. Wade, January 27, 1862, Stanton Papers, LC; "Federal Generals and a Good Press," 291. For a partial defense of Lincoln's order, see Williams, *Lincoln and His Generals,* 62.

32. Strong, *Diary,* 3:203; *MCWP,* 156–60; Trumbull, "Trumbull Correspondence," 103; *Chicago Tribune,* February 1, 1862; *OR,* 5:41; Gorham, *Life and Public Services of Edwin M. Stanton,* 1:336.

33. *CWL,* 5:115, 118–19; *OR,* 5:41; *Washington Evening Star,* February 1, 1862.

34. *MCWP,* 163–70. For useful secondary accounts analyzing the strategy, see Hattaway and Jones, *How the North Won,* 93–96; Sears, *McClellan,* 149–51; Rafuse, *McClellan's War,* 178–82; and Reed, *Combined Operations,* 104–7.

35. *OR,* 5:45; Stoddard, *Dispatches from Lincoln's White House,* 55; Nicolay and Hay, *Lincoln,* 5:166.

36. Tap, *Over Lincoln's Shoulder,* 55–69; Sears, *McClellan,* 144–46; Daly, *Diary of a Union Lady,* 105; *MCWP,* 173; Bates, *Diary,* 229; *Chicago Tribune,* February 15, 1862.

37. Gurowski, *Diary,* 1:156, 161; *Boston Herald,* January 31, 1862; *Congressional Globe,* 37th Cong., 2nd sess., 569–74; *New York Daily Tribune,* February 6, 1862; *New York Times,* February 18, 1862; Cox, *Speech of Hon. S. S. Cox, of Ohio, Vindication of Gen. McClellan,* 3–11; Samuel L. M. Barlow to Henry D. Bacon, February 3, 9, 1862, Barlow Letterbook 7, BPHL,

reel 6; Smith, *Autobiography*, 31; Joseph Medill to AL, February 9, 1862, ALPLC; Daly, *Diary of a Union Lady*, 98; Tap, *Over Lincoln's Shoulder*, 111.

38. Swinton, *Army of the Potomac*, 80; *Chicago Tribune*, February 6, 1862; *New York Times*, February 8, 1862; Bryant, *Letters*, 4:255; *New York Daily Tribune*, February 6, 1862; Hamlin, *Life and Times of Hannibal Hamlin*, 441; *New York Herald*, February 8, 10, 1862.

39. Burlingame, *Lincoln*, 2:285–86, 295; *CWL*, 5:130; *New York Daily Tribune*, February 6, 1862; Olmsted, *Papers*, 4:258; Browning, *Diary*, 1:529.

40. *CWL*, 5:130; *MCWP*, 171–72; *New York Times*, February 13, 15, 18, 25, 1862; Bacon and Howland, *My Heart toward Home*, 147; Cleaver, *Your Affectionate Son*, 113–14; *Boston Daily Advertiser*, February 17, 1862; S. P. Hanscom to James Gordon Bennett, February 16, 1862, Bennett Papers, LC. For an excellent account of McClellan's role in western-theater operations during this period, including his dealing with the rival ambitions of Halleck and Buell, see Rafuse, *McClellan's War*, 182–88.

41. Stoddard, *Dispatches from Lincoln's White House*, 60–61.

42. Gorham, *Life and Public Services of Edwin M. Stanton*, 1:285–86; *Chicago Tribune*, February 25, 1862; Dana, *Recollections of the Civil War*, 9–10; *Boston Daily Advertiser*, February 19, 21, 1862; *New York Times*, February 21, 24, 26–28, 1862; *Washington Evening Star*, February 21, 24, 1862; Edwin M. Stanton to Charles A. Dana, February 23, 1862, Dana Papers, LC; S. Deming to Samuel L. M. Barlow, February 22, 1862, BPHL; Barlow to Edwin M. Stanton, February 22, 1862; and Barlow to GBM, February 25, 1862, Barlow Letterbook 7, ibid.; Hay, *Lincoln's Journalist*, 225–28. In the February 23 letter to Dana, Stanton unleashed this scornful blast: "Was it not a funny sight to see a certain Military hero in the telegraph office at Washington last Sunday organizing victory, and by sublime military combinations capturing Fort Donelson Six hours after Grant & Smith had taken it sword in hand & had victorious possession! It would be a picture worthy of Punch."

43. *New York Times*, March 3, 1862; Patrick, *Inside Lincoln's Army*, 45–46; *Washington Evening Star*, February 26, 1862; *New York Herald*, February 19, 1862; *New York Daily Tribune*, February 22, 1862; De Peyster, *Personal and Military History of Philip Kearny*, 226; Guiney, *Commanding Boston's Irish Ninth*, 70; Duff, *To Petersburg*, 37–38; Rusling, *Men and Things I Saw in Civil War Days*, 215.

44. Chase, *Yours for the Union*, 63; Hazelton, *Army of the Potomac*, 46; Medill and Medill, *Family and Nation under Fire*, 58–59; *New York Times*, February 21, 1862; *New York Herald*, February 22, 1862; *Washington Evening Star*, February 12, 1862; Meade, *Life and Letters*, 1:246; SPHJ, February 18, 1862, reel 7; Strong, *Diary*, 3:208.

45. *CCW*, 1:84–87; Detroit Post and Tribune, *Zachariah Chandler*, 226–27; *Chicago Tribune*, February 22, 1862; *Washington National Republican*, February 24, 1862.

46. Bates, *Diary*, 233; Nicolay, *With Lincoln in the White House*, 71; *MCWP*, 187; Keckley, *Behind the Scenes*, 110; Shenk, *Lincoln's Melancholy*, 175–81. For an extremely useful account of the illness of the Lincolns' boys, Willie's funeral, and the family's grief, see Burlingame, *Lincoln*, 2:297–302.

47. Beatie, *Army of the Potomac*, 2:549–50, 567–68, 3:1–6; Schuckers, *Life and Public Services of Salmon Portland Chase*, 446; *MOS*, 192; *MCWP*, 191–92; Kelley, *Lincoln and Stanton*, 22.

48. Strother, *Virginia Yankee in the Civil War,* 4; Beatie, *Army of the Potomac,* 3:6–10; *MCWP,* 191–92; GBM, "Peninsular Campaign," 165.

49. *OR,* 5:728–29; *MCWP,* 192; Schuckers, *Life and Public Services of Salmon Portland Chase,* 446; Nicolay, *With Lincoln in the White House,* 72–73; Horace White to Joseph Medill, March 3, 1862, Charles H. Ray Papers, Henry E. Huntington Library; Sears, *McClellan,* 158. For a sharp critique of Stanton's role, see Marvel, *Lincoln's Autocrat,* 168–69.

50. *MCWP,* 193–95; *MOS,* 195; Sumner, *Selected Letters,* 2:103.

51. *MCWP,* 195–96; Henry W. Halleck to his wife, January 15, 1862, Halleck Papers, Schoff Civil War Collection, Clements Library, University of Michigan; Kelley, *Lincoln and Stanton,* 29; Trefousse, *Benjamin Franklin Wade,* 170; Peskin, "Two White House Visits," 157–58.

52. Meade, *Life and Letters,* 1:248–49; Patrick, *Inside Lincoln's Army,* 48–49; Samuel L. M. Barlow to Henry D. Bacon, February 25, 1862, Barlow Letterbook 7, BPHL, reel 7.

53. *MOS,* 196; SPHJ, March 4, 1862, reel 7; Norton, *Army Letters,* 56–57; Kearny, *Letters from the Peninsula,* 30; Patrick, *Inside Lincoln's Army,* 48–49.

54. *OR,* 5:49–50; *MOS,* 195–96.

55. Sears, *McClellan,* 159. There is a possibility that McDowell may also have shared some information with McClellan's enemies. Williams, *Lincoln and the Radicals,* 117–18.

56. William B. Franklin, "The Great Crime of the War," in *Annals of the War,* 79–80; Naglee, *Peninsular Campaign,* 2; SPHJ, March 8, 1862, reel 7; Heintzelman to John G. Barnard, October 14, 1864, Heintzelman Papers, LC, reel 10; *New York Herald,* December 4, 1864.

57. John G. Barnard to Samuel Peter Heintzelman, October 2, 1864; and Heintzelman to Barnard, October 14, 1863, Heintzelman Papers, LC, reel 10; SPHJ, March 8, 1862, reel 7; *New York Herald,* December 4, 1864; Samuel Peter Heintzelman to AL, March 8, 1862; and John G. Barnard to Edward D. Townsend, October 3, 1864, ALPLC; Naglee, *Peninsular Campaign,* 2; Franklin, "Great Crime of the War," 80; Hay, *Inside Lincoln's White House,* 35. Stanton was including McClellan and Marcy along with the eight generals who had voted with them.

58. SPHJ, March 8, 1862, reel 7; John G. Barnard to Samuel Peter Heintzelman, October 2, 1864, Heintzelman Papers, LC, reel 10; Naglee, *Peninsular Campaign,* 3; Kelley, *Lincoln and Stanton,* 33; comte de Paris, *Voyage en Amérique,* 319; Samuel L. M. Barlow to W. H. Clement, March 8, 1862, Barlow Letterbook 7, BPHL, reel 7.

59. *New York Daily Tribune,* September 10, October 12, 1861; *Washington National Republican,* October 16, 1861; SPHJ, February 21, 1862, reel 7; Julian, *Political Recollections,* 204–5; *CCW,* 1:6–7, 86–88.

60. *CWL,* 1:149–50; *OR,* 5:50; Keyes, *Fifty Years' Observation,* 437–38. For differing assessments of Lincoln's decision, see Williams, *Lincoln Finds a General,* 1:144–45; Murray and Hsieh, *Savage War,* 171; and Rafuse, *McClellan's War,* 191–92. For a more general critique of Lincoln's difficulties in trying to direct the actions of his generals, see Pryor, "Conflict, Chaos, and Confidence," 45–50.

61. *OR,* 5:18, 739–41, 755; *MCWP,* 200; SPHJ, March 11, 1862, reel 7.

62. *CWL,* 5:151; *Washington National Republican,* March 12, 1862; *MOS,* 162–63.

63. Nicolay and Hay, *Lincoln,* 5:173; Dahlgren, *Memoir of John A. Dahlgren,* 559; Nicolay, *With Lincoln in the White House,* 74–75; Welles, *Diary,* 1:61–65; Browning, *Diary,* 1:533.

64. GBM to Randolph Marcy, March 9, 1862; Marcy to GBM, March 11, 1862; and Fitz John Porter to Marcy, March 10, 1862, MPLC; *OR*, 5:51; *Boston Daily Advertiser*, March 13, 1862; comte de Paris, *Voyage en Amérique*, 327; Pearson, *James S. Wadsworth*, 113; Joinville, *Army of the Potomac*, 24–25; *MCWP*, 201–3.

65. *OR*, 5:55–56, 750; *MCWP*, 207; *CCW*, 1:598; *CWL*, 5:157–58.

66. *MCWP*, 209–10; Randolph B. Marcy to GBM, March 14, 1862, MPLC; Bates, *Diary*, 239–40; Weld, *Diary and Letters*, 72; comte de Paris, *Voyage en Amérique*, 332; Barlow to Henry D. Bacon, March 15, 1862, Barlow Letterbook 7, BPHL, reel 7; *OR*, 5:752.

67. *OR*, 5:53–54; comte de Paris, *Voyage en Amérique*, 329–31; Beatie, *Army of the Potomac*, 3:87–88; Snell, *From First to Last*, 87; Jesse Gove Journal, March 12, 1862, LC; SPHJ, March 13, 1862, reel 7; *CCW*, 1:242–50; Barlow, *"Fear Was Not in Him,"* 51.

68. Edge, *McClellan and the Campaign on the Yorktown Peninsula*, 11; Tap, *Over Lincoln's Shoulder*, 114; Castleman, *Army of the Potomac*, 114; Burlingame, *Lincoln*, 2:305; Kearny, *Letters from the Peninsula*, 36; [Nathaniel Hawthorne], "Chiefly about War-Matters. By a Peaceable Man," *Atlantic Monthly* 10 (July 1862): 45.

69. Weld, *Diary and Letters*, 68; Lee, *Wartime Washington*, 109; Fessenden, *Life and Public Services of William Pitt Fessenden*, 1:261; *New York Daily Tribune*, March 12–13, 1862; Kearny, *Letters from the Peninsula*, 34, 37–38. For general summaries of the criticism, see Strong, *Diary*, 3:214; and [Hawthorne], "Chiefly about War-Matters," 51–52.

70. *Chicago Tribune*, March 12, 1862; *New York Daily Tribune*, March 13, 18, 1862; James M. Ashley to Horace Greeley, March 25, 1862, Greeley Papers, LC; H. Calkin to S. P. Hanscom, March 12, 1862, Bennett Papers, LC; *Liberator* (Boston), March 28, 1862; Julian, *Political Recollections*, 205–6; Burlingame, *Lincoln*, 2:305; Adam Gurowski to Zachariah Chandler, March 12, 1862, Chandler Papers, LC.

71. Meade, *Life and Letters*, 1:250–51; Samuel L. M. Barlow to John R. Thompson, March 17, 1862; and Barlow to Henry D. Bacon, March 15, 1862, Barlow Letterbook 7, BPHL, reel 7.

72. *New York Herald*, March 13, 1862; *Lamoille Newsdealer (Hyde Park, VT)*, March 21, 1862; *Louisville (KY) Daily Journal*, February 25, 1862; Dwight, *Life and Letters*, 211–12; Johnson, *Civil War Letters*, 97.

73. Stedman and Gould, *Life and Letters of Edmund Clarence Stedman*, 1:268–69; *New York Times*, March 14, 1862; Joseph C. G. Kennedy to AL, March 15, 1862, ALPLC.

74. *CWL*, 5:155; Flower, *Edwin McMasters Stanton*, 140; Hay, *Inside Lincoln's White House*, 36; Bates, *Diary*, 229; Nicolay and Hay, *Lincoln*, 5:179; Rafuse, *McClellan's War*, 194–95.

75. Comte de Paris, *Voyage en Amérique*, 225, 334–35; Meade, *Life and Letters*, 1:250; Wainwright, *Diary of Battle*, 26; Patrick, *Inside Lincoln's Army*, 51; *New York Times*, March 13–14, 1862; *New York Herald*, March 14, 1862; *MCWP*, 206–7.

6. HALTING PLANS

1. *MCWP*, 211.

2. Marshall, *War of the People*, 67; Wainwright, *Diary of Battle*, 28; *New York Times*, March 16–17, 1862; *Boston Herald*, March 19, 1862; *Boston Daily Advertiser*, March 17, 1862; *Chicago Tribune*, March 17, 1862.

3. Proceedings of the War Board, March 13, 1862, Stanton Papers, LC; George Gibbs to GBM, March 13, 1862, MPLC; Flower, *Edwin McMasters Stanton,* 141. One prominent Republican politician later described Stanton taking on such an expansive role in military policy to have been an "egregious blunder." Blaine, *Twenty Years of Congress,* 1:367–68. For a more positive view, see Hattaway and Jones, *How the North Won,* 119–24.

4. Hitchcock, *Fifty Years in Camp and Field,* 438–40; Proceedings of the War Board, March 18, 1862, Stanton Papers, LC. For a full account of Stanton's maneuvers with Hitchcock, see Marvel, *Lincoln's Autocrat,* 172–76.

5. French, *Witness to the Young Republic,* 391–92; *Washington Evening Star,* March 17, 1862; Naglee, *Peninsular Campaign,* 3; Edmund C. Stedman to GBM, March 17, 1862, MPLC; *MCWP,* 214; Gould, *Civil War Journals,* 107; Donaldson, *Inside the Army of the Potomac,* 49; Meade, *Life and Letters,* 1:253; George Gordon Meade to Margaret Meade, March 18, 1862, Meade Papers, Historical Society of Pennsylvania.

6. Swinton, *Army of the Potomac.* 94; McClure, *Lincoln and Men of War-Times,* 213–14; Hattaway and Jones, *How the North Won,* 143–46.

7. George Gibbs to GBM, March 13, 1862, MPLC; Rafuse, *McClellan's War,* 197; Bates, *Diary,* 240–41; *MCWP,* 213; *New York Times,* March 17, 1862; *Boston Daily Advertiser,* March 18, 1862; Stedman and Gould, *Life and Letters of Edmund Clarence Stedman,* 1:273. John Hennessy has made the important point that the Army of the Potomac from the outset faced intense political scrutiny, which in turn made its leadership preternaturally cautious. Hennessy, "Conservatism's Dying Ember: Fitz John Porter and the Union War, 1862," in Rafuse, *Corps Commanders in Blue,* 20.

8. *New York Herald,* March 20, 1862; Fitz John Porter to Manton Marble, March 17, 1862, Marble Papers, LC, reel 1; Swinton, *Army of the Potomac,* 99–100; Nevins, *War for the Union,* 2:48; Sears, *To the Gates of Richmond,* 23.

9. McAllister, *Civil War Letters,* 127; comte de Paris, *Voyage en Amérique,* 352–53; Faller and Faller, *Dear Folks at Home,* 63; *OR: Supplement,* 2:22–23; *OR,* 11(3):10, 14–15, 17–18, 29; Weld, *Diary and Letters,* 89; Bacon and Howland, *My Heart toward Home,* 160.

10. *MCWP,* 215–16; *OR,* 11(3):9, 18, 24–25; Dahlgren, *Memoir of John A. Dahlgren,* 361–62 *CCW,* 1:630–31.

11. *Boston Herald,* March 19, 1862; *New York Times,* March 18, 1862; *OR,* 51(1):557; Julian, *Political Recollections,* 210; Stoddard, *Dispatches from Lincoln's White House,* 65–66; *Chicago Tribune,* April 1, 1862; George Gordon Meade to Margaret Meade, March 31, 1862, Meade Papers, Historical Society of Pennsylvania; Johnson, "Sensitivity and Civil War," 446.

12. Patrick, *Inside Lincoln's Army,* 53; Dwight, *Life and Letters,* 215; Gould, *Civil War Journals,* 108; *Boston Herald,* March 21, 24, 29, 1862; James A. Dix to Manton Marble, March 21, 1862, Marble Papers, LC, reel 1.

13. *Boston Post,* n.d., in *Washington Evening Star,* March 21, 1862; *Boston Traveler,* n.d. in *Liberator* (Boston), March 28, 1862; *Washington National Republican,* March 24, 1862; *Chicago Tribune,* March 29, 1862.

14. *OR,* 5:58–59, 11(3):52; *MOS,* 163–66; *CWL,* 5:175–76; Hay, *At Lincoln's Side,* 18; *MCWP,* 219–20. For critiques of Lincoln's decision, see Upton, *Military Policy of the United States,* 297; and Williams, *Lincoln and His Generals,* 77.

15. *MCWP,* 222–223; Proceedings of the War Board, March 27, 1862, Stanton Papers, LC; *OR,* 11(3):60–62. For standard criticisms of McClellan's misleading claims and failure to explain his reasoning to the Lincoln administration, see Williams, *Lincoln and His Generals,* 79–80; and Sears, *McClellan,* 170–72. For more favorable assessments, see Rafuse, *McClellan's War,* 202–3, 205–6; and Rowland, "Heaven Save a Country," 7–8.

16. *MOS,* 226; Nevins, *War for the Union,* 2:45n; *New York Times,* March 26–27, 1862; comte de Paris, *Voyage en Amérique,* 373.

17. Hattaway and Jones, *How the North Won,* 98; McClellan, *Oration,* 6, 20; *New York Times,* April 2, 1862.

18. *OR,* 11(3):32, 12(3):16; *MCWP,* 220–21.

19. *OR,* 5:747, 749–50, 754, 11(3):14, 18, 24–25, 27–29, 38–39, 65; *MCWP,* 212–13; Beatie, *Army of the Potomac,* 3:223–31, 287–91; *CWL,* 5:164; Cannon, *Personal Reminiscences,* 145–52.

20. *OR: Supplement,* 2:28; *OR,* 11(1):6, 11(3):63; Noe, *Howling Storm,* 130; *MCWP,* 224–27. McClellan later complained that the navy had refused to supply the gunboats necessary to attack Confederate batteries at Yorktown and Gloucester. *OR,* 11(1):8; GBM, "The Peninsular Campaign," in Johnson and Buel, *Battles and Leaders,* 2:169.

21. GBM to Samuel P. Heintzelman, April 4, 1862, Heintzelman Papers, LC, reel 9; Sears, *To the Gates of Richmond,* 35; Beatie, *Army of the Potomac,* 3:291–95; Donaldson, *Inside the Army of the Potomac,* 58; Abbott, *Fallen Leaves,* 109; *MCWP,* 228.

22. *New York Times,* March 30, April 2, 1862; Mayo, *Civil War Letters,* 201–2; Kearny, *Letters from the Peninsula,* 41–42; Strong, *Diary,* 3:215.

23. Hay, *At Lincoln's Side,* 19; *CWL,* 5:179; Burlingame, *Lincoln,* 2:209; William B. Franklin to GBM, April 7, 1862, MPLC; Beatie, *Army of the Potomac,* 3:340–47; *CCW,* 1:13, 17; *OR,* 11(3):66, 67–68; McClellan, "Peninsular Campaign," 170. For critiques of Lincoln's decisions, see Webb, *Peninsula,* 180; Mark Grimsley, "Lincoln as Commander in Chief: Forays into Generalship," in Engle, *War Worth Fighting,* 66.

24. *OR,* 11(3):73, 11(1):5–6, 10; *MCWP,* 230; Chase, *Papers,* 3:176–77; Meade, *Life and Letters,* 1:256–57; *OR: Supplement,* 2:29–30; Joinville, *Army of the Potomac,* 41. For a critique of McClellan's reasoning, see Sears, *McClellan,* 175–77.

25. *MOS,* 70–71; Patrick, *Inside Lincoln's Army,* 59; comte de Paris, *Voyage en Amérique,* 367; *CCW,* 1:255–61; *OR,* 12(1):277. For varying defenses for Lincoln's decision, see Sears, *McClellan,* 176–78; and Hattaway and Jones, *How the North Won,* 174–76.

26. *OR: Supplement,* 2:29–30; Beatie, *Army of the Potomac,* 3:322–40; *MCWP,* 228; *OR,* 11(1):6–7; *CCW,* 1:393, 428–29; Joinville, *Army of the Potomac,* 38; Ethan Allen Hitchcock, "Notes upon the Report of Major General George B. McClellan," n.d., Hitchcock Papers, LC, 38–40; Browning and Silver, *Environmental History,* 53–54; GBM, "Peninsular Campaign," 171. For a perceptive and scientifically grounded analysis of the influence of rain and mud on the Peninsula Campaign, see Kenneth W. Noe, "'I Am Completely Checked by the Weather': George B. McClellan, Weather, and the Peninsula Campaign," in Bledsoe and Lang, *Upon the Fields of Battle,* 45–70.

27. *MCWP,* 216–17, 229; *OR,* 11(3):80–81, 51(1):564–65; Reed, *Combined Operations,* 142–47. Historian Joseph Glatthaar has argued that McClellan's behavior on the Peninsula—exaggerating enemy numbers, repeatedly calling for more resources, and blaming others for

any failures—established a pattern for the rest of his military career. Glatthaar, *Partners in Command,* 60.

28. *OR: Supplement,* 2:30; Jonas D. Richardson to "Dear Parents and Brother," April 7, 1862, Richardson Correspondence, Bentley Library, University of Michigan; Regan, *Lost Civil War Diaries,* 45; *New York Times,* April 9, 1862; *MOS,* 308; *MCWP,* 230; Keyes, *Fifty Years' Observation,* 446; *CCW,* 1:566, 600; comte de Paris, *Civil War in America,* 1:265–66. For the logistical difficulties that plagued McClellan's advance, see William J. Miller, "Scarcely Any Parallel in History: Logistics, Friction, and McClellan's Strategy for the Peninsula Campaign," in Miller, *Peninsula Campaign,* 2:141–45.

29. *CWL,* 5:182; Dahlgren, *Memoir of John A. Dahlgren,* 363; Hay, *At Lincoln's Side,* 19; Hay, *Lincoln's Journalist,* 242–44; Browning, *Diary,* 1:537–38; *MCWP,* 234. Even Keyes, never a great supporter of McClellan, thought the Army of the Potomac needed more men for the campaign, especially given the absence of naval assistance, and wrote a long letter of complaint to New York senator Ira Harris in which he criticized the government for removing McDowell and other units from McClellan's control. *OR,* 11(1):13–14. During this same period, the president joked with a visitor requesting a pass through Union lines to Richmond that he had given "McClellan and more than two hundred thousand others passes to Richmond, and not a single one of 'em has yet gotten there!" On another occasion, Lincoln sharply noted that McClellan was undoubtedly a good engineer with a "special talent for developing a *stationary* engine." Browne, *Every-Day Life of Abraham Lincoln,* 491; Carpenter, *Six Months at the White House,* 255.

30. *New York Herald,* April 6, 1862; *Boston Daily Advertiser,* April 7, 1862; Browning, *Diary,* 1:538; Jacob B. Rister to Benjamin F. Wade, March 30, 1862, Wade Papers, LC; Thomas Ewing to AL, April 9, 1862, ALPLC; Janney, *Civil War Period Journals,* 108; Samuel L. M. Barlow to Henry D. Bacon, April 10, 1862, Barlow Letterbook 7, BPHL, reel 7. Ironically, the secretary of war, perhaps spurred by recent victories and overconfidence, had closed the recruiting offices even as McClellan was heading for the Peninsula. Done only days before the war's first great bloodletting at the Battle of Shiloh, this badly timed move defies ready explanation. Marvel, *Lincoln's Autocrat,* 179–80; Nevins, *War for the Union,* 2:63–64.

31. Burlingame, *Lincoln,* 2:305; *Chicago Tribune,* April 7, 1862; Drake McKay to Zachariah Chandler, April 9, 1862, Chandler Papers, LC; A. H. Hood, Thaddeus Stevens, April 14, 1862, Stevens Papers, LC.

32. *New York Times,* April 7, 1862; Francis P. Blair Sr. to GBM, April 12, 1862; and C. M. Harmon to GBM, April 8, 1862, MPLC; *Boston Herald,* April 9, 1862; *New York Herald,* April 10, 1862; Stedman and Gould, *Life and Letters of Edmund Clarence Stedman,* 1:274; *Boston Daily Advertiser,* April 1, 1862; Jacob B. Rister to Benjamin F. Wade, March 30, 1862, Wade Papers, LC.

33. *MCWP,* 232, 235; *New York Times,* April 8, 1862; SPHJ, April 8, 1862, reel 7; *OR,* 11(3):78–79; *MOS,* 309.

34. John W. Patterson to his wife, April 13, 1862, Patterson Papers, FSNMP; Chase, *Yours for the Union,* 75–76; George M. Redlon to his father, April 13, 1862, Redlon Letters, Maine Historical Society; Haydon, *For Country, Cause, & Leader,* 220–21; Castleman, *Army of the Potomac,* 115; Colby, *Civil War Papers,* 110; Guiney, *Commanding Boston's Irish Ninth,* 92–93; Dyer, *Journal of a Civil War Surgeon,* 18.

35. Bates, *Diary*, 248–49; *CWL*, 5:184–85; Montgomery Blair to GBM, April 9, 1862, MPLC; Browning, *Diary*, 1:540; Patrick, *Inside Lincoln's Army*, 66; Hay, *At Lincoln's Side*, 20.

36. *MCWP*, 231, 237; *OR*, 11(1):14–15, 11(3):86, 91; Burlingame, *Lincoln*, 2:311; Snell, *From First to Last*, 92; William B. Franklin to GBM, April 7, 1862, MPLC.

37. Fishel, "Pinkerton and McClellan," 126–27; *CCW*, 1:17–18; E. J. Allen [Allan Pinkerton] to GBM, April 7, 1862, MPLC; Barlow, *"Fear Was Not in Him,"* 57. See the useful sorting of numbers in Sears, *McClellan*, 179; for the entire campaign, see Williams, *Lincoln and His Generals*, 87–91.

38. *MCWP*, 238; *New York Times*, April 12, 1862; L. A. Whitely to James Gordon Bennett, April 14, 1862, Bennett Papers, LC; Donaldson, *Inside the Army of the Potomac*, 60; Rhodes, *All for the Union*, 62–63.

39. *CCW*, 1:347–48; *OR*, 11(1):129–30; Kearny, *Letters from the Peninsula*, 45, 50; Michie, *General McClellan*, 245–46; Favill, *Diary of a Young Officer*, 79.

40. From the outset, rainy weather had often turned roads into impassable mud and later made the siege of Yorktown much more difficult. Browning and Silver, *Environmental History*, 56–59; Noe, *Howling Storm*, 131–33.

41. Warren Lee Goss, "Yorktown and Williamsburg," in Johnson and Buel, *Battles and Leaders*, 2:193; *OR*, 11(3):97–100, 103, 107–8, 110–11; SPHJ, April 14, 16, 1862, reel 7; Fitz John Porter to Manton Marble, April 18, 1862, Marble Papers, LC, reel 1.

42. Rafuse, *McClellan's War*, 206–7; Michie, *General McClellan*, 248; Weld, *Diary and Letters*, 99; *MOS*, 286–90; *MCWP*, 240; Hitchcock, *Fifty Years in Camp and Field*, 441; E. A. Hitchcock to Edwin M. Stanton, April 19, 1862, Stanton Papers, LC; Sears, *McClellan*, 179–80.

43. *MCWP*, 239, 241–42, 244–45; Rafuse, *McClellan's War*, 208–9; Biddle, "Recollections of McClellan," 464–65; Hagerman, "Professionalization of George B. McClellan," 125–26; *CCW*, 1:601; Wainwright, *Diary of Battle*, 44; Hays, *Life and Letters*, 208–9; Norton, *Army Letters*, 69–70; Weld, *Diary and Letters*, 101.

44. *Boston Daily Advertiser*, April 23, 1862, *New York Times*, April 23, 25, 1862; *MCWP*, 245–47; *OR*, 11(3):121, 123, 125, 51(1):584; Regan, *Lost Civil War Diaries*, 46; Dickey, *Eighty-Fifth Regiment Pennsylvania Volunteer Infantry*, 32; *MOS*, 314; SPHJ, April 28, 1862, reel 7; *OR: Supplement*, 2:40.

45. Morris E. Boss to "Dear Parents and all," April 18, 1862, Union Soldier Letters, A. S. Williams Collection, University of Alabama, Tuscaloosa; Regan, *Lost Civil War Diaries*, 46; Norton, *Army Letters*, 65; Chase, *Yours for the Union*, 85; John W. Patterson to his wife, April 23, 1862, Patterson Papers, FSNMP; Hays, *Life and Letters*, 210; Murray, *Letters from Berdan's Sharpshooters*, 23.

46. *Chicago Tribune*, April 24, 1862; Samuel L. M. Barlow to George B. McClellan, April 14, 1862, Barlow Letterbook 7, BPHL, reel 7; *New York Herald*, April 15, 23, 1862; Strong, *Diary*, 3:217; Edward Everett to "Wise," April 20, 1862, MPLC.

47. Fitz John Porter to Manton Marble, April 26, 1862, Marble Papers, LC, reel 1; Bowen, *From Ball's Bluff to Gettysburg*, 91; Mayo, *Civil War Letters*, 203. Elizabeth Blair Lee (daughter of Francis Preston Blair Sr.) noted how Chandler's wife strongly denounced McClellan and that both Senator Lyman Trumbull of Illinois and his wife were "too bitter to visit with pleasure." Lee, *Wartime Washington*, 138–39.

48. Nicolay and Hay, *Lincoln,* 5:366; McClure, *Lincoln and Men of War-Times,* 176n; Viele, "A Trip with Lincoln, Chase, and Stanton," 813–14; Marvel, *Lincoln's Autocrat,* 166; Bates, *Lincoln in the Telegraph Office,* 38–39, 108–9; *OR,* 11(3):103, 11(1):383.

49. *New York Times,* April 16, 20, 1862; *Boston Daily Advertiser,* April 18–19, 21, 1862; Shaw, *Blue-Eyed Child of Fortune,* 195; Weld, *Diary and Letters,* 103; *OR: Supplement,* 2:37; David Davis to Joseph Holt, April 28, 1862, Holt Papers, LC; *Boston Herald,* April 18, 1862; *New York Daily Tribune,* April 23, 1862; "Command of the Army," *Harper's Weekly,* April 12, 1862, 226.

50. *Boston Daily Advertiser,* April 16, 22, May 2, 1862; Stoddard, *Dispatches from Lincoln's White House,* 71–72, 73, 75; Hay, *Lincoln's Journalist,* 245–46; *New York Herald,* April 21, 1862; Bates, *Diary,* 253; Sumner, *Selected Letters,* 2:110, 112.

51. *MCWP,* 250–52; *CWL,* 5:203; *New York Times,* April 27, 29, May 1, 1862; Strong, *Diary,* 3:222; *OR,* 11(3):129, 131, 153, 11(1):268; *OR: Supplement,* 2:43–44; comte de Paris, *Voyage en Amérique,* 318. Because of recent successes in the West and the advance on the Peninsula, McClellan's strongest editorial supporter headlined, "The End of the War Near at Hand." *New York Herald,* April 30, 1862.

52. Weld, *Diary and Letters,* 104; Gould, *Civil War Journals,* 120; Bowen, *From Ball's Bluff to Gettysburg,* 95; Forrest Little to his parents, May 2, 1862, Little Letters, Saint Mary's College; Jonas D. Richardson to his parents and brother, May 4, 1862, Richardson Correspondence, Bentley Library, University of Michigan; Hays, *Life and Letters,* 215.

53. *OR,* 11(1):18, 11(3):134; Wainwright, *Diary of Battle,* 44; Auchmuty, *Letters of Richard Tylden Auchmuty,* 51–52; *MCWP,* 253–58. Ironically, Assistant Secretary of the Navy Gustavus Fox now decided that a couple of gunboats could have neutralized the Yorktown batteries after all. Fox, *Confidential Correspondence,* 1:266. Historian Glenn Brasher has argued that the Confederate works at Yorktown—built by impressed slaves—delayed McClellan and affected the outcome of the Peninsula Campaign and especially its influence on the slavery question. Brasher, *Peninsula Campaign & the Necessity of Emancipation,* 100–101.

54. Joinville, *Army of the Potomac,* 47–48; Gurowski, *Diary,* 1:201–2; John Worthington Ames to his father, May 5, 1862, Ames Papers, Coco Collection, Harrisburg Civil War Roundtable Collection, AHEC; *New York Times,* May 2, 1862; Bowen, *Dear Friends at Home,* 82; Brandegee, *Charlie's Civil War,* 56; Johnson, "Sensitivity and Civil War," 557–58; *OR,* 11(1):321.

55. *New York Times,* May 7, 1862; Dahlgren, *Memoir of John A. Dahlgren,* 366; *Washington Evening Star,* May 5, 1862; *Washington National Republican,* May 5, 1862; Oliver Otis Howard to Elizabeth Howard, April 13, 1862, Howard Papers, Bowdoin College; Frémont, *Letters,* 323.

7. RECRIMINATIONS

1. *CWL,* 5:207, 209–10; Burlingame, *Lincoln,* 2:312–13; *OR,* 11(3):138, 145; P. H. Watson to Edwin Stanton, May 9, 1862, Stanton Papers, LC. For a pointed and persuasive argument that it was a great mistake on McClellan's part not to meet with Lincoln on the Peninsula, see Sears, *Lincoln's Lieutenants,* 210.

2. Chase, *Papers,* 3:197; *Boston Daily Advertiser,* May 16, 1862; *MCWP,* 253; Bacon and Howland, *My Heart toward Home,* 191; Gilbert Thompson Journal, May 4, 1862, LC; *OR,*

11(1):22; *CCW,* 1:430, 577; Webb, *Peninsula,* 71–72; Ethan Allen Hitchcock, "Notes upon the Report of General George B. McClellan," n.d., Hitchcock Papers, LC, 46–47.

3. Sears, *To the Gates of Richmond,* 70–82; Wainwright, *Diary of Battle,* 57; *OR,* 11(1):130, 449, 11(3):143; Hard, *Eighth Cavalry Regiment, Illinois Volunteers,* 113; Joinville, *Army of the Potomac,* 55; *CCW,* 1:430.

4. *MCWP,* 256–58; *OR: Supplement,* 2:52, 54; Hebert, *Fighting Joe Hooker,* 89–90; Kearny, *Letters from the Peninsula,* 60, 74–75; Osborn, *No Middle Ground,* 22, 30–31; Philip Kearny to Oliver S. Halstead, May 15, 1862, ALPLC. For a full discussion of the generalship at Williamsburg and the fallout afterward, see Sears, *Lincoln's Lieutenants,* 204–8.

5. *New York Times,* May 7, 1862; Daly, *Diary of a Union Lady,* 127; *Washington National Republican,* May 13, 1862; *New York Herald,* May 8, 10–11, 1862. A skeptical Ohio woman, who followed the war news closely, sarcastically wondered if McClellan, despite the victory at Williamsburg, would "wait another year before he does anything of importance." Janney, *Civil War Period Journals,* 117.

6. Burlingame, *Lincoln,* 2:314; Nicolay, *With Lincoln in the White House,* 77; Seward, *Seward at Washington,* 95; Chase, *Papers,* 1:345; Schuckers, *Life and Public Services of Salmon Portland Chase,* 435–36; Hay, *Lincoln's Journalist,* 260–61.

7. *Washington National Republican,* May 7, 9, 1862; *Boston Herald,* May 8, 1862; *Chicago Tribune,* May 10, 1862.

8. Hyde, *Civil War Letters,* 4–5; Moore, *Rebellion Record,* 5 (Rumors and Incidents):26; Murray, *Seneca County Troops,* 26; *MCWP,* 255; *CCW,* 1:20, 353–54, 578, 604; *OR,* 11(1):130, 11(3):146; Browning and Silver, *Environmental History,* 56–59; Noe, *Howling Storm,* 136–39.

9. *MOS,* 353; Sears, *McClellan,* 184; *OR,* 11(3):146–47, 151; *New York Times,* May 8, 1862.

10. *MCWP,* 258–60.

11. *CWL,* 5:207–8; Rafuse, *McClellan's War,* 211–12; *OR: Supplement,* 2:40, 56; Sears, *Lincoln's Lieutenants,* 208–9.

12. Donaldson, *Inside the Army of the Potomac,* 76; Duff, *To Petersburg,* 56; Glaza-Herrington, *Dear Brother and Sister,* 285–86; French, *Witness to the Young Republic,* 396–97; *Washington Evening Star,* May 8, 1862; *Boston Herald,* May 9, 1862; Samuel L. M. Barlow to GBM, May 10, 1862, Barlow Letterbook 7, BPHL, reel 7.

13. *Congressional Globe,* 37th Cong., 2nd sess., 2041; *New York Times,* May 10, 16, 1862; Meade, *Life and Letters,* 1:266; John Gibbon to his wife, May 11, 1862, Gibbon Papers, Historical Society of Pennsylvania; Samuel L. M. Barlow to Stewart Van Vliet, May 10, 1862, Barlow Letterbook 7, BPHL, reel 7.

14. Palfrey, "Period Which Elapsed," 167–68; *MOS,* 354; *MCWP,* 260–62; *OR,* 11(3):166.

15. Macnamara, *Ninth Regiment Massachusetts Volunteer Infantry,* 84–85; Jesse Gove Journal, May 11, 1862, Gove Family Papers, LC; Auchmuty, *Letters of Richard Tylden Auchmuty,* 54; *OR: Supplement,* 2:119; McFadden, *Aunt and the Soldier Boys,* 22; Hays, *Life and Letters,* 216; *OR,* 11(3):169–70, 174; *MCWP,* 264–65.

16. *OR,* 11(3):66, 107, 149–50, 169–70, 174–74; Patrick, *Inside Lincoln's Army,* 67; comte de Paris, *Voyage en Amérique,* 399–400; *New York Times,* May 11, 1862; William H. Seward to AL, May 15, 1862, ALPLC; *MCWP,* 267; *CWL,* 5:216.

17. *OR,* 11(1):27–28; *CWL,* 5:219–20; *CCW,* 1:261–64; Irvin McDowell to C. A. Hechscher, June 17, 1862, copy, BPHL; John Tucker to Edwin M. Stanton, May 20, 1862, Stanton Papers, LC; John W. Ames to his father, May 24, 1862, Ames Papers, Coco Collection, Harrisburg Civil War Round Table Collection, AHEC; *OR: Supplement,* 2:58. For secondary accounts of Lincoln's decision and McClellan's response, see Rafuse, *McClellan's War,* 212–16; and Sears, *Lincoln's Lieutenants,* 216–17. For an argument that the addition of McDowell to McClellan's army would likely have changed the course of the campaign, see Mark Grimsley, "Lincoln as Commander in Chief: Forays into Generalship," in Engle, *War Worth Fighting,* 81.

18. *MCWP,* 269; Fitz John Porter to Manton Marble, May 21, 1862, Marble Papers, LC, reel 1; Heman Dyer to Edwin M. Stanton, May 16, 1862, Stanton Papers, LC; *OR,* 19(2):725–28; *New York Times,* May 20, 1862.

19. Fessenden, *Life and Public Services of William Pitt Fessenden,* 1:260–61; *Chicago Tribune,* May 17, 19, 1862; *Boston Daily Advertiser,* May 19, 1862; *Washington Evening Star,* May 17, 27, 1862; Chase, *Papers,* 3:203; Nicolay, *With Lincoln in the White House,* 78.

20. *OR,* 11(3):179–80, 182, 184; *MOS,* 394; Winslow, *John Sedgwick,* 13; John E. Wool to GBM, May 24, 1862, MPLC; *New York Times,* May 22, 24, 1862; *Chicago Tribune,* May 23, 1862; Castleman, *Army of the Potomac,* 147. On the importance and use of intelligence provided by runaway slaves to the Army of the Potomac before and during the Peninsula Campaign, see Brasher, *Peninsula Campaign & the Necessity of Emancipation,* 82–85, 119–21, 127–31, 167–69, 182–83.

21. William Watts Folwell Diary, May 18, 1862, University of Minnesota Archives; Northup and Northup, *Drifting to an Unknown Future,* 32; McAllister, *Civil War Letters,* 163; *MCWP,* 269–74; Samuel P. Heintzelman to Henry Wilson, May 21, 1862, Heintzelman Papers, LC, reel 9.

22. *CWL,* 5:232–33; Browning, *Diary* 1:546–47; *OR,* 51(1):75, 12(3):219–21; *CCW,* 1:264–69. Mark Grimsley has characterized Lincoln's intervention in the Valley Campaign as a "well intentioned but misguided military adventure." Grimsley, "Lincoln as Commander in Chief," 84. For other assessments in varying degrees critical of both Lincoln and McClellan, see Williams, *Lincoln and His Generals,* 102–5; and Sears, *McClellan,* 187–91.

23. *CWL,* 5:231–32; *MCWP,* 275; *OR,* 11(1):30–31.

24. GBM, "The Peninsular Campaign," in Johnson and Buel, *Battles and Leaders,* 2:180; Fishel, *Secret War for the Union,* 154–57; John Tucker to Edwin M. Stanton, May 22, 1862, Stanton Papers, LC.

25. *CWL,* 5:235–37; *MCWP,* 275–76.

26. Nicolay, *With Lincoln in the White House,* 78–79; *OR,* ser. 3, 2:70; Chase, *Papers,* 2:204; Fessenden, *Life and Public Services of William Pitt Fessenden,* 1:262–63.

27. *CWL,* 5:239; *OR,* 11(1):32, 11(3):192; *MCWP,* 277.

28. *MCWP,* 277–78.

29. *Boston Herald,* May 27, 1862; *New York Times,* May 27, 1862; *Washington Daily National Intelligencer,* May 26, 1862; *Chicago Tribune,* May 26, 1862; McFadden, *Aunt and the Soldier Boys,* 24; Brewster, *When This Cruel War Is Over,* 141; Henry A. McAllister to "My Friend Ann," June 1, 1862, Robinson Family Papers, Rokeby Museum; *Boston Daily Advertiser,* May 24, 1862; *Washington Evening Star,* May 31, 1862.

30. *Washington Evening Star*, May 28, 1862; Sumner, *Selected Letters*, 2:114–15; *Principia* (New York), May 22, 1862; Gillam, *Letters*, 162–64; John W. Ames to his father, May 18, 1862, Ames Papers, Coco Collection, Harrisburg Civil War Roundtable Collection, AHEC. Phil Kearny believed that McClellan would secretly negotiate with southerners to win support in the next presidential election. Kearny, *Letters from the Peninsula*, 87–88.

31. *OR*, 11(1):33, 679; GBM, "Peninsular Campaign," 175–76; Snell, *From First to Last*, 122; Joinville, *Army of the Potomac*, 68–69; *New York Times*, May 28, 1862; *MCWP*, 279–80; *MOS*, 397.

32. *OR*, 11(1):36; *CWL*, 5:244–45; *MCWP*, 279–80.

33. *MCWP*, 278, 281; Sears, *To the Gates of Richmond*, 95–96; Swinton, *Army of the Potomac*, 130–31; Noe, *Howling Storm*, 139–40; Hagerman, "Professionalization of George B. McClellan," 127; *New York Times*, May 29, 1862; *OR*, 12(3):275–76.

34. *MOS*, 365, 377–93. 397–98; *OR*, 11(1):38, 11(3):203; Thompson, *Civil War to the Bloody End*, 208; *OR: Supplement*, 2:65; *CCW*, 1:352, 432; *MCWP*, 284; Sears, *To the Gates of Richmond*, 141; Ellis, *Leaves from the Diary of an Army Surgeon*, 56.

35. *MCWP*, 285–86; Kearny, *Letters from the Peninsula*, 92; Rusling, *Men and Things I Saw in Civil War Days*, 26; *CCW*, 1:22, 366, 445; *OR*, 11(1):130–31; *OR: Supplement*, 2:68, 70–71; Thompson, *Civil War to the Bloody End*, 217–18; Erasmus D. Keyes to Randolph B. Marcy, June 6, 1862, MPLC; *Boston Herald*, June 1, 1862; Weld, *Diary and Letters*, 109; *Chicago Tribune*, June 4, 1862.

36. *OR*, 11(1):42, 44; Joinville, *Army of the Potomac*, 79–80; Haydon, *For Country, Cause, & Leader*, 244–45; McAllister, *Civil War Letters*, 169; *Boston Daily Advertiser*, May 30, 1862; *New York Herald*, June 3, 1862; Sears, *To the Gates of Richmond*, 160–61.

37. *MCWP*, 286–88; Weld, *Diary and Letters*, 111; Murray, *Letters from Berdan's Sharpshooters*, 56; Waters Whipple Braman to his uncle, June 5, 1862, Braman Letters, NYM-MVRC; *OR*, 11(1):44. For an echo of McClellan's ruminations about the costs of battle, see Twichell, *Civil War Letters*, 140. For critiques, see Williams, *Lincoln and His Generals*, 107; and Sears, *Lincoln's Lieutenants*, 230.

38. *CWL*, 5:257–58; *OR*, 11(1):45; *MOS*, 288; *MCWP*, 288; *New York Times*, June 2–3, 1862; *Chicago Tribune*, June 3, 1862. For details on the continuing weather problems, consequent health problems, and an assessment of environmental influences on the campaign, see Noe, *Howling Storm*, 141–43; and Browning and Silver, *Environmental History*, 61–66.

39. *MCWP*, 288–89; *OR*, 11(1):45–46; *MOS*, 399.

40. Browning, *Diary*, 1:548–49; Seward, *Seward at Washington*, 98; Nicolay, *With Lincoln in the War House*, 80; Bates, *Diary*, 260; Christopher P. Wolcott to "My Dear Wife," June 1, 1862, in "Edwin M. Stanton: A Biographical Sketch by His Sister," n.d., Ohio Historical Society.

41. *OR*, 11(3):216, 219; *MCWP*, 289–92; Edge, *McClellan and the Campaign on the Yorktown Peninsula*, 159; *OR: Supplement*, 2:72. On the failure of Lincoln and Stanton (and some historians) to appreciate the importance of weather in military campaigns, see Kenneth W. Noe, "'I Am Completely Checked by the Weather': George B. McClellan, Weather, and the Peninsula Campaign," in Bledsoe and Lang, *Upon the Fields of Battle*, 47–48.

42. *OR*, 11(3):220–21, 223; *MCWP*, 293–96; Sears, *To the Gates of Richmond*, 162; *New York Times*, June 9, 12, 1862.

43. *New York Times,* June 4, 1862; *Boston Herald,* June 13, 1862; Brandegee, *Charlie's Civil War,* 60, 64; John Bigelow to "Dear Judge," June 15, 1862, Bigelow Collection, New-York Historical Society; *Boston Daily Advertiser,* June 4, 1862; *MCWP,* 296–97; Regan, *Lost Civil War Diaries,* 61; Edge, *McClellan and the Campaign on the Yorktown Peninsula,* 159–60; Perkins, "Civil War Diary," 155; Johnson, *Civil War Letters,* 115.

44. Dodge, *On Campaign with the Army of the Potomac,* 9; *MCWP,* 297–98; Joseph C. G. Kennedy to GBM, June 12, 1862, MPLC; *OR,* 11(1):47; Christopher P. Wolcott to "My Dear Wife," June 11, 1862, in "Edwin M. Stanton: A Biographical Sketch by His Sister."

45. Dyer, *Journal of a Civil War Surgeon,* 25; Favill, *Diary of a Young Officer,* 123; Kearny, *Letters from the Peninsula,* 101, 113; Sumner, *Selected Letters,* 2:118; Strong, *Diary,* 3:229.

46. John F. Reynolds to Ellie Reynolds, June 4, 10, 1862, Reynolds Family Papers, Franklin and Marshall College; Sedgwick, *Correspondence,* 2:50; Murray, *Letters from Berdan's Sharpshooters,* 62;

47. *MCWP,* 299–301; *MOS,* 404; E. J. Allen [Allan Pinkerton] to Andrew Porter, June 15, 1862, MPLC; Nicolay and Hay, *Lincoln,* 5:414–15; *OR: Supplement,* 2:77. The long supply lines, muddy roads, and construction of bridges put heavy demands on the engineers. Army, *Engineering Victory,* 123–26.

48. *Alexandria (VA) Gazette,* June 6, 1862; *New York Times,* June 3, 18, 1862; *Chicago Tribune,* June 11, 1862; *Washington Evening Star,* June 12, 1862; L. A. Whitely to James Gordon Bennett, June 15, 1862, Bennett Papers, LC.

49. Dodge, *On Campaign with the Army of the Potomac,* 14, 17; Meade, *Life and Letters,* 1:275; Gillam, *Letters,* 179; Johnson, *Civil War Letters,* 118; Cleaver, *Your Affectionate Son,* 138; Perkins, "Letters Home," 114.

50. *OR,* 11(1):1052–60; *MCWP,* 300; Kearny, *Letters from the Peninsula,* 110. Key saw himself as a political adviser to McClellan, was frequently in contact with Chase, and believed that the army rather than the civilian authorities should bring about emancipation. Styple, *McClellan's Other Story,* 131–33.

51. *New York Daily Tribune,* June 18, 1862; *New York Times,* May 31, June 8, 17, 1862; *Washington National Republican,* July 1, 1862; Edwin Stanton to George B. McClellan, June 7–8, 9, 1862; and McClellan to Stanton, June 8, 1862, Stanton Papers, LC; Marvel, *Lincoln's Autocrat,* 201; Samuel L. M. Barlow to B. Stark, June 28, 1862, Barlow Letterbook 7, BPHL, reel 7; *MOS,* 406–7; *MCWP,* 306.

52. Sears, *To the Gates of Richmond,* 168–72; Strong, *Diary,* 3:231.

53. Irvin McDowell to AL, June 15, 1862; and Winfield Scott to AL, June 24, 1862, ALPLC; *CWL,* 5:272–73, 276; Daly, *Diary of a Union Lady,* 147; Irvin McDowell to his wife, June 15, 1862, McDowell Letters, FSNMP; *OR,* 51(1):79; *MCWP,* 302–3. Even Greeley's *Tribune* recommended sending every available regiment to McClellan. *New York Daily Tribune,* June 19, 1862.

54. *New York Herald,* June 26, 1862; *New York Times,* June 25, 1862; Strong, *Diary,* 3:233; Stoddard, *Dispatches from Lincoln's White House,* 82; Horatio Woodman to Edwin M. Stanton, June 22, 1862, Stanton Papers, LC; Joseph Holt to Theodore S. Bell, June 21, 1862, Civil War Letters Collection, New-York Historical Society; Samuel L. M. Barlow to George B. McClellan, June 17, 1862, Barlow Letterbook 7, BPHL, reel 7; *MCWP,* 305; Kearny, *Letters*

from the Peninsula, 108–10; Hay, *Inside Lincoln's White House,* 231–32; Weld, *Diary and Letters,* 120–21.

55. James W. Riggs to AL, June 17, 1862, ALPLC; Israel Washburn to William H. Seward, July 2, 1862, Stanton Papers, LC; Browning, *Diary,* 1:552; Chase, *Papers,* 3:211–14; *New York Daily Tribune,* June 19, 1862; *Chicago Tribune,* June 23, 1862.

56. *New York Herald,* June 26, 1862; *New York Times,* June 20–21, 1862; *New York World,* June 21, 1864; Meade, *Life and Letters,* 1:277–78; Gillam, *Letters,* 184; *MCWP,* 304; *OR,* 11(3):238–39; Fitz John Porter to Manton Marble, June 20, 1862, Marble Papers, LC, reel 1.

57. *MCWP,* 306–12; *OR: Supplement,* 2:80; Sears, *McClellan,* 204–5; *OR,* 11(1):49, 268.

58. *OR: Supplement,* 2:82; *MCWP,* 312–15, 317; *New York Herald,* July 1, 1862; *OR,* 11(3):257. In the evening, Stanton again tried to reassure McClellan that he wished for him "success and good fortune (and I have never had any other feeling)." *OR,* 11(3):259.

59. Swinton, *Army of the Potomac,* 146–48; *OR,* 11(1):53–55; *CWL,* 5:286.

60. *OR,* 11(1):117–18, 11(3):265; Fitz John Porter, "Hanover Court House and Gaines's Mill," in Johnson and Buel, *Battles and Leaders,* 2:331, 342–42; *MCWP,* 318–21; Sears, *To the Gates of Richmond,* 215–17; *OR: Supplement,* 2:83–84; *CCW,* 1:355. For varying assessments of McClellan decision making, see Sears, *To the Gates of Richmond,* 206, 215–17; and Rafuse, *McClellan's War,* 223–25. For a carefully detailed account (that weighs a great deal of fragmentary and contradictory postwar evidence) with an emphasis on what McClellan expected from Porter's forces, which would bear the brunt of initial Confederate attacks, see Marvel, *Radical Sacrifice,* 160–65.

61. *MCWP,* 322–23. Beginning in 1887 with a statement from McClellan's literary executor, followed by the publication of a memoir by War Department telegraph operator David Homer Bates in 1907, there were claims that the last paragraph of McClellan's dispatch had been suppressed either by Stanton or by his supervisor of telegraphic messages, Colonel Edward Sanford. Instead, as historian William Marvel has persuasively argued, it is likely that both Stanton and Lincoln saw the dispatch, so the gulf between McClellan and the administration only widened. *MOS,* 10–11; Bates, *Lincoln in the Telegraph Office,* 108–10; Marvel, *Lincoln's Autocrat,* 208–9.

62. Nicolay and Hay, *Lincoln,* 5:443; Browning, *Diary,* 1:352. See the fine assessment of this meeting's importance in Pinsker, *Lincoln's Sanctuary,* 23–25.

8. THE BATTLE IS JOINED

1. *CWL,* 5:289–92; Nicolay, *With Lincoln in the White House,* 83; *OR,* 11(3):271. Assistant Secretary of the Navy Gustavus Fox recommended drafting one hundred thousand militia to be trained in Washington and then sent to McClellan for an advance on Richmond. Fox, *Confidential Correspondence,* 2:329.

2. *CWL,* 5:287, 290; Cozzens, *General John Pope,* 71–78; John Pope, "The Second Battle of Bull Run," in Johnson and Buel, *Battle and Leaders.* 2:452–54; Pope, *Military Memoirs,* 119.

3. GBM, "The Peninsular Campaign" in Johnson and Buel, *Battles and Leaders,* 2:182; *MCWP,* 324; *MOS,* 426; *OR: Supplement,* 2:85; Sears, *McClellan,* 216; Charles C. Fulton to AL, June 29, 1862, ALPLC; *CWL,* 5:292–93.

4. *CCW,* 1:356, 436–37, 592; Castleman, *Army of the Potomac,* 168–69; *MOS,* 426–28; Sears, *To the Gates of Richmond,* 265; Rafuse, *McClellan's War,* 226; Joinville, *Army of the Potomac,* 93; William B. Franklin, "Rear-Guard Fighting during the Change of Base," in Johnson and Buel, *Battles and Leaders,* 2:370–71.

5. *OR,* 11(1):120; Rafuse, *McClellan's War,* 227; *MOS,* 428–34; Franklin, "Rear-Guard Fighting," 377; Sears, *To the Gates of Richmond,* 278–81; Sears, *McClellan,* 218–19; *Official Records of the Union and Confederate Navies,* ser. 1, 7:709; *MCWP,* 325–26. For a detailed account of McClellan's movements, see Burton, *Extraordinary Circumstances,* 242–44. Burton, Sears, and Rafuse all present telling critiques of what they interpret as a dereliction of command responsibility.

6. Dahlgren, *Memoir of John A. Dahlgren,* 374–75; Burlingame, *Lincoln,* 2:322; *CWL,* 5:295–97; *OR,* 11(3):276–77, 280; Seward, *Seward at Washington,* 102.

7. *MCWP,* 327–28; *CCW,* 1:357–58, 364, 436–37, 449, 573; Joinville, *Army of the Potomac,* 95–96; Keyes, *Fifty Years' Observation,* 482–83; Fitz John Porter, "The Battle of Malvern Hill," in Johnson and Buel, *Battles and Leaders,* 2:414; William F. Biddle to John C. Ropes, March 27, 1895, Ropes Papers, Boston University; Sears, *To the Gates of Richmond,* 309, 320, 336; Fitz John Porter to GBM, July 1, 1862, MPLC ; *OR,* 51(1):712–13. McClellan's account says little about what he did on July 1. GBM, "Peninsular Campaign," 186–87; *MOS,* 434–437.

8. *CWL,* 5:298, 301.

9. *MCWP,* 329, 333; George L. Kilmer, "The Army of the Potomac at Harrison's Landing," in Johnson and Buel, *Battles and Leaders,* 2:427; *CCW,* 1:26, 365; *MOS,* 481–82; Edwin Stanton to David Hunter, June 3, 1862, Stanton Papers, LC; *OR,* 11(3):290–91, 294; *CWL,* 5:303; Noe, *Howling Storm,* 157–58; Burton, *Extraordinary Circumstances,* 371–72.

10. *CWL,* 5:305–6; *MCWP,* 334–38. For an analysis of McClellan's accomplishments, see Rafuse, *McClellan's War,* 230–31.

11. Porter, "Battle of Malvern Hill," 426–27; *MCWP,* 339; Dodge, *On Campaign with the Army of the Potomac,* 52; Hays, *Life and Letters,* 249; Favill, *Diary of a Young Officer,* 154. McClellan kept promising active operations or even a battle soon. *OR,* 11(3):298–99; *MCWP,* 340.

12. Gilbert Thompson Journal, July 6, 1862, LC; Truman Seymour to Ira Harris, July 7, 1862, Civil War Letters Collection, New-York Historical Society; Fry, *Republic in the Ranks,* 15, 37; Krom, *First Minnesota,* 234; Ellis, *Leaves from the Diary of an Army Surgeon,* 163–64; Patrick, *Inside Lincoln's Army,* 103–4; French, *Witness to the Young Republic,* 401; Newman, "A Democrat in Lincoln's Army," 160; William T. H. Brooks to his father, July 5, 1862, Brooks Papers, AHEC; Bowen, *Dear Friends at Home,* 122–23; Haydon, *For County, Cause, & Leader,* 263–64; Dexter, *Seymour Dexter,* 73–74.

13. Bennett, *Musket and Sword,* 62–63; Breyfogle, *Story,* 185–86; Rusling, *Men and Things I Saw in Civil War Days,* 262; Favill, *Diary of a Young Officer,* 156–57; Barlow, *"Fear Was Not in Him,"* 91, 93–94; Osborn, *No Middle Ground,* 62; Castleman, *Army of the Potomac,* 178; Hadley, "Indiana Soldier in Love and War," 216.

14. Greene, *Letters to My Wife,* 31; Gaff, *On Many a Bloody Field,* 141; Young, *Dear Delia,* 79–80; Chase, *Yours for the Union,* 114.

15. *Boston Daily Advertiser,* July 2, 4, 7, 1862; Olmsted, *Papers,* 4:390–91; Gallman, *Ca-*

cophony of Politics, 75; Norton, *Army Letters,* 98; John Darragh Wilkins to his wife, July 9, 1862, Wilkins Papers, Schoff Civil War Collection, Clements Library, University of Michigan.

16. *New York Daily Tribune,* July 4, 1862; *Chicago Tribune,* July 10, 1862; *Boston Daily Advertiser,* July 5, 1862; Samuel L. M. Barlow to Mary Ellen McClellan, July 2, 1862, Barlow Letterbook 7, BPHL, reel 7.

17. *Boston Herald,* July 2, 1862; *Boston Daily Advertiser,* July 2, 1862; *Chicago Tribune,* July 3, 1862; *New York Herald,* July 6, 1862; *Louisville (KY) Daily Journal,* July 4, 1862; *New York Times,* July 10, 1862; *Washington Evening Star,* July 10, 1862.

18. Strong, *Diary,* 3:233, 234–35, 236–37; Virginia L. Woodbury Diary, June 29, 1862, Woodbury Papers, LC; *New York Times,* July 1, 2, 4, 1862; French, *Witness to the Young Republic,* 400–401; Horace Greeley to Joshua R. Giddings, June 29, 1862, Giddings Papers, Ohio Historical Society, reel 5.

19. Fessenden, *Life and Public Services of William Pitt Fessenden,* 1:263–64; Joshua R. Giddings to Grotius Giddings, July 3, 1862, Giddings Papers, Ohio Historical Society, reel 5; *Washington Evening Star,* July 7, 1862; Swinton, *Army of the Potomac,* 169–70.

20. Browning, *Diary,* 1:556–57; *New York Times,* July 6, 1862; Nicolay, *With Lincoln in the White House,* 84; Burlingame, *Lincoln,* 2:324; *Addresses Delivered at the Lincoln Dinner,* 307–8; Wilson and Davis, *Herndon's Informants,* 189–90; Nicolay, *Oral History of Abraham Lincoln,* 83–84.

21. *New York Herald,* July 4, 1862; John P. Sanderson to AL, July 4, 1862, ALPLC; McClure, Lamphier, and Kregar, *"Spur Up your Pegasus,"* 207; Schuckers, *Life and Public Services of Salmon Portland Chase,* 448; Oberholtzer, *Jay Cooke,* 1:197–98; Seward, *Seward at Washington,* 113–14; Strong, *Diary,* 3:234–35; Fessenden, *Life and Public Services of William Pitt Fessenden,* 1:263–64; Gurowski, *Diary,* 1:256.

22. *New York Herald,* July 10, 11, 14, 1862; Nicolay, *With Lincoln in the White House,* 85; *New York Daily Tribune,* July 10, 1862; *New York Times,* July 11, 1862; Wormeley, *Other Side of War,* 189; *OR: Supplement,* 2:93; *OR,* 11(3):307; Macnamara, *Ninth Regiment Massachusetts Volunteer Infantry,* 172; Sears, *McClellan,* 227; Robertson, *Diary of the War,* 42; Fuller, *Recollections of the War of 1861,* 46; Twichell, *Civil War Letters,* 165–66.

23. *CWL,* 309–12; Keyes, *Fifty Years' Observation,* 486–87; *OR,* 11(3):313–14; *OR: Supplement,* 2:94.

24. *MCWP,* 341, 348–49.

25. *MCWP,* 304; *CWL,* 5:279–80; *OR,* 11(1):48.

26. *MCWP,* 344–45. On July 12, during a meeting at the White House, Lincoln appealed to border-state representatives to support a policy of compensated emancipation. Whether this had some connection with McClellan's recommendations is unclear. *CWL,* 317–19; Gideon Welles to Montgomery Blair, November 23, 1873, Blair Family Papers, LC.

27. *MCWP,* 346; *MOS,* 487; Cox, *Military Reminiscences,* 1:357–58. For a largely favorable treatment of the Harrison's Landing letter, see Randall, *Lincoln the President,* 2:102–4. The sharpest historical critiques began with Nicolay and Hay, *Lincoln,* 5:449–52. For especially strong criticism of McClellan, see Nevins, *War for the Union,* 2:160. For more evenhanded treatment, see Williams, *Lincoln and His Generals,* 132–33; Paludan, *Presidency of Abraham Lincoln,* 140–41; and Cooling, *Counter-Thrust,* 15–17. More broadly speaking, the Civil War

illustrates the great difficulty in neatly separating military activity from political activity. For useful comments on the theory involved, see Risa Brooks, "The Paradoxes of Huntingtonian Professionalism," in Beehner, Brooks, and Mauer, *Reconsidering American Civil-Military Relations*, 20–31.

28. *MOS*, 446–47; Nicolay, *With Lincoln in the White House*, 85; *Boston Herald*, July 12, 1862; *Washington National Republican*, July 12, 1862; *New York Times*, July 12, 1862; Burlingame, *Lincoln*, 2:230; Browning, *Diary*, 1:557, 559–60; *CWL*, 5:322.

29. *MCWP*, 357; *OR*, ser. 2, 4:221. Quartermaster General Meigs was probably the source of Lincoln's 160,000 figure. *CCW*, 1:295–97.

30. Browning, *Diary*, 1:558; Pope, *Military Memoirs*, 122–23; Flower, *Edwin McMasters Stanton*, 171; Edwin Stanton to Randolph B. Marcy, July 5, 1862, MPLC.

31. Edwin Stanton to GBM, July 5, 1862, MPLC; *MCWP*, 346–47.

32. "Edwin M. Stanton: A Biographical Sketch by His Sister," n.d., Ohio Historical Society, 157; Goodwin, *Team of Rivals*, 448; Marvel, *Lincoln's Autocrat*, 211; Schuckers, *Life and Public Services of Salmon Portland Chase*, 447–48.

33. Stoddard, *Dispatches from Lincoln's White House*, 85; *Daily Cleveland Herald*, July 8, 1862; *New York Times*, July 4, 21, 1862; *New York Herald*, July 4, 1862; Gurowski, *Diary*, 1:228–29; *OR*, ser. 3, 2:219; Daly, *Diary of a Union Lady*, 160; Orville Hickman Browning to AL, August 11, 1862, ALPLC.

34. *New York Times*, July 10, 1862; *Boston Daily Advertiser*, July 5, 1862; Strong, *Diary*, 3:239; Olmsted, *Papers*, 381–82, 402; *New York Herald*, July 7, 1862; Albert Cross Diary, July 14, 1862, Special Collections, University of Iowa, Iowa City.

35. John Gibbon to his wife, July 5, 1862, Gibbon Papers, Historical Society of Pennsylvania; *New York Herald*, June 3, 1862; Hodge, *Life of Charles Hodge*, 475; Wilson, "Types and Traditions of the Old Army," 556; *CWL*, 5:312–13; Burlingame, *Lincoln*, 2:369–70; Marszalek, *Commander of All Lincoln's Armies*, 127–28; Hay, *Inside Lincoln's White House*, 191–92.

36. Wilson, "Types and Traditions of the Old Army," 556–57; *MCWP*, 354–55, 361, 364–65, 367, 374; Samuel L. M. Barlow to Henry D. Bacon, July 19, 1862; and Barlow to McClellan, July 18, 1862, Barlow Letterbook 7, BPHL, reel 7.

37. *OR*, 11(3):295; *MCWP*, 342–43; *CCW* 1:279–80; Wilkes, *McClellan: From Ball's Bluff to Antietam*, 5–8; Pope, "Second Battle of Bull Run," 455–56; Chase, *Papers*, 1:350; William H. Kindig to Henry A. Bitner, July 21, 1862, Bitner Papers, University of Virginia; Matsui, *First Republican Army*, 33, 73.

38. Cozzens, *General John Pope*, 85–86; Sears, *Civil War: The Second Year*, 329–31; *MCWP*, 368. Engineer Barnard—no great fan of McClellan and agreed with Lincoln that the Army of the Potomac should be withdrawn from the Peninsula—expected for Pope that "downfall which commonly follows empty conceit when it is charged with weighty affairs." Fox, *Confidential Correspondence*, 2:323–25.

39. Olmsted, *Papers*, 4:397; *OR*, 11(3):320, 332; Breyfogle, *Story*, 188; *Boston Herald*, July 21, 1862; Fry, "McClellan's Epidemic," 7–18. On the effects of the heat and humidity, see Noe, *Howling Storm*, 159–61; and Browning and Silver, *Environmental History*, 62–64.

40. Kearny, *Letters from the Peninsula*, 125; J. G. Barnard to GBM, July 2, 1862; and GBM to Mary Ellen McClellan, July 15, 1862, MPLC; Olmsted, *Papers*, 4:397; *MCWP*, 353, 358–59,

360–68. On July 20, the Army of the Potomac had slightly over 100,000 men "present for duty" but still nearly 40,000 "absent." *OR,* 11(3):329.

41. Rhodes, *All for the Union,* 74; Chase, *Yours for the Union,* 117; Roy, *Recollections of a Prisoner of War,* 116–17; Acton, "Dear Mollie," 36; Faller and Faller, *Dear Folks at Home,* 81; Spiegel, *Your True Marcus,* 126, 133.

42. Murray, *Ontario County Troops,* 45–46; Norton, *Army Letters,* 101–2; Murray, *Letters from Berdan's Sharpshooters,* 90; Whitman, *Civil War Letters,* 59; Bowen, *Dear Friends at Home,* 125–26; Acton, "Dear Mollie," 37; *Pittsburg Evening Chronicle,* July 25, 1862; Bowen, *From Ball's Bluff to Gettysburg,* 115–16; Matsui, *First Republican Army,* 146. Some of this commentary reflected signs of growing political divisions in the army between Republican- and Democratic-leaning volunteers. Fry, *Republic in the Ranks,* 39–41, 44–45. John G. Barnard had grown increasingly critical of McClellan but still believed that Little Mac's plans had been "upset and perverted. *Everybody* seems to have had a hand in meddling—the President—Secretaries of State, Treasury, as well as of war and I know not how many others. . . . [H]ad McDowell *come with us* as was intended we would have been in Richmond in 3 or 4 weeks." Fox, *Confidential Correspondence,* 2:330.

43. Fry, "McClellan's Epidemic," 18–23; Sears, *Lincoln's Lieutenants,* 273; Barlow, *"Fear Was Not in Him,"* 99; Smith, *Swamp Doctor,* 25; *Boston Herald,* July 21, 1862.

44. Zachariah Chandler to his wife, July 6, 1862, Chandler Papers, LC; *Congressional Globe,* 37th Cong., 2nd sess., pt. 4, 3134, 3149, 3219–26; *New York Times,* July 11, 1862.

45. Zachariah Chandler to his wife, July 11, 1862, Chandler Papers, LC; *Washington Evening Star,* July 9, 1862; *Washington National Republican,* July 10, 1862; *Principia* (New York), July 10, 1862.

46. *CCW,* 1:102; *Congressional Globe,* 37th Cong., 2nd sess., pt. 4, 3386–92. This speech soon appeared as a pamphlet: Chandler, *Conduct of the War.*

47. Detroit Post and Tribune, *Zachariah Chandler,* 238–39; "Hon. Z. Chandler," 202; George, *Zachariah Chandler,* 81–82n; Thomas and Hyman, *Stanton,* 212; *McClellan's Campaign,* 3–12; Samuel L. M. Barlow to George B. McClellan, July 18, 1862, Barlow Letterbook 7, BPHL, reel 7; *MCWP,* 369; Ambrose E. Burnside to GBM, July 15, 1862, MPLC.

48. *Chicago Tribune,* July 13, 25, 1862; Bacon and Howland, *My Heart toward Home,* 270; *New York Times,* July 14, 1862; *Boston Herald,* July 18, 1862; *Liberator* (Boston), July 18, 1862; Charles Francis Adams Diary, July 19, 1862, Massachusetts Historical Society; Morris Kimball to Zachariah Chandler, July 23, 1862, Chandler Papers, LC; Neely, *Union Divided,* 71.

49. Denslow, *Frémont and McClellan,* 3–29; Stuart McKee to Richard Yates, July 18, 1862, Yates Family Papers, Abraham Lincoln Presidential Library; *New York Times,* July 22, 1862; J. Eastman Johnson to Zachariah Chandler, July 15, 1862, Chandler Papers, LC. McClellan told a New York senator that his army had provided both protection and employment for slaves who came into his lines, but "the supply of these operatives has thus far been insufficient for our wants." *MCWP,* 353.

50. Olmsted, *Papers,* 4:399; *Boston Daily Advertiser,* July 9, 14, 25, 1862; *Proceedings of the Mass Meeting of Loyal Citizens,* 53–55; *New York Herald,* July 15, 25, 1862; *New York Times,* July 17, 1862.

51. *Boston Herald,* July 14, 1862; *New York Times,* July 17, 1862; *Washington National Republican,* July 14, 1862; Robert H. McCurdy and James W. White to AL, July 14, 1862; and William D. Kelley to AL, July 23, 1862, ALPLC; Stoddard, *Lincoln's White House Secretary,* 288; Hay, *At Lincoln's Side,* 22; *Chicago Tribune,* July 22, 1862; Chase, *Papers,* 1:350–51, 3:229–30; Francis P. Blair to Francis P. Blair Jr., July 25, 1862, Blair Family Papers, LC.

52. *MCWP,* 351, 362; Alfred Pleasonton to Joseph Holt, July 14, 1862, Holt Papers, LC; *OR: Supplement,* 2:96–97.

53. Browning, *Diary,* 1:563; Strother, *Virginia Yankee in the Civil War,* 69; *Boston Daily Advertiser,* July 23, 1862; *New York Herald,* July 24, 1862; Hoffman, *Vermont Cavalryman in War and Love,* 126; J. W. Alsop to GBM, July 24, 1862, MPLC. There was some speculation that Halleck's appointment might lead to McClellan's resignation, but he assured one friend that this was not the case. McClellan later described how Halleck, upon his arrival in Washington, had warned him to be wary of Stanton. At the same time, Stanton had told him that Halleck was a man devoid of principle. William Aspinwall to Mary Ellen McClellan, July 24, 1862; and Aspinwall to GBM, July 24, 1862, MPLC; *MCWP,* 371; *MOS,* 137.

54. *OR,* 11(3):337–38, 12(2):5; Sears, *McClellan,* 239–41; *CCW,* 1:638. At this time, Petersburg was lightly defended and might have been easy pickings. Grant would adopt such a strategy two years later.

55. Wilson, "Types and Traditions of the Old Army," 557; *OR,* 11(3):338–39; *OR: Supplement,* 2:98–99; Meigs, "General M. C. Meigs on the Conduct of the War," 293–94.

56. Swinton, *Army of the Potomac,* 170–71; *OR,* 11(3):340–41; Wilson, "Types and Traditions of the Old Army," 557; *Chicago Tribune,* July 21, 1862; *New York Herald,* July 28, 1862; *Boston Herald,* July 31, 1862.

57. GBM, "From the Peninsula to Antietam: Posthumous Notes," in Johnson and Buel, *Battles and Leaders,* 2:548; *MCWP,* 370–71, 373–74, 375; Fishel, "Pinkerton and McClellan," 129; William Watts Folwell Diary, July 24, 1862, University of Minnesota Archives; Stowe, "Life with the 15th Mass.," 49; *MOS,* 455; *New York Times,* July 30, 1862; *New York Herald,* July 31, 1862, For details on the Army of the Potomac's activities in late July and early August, see Rafuse, *McClellan's War,* 248–50. For an assessment of a possible move on Petersburg, see Cooling, *Counter-Thrust,* 28–31.

58. Bright and Bright, *"Respects to All,"* 37–38; Virginia L. Woodbury Diary, August 3, 1862, Woodbury Papers, LC; Perkins, "Letters Home," 120; Robert S. Robertson to his parents, August 1, 1862, Robertson Papers, FSNMP; *New York Herald,* July 29, 1862.

59. Brewster, *When This Cruel War Is Over,* 178; Dyer, *Journal of a Civil War Surgeon,* 31; *National Antislavery Standard* (New York), July 26, 1862; Wilkes, *McClellan: From Ball's Bluff to Antietam,* 8–17; Janney, *Civil War Period Journals,* 131–32; Trefousse, *Benjamin Franklin Wade,* 173; *New York Times,* July 28, August 1, 1862.

60. Strong, *Diary,* 3:244–45; Jellison, *Fessenden,* 150; Harrison G. O. Blake to AL, July 28, 1862; and John Hutchins to AL, July 31, 1862, ALPLC; *Liberator* (Boston), July 25, 1862.

61. Chase, *Papers,* 1:353–54, 358; Caleb B. Smith to Edwin M. Stanton, July 29, 1862, Stanton Papers, LC; *Washington National Republican,* August 2, 1862; Nicolay and Hay, *Lincoln,* 6:3.

62. *MCWP,* 372, 375, 376–78; *OR: Supplement,* 2:99–100; *OR,* 11(1):76–77. McClellan failed to answer this dispatch about the removal of the sick. Ibid., 79.

63. *OR,* 11(3):343.

64. *MCWP,* 380–81.

65. *MCWP,* 382–83; Mary Ellen McClellan to GBM, August 3, 1862; and Ambrose E. Burnside to GBM, August 2, 1862, MPLC

66. *OR,* 11(1):77, 80–81; *MCWP,* 383–85. For army reaction to the withdrawal order, see *OR: Supplement,* 2:102; and Powell, *Fifth Army Corps,* 192.

9. SHELVED AND RETURNED

1. *OR,* 11(1):82–83, 11(3):359–60.

2. *OR,* 11(1):78–79, 84–85, 11(3):355; Wilson, "Types and Traditions of the Old Army," 557.

3. *MCWP,* 389–90; Fitz John Porter to Manton Marble, August 10, 1862, Marble Papers, LC, reel 1; *OR: Supplement,* 2:105; Fry, "McClellan's Epidemic," 24; Chase, *Yours for the Union,* 130; Abbott, *Fallen Leaves,* 134.

4. Cozzens, *General John Pope,* 77, 80–82, 87–88.

5. Herman Hattaway and Archer Jones describe Cedar Mountain as an "ill-fought battle, mismanaged by both sides." Hattaway and Jones, *How the North Won,* 223.

6. John P. Hatch to his father, August 9, 1862, Hatch Papers, LC; L. A. Whitely to James Gordon Bennett, July 29, 1862, Bennett Papers, LC; Fitz John Porter to Manton Marble, August 10, 1862, Marble Papers, LC, reel 1; *OR,* 11(1):85–86; *MOS,* 466.

7. *MCWP,* 387–88; Fitz John Porter to Manton Marble, August 5, 1862, Marble Papers, LC, reel 1; *OR: Supplement,* 2:104; Samuel L. M. Barlow to GBM, August 9. 1862, MPLC. On August 9, McClellan issued a lengthy order, dealing with civilian property and slaves, that won warm support from friendly editors and no doubt confirmed the suspicions of his critics. *OR,* 11(3):362–64; *New York Herald,* August 14, 1862; *Boston Daily Advertiser,* August 15, 1862.

8. Chase, *Papers,* 1:243–44; Schuckers, *Life and Public Services of Salmon Portland Chase,* 448–49; Seward, *Seward at Washington,* 121; *Washington National Republican,* August 7, 13, 1862; Vallandigham, *Speeches, Arguments, Addresses, and Letters,* 395, 409.

9. Dahlgren, *Memoir of John A. Dahlgren,* 378; French, *Witness to the Young Republic,* 405; *CWL,* 5:358–59; Chase, *Papers,* 1:360; *Washington Daily National Intelligencer,* August 6, 7, 1862; *Boston Daily Advertiser,* August 8, 1862; *New York Herald,* August 8, 1862. According to one abolitionist editor, Lincoln was still "sailing in the same boat with McClellan and Halleck." Another fretted that recent troop levies would do little good so long as McClellan retained command. *Liberator* (Boston), August 8, 1862; *National Antislavery Standard* (New York), August 9, 1862.

10. Margaret S. Heintzelman to AL, August 9, 1862, ALPLC; *OR: Supplement,* 2:109; *MCWP,* 390–91; Wainwright, *Diary of Battle,* 87; *Boston Daily Advertiser,* August 13, 1862.

11. *OR,* 11(1):87; *MCWP,* 391–92.

12. Fitz John Porter to "My dear Howard," August 12, 1862, Porter Papers, LC, reel 2; Wainwright, *Diary of Battle,* 83; Norton, *Army Letters,* 117; Haydon, *For County, Cause, & Leader,* 270; Smith, *Swamp Doctor,* 40; Meade, *Life and Letters,* 1:302–3.

13. *OR*, 11(1):24, 88–89, 12(3):578–79; *MOS*, 467–68; *New York Times*, August 15, 1862; *New York Herald*, August 19, 1862; *Boston Daily Advertiser*, August 19, 1862. For assessments largely favorable to McClellan on this point, including from scholars whose overall views of the general's performance are much more critical, see Michie, *General McClellan*, 381–82; Sears, *McClellan*, 246–47; and Rafuse, *McClellan's War*, 251–52.

14. *MCWP*, 394–96; Meade, *Life and Letters*, 1:304 *OR*, 11(1):90, 12(3):590, 594–95; Marvel, *Burnside*, 105. According to the few surviving letters, Nelly generally reinforced McClellan's opinions on Pope, Halleck, Lincoln, Stanton, and his own generalship. Mary Ellen McClellan to GBM, August 23, 1862, MPLC.

15. *OR*, 12(3):599, 606–7, 11(3):379–80; *MCWP*, 397.

16. *MOS*, 469–70; *MCWP*, 397–99; *OR*, 11(1):92, 12(3), 615–16. Halleck reported to Stanton that some corps in the Army of the Potomac had advanced quickly but that "the delays of others were neither creditable nor excusable." *OR*, 12(2):7–8. Some Potomac soldiers expected their commander soon to be gone and criticized him for blaming any failures on Washington. Others repeated the familiar complaints that Little Mac always seemed to be entrenching and even concluded that the entire Peninsula Campaign had been a disgrace. Favill, *Diary of a Young Officer*, 174; Trobriand, *Our Noble Blood*, 68; Colby, *Civil War Papers*, 134.

17. *MOS*, 508; *New York Times*, August 24, 1862; *OR*, 12(3):645–46, 659–60, 672–73, 11(1):94; Ropes, *Army under Pope*, 153–54; *MCWP*, 405–6.

18. *OR*, 11(1):94–95, 12(3):688–92; *MCWP*, 406–10; *CWL*, 5:396. Halleck denied having made any disparaging remarks about McClellan concerning the Confederate raid on Manassas. *OR*, 12 (3):690. For varying assessments of McClellan's actions on August 27, see Sears, *McClellan*, 250–51; and Rafuse, *McClellan's War*, 258–61.

19. Castleman, *Army of the Potomac*, 193, 203; Alexander S. Webb to his father, August 14, 1862, Webb Papers, Sterling Library, Yale University; *OR: Supplement*, 2:106–7, 109; Cox, *Military Reminiscences*, 1:241–42; Haupt, *Reminiscences*, 98–99.

20. *OR*, 11(1):97, 12(3):706–12; *MCWP*, 411–14.

21. *OR*, 11(1):100, 12(3):722–23; *MCWP*, 415, 417; *CWL*, 5:399.

22. *MCWP*, 417–18; *OR*, 12(3):723–24. For defenses of McClellan's dealings with Pope and excuses for the controversial telegram to Lincoln, see Upton, *Military Policy of the United States*, 353–61; and Hassler, *McClellan*, 204–12. For more critical and persuasive assessments that still stop short of saying that McClellan wanted Pope defeated, see Sears, *McClellan*, 251–54; Rafuse, *McClellan's War*, 263–66, 271–72; and Cozzens, *General John Pope*, 107–9.

23. John Pope to AL, August 30, 1862, ALPLC; *OR*, 12(3):741, 744–47, 11(1):101; *MCWP*, 419–22. For the role of transportation bottlenecks in the various troop movements on August 30, see Cooling, *Counter-Thrust*, 127.

24. Welles, *Diary*, 1:83; Hay, *Lincoln's Journalist*, 291; *Chicago Tribune*, August 18, 1862; Gurowski, *Diary*, 1:250; Chase, *Papers*, 1:363; William Watts Folwell Diary, August 22, 1862, University of Minnesota Archives; Janney, *Civil War Period Journals*, 138; *Washington Evening Star*, August 22, 1862; *Chicago Tribune*, August 23, 27, 1862; *Boston Herald*, August 20, 23, 1862.

25. *MCWP*, 422–26; *OR*, 11(1):102–3, 12(3):773.

26. Mary Ellen McClellan to GBM, August 30, 1862, MPLC; Welles, *Diary*, 1:83; SPHJ, August 22, 1862, reel 7; Olmsted, *Papers*, 4:413–14.

27. *OR,* 12(3):706, 739–41; Chase, *Papers,* 1:366.

28. *Cincinnati Gazette,* n.d., in *Chicago Tribune,* August 28, 1862; Cullom, *Fifty Years of Public Service,* 92; Israel Washburn Jr. to AL, August 28, 1862, ALPLC.

29. Chase, *Papers,* 3:255; Schuckers, *Life and Public Services of Salmon Portland Chase,* 449–50; Strother, *Virginia Yankee in the Civil War,* 97. McDowell was convinced that many officers in the Army of the Potomac who "came to us [i.e., the Army of Virginia] did so with a grudge and without any heart for the work. They wanted us to fall behind the works at Washington where we should come under McClellan's orders." Irvin McDowell to his wife, September 4, 1862, McDowell Letters, FSNMP.

30. Flower, *Edwin McMasters Stanton,* 176–77; Edwin M. Stanton, Salmon P. Chase, Caleb B. Smith, and Edward Bates to AL, n.d., 1862, Stanton Papers, LC; Chase, *Papers,* 1:366–67; Welles, *Diary,* 1:93–98; Hay, *Inside Lincoln's White House,* 37.

31. Welles, *Diary,* 1:99; Hay, *Inside Lincoln's White House,* 37–38.

32. *OR,* 12(3):786–87, 12(2):82–83, 19(1):36; Schurz, *Reminiscences,* 2:379; Cox, *Military Reminiscences,* 1:242–43; *MCWP,* 428.

33. Nicolay and Hay, *Lincoln,* 6:21; *OR,* 11(1):104; *MCWP,* 427; Raymond, "Extracts from the Journal of Henry J. Raymond," 423; J. E. Edwards to GBM, April 12, 1883, MPLC.

34. Warden, *Life and Public Services of Salmon Portland Chase,* 457; Welles, *Diary,* 1:100–102; *Washington National Republican,* September 1, 1862; Chase, *Papers,* 1:367–69.

35. Schuckers, *Life and Public Services of Salmon Portland Chase,* 450; Gideon Welles to Montgomery Blair, November 23, 1873, Blair Family Papers, LC; Bates copy of remonstrance against McClellan, September 2, 1862, ALPLC; Flower, *Edwin McMasters Stanton,* 178–79; *New York Evening Post,* July 13, 1891; *CCW,* 1:438; *MOS,* 534; *MCWP,* 428; *CWL,* 5:486; Chase, *Papers,* 1:368; Welles, *Diary,* 1:101–2. Chase later compared Lincoln's reinstatement of McClellan to "the case of the woman who after yielding everything but the last favor could hardly help yielding that also." Burlingame, *Lincoln,* 2:378.

36. Stevens, *Selected Papers,* 1:320–21; *Boston Daily Advertiser,* September 2, 1862; Wilkes, *McClellan: From Ball's Bluff to Antietam,* 20–21; Reid, *Radical View,* 1:223; Janney, *Civil War Period Journals,* 140; *Washington National Republican,* September 1, 1862; *New York Times,* September 2, 1862.

37. Oberholtzer, *Jay Cooke,* 1:202–4; *Chicago Tribune,* August 30, 1862; *New York Times,* September 4, 1862; *New York Herald,* September 4, 1862; Burlingame, *Lincoln,* 2:379.

38. Strong, *Diary,* 3:252; Rafuse, *McClellan's War,* 266; John Worthington Ames to his mother, September 5, 1862, Ames Papers, Coco Collection, Harrisburg Civil War Round Table Collection, AHEC; Child, *Fifth New Hampshire,* 116–17; Becker and Thomas, *Hearth and Knapsack,* 45; Hyde, *Civil War Letters,* 44; Edwards, *Dear Friend Anna,* 31.

39. William Clark Hawes Diary, August 31, 1862, Massachusetts Historical Society; Dexter, *Seymour Dexter,* 81; Thomas Carleton Cheney to David Gilchrist, September 5, 1862, Cheney Papers, University of New Hampshire; William Watts Folwell Diary, September 7, 1862, University of Minnesota Archives; Wainwright, *Diary of Battle,* 90; Macnamara, *Ninth Regiment Massachusetts Volunteer Infantry,* 198, 201; Miller, *Drum Taps in Dixie,* 38–39; Ellis, *Leaves from the Diary of an Army Surgeon,* 214; Mann, *Fighting with the Eighteenth*

Massachusetts, 96–97; Dawes, *Service with the Sixth Wisconsin,* 75–76; Marshall, *War of the People,* 103–4.

40. Jacob S. Kiester to his father, August 31, 1862, Kiester Letters, Civil War Miscellaneous Collection, AHEC; Bowen, *Dear Friends at Home,* 144; Hayes, *Diary and Letters,* 2:340–41; Weld, *Diary and Letters,* 135–36; Meade, *Life and Letters,* 1:307.

41. *Washington Evening Star,* September 3, 1862; *MCWP,* 428–30; *MOS,* 535–37; *OR,* 11(1):105, 12(3):797; Cox, *Military Reminiscences,* 1:243–44.

42. *CWL,* 5:404; Marszalek, *Commander of All Lincoln's Armies,* 146–47; *OR,* 19(1):38; Sears, *McClellan,* 273–80; Rafuse, *McClellan's War,* 274–75; *MCWP,* 435; Joseph Hooker to Randolph Marcy, September 5, 1862, MPLC.

43. Chase, *Papers,* 1:369–70, 372; Cozzens, *General John Pope,* 196–202; *OR,* 12(3):809, 811–13, 816–26; John Pope to Edwin M. Stanton, September 5, 1862, Stanton Papers, LC; John Pope to Richard Yates, September 21, 1862, Yates Family Papers, Abraham Lincoln Presidential Library.

44. Hay, *Inside Lincoln's White House,* 38–39; Welles, *Diary,* 1:107; Chase, *Papers,* 1:370; *New York World,* September 2, 5, 1862; August Belmont to AL, September 4, 1862, ALPLC; Seward, *Seward at Washington,* 126–27.

45. *New York Herald,* September 4–5, 1862; *Boston Daily Advertiser,* September 5, 1862; E. Ball to John T. Shyrock, September 5, 1862, Shyrock Papers, Western Reserve Historical Society, Cleveland; Burlingame, *Lincoln,* 378–79; Stedman and Gould, *Life and Letters of Edmund Clarence Stedman,* 1:281–82; *New York Times,* September 6, 1862.

46. *MCWP,* 436–37; *CWL,* 5:407; Welles, *Diary,* 1:111; Gurowski, *Diary,* 1:264; John Worthington Ames to his mother, September 6, 1862, Ames Papers, Coco Collection, Harrisburg Civil War Round Table Collection, AHEC; Bliss, "Chaos Still Reigns in This Camp," 24. On McClellan's reorganizing efforts, see Sears, *Lincoln's Lieutenants,* 546–551.

47. *CCW,* 1:438–39; Hartwig, *To Antietam Creek,* 133–52; *MCWP,* 437–38; *OR,* 19(1):39; Castleman, *Army of the Potomac,* 218; *OR: Supplement,* 3:437–38. Hartwig analyzes leadership problems in this reorganized army while observing that McClellan's staff was highly capable.

48. Welles, *Diary,* 1:111–18; Chase, *Papers,* 1:375; John Batchelder Bailey Journal, September 10–13, 1862, New Hampshire Historical Society; Montgomery Blair to unknown, September ?, 1862, Blair Family Papers, LC; Trefousse, *Radical Republicans,* 200; D. S. Linegar to Richard Yates, September 9, 1862, Yates Family Papers, Abraham Lincoln Presidential Library; Zachariah Chandler to P. W. Watson, September 10, 1862, Stanton Papers, LC; Chandler to Lyman Trumbull, September 10, 1862, Trumbull Papers, LC, reel 12.

49. Welles, *Diary,* 1:118–22; Slotkin, *Long Road to Antietam,* 178–80; *New York Daily Tribune,* September 13, 1862; *Chicago Tribune,* September 11, 1862; Strong, *Diary,* 3:254.

50. [Belmont], *A Few Letters and Speeches,* 105–6; *Washington Daily National Intelligencer,* September 8, 1862; J. F. Wilson to James Gordon Bennett, September 8, 1862, Bennett Papers, LC; *Washington Evening Star,* September 11, 1862; *New York Herald,* September 9, 11, 1862.

51. Hays, *Life and Letters,* 273; James J. Gillette to his mother, September 8, 1862, Gillette

Papers, LC; Oliver Otis Howard to Elizabeth Howard, September 10, 1862, Howard Papers, Bowdoin College; Gould, *Hiram G. Berry,* 207.

52. Hartwig, *To Antietam Creek,* 172–76; *OR,* 19(2):201, 210, 212; *MCWP,* 438–39; Strother, *Virginia Yankee in the Civil War,* 120–21; GBM, "From the Peninsula to Antietam: Posthumous Notes," in Johnson and Buel, *Battles and Leaders,* 2:551–52; Wilson, "Types and Traditions of the Old Army," 559. For a detailed account of McClellan's advance into Maryland, see Rafuse, *McClellan's War,* 282–88.

53. Strother, *Virginia Yankee in the Civil War,* 103; *MCWP,* 439–445, 447; Hartwig, *To Antietam Creek,* 181–82. The enemy numbers that McClellan reported, based on information from civilians and other less than reliable sources, were roughly triple Lee's actual strength. Fishel, *Secret War for the Union,* 213–22; Sears, *McClellan,* 276–78.

54. *OR: Supplement,* 3:439; *CWL,* 5:415; *MOS,* 569; *MCWP,* 446–47; *OR,* 19(1):42.

55. Hartwig, *To Antietam Creek,* 196–202; *CWL* 5:418; Nathaniel P. Banks to AL, September 12, 1862, ALPLC; *MCWP,* 448–49. For a good analysis of Lincoln and McClellan's differing objectives at this point, see Cooling, *Counter-Thrust,* 184–86.

56. Strother, *Virginia Yankee in the Civil War,* 105; Steiner, *Report,* 24–25; Gibbon, *Personal Recollections,* 74; Sears, *Lincoln's Lieutenants,* 357; Marvel, *Lincoln's Darkest Year,* 193; *OR,* 19(1):26; Hartwig, *To Antietam Creek,* 282–87; *MCWP,* 453 Rafuse, *McClellan's War,* 291–93; Hassler, *McClellan,* 245–46; Fishel, *Secret War for the Union,* 222–40. John Gibbon later recalled McClellan declaring, "Here is a paper with which if I cannot whip 'Bobbie Lee,' I will be willing to go home." Gibbon, *Personal Recollections,* 73.

57. *OR,* 19(2):280–81.

58. *MCWP,* 454–57. For a detailed and balanced critique of McClellan's plans, see Hartwig, *To Antietam Creek,* 286–91. For a pointed argument that the importance of the Lost Order has been exaggerated and that McClellan should be exonerated from the charge of responding too slowly, see Stotelmyer, *Too Useful to Sacrifice,* 4–45. Historians have sharply disagreed over the timing of McClellan's note to Lincoln, and the evidence is admittedly ambiguous. Sears, "Curious Case of the Lost Order," 30–40, 73; "The Lost Order," 4. The author is greatly indebted to William Marvel for assistance in sifting through the details.

59. *Chicago Tribune,* September 12, 1862; Garfield, *Wild Life of the Army,* 134; Daly, *Diary of a Union Lady,* 171; *Boston Daily Advertiser,* September 12, 1862; Olmsted, *Papers,* 4:415; Strong, *Diary,* 3:256; *OR,* ser. 3, 2:543–44.

60. Burlingame, *Lincoln,* 2:377; Reid, *Radical View,* 1:227; Chase, *Papers,* 1:381–82; Welles, *Diary,* 1:124–30; Lee, *Wartime Washington,* 177. For border-state support of Lincoln's reinstatement of McClellan and discontent with the cabinet—especially Stanton—see Garrett Davis, John B. Huston, and Richard A. Buckner to AL, September 6, 1862; and Garrett Davis to AL, September 7, 1862, ALPLC.

10. VICTORY, DELAY, AND DANGER

1. George W. Quimby to his sister, September 13, 1862, Quimby Letters, University of Vermont; Ritchie, *Four Years in the First New York Light Artillery,* 87; *Chicago Tribune,*

September 15, 1862; Morse, "From Second Bull Run to Antietam," 273–74; Hitchcock, *War from the Inside,* 39–40. See also the soldier comments cited in chapter 9.

2. *OR,* 19(1):27, 53, 19(2):289; *MCWP,* 457–61; Morse, "From Second Bull Run to Antietam," 273–74; Waters Whipple Braman to "Dear Uncle & Aunt," September 16, 1862, Braman Letters, NYMMVRC; Strother, "Personal Recollections of the War," 277–78. For a detailed, perceptive, and judicious account of the fight, see Hartwig, *To Antietam Creek,* 300–477. For differing assessments of McClellan's orders and movements on September 14, see Sears, *McClellan,* 286–290; Rafuse, *McClellan's War,* 294–99; and Cooling, *Counter-Thrust,* 209–13, 217–20.

3. Hartwig, *To Antietam Creek,* 490–92; *OR,* 19(1):28–29; Patrick, *Inside Lincoln's Army,* 146; *MCWP,* 461–62; Cox, *Military Reminiscences,* 1:381–84; Marvel, *Burnside,* 123–26; Gibbon, *Personal Recollections,* 78–79; Biddle, "Recollections of McClellan," 462–63. McClellan even reported this victory to Winfield Scott, who responded: "Bravo my dear General. Twice more & it's done." *MCWP,* 464; Winfield Scott to GBM, September 16, 1862, MPLC.

4. *MCWP,* 464–65; Cox, *Military Reminiscences,* 1:298–300; Hartwig, *To Antietam Creek,* 492–94; *OR,* 19(1):29, 53–54; *MOS,* 587. For a critique of McClellan's failing to take advantage of his success at South Mountain and the Confederates' dispersed forces, see Sears, *Lincoln's Lieutenant's,* 369–75. For a clear account of McClellan's actions that day with little evaluation, see Rafuse, *McClellan's War,* 300–307. For a detailed defense, see Stotelmyer, *Too Useful to Sacrifice,* 92–142. Richard Slotkin has speculated that had McClellan attacked on September 15, Lee might well have retreated back across the Potomac and deprived the Federals of an opportunity to win a significant victory. Slotkin, *Long Road to Antietam,* 217–22.

5. Henry C. Bowen to Salmon P. Chase, September 13, 1862, Chase Papers, LC; Chase, *Papers,* 1:386, 389; Seward, *Seward at Washington,* 131; Welles, *Diary,* 1:130; Richard Yates to AL, September 15, 1862, ALPLC; *CWL,* 425–26.

6. Stedman and Gould, *Life and Letters of Edmund Clarence Stedman,* 1:284; *New York Herald,* September 14–15, 1862; *Boston Daily Advertiser,* September 16, 1862; *Boston Herald,* September 15, 1862. One newspaper friendly to McClellan even reported that the general and the secretary of war had now reconciled their differences. *Boston Daily Advertiser,* September 15, 1862.

7. On the terrain, see Sears, *Landscape Turned Red,* 168–69.

8. *MCWP,* 465–6; *OR,* 19(1):29–30, 41, 54–55, 217–18, 19(2):311; Palfrey, *Antietam and Fredericksburg,* 56–57; Hartwig, *To Antietam Creek,* 482–96, 606–7; Carman, *Maryland Campaign,* 2:21; Cox, *Military Reminiscences,* 1:303–5. See also the helpful analysis in Sears, *McClellan,* 296–302; Rafuse, *McClellan's War,* 308–9; and Slotkin, *Long Road to Antietam,* 224–28. Delays in deploying the Ninth Corps may have reflected McClellan's loss of confidence in Burnside. Cox, *Military Reminiscences,* 1:384.

9. *OR,* 19(1):55, 275, 51(1):839; Hartwig, *To Antietam Creek,* 638–45. Hartwig's analysis of McClellan's options in moving his troops on September 16 in preparation for battle the following day is superb. For a detailed critique of McClellan's ambiguous battle plan, see Slotkin, *Long Road to Antietam,* 241–51.

10. Carman, *Maryland Campaign,* 2:44–51; Child, *Fifth New Hampshire,* 120; Cox, *Military Reminiscences,* 1:311, 323–24, 328–29, 335–36; William B. Franklin, "Notes on Cramp-

ton's Gap and Antietam," in Johnson and Buel, *Battles and Leaders,* 2:597; Sears, *McClellan,* 309–10; Rafuse, *McClellan's War,* 314–21. Thomas Clemens has cast serious doubt on the often-repeated tale that McClellan was still sleeping as the battle began. Carman, *Maryland Campaign,* 2:171–72n.

11. Lossing, *Pictorial Field Book,* 2:476; Weigley, *Great Civil War,* 153–54; Sears, *McClellan,* 307; Murray, *New Yorkers in the Civil War,* 67–68; Strother, *Virginia Yankee in the Civil War,* 110; Strother, "Personal Recollections of the War," 282–83.

12. Sears, *Landscape Turned Red,* 261–62.

13. Wilson, *Under the Old Flag,* 1:112–14; Franklin, "Notes on Crampton's Gap and Antietam," 597; Sears, *McClellan,* 315–17; Sears, *Landscape Turned Red,* 314–16; Strother, "Personal Recollections of the War," 284; *OR,* 19 (1):30–31, 62; *MCWP,* 467; Edward H. Wright to Fitz John Porter, March 3, 1892, Porter Papers, LC, reel 2. For a vigorous defense of Burnside's performance, see Marvel, *Burnside,* 130–50. For a defense (though not an uncritical one) of McClellan's afternoon hesitancy, see Rafuse, *McClellan's War,* 321–27.

14. Castleman, *Army of the Potomac,* 228–29; Franklin, "Notes on Crampton's Gap and Antietam," 597; *CCW,* 1:627, 642; *OR,* 19(1):32; *MCWP,* 468. On McClellan and enemy numbers during the Antietam Campaign, see Fishel, "Pinkerton and McClellan," 132–33, 137. But historians have also overestimated the size of McClellan's available forces. Compare Sears, *McClellan,* 301–5, to Hartwig, *To Antietam Creek,* 593.

15. *MCWP,* 469, 473; *OR,* 19(1):32, 65; *CCW,* 1:441; Styple, *Generals in Bronze,* 194; Strother, *Virginia Yankee in the Civil War,* 112; Strother, "Personal Recollections of the War," 285; *MOS,* 618–19; Swinton, *Army of the Potomac,* 222–23. For a description by a junior officer of the field the day after the battle, see John C. Whiteside to his mother, October 4, 1862, Whiteside Letter, Bentley Library, University of Michigan.

16. Strother, "Personal Recollections of the War," 287; *MCWP,* 469–70, 473; Snell, *From First to Last,* 197; Slotkin, *Long Road to Antietam,* 344–52.

17. Ira Harris to GBM, September 28, 1862, MPLC; Harris to AL, October 2, 1862, ALPLC; *MCWP,* 467, 473, 475, 477; *OR,* 19(1):68, 19(2):247.

18. Edwin M. Stanton to Zachariah Chandler, September 18, 1862, Chandler Papers, LC; Chase, *Papers,* 1:392, 3:275–76, 278; Montgomery Blair to Francis Preston Blair Jr., September 17, 1862, Blair Family Papers, LC; Montgomery Blair to GBM, September 19, 1862, MPLC; Welles, *Diary,* 1:139–40, 142; Lee, *Wartime Washington,* 182, 185; Seward, *Seward at Washington,* 132.

19. *Boston Daily Advertiser,* September 19, 1862; *New York Herald,* September 20, 1862; *Boston Herald,* September 22, 1862, *New York Daily Tribune,* September 19, 20, 22, 29, 1862; Reid, *Radical View,* 1:232.

20. John Pope to Richard Yates, September 21, 1862, Yates Family Papers, Abraham Lincoln Presidential Library; Gurowski, *Diary,* 1:274–75; Garfield, *Wild Life of the Army,* 139.

21. *New York Herald,* September 23, 1862; *New York World,* September 20, 1862; *Louisville (KY) Daily Journal,* September 23, 1862; Stoddard, *Dispatches from Lincoln's White House,* 103; T. J. Barnett to Samuel L. M. Barlow, September 19, 1862, BPHL; Olmsted, *Papers,* 4:418–20.

22. Engle, *Gathering to Save a Nation,* 227–34; Lathrop, *Life and Times of Samuel J. Kirkwood,* 228–30; Welles, *Diary,* 1:53; *New York Herald,* September 25, 1862.

23. Bowen, *Dear Friends at Home,* 157; Fry, *Republic in the Ranks,* 51; Wightman, *From Antietam to Fort Fisher,* 44–45; Alexander S. Webb to his father, September 24, 1862, Webb Papers, Yale University; Charles N. Tenney to Adelaide E. Case, September 25, 1862, Nettleton Civil War Collection, University of Virginia; Norton, *Army Letters,* 122–23; Young, *Dear Delia,* 98–99.

24. Chase, *Yours for the Union,* 146; Nichols, *"Your Soldier Boy Samuel,"* 27; Waters Whipple Braman to "Dear Uncle," September 18, 25, 1862, Braman Letters, NYMMVRC; John W. Patterson to his wife, September 22, 1862, Patterson Papers, FSNMP; Thomas Carleton Cheney to Luther Cheney, September 22, 1862, Cheney Papers, University of New Hampshire; H. B. Whipple to GBM, September 23, 1862, MPLC; Black, *Yankee Horseman in the Shenandoah Valley,* 29–30. In an excellent essay, Brooks D. Simpson argues that the Army of the Potomac by this time had absorbed McClellan's caution, hesitation, and suspicion toward official Washington. Simpson, "General McClellan's Bodyguard: The Army of the Potomac after Antietam," in Gallagher, *Antietam Campaign,* 44–73.

25. Gerrish, *Army Life,* 40; Mayo, *Civil War Letters,* 218; Carter, *Four Brothers in Blue,* 131; Favill, *Diary of a Young Officer,* 191; Castleman, *Army of the Potomac,* 231–32, 234; Nevins, *War for the Union,* 2:230; Holt, *Surgeon's Civil War,* 27; William Watts Folwell Diary, September 28, 1862, University of Minnesota Archives.

26. Welles, *Diary,* 1:148–49; Chase, *Papers,* 1:400–401, 403; Garfield, *Wild Life of the Army,* 141–42; Burlingame, *Lincoln,* 2:428.

27. Lamon, *Recollections of Abraham Lincoln,* 289; Prince de Joinville to William H. Seward, September 19, 1862, ALPLC; Endicott, "Reminiscences of Seventy-Five Years," 225; Herndon and Weik, *Herndon's Lincoln,* 83; Welles¸ *Diary,* 1:46; *CWL,* 5:442–43; *New York Times,* October 4, 1862; Hay, *Lincoln's Journalist,* 318; Hay, *Inside Lincoln's White House,* 41. Richard Slotkin lends some credence to these reports of a conspiracy but considers McClellan too weak to carry out any bold move against the government. Slotkin, *Long Road to Antietam,* 367–71.

28. *OR,* 19(1):67–71, 19(2):354; *CCW,* 1:369; *MCWP,* 477.

29. *MCWP,* 480–83, 486; *OR,* 19(1):82, 19(2):360; *New York Herald,* September 26, 1862; *New York World,* September 30, 1862; *Washington Evening Star,* October 1, 1862. There were reports that discord between McClellan and Halleck was growing. As historian John Marszalek has cogently observed, "McClellan overwhelmed Halleck and made him feel powerless through his determined stubbornness and his disdain for Halleck's suggestions." *Chicago Tribune,* October 1, 1862; *OR,* 52(1):717; Marszalek, *Commander of All Lincoln's Armies,* 352–53.

30. "Lincoln Visits the Army of the Potomac"; *CWL,* 7:538; *MCWP,* 487–88; *MOS,* 654; *New York Herald,* October 5, 1862.

31. Wainwright, *Diary of Battle,* 110; Strother, *Virginia Yankee in the Civil War,* 121; *MOS,* 654; *New York Herald,* October 7, 1862. A story that Lincoln had requested his sometime bodyguard Ward Hill Lamon to sing a silly song while the two of them, along with McClellan, were on the Antietam battleground later circulated during the 1864 presidential campaign. Apparently Lamon did sing something (he later said it was a "sad song'), but the

tale undoubtedly fit into Lincoln's reputation for light humor and his critics' insistence on the president's crude manners. *CWL*, 7:549; Lamon, *Recollections of Abraham Lincoln*, 144–51.

32. Browne, *Every-Day Life of Abraham Lincoln*, 523–25; *New York Herald*, October 7, 1862; Small, *Road to Richmond*, 50–51; Stone, *Personal Recollections*, 96; *Under the Maltese Cross*, 78; Wightman, *From Antietam to Fort Fisher*, 48.

33. Regan, *Lost Civil War Diaries*, 96; Mann, *Fighting with the Eighteenth Massachusetts*, 106; Carter, *Four Brothers in Blue*, 136–37; Geary, *Politician Goes to War*, 58–59; Pardington, *Dear Sarah*, 19–20; Gaff, *On Many a Bloody Field*, 197; Hitchcock, *From Ashby to Andersonville*, 26; Strother, *Virginia Yankee in the Civil War*, 121–22; Wainwright, *Diary of Battle*, 109.

34. "Lincoln Visits the Army of the Potomac"; *New York Times*, October 4, 1862; Dawes, *Service with the Sixth Wisconsin Infantry*, 100; Lamson, *From Maine to the Wilderness*, 26, 28; Ellis, *Leaves from the Diary of an Army Surgeon*, 306–7; *New York Herald*, October 7, 1862.

35. "Lincoln Visits the Army of the Potomac"; Lamon, *Recollections of Abraham Lincoln*, 148; *New York Herald*, October 5, 7, 1862; *MOS*, 627–28, 654; *OR*, 19(1):71–72; Meade, *Life and Letters*, 1:317; *MCWP*, 489–90; Burlingame, *Lincoln*, 2:426.

36. Nicolay, *Oral History of Abraham Lincoln*, 16; *CWL*, 5:448; Burlingame, *Lincoln*, 2:426; Nicolay and Hay, *Lincoln*, 6:142. John Hay wrote an anonymous newspaper article berating McClellan for timidity and inaction; McClellan had proven to be a general always asking for reinforcements but never satisfied. Hay, *Lincoln's Journalist*, 314–16.

37. Kelley, *Lincoln and Stanton*, 75; Chase, *Papers*, 1:411, 416–17; Jesse K. DuBois to AL, October 6, 1862, ALPLC; Burlingame, *Lincoln*, 2:424; Welles, *Diary*, 1:160–61; T. J. Barnett to Samuel L. M. Barlow, October 6, 1862, BPHL; *New York Times*, October 7, 1862.

38. *New York Herald*, October 7, 1862; Slotkin, *Long Road to Antietam*, 382–83; *Washington Daily National Intelligencer*, October 10, 1862; *OR*, 19(1):10–11, 83, 19(2):380, 395–96; Snell, *From First to Last*, 200; Meade, *Life and Letters*, 1:317–18; *MCWP*, 492–93; Wilson, "Types and Traditions of the Old Army," 559.

39. Hagerman, "Professionalization of George B. McClellan," 130; Cooling, *Counter-Thrust*, 275; *OR*, 19(1):74, 76–78, 19(2):347; Curtis, *McClellan's Last Service to the Republic*, 68–75; Hirst, *Boys from Rockville*, 31; Richard B. Irwin, "The Removal of McClellan," in Johnson and Buel, *Battles and Leaders*, 3:102–3; *Boston Herald*, October 8, 1862. For a detailed examination of the supply problems that strongly defends McClellan, see Stotelmyer, *Too Useful to Sacrifice*, 203–4, 210–16, 228–42.

40. Garfield, *Wild Life of the Army*, 153, 157; Oliver P. Morton to AL, October 7, 1862, ALPLC; Olmsted, *Papers*, 4:435–36; *New York Times*, October 1, 1862; Child, *Selected Letters*, 416–17.

41. Gurowski, *Diary*, 1:289; Stoddard, *Dispatches from Lincoln's White House*, 112; *New York Times*, October 2, 1862; Olmsted, *Papers*, 4:429–31, 449–51; *Boston Daily Advertiser*, October 2, 1862; Peoples Party (Massachusetts), *Proceedings of the Convention*, 18, 25.

42. *New York Times*, October 1, 1862; John C. Whiteside to "Dear Mother," October 4, 1862, Whiteside Letter, Bentley Library, University of Michigan; Rhodes, *All for the Union*, 84; Wainwright, *Diary of Battle*, 114–15; Bowen, *Dear Friends at Home*, 163–64; Hayes, *Diary and Letters*, 2:361.

43. *Boston Daily Advertiser,* September 29, 1862; J. W. Alsop to GBM, September 30, 1862; Montgomery Blair to GBM, September 27, 1862; and Francis Preston Blair Sr. to GBM, September 30, 1862, MPLC; Francis Preston Blair Sr. to Francis Preston Blair Jr., October 3, 1862, Blair Family Papers, LC; Cox, *Military Reminiscences,* 1:355–56.

44. Sears, *Civil War: The Second Year,* 538, 543–49; L. A. Whiteley to James Gordon Bennett, September 24, 1862, Bennett Papers, LC; "George Breck's Civil War Letters,'" in McKelvey, *Rochester in the Civil War,* 109; Norton, *Army Letters,* 125–26.

45. *MCWP,* 481–82, 489; Cochrane, *American Civil War,* 28–29; Smith, *Autobiography,* 57–58; Hay, *Inside Lincoln's White House,* 360–61; Cox, *Military Reminiscences,* 1:358–64.

46. *MCWP,* 493–94.

47. *New York Daily Tribune,* October 9, 1862; *Boston Daily Advertiser,* October 9, 1862; *New York Herald,* October 10, 1862; *Boston Herald,* October 11, 1862; *Chicago Tribune,* October 9, 15, 1862; *New York Times,* October 13, 1862; Welles, *Diary,* 1:162–63.

48. Garfield, *Wild Life of the Army,* 160–61; Hamlin, *Life and Times of Hannibal Hamlin,* 442–43; Medill and Medill, *Family and Nation under Fire,* 18–19; Starr, *Reporting the Civil War,* 124. For signs of growing Republican sentiment in the Army of the Potomac, see Fry, *Republic in the Ranks,* 56–58.

49. *New York Herald,* September 19, 1862; *CWL,* 5:452; *New York Times,* October 12, 14, 1862; *MCWP,* 501.

50. Strong, *Diary,* 3:265; *Chicago Tribune,* October 10, 1862; *New York Times,* October 14, 16, 19, 1862; Fiske, *Mr. Dunn Browne's Experiences in the Army,* 21–22; Fry, *Republic in the Ranks,* 59–60. One irony, as pointed out by an abolitionist editor, was that McClellan's failure to take Richmond "saved the rebellion for the time, and destroyed slavery for all time." *National Antislavery Standard* (New York), October 11, 1862.

51. *MCWP,* 497–98; *New York Times,* October 12, 1862; Nicolay, *With Lincoln in the White House,* 89; Welles, *Diary,* 1:169–70.

52. *CWL,* 5:460–61; *MCWP,* 499; Welles, *Diary,* 1:176–77; Gurowski, *Diary,* 1:299.

53. *MCWP,* 485–86, 500, 504; *Boston Daily Advertiser,* October 13, 23, 1862; *New York Times,* October 18–19, 22, 1862; *OR,* 19(1):12–13, 15–18, 20, 75; "George Breck's Civil War Letters," 109; *Washington Evening Star,* October 24, 1862; *New York Herald,* October 23, 1862; Rafuse, *McClellan's War,* 356–57. According to one newspaper, once the Army of the Potomac received the requested shoes, "a brand new excuse will have to be invented." *New York Times,* October 20, 1862.

54. Du Pont, *Samuel Francis Du Pont,* 2:248; Nicolay, *With Lincoln in the White House,* 89; *OR,* 19(1):81; Stoddard, *Dispatches from Lincoln's White House,* 116–17; Meade, *Life and Letters,* 1:320.

55. Meade, *Life and Letters,* 1:318–19; *Chicago Tribune,* October 14, 1862; *Washington National Republican,* October 18, 1862; *New York Times,* October 24, 1862; "M" [Randolph B. Marcy] to Samuel L. M. Barlow, October 21, 1862, BPHL.

56. Gibbon, *Recollections,* 92; *New York Herald,* October 10, 1862; *Boston Daily Advertiser,* October 21, 1862; "M" [Randolph B. Marcy] to Samuel L. M. Barlow, October 21, 1862, BPHL; Darius N. Couch, "Right Grand Division," in Johnson and Buel, *Battles and Leaders,* 3:105–6.

11. THE LAST CAMPAIGN, THE POLITICS OF REMOVAL, AND THE NOT-SO-FINAL FAREWELL

1. Charles Francis Adams Diary, October 22, 1862, Adams Family Papers, Massachusetts Historical Society; Strong, *Diary,* 3:267; William Cullen Bryant to AL, October 22, 1862; and Horace White to AL, October 22, 1862, ALPLC; Burlingame, *Lincoln,* 2:429; Chase, *Papers,* 3:306.

2. *MCWP,* 495, 505; Rafuse, *McClellan's War,* 360–62; T. J. Barnett to Samuel L. M. Barlow, October 24, 1862, BPHL; *Washington Evening Star,* October 24, 1862; *OR,* 19(2):470. Just as McClellan was finally prepared to move, rain and storms interfered, and soon the weather turned decidedly cold. Noe, *Howling Storm,* 180–81.

3. *Boston Daily Advertiser,* October 25, 1862; *Washington National Republican,* October 25, 1862; *OR,* 19(1):21–24, 19(2):492–93; Fitz John Porter to Seth Williams, October 28, 1862, Thomas Dolan Telegrams, New-York Historical Society; Sears, *McClellan,* 332–33.

4. *OR,* 19(1):15, 18–20, 72 77–80, 19(2):421–24; *MCWP,* 495, 499, 504; Meade, *Life and Letters,* 1:320.

5. *OR,* 19(2), 484–85, 490–91; *CWL,* 5:474, 477, 479; *MCWP,* 508; Rafuse, *McClellan's War,* 362–63. Historian Craig Symonds has observed that Lincoln may have quickly regretted sending his sarcastically worded dispatch to McClellan, realizing it would do little good. Symonds, *Lincoln and His Admirals,* 265–66. For a judicious assessment of the cavalry situation, see Starr, *Union Cavalry,* 1:301–2, 309–22.

6. *New York Herald,* October 25, 1862; *New York Times,* October 28–29, 1862; T. J. Barnett to Samuel L. M. Barlow, October 27, 1862, BPHL; *OR: Supplement,* 3:449; John Darragh Wilkins to his wife, October 26, 1862, Wilkins Papers, Schoff Civil War Collection, Clements Library, University of Michigan; *Boston Daily Advertiser,* October 29, 1862; *Boston Herald,* October 23–25, 1862.

7. *Boston Herald,* October 27, 1862; Garfield, *Wild Life of the Army,* 169; Emerson, *Life and Letters of Charles Russell Lowell,* 231; Child, *Selected Letters,* 418; Hay, *At Lincoln's Side,* 27.

8. *New York Times,* October 14, 21, 23, 29, 1862; *Boston Daily Advertiser,* October 25, 1862; *Dayton (OH) Daily Empire,* November 13, 1862; Robert S. Robertson to his parents, October 17, 1862, Robertson Papers, FSNMP; *MCWP,* 501; Stedman and Gould, *Life and Letters of Edmund Clarence Stedman,* 1:291–92.

9. Parker, *Letter to the People of Massachusetts,* 4; Burlingame, *Lincoln,* 2:429–30; Schuckers, *Life and Public Services of Salmon Portland Chase,* 458–59; Nicolay, *With Lincoln in the White House,* 90.

10. *OR,* 19(1):84–87, 19(2):501, 51(1):897–98; *MCWP,* 511–13; Favill, *Diary of a Young Officer,* 198; Gray and Ropes, *War Letters,* 9; Rafuse, *McClellan's War,* 364; *CWL,* 5:479, 481.

11. *MCWP,* 514–16.

12. *Under the Maltese Cross,* 86; Gibbon, *Personal Recollections,* 94; Weld, *Diary and Letters,* 146–47; *OR,* 19(2):531; Waters Whipple Braman to "Dear Cousin Abbie," October 29, 1862, Braman Letters, NYMMVRC; Alexander S. Webb to his father, October 29, 1862, Webb Papers, Sterling Library, Yale University; Geary, *Politician Goes to War,* 66; *New York Times,* October 27, 30, November 5, 6, 8, 1862; *Chicago Tribune,* October 28, 1862; *New York Herald,* November 8, 1862.

13. Oliver S. Halsted to John G. Nicolay, November 7, 1862, ALPLC; *OR*, 19(1):7–9; Stedman and Gould, *Life and Letters of Edmund Clarence Stedman*, 1:291; *New York Times*, October 31, 1862; *South Bend (IN) Register*, n.d., in *Chicago Tribune*, November 3, 1862; *Cleveland Daily Herald*, November 3, 1862.

14. *OR*, ser. 3, 2:703–4; *MCWP*, 488, 516. See the excellent assessment of Halleck during this period in Marszalek, *Commander of All Lincoln's Armies*, 153–54.

15. Mary Todd Lincoln to AL, November 2, 1862, ALPLC; Stearns, *Life and Public Services of George Luther Stearns*, 270–71; *MCWP*, 517; Nicolay, *With Lincoln in the White House*, 90; Burlingame, *Lincoln*, 2:249. See also Sanitary Commission official Mary Livermore's account of a conversation in which Lincoln supposedly said he was tired of hearing about "strategy" when the war could only be ended by "hard desperate fighting." Livermore, *My Story of the War*, 555–57.

16. Welles, *Diary*, 1:179–80; *New York Herald*, November 5, 1862; Stedman and Gould, *Life and Letters of Edmund Clarence Stedman*, 1:294; Small, *Road to Richmond*, 53; Donaldson, *Inside the Army of the Potomac*, 158; Hugh Henry to his sister, November 7, 1862, Henry Family Papers, University of Vermont.

17. *New York Times*, November 5–7, 11, 1862; *Washington National Republicans*, November 7, 1862; Oliver Halstead Jr. to John G. Nicolay, November 7, 1862, ALPLC; *Chicago Tribune*, November 8, 1862; Lyman Trumbull to Zachariah Chandler, November 9, 1862, Chandler Papers, LC. For a negative assessment of McClellan's campaign after Antietam, see Sears, *McClellan*, 337–40. For a much more positive evaluation, see Rafuse, *McClellan's War*, 371, 379–81.

18. Typically enough, Halleck later disclaimed either favoring or opposing McClellan's removal. But shortly after Lincoln issued the order, he told his wife that Little Mac had to go because otherwise "he would have broken down the government." Henry W. Halleck to C. P. Buckingham, December 22, 1862, Halleck Letters, Abraham Lincoln Presidential Library; Henry W. Halleck to his wife, November 9, 1862, Halleck Letters, Schoff Civil War Collection, Clements Library, University of Michigan.

19. *CWL*, 5:485–86; Francis Preston Blair Sr. to Francis Preston Blair Jr., November 7, 1862; and Francis Preston Blair Sr. to Montgomery Blair, March 2, 1863, Blair Family Papers, LC; Virginia L. Woodbury Diary, November 14, 1862, Woodbury Papers, LC, reel 1; *New York Times*, November 10, 1862. Lincoln also ordered the removal of Porter from corps command.

20. *MCWP*, 519–20; Haupt, *Reminiscences*, 156–57.

21. Marvel, *Burnside*, 99, 111, 159–60; *MCWP*, 520.

22. *MCWP*, 520–21; Teall, "Ringside Seat at Fredericksburg," 21.

23. George G. Meade to Margaret Meade, November 7, 8, 9, 1862, Meade Papers, Historical Society of Pennsylvania; Snell, *From First to Last*, 203; *New York Daily Tribune*, November 11, 1862; Oliver Otis Howard to his wife, November 8, 1862; and Howard to Charles Howard, November 9, 1862, Howard Papers, Bowdoin College; Ford, *Cycle of Adams Letters*, 1:194; Hsieh, *West Pointers in the Civil War*, 169; Haley, *Rebel Yell and the Yankee Hurrah*, 50; Villard, *Memoirs*, 1:336; Fitz John Porter to Manton Marble, November 9, 1862, Marble Papers, LC, reel 1; Patrick, *Inside Lincoln's Army*, 173.

24. Strother, *Virginia Yankee in the Civil War*, 127; "George Breck's Civil War Letters," in McKelvey, *Rochester in the Civil War*, 110; Waters W. Braman to "Dear Abbie," November 11,

1862, Braman Letters, NYMMVRC; Haydon, *For Country, Cause, & Leader,* 286; Charles E. Bowers to "Lydia," November 11, 1862, Bowers Papers, Massachusetts Historical Society; Wainwright, *Diary of Battle,* 124; John S. Crocker to "Dear Harriette," November 8, 1862, Crocker Papers, Brockett Collection, Cornell University.

25. Oliver, "Robert Oliver, Jr., and the Oswego County Regiment," 288; Benjamin F. Ashenfelter to his mother, November 12, 1862, Ashenfelter Letters, Harrisburg Civil War Round Table Collection, AHEC; Robert S. Robertson to his parents, November 12, 1862, Robertson Papers, FSNMP; George W. Quimby to his parents, November 14, 1862, Quimby Letters, University of Vermont.

26. Albert E. Higley to his father, November 21, 1862, Higley Diary and Letters, FSNMP; Charles H. Eager to his wife, Eager Letters, Lewis Leigh Collection, AHEC; Waters Whipple Braman to "Dear Libbie," November 11, 1862, Braman Letters, NYMMVRC; Edward K. Russell to his mother, December 1, 1862, Russell Collection, FSNMP; Norton, *Army Letters,* 288.

27. Brandegee, *Charlie's Civil War,* 111; John W. Patterson to his wife, November 19, 1862, Patterson Papers, FSNMP; Donaldson, *Inside the Army of the Potomac,* 162–63; John Darragh Wilkins to his wife, November 13, 1862, Wilkins Papers, Schoff Civil War Collection, Clements Library, University of Michigan; Jonathan Burrell to his brother and sister, November 11, 1862, Burrell Papers, New York State Library.

28. Robertson, *Diary of the War,* 66; T. W. Eagan to GBM, November 15, 1862, MPLC; James E. Decker to his father, November 10, 1862, Decker Letters, FSNMP; Smith, *118th Pennsylvania,* 107–8; Bowen, *Dear Friends at Home,* 186; Duff, *To Petersburg,* 92; Dyer, *Journal of a Civil War Surgeon,* 50.

29. Regan, *Lost Civil War Diaries,* 104; Charles E. Bowers to "Lydia," November 11, 1862, Bowers Papers, Massachusetts Historical Society; John S. Crocker to his wife, November 13, 1862, Crocker Papers, Brockett Collection, Cornell University; *Minnesota in the Civil and Indian Wars,* 1:28–29; Thomas, *Civil War Letters,* 111–12; Dawes, *Service with the Sixth Wisconsin,* 105; Abbott, *Fallen Leaves,* 142–43; *New York Times,* November 13, 1862; Rhodes, *All for the Union,* 88.

30. *New York Times,* November 13, 1862; Beidelman, *Civil War Letters,* 145; John F. Reynolds to his sister, November 30, 1862, Reynolds Family Papers, Franklin and Marshall College; Fry, *Republic in the Ranks,* 62–63; Judson, *Eighty-Third Regiment Pennsylvania Volunteers,* 98; Duff, *To Petersburg,* 89.

31. Egbert M. Rogers to his sisters, November 26, 1862, Rogers Papers, New York State Library; Charles E. Bowers to "Lydia," November 11, 1862, Bowers Papers, Massachusetts Historical Society; Edwards, *Dear Friend Anna,* 39–40; Fry, *Republic in the Ranks,* 62; Bennett, *Musket and Sword,* 108–9; Nichols, *"Your Soldier Boy Samuel,"* 48.

32. Dyer, *Journal of a Civil War Surgeon,* 47; E. Risby to unknown, n.d., 1862, Miscellaneous Civil War Letters, Hamilton College Library; Strother, *Virginia Yankee in the Civil War,* 129; Osborn, *No Middle Ground,* 88; Gray and Ropes, *War Letters,* 19; Josiah C. Fuller to his wife, November 13, 1862, Fuller Papers, Massachusetts Historical Society. For additional examples in the First and Third Corps, see Fry, *Republic in the Ranks,* 61.

33. Moulton, *Fort Lyon to Harper's Ferry,* 57; Cleaver, *Your Affectionate Son,* 150; Castleman, *Army of the Potomac,* 240–42; Bolton, *Civil War Journal,* 96; *New York Times,* November 13, 1862; Hays, *Life and Letters,* 279; Duff, *To Petersburg,* 91–92.

34. *New York Times,* November 11–12, 14, 1862; *New York Herald,* November 12, 1862; Patrick, *Inside Lincoln's Army,* 173–74; Meade, *Life and Letters,* 1:325–26; John S. Crocker to his wife, November 13, 1862, Crocker Papers, Brockett Collection, Cornell University.

35. Wainwright, *Diary of Battle,* 125; Louis N. Tucker to "Dear John," November 14, 1862, Porter Papers, LC, reel 2; Charles E. Bowers to "Lydia," November 10, 1862, Bowers Papers, Massachusetts Historical Society; Charles H. Salter to Isabella Duffield, November 14, 1862, Divie Bethune Duffield Papers, Burton Historical Collection, Detroit Public Library; Donaldson, *Inside the Army of the Potomac,* 164–65; Nash, *Forty-Fourth New York,* 110; Smith, *118th Pennsylvania,* 107–8n.

36. McCarter, *My Life in the Irish Brigade,* 67; Tyler, *Recollections of the Civil War,* 56–57; Willsey, *Civil War Diary,* 57; John Bigelow to "Dear Judge," November 10, 1862, Bigelow Collection, New-York Historical Society; Southwick, *Duryee Zouave,* 93–94; Heffelfinger, "Dear Sister Jennie," 215; Waters Whipple Braman to "Dear Libbie," November 11, 1862, Braman Letters, NYMMVRC; Frank M. Carron to his mother, November 10, 1862, Carron Papers, FSNMP; Teall, "Ringside Seat at Fredericksburg," 20–21.

37. William Adams Moore to his father, November 18, 1862, Moore Correspondence, New Hampshire Historical Society; Perkins, "Letters Home," 129; Charles E. Bowers to "Lydia," November 10, 1862, Bowers Papers, Massachusetts Historical Society; Strathern, *Civil War Letters,* 88; John S. Crocker to his wife, November 10, 1862, Crocker Papers, Brockett Collection, Cornell University; Robert S. Robertson to his parents, November 10, 1862, Robertson Papers, FSNMP; Lewis Masonheimer Diary, November 10, 1862, Harrisburg Civil War Round Table Collection, AHEC; *MCWP,* 522.

38. *MCWP,* 522; Donaldson, *Inside the Army of the Potomac,* 161–62, 164; Hirst, *Boys from Rockville,* 37; Smith, *118th Pennsylvania,* 107; Robertson, *Diary of the War,* 67–68; Johnson, *Civil War Letters,* 27–28; Louis Fortesque to "Friend Sam," November 13, 1862, Fortesque Letters, Dreer Collection, AHEC; Edward H. C. Taylor to his sister, November n.d., 1862, Taylor Civil War Letters, Hobart and Smith Colleges; Heffley and Heffley, *Civil War Diaries,* 11; *New York Herald,* November 12, 1862.

39. *New York Times,* November 14, 1862; Edwin O. Wentworth to his father, November 10, 1862, Wentworth Papers, LC; Thomas H. Mann to unknown, ca. November 7–9, 1862, Mann Papers, Brown Military Collection, Brown University; John W. Patterson to his wife, November 19, 1862, Patterson Papers, FSNMP.

40. *New York Herald,* November 12, 1862; Sears, *McClellan,* 343; *MCWP,* 521; *New York Times,* November 11, 19, 1862; Strother, "Personal Recollections of the War," 582; *Philadelphia Press,* n.d., in *New York Herald,* November 13, 1862.

41. *MCWP,* 525; *New York Times,* November 13–14, 1862; *Boston Herald,* November 15, 1862; *New York Herald,* November 14, 1862. For claims that the crowds were small and there had been attempts to bring in many more people, see *New York Times,* November 16, 19, 1862.

42. *New York Times,* November 10–11, 18, 1862; *National Antislavery Standard* (New York), November 15, 1862; *Liberator* (Boston), November 21, 1862; *Principia* (New York), November 13, 1862; Gurowski, *Diary,* 1:313–14; *Cincinnati Gazette,* n.d., in *Washington National Republican,* November 15, 17, 1862; *Chicago Tribune,* November 10, 12, 1862; *Boston Herald,* November 11, 1862. Although she was sorry to see McClellan go and acknowledged

that her brother Montgomery Blair had opposed Lincoln's decision "bitterly," Elizabeth Blair Lee had decided that the general was simply "too slow." At the same time, she predicted that "persecution" might make him into a presidential candidate and remained appreciative of what he had accomplished with "a vanquished & demoralized Army" during the Antietam Campaign. Lee, *Wartime Washington,* 203.

43. *Washington National Republican,* November 10, 1862; *New York Times,* November 11, 13, 1862; *Chicago Tribune,* November 27, 1862; Garfield, *Wild Life of the Army,* 176; Engle, *Gathering to Save a Nation,* 251; Daniel S. Dickinson to AL, November 9, 1862, ALPLC; Medill and Medill, *Family and Nation under Fire,* 125; Forbes, *Letters and Recollections,* 1:336–37.

44. *New York Herald,* November 10, 12, 13, 1862; *Boston Daily Advertiser,* November 11, 13, 1862; Adelaide E. Case to Charles N. Tenney, November 16, 1862, Nettleton Civil War Collection, University of Virginia.

45. *New York Herald,* November 10, 17 1862; *New York World,* November 10–11, 1862. An Episcopal priest in Hartford, who reported that Connecticut's Republican governor, William A. Buckingham, had ordered an artillery salute to celebrate McClellan's removal, believed that the general had been sacrificed to assuage abolitionist anger over the recent elections. William Jarvis to "My Dear William," November 10, 1862, Jarvis Letters, Connecticut Historical Society.

46. *Chicago Tribune,* November 14, 19, 1862; *Washington National Republican,* November 11, 13, 1862; Turner, *Freedom's Witness,* 83; *New York Times,* November 10, 11, 22, 1862; "Causes of the Removal of Gen. McClellan," *Old Guard* 1 (January 1863): 39.

47. *Chicago Tribune,* December 5, 1862; *New York Herald,* November 10, 1862; Lee, *Wartime Washington,* 204; Janney, *Civil War Period Journals,* 161; Nicolay, *With Lincoln in the White House,* 93. After his removal, McClellan received notes praising his course from cautious conservatives not aligned with Democratic Party leaders. John A. Dix to Mrs. Dix, November 17, 1862; and Edward Everett to GBM, November 17, 1862, MPLC; *New York Times,* November 11, 1862.

12. WAITING GAME

1. *New York Times,* November 21, 22, 25, 1862; *New York Herald,* November 21, 25, 1862.

2. *New York Herald,* November 22, 1862.

3. *New York Times,* November 26, 28, December 15, 1862, March 18, 1863; *New York Herald,* November 26, December 4, 1862; Lauderdale, *Wounded River,* 150.

4. *New York Times,* December 4, 27, 1862, January 5, 6, 17, 1863; *New York Herald,* January 27, 1863; *Chicago Tribune,* March 7, 1863; *MCWP,* 535, 542; Myers, *Study in Personality,* 405–6.

5. Sears, *McClellan,* 350; *Washington Daily National Republican,* January 19, February 3, 1863; *Boston Herald,* January 29, February 3, 4, 1863; *New York Times,* January 29, February 3, 4, 6, 1863; *MCWP,* 536, 543; *New York Herald,* January 29, 1863; *Boston Post,* January 29–31, February 2, 3, 7, 1863, in *New York Herald,* January 30, 31, February 1, 3, 4, 8, 1863; *Washington Evening Star,* February 3, 1863; George T. Curtis to William C. Prime, February 6, 1863, MPLC. For particularly sour assessments of McClellan's visit to Boston, see

Gray and Ropes, *Civil War Letters,* 83; *Liberator* (Boston), February 13, 1863; and *National Antislavery Standard* (New York), February 21, 1863. The *Chicago Tribune* thought that McClellan's travels in the East meant that he already imagined himself to be "the Copperhead candidate for President in 1864." *Chicago Tribune,* February 11, 1863.

6. *OR,* 12(2):4–8; *Washington National Republican,* December 8, 1862; Zachariah Chandler to his wife, December 4, 1862, Chandler Papers, LC; *New York Herald,* December 5, 1862; [Prime], *General H. W. Halleck's Report,* 3–22.

7. *OR,* 12(1):39–40, 91–101; *New York Times,* December 8, 11, 1862; *Washington Daily National Intelligencer,* December 10, 17, 1862; *New York Daily Tribune,* January 17, 1863; *New York Herald,* December 10–11, 1862. Reacting to McClellan's testimony, War Board chairman Hitchcock tartly observed: "It is the old story over again; he commits the blunder and then tries to throw the blame on others." Ethan Allen Hitchcock to Mary Mann, December 16, 1862, Hitchcock Papers, LC.

8. *New York Times,* December 5, 1862; *New York Herald,* January 19, 1863; Alexander S. Webb to his father, November 26, 1862, Webb Papers, Sterling Library, Yale University; *OR,* 12(2):1016–19. Some of McClellan's political supporters in New York City also tried and failed to get the board of aldermen to pass resolutions in Porter's favor. *New York Times,* January 27, 1863. Zach Chandler told his wife at least twice that Porter should have been shot. Zachariah Chandler to his wife, January 22, February 7, 1863, Chandler Papers, LC. For a finely detailed account that sifts through a mountain of evidence on the case, see Marvel, *Radical Sacrifice.*

9. *OR,* 21:774; Brewster, *When This Cruel War Is Over,* 193; Young, *Dear Delia,* 119–20.

10. John Darraugh Wilkins to his wife, November 26, 1862, Wilkins Papers, Schoff Civil War Collection, Clements Library, University of Michigan; John H. Remington to his mother, December 14, 1862, Remington Papers, Rhode Island Historical Society; White, *Emancipation, the Union Army, and the Reelection of Abraham Lincoln,* 49; Bright and Bright, *"Respects to All,"* 34; Walker, *Quite Ready to Be Sent Somewhere,* 65.

11. Willet Raynor to Zachariah Chandler, December 4, 1862, Chandler Papers, LC; *New York Times,* November 29, December 13, 1862; *Chicago Tribune,* November 19, December 16, 1862; Gray and Ropes, *War Letters,* 42–43; *Liberator* (Boston), December 12, 1862; *Boston Herald,* December 18, 1862.

12. *New York Herald,* November 26, 29, December 5, 1862; *New York Times,* November 29, December 9, 12, 1862; Stoddard, *Dispatches from Lincoln's White House,* 121.

13. Daniel Read Larned to "My Dear Henry," November 22, 1862, Larned Papers, LC; *New York Herald,* December 8, 1862; Moe, *Last Full Measure,* 205; Strother, *Virginia Yankee in the Civil War,* 130. One newspaper claimed that the Radicals hoped to replace Burnside with Frémont. *New York Herald,* November 28, 1862.

14. Zerah Coston Monks to Hannah T. Rohrer, December 21, 1862, Monks-Rohrer Letters, Special Collections, Emory University; William Wirt Henry to Mary Jane Henry, December 19, 1862, Henry Family Papers, Vermont Historical Society; Parker, *Henry Wilson's Regiment,* 237; James Jenkins Gillette to his mother, December 17, 1862, Gillette Papers, LC; Patrick, *Inside Lincoln's Army,* 193; Henry Welch to his father, December 21, 1862, Welch Letters, Hamilton College Library; *Washington Evening Star,* January 14, 1863. The mere rumor of McClellan's return seemed to inspire troops who had become despondent after Fredericksburg. Goddard, *Good Fight That Didn't End,* 120.

15. *New York Herald,* December 17, 1862; Albert B. Williams to his father, December 29, 1862, Williams Letters, Rhees Library, University of Rochester, Rochester, NY; Brandegee, *Charlie's Civil War,* 130.

16. John H. Van Ingen [8th New York Cavalry] to "My own dear Goodie," December 15, 1862, www.mqamericana.com/Museum_Quality_Americana.html (item removed); Richards, *Village Life in America,* 149–51; *New York Herald,* December 17, 1862; W. C. Barry to James Gordon Bennett, December 28, 1862, Bennett Papers, LC; Thomas H. Mann to "Friends of the Lyceum," January 20[?], 1863, Mann Papers, Brown Military Collection, Brown University; Ripley, *Vermont General,* 67; Geary, *Politician Goes to War,* 88. One thoughtful volunteer believed authorities in Washington were just too proud to admit that McClellan's removal had been a mistake. Gray and Ropes, *War Letters,* 57. One editor suggested that the disaster at Fredericksburg provided further evidence about the James River being the proper approach to Richmond. *New York Herald,* December 19, 1862.

17. William Withington to his sister Lucy, December 23, 1862, Withington Papers, Bentley Library, University of Michigan; George Washington Lambert Diary, December 15, 1862, Indiana Historical Society; McWhirter, *Battle Hymns,* 95–96; Moore, *Rebellion Record,* 6 (Documents):96; Henry W. Beecham to his mother, December 19, 1862, Beecham Letters, Wisconsin Historical Society; Walter Phelps to his wife, December 27, 1862, Phelps Letters, FSNMP; Cyrus J. Hardaway to his mother, December 17, 1862, Hardaway Letters, FSNMP; Bowen, *From Ball's Bluff to Gettysburg,* 142; Caleb H. Beal to his parents, December 23, 1862, Beal Papers, Massachusetts Historical Society; James E. Decker to his sister, December 17, 1862, Decker Letters, Civil War Document Collection, AHEC.

18. Chase, *Yours for the Union,* 184–85; Dodge, *On Campaign with the Army of the Potomac,* 120; Henry H. Young to his mother, December 29, 1862, Young Papers, Civil War Miscellaneous Collection, AHEC; William Hamilton to his mother, December 24, 1862, Hamilton Papers, LC; George A. Marden Diary, December 16, 1862, Dartmouth College Library; William H. Brown to his brother, December 27, 1862, Brown Letters, Civil War Collection, Brown University; *Fifth Annual Report of the Chief of the Bureau of Military Statistics,* 725–26; William Patterson to his mother, December 24, 1862, Patterson Letters, Harrisburg Civil War Round Table Collection, AHEC; Whittemore, *"But God Has So Ordered It,"* 227; Samuel W. Eaton to Eddie Eaton, December 15, 1862, Eaton Papers, Wisconsin Historical Society; Cutler, *Life and Times Ephraim Cutler,* 296–97. For pointed comparisons of Burnside and McClellan that much favored the latter, see Bowen, *Dear Friends at Home,* 209–10; and Donaldson, *Inside the Army of the Potomac,* 199.

19. Herman Haupt to AL, December 22, 1862, Stanton Papers, LC; Bates, *Diary,* 270; Francis Preston Blair to AL, December 18, 1862, ALPLC; *Chicago Tribune,* December 18, 1862; Browning, *Diary,* 1:601; Francis Preston Blair to Montgomery Blair, January 30, 1863, Blair Family Papers, LC; *New York Herald,* December 22, 1862. Although maintaining that Lincoln's course in removing McClellan had been vindicated, one newspaper conceded that "a share of the men who call themselves loyal, together with all those whose loyalty is properly doubted," continued to argue that McClellan had been "abused" and should return. *Chicago Tribune,* January 22, 1863.

20. Peifer, *Bethlehem Boy,* 129; Watson, *Letters of a Civil War Surgeon,* 76; William Pat-

terson to his mother, December 24, 1862, Patterson Letters, Harrisburg Civil War Round Table Collection, AHEC; Dexter, *Seymour Dexter,* 130; Halsey, *Brother against Brother,* 97–98; *Harrisburg (PA) Patriot and Union,* January 12, 1863; "Civil War Letters of Francis Edwin Pierce of the 108th New York Volunteer Infantry," in McKelvey, *Rochester in the Civil War,* 166; Charles H. Eager to his wife, December 16, 1862, Eager Letters, Leigh Collection, AHEC; Moore, *Rebellion Record* 6 (Documents):95–96.

21. George A. Marden Diary, December 19, 1862, Dartmouth College Library; Reuben W. Schell to his father, December 31, 1862, Schell Letters, FSNMP; Allen, "Civil War Letters," 571; R. S. Robertson to his mother, December 24, 1862, Robertson Papers, FSNMP; Henry C. Ropes to "Dear John," December 20, 1862, Ropes Papers, Boston Public Library; Ford, *Cycle of Adams Letters,* 1:241; Thomas H. Mann to "Friends at Home," January 4, 1863, Mann Papers, Brown Military Collection, Brown University.

22. George Barnard to his father, December 18, 1862, Barnard Papers, Massachusetts Historical Society; *New York Irish-American,* December 27, 1862; Abbot, *Fallen Leaves,* 149, 158; Carter, *Four Brothers in Blue,* 210–11; Russ, "Civil War Letters Concerning Members of Co. G, 174th Reg., P.V.I.," 189; Russell, "Aftermath of Prairie Grove," 355.

23. L. B. Halven to Simeon Whiteley, December 16, 1862, Whiteley Papers, Abraham Lincoln Presidential Library; Gray and Ropes, *War Letters,* 49–54, 67–68; Guiney, *Commanding Boston's Irish Ninth,* 163; Castleman, *Army of the Potomac,* 274; Dyer, *Journal of a Civil War Surgeon,* 59; Harris and Niflot, *Dear Sister,* 65; William R. Williams to his wife, December 26, 1862, Williams Letters, Civil War Miscellaneous Collection, AHEC; Hays, *Life and Letters,* 392; John W. Ames to his mother, December 29, 1862, Ames Papers, Coco Collection, Harrisburg Civil War Roundtable Collection, AHEC. A perceptive New York diarist thought McClellan was hurting himself by too close an association with "ultra-Democrats." Daly, *Diary of a Union Lady,* 212.

24. Snell, *From First to Last,* 228; William B. Franklin to George B. McClellan, December 23. 1862, MPLC; Raymond, "Extracts from the Journal of Henry J. Raymond," 420; Sherman, *Sherman's Civil War,* 348; Hsieh, *West Pointers and the Civil War,* 170; Browning, *Diary,* 1:611; Gouverneur K. Warren to William Warren, December 18, 1862, Warren Papers, New York State Library.

25. Hayes, *Diary and Letters,* 2:378; Burlingame, *Lincoln,* 1:431; Gurowski, *Diary,* 2:42; *Pittsburgh Daily Dispatch,* January 22, 1863.

26. *MCWP,* 531, 533–34; *New York Daily Tribune,* January 8, 1863; *Carrier's Address of the New York World;* Peterson, *Military Review of the Campaign in Virginia and Maryland;* Cox, *Meaning of the Elections of 1862,* 7–8; Frederick A. Conkling to Horace Greeley, December 16, 1862, Greeley Papers, LC. In a speech at Newark, New Jersey, Clement Vallandigham stated that the politicians had gotten rid of McClellan, the country's most capable general. *New York Times,* February 15, 1863.

27. Perry, *Life and Letters of Henry Lee Higginson,* 175; Edwards, *Of Singular Genius,* 230; Hodge, *Life of Charles Hodge,* 475; Charles Francis Adams Diary, February 16, 1863, Massachusetts Historical Society; *New York Times,* January 30, 1863; *New York Herald,* January 29, February 2, 1863; Francis Preston Blair to AL, December 18, 1862, ALPLC; Walker, *Quite Ready to Be Sent Somewhere,* 79; *MCWP,* 530; Browning, *Diary,* 1:612–13. McClellan's

appearance in Washington attracted crowds of sightseers and created more speculation about his immediate future. Brooks, *Washington in Lincoln's Time,* 14–15.

28. *New York Herald,* December 26, 1862, January 10, 16, 1863; *New York World,* December 19, 1862; *Columbus (OH) Gazette,* January 23, 1863; Williams, *Lincoln and the Radicals,* 239–40.

29. *New York Herald,* December 26, 1862, January 16, 19, 21, 23, February 2, 1863; *New York Times,* December 30, January 2, 1863; Horatio Nelson Taft Diary, January 2, 1863, LC; *Louisville (KY) Daily Journal,* December 24, 1862.

30. Garfield, *Wild Life of the Army,* 201–2; *Pittsburgh Daily Dispatch,* December 19, 1862; Cutler, *Life and Times of Ephraim Cutler,* 296–97; E. H. Eldredge to John H. B. McClellan, November 28, 1862, MPLC; Stoddard, *Dispatches from Lincoln's White House,* 127; *Chicago Tribune,* January 22, 1863; Gurowski, *Diary,* 2:42; Zachariah Chandler to his wife, January 22, 1863, Chandler Papers, LC; Stevens, *Selected Papers,* 1:367.

31. Rable, *Fredericksburg! Fredericksburg!,* 322–32; Burlingame, *Lincoln,* 2:446, 448–57; Browning, *Diary,* 1:600–601; Brooks, *Lincoln Observed,* 13.

32. Burlingame, *Lincoln,* 2:448–50, 474–77, 485–87; Rable, *Fredericksburg! Fredericksburg!,* 390–91, 401–2, 421–23.

33. Dexter, *Seymour Dexter,* 131; Walker, *Quite Ready to Be Sent Somewhere,* 84; John W. Patterson to his wife, January 28, 1863, Patterson Papers, FSNMP; Charles Kinsman to Emeline Quimby, February 8, 1863, Quimby Letters, University of Vermont.

34. *New York Herald,* January 27, 1863; Charles H. Eager to his wife, January 27, 1863, Eager Letters, Leigh Collection, AHEC; Watson, *Letters of a Civil War Surgeon,* 78; Ambrose F. Cole to his wife, February 21, 1863, Cole Letters, FSNMP; Rich, "Quaker Soldier," 281–82; Wightman, *From Antietam to Fort Fisher,* 106. Republicans expected Hooker to root out the McClellan influence in the Army of the Potomac. Thaddeus Stevens hoped that the "citizen soldiers" would resist the siren calls from Democratic officers and disloyal newspapers that only McClellan could achieve victory. *Boston Herald,* February 7, 1863; Stevens, *Selected Papers,* 1:365.

35. Moore, *Rebellion Record,* 6 (Diary of Events):51; Browning, *Diary,* 1:620–21; John Fay to "Dear Aunt Martha," February 2, 1863, Fay Letter, FSNMP; A. D. Slade, *A. T. A. Torbert,* 57; John W. Patterson to his father, February 9, 1863, Patterson Papers, FSNMP; Allan L. Bevan to his sister, March 20, 1863, Bevan Correspondence, Civil War Document Collection, AHEC; Adam Fair to Jacob Lowenberg, March 12, 1863, Adam Fair Letters, State Historical Society of Iowa, Des Moines; Taylor, *Civil War Letters of Joseph K. Taylor,* 93–94; James A. Carman to his uncle, February 18, 1863, Carman Family Collection, AHEC; Thomas H. Mann to his mother, March 4, 1863, Mann Papers, Brown Military Collection, Brown University; Mayo, *Civil War Letters,* 227; Bonsall, *Well Satisfied with My Position,* 98. For contrary reports claiming waning enthusiasm for McClellan and speculating about a possible court-martial for the general, see Osborn, *No Middle Ground,* 106; *New York Times,* February 23, April 10, 1863; and James Cornell Biddle to his wife, April 13, 1863, Biddle Letters, Historical Society of Pennsylvania.

36. *New York Herald,* February 8, 19, 1863; *Louisville (KY) Daily Journal,* February 9, 1863; *New York Daily Tribune,* February 9, 12, 1863; *New York Times,* January 22, Feb-

ruary 5, 8, 1863; *Chicago Tribune,* February 10, 20, 1863; Zachariah Chandler to his wife, January 22, February 10, 1863, Chandler Papers, LC; Wilkes, *McClellan: From Ball's Bluff to Antietam,* 31–35; Garfield, *Wild Life of the Army,* 235. The caucus of Republican senators that had moved against Seward in December 1862 claimed that the secretary of state had both resisted the Emancipation Proclamation and the removal of McClellan. Word came to Fitz John Porter, however, that Seward was hostile to McClellan and had prevented Stanton from leaving the cabinet. *New York Times,* December 22, 1862; Fitz John Porter to William C. Prime, July 7, 1863, Porter Papers, LC, reel 3.

37. Stevens, *Selected Papers,* 1:378–39; Julian, *Speeches on Political Questions,* 198–201; Richardson, *Secret Service,* 323–24; *Washington Daily National Republican,* January 21, 1863; Samuel M Shaw to Thurlow Weed, February 15, 1863, ALPLC; Browning, *Diary,* 1:619.

38. *Springfield (IL) Journal,* n.d., in *Chicago Tribune,* March 26, 1863; *MCWP,* 540; *OR: Supplement,* 4:452; Wilkes, *McClellan: From Ball's Bluff to Antietam,* 35–39; Williams, *Lincoln and the Radicals,* 246–47; Zachariah Chandler to his wife, March 31, 1863, Chandler Papers, LC; *Chicago Tribune,* April 2, 7, 1863; *New York Daily Tribune,* April 6, 7, 1863; *New York Times,* April 6, 7, 1863; Swisshelm, *Crusader and Feminist,* 212–16; *Boston Herald,* April 20, 1863. Such Republican alarm incited only ridicule from the opposition, including comments about how, with Hooker in command, delays suddenly seemed more tolerable. *New York Herald,* February 16, 1863; *Washington Weekly National Intelligencer,* March 5, April 9, 1863.

39. Marvel, *Great Task Remaining,* 26–29; Gould, *Civil War Journals,* 264; Dyer, *Journal of a Civil War Surgeon,* 69; William Watts Folwell Diary, April 6, 1863, University of Minnesota Archives; Williams, *Lincoln and His Generals,* 250; Tap, *Over Lincoln's Shoulder,* 163; *New York Herald,* April 3, 9, 10, 1863; *Boston Daily Advertiser,* April 7, 1863; Walker, *Quite Ready to Be Sent Somewhere,* 114. For a Democratic defense of McClellan and attack on the committee, see Flagg, *Speech of Hon. William J. Flagg,* 6–15. Old-line Whig and conservative Edward Everett recommended that McClellan have a "first-rate lawyer" go over the committee report to "cover" his critics with "confusion." He expected McClellan to be recalled as general in chief. Edward Everett to GBM, May 8, 1863, MPLC.

40. *New York Times,* February 4, 5, 14, 20, 25, 1863.

41. *New York Herald,* February 11–13, 18–20, 23, April 8, 1863; George Hill to his parents, February 11, 1863, Hill Correspondence, Civil War Document Collection, AHEC; *New York Times,* February 12, 13, 17, 18, 20, 24, 28, March 7, 1863; *Washington Daily National Republican,* February 17, 18, March 6, 1863; *Washington Daily National Intelligencer,* May 27, 1863; Edward Everett to GBM, February 20, 1863, MPLC; *MCWP,* 537; seating chart and menu, May 19. 1863, Marble Papers, LC, reel 2. On hearing that McClellan had joined a church in New York, abolitionist speaker Anna Dickinson sarcastically commented that "she hoped he would obey holy orders better than he ever did military orders." *New York Herald,* April 22, 1863. At this point, McClellan offered little encouragement to Democratic wirepullers. Gallman, *Cacophony of Politics,* 189–90.

42. Brooks, *Lincoln Observed,* 50; Brooks, *Washington in Lincoln's Time,* 57–58; John Sherman to William T. Sherman, May 7, 1863, Sherman Papers, LC.

43. Hyde, *Civil War Letters,* 77; Charles Francis Adams Diary, June 7, 1863, Massachusetts Historical Society; Grandchamp, *Boys of Adams' Battery G,* 125; *Washington Weekly*

National Intelligencer, June 18, 1863; George Armstrong Custer to GBM, May 6, 1863, MPLC; Marshall Phillips to his wife, May 11, 1863, Phillips Correspondence, Maine Historical Society; C. W. Buckingham to unknown, May 30, 1863, Bennett Papers, LC; Perry, *Letters from a Surgeon,* 41; Brewster, *When This Cruel War Is Over,* 233; Marvel, *Great Task Remaining,* 66; Henry C. Ropes to his mother, May 9, 1863, Ropes Papers, Boston Public Library.

44. John Gibbon to GBM, May 6, 18, 1863; Jacob D. Cox to GBM, March 14, 1863; and M. F. McMahon to GBM, May 13, 1863, MPLC; Abbott, *Fallen Leaves,* 181.

45. *New York Times,* May 9, 1863; *Boston Herald,* May 12, 1863; James A. Hamilton to AL, May 11, 1863; and Francis Preston Blair to AL, May 17, 1863, ALPLC; Beck, "Letters of a Civil War Surgeon," 153; Hays, *Life and Letters,* 392; Brooks, *Lincoln Observed,* 46; Zachariah Chandler to his wife, May 20, 1863, Chandler Papers, LC; Brooks, *Washington in Lincoln's Time,* 16, 58–59.

46. *Chicago Tribune,* May 16, June 6, 17, 1863; *Boston Herald,* May 15, June 17, 1863; *New York Herald,* May 15, June 2, 19, 1863; *Washington Evening Star,* May 15, 1863; *Washington National Republican,* June 4, 1862; *New York Times,* June 4, 12, 13, 17, 18, 21, 1863; Charles F. Dunham to James Lawrence, February 23, 1863; Charles C. Fulton to GBM, May 29, 1863; Thurlow Weed to GBM, June 12, 1863; and Horatio Seymour to GBM, June 15, 1863, MPLC; *MCWP,* 548–50. For competing claims about who cheered for McClellan during a political meeting in Utica and during his visit to Albany, see *New York Herald,* May 28, 30, 31, 1863; *Boston Daily Advertiser,* May 28, 1863; *New York Times,* May 30, 1863.

47. *New York Herald,* June 17–19, 22, 24, 1863; *Boston Herald,* June 19, 1863; *Chicago Tribune,* June 19, 1863; *New York Times,* June 19, 20, 1863; T. J. Barnett to Samuel L. M. Barlow, June 19, 1863, BPHL; Lee, *Wartime Washington,* 277; *New York Tablet,* June 27, 1863; *Washington Daily National Intelligencer,* June 18, 25, 1863.

48. Edgar Cowan to AL, June 17, 1863; James Dixon to AL, June 28, 1863; Edward Everett to AL, June 16, 1863; Thomas S. McIncron to AL, June 22, 1863; and S. F. Miller to AL, June 29, 1863, ALPLC; Richard H. Rush to GBM, June 18, 1863; and Edward Everett to GBM, June 18, 1863, MPLC; *OR,* 27(3):168, 391, 409, 435; T. J. Barnett to Samuel L. M. Barlow, July 2, 1863, BPHL; Charles Francis Adams Diary, June 27, July 8, 1863, Massachusetts Historical Society. In Philadelphia and New York, local legislative bodies passed resolutions calling for McClellan's return to command. *Boston Daily Advertiser,* July 2, 1863; *New York Times,* July 3, 1863.

49. John E. Thomson to AL, June 30, 1863; Edwin D. Morgan to AL, July 1, 1863; Philadelphia Common Council to AL, July 2, 1863; Joseph P. Bradley and Marcus L. Ward to AL, July 2, 1862; and Alexander K. McClure to AL, June 30, 1863, ALPLC; Alexander K. McClure to Ida Tarbell, February 19, 1899, Tarbell Collection Lincolnania, Allegheny College; *New York Times,* July 2, 1862. Yet McClure also worried that Lincoln had waited too long to bring back McClellan and thought it might be a political gift to the Democrats should the newly appointed commander of the Army of the Potomac, Major General George Gordon Meade, fail to defeat Lee. Alexander K. McClure to Lincoln, July 1, 1863, ALPLC.

50. *CWL,* 6:311–12; McClure, *Recollections of Half a Century,* 318–19; Welles, *Diary,* 1:345; *New York Herald,* June 17, 1863; *New York Times,* June 17, 1863; *New York Daily Tribune,* June 23, 1863; *Boston Herald,* July 1, 1863; Cornelius A. Walborn to Edwin M. Stanton, June 28, 1863; and William D. Kelley to AL, June 30, 1863, ALPLC; Stevens, *Selected Papers,*

1:398–99. There were reports that both Thurlow Weed and Horatio Seymour were working to restore McClellan to command. William A. Hall to Salmon P. Chase, May 22, 1863; and James W. Stone to Chase, June 29, 1863, Chase Papers, LC. Weed later said that in March he had recommended that McClellan replace Halleck. *New York Times*, July 13, 1863.

51. Wainwright, *Diary of Battle*, 223; Patrick, *Inside Lincoln's Army*, 263; Donaldson, *Inside the Army of the Potomac*, 283; Spiegel, *Your True Marcus*, 294, 297; McCalmont, *Extracts from Letters*, 43; Olsen, *Upon the Tented Field*, 129; Weld, *Diary and Letters*, 227–28.

52. Burlingame, *Lincoln*, 2:499–503.

53. Wainwright, *Diary of Battle*, 229; *Louisville (KY) Daily Journal*, June 30, 1863; A. Boyd Hamilton to his mother, June 30, 1863, Hamilton Papers, LC; *New York Herald*, July 1, 1863; *Chicago Tribune*, July 1, 1863; William Wirt Henry to Mary Jane Henry, July 1, 1863, Henry Family Papers, Vermont Historical Society; Hayward, *Last to Leave the Field*, 157–58; Strother, *Virginia Yankee in the Civil War*, 188.

54. William Stow to "Dear Friends," July 6, 1863, Stow Papers, University of Vermont; Parker, *Henry Wilson's Regiment*, 331; Goss, *Recollections of a Private*, 179; Macnamara, *Ninth Regiment Massachusetts Volunteer Infantry*, 315; Donaldson, *Inside the Army of the Potomac*, 298; Cheek and Pointon, *Sauk County Riflemen*, 70; Graham, "On to Gettysburg," 473–74; Spear, *Civil War Recollections*, 215; Fitz John Porter to Manton Marble, July 22, 1863, Marble Papers, LC, reel 2; Gerrish, *Army Life*, 242; Wainwright, *Diary of Battle*, 242; *OR: Supplement*, 5:190; Olmsted, *Papers*, 4:638–40; Samuel L. M. Barlow to GBM, August 8, 1863, MPLC; *MCWP*, 550.

55. *MCWP*, 551; George Gordon Meade to GBM, July 4, 1863, MPLC; Charles H. Salter to Isabella Duffield, July 29, 1863, Divie Bethune Duffield Papers, Burton Historical Collection, Detroit Public Library; *National Antislavery Standard* (New York), July 11, 1863; *New York Times*, July 9, 1863; *OR*, 27 (3):552–53.

56. Strong, *Diary*, 3:330; Emerson, *Life and Letters of Charles Russell Lowell*, 274, 278; Wainwright, *Diary of Battle*, 266; Buffalo Common Council to AL, July 16, 1863, Papers of Abraham Lincoln Project, Springfield, IL; *Boston Daily Advertiser*, July 23, 1863; *Chicago Tribune*, July 23, 1863; Gurowski, *Diary*, 2:269; James Lawrence to GBM, July 24, 1863; Edward Everett to GBM, July 25, 1863; and William Dennison to GBM, August 4, 1863, MPLC; *MCWP*, 552, 555; *New York Herald*, July 20, 1863; Sears, *McClellan*, 355–56.

13. A DIFFERENT ARENA OF CONFLICT

1. *Washington Daily National Intelligencer*, July 13, 1863; *New York Herald*, July 16, 21, 23, 28, September 3, 1863; Fitz John Porter to Manton Marble, July 13, 1863, Marble Papers, LC, reel 2; *Boston Daily Advertiser*, July 16, 1863; *New York Times*, August 2, 1863; *Boston Post*, n.d., in *Washington Daily National Intelligencer*, August 10, 1863. For a sharply worded rejection of any comparisons between Meade and McClellan, see *New York Times*, August 12, 1863.

2. *Washington Daily National Intelligencer*, August 11, 1863; *Washington Daily National Republican*, August 12, 1863; *Washington Evening Star*, August 17, 1863; *New York Times*, August 14, 23, 1863; *MCWP*, 555–56. In early September, McClellan reviewed troops on

Staten Island and made brief remarks about the Peninsula and Antietam Campaigns. The soldiers warmly greeted the general, who shook hands for over an hour, while a colonel offered a champagne toast to "Our army's love, our country's hope." *New York Times,* September 9, 1863; *Washington Daily National Intelligencer,* September 12, 1863; *New York Herald,* September 9, 1863.

3. Sedgwick, *Correspondence,* 2:155; Chase, *Papers,* 1:449; *New York Daily Tribune,* August 31, 1863; Meade, *Life and Letters,* 1:145; Marvel, *Lincoln's Autocrat,* 299–300; *OR,* 29(2):227, 261–62; Wainwright, *Diary of Battle,* 284; Patrick, *Inside Lincoln's Army,* 291; *Chicago Tribune,* October 1, 1863.

4. Abbott, *Fallen Leaves.,* 213; Regan, *Lost Civil War Diaries,* 164–65; Chase, *Yours for the Union,* 291–92; Waters Whipple Braman to "Cousin Em," October 28, 1863, Braman Letters, NYMMVRC; Wainwright, *Diary of Battle,* 282–86; Mann, *Fighting with the Eighteenth Massachusetts,* 194; *Liberator* (Boston), October 2, 1863; *New York Herald,* October 5, 1863; *Chicago Tribune,* October 1, 1863; Perkins, *Three Years a Soldier,* 129; Eddy, *Sixtieth Regiment New York State Volunteers,* 281–84; Lyman, *Meade's Army,* 44; Patrick, *Inside Lincoln's Army,* 291; Rawle, *Blue-Blooded Cavalryman,* 88; Arthur McClellan to GBM, September 26, 1863, MPLC. A surgeon who had no use for McClellan claimed that although some officers might have supported the testimonial, the enlisted men "had no heart in it." Dyer, *Journal of a Civil War Surgeon,* 122–23. For a perceptive account of the controversy, see Fry, *Republic in the Ranks,* 111–17.

5. Thomas H. Mann to "Friends at Home," September 25, 1863, Mann Papers, Brown Military Collection, Brown University; Hay, *Inside Lincoln's White House,* 79–80; Samuel L. Barlow to GBM, September 9, 1863, Letterbook 8, BPHL, reel 7.

6. S. L. M. Barlow to GBM, September 28, 1863, Letterbook 8, BPHL, reel 7; *MCWP,* 558–59; *Chicago Tribune,* October 13, 1863; *Washington Daily National Republican,* October 14, 1863; Welles, *Diary,* 1:469, 471; Strong, *Diary,* 3:364. On the Pennsylvania governor's race, including efforts to make Woodward out to be an arch Copperhead, see White, *Emancipation, the Union Army, and the Reelection of Abraham Lincoln,* 26–35; and Neely, *Lincoln and the Democrats,* 93–95. For a wonderfully detailed and penetrating account of the Pennsylvania context, see Gallman, *Cacophony of Politics,* 188–99.

7. *New York Times,* October 14, 1863; D. Salomon to Manton Marble, November 12, 1863; Manton Marble to GBM, November 11, 1863; and E. H. Eldredge to GBM, December 4, 1863, MPLC; Dyer, *Journal of a Civil War Surgeon,* 124; Wainwright, *Diary of Battle,* 294; Mann, *Fighting with the Eighteenth Massachusetts,* 195; James Baldwin Burrows to his brother, December 29, 1863, Burrows Correspondence, Civil War Document Collection, AHEC; Fry, *Republic in the Ranks,* 126; Gray and Ropes, *War Letters,* 251; *Chicago Tribune,* October 21, November 3, 1863.

8. Hay, *Inside Lincoln's White House,* 132–33; Zachariah Chandler to AL, November 15, 1863, ALPLC.

9. *MCWP,* 560–62; John Jacob Astor to GBM, November 19, 1863, MPLC.

10. *MCWP,* 563; *New York Herald,* December 8, 17, 1863; *Washington Weekly National Intelligencer,* December 24, 1863. One Republican editor believed that efforts to promote Grant as a presidential candidate was designed to "kill him off" and get him out of McClellan's

way. "McClellan is a political myth," he added. *Washington Daily National Republican,* December 30, 1863.

11. Sears, *McClellan,* 352–53; *Chicago Tribune,* September 7, 1863; *New York Journal of Commerce,* n.d., in *Washington Weekly National Intelligencer,* September 24, 1863.

12. Gurowski, *Diary,* 3:102–10; *New York Times,* January 6, 1864; Lowell, "General McClellan's Report," 554–64; *Chicago Tribune,* January 9, 1864. At the same time, some Republican soldiers had begun publishing works sharply critical of the Union high command in general and McClellan in particular. Fry, *Republic in the Ranks,* 147–54.

13. *New York Times,* February 27–April 18, 1864; Swinton, *"Times" Review of McClellan.* For the importance of Republican critiques of McClellan's military record in the coming presidential campaign, see Neely, *Union Divided,* 80–88.

14. Fitz John Porter to Manton Marble, December 24, 1863, Marble Papers, LC; *New York Journal of Commerce,* n.d., in *Alexandria (VA) Gazette,* February 2, 1864; Francis P. Blair Sr. to Montgomery Blair, March 2, 1863, Blair Family Papers, LC; Marvel, *Great Task Remaining,* 276; Thomas H. Mann to "Dear Friends at Home," March 14, 1864, Mann Papers, Brown Military Collection, Brown University; Abbott, *Fallen Leaves,* 239; Wainwright, *Diary of Battle,* 330–31; "George Breck's Civil War Letters," in McKelvey, *Rochester in the Civil War,* 136–37.

15. Zorn, *Sergeant's Story,* 93; *Boston Daily Advertiser,* December 25, 1863; Hiram Ketchum to Samuel F. B. Morse, January 23, 1864, Morse Papers, LC; *New York Times,* March 18, 1864.

16. *New York Times,* January 4, March 19, 1864; *Chicago Tribune,* February 5, 1864. An 1861 phrenological reading based only on a portrait of McClellan had been entirely favorable, but an 1864 reading based on a likeness found in a biography was more mixed, declaring the general to be not only intelligent and ambitious but also passive and cautious. "Maj. Gen. George B. McClellan," *American Phrenological Journal* 34 (September 1861): 49–51; "George B. McClellan," ibid. 40 (November 1864): 144–45.

17. *New York Herald,* January 6, February 1, 3, 26, 1864.

18. *New York Herald,* January 21, 1864; *New York Times,* February 5, April 5, 1864; *Washington Daily National Republican,* March 15, 1864.

19. *New York Herald,* January 15, 1864; Hiram Ketchum to GBM, March 9, 1864, MPLC; Ketchum, *General McClellan's Peninsula Campaign,* 3–13, 21–32, 51.

20. [McClellan], "Coming Campaign Foreshadowed," 193–94; [McClellan], "Coming Campaign in the West," 209–10; Lowell, "General McClellan's Report," 344.

21. *New York Times,* April 5–17, 19–24, 1864; *New York Herald,* April 23, 1864; *Chicago Tribune,* April 29, 1864. For a more detailed account and excellent political analysis, see Gallman, *Cacophony of Politics,* 214–17.

22. *New York Times,* March 27, 1864.

23. *Chicago Tribune,* February 15, March 22, 1864; *New York Times,* March 13, April 18, 1864; Strother, *Virginia Yankee in the Civil War,* 212. Republicans also repeatedly pointed to McClellan's Woodward letter. Gallman, *Cacophony of Politics,* 229–31.

24. *Chicago Tribune,* March 9, 10, 13, 1864; *New York Times,* March 12, 14, 1864; *Washington Evening Star,* March 9, 1864; *New York Herald,* March 21, 1864; *MCWP,* 568–70; Sears, *McClellan,* 361–62. Even the Joint Committee on the Conduct of the War decided that

the witness who supposedly could confirm that McClellan had met with Lee was a "man of such character that no confidence could be placed in any statement he might make under oath." *CCW,* 4:xx–xxi.

25. George G. Pardee[?] to GBM, December 31, 1863, MPLC; *New York Times,* March 11, 1864; Gurowski, *Diary,* 3:199; *New York Herald,* March 25, April 19, 1864; *Boston Herald,* April 20, 22, 1864; *Boston Daily Advertiser,* April 22, May 3, 1864; Luigi Palma di Cesnola to Hiram Hitchcock, May 28, 1864, Cesnola Papers, Dartmouth College Library; McCalmont, *Extracts from Letters,* 78–79; *CCW,* 4:375; Thomas H. Mann to "Members of the Lyceum," April 25, 1864, Mann Papers, Brown Military Collection, Brown University.

26. *New York Herald,* April 1, 1864; Montgomery Blair to Samuel L. M. Barlow, April 28, May 1, 11, 1864; and Barlow to Blair, April 26, 1864, BPHL; *MCWP,* 574–75. According to a *New York Times* correspondent in Washington, Lincoln had early in April denied a newspaper report that the Blair family had recommended that McClellan be placed in charge of the Washington defenses. *New York Times,* April 1, 1864.

27. Samuel L. M. Barlow to Montgomery Blair, April 26, 1864, BPHL; Welles, *Diary,* 2:28–29; Fehrenbacher and Fehrenbacher, *Recollected Words of Abraham Lincoln,* 203; Burlingame, *Lincoln,* 2:626–27.

28. *MCWP,* 575–76; Gilbert Thompson Journal, June 29, 1864, LC; *New York Times,* May 6, 14, 20, 22, June 1, 13, 1864; *Chicago Tribune,* June 6, 1864.

29. Lyman, *Meade's Headquarters,* 141–42; Luigi Palma di Cesnola to "My Dear Friend," June 28, 1864, Cesnola Papers, Dartmouth College Library; James K. Hale to his brother, June 19, 1864, Hale Letters, Schoff Civil War Collection, Clements Library, University of Michigan; Wainwright, *Diary of Battle,* 391, 412, 419; Poe, *My Dear Nelly,* 224, 227.

30. *New York Daily Tribune,* July 25, 1864; Hyde, *Civil War Letters,* 133, 136; Crotty, *Four Years Campaigning,* 134; *Star of the North* (Bloomsburg, PA), June 6, 1864; Chase, *Yours for the Union,* 354–55; Holmes, "Civil War Letters." 126.

31. *New York Times,* June 16, 1864; McClellan, *Oration,* 5, 6, 20, 23–24; *MCWP,* 580–81.

32. Strong, *Diary,* 3:459; Samuel L. M. Barlow to GBM, June 16, 1864; and Manton Marble to GBM, June 16, 1864, MPLC; Wainwright, *Diary of Battle,* 431; Abbott, *Family Letters,* 72–73; *New York Herald,* June 25, 1864; McClellan, *Oration,* 5; *Chicago Tribune,* July 9, 1864; *New York Freeman's Journal and Catholic Register,* June 25, 1864. A Vermont enlisted man complained about Stanton dismissing the officer who had invited McClellan to speak. In fact, on Stanton's orders, the entire committee that had arranged for McClellan's appearance faced disciplinary action. Charles C. Morey to his parents, July 8, 1864, Stuart Goldman Collection, AHEC; *MCWP,* 582; *New York Herald,* July 1, 2, August 2, 1864.

33. Katz, *August Belmont,* 125–26; Manton Marble to James W. Hall, March 10, 1864, Marble Papers, LC, reel 3; Samuel S. Cox to Franklin Pierce, March 17, 1864, Pierce Papers, LC; *New York Freeman's Journal and Catholic Register,* March 26, 1864; *New York Times,* June 13, 1864. For an interpretation that emphasizes not only the Democrats' drive for unity in 1864 but also the persistence of factionalism, see Silbey, *Respectable Minority,* 116–23.

34. Dean Richmond to Manton Marble, June 16, 1864; Samuel S. Cox to Marble, June 22, 1864; and William Cassidy to Marble, June 25, 1864, Marble Papers, LC, reel 3; Samuel L. M. Barlow to GBM, June 16, 1864, MPLC; *MCWP,* 577–80.

35. Luigi Palma di Cesnola to "My Dear Friend," July 7, 1864, Cesnola Papers, Dartmouth College Library; *New York Herald,* July 1, 1864, Edwin D. Morgan to AL, July 27, 1864, ALPLC.

36. *New York Times,* October 10, 1864; Nicolay and Hay, *Lincoln,* 9:247–49; Francis P. Blair Sr. to AL, July n.d., 1864, ALPLC; Sears, *McClellan,* 364–66; *MCWP,* 583–85.

37. *New York Herald,* July 14, 16, 23, 27, August 2, 9 1864; *New York Times,* August 4, 5, 7, 1864; *Washington Daily National* Intelligencer, August 1, 12, 1864; Rhodes, *History of the United States,* 4:507n; Grant, *Papers,* 11:253; Patrick, *Inside Lincoln's Army,* 410; Vincent, *Your Affectionate Son,* 193; Reinhart, *Yankee Dutchmen,* 190; Amos Myers to AL, August 4, 1864; and John L. Scott to AL, August 4, 1864, ALPLC; *CWL,* 7:470. For a useful discussion of the thin evidence on Lincoln's thinking about this question, see John Y. Simon, "Grant, Lincoln, and Unconditional Surrender," in Boritt, *Lincoln's Generals,* 178–81.

38. Naglee, *Peninsular Campaign,* 6; *New York Times,* October 4, 10, 1864; *MCWP,* 582–86.

39. For a useful account of McClellan's deficiencies as a presidential candidate, see Neely, *Lincoln and the Democrats,* 124–26.

40. T. J. Barnett to Samuel L. M. Barlow, March 20, 1864; and Barlow to GBM, May 18, 1864, BPHL

41. *New York Times,* July 6, 9, August 11, 1864; *New York Herald,* August 5, 9–11, 1864; *Boston Daily Advertiser,* August 13, 1864.

42. *MCWP,* 579–80, 586.

43. *Washington Daily National Republican,* August 17, 1864; *New York Daily Tribune,* August 13, 1864; Long, *Jewel of Liberty,* 180–82; *New York Times,* July 27, 1864. Some McClellan supporters hoped to pick up support from the Frémont faction, and anti-Lincoln Republicans even hoped that if Frémont bowed out, the president would agree to do so as well. Once Frémont withdrew from the contest in September and Blair left the cabinet, Radicals such as Chandler and Wade were certainly pleased, whatever their continuing reservations about Lincoln. Max Langenschwarz to GBM, August 10, 1864; and Randolph B. Marcy to GBM, September 13, 1864, MPLC; *New York Times,* September 23, 1864; Zachariah Chandler to his wife, September 8, 1864; and Benjamin F. Wade to Chandler, October 2, 1864, Chandler Papers, LC.

44. James Hall to GBM, July 18, 1864; James Harrison to GBM, August 12, 1864; Amasa Parker to GBM, July 24, 1862; George W. Morgan to GBM, August 12, 1864; and A. C. Niven to GBM, August 17, 1864, MPLC; *MCWP,* 586; Strong, *Diary,* 3:477; *New York Freeman's Journal and Catholic Register,* August 13, 1864; Marvel, *Tarnished Victory,* 160; Standard and Standard, *This Infernal War,* 214; Biddlecom, *No Freedom Shrieker,* 206; *New York Times,* August 21, 1864. For comments of soldiers committed to McClellan before the Chicago convention, see Ward, "Campaign of 1864," 192; Spurgeon, *Kansas Soldier at War,* 141; and William Boston to "Dear Aunt," August 1, 1864, Boston Letters, Bentley Library, University of Michigan.

45. J. W. Fitch to George Morgan, August 10, 1864; and Samuel S. Cox to GBM, August 4, 1864, MPLC; *New York Times,* August 16, 24, 1864; Noah Brooks to John G. Nicolay, August 29, 1864, ALPLC. For a prescient warning from a Union officer to Cox about the danger of nominating McClellan on a peace platform, see Ward, "Campaign of 1864," 190–92.

46. Haley, *Rebel Yell and the Yankee Hurrah,* 193; Tidd, *Dear Friend Amelia,* 128–29; Marvel, *Tarnished Victory,* 160; Johnson, *Papers,* 7:37; Spurgeon, *Kansas Soldier at War,* 141; Benjamin Rush to GBM, July 18, 1864; and Randolph B. Marcy to GBM, August 12,

1864, MPLC. For a detailed, contemporary assessment of army opinion, see David Cameron to GBM, August 30, 1864, ibid.

47. Henry S. Jay to "Dear Mary," August 26, 1864; and Jay to "Dear Nancy," August 29, 1864, Civil War Document Collection, AHEC; Reid, *Uncommon Soldiers*, 181–82; Solomon L. Mershow to GBM, August 12, 1864; Joel Parker to GBM, August 27, 1864; Manton Marble to GBM, August n.d., 1864; S. L. M. Barlow to unknown, August 27, 1864; and Barlow to GBM, August 28, 1864, MPLC; John Berry to S. L. M. Barlow, August 12, 1864, BPHL; Charles A. Dana to James S. Pike, August 8, 1864, Pike Letters, University of Maine; Samuel L. M. Barlow to Manton Marble, August 21, 24, 26, 1864, Marble Papers, LC, reel 4; *New York Herald*, August 27, 1864. For speculation (likely with some foundation) that some New Yorkers were plotting with Peace Democrats to make Seymour the nominee, see H. S. Lansing to GBM, August 28, 1864; and George Morgan to GBM, September 1, 1864, MPLC; and *New York Herald*, August 24, 1864. For a critique of several blunders made by McClellan's chief backers, see Sears, *McClellan*, 371–74.

48. *Official Proceedings*, 3–4, 10. On the factional maneuvering preceding and during the convention between what has been termed the "Legitimists" and the "Purists," see Silbey, *Respectable Minority*, 124–30.

49. S. L. M. Barlow to GBM, August 29, 1864, MPLC; McPherson, *Political History*, 423; *Official Proceedings*, 27.

50. *Official Proceedings*, 29–42; *New York Times*, August 31, 1864. For an account of McClellan's role in the Maryland arrests, see Marvel, *Mr. Lincoln Goes to War*, 195–99. One former legislator who had been arrested and imprisoned promised McClellan his "hearty and honest support in the coming campaign." James W. Maxwell to GBM, September 6, 1864, MPLC. For an effort to find out whether McClellan had recommended or approved the arrests, see John W. Forney to Lincoln, September 1, 1864, ALPLC.

51. *Official Proceedings*, 43–50; *New York Times*. September 1, 1864.

52. *New York Times*, September 1–4, 7, 1864; *Boston Daily Advertiser*, September 2, 1864; *Washington Daily National Republican*, September 3, 1864; *Alexandria (VA) Gazette*, September 2, 1864; Katz, *August Belmont*, 132–33.

53. *MCWP*, 587; *New York World*, September 1, 1864; Samuel L. M. Barlow to GBM, August 31, 1864; and John V. L. Pruyn to GBM, August 31, 1864, MPLC; *Newark Advertiser*, n.d., in *New York Times*, September 3, 1864.

54. Clement L. Vallandigham to GBM, September 4, 1864; and Hiram White to GBM, September 7, 1864, MPLC; William Cassidy to S. L. M. Barlow, September 5, 1864, BPHL; *New York Herald*, September 4, 1864.

55. Samuel L. M. Barlow to Washington McLean, September 2, 1864, copy; William J. Danes to GBM, September 2, 1864; James Gallatin to GBM, September 6, 1864; and Peter Abel to GBM, September 7, 1864, MPLC.

56. C. P. Osborne to GBM, September 6, 1864; John H. Dey to GBM, August 31, 1864; Hiram Ketchum to GBM, September 1, 1864; and L. Edgerton to GBM, September 3, 1864, MPLC. On the wartime critique of political partisanship, see Neely, *Union Divided;* and Smith, *No Party Now.*

57. Samuel L. M. Barlow note, ca. August 31, 1864; Joseph B. Stewart to GBM, September 1, 1864; Barlow to GBM, September 1, 1864; August Belmont to GBM, September 3, 1864; and William E. Dodge to unknown, September 1, 1864, MPLC.

58. William Gray to GBM, September 1, 1864; J. T. Moulton to GBM, September 5, 1864; Henry Moore to GBM, September 6, 1864; John Robinson to GBM, September 5, 1864; Jonathan H. White to GBM, September 4, 1864; Charles Davies to GBM, September 3, 1864; John Graham to GBM, September 5, 1864; and W. A. Stephens to GBM, September 2, 1864, MPLC.

59. George T. Curtis to GBM, September 1, 1864; William H. Aspinwall to GBM, September 4, 1864; James Dixon et al. to GBM, September 8, 1864; and John Whiting to GBM, September 1, 1864, MPLC.

60. E. H. Kettell to GBM, September 5, 1864; Isaac J. Wistar to GBM, September 3, 1864; and William J. Danes to GBM, September 2, 1864, MPLC.

61. Samuel L. M. Barlow to GBM, September 3, 1864, MPLC; *MCWP*, 590–93, 595–96. For the view that McClellan's commitment to the Union at this time was wavering, see Wilson, "McClellan's Changing Views," 498–505. For a persuasive refutation of this argument, see Sears, "McClellan and the Peace Plank of 1864," 57–64.

62. George W. Morgan to GBM, September 8, 1864; George T. Curtis to GBM, September 8, 1864; Edward Kemble to GBM, September 9, 1864; Sidney Deming to GBM, September 10, 1864; Daniel W. Voorhees to GBM, September 14, 1864; and Amos Kendell to GBM, September 10, 1864, MPLC; *MCWP*, 598.

63. Samuel S. Cox to GBM, September 8[?], September 21, 1864; S. L. M. Barlow to GBM, September 12, 1864; George H. Pendleton to August Belmont, copy, August 27, 1864; William S. Garvin to GBM, September 18, 1864; and W. H. Flag to GBM, September 11, 1864, MPLC; *New York World*, n.d., in *Alexandria (VA) Gazette*, September 14, 1864; *New York Herald*, September 11, 1864; *New York Freeman's Journal and Catholic Register*, September 17, 1864.

64. *Washington Evening Star*, September 9, 12, 13, 1864; *New York Times*, September 12, 1864; McPherson, *Political History*, 421; Silbey, *Respectable Minority*, 136–37; *Chicago Tribune*, September 10, 1864; Johnson, *Papers*, 7:155; Hunt, *Israel, Elihu, and Cadwallader Washburn*, 231; Hiram White to GBM, September 7, 1864, MPLC.

65. Curtis, *Address at Philadelphia*, 2–5; *New York Tablet*, September 24, 1864; Hodge, *Life of Charles Hodge*, 480–81; Frothingham, *Edward Everett*, 462; T. Jefferson Coolidge to GBM, September 19, 1864, MPLC.

66. *Washington National Republican*, September 9, 14, 1864; Strong, *Diary*, 3:484; Sumner, *Charles Sumner*, 11:428–29; *New York Times*, September 12, 1864.

67. *New York Times*, September 11, 13, 16, 18, 20, 23, October 7, 1864; *Chicago Tribune*, September 18, 1864.

68. Sumner, *Charles Sumner*, 11:427–28. Chang and Eng Bunker were the most widely publicized conjoined twins of this period.

69. *New York Times*, September 10, 15, 30, 1864; "McClellan's Letter," *Harper's Weekly*, September 24, 1864; *Boston Daily Advertiser*, October 11, 1864; *New York Daily Tribune*, September 9, 10, 1864.

14. THE FINAL BATTLE

1. *CWL,* 7:514.

2. Burlingame, *Lincoln,* 2:659–65; *CWL,* 7:433–34; *American Annual Cyclopaedia, 1864,* 307–10.

3. Schurz, *Reminiscences,* 3:103–4; Butler, *Private and Official Correspondence,* 5:35; *CWL,* 7:506–7; Brooks, *Washington in Lincoln's Time,* 180.

4. The Republicans had dubbed their party conclave the National Union Convention, hoping to attract the support of War Democrats.

5. Theodore Tilton to Anna E. Dickinson, July 13, 1864, Dickinson Papers, LC; Du Pont, *Samuel Francis Du Pont,* 3:370; Burlingame, *Lincoln,* 2:664; Long, *Jewel of Liberty,* 192–94; Butler, *Private and Official Correspondence,* 5:67–68; *New York Sun,* June 30, 1889; Thurlow Weed to William H. Seward, August 22, 1864; and Henry J. Raymond to AL, August 22, 1864, ALPLC. Some Republicans feared that Lincoln might succumb to pressure to open peace talks with the Rebels. *New York Herald,* August 29, 1864; Forbes, *Letters and Recollections,* 2:102–3.

6. Burlingame, *Lincoln,* 2:680; *New York Sun,* July 30, 1889; Hay, *At Lincoln's Side,* 92.

7. *New York Sun,* June 30, 1889; Burlingame, *Lincoln,* 2:666; Nicolay, *With Lincoln in the White House,* 155.

8. *New York Sun,* June 30, 1889; Tarbell, *Lincoln,* 2:200–201; Burlingame, *Lincoln,* 2:665–67; George Wilkes to Elihu B. Washburne, August 31, 1864, Washburne Papers, LC; Thurlow Weed to William H. Seward, September 10, 1864, ALPLC.

9. Welles, *Diary,* 2:129–30; Chandler, "Chandler's Part in the Reelection of Lincoln," 272. Massachusetts senator Henry Wilson warned Lincoln of serious grumbling about the cabinet and the malign influence of the Blair family. Wilson to AL, September 5, 1864, ALPLC.

10. Welles, *Diary,* 2:135; Gideon Welles to his wife, September 4, 1864, Welles Papers, LC; Thurlow Weed to William H. Seward, September 10, 1864, ALPLC; Nicolay, *With Lincoln in the White House,* 157; Theodore Tilton to Anna E. Dickinson, September 3, 1864, Dickinson Papers, LC; Sumner, *Selected Letters,* 2:253; Burlingame, *Lincoln,* 2:689–90. There were a few holdouts. Abolitionist Wendell Phillips reportedly said he would "sooner cut his right hand off than vote for Lincoln." Lillie B. Chase to Anna E. Dickinson, September 19, 1864, Dickinson Papers, LC.

11. *New York Times,* September 8, 1864; *Washington Post,* August 16, 1891; Thompson, "Talk with President Lincoln."

12. Noah Brooks to John G. Nicolay, September 2, 1864; Henry Wilson to AL, September 5, 1864; and Samuel F. George to AL, September 7, 1864, ALPLC; McCalmont, *Extracts from Letters,* 96–96; Greene, *Letters from a Sharpshooter,* 252–53.

13. White, *Emancipation, the Union Army, and the Reelection of Abraham Lincoln,* 103; Waters Whipple Braman to "Cousin Abbie," September 6, 1864, Braman Letters, NYMMVRC; Wightman, *From Antietam to Fort Fisher,* 212. Wainwright, *Diary of Battle,* 473.

14. Wainwright, *Diary of Battle,* 460–61; Hayes, *Diary and Letters,* 2:504–5; Lane, *Soldier's Diary,* 197; Davis, *Lincoln's Men,* 206.

15. White, "White Papers," 265–66; Parks, *Civil War Letters,* 36; Charles M. Smith to his father, September 14, 1864, Smith Papers, Wisconsin Historical Society; James Coe to

Robert Crouse, September 1, 1864, Crouse Papers, Bentley Library, University of Michigan; Bonner, *Soldier's Pen,* 141; White, *Emancipation, the Union Army, and the Reelection of Abraham Lincoln,* 110.

16. Elmer D. Wallace to his mother, September 2, 1864, Wallace Papers, Bentley Library, University of Michigan; Henry McKendree Ewing to Nan Ewing, September 6, 1864, Ewing Family Papers, Archives of Michigan, Michigan History Center, Lansing; Standard and Standard, *This Infernal War,* 214, 216.

17. Finley Anderson to GBM, September 6, 1864, MPLC; John [Aughe?] to unknown, September 14, 1864, Hunter Papers, Ohio Historical Society; Leander Harris to "my darling Emmy," September 10, 1864, Harris Letters, Dartmouth College Library; George Stearns to his mother, September 18, 1864, Stearns Papers, New Hampshire Historical Society; Evans Blake to Elihu Washburne, September 30, 1864, Washburne Papers, LC.

18. Connolly, *Three Years in the Army of the Cumberland,* 261; Lane, *Soldier's Diary,* 205; Finley Anderson to Frederic Hudson, September 10, 1864, Bennett Papers, LC; John Earnest to Richard Yates, September 16, 1864, Yates Family Papers, Abraham Lincoln Presidential Library; Resolutions of Co. M, 5th Illinois Cavalry, September 16, 1864, Mason Brayman Papers, Chicago Historical Society; Rawle, *Blue-Blooded Cavalryman,* 189; Post, *Soldier's Letters,* 416. Nor could many soldiers stomach the Democrat's vice-presidential nominee. Some men who said they would have voted for McClellan refused to do so with Pendleton on the ticket, a sentiment that received further amplification in the press. M. H. Hart to "Friends Alpha & Sarah," September 15, 1864, Civil War Letters, Chautauqua County Historical Society; Reid, *Uncommon Soldiers,* 186; *Philadelphia Press,* September 27, 1864. Manton Marble advised McClellan to write no more political letters. The editor also acknowledged that the platform had done political damage. Manton Marble to GBM, September 12, 1864, MPLC.

19. White, *Emancipation, the Union Army, and the Reelection of Abraham Lincoln,* 106; Kamphoefner and Helbich, *Germans in the Civil War,* 443; Glatthaar, *March to the Sea and Beyond,* 47; Taylor, *Letters Home to Sarah,* 115; *New York Times,* September 17, 1864.

20. Long, *Hard Times,* 133; Bacon and Howland, *Letters of a Family,* 2:626–27; James Helme Rickard to his brother, September 12, 1864, Rickard Letters, American Antiquarian Society; Cram, *Soldiering with Sherman,* 140.

21. Edgcomb, "Dear Brother Isaac," 15; Fleming, "Palace Guard View of Lincoln," 35–36; George Benton Codman to his sister, September 11, 1864, Codman Letters, Dartmouth College Library; Henry W. Owen to "Friend Emma," September 14, 1864, Owen Correspondence, Civil War Document Collection, AHEC; Biddlecom, *No Freedom Shrieker,* 215–16.

22. *Washington Daily National Intelligencer,* September 2, 1864; *New York Times,* September 4, 1864; Johnson, *Papers,* 7:151; [Belmont], *A Few Letters and Speeches,* 110–11; Winthrop, *Speech of Hon. Robert C. Winthrop,* 6.

23. *New York World,* September 6, October 1, 1864; George Ticknor Curtis to Manton Marble, September 28, 1864, Marble Papers, LC, reel 4; *Boston Daily Advertiser,* September 19, 1864; *New York Times,* September 15, 16, 1864; "McClellan and Lincoln," *Old Guard* 2 (October 1864): 224.

24. W. B. Lawrence to Franklin Pierce, October 17, 1864, Pierce Papers, LC; Zornow, *Lincoln and the Party Divided,* 137–38; *Cincinnati Convention,* 2–3, 6–13; *New York Herald,*

October 27, 1864. Mark Neely has pointed out that the Democratic call for an armistice and convention of states posed insuperable constitutional and practical problems. Neely, *Lincoln and the Democrats,* 164–66.

25. *New York Herald,* September 17, 1864; *MCWP,* 598–99, 601, 606, 610; Sears, *McClellan,* 380, 382–83. McClellan's running mate did even less, making but one brief late-October speech—after Republicans had for weeks ridiculed his silence. Even then, Pendleton simply offered general criticisms of the Lincoln administration while approvingly quoting McClellan and repeatedly invoking the word "Union." *New York Times,* October 25, 1864.

26. In early October, there were some new revelations about this supposed offer and some back and forth in the press. *Washington Daily National Intelligencer,* October 3, 8, 12, 1864; *New York Times,* October 10, 1864.

27. Freidel, *Union Pamphlets,* 2:1078, 1080–81, 1088–89, 1091–92. McClellan praised Winthrop for his "calm dignified & able & exhaustive exposition of the questions at issue. Would that the whole contest could be conducted in the spirit with which you approach it!" *MCWP,* 615–16.

28. Freidel, *Union Pamphlets,* 2:1097, 1101; *Washington Weekly National Intelligencer,* October 27, 1864. See also the careful analysis in Gallman, *Cacophony of Politics,* 250–54.

29. Neely, *Lincoln and the Democrats,* 128–33. For exceptions, see John H. Van Erie to GBM, September 14, 1864; and Isaac Metzler to GBM, September 26, 1864, MPLC. For the point that some campaign songs and cartoons clearly played to racial fears, see Gallman, *Cacophony of Politics,* 255–60.

30. Thomas H. Clark to GBM, October 10, 1864; Robert J. Wright to GBM, October 13, 1864; and D. Webster Dixon to GBM, September 20, 1864, MPLC; Samuel S. Cox to Manton Marble, January 13, 1865; James Guthrie to Samuel S. Cox, January 22, 1865; and Dean Richmond to Marble. January 23, 1865, Marble Papers, LC, reel 5.

31. Seward, *Issues of the Conflict,* 6; Lucius Fairchild to AL, September 13, 1864, ALPLC.

32. Neil, *Alexander Neil and the Last Shenandoah Valley Campaign,* 63; *New York Times,* October 7, 1864; Henry H. Elliott to Gideon Welles, September 3, 1864, Welles Papers, LC; Biddlecom, *No Freedom Shrieker,* 228; *New York Daily Tribune,* September 23, 1864. In its usually unpredictable manner, the *Tribune*'s archrival, the *New York Herald,* declared that both Lincoln and McClellan stood on solidly Union platforms and that Union victories would help drive the Copperheads out of the Democratic Party. James Gordon Bennett had favored Grant as a presidential candidate, but the *Herald* sounded increasingly neutral while discounting McClellan's chances of election. A rumored visit from McClellan had evidently failed to win Bennett's editorial backing. *New York Herald,* September 2, 11, 16, 22, 1864; Albert Ramsey to GBM, October 18, 1864, MPLC; William O. Bartlett to AL, November 5, 1864, ALPLC.

33. Henry Winter Davis to Zachariah Chandler, August 24, 1864, Chandler Papers, LC; Wade, *Facts for the People; New York Times,* September 1, 5, 12, October 20, 1864; *McClellan's Military Career; Liberator* (Boston), October 21, 1864; Johnson, *Papers,* 7:237; *Washington Daily National Republican,* September 2, 1864. For an assessment of Republican assaults on McClellan's military record, see Neely, *Union Divided,* 79–83.

34. Gurowski, *Diary,* 3:329; Swinton, *A Few Plain Words,* 5; *Chicago Tribune,* October 23, 1864.

35. *Chicago Tribune,* September 23, 24, 1864; *New York Daily Tribune,* September 26, 1864; *Washington Daily National Republican,* September 28, October 15, 18, November 5, 1864; *New York Times,* October 21, 1864; Neely, *Union Divided,* 82–83. Republicans also downplayed McClellan's contributions to the strategic victory at Antietam. Even Montgomery Blair, who had left the cabinet in September 1864, made a speech that, while offering an unusually balanced assessment of McClellan's military record, nevertheless strongly defended Lincoln's decision to remove him from command. *Chicago Tribune,* October 1, 1864; *New York Times,* October 16, 1864.

36. *Washington Weekly National Intelligencer,* September 1, 1864; *Page of History,* 1–4; Neely, *Union Divided,* 83–88; *New York Herald,* September 13, 14, 21, 1864; *New York World,* October 1, 1864.

37. *New York Times,* September 6, 8, 24, 1864; *Washington Daily National Republican,* September 8, 1864; *Washington Evening Star,* September 21, 1864; Squier, *This Wilderness of War,* 77. A Washington newspaper wrote darkly about the role of August Belmont, who was supposedly financed by the Rothschilds and British gold. *Washington Daily National Republican,* September 8, October 6, 1864.

38. *New York Times,* September 7, 23, November 7, 1864; Hamilton, *Coercion Completed,* 14–24; Bristed, *Cowards' Convention,* 2; *"Only Alternative,"* 19; *New York Daily Tribune,* October 5, 1864. For a refutation of these charges that sought to reduce the peace faction to an insignificant minority, see *Washington Weekly National Intelligencer,* October 20, 1864.

39. *Washington Daily National Republican,* September 12, 1864; *Chicago Tribune,* September 30, 1864; *New York World,* September 5, 1864; *New York Times,* September 16, October 4, 24, 1864; Elmer D. Wallace to his mother, October 16, 1864, Wallace Papers, Bentley Library, University of Michigan; Marshall, *Army Life,* 402–3; John F. Lane to "Dear Ellen," September 21, 1864, Crist Manuscripts, Lilly Library, Indiana University.

40. *Boston Daily Advertiser,* October 7, 1864; Johnson, *Papers,* 7:270; *Chicago Tribune,* September 10, October 29, 1864; William Hughes to AL, October 17, 1864; Edgar Conkling to AL, September 28, October 20, 1864; and P. Wellington to AL, October 16, 1864; ALPLC; Edgar Conkling to Joseph Holt, November 8, 1864, Holt Papers, LC; Edward A. Wild to Edward W. Kinsley, October 27, 1864, Kinsley Papers, University of Massachusetts. At the same time, Republicans cited the dangers of states' rights ideology, appealed to working-class values (along with fear of southern slaveholders), and claimed to be faithful constitutionalists in casting their appeal to certain ethnic groups without harping on questions of loyalty. Lieber, *Lincoln or McClellan.*

41. Bates, *Diary,* 423; Samuel L. M. Barlow to GBM, September 23, 1864, MPLC; *Chicago Tribune,* September 3, 1864; *Boston Daily Advertiser,* September 17, 1864; *MCWP,* 602–3.

42. *New York Herald,* November 7, 1864; *New York Times,* October 15, 1864; *Boston Daily Advertiser,* October 15, 1864; *Chicago Tribune,* October 1, 1864; Miller, *Fighting for Liberty and Right,* 263; *Washington Daily National Republican,* November 2, 1864; Stevens, *Selected Papers,* 1:502.

43. Caleb Blanchard to "Dear Mattie," October 20, 1864, Blanchard Papers, Connecticut Historical Society; Morris Conklin to Eron Thomas, October 20, 1864, Civil War Collection, American Antiquarian Society; Anderson, *They Died to Make Men Free,* 234; Tapert, *Brothers' War,* 224.

44. *New York Times,* October 13, 15, 16, 1864; B. M. Shirley to Joseph Holt, October 4, 1864, Holt Papers, LC; George Tobey Anthony to his brother, October 24, 1864, Anthony Papers, Clements Library, University of Michigan; Plotow, *For Their Letters,* 163. In Ohio, there were reports of the balloting closing early at army camps if the soldiers were not voting Republican; agents distributing Democratic ballots were reportedly driven away. Samuel S. Cox to GBM, October 11, 1864, MPLC.

45. Fry, *Republic in the Ranks,* 161, 173; *Louisville (KY) Daily Journal,* September 19, 1864; *New York Herald,* September 30, 1864; *Gettysburg (PA) Compiler,* November 5, 1864; Davis, *Lincoln's Men,* 208–9; *MCWP,* 612–13.

46. Manton Marble to GBM, September 12, 1864; and E. H. Kettell to GBM, September 24, 1864, MPLC; Edwin D. Morgan to Edwin M. Stanton, September 15, 1864, Stanton Papers, LC.

47. *OR,* 38(5):857; *New York Times,* September 17, October 26, 1864; *New York Herald,* September 29, 1864; Fry, *Republic in the Ranks,* 165–66; Meade, *Life and Letters,* 2:232, 244–45; Sherman, *Sherman's Civil War,* 742–43.

48. Wainwright, *Diary of Battle,* 477; Williams, *From the Cannon's Mouth,* 347–48; *Ebensburg (PA) Democrat and Sentinel,* November 9, 1864; Poremba, *If I Am Found Dead,* 210; James Cornell Biddle to his wife, October 14, 1864, Biddle Letters, Historical Society of Pennsylvania; Patrick, *Inside Lincoln's Army,* 433.

49. Fry, *Republic in the Ranks,* 166–70; Henry Lieberman to GBM, October 8, 1864; and Horatio Seymour to GBM, October 23, 1864, MPLC; *New York Times,* November 6, 1864. For analysis of some of the violent confrontations, see Blair, *With Malice toward Some,* 222–24.

50. Tidd, *Dear Friend Amelia,* 134–35; Styple, *Writing and Fighting the Civil War,* 301–2; *Washington Daily National Intelligencer,* October 7, 1864; Guarneri, *Lincoln's Informer,* 315; McKelvy, "Soldier Voting in 1864," 392–93; *CWL,* 8:11. For Democratic anticipation of election fraud based on the Lincoln administration's control of post offices and the telegraph, see *New York World,* September 19, 1864.

51. *OR,* ser. 3, 4:751–52. In some states, soldiers would have to return home to cast their ballots, but other states authorized voting in the field. Most notably, Indiana, Illinois, and New Jersey failed to do so. Winther, "Soldier Vote in the Election of 1864," 440–47.

52. Winther, "Soldier Vote in the Election of 1864," 449–51; McSeveney, "Re-electing Lincoln," 147–48; Horatio Seymour to GBM, September 30, 1864, MPLC; Edwin Stanton to Horatio Seymour, October 6, 1864; and Stanton to George H. Thomas, October 22, 1864, Letterbook, Stanton Papers, LC.

53. Meade, *Life and Letters,* 2:233–34, 239–40; James Henry Wickes to his father, October 18, 1864, Wickes Papers, Boston Public Library; McKelvy, "Soldier Voting in 1864," 403–4; "George Breck's Civil War Letters," in McKelvey, *Rochester in the Civil War,* 140–41; *New York Times,* November 12, 1864; Voris, *Citizen-Soldier's Civil War,* 232; Winther, "Soldier Vote in the Election of 1864," 454.

54. Fry, *Republic in the Ranks*, 172–74; Chandler, *Soldier's Right to Vote*, 3–4; *New York Times*, October 28, 1864.

55. Trimble, *Brothers 'til Death*, 117; John H. Ferry to GBM, October 3, 1864; and George M. Buck to GBM, November 10, 1864, MPLC; Lyman, *Meade's Headquarters*, 247–48; White, *Emancipation, the Union Army, and the Reelection of Abraham Lincoln*, 117–23; Styple, *Writing and Fighting the Civil War*, 297; Blair, *With Malice toward Some*, 227–28; *New York World*, November 4, 1864; McFadden, *Aunt and the Soldier Boys*, 152.

56. *New York Times*, October 23, 25, 27–29, 1864; Ritner and Ritner, *Love and Valor*, 384; Mohr, *Cormany Diaries*, 490; Elmer D. Wallace to his parents, November 9, 1864, Wallace Papers, Bentley Library, University of Michigan; Matrau, *Letters Home*, 100; William D. Butler to "James and the folks," October 26, 1864, Civil War Letters Collection, New-York Historical Society; *Philadelphia Press*, October 21, 1864; Biddlecom, *No Freedom Shrieker*, 242. Soldiers from states that did not permit voting in the field held their own straw votes. These often favored Lincoln. Levi Ross Diary, October 31, 1864, Abraham Lincoln Presidential Library; Miller, *Fighting for Liberty and Right*, 271.

57. Musser, *Soldier Boy*, 159, 161; Thomas, *Civil War Letters*, 259; Matrau, *Letters Home*, 100.

58. Chase, *Yours for the Union*, 376; White, *Emancipation, the Union Army, and the Reelection of Abraham Lincoln*, 114, 117; Blauvelt, *Civil War Letters*, 60.

59. For differing interpretations and important statistical analysis of the soldier vote, see White, *Emancipation, the Union Army, and the Reelection of Abraham Lincoln*, 112–14, 126–27; Fry, *Republic in the Ranks*, 178–79.

60. White, *Emancipation, the Union Army, and the Reelection of Abraham Lincoln*, 8–9, 109, 115–17. For the state and army election returns, see *OR*, 42(3):560–61, 565–66, 568–70, 574, 576–78; *Tribune Almanac and Political Register for 1865*, 46–67; White, *Emancipation, the Union Army, and the Reelection of Abraham Lincoln*, 171–76; and Fry, *Republic in the Ranks*, 208–25.

61. *CWL*, 8:75.

62. *CWL*, 8:3–4, 46. Because of the Electoral College, as historian William Marvel has pointed out, the election was much closer than Lincoln's strong showing in the popular vote and even in the electoral vote indicated: "Had fewer than forty-two thousand wavering War Democrats changed their votes in six close states—representing barely 1 percent of the total votes cast and less than the total of McClellan's surplus majorities in the three states he did win—McClellan would have taken the presidency with an electoral victory of 120–114." Marvel, *Tarnished Victory*, 225.

63. *CWL*, 8:53.

64. Brooks, *Lincoln Observed*, 142–43; Hay, *Inside Lincoln's White House*, 243; *CWL*, 8:108–10, 124, 128–30. For more details about Lincoln on Election Day, see the fine account in Burlingame, *Lincoln*, 2:722–23.

65. Hay, *Inside Lincoln's White House*, 247–48; *CWL*, 8:100–101.

66. *CWL*, 8:149–50; Brooks, *Washington in Lincoln's Time*, 219.

67. For Lincoln as a Whig, see the classic essay, "Abraham Lincoln: Whig in the White House" in Donald, *Lincoln Reconsidered*, 187–208.

68. *Chicago Tribune,* September 28,1864; *Washington Daily National Republican,* September 29, 1864; *New York Times,* October 27, 1864; *MCWP,* 418; A. F. Randolph to William H. Seward, November 13, 1862, ALPC; *Washington Daily National Intelligencer,* November 14, 1862.

69. Samuel L. M. Barlow to GBM, November 9, 1864; and Manton Marble to GBM, November 13, 18, 1864, MPLC; *Washington Daily National Intelligencer,* November 17, 1864; *MCWP,* 618–25; Sears, *McClellan,* 384–86. Some Democrats predictably pointed to fraud and intimidation to explain why so many soldiers failed to support McClellan. His old comrade William Franklin believed that the general had been the victim of "electioneering tricks." *Louisville (KY) Daily Journal,* November 4, 1864; Fry, *Republic in the Ranks,* 178; William B. Franklin to GBM, November 25, 1864, MPLC.

70. *New York Freeman's Journal and Catholic Register,* November 19, 1864; *New York Times,* January 10, 1865; Katz, *Belmont,* 150–52; *Washington Daily National Republican,* November 17, 1864; *Boston Daily Advertiser,* November 16, 1864; "The Election," *Harper's Weekly,* November 19, 1864, 738; *Liberator* (Boston), November 18, 1864; Neely, *Union Divided,* 169.

71. Daly, *Diary of a Union Lady,* 329–30; W. G. Murray to GBM, December 14, 1864, MPLC; *New York Times,* January 12, 20, 1865; *Washington Evening Star,* January 20, 1865.

72. *Washington Daily National Intelligencer,* January 27, February 21, March 11, April 7, 1865; *New York Times,* March 2, 1865; *Washington Evening Star,* March 9, 1865; *Boston Daily Advertiser,* March 3, 1865; *Washington National Republican,* May 2, 1865; *MCWP,* 629.

73. *MCWP,* 630–31; GBM Diary, April 14, 16, 1865, MPLC.

74. Johnson, *"God's Ways Unsearchable,"* 4. On the mythic quality of the story, see Grimsley, "Lincoln-McClellan Relationship," 63–81.

BIBLIOGRAPHY

PRIMARY SOURCES

Manuscripts

Abraham Lincoln Presidential Library, Springfield, Illinois
    Henry W. Halleck Letters
    Levi Ross Diary
    Simeon Whiteley Papers
    Yates Family Papers
Allegheny College, Meadville, Pennsylvania
    Ida M. Tarbell Collection of Lincolnania
American Antiquarian Society, Worcester, Massachusetts
    Civil War Collection
    Comey Family, Civil War Papers
    James Helme Rickard Letters
    Henry Rogers Smith Letters
Boston Public Library, Boston, Massachusetts
    Henry C. Ropes Papers
    Henry W. Tisdale Diary
    James Wickes Papers
Boston University, Boston, Massachusetts
    John C. Ropes Collection
Bowdoin College Library, Brunswick, Maine
    Oliver Otis Howard Papers
Brown University, Special Collections, John Hay Library, Providence, Rhode Island
    William H. Brown Letters, Civil War Collection
    Thomas H. Mann Papers, Anne S. K. Brown Military Collection
Chautauqua County Historical Society, Westfield, New York
    Civil War Letters

Connecticut Historical Society, Hartford
Caleb and Horatio Blanchard Papers
William Jarvis Letters
Cornell University, Department of Archives and Manuscripts, Ithaca, New York
John S. Crocker Papers, Frank S. Brockett Collection
Dartmouth College Library, Special Collections, Dartmouth, New Hampshire
Luigi Palma di Cesnola Papers
George Benton Codman Letters
Leander Harris Letters
George A. Marden Diary
Detroit Public Library
Divie Bethune Duffield Papers, Burton Historical Collection
Duke University, Rubenstein Rare Book and Manuscript Library, Durham, North Carolina
James Gordon Bennett Papers
Darius Starr Papers
Emory University, Archives and Special Collections, Atlanta, Georgia
Monks-Rohrer Letters
Franklin and Marshall College, Special Collections, Lancaster, Pennsylvania
Reynolds Family Papers
Fredericksburg and Spotsylvania National Military Park, Virginia
Adam C. Baum Papers
Francis M. Carron Papers
George T. Chapin Letters
Ambrose F. Cole Letters
Samuel V. Dean Letters
James E. Decker Letters
James Fay Letter
Cyrus J. Hardaway Letters
William L. Heermance Letters
Albert E. Higley Dairy and Letters
William H. Jackson Letters
Irvin McDowell Letters
John W. Patterson Papers
Walter Phelps Letters
Robert S. Robertson Letters
Kirby Smith Russell Collection
Benneville and Reuben Schell Letters
Darius Starr Papers

Edward W. Steffan Letters
Joseph P. Vickers Papers
Hamilton College Library, Special Collections, Clinton, New York
Miscellaneous Civil War Letters
George W. Pearl Letters
Henry Welch Letters
Historical Society of Pennsylvania, Philadelphia
James Cornell Biddle Letters
John Gibbon Papers
George Gordon Meade Papers
Hobart and William Smith Colleges, Geneva, New York
Edward H. C. Taylor Civil War Letters
Henry E. Huntington Library, San Marino, California
Samuel L. M. Barlow Papers
Charles H. Ray Papers
Indiana Historical Society, Indianapolis
George Washington Lambert Diary
Indiana University, Lilly Library, Bloomington
Crist Manuscripts
Library of Congress
James Gordon Bennett Papers
Blair Family Papers
Zachariah Chandler Papers
Salmon P. Chase Papers
Anna E. Dickinson Papers
John William Draper Family Papers
William B. Franklin Papers
James G. Gillette Papers
Gove Family Papers
Horace Greeley Papers
William Hamilton Papers
John P. Hatch Papers
Samuel Peter Heintzelman Papers
Ethan Allen Hitchcock Papers
Joseph Holt Papers
Daniel Read Larned Papers
Abraham Lincoln Papers
Manton Marble Papers
George B. McClellan Papers
Samuel F. B. Morse Papers

Franklin Pierce Papers
Fitz John Porter Papers
William T. Sherman Papers
Edwin M. Stanton Papers
Thaddeus Stevens Papers
Horatio Nelson Taft Diary
Gilbert Thompson Journal
Benjamin F. Wade Papers
Elihu B. Washburne Papers
Gideon Welles Papers
Levi Woodbury Papers
Maine Historical Society, Portland
James Brown Papers
Marshall Phillips Correspondence
George M. Redlon Letters
Massachusetts Historical Society, Boston
Charles Francis Adams Diary
Caleb H. Beal Papers
Charles Bowers Papers
Josiah C. Fuller Papers
William Clark Hawes Diary
New Hampshire Historical Society, Concord
John Batchelder Bailey Journal
William Adams Moore Correspondence
George Stearns Papers
New-York Historical Society
Bigelow Collection
Civil War Letters Collection
Thomas Dolan Telegrams
New York Military Museum and Veterans Research Center, Saratoga Springs
Waters Whipple Braman Letters
New York Public Library
Henry J. Raymond Papers
New York State Library, Albany
Jonathan Burrell Papers
Egbert M. Rogers Papers
Gouverneur K. Warren Papers
Ohio Historical Society, Columbus
"Edwin M. Stanton: A Biographical Sketch by His Sister, Pamphila Stanton Wolcott."

Joshua R. Giddings Papers
William F. Hunter Jr. Papers
Rhode Island Historical Society, Providence
James H. Remington Papers
Rokeby Museum, Ferrisville, Vermont
Robinson Family Papers
Saint Mary's College, Rare Book and Manuscript Collection, Moraga, California
Forrest Little Letters
U.S. Army Heritage and Education Center, Carlisle, Pennsylvania
William T. H. Brooks Papers
Carman Family Collection
Civil War Document Collection
Allan L. Bevan Correspondence
Samuel Brooks Correspondence
James Baldwin Burrows Correspondence
James E. Decker Letters
Edmund Hawley Correspondence
George Hill Jr. Correspondence
Henry S. Jay Correspondence
Henry W. Owen Correspondence
Civil War Miscellaneous Collection
Samuel J. Alexander Papers
Jacob S. Kiester Letters
William B. Williams Letters
Henry H. Young Papers
Civil War Times Illustrated Collection
Charles H. Eager Letters, Lewis Leigh Collection
Louis R. Fortesque Letters, Dreer Collection
Stuart Goldman Collection
Harrisburg Civil War Round Table Collection
John Worthington Ames Papers, Gregory Coco Collection
Benjamin F. Ashenfelter Letters
Lewis Masonheimer Diary
Isaac Morrow Letters
William Patterson Letters
U.S. Military Academy, West Point, New York
Fitz John Porter Papers
University of Maine, Orono
James S. Pike Letters

University of Massachusetts, Amherst
    Edward W. Kinsley Papers
University of Michigan, Bentley Library, Ann Arbor
    William Boston Letters
    Robert Crouse Papers
    George Lockley Diary
    John Monteith Papers
    Jonas D. Richardson Correspondence
    John B. Stickney Papers
    Elmer D. Wallace Papers
    John Whiteside Letter
    William Withington Papers
University of Michigan, Clements Library, Ann Arbor
    Schoff Civil War Collection
        George T. Anthony Papers
        James K. Hale Letters
        Henry W. Halleck Papers
        John Darragh Wilkins Papers
University of Minnesota Archives, Minneapolis
    William Watts Folwell Diary
University of New Hampshire, Special Collections and Archives, Durham
    Thomas Carleton Cheney Papers
University of Vermont, Silver Special Collections Library, Burlington
    William Wirt Henry Family Papers
    George W. Quimby Letters
    William Stow Papers
University of Virginia, Special Collections, Charlottesville
    Henry A. Bitner Papers
    Corrine Carr Nettleton Civil War Collection
Vermont Historical Society, Barre
    Henry Family Papers
Wisconsin Historical Society, Madison
    Henry J. Beecham Letters
    Edward Dwight Eaton Papers
    Charles M. Smith Papers
Yale University, Sterling Library, New Haven, Connecticut
    Charles Morgan Coit Papers
    Alexander S. Webb Papers

Newspapers and Periodicals

Alexandria (VA) Gazette
Boston Daily Advertiser
Boston Herald
Chicago Tribune
Columbus (OH) Gazette
Daily Cleveland Herald
Dayton (OH) Daily Empire
Ebensburg (PA) Democrat and Sentinel
Frank Leslie's Illustrated Newspaper
Harper's Weekly
Gettysburg (PA) Compiler
Lamoille Newsdealer (Hyde Park, VT)
Liberator (Boston)
Louisville (KY) Daily Journal
National Antislavery Standard (New York)
New York Daily Tribune
New York Freeman's Journal and Catholic Register
New York Herald
New York Sun
New York Tablet
New York Times
New York World
Philadelphia Press
Principia (New York)
Star of the North (Bloomsburg, PA)
Washington Daily National Intelligencer
Washington Evening Star
Washington National Republican

Books

Abbott, Henry Larcom. *Family Letters of General Henry Larcom Abbott, 1841–1927.* Edited by Catherine C. Abbott. Gettysburg, PA: Thomas, 2001.

Abbott, Henry Livermore. *Fallen Leaves: The Civil War Letters of Henry Livermore Abbott.* Edited by Robert Garth Scott. Kent, OH: Kent State University Press, 1991.

Addresses Delivered at the Lincoln Dinner of the Republican Club of New York in Response to the Toast Abraham Lincoln, 1887–1909. New York: Republican Club of the City of New York, 1909.

American Annual Cyclopaedia and Register of Important Events of the Year 1864. New York: D. Appleton, 1872.

Ankeny, Henry G. *Kiss Josey for Me!* Edited by Florence Marie Ankeny Cox. Santa Ana, CA: Friis-Pioneer, 1974.

Annals of the War Written by Leading Participants North and South. Dayton, OH: Morningside, 1988.

Antietam. *McClellan and Fremont: A Reply to "Fremont and McClellan, Their Political and Military Careers Reviewed."* New York: Sinclair Toussey, 1862.

Applegate, John S. *Reminiscences and Letters of George Arrowsmith of New Jersey, Late Lieutenant-Colonel of the One Hundred and Fifty-Seventh Regiment, New York State Volunteers*. Red Bank, NJ: John H. Cook, 1893.

Arnold, Isaac N. *Life of Abraham Lincoln*. Chicago: A. C. McClurg, 1884.

Auchmuty, Richard Tylden. *Letters of Richard Tylden Auchmuty, Fifth Corps, Army of the Potomac*. Edited by E.S.A. N.p.: Privately printed, n.d.

Averell, William Woods. *Ten Years in the Saddle: The Memoir of William Woods Averell*. Edited by Edward K. Eckert and Nicholas J. Amato. San Rafael, CA: Presidio, 1978.

Bacon, Georgeanna Woolsey, and Eliza Woolsey Howland, comps. *Letters of a Family during the War for the Union, 1861–1865*. 2 vols. N.p., 1899.

———, comps. *My Heart toward Home: Letters of a Family during the Civil War*. Edited by Daniel John Hoisington. Roseville, MN: Edinborough, 2001.

Barlow, Francis C. *"Fear Was Not in Him": The Civil War Letters of Major General Francis C. Barlow, U.S.A.* Edited by Christian G. Samito. New York: Fordham University Press, 2004.

Barnard, J. G. *The Peninsular Campaign and Its Antecedents as Developed by the Report of Maj. Gen. Geo. B. McClellan, and Other Published Documents*. New York: D. Van Nostrand, 1864.

Barrett, Orvey S. *Reminiscences, Incidents, Battles, March and Camp Life of the Old 4th Michigan in War of Rebellion, 1861 to 1864*. Detroit: W. S. Outler, 1888.

Bates, David Homer. *Lincoln in the Telegraph Office: Recollections of the United States Military Telegraph Corps during the Civil War*. New York: Century, 1907.

Bates, Edward. *Diary of Edward Bates, 1859–1866*. Edited by Howard K. Beale. Washington: Government Printing Office, 1933.

Beatty, John. *The Citizen-Soldier; or, Memoirs of a Volunteer*. Cincinnati: Wilstach, Baldwin, 1872.

Becker, Carl M., and Ritchie Thomas, eds. *Hearth and Knapsack: The Ladley Letters, 1857–1880*. Athens: Ohio University Press, 1988.

Beidelman, George Washington. *The Civil War Letters of George Washington Beidelman*. Edited by Catherine H. Vanderslice. New York: Vantage, 1978.

[Belmont, August]. *A Few Letters and Speeches of the Late Civil War.* New York: Privately printed, 1870.

Bennett, Edwin Clark. *Musket and Sword; or, The Camp, March, and Firing Line in the Army of the Potomac.* Boston: Coburn, 1900.

Benton, Cora Beach. *Hard Breathing Days: The Civil War Letters of Cora Beach Benton.* Edited by Thomas R. Tabor. Albion, NY: Almeron, 2003.

Biddlecom, Charles. *No Freedom Shrieker: The Civil War Letters of Charles Biddlecom.* Edited by Katherine M. Aldridge. Ithaca, NY: Paramount Market, 2012.

Black, John H. *A Yankee Horseman in the Shenandoah Valley: The Civil War Letters of John H. Black, Twelfth Pennsylvania Cavalry.* Edited by David J. Coles and Stephen D. Engle. Knoxville: University of Tennessee Press, 2012.

Blaine, James G. *Twenty Years of Congress: From Lincoln to Garfield.* 2 vols. Norwich, CT: Henry Bill, 1884.

Blauvelt, Isaac E. *Civil War Letters of Isaac E. Blauvelt, Friends and Other Suitors.* Edited by Charles E. Finsley. Cedar Hill, TX: Kings Creek, 1997.

Bolton, William J. *The Civil War Journal of Colonel William J. Bolton, 51st Pennsylvania, April 20, 1861–August 2, 1865.* Edited by Richard A. Sauers. Conshohocken, PA: Combined, 2000.

Bonner, Robert E. *The Soldier's Pen: Firsthand Impressions of the Civil War.* New York: Hill and Wang, 2006.

Bonsall, Spencer. *Well Satisfied with My Position: The Civil War Journal of Spencer Bonsall.* Edited by Michael A. Flannery and Katherine H. Oomens. Carbondale: Southern Illinois University Press, 2007.

Boutwell, George S. *Emancipation: Its Justice, Expediency and Necessity, as the Means of Securing a Speedy and Permanent Peace: An Address Delivered by Hon. George S. Boutwell, in Tremont Temple, Boston, under the Auspices of the Emancipation League, December 16, 1861.* Boston: Wright & Potter, Printers, 1861.

Bowen, Charles T. *Dear Friends at Home: The Civil War Letters and Diaries of Sergeant Charles T. Bowen, Twelfth United States Infantry, First Battalion, 1861–1864.* Edited by Edward K. Cassedy. Baltimore: Butternut and Blue, 2001.

Bowen, Roland E. *From Ball's Bluff to Gettysburg . . . and Beyond: The Civil War Letters of Private Roland E. Bowen, 15th Massachusetts Infantry, 1861–1864.* Edited by Gregory A. Coco. Gettysburg, PA: Thomas, 1994.

Bradley, Leverett. *Leverett Bradley: A Soldier Boy's Letters, 1862–1865.* Boston: [Everett], 1905.

Brandegee, Charles. *Charlie's Civil War: A Private's Trial by Fire in the 5th New York Volunteers—Duryée Zouaves and 146th New York Infantry.* Edited by Charles Brandegee Livingstone and Brian Pohanka. Gettysburg, PA: Thomas, 1997.

Brewster, Charles Harvey. *When This Cruel War Is Over: The Civil War Letters of Charles Harvey Brewster.* Edited by David W. Blight. Amherst: University of Massachusetts Press, 1992.

Breyfogle, Joshua D. *The Story of Joshua D. Breyfogle, Private, 4th Ohio Infantry (10th Ohio Cavalry) and the Civil War.* Edited by George E. Carter. Lewiston, NY: Edward Mellen, 2001.

Bright, Michael, and Adam Bright. *"Respects to All": Letters of Two Pennsylvania Boys in the War of the Rebellion.* Edited by Aida Craig Truxall. Pittsburgh: University of Pittsburgh Press, 1962.

Bristed, Charles Astor. *The Cowards' Convention.* New York: Loyal Publication Society, 1864.

Brooks, Noah. *Abraham Lincoln.* Washington: National Tribune, 1888.

———. *Lincoln Observed: Civil War Dispatches of Noah Brooks.* Edited by Michael Burlingame. Baltimore: Johns Hopkins University Press, 1998.

———. *Washington in Lincoln's Time.* New York: Century, 1895.

Browne, Francis Fisher. *The Every-Day Life of Abraham Lincoln.* Minneapolis: Northwestern, 1887.

Browning, Orville Hickman. *Diary of Orville Hickman Browning.* Edited by Theodore Calvin Peace and James G. Randall. 2 vols. Springfield: Illinois State Historical Library, 1925–33.

Bryant, William Cullen. *The Letters of William Cullen Bryant.* Edited by William Cullen Bryant II and Thomas G. Voss. 6 vols. New York: Fordham University Press, 1975–92.

Buchanan, James. *The Works of James Buchanan.* Edited by John Bassett Moore. 12 vols. Philadelphia: J. B. Lippincott, 1911.

Butler, Benjamin F. *Private and Official Correspondence of Gen. Benjamin F. Butler, during the Period of the Civil War.* 5 vols. Norwood, MA: Plimpton, 1917.

Campbell, Alexander, and James Campbell. *"Him on One Side and Me on the Other": The Civil War Letters of Alexander Campbell, 79th New York Infantry Regiment, and James Campbell, 1st South Carolina Battalion.* Edited by Terry A. Johnston Jr. Columbia: University of South Carolina Press, 1999.

Cannon, LeGrand B. *Personal Reminiscences of the Rebellion, 1861–1866.* New York: Burr Printing House, 1895.

Carman, Ezra A. *The Maryland Campaign of September 1862.* Edited by Thomas G. Clemens. 3 vols. El Dorado Hills, CA: Savas Beatie, 2010–17.

Carpenter, F. B. *Six Months at the White House with Abraham Lincoln.* New York: Hurd and Houghton, 1866.

The Carrier's Address of the New York World, January 1st, 1863. New York: Isaac J. Oliver, 1863.

Carter, Robert Goldthwaite. *Four Brothers in Blue or Sunshine and Shows of the War of the Rebellion: A Story of the Great Civil War from Bull Run to Appomattox.* Austin: University of Texas Press, 1978.

Castleman, Alfred L. *The Army of the Potomac, behind the Scenes: A Diary of Unwritten History.* Milwaukee: Strickland, 1863.

Chandler, William E. *The Soldier's Right to Vote. Who Opposes It? Who Favors It?; or, The Record of the McClellan Copperheads against Allowing the Soldier Who Fights, the Right to Vote while Fighting.* Washington: Lemuel Towers, 1864.

Chandler, Zachariah. *Conduct of the War: Speech of Hon. Z. Chandler of Mich., in the Senate of the United States, Wednesday, July 16, 1862.* Washington: Scammel, 1862.

Chase, John W. *Yours for the Union: The Civil War Letters of John W. Chase, First Massachusetts Light Artillery.* Edited by John S. Collier and Bonnie B. Collier. New York: Fordham University Press, 2004.

Chase, Salmon P. *The Salmon P. Chase Papers.* Edited by John Niven. 5 vols. Kent, OH: Kent State University Press, 1993–98.

Cheek, Philip, and Mair Pointon. *History of the Sauk County Riflemen Known as Company "A," Sixth Wisconsin Veteran Volunteer Infantry, 1861–1865.* Madison, WI: Democrat Print, 1909.

Child, Lydia Maria. *Lydia Maria Child: Selected Letters, 1817–1880.* Edited by Milton Meltzer and Patricia G. Holland. Amherst: University of Massachusetts Press, 1982.

Child, William. *A History of the Fifth New Hampshire Regiment New Hampshire Volunteers, in the American Civil War, 1861–1865.* Bristol, NH: R. W. Musgrove, 1893.

Christie, Thomas, and William Christie. *Brother of Mine: Civil War Letters of Thomas and William Christie.* Edited by Hampton Smith. Minneapolis: Minnesota Historical Society Press, 2011.

Cincinnati Convention, October 18, 1864, for the Organization of a Peace Party upon State-Rights, Jeffersonian, Democratic Principles and for the Promotion of Peace and Independent Nominations for President and Vice-President of the United States. [Cincinnati(?): N.p., 1864].

Clarke, Hermon. *Back Home in Oneida: Hermon Clarke and His Letters.* Edited by Harry F. Jackson and Thomas F. O'Donnell. Syracuse, NY: Syracuse University Press, 1965.

Cleaver, James. *Your Affectionate Son: Letters from a Civil War Soldier.* Edited by Milean Ruff Daugherty. Tarentum, PA: Word Association, 2011.

Cochrane, John. *American Civil War. Memories of Incidents Connected with the Origin of the Rebellion That Threatened the Existence of the National Government.* New York: Rogers and Sherwood, 1879,

——. *War for the Union: Memoir of Gen. John Cochrane.* New York: N.p., 1876.

Coffin, Charles Carleton. *The Boys of '61; or, Four Years of Fighting*. Boston: Dana Estes, 1899.

Colby, Newton T. *The Civil War Papers of the Lt. Colonel Newton T. Colby, New York Infantry*. Edited by William E. Hughes. Jefferson, NC: McFarland, 2003.

Comte de Paris, Louis Phillipe Albert d'Orléans. *Voyage en Amérique, 1861–1862: Un prince français dans la guerre de Sécession*. Edited by Farid Ameur. Paris: Perrin/Fondation Saint-Louis, 2011.

———. *History of the Civil War in America*. 4 vols. Philadelphia: Porter and Coates, 1875–88.

Connolly, James A. *Three Years in the Army of the Cumberland*. Edited by Paul M. Angle. Bloomington: Indiana University Press, 1959.

Corby, William. *Memoirs of Chaplain Life: Three Years with the Irish Brigade in the Army of the Potomac*. Edited by Lawrence Frederick Kohl. New York: Fordham University Press, 1992.

Cox, Jacob Dolson, *Military Reminiscences of the Civil War*. 2 vols. New York: Charles Scribner's Sons, 1900.

Cox, Samuel Sullivan. *Meaning of the Elections of 1862: Speech of Hon. S. S. Cox of Ohio, Delivered in the House of Representatives, December 15, 1862*. Washington: L. Towers, [1862].

———. *Speech of Hon. S. S. Cox, of Ohio, Vindication of Gen. McClellan from the Attacks of Congressional War Critics, . . . January 31, 1862*. Washington: Towers Printers, 1862.

Cozzens, Peter, ed. *Battles and Leaders of the Civil War, Volume 6*. Urbana: University of Illinois Press, 2004.

Cram, George F. *Soldiering with Sherman: Civil War Letters of George F. Cram*. Edited by Jennifer Cain Bohrnstedt. DeKalb: Northern Illinois University Press, 2000.

Crotty, D. G. *Four Years Campaigning in the Army of the Potomac*. Grand Rapids, MI: Dygert Brothers, 1874.

Cullom, Shelby M. *Fifty Years of Public Service*. Chicago: A. C. McClurg, 1911.

Curtis, George Ticknor. *Address of Hon. George Ticknor Curtis at Philadelphia, Sept. 30, 1864*. New York: N.p., 1864.

———. *McClellan's Last Service to the Republic, together with a Tribute to His Memory*. New York: D. Appleton, 1886.

Custer, Elizabeth Bacon. *The Civil War Memories of Elizabeth Bacon Custer*. Austin: University of Texas Press, 1994.

Dahlgren, Madeline Vinton. *Memoir of John A. Dahlgren, Rear Admiral United States Navy*. Boston: James R. Osgood, 1882.

Daly, Mary Lydig. *Diary of a Union Lady, 1861–1865*. Edited by Harold Earl Hammond. New York: Funk and Wagnalls, 1962.

Dana, Charles A. *Recollections of the Civil War*. New York: D. Appleton, 1898.

Dawes, Rufus. *Service with the Sixth Wisconsin Volunteers.* Dayton, OH: Morningside, 1984.

Denslow, Van Buren. *Frémont and McClellan, Their Political and Military Careers Reviewed.* Yonkers, NY: Semi-Weekly Clarion, 1862.

Dexter, Seymour. *Seymour Dexter, Union Army: Journal and Letters of Civil War Service in Company K, 23rd New York Volunteer Regiment of Elmira.* Edited by Carl A. Morrell. Jefferson, NC: McFarland, 1996.

Dicey, Edward. *Spectator of America.* Edited by Herbert Mitang. Chicago: Quadrangle Books, 1971.

Dickerson, Frank. *Dear Father: The Civil War Letters of Lt. Frank Dickerson, a Son of Belfast Maine.* Edited by H. Draper Hunt. Unity, ME: North Country, 1992.

Dix, John Adam. *Memoirs of John Adams Dix.* Edited by Morgan Dix. 2 vols. New York: Harper and Brothers, 1883.

Dodge, Theodore Ayrault. *On Campaign with the Army of the Potomac: The Civil War Journal of Theodore Ayrault Dodge.* Edited by Stephen W. Sears. New York: Cooper Square, 2001.

Donaldson, Francis Adams. *Inside the Army of the Potomac: The Civil War Experience of Captain Francis Adams Donaldson.* Edited by J. Gregory Acken. Mechanicsburg, PA: Stackpole Books, 1998.

Doster, William E. *Lincoln and Episodes of the War.* New York: G. P. Putnam's Sons, 1915.

Drake, George. *The Mail Goes Through; or, the Civil War Letters of George Drake (1846–1918).* Edited by Julia A. Drake. San Angelo, TX: Anchor, 1964.

Duff, Levi Bird. *To Petersburg with the Army of the Potomac: The Civil War Letters of Levi Bird Duff, 105th Pennsylvania Volunteers.* Edited by Jonathan E. Helmreich. Jefferson, NC: McFarland, 2009.

Du Pont, Samuel Francis *Samuel Francis Du Pont: A Selection from His Civil War Letters.* Edited by John D. Hayes. 3 vols. Ithaca, NY: Published for the Eleutherian Mills Historical Library by the Cornell University Press, 1969.

Dwight, Wilder. *Life and Letters of Wilder Dwight, Lieut.-Col. Second Mass. Inf. Vols.* Boston: Ticknor and Fields, 1868.

Dyer, J. Franklin. *The Journal of a Civil War Surgeon.* Edited by Michael B. Chesson. Lincoln: University of Nebraska Press, 2003.

Eddy, Richard. *History of the Sixtieth Regiment New York State Volunteers.* Philadelphia: Published by the author, 1864.

Edge, Frederick Milnes. *Major-General McClellan and the Campaign on the Yorktown Peninsula.* London: Trubner, 1865.

Edwards, Abial Hall. *Dear Friend Anna: The Civil War Letters of a Common Soldier from Maine.* Edited by Beverly Hayes Kalgren and James L. Crouthamel. Orono: University of Maine Press, 1992.

Ellet, Charles, Jr. *The Army of the Potomac, and Its Mismanagement.* New York: Ross and Tousey, 1862.

——. *Military Incapacity and What It Costs the Country.* New York: Ross and Tousey, 1862.

Ellis, Thomas T. *Leaves from the Diary of an Army Surgeon; or, Incidents of Field Camp, and Hospital Life.* New York: John Bradburn, 1863.

Faller, Leo W., and John I. Faller. *Dear Folks at Home: The Civil War Letters of Leo W. and John I. Faller with an Account of Andersonville.* Edited by Milton E. Flower. Carlisle, PA: Cumberland County Historical Society, 1963.

Favill, Josiah Marshall. *Diary of a Young Officer: Serving with the Armies of the United States during the War of the Rebellion.* Chicago: R. R. Donnelley and Sons, 1909.

Fehrenbacher, Don E., and Elizabeth Fehrenbacher, *Recollected Words of Abraham Lincoln.* Stanford, CA: Stanford University Press, 1996.

Field, Maunsell B. *Memories of Many Men and of Some Women.* New York: Harper Brothers, 1874.

Fifth Annual Report of the Chief of the Bureau of Military Statistics. Albany, NY: C. Van Benthugsen, 1868.

Fiske, Samuel J. *Mr. Dunn Browne's Experiences in the Army: The Civil War Letters of Samuel W. Fiske.* Edited by Stephen W. Sears. New York: Fordham University Press, 1998.

Flagg, William J. *Speech of Hon. William J. Flagg of Hamilton County, Delivered in the Ohio House of Representatives, March 25, 1863.* N.p., 1863.

Forbes, John Murray. *Letters and Recollections of John Murray Forbes.* Edited by Sarah Forbes Hughes. 2 vols. Boston: Houghton Mifflin, 1900.

Ford, Worthington Chauncey, ed. *Cycle of Adams Letters, 1861–1865.* 2 vols. Boston: Houghton Mifflin, 1920.

Fortescue, Louis R. *Service with the Signal Corps: The Civil War Memoir of Louis R. Fortescue.* Edited by J. Gregory Acken. Knoxville: University of Tennessee Press, 2015.

Fox, Gustavus, *Confidential Correspondence of Gustavus Vasa Fox, Assistant Secretary of the Navy, 1861–1865* New York: De Vinne, 1918.

Freidel, Frank, ed. *Union Pamphlets of the Civil War, 1861–1865.* 2 vols. Cambridge, MA: Harvard University Press, 1967.

Frémont, Jessie Benton. *The Letters of Jessie Benton Frémont.* Edited by Pamela Herr and Mary Lee Spence. Urbana: University of Illinois Press, 1993.

French, Benjamin Brown. *Witness to the Young Republic: A Yankee's Journal, 1828–1870.* Edited by David B. Cole and John J. McDonough. Hanover, NH: University Press of New England, 1989.

Fuller, Charles A. *Personal Recollections of the War of 1861*. Sherburne, NY: News Job Printing House, 1906.

Garfield, James A. *Wild Life of the Army: The Civil War Letters of James A. Garfield*. Edited by Frederick D. Williams. East Lansing: Michigan State University Press, 1964.

Geary, John White. *A Politician Goes to War: The Civil War Letters of John White Geary*. Edited by William Alan Blair. University Park: Pennsylvania State University Press, 1995.

Gerrish, Theodore. *Army Life: A Private's Reminiscences of the Civil War*. Portland, ME: Hoyt, Fogg, and Donham, 1882.

Gibbon, John. *Personal Recollections of the Civil War*. New York: G. P. Putnam's Sons, 1928.

Gillam, Chandler B. *Letters of a Civil War Soldier: Chandler B. Gillam, 28th New York Volunteers, with Diary of W. L. Hicks*. Edited by Ellen C. Collier. [Philadelphia]: Xlibris, 2005.

Gilmore, James R. *Personal Recollections of Abraham Lincoln and the Civil War*. Boston: L. C. Page, 1898.

Glaza-Herrington, Linda. *Dear Brother and Sister: Smith-Haviland-Cadwell: Fourth Michigan Volunteer Infantry Civil War Letters*. Grand Rapids, MI: Schuler Books and Music, 2012.

Goddard, Henry P. *The Good Fight That Didn't End: Henry P. Goddard's Accounts of Civil War and Peace*. Edited by Calvin Goddard Zon. Columbia: University of South Carolina Press, 2008.

Goss, Warren Lee. *Recollections of a Private: A Story of the Army of the Potomac*. New York: Thomas Y. Crowell, 1890.

Gould, Edward K. *Major General Hiram G. Berry*. Rockland, ME: Press of the Courier Gazette, 1899.

Gould, John Mead. *The Civil War Journals of John Mead Gould, 1861–1866*. Edited by William B. Jordan. Baltimore: Butternut and Blue, 1997.

Grant, Ulysses S. *The Papers of Ulysses S. Grant*. 32 vols. Carbondale: Southern Illinois University Press, 1967–2012.

Gray, John Chipman, and John Codman Ropes. *War Letters, 1862–1865*. Boston: Houghton Mifflin, 1927.

Greene, J. Harvey. *Letters to My Wife: A Civil War Diary from the Western Front*. Edited by Sharon L. D. Kraynek. Apollo, PA: Closson, 1995.

Greene, William B. *Letters from a Sharpshooter: The Civil War Letters of William B. Greene, Co. G., Berdan's Sharpshooters*. Edited by William H. Hastings. Belleville, WI: Historic Publications, 1993.

Griffin, James B. *A Gentleman and Officer: A Military and Social History of*

James B. Griffin's Civil War. Edited by Judith N. McArthur and Orville Vernon Burton. New York: Oxford University Press, 1996.

Guiney, Patrick R. *Commanding Boston's Irish Ninth: The Civil War Letters of Colonel Patrick R. Guiney, Ninth Massachusetts Volunteer Infantry.* Edited by Christopher G. Samito. New York: Fordham University Press, 1998.

A Gun Manufacturer. *A Review of the Report of the Commission on Ordnance and Ordnance Stores: With a Few Comments upon the Present Administration of the War Department.* N.p., 1862.

Gurowski, Adam. *Diary.* 3 vols. New York: Burt Franklin, 1968.

Haley, John W. *The Rebel Yell and the Yankee Hurrah: The Civil War Journal of a Maine Volunteer.* Edited by Ruth L. Silliker. Camden, ME: Down East Books, 1985.

Halsey, Edmund. *Brother against Brother: The Lost Civil War Diary of Lt. Edmund Halsey.* Edited by Bruce Chadwick. Secaucus, NJ: Birth Lane, 1997.

Hamilton, James A. *Reminiscences of James A. Hamilton; or, Men and Events, at Home and Abroad, during Three Quarters of a Century.* New York: Charles Scribner, 1869.

Hamilton, John C. *Coercion Complete, or Treason Triumphant.* New York: William G. Bryant, 1864.

[Hancock, Almira]. *Reminiscences of Winfield Scott Hancock, by His Wife.* New York: C. L. Webster, 1887.

Hard, Abner. *History of the Eighth Cavalry Regiment, Illinois Volunteers.* Dayton, OH: Morningside, 1984.

Harris, Robert F., and John Niflot, ed. *Dear Sister: The Civil War Letters of the Brothers Gould.* Westport, CT: Praeger, 1998.

The Harrison's Bar Letter of Gen. McClellan. Opinions of James Guthrie, John Van Buren, Reverdy Johnson, &c. New York: N.p., 1864.

Hartwell, John F. L. *To My Beloved Wife and Boy at Home: The Letters and Diaries of Orderly Sergeant John F. L. Hartwell.* Edited by Ann Hartwell Britton and Thomas J. Reed. Madison, NJ: Fairleigh Dickinson University Press, 1997.

Harwell, Richard B., ed. *The Union Reader: As the North Saw the War.* New York: Longmans, Green, 1958.

Haupt, Herman. *Reminiscences of General Herman Haupt.* Milwaukee, WI: Wright and Joys, 1901.

Hawthorne, Julian. *Hawthorne and His Wife: A Biography.* 2 vols. Boston: Houghton Mifflin, 1891.

Hay, John. *At Lincoln's Side: John Hay's Civil War Correspondence and Selected Writings.* Edited by Michael Burlingame. Carbondale: Southern Illinois University Press, 2000.

———. *Inside Lincoln's White House: The Complete Civil War Diary of John Hay*. Edited by Michel Burlingame and John R. Turner Ettlinger. Carbondale: Southern Illinois University Press, 1997.

———. *Lincoln's Journalist: John Hay's Anonymous Writings for the Press, 1860–1864*. Edited by Michael Burlingame. Carbondale: Southern Illinois University Press, 1998.

Haydon, Charles B. *For Country, Cause, & Leader: The Civil War Journal of Charles B. Haydon*. Edited by Stephen W. Sears. New York: Ticknor and Fields, 1993.

Hayes, Rutherford Birchard. *Diary and Letters of Rutherford Birchard Hayes*. 5 vols. Columbus: Ohio State Archaeological and Historical Society, 1922–26.

Hays, Alexander. *Life and Letters of Alexander Hays*. Edited by George Thornton Fleming. Pittsburgh: N.p., 1919.

Hayward, Ambrose Henry. *Last to Leave the Field: The Life and Letters of First Sergeant Ambrose Henry Hayward, 28th Pennsylvania Volunteer Infantry*. Edited by Timothy J. Orr. Knoxville: University of Tennessee Press, 2010.

Heffley, Albert, and Cyrus P. Heffley. *Civil War Diaries of Capt. Albert Heffley and Lt. Cyrus P. Heffley, Co. F, 142nd Regt. Penna. Vol., Army of the Potomac*. Apollo, PA: Closson Press, 2000.

Herndon, William H. *Brief Analysis of Lincoln's Character: A Letter to J. E. Remsburg, Oak Mills, Kansas, from W. H. Herndon, Springfield, Illinois, September 10, 1887*. N.p.: Privately printed, 1917.

———. *Herndon on Lincoln: Letters*. Edited by Douglas L. Wilson and Rodney O. Davis. Urbana: University of Illinois Press, 2016.

Herndon, William H., and Jesse W. Weik. *Herndon's Lincoln*. Edited by Douglas L. Wilson and Rodney O. Davis. Urbana: University of Illinois Press, 2006.

Hirst, Benjamin. *The Boys from Rockville: Civil War Narratives of Sgt. Benjamin Hirst, Company D, 14th Connecticut Volunteers*. Edited by Robert L. Bee. Knoxville: University of Tennessee, 1998.

History of the Twenty-Third Pennsylvania Volunteer Infantry, Birney's Zouaves. [Philadelphia: N.p., 1904].

Hitchcock, Ethan Allen. *Fifty Years in Camp and Field: Diary of Major-General Ethan Allen Hitchcock*. Edited by W. A. Croffut. New York: G. P. Putnam's Sons, 1909.

Hitchcock, Frederick L. *War from the Inside: The Story of the 132nd Regiment Pennsylvania Volunteer Infantry in the War for the Suppression of the Rebellion, 1862–1863*. Philadelphia: J. B. Lippincott, 1904.

Hitchcock, George A. *From Ashby to Andersonville: The Civil War Diary and Reminiscences of George A. Hitchcock, Private, Company A, 21st Massachusetts Infantry*. Edited by Ronald G. Watson. Campbell, CA: Savas, 1997.

Hoffman, Elliott W., ed. *A Vermont Cavalryman in War and Love: The Civil War Letters of Brevet Major General Williams Wells and Anna Richardson*. Lynchburg, VA: Schroeder, 2007.

Holt, Daniel M. *A Surgeon's Civil War: The Letters and Diary of Daniel M. Holt, M.D.* Edited by James M. Greiner, Janet L. Coryell, and James R. Smither. Kent, OH: Kent State University Press, 1994.

Hotchkiss, Jedediah. *Make Me a Map of the Valley: The Civil War Journal of Stonewall Jackson's Topographer*. Edited by Archie P. McDonald. Dallas: Southern Methodist University Press, 1973.

Household Reading: Selections from the Congregationalist, 1849–1866. Boston: Galen James, 1867.

Howard, Oliver Otis. *Autobiography of Oliver Otis Howard, Major General United States Army*. 2 vols. New York: Baker and Taylor, 1907.

Hunt, Gaillard, ed. *Israel, Elihu, and Cadwallader Washburn: A Chapter in American Biography*. New York: Macmillan, 1925.

Hyde, Thomas W. *Civil War Letters*. N.p.: John H. Hyde, 1933.

———. *Following the Greek Cross; or, Memories of the Sixth Army Corps*. Boston: Houghton Mifflin, 1894.

Ingersoll, Joseph Reed. *Secession: A Folly and a Crime*. Philadelphia: King and Baird, 1862.

Janney, Paulina Stevens. *The Civil War Period Journals of Paulina Stevens Janney, 1859–1866*. Edited by Christie Hill Russell. Baltimore: Gateway, 2007.

Johnson, Andrew. *The Papers of Andrew Johnson*. 16 vols. Edited by Leroy P. Graf et al. Knoxville University of Tennessee Press, 1967–2000.

Johnson, Charles F. *The Civil War Letters of Charles F. Johnson, Invalid Corps*. Edited by Fred Pelka. Amherst: University of Massachusetts Press, 2004.

Johnson, Herrick. *"God's Ways Unsearchable": A Discourse, on the Death of President Lincoln, Preached before the Third Presbyterian Congregation, in Mozart Hall, Pittsburgh, Pa., Sunday April 23, 1865*. Pittsburgh: W. G. Johnston, 1865.

Johnson, Robert Underwood, and Clarence Clough Buel, eds. *Battles and Leaders of the Civil War*. 4 vols. New York: Castle Books, 1956.

Joinville, Prince de. *The Army of the Potomac: Its Organization, Its Commander, Its Campaigns*. Translated by William Henry Hurlbert. New York: Anson D. F. Randolph, 1862.

Judson, Amos M. *History of the Eighty-Third Regiment Pennsylvania Volunteers*. Erie, PA: B. F. H. Lynn, [1865].

Julian, George W. *Political Recollections, 1840 to 1872*. Chicago: Jansen, McClurg, 1884.

———. *Speeches on Political Questions*. New York: Hurd and Houghton: 1872.

Kamphoefner, Walter D., and Wolfgang Helbich, eds. *Germans in the Civil War:*

The Letters They Wrote Home. Chapel Hill: University of North Carolina Press, 2006.

Kearny, Philip. *Letters from the Peninsula: The Civil War Letters of General Philip Kearny.* Edited by William B. Styple. Kearny, NJ: Belle Grove, 1988.

Keckley, Elizabeth. *Behind the Scenes; or, Thirty Years a Slave, and Four Years in the Lincoln White House.* New York: G. W. Carleton, 1868.

Kelley, William D. *Lincoln and Stanton: A Study of the War Administration of 1861 and 1862, with Special Consideration of Some Recent Statements of Gen. Geo. B. McClellan.* New York: G. P. Putnam's Sons, 1885.

Ketchum, Hiram. *General McClellan's Peninsula Campaign.* New York: N.p., 1864.

Keyes, Erasmus Darwin. *Fifty Years' Observation of Men and Events Civil and Military.* New York: Charles Scribner's Sons, 1884.

King, Horatio. *Turning on the Light: A Dispassionate Survey of President Buchanan's Administration from 1860 to Its Close.* Philadelphia: J. B. Lippincott, 1895.

Lamon, Ward Hill. *Recollections of Abraham Lincoln, 1847–1865.* Edited by Dorothy Lamon. Chicago: A. C. McClurg, 1911.

Lamson, William. *From Maine to the Wilderness: The Civil War Letters of Private William Lamson, 20th Maine Infantry.* Edited by Roderick M. Engert. Orange, VA: Publisher's Press, 1993.

Lane, David. *A Soldier's Diary; the Story of a Volunteer, 1862–1865.* Jackson[?], MI: N.p., 1905.

Lauderdale, John Vance. *The Wounded River: The Civil War Letters of John Vance Lauderdale, M.D.* Edited by Peter Josyph. East Lansing: Michigan State University Press, 1993.

"Leave Pope to Get Out of His Scrape." Washington: McGill and Witherow, 1864.

Le Duc, William G. *Recollections of a Civil War Quartermaster.* Edited by Augustine V. Gardner. St. Paul, MN: North Central, 1963.

Lee, Elizabeth Blair. *Wartime Washington: The Civil War Letters of Elizabeth Blair Lee.* Edited by Virginia Jeans Laas. Urbana: University of Illinois Press, 1991.

Lieber, Francis. *Lincoln or McClellan. Appeal to the Germans in America.* New York: Loyal Publication Society, 1864.

Lincoln, Abraham. *The Collected Works of Abraham Lincoln.* Edited by Roy P. Basler. 8 vols. New Brunswick, NJ: Rutgers University Press, 1953.

Livermore, Mary. *My Story of the War.* Hartford, CT: A. D. Worthington, 1889.

Long, Hezekiah. *Hard Times, Hard Bread, and Harder Coffee: The Civil War Correspondence of Hezekiah Long, Company F., 20th Maine Infantry.* Edited by Richardson's Civil War Round Table. Northport, ME: Richardson's Civil War Round Table, 2008.

Lossing, Benson J. *Pictorial Field Book of the Civil War.* 3 vols. Baltimore: Johns Hopkins University Press, 1997.

Lyman, Theodore. *Meade's Army: The Private Notebooks of Lt. Col. Theodore Lyman.* Edited by David W. Lowe. Kent, OH: Kent State University Press, 2007.

———. *Meade's Headquarters, 1863–1865: Letters of Colonel Theodore Lyman from the Wilderness to Appomattox.* Edited by George R. Agassiz. Boston: Atlantic Monthly, 1922.

Macnamara, Daniel George. *History of the Ninth Regiment Massachusetts Volunteer Infantry.* Boston: E. B. Stillings, 1899.

Major-General George B. McClellan, from August 1st 1861 to August 1st, 1862. New York: H. Dexter, 1862.

Mann, Thomas H. *Fighting with the Eighteenth Massachusetts: The Civil War Memoir of Thomas H. Mann.* Edited by John J. Hennessy. Baton Rouge: Louisiana State University Press, 2000.

Marshall, Albert O. *Army Life: From a Soldier's Journal.* Joliet, IL: Chicago Legal News 1884.

Marshall, Jeffrey D., ed. *A War of the People: Vermont Civil War Letters.* Hanover, NH: University Press of New England, 1999.

Matrau, Henry. *Letters Home: Henry Matrau of the Iron Brigade.* Edited by Marcia Reid-Green. Lincoln: University of Nebraska Press, 1993.

Matthews, James Mero. *Soldiers in Green: Civil War Diaries of James Mero Matthews, 2nd U.S. Sharpshooters.* Edited by Peter Dalton. Sandy Point, ME: Richardson's Civil War Round Table, 2002.

Mayo, Perry. *The Civil War Letters of Perry Mayo.* Edited by Robert W. Hodge. East Lansing, MI: [Museum, Michigan State University], 1967.

McAllister, Robert. *The Civil War Letters of General Robert McAllister.* Edited by James I. Robertson Jr. New Brunswick, NJ: Rutgers University Press, 1965.

McCalmont, Alfred B. *Extracts from Letters Written by Alfred B. McCalmont, 1862–1865, from the Front during the War of the Rebellion.* N.p., 1908.

McCarter, William. *My Life in the Irish Brigade: The Civil War Memoirs of Private William McCarter, 116th Pennsylvania Volunteer Infantry.* Edited by Kevin E. O'Brien. Campbell, CA: Savas, 1996.

McClellan, George B. *The Armies of Europe.* Philadelphia: J. B. Lippincott, 1861.

———. *The Civil War Papers of George B. McClellan: Selected Correspondence, 1860–1865.* Edited by Stephen W. Sears. New York: Ticknor and Fields, 1989.

———. *The Mexican War Diary and Correspondence of George B. McClellan.* Edited by Thomas W. Cutrer. Baton Rouge: Louisiana State University Press, 2009.

———. *The Mexican War Diary of General George B. McClellan.* Edited by William Starr Myers. Princeton, NJ: Princeton University Press, 1917.

———. *McClellan's Own Story.* New York: Charles L. Webster, 1887.

———. *Oration by Gen. George B. McClellan.* New York: C. S. Westcott, 1864.

McClellan's Campaign. Reprinted from the World of August 7, 1862. New York, Anson D. F. Randolph, 1862.

McClellan's Military Career Reviewed and Exposed: The Military Policy of the Administration Set Forth and Vindicated. Washington: Union Congressional Committee, 1864.

McClure, Alexander K. *Abraham Lincoln and Men of War-Times: Some Personal Recollections of War and Politics during the Lincoln Administration.* Philadelphia: Times, 1892.

———. *Recollections of Half a Century.* Salem, MA: Salem, 1902.

McClure, J. B., ed. *Anecdotes and Stories of Abraham Lincoln.* Chicago: Rhodes and McClure, 1884.

McClure, James P., Peg A. Lamphier, and Erika M. Kreger, eds. *"Spur Up Your Pegasus": Family Letters of Salmon, Kate, and Nettie Chase, 1844–1873.* Kent, OH: Kent State University Press, 2009.

McCulloch, Hugh. *Men and Measures of Half a Century.* New York: Charles Scribner's Sons 1888.

McFadden, Janice Bartlett Reeder. *Aunt and the Soldier Boys from Cross Creek Village, Pennsylvania, 1856–1866.* Santa Cruz, CA: Moore's Graphic Arts, 1970.

McKelvey, Blake, ed. *Rochester in the Civil War.* Rochester, NY: Rochester Historical Society, 1944.

McPherson, Edward. *Political History of the United States during the Great Rebellion.* 4th ed. Washington: James G. Chapman, 1882.

Meade, George. *The Life and Letters of George Gordon Meade.* 2 vols. New York: Charles Scribner's Sons, 1913.

Medill, William, and Joseph. *A Family and Nation under Fire: The Civil War Letters and Journals of William and Joseph Medill.* Edited by Georgiann Baldino. Kent, OH: Kent State University Press, 2018.

Melville, Herman. *Battle-Pieces and Aspects of the War.* New York: Harper and Brothers, 1866.

Meyers, Augustus. *Ten Years in the Ranks.* New York: Stirling, 1914.

Miller, Delavan S. *Drum Taps in Dixie: Memories of a Drummer Boy, 1861–1865.* Watertown, NY: Hungerford-Holbrook, 1905.

Miller, William Bluffton. *Fighting for Liberty and Right: The Civil War Diaries of William Bluffton Miller, First Sergeant, Company K, Seventy-Fifth Indiana Volunteer Infantry.* Edited by Jeffrey L. Patrick and Robert J. Willey. Knoxville: University of Tennessee Press, 2005.

Mills, Charles J. *Through Blood and Fire: The Civil War Letters of Major Charles J. Mills, 1862–1865.* Edited Gregory A. Coco. Gettysburg, PA: Privately printed, 1982.

Minnesota in the Civil and Indian Wars. 2 vols. St. Paul: Pioneer, 1890–93.

Moats, Virgil H. *Shiloh to Vicksburg: Dear Eliza, an Eyewitness Account in the Civil War Letters of Major Virgil H. Moats.* Edited by Edward L. Walker. Pebble Beach, CA: Hedgehog, [1984].

Mohr, James C., ed. *The Cormany Diaries: A Northern Family in the Civil War.* Pittsburgh, PA: University of Pittsburgh Press, 1982.

Moore, Frank A., ed. *The Rebellion Record: A Diary of American Events.* 12 vols. New York: Arno, 1977.

Moulton, Charles H. *Fort Lyon to Harper's Ferry: On the Border of North and South with "Rambling Jour": The Civil War Letters of Newspaper Dispatches of Charles H. Moulton (34th Mass. Vol. Inf.).* Edited by Lee C. Drickamer and Karen D. Drickamer. Shippensburg, PA: White Mane, 1987.

Murray, R. L. *Letters from Berdan's Sharpshooters.* Wolcott, NY: Benedum Books, 2005.

———. *Madison County Troops in the Civil War.* Wolcott. NY: Benedum Books, 2004.

———. *New Yorkers in the Civil War: A Historic Journal, Volume 3.* Wolcott, NY: Benedum Books, 2004.

———. *Ontario County Troops in the Civil War: Volume Two—Canandaigua Area Troops.* Wolcott, NY: Benedum Books, 2003.

———. *Seneca County Troops in the Civil War.* Wolcott, NY: Benedum Books, 2005.

———. *Yates County Troops in the Civil War.* Wolcott, NY: Benedum Books, 2006.

Musser, Charles O. *Soldier Boy: The Civil War Letters of Charles O. Musser, 29th Iowa.* Edited by Barry Popchock. Iowa City: University of Iowa Press, 1995.

Naglee, Henry Morris. *The Peninsular Campaign. A Secret and Important Chapter in the History of the War.* Philadelphia: N.p., 1864.

———. *The Two Letters of Gen. H. M. Naglee about Gen. McClellan.* New York: N.p., 1864.

Nash, Eugene Arus. *A History of the Forty-Fourth New York Volunteer Infantry in the Civil War.* Chicago: R. R. Donnelley, 1910.

Neil, Alexander. *Alexander Neil and the Last Shenandoah Valley Campaign: Letters of Army Surgeon to His Family, 1864.* Edited by Richard R. Duncan. Shippensburg, PA: White Mane, 1996.

Nichols, Samuel. *"Your Soldier Boy Samuel": Civil War Letters of Lieut. Samuel Edmund Nichols.* Edited by Charles Sterling Underhill. Buffalo, NY: Privately printed, 1929.

Nicolay, Helen. *Personal Traits of Abraham Lincoln.* New York: Century, 1912.

Nicolay, John G. *An Oral History of Abraham Lincoln: John G. Nicolay's Interviews and Essays.* Edited by Michael Burlingame. Carbondale: Southern Illinois University Press, 1996.

———. *With Lincoln in the White House: Letters, Memoranda, and Other Writings of John G. Nicolay, 1860–1865.* Edited by Michael Burlingame. Carbondale: Southern Illinois University Press, 2000.

Nicolay, John G., and John Hay. *Abraham Lincoln: A History.* 10 vols. New York: Century, 1890.

Northup, James E., and Samuel W. Northup. *Drifting to an Unknown Future: The Civil War Letters of James E. Northup and Samuel W. Northup.* Edited by Robert C. Steensma. Sioux Falls, SD: Center for Western Studies, Augustana College, 2000.

Norton, Oliver Willcox. *Army Letters, 1861–1865.* Chicago: O. L. Denning, 1903.

Official Proceedings of the Democratic National Convention, Held in 1864 at Chicago. Chicago: Times Steam Book and Job Printing House, 1864.

Official Records of the Union and Confederate Navies in the War of the Rebellion. 31 vols. Washington: Government Printing Office, 1894–1922.

Oldroyd, Osborn H., ed. *The Lincoln Memorial Album—Immortelles.* New York: G. W. Carlton, 1882.

Olmsted, Frederick Law. *The Papers of Frederick Law Olmsted.* 7 vols. to date. Baltimore: Johns Hopkins University Press, 1977–.

Olsen, Bernard, ed. *Upon the Tented Field.* Red Bank, NJ: Historic Projects, 1993.

The "Only Alternative": A Tract for the Times by a Plain Man. Philadelphia: Henry B. Ashmead, 1864.

Opdycke, Emerson. *The Battle for God and the Right: The Civil War Letterbooks of Emerson Opdycke.* Edited by Glenn V. Longacre and John E. Haas. Urbana: University of Illinois Press, 2003.

Osborn, Thomas Ward. *No Middle Ground: Thomas Ward Osborn's Letters from the Field (1862–1864).* Edited by Herb S. Crumb and Katherine Dhalle. Hamilton, NY: Edmonston, 1983.

A Page of History: From the N.Y. Journal of Commerce. New York: Society for the Diffusion of Political Knowledge, 1864.

Palfrey, Francis Winthrop. *The Antietam and Fredericksburg.* New York: Charles Scribner's Sons, 1882.

Papers of the Military Historical Society of Massachusetts. 15 vols. Wilmington, NC: Broadfoot, 1989.

Pardington, John H. *Dear Sarah: Letters Home from a Soldier of the Iron Brigade.* Edited by Coralou Peel Lassen. Bloomington: Indiana University Press, 1999.

Parker, Joel. *Letter to the People of Massachusetts.* Cambridge, MA: H. O. Houghton, 1862.

Parker, John Lord. *Henry Wilson's Regiment: History of the Twenty-Second Massachusetts Infantry, the Second Company Sharpshooters, and Then Third Light Battery in the War of the Rebellion.* Boston: Press of Rand Avery, 1887.

Parks, George. *The Civil War Letters of Private George Parks, Co. C, 24th New York Volunteers.* Edited by Joseph M. Overfield. Buffalo, NY: Gallagher Printing, 1992.

Patrick, Marsena, *Inside Lincoln's Army: The Diary of Marsena Rudolph Patrick, Provost Marshal General, Army of the Potomac.* Edited by David S. Sparks. New York: Thomas Yoseloff, 1964.

Peck, Marcus. *Marcus Peck: Letters of a Civil War Soldier and His Family.* Edited by Eve H. Gemmill and Marie E. Hoffman. Poestenkill, NY: Poestenkill Historical Society, 1993.

Peifer, James A. *Bethlehem Boy: The Civil War Letters and Diary of James A. Peifer.* Edited by Carolyn W. Abel and Patricia N. McAndrew. Bethlehem, PA: Moon Trail Books, 2007.

People's Party (Massachusetts). *Proceedings of the Convention of the People of Massachusetts: Holden at Faneuil Hall, Boston, October 7, 1862.* Boston: C. J. Peters, 1862.

Perkins, George. *Three Years a Soldier: The Diary and Newspaper Correspondence of Private George Perkins, Sixth New York Independent Battery, 1861–1864.* Edited by Richard N. Griffin. Knoxville: University of Tennessee Press, 2006.

Perry, John Gardner. *Letters from a Surgeon of the Civil War.* Edited by Martha Derby Perry. Boston: Little, Brown, 1906.

Peterson, Frederick A. *Military Review of the Campaign in Virginia and Maryland in 1862.* New York: S. Tousey, H. Dexter, [1863]

Pettit, Frederick. *Infantryman Pettit: The Civil War Letters of Corporal Frederick Pettit: Late of Company C, 100th Pennsylvania Volunteer Infantry Regiment "The Roundheads," 1862–1864.* Shippensburg, PA: White Mane, 1990.

Pickrell, W. N. *History of the Third Indiana Cavalry.* Indianapolis: [Aetna Printing], 1906.

Pisani, Camille Ferri. *Prince Napoleon in America, 1861: Letters from His Aide-de-camp.* Translated by Georges J. Joyaux. Bloomington: Indiana University Press, 1959.

Plotow, Mark. *For Their Letters, for Their Words: Illinois Soldiers Write Home.* Carbondale: Southern Illinois University Press, 2019.

Poe, Orlando M. *My Dear Nelly: The Selected Civil War Letters of General Orlando M. Poe to His Wife Eleanor.* Edited by Paul Taylor. Kent, OH: Kent State University Press, 2020.

Pope, John. *The Military Memoirs of General John Pope.* Edited by Peter Cozzens and Robert I. Girardi. Chapel Hill: University of North Carolina Press, 1998.

Poremba, David Lee, ed. *If I Am Found Dead: Michigan Voices from the Civil War.* Ann Arbor, MI: Ann Arbor Media Group, 2006.

Porter, Horace. *Campaigning with Grant.* New York: Century, 1897.

Post, Lydia M. *Soldiers' Letters: From Camp, Battle-field, and Prison.* New York: Bunce and Huntington, 1865.

Prentiss, George L. *The Free Christian State and the Present Struggle: An Address Delivered before the Association of the Alumni of Bowdoin College, August 8, 1861.* New York: John A. Gray, 1861.

Priest, D. D. *Shouts and Whispers: The Civil War Correspondence of D. D. Priest of Mount Holly, Vermont.* Edited by Nancy D. Wilson. Manchester Center, VT: Shires, 2011.

Prim, Juan. *General McClellan and the Army of the Potomac.* New York: John Bradburn, 1864.

[Prime, W. C.]. *General H. W. Halleck's Report Reviewed in the Light of the Facts.* New York: Anson D. F. Randolph, 1862.

Proceedings of the Mass Meeting of Loyal Citizens, on Union Square, New York, 15th Day of July, 1862. New York: George F. Nesbitt, 1862.

Rawle, William Brooke. *Blue-Blooded Cavalryman: Captain William Brooke Rawle in the Army of the Potomac, May 1863–August 1865.* Edited by J. Gregory Acken. Kent, OH: Kent State University Press, 2019.

Raymond, Henry J. *The Life and Public Services of Abraham Lincoln.* New York: Derby and Miller, 1865.

Regan, Timothy J. *The Lost Civil War Diaries: The Diaries of Corporal Timothy J. Regan.* Victoria, Canada: Tafford, 2003.

Reid, Harvey. *Uncommon Soldiers: Harvey Reid and the 22nd Wisconsin March with Sherman.* Edited by Frank L. Byrne. Knoxville: University of Tennessee Press, 2001.

Reid, Whitelaw. *A Radical View: The "Agate" Dispatches of Whitelaw Reid, 1861–1865.* Edited by James G. Smart. 2 vols. Memphis, TN: Memphis State University Press, 1976.

Reinhart, Joseph R., ed. *Yankee Dutchmen under Fire: Civil War Letters from the 82nd Illinois Infantry.* Kent, OH: Kent State University Press, 2013.

Report of the Joint Committee on the Conduct of the War. 8 vols. Wilmington, NC: Broadfoot, 1998–2000.

Rhodes, Elisha Hunt. *All for the Union: The Civil War Diary and Letters of Elisha Hunt Rhodes.* New York: Orion Books, 1985.

Rice, Allen Thorndike. *Reminiscences of Abraham Lincoln by Distinguished Men of His Time.* New York: North American Review, 1889.

Richards, Carolina Cowles. *Village Life in America, 1852–1872.* Gansevoort, NY: Corner House Historical Publications, 1997.

Richards, G. W. *A Brief History of the Rebellion, and a Life of Gen. McClellan; Containing Some Facts Never before Published.* Philadelphia: J. Magee, 1862.

Richardson, Albert D. *The Secret Service, the Field, the Dungeon, and the Escape.* Hartford, CT: American, 1865.

Riddle, Albert Gallatin. *Recollections of War Times: Reminiscences of Men and Events in Washington.* New York: G. P. Putnam's Sons, 1895.

Ripley, Edward Hastings. *Vermont General: The Unusual War Experiences of Edward Hastings Ripley.* Edited by Otto Eisenschiml. New York: Devin-Adair, 1960.

Ritchie, Donald F. *Four Years in the First New York Light Artillery: The Papers of David F. Ritchie.* Edited by Norman L. Ritchie. Hamilton, NY: Edmonston, 1997.

Ritner, Jacob, and Emeline Ritner. *Love and Valor: Intimate Civil War Letters between Captain Jacob and Emeline Ritner.* Edited by Charles F. Larimer. Western Springs, IL: Sigourney, 2000.

Robertson, Robert S. *Diary of the War.* Edited by Charles N. Walker and Rosemary Walker. Fort Wayne, IN: N.p., 1965.

Ropes, John Codman. *The Army under Pope.* New York: Charles Scribner's Sons, 1881.

Roy, Andrew. *Recollections of a Prisoner of War.* 2nd ed. rev. Columbus, OH: J. L. Trauger, 1909.

Rusling, James Fowler. *Men and Things I Saw in Civil War Days.* New York: Methodist Book Concern, 1914.

Russell, William Howard. *My Diary North and South.* 2 vols. New York: Harper and Brothers, 1863.

———. *My Diary North and South.* Edited by Eugene Berwanger. New York: Alfred A. Knopf, 1988.

———. *William Howard Russell's Civil War: Private Diary and Letters, 1861–1862.* Athens: University of Georgia Press, 1992.

Schuckers, J. W. *The Life and Public Services of Salmon Portland Chase.* New York: D. Appleton, 1874.

Schurz, Carl. *The Reminiscences of Carl Schurz.* 3 vols. New York: McClure, 1907–8.

Searle, L. C., Mrs. *Washington, Our Example. The Father of a Nation Will Restore It to Peace.* Philadelphia: James Challen and Son, 1865.

Sears, Stephen W., ed. *The Civil War: The Second Year by Those Who Lived It.* New York: Library of America, 2012.

Sedgwick, John. *The Correspondence of John Sedgwick.* 2 vols. New York: Printed for Carl and Ellen Battelle Stoeckel, 1902.

Seward, Frederick W. *Reminiscences of a War-Time Statesman and Diplomat, 1830–1915.* New York: G. P. Putnam's Sons, 1916.

———. *Seward at Washington, as Senator and Secretary of State: A Memoir of His Life, with Selections from his Letters, 1861–1872.* New York: Derby and Miller, 1891.

Seward, William H. *Issues of the Conflict—Terms of Peace: Speech of William H. Seward on the Occasion of the Fall of Atlanta, at Auburn, Saturday, September 3, 1864*. N.p., 1864.

Shaw, Robert Gould. *Blue-Eyed Child of Fortune: The Civil War Letters of Colonel Robert Gould Shaw*. Edited by Russell Duncan. Athens: University of Georgia Press, 1992.

Sherman, William T. *Sherman's Civil War: Selected Correspondence of William T. Sherman, 1860–1865*. Edited by Brooks D. Simpson and Jean V. Berlin. Chapel Hill: University of North Carolina Press, 1999.

Shortell, Michael. *The Civil War Letters of Corporal Michael Shortell, Company G, 7th Wisconsin Infantry*. Compiled by Mary Wanty Frazer. Bowie, MD: M. W. Frazer, 1992.

Sketches of War History, 1861–1865, Papers Prepared for the Ohio Commandery of the Military Order of the Loyal Legion of the United States, 1888–1890. 8 vols. Wilmington, NC: Broadfoot, 1991.

Small, Abner. *Road to Richmond: The Civil War Memoirs of Major Abner R. Small of the Sixteenth Maine Volunteers*. Edited by Harold Adams Small. Berkeley, CA: University of California Press, 1939.

Smith, J. L. *History of the 118th Pennsylvania Volunteers, Corn Exchange Regiment*. Philadelphia: J. L. Smith, 1905.

Smith, Thomas W. *"We Have It Damn Hard Out Here": The Civil War Letters of Sergeant Thomas W. Smith, 6th Pennsylvania Cavalry*. Edited by Eric J. Wittenberg. Kent, OH: Kent State University Press, 1999.

Smith, William F. *Autobiography of Major General William F. Smith, 1861–1864*. Edited by Herbert M. Schiller. Dayton, OH: Morningside, 1990.

Smith, William Mervale. *Swamp Doctor: The Diary of a Union Surgeon in the Virginia and North Carolina Marshes*. Edited by Thomas P. Lowry. Mechanicsburg, PA: Stackpole Books, 2001.

Southwick, Thomas P. *A Duryee Zouave*. Brookneal, VA: Shroeder, 1995.

Spear, Ellis. *The Civil War Recollections of General Ellis Spear*. Edited by Abbot Spear, Andrea C. Hawkes, Marie H. McCosh, Craig L. Symonds, and Michael H. Alpert. Orono: University of Maine Press, 1997.

Spiegel, Marcus M. *Your True Marcus: The Civil War Letters of a Jewish Colonel*. Edited by Frank L. Byrne and Jean Powers Soman. Kent, OH: Kent State University Press, 1985.

Spurgeon, Ken, ed. *A Kansas Soldier at War: The Civil War Letters of Christian and Elise Dubach Isely*. Charleston, SC: History Press, 2013.

Squier, George W. *This Wilderness of War: The Civil War Letters of George W. Squier, Hoosier Volunteer*. Edited by Julie A. Doyle, John David Smith, and Richard M. McMurry. Knoxville: University of Tennessee Press, 1998.

Standard, William, and Jane Standard. *This Infernal War: The Civil War Letters of William and Jane Standard.* Edited by Timothy Mason Roberts. Kent, OH: Kent State University Press, 2018.

Stanton, Elizabeth Cady. *Elizabeth Cady Stanton as Revealed in Her Letters, Diary, and Reminiscences.* Edited by Theodore Stanton and Harriot Stanton Blatch. 2 vols. New York: Harper and Brothers, 1922.

Stearns, Amos E. *The Civil War Diary of Amos E. Stearns, a Prisoner at Andersonville.* Edited by Leon Basile. Rutherford, NJ: Fairleigh Dickinson University Press, 1981.

Stedman, Laura, and George M. Gould. *Life and Letters of Edmund Clarence Stedman.* 2 vols. New York: Moffat, Yard, 1910.

Steiner, Lewis Henry. *Report of Lewis H. Steiner, M.D., Inspector of the Sanitary Commission, Containing a Diary Kept during the Rebel Occupation of Frederick, Md., and an Account of the Operations of the U.S. Sanitary Commission during the Campaign in Maryland, September 1862.* New York: Anson D. F. Randolph, 1862.

Stephens, C. A. *Berdan's United States Sharpshooters in the Army of the Potomac.* Dayton, OH: Morningside, 1984.

Stevens, Hazard. *The Life of Isaac Ingalls Stevens.* 2 vols. Boston: Houghton Mifflin, 1900.

Stevens, Thaddeus. *The Selected Papers of Thaddeus Stevens.* 2 vols. Pittsburgh: University of Pittsburgh Press, 1997.

Stewart, Alexander Morrison. *Camp, March, and Battlefield; or, Three Years and a Half with the Army of the Potomac.* Philadelphia: J. B. Rodgers, 1865.

Stoddard, William O. *Dispatches from Lincoln's White House: The Anonymous Civil War Journalism of Presidential Secretary William O. Stoddard.* Edited by Michael Burlingame. Lincoln: University of Nebraska Press, 2002.

———. *Inside the White House in War Times: Memoirs and Reports of Lincoln's Secretary.* Lincoln: University of Nebraska Press, 2000.

———. *Lincoln's White House Secretary: The Adventurous Life of William O. Stoddard.* Edited by Harold Holzer. Carbondale: Southern Illinois University Press, 2007.

Stone, James Madison. *Personal Recollections of the Civil War, by One Who Took Part in It as a Private Solder in the 21st Volunteer Regiment of Infantry from Massachusetts.* Boston: Published by the author, 1918.

Strathern, John H. *The Civil War Letters of Cpl. John H. Strathern, Eighth Pennsylvania Reserve Volunteer Corps.* Edited by Marlene C. Bumbera. Apollo, PA: Closson, 1994.

Strong, George Templeton. *The Diary of George Templeton Strong.* 4 vols. Edited by Allan Nevins and Milton Halsey Thomas. New York: Macmillan, 1952.

Strother, David Hunter. *A Virginia Yankee in the Civil War: The Diaries of David Hunter Strother.* Edited by Cecil D. Eby Jr. Chapel Hill: University of North Carolina Press, 1961.

Stuckenberg, John H. W. *"I'm Surrounded by Methodists": Diary of John H. W. Stuckenberg, Chaplain of the 145th Pennsylvania Volunteer Infantry.* Edited by David T. Hedrick and Gordon Barry Davis Jr. Gettysburg, PA: Thomas, 1995.

Styple, William B., ed. *Generals in Bronze: Interviewing the Commanders of the Civil War.* Kearny, NJ: Belle Grove, 2005.

——, ed. *Writing and Fighting the Civil War: Soldier Correspondence to the New York Sunday Mercury.* Kearny, NJ: Belle Grove, 2000.

Sumner, Charles. *Charles Sumner: His Complete Works.* 20 vols. Boston: Lee and Shepard, 1900.

——. *The Selected Letters of Charles Sumner.* Edited by Beverly Wilson Palmer. 2 vols. Boston: Northeastern University Press, 1990.

Supplement to the Official Records of the Union and Confederate Armies. 100 vols. Wilmington, NC: Broadfoot, 1994–2001.

Swinton, William. *Campaigns of the Army of the Potomac.* Secaucus, NJ: Blue and Grey, 1988.

——. *A Few Plain Words with the Rank and File of the Union Armies.* [Washington]: Printed by L. Towers for the Union Congressional Committee, 1864.

——. *The "Times" Review of McClellan: His Military Career Reviewed and Exposed.* New York: N.Y. Times, 1864.

Swisshelm, Jane Grey. *Crusader and Feminist: Letters of Jane Grey Swisshelm, 1858–1865.* Edited by Arthur J. Larsen. St. Paul: Minnesota Historical Society, 1934.

Tapert, Annette. *The Brothers' War: Civil War Letters to Their Loved Ones from the Blue and Gray.* New York: Times Books, 1988.

Taylor, Guy C. *Letters Home to Sarah: The Civil War Letters of Guy C. Taylor, 36th Wisconsin Volunteers.* Edited by Kevin Alderson and Patsy Alderson. Madison: University of Wisconsin Press, 2012.

Taylor, Joseph K. *The Civil War Letters of Joseph K. Taylor of the Thirty-Seventh Massachusetts Volunteer Infantry.* Edited by Kevin C. Murphy. Lewiston, NY: Edward Mellen, 1998.

Thomas, James B. *The Civil War Letters of First Lieutenant James B. Thomas, Adjutant, 107th Pennsylvania Volunteers.* Edited by Mary Warner Thomas and Richard A. Sauers. Baltimore: Butternut and Blue, 1995.

Tidd, John. *Dear Friend Amelia: The Civil War Letters of Private John Tidd.* Edited by Mary Jordan and Joyce Hatch. Ithaca, NY: Six Mile Creek, 2011.

Townsend, E. D. *Anecdotes of the Civil War in the United States.* New York: D. Appleton, 1884.

Townsend, George Alfred. *Rustics in Rebellion: A Yankee Reporter on the Road to Richmond, 1861–1865.* Chapel Hill: University of North Carolina Press, 1950.

The Tribune Almanac and Political Register for 1865. New York: Tribune Association, 1864.

Trimble, Richard M., ed. *Brothers 'til Death: The Civil War Letters of William, Thomas, and Maggie Jones, 1861–1865.* Macon, GA: Mercer University Press, 2000.

Trobriand, Régis de. *Four Years with the Army of the Potomac.* Translated by George K. Dauchy. Boston: Ticknor, 1889.

———. *Our Noble Blood: The Civil War Letters of Major-General Régis de Trobriand.* Translated by Nathalie Chartrain. Edited by William B. Styple. Kearny, NJ: Belle Grove, 1997.

Turner, Henry McNeal. *Freedom's Witness: The Civil War Correspondence of Henry McNeal Turner.* Edited by Jean Lee Cole. Morgantown: West Virginia University Press, 2013.

Turner, Justin G., and Linda Levitt Turner. *Mary Todd Lincoln: Her Life and Letters.* New York: Alfred A. Knopf, 1972.

Twichell, Joseph Hopkins. *The Civil War Letters of Joseph Hopkins Twichell: A Chaplain's Story.* Edited by Peter Messent and Steve Courtney. Athens: University of Georgia Press, 2006.

Tyler, Mason Whiting. *Recollections of the Civil War.* Edited by William S. Tyler. New York: G. P. Putnam's Sons, 1912.

Tyler, Moses Coit. *Moses Coit Tyler, 1835–1900: Selections from His Letters and Diaries.* Edited by Jessica Austen. New York: Doubleday, 1911.

Under the Maltese Cross: Antietam to Appomattox, the Loyal Uprising in Western Pennsylvania, Campaigns 155th Pennsylvania Regiment Narrated by Rank and File. Akron, OH: Werner, 1910.

Upton, Emory. *The Military Policy of the United States.* Washington: Government Printing Office, 1912.

Vallandigham, Clement L. *Speeches, Arguments, Addresses, and Letters of Clement L. Vallandigham.* New York: J. Walter, 1864.

Villard, Henry. *Lincoln on the Eve of '61.* Edited by Harold G. and Oswald Garrison Villard. New York: Alfred A. Knopf, 1941.

———. *Memoirs of Henry Villard, Journalist and Financier.* 2 vols. New York: Houghton Mifflin, 1904.

Vincent, Charles Macreading. *Your Affectionate Son: Civil War Diaries and Letters by a Soldier from Martha's Vineyard.* Edited by Marian Ragan Halperin. N.p.: Martha's Vineyard Museum, 2008.

Voris, Alvin C. *A Citizen-Soldier's Civil War: The Letters of Brevet Major General Alvin C. Voris.* Edited by Jerome Mushkat. DeKalb: North Illinois University Press, 2002.

Wade, Benjamin F. *Facts for the People: Ben Wade on McClellan.* Cincinnati: C. Clark, 1864.

——. *Traitors and Their Sympathizers: Speech of Hon. B. F. Wade of Ohio in the Senate of the United States, April 21, 1862.* [Washington: Scammell, 1862].

Wainwright, Charles S. *A Diary of Battle: The Personal Journals of Colonel Charles S. Wainwright, 1861–1865.* Edited by Allan Nevins. New York: Harcourt, Brace, and World, 1962.

Walker, Aldace Freeman. *Quite Ready to be Sent Somewhere: The Civil War Letters of Aldace Freeman Walker.* Edited by Tom Ledoux. Victoria, Canada: Trafford, 2002.

Ward, Joseph R. *An Enlisted Man's View of the Civil War: The Wartime Papers of Joseph R. Ward, 39th Illinois Volunteer Infantry.* Edited by D. Duane Cummins and Daryl Hohweiler. West Lafayette, IN: Belle, 1981.

War of the Rebellion: A Compilation of the Official Records of the Union and Confederate Armies. 128 vols. Washington: Government Printing Office, 1880–1901.

Watson, William. *Letters of a Civil War Surgeon.* Edited by Paul Fatout. West Lafayette, IN: Purdue University Press, 1996.

Webb, Alexander S. *The Peninsula: McClellan's Campaign of 1862.* New York: Charles Scribner's Sons, 1881.

Weld, Stephen Minot. *War Diary and Letters of Stephen Minot Weld, 1861–1865.* Boston: Massachusetts Historical Society, 1979.

Welles, Gideon. *Diary of Gideon Welles: Secretary of the Navy under Lincoln and Johnson.* Edited by Howard K. Beale. 3 vols. New York: W. W. Norton, 1960.

——. *Lincoln and Seward.* New York: Sheldon, 1874.

White, Daniel. *Dear Wife: Letters of a Civil War Soldier.* Edited by Jack C. Davis. Louisville, KY: Sulgrave, 1991.

Whiteaker, Larry H., and W. Calvin Dickinson, eds. *Civil War Letters of the Tenure Family, Rockland County, N.Y., 1862–1865.* New York: Historical Society of Rockland County, 1990.

Whitman, George Washington. *Civil War Letters of George Washington Whitman.* Edited by Jerome M. Loving. Durham, NC: Duke University Press, 1975.

Whittemore, Harrison. *"But God Has So Ordered It": The Civil War Diaries of Sgt. Harrison Whittemore, 1st Massachusetts Infantry, Company K.* Edited by Lee Ward. Independence, MO: Two Trails, 2005.

Wightman, Edward King. *From Antietam to Fort Fisher: The Civil War Letters of Edward King Wightman, 1862–1865.* Edited by Edward G. Longacre. Rutherford, NJ: Associated University Press, 1985.

Wilkes, George. *McClellan: From Ball's Bluff to Antietam.* New York: Sinclair Tousey, 1863.

——. *McClellan: Who He Is and What He Has Done.* New York: Sinclair Tousey, 1862.

Willcox, Orlando B. *Forgotten Valor: The Memoirs, Journals, and Civil War Letters of Orlando B. Willcox.* Edited by Robert Garth Scott. Kent, OH: Kent State University Press, 1999.

Williams, Alpheus S. *From the Cannon's Mouth: The Civil War Letters of General Alpheus S. Williams.* Edited by Milo M. Quaife. Detroit: Wayne State University Press, 1959.

Wills, Charles W. *Army Life of an Illinois Soldier.* Compiled by Mary E. Kellogg. Carbondale: Southern Illinois University Press, 1996.

Willsey, Berea M. *The Civil War Diary of Berea M. Willsey: The Intimate Daily Observations of a Massachusetts Volunteer in the Union Army, 1862–1864.* Edited by Jessica H. Demay. Bowie, MD: Heritage Books, 1995.

Wilson, Douglas L., and Rodney O. Davis, eds. *Herndon's Informants: Letters, Interviews, and Statements about Abraham Lincoln.* Urbana: University of Illinois Press, 1998.

Wilson, James Harrison. *Under the Old Flag.* 2 vols. New York: D. Appleton, 1912.

Winthrop, Robert C. *Speech of Hon. Robert C. Winthrop, at the Great Ratification Meeting in Union Square, New York, September 17, 1864.* [New York: N.p., 1864].

Wister, Sarah Butler. *Walter S. Newhall, a Memoir.* Philadelphia: C. Sherman, 1864.

Wormeley, Katherine Prescott. *The Other Side of War with the Army of the Potomac.* Boston: Ticknor, 1889.

Wright, James A. *No More Gallant a Deed: A Civil War Memoir of the First Minnesota Volunteers.* Edited by Steven J. Keillor. Minneapolis: Minnesota Historical Society, 2001.

Young, Henry F. *Dear Delia: The Civil War Letters of Captain Henry F. Young, Seventh Wisconsin Infantry.* Edited by Micheal J. Larson and John David Smith. Madison: University of Wisconsin Press, 2019.

Young, John Russell. *Around the World with General Grant.* 2 vols. New York: American News, 1879.

Zorn, Jacob J. *A Sergeant's Story: Civil War Diary of Jacob J. Zorn, 1862–1865.* Edited by Barbara M. Croner. Apollo, PA: Closson, 1999.

Articles and Chapters

Acton, Edward A. "'Dear Mollie': Letters of Captain Edward A. Acton to His Wife, 1862." Edited by Mary Acton Hammond. *Pennsylvania Magazine of History and Biography* 89 (January 1965): 3–51.

Allen, Winthrop S. G. "Civil War Letters of Winthrop S. G. Allen." *Journal of the Illinois State Historical Society* 24 (October 1931): 553–77.

Beale, Joseph Boggs. "Education of an Artist: The Diary of Joseph Boggs Beale,

1856–1862." *Pennsylvania Magazine of History and Biography* 97 (October 1973): 485–510.

Beck, E. W. H. "Letters of a Civil War Surgeon." *Indiana Magazine of History* 27 (June 1931): 132–63.

Biddle, William F. "Recollections of McClellan." *United Service* 11 (May 1894): 460–69.

Black, Jeremiah S. "Mr. Black to Mr. Wilson." *Galaxy* 11, no. 2 (February 1871): 257–276.

———. "Senator Wilson and Edwin M. Stanton." *Galaxy* 9, no. 6 (June 1870): 817–31.

Bliss, George N. "Chaos Still Reigns in This Camp—Letters of Lieutenant George N. Bliss, 1st New England Cavalry, March–September 1862." Edited by Edward G. Longacre. *Rhode Island History* 36 (February 1977): 14–24.

Boots, E. N. "Civil War Letters of E. N. Boots in 1862." Edited by Wilfred W. Black and E. N. Boots. *Virginia Magazine of History and Biography* 69 (April 1961): 194–209.

Bunten, Sirene. "A Civil War Diary from French Creek: Selections from the Diary of Sirene Bunten." Edited by Stephen Cresswell. *West Virginia History* 48 (1989): 131–41.

Capron, Thaddeus H. "War Diary of Thaddeus H. Capron, 1861–1865." *Journal of the Illinois State Historical Society* 12 (October 1919): 330–406.

Chandler, Zachariah. "Zachariah Chandler's Part in the Reelection of Abraham Lincoln." *Mississippi Valley Historical Review* 22 (September 1935): 267–76.

Clark, Charles A. "General McClellan." In *War Sketches and Incidents as Related by the Companions of the Iowa Commandery, Military Order of the Loyal Legion of the United States,* 2:9–47. Wilmington, NC: Broadfoot, 1994.

Coffin, Gorham. "Civil War Letters of Gorham Coffin." Edited by Herbert A. Wisbey Jr. *Essex Institute Historical Collections* 93 (January 1957): 58–92.

"Commemoration of the Lincoln Centenary by the Ohio Commandery of the Military Order of the Loyal Legions of the United States." In *Sketches of War History,* 7:283–313.

Cunningham, David. "Major Cunningham's Journal, 1862." Edited by Elizabeth Cometti. *West Virginia History* 34 (January 1973): 187–211.

Edgcomb, George. "'Dear Brother Isaac . . .': Letters from George Edgcomb, 15th New York Engineers." Edited by Edmund Raus. *Military Images* 8 (May–June 1987): 14–15.

Endicott, William. "Reminiscences of Seventy-Five Years." *Proceedings of the Massachusetts Historical Society,* 3rd ser., 46 (November 1912): 208–33.

"Federal Generals and a Good Press." *American Historical Review* 39 (January 1934): 284–97.

Fleming, John H. "A Palace Guard View of Lincoln (The Civil War Letters of John H. Fleming.)" Edited Christian Brun. *Soundings: Collections of the University [of California at Santa Barbara] Library* 3 (December 1971): 18–39.

Fry, James B. "McClellan and His 'Mission': A Study." *Century* 6 (October 1894): 931–46.

Graham, Ziba B. "On to Gettysburg: Ten Days from My Diary of 1863. A Paper Read before the Commandery of the State of Michigan . . . March 2, 1889." In *War Papers Read before the Commandery of the State of Michigan, Military Order of the Loyal Legion of the United States,* 1:467–82. Wilmington, NC: Broadfoot, 1993.

Griner, Joseph Addison. "The Civil War of a Pennsylvania Trooper." Edited by Daniel H. Woodward. *Pennsylvania Magazine of History and Biography* 87 (January 1963): 39–62.

Hadley, John Vestal. "An Indiana Soldier in Love and War: The Civil War Letters of John V. Hadley." Edited by James I. Robertson Jr. *Indiana Magazine of History* 59 (September 1963): 189–288.

Heffelfinger, Jacob. "'Dear Sister Jennie,' 'Dear Brother Jacob': Correspondence between a Northern Soldier and His Sister." Edited by Florence C. McLaughlin. *Western Pennsylvania Historical Magazine* 60 (April 1977): 109–43.

Holmes, James Rush. "The Civil War Letters of James Rush Holmes." Edited by Ida Bright Adams. *Western Pennsylvania Historical Magazine* 44 (June 1961): 105–27.

"Hon. Z. Chandler—His Services and Events of the Period." *Republic* 4 (April 1875): 193–208.

"An Iowa Woman in Washington, D.C., 1861–1865." *Iowa Journal of History* 52 (January 1954): 61–90.

King, Charles. "A Boy's Recollections of Our Great Generals." In *War Papers, Being Papers Read before the Commandery of the State of Wisconsin, Military Order of the Loyal Legion of the United States,* 3:125–39. Wilmington, NC: Broadfoot, 1993.

Lazear, Bazel F. "The Civil War Letters of Colonel Bazel F. Lazear." Edited by Vivian Kirkpatrick McLarty. *Missouri Historical Review* 44 (April, July 1950): 254–73, 387–401; 45 (October 1950): 47–63.

Legate, George H. "Never Defeated Yet." Edited by Paul Kallina. *Lincoln Herald* 89 (Fall 1987): 117–22.

Leonard, James H. "Letters of a Fifth Wisconsin Volunteer." Edited by R. G. Plumb. *Wisconsin Magazine of History* 3 (September 1919): 52–83.

"Lincoln Visits the Army of the Potomac." *Lincoln Lore* 1277, September 28, 1953.

Lowell, James Russell. "General McClellan's Report." *North American Review* 98 (April 1864): 550–66.

McClellan, George B. "General Jomini." *Galaxy* 7 (June 1869): 874–88.

[McClellan, George B.]. "The Coming Campaign Foreshadowed." *Round Table* 1, March 12, 1864, 193–94.

———. "The Coming Campaign in the West." *Round Table* 1, March 19, 1864, 209–10.

McKelvy, David. "Soldier Voting in 1864: The David McKelvy Diary." Edited by Margaret McKelvy Bird and Daniel W. Crofts. *Pennsylvania Magazine of History and Biography* 115 (July 1991): 371–413.

Meigs, Montgomery. "General M. C. Meigs on the Conduct of the War." *American Historical Review* 26 (January 1921): 285–303.

Morse, Charles F. "From Second Bull Run to Antietam." In *War Papers and Personal Reminiscences Read before the Commandery of the State of Missouri, Military Order of the Loyal Legion of the United States,* 1:268–86. St. Louis: Becktold, 1892.

Newman, Simon P. "A Democrat in Lincoln's Army: The Civil War Letters of Henry P. Hubbell." *Princeton University Library Chronicle* 50 (Winter 1989): 155–68.

Oliver, Robert, Jr. "Robert Oliver, Jr., and the Oswego County Regiment." Edited by Charles M. Snyder. *New York History* 38 (July 1957): 276–93.

Palfrey, Francis W. "The Period Which Elapsed between the Fall of Yorktown and the Beginning of the Seven Days' Battles." In *Papers of the Military Historical Society of Massachusetts,* 1:155–215.

Palfrey, John C. "The Siege of Yorktown." In *Papers of the Military Historical Society of Massachusetts,* 1:91–152.

Perkins, Charles C. "The Civil War Diary of Pvt. Charles C. Perkins, 1st Massachusetts Infantry Regiment, June 4–July 4, 1862." Edited by Richard J. Sommers. In Miller, *Peninsula Campaign,* 1:144–76.

Perkins, Charles E. "Letters Home: Sergeant Charles E. Perkins in Virginia, 1862." Edited by Ray Henshaw and Glenn W. LaFantasie. *Rhode Island History* 39 (November 1980): 107–31.

Perry, Aaron F. "A Chapter in Interstate Diplomacy." In *Sketches of War History,* 3:333–63.

Peskin, Alan, ed. "Two White House Visits: Congressman James H. Campbell Prods President Lincoln and Shares 'a Dish of Gossip with the First Lady,'" *Lincoln Herald* 94 (Winter 1992): 157–58.

Raymond, Henry W., ed. "Extracts from the Journal of Henry J. Raymond." *Scribner's Monthly* 19 (January, March 1880): 419–24, 703–10.

Rich, James B. "Quaker Soldier: Letters of James B. Rich to Sue J. Sheppard (1862–1864)." *Bulletin of the Historical Society of Montgomery County* 25 (Spring 1987): 275–307.

Russ, William A., Jr., ed. "Civil War Letters Concerning Members of Co. G, 174th Reg., P.V.I." *Susquehanna University Studies* 5 (May 1955): 179–220.

Russell, Ira. "The Aftermath of Prairie Grove: Union Letters from Fayetteville." Edited by William L. Shea. *Arkansas Historical Quarterly* 47 (Winter 1988): 345–61.

Russell, William Howard. "Recollections of the Civil War—V." *North American Review* 166 (June 1898): 740–50.

Scott, Eben Greenough. "General McClellan." *Atlantic Monthly* 70 (July 1892): 1–14.

Stowe, Jonathan P. "Life with the 15th Mass." *Civil War Times Illustrated* 11 (August 1972): 4–11, 48–54.

Strother, D. H. "Personal Recollections of the War by a Virginian [Tenth Paper] Antietam." *Harper's New Monthly Magazine* 36 (February 1868): 273–91, 567–82.

Taylor, Isaac Lyman. "Campaigning with the First Minnesota, a Civil War Diary." Edited by Hazel C. Wolf. *Minnesota History* 25 (September 1944): 224–57.

Teall, William W. "Ringside Seat at Fredericksburg." *Civil War Times Illustrated* 4 (May 1965): 17–34.

Thompson, Joseph P. "A Talk with President Lincoln." *Congregationalist,* March 30, 1866, 50–51.

Truesdell, S. N. "Pale Cheeks but No Trembling Hands: Civil War Letters of a Connecticut Soldier." Edited by Henry M. Adams. *Lincoln Herald* 55 (1953): 36–41.

Trumbull, Lyman. "A Statesman's Letters of the Civil War Period." *Journal of the Illinois State Historical Society* 2 (July 1909): 43–50.

———. "Trumbull Correspondence." *Mississippi Valley Historical Review* 1 (June 1914): 101–8.

Viele, Egbert L. "A Trip with Lincoln, Chase, and Stanton." *Scribner's Monthly* 6 (October 1878): 813–23.

Vliet, John. "A Brooklyn Soldiers a Century Ago." Edited by David M. Cory. *Journal of Long Island History* 3, no. 2 (1962): 29–54.

Ward, Durbin. "The Presidential Campaign of 1864 as Viewed by a Federal Army Colonel." Edited by David Lindsey. *Georgia Historical Quarterly* 39 (June 1955): 187–92.

White, Herman Lorenzo. "The White Papers: Letters (1861–1865) of Pvt. Herman Lorenzo White, 22nd Regiment Massachusetts Volunteers." Edited by Kathleen Kroll and Charles Moran. *Massachusetts Review* 18 (Summer 1977): 248–70.

Willoughby, Charles H. "Extracts from Journal of Charles H. Willoughby, Private Company C, Thirty-Fourth New York Volunteers." *Fifth Annual Report of the New York State Bureau of Military Statistics* (1868): 473–543.

Wilson, Henry. "Edwin M. Stanton" *Atlantic Monthly* 25 (February 1870): 234–45.

Wilson, James Grant. "Types and Traditions of the Old Army. II: General Halleck—A Memoir." *Journal of the Military Service Institution of the United States* 36 (1905): 537–59.

SECONDARY WORKS

Books

Adams, Michael C. C. *Living Hell: The Dark Side of the Civil War.* Baltimore: Johns Hopkins University Press, 2014.

Anderson, William M. *They Died to Make Men Free: A History of the 19th Michigan in the Civil War.* Berrien Springs, MI: Hardscabble Books, 1980.

Andrews, J. Cutler *The North Reports the Civil War.* Pittsburgh: University of Pittsburgh Press, 1955.

Army, Thomas F., Jr. *Engineering Victory: How Technology Won the Civil War.* Baltimore: Johns Hopkins University Press, 2016.

Baker, Jean H. *The Lincoln Marriage: Beyond the Battle of Quotations.* Gettysburg, PA: Fortenbaugh Memorial Lecture, 1999.

———. *Mary Todd Lincoln, a Biography.* New York: W. W. Norton, 1987.

Beatie, Russel H. *The Army of the Potomac.* 3 vols. Cambridge, MA: DaCapo, 2002 (vols. 1–2); New York: Savas Beatie, 2007 (vol. 3).

Beehner, Lionel, Risa Brooks, and Donald Mauer, eds. *Reconsidering American Civil-Military Relations: The Military, Society, Politics, and Modern War.* New York: Oxford University Press, 2021.

Blair, William A. *With Malice toward Some: Treason and Loyalty in the Civil War Era.* Chapel Hill: University of North Carolina Press, 2014.

Bledsoe, Andrew S., and Andrew F. Lang, eds. *Upon the Fields of Battle: Essays on the Military History of the American Civil War.* Baton Rouge: Louisiana State University Press, 2018.

Boritt, Gabor S., ed. *Lincoln's Generals.* New York: Oxford University Press, 1994.

Brandt, Nat. *Mr. Tubbs' Civil War.* Syracuse, NY: Syracuse University Press, 1996.

Brasher, Glenn David. *The Peninsula Campaign & the Necessity of Emancipation: African Americans & Their Fight for Freedom.* Chapel Hill: University of North Carolina Press, 2012.

Browning, Judkin, and Timothy Silver. *An Environmental History of the Civil War.* Chapel Hill: University of North Carolina Press, 2020.

Burlingame, Michael. *Abraham Lincoln: A Life.* 2 vols. Baltimore: Johns Hopkins University Press, 2008.

———. *The Inner World of Abraham Lincoln.* Urbana: University of Illinois Press, 1994.

Cain, Marvin R. *Lincoln's Attorney General: Edward Bates of Missouri.* Columbia: University of Missouri Press, 1965.

Carwardine, Richard. *Lincoln: A Life of Purpose and Power.* New York: Alfred A. Knopf, 2003.

Catton, Bruce. *Mr. Lincoln's Army.* New York: Doubleday, 1951.

——. *Terrible Swift Sword.* Garden City, NY: Doubleday, 1963.

Clapp, Margaret. *Forgotten First Citizen: John Bigelow.* Boston: Little, Brown, 1947.

Clinton, Catherine. *Mrs. Lincoln, a Life.* New York: Harper, 2009.

Cohen, Elliott A. *Supreme Command: Soldiers, Statesmen, and Leadership in Wartime.* New York: Free Press, 2002.

Cooling, Benjamin Franklin. *Counter-Thrust: From the Peninsula to the Antietam.* Lincoln: University of Nebraska Press, 2007.

——. *Symbol, Sword, and Shield: Defending Washington during the Civil War.* Rev. 2nd ed. Shippensburg, PA: White Maine, 1991.

Cooper, William J. *We Have the War upon Us: The Onset of the Civil War, November 1860–April 1861.* New York: Alfred A. Knopf, 2012.

Cozzens, Peter. *General John Pope: A Life for the Nation.* Urbana: University of Illinois Press, 2000.

Craig, Gordon A. *The Politics of the Prussian Army, 1640–1945.* New York: Oxford University Press, 1956.

Crofts, Daniel W. *A Secession Crisis Enigma: William Henry Hurlbert and "The Diary of a Public Man."* Baton Rouge: Louisiana State University Press, 2010.

Cushman, Stephen. *The General's Civil War: What Their Memoirs Can Teach Us Today.* Chapel Hill: University of North Carolina Press, 2021.

Cutler, Julia P. *Life and Times of Ephraim Cutler.* Cincinnati: Robert Clarke, 1890.

Davis, William C. *Lincoln's Men: How President Lincoln Became Father to an Army and a Nation.* New York: Free Press, 1999.

De Peyster, John Watts. *Personal and Military History of Philip Kearny.* New York: Rice and Gage, 1869.

Detroit Post and Tribune. *Zachariah Chandler: An Outline Sketch of His Life and Public Services.* Detroit: Post and Tribune, 1880.

Dickey, Luther S. *History of the Eighty-Fifth Regiment Pennsylvania Volunteer Infantry.* New York: J. C. and W. E. Powers, 1915.

Dirck, Brian. *Lincoln the Lawyer.* Urbana: University of Illinois Press, 2007.

Donald, David Herbert. *Charles Sumner and the Rights of Man.* New York: Alfred A. Knopf, 1970.

——. *Lincoln.* New York: Simon and Schuster, 1995.

——. *Lincoln Reconsidered: Essays on the Civil War Era.* Rev. ed. New York: Alfred A. Knopf, 1956.

——. *"We Are Lincoln Men": Abraham Lincoln and His Friends.* New York: Simon and Schuster, 2003.

Ecelbarger, Gary L. *Frederick W. Lander: The Great Natural American Soldier.* Baton Rouge: Louisiana State University Press, 2000.

Edwards, Robert. *Of Singular Genius, of Singular Grace: A Biography of Horace Bushnell.* Cleveland: Pilgrim, 1992.

Emerson, Edward Waldo. *Life and Letters of Charles Russell Lowell.* Columbia: University of South Carolina Press, 2005.

Engle, Stephen D. *Gathering to Save a Nation: Lincoln and the War Governors.* Chapel Hill: University of North Carolina Press, 2016.

——, ed. *The War Worth Fighting For: Abraham Lincoln's Presidency and Civil War America.* Gainesville: University Press of Florida, 2015.

Fessenden, Francis. *Life and Public Services of William Pitt Fessenden.* 2 vols. Boston: Houghton Mifflin, 1907.

Fishel, Edwin C. *The Secret War for the Union: The Untold Story of Military Intelligence in the Civil War.* Boston: Houghton Mifflin, 1996.

Flower, Frank Abial. *Edwin McMasters Stanton: The Autocrat of Rebellion, Emancipation, and Reconstruction.* Boston: George M. Smith, 1905.

Frothingham, Paul Revere. *Edward Everett: Orator and Statesman.* Boston: Houghton Mifflin, 1925.

Fry, Zachary A. *A Republic in the Ranks: Loyalty and Dissent in the Army of the Potomac.* Chapel Hill: University of North Carolina Press, 2020.

Gaff, Alan D. *On Many a Bloody Field: Four Years in the Iron Brigade.* Bloomington: Indiana University Press, 1996.

Gallagher, Gary W., ed. *The Antietam Campaign.* Chapel Hill: University of North Carolina Press, 1999.

Gallman, J. Matthew. *America's Joan of Arc: The Life of Anna Elizabeth Dickinson.* New York: Oxford University Press, 2006.

——. *The Cacophony of Politics: Northern Democrats and the American Civil War.* Charlottesville: University of Virginia Press, 2021.

George, Sister Mary Karl. *Zachariah Chandler: A Political Biography.* East Lansing: Michigan State University Press, 1969.

Glatthaar, Joseph T. *The March to the Sea and Beyond: Sherman's Troops in the Savannah and Carolinas Campaigns.* New York: New York University Press, 1986.

——. *Partners in Command: The Relationship between Leaders in the Civil War.* New York: Free Press, 1994.

Goodwin, Doris Kearns. *Team of Rivals: The Political Genius of Abraham Lincoln.* New York: Simon and Schuster, 2005.

Gorham, George Congdon. *Life and Public Services of Edwin M. Stanton.* 2 vols. Boston: Houghton, Mifflin, 1899.

Gould, Edward Kalloch. *Major-General Hiram G. Berry.* Rockland, ME: Press of the Courier-Gazette, 1899.

Grandchamp, Robert *The Boys of Adams' Battery G: The Civil War through the Eyes of a Union Light Artillery Unit.* Jefferson, NC: McFarland, 2009.

Green, Jeffrey W. *McClellan and the Union High Command, 1861–1863.* Jefferson, NC: McFarland, 2017.

Grimsley, Mark. *The Hard Hand of War: Union Military Policy toward Southern Civilians, 1861–1865.* Cambridge: Cambridge University Press, 1995.

Guarneri, Carl J. *Lincoln's Informer: Charles A. Dana and the Inside Story of the Union War.* Lawrence: University Press of Kansas, 2019.

Guelzo, Allen C. *Abraham Lincoln: Redeemer President.* Grand Rapids, MI: William B. Eerdmans, 1999.

Hamlin, Charles Eugene. *The Life and Times of Hannibal Hamlin.* Cambridge, MA: Riverside, 1899.

Harris, Wilmer C. *Public Life of Zachariah Chandler, 1851–1875.* Lansing: Michigan Historical Commission, 1917.

Hartwig, D. Scott. *To Antietam Creek: The Maryland Campaign of September 1862.* Baltimore: Johns Hopkins University Press, 2012.

Hassler, Warren W., Jr. *General George B. McClellan: Shield of the Union.* Baton Rouge: Louisiana State University Press, 1957.

Hattaway, Herman, and Archer Jones. *How the North Won: A Military History of the Civil War.* Urbana: University of Illinois Press, 1983.

Hearn, Chester G. *Lincoln and McClellan at War.* Baton Rouge: Louisiana State University Press, 2012.

Hebert, Walter H. *Fighting Joe Hooker.* Indianapolis: Bobbs-Merrill, 1944.

Heleniak, Roman J., and Lawrence L. Hewitt, eds. *The Confederate High Command and Related Topics.* Shippensburg, PA: White Mane, 1990.

Hoadley, John Chipman. Memorial of Henry Sanford Gansevoort. Boston: Franklin, 1875.

Hodge, Alexander A. *The Life of Charles Hodge, D.D.* London: T. Nelson, 1881.

Holland, J. G. *Life of Abraham Lincoln.* Springfield, MA: Gurdon Bill, 1866.

Holzer, Harold. *Lincoln President-Elect: Abraham Lincoln and the Great Secession Winter, 1860–1861.* New York: Simon and Schuster, 2008.

Hooper, Candace Shy. *Lincoln's Generals' Wives: Four Women Who Influenced the Civil War—for Better and for Worse.* Kent, OH: Kent State University Press, 2016.

Howe, M. A. DeWolfe. *The Life and Letters of George Bancroft.* 2 vols. New York: Scribner's, 1908.

Hsieh, Wayne Wei-siang. *West Pointers and the Civil War: The Old Army in War and Peace.* Chapel Hill: University of North Carolina Press, 2009.

Huntington, Samuel P. *The Soldier and the State: The Theory and Practice of Civil-Military Relations.* Cambridge, MA: Harvard University Press, 1959.

Jellison, Charles A. *Fessenden of Maine: Civil War Senator.* Syracuse, NY: Syracuse University Press, 1962.

Johnson, Timothy D. *Winfield Scott: The Quest for Military Glory.* Lawrence: University Press of Kansas, 1998.

Katz, Irving. *August Belmont: A Political Biography.* New York: Columbia University Press, 1968.

King, Willard L. *Lincoln's Manager: David Davis.* Cambridge, MA: Harvard University Press, 1960.

Krom, Richard G. *The First Minnesota . . . Second to None.* Rochester, MN: Published by the author, 2010.

Lamers, William M. *The Edge of Glory: A Biography of General Williams S. Rosecrans.* New York: Harcourt, Brace, and World, 1961.

Lathrop, H. W. *The Life and Times of Samuel J. Kirkwood: Iowa's War Governor.* Iowa City: Published by the author, 1893.

Leech, Margaret. *Reveille in Washington, 1860–1865.* New York: Harper and Brothers, 1941.

Long, David E. *The Jewel of Liberty: Abraham Lincoln's Re-Election and the End of Slavery.* Mechanicsburg, PA: Stackpole Books, 1994.

Manning, Chandra. *What This Cruel War Was Over: Soldiers, Slavery, and the Civil War.* New York: Alfred A. Knopf, 2007.

Marszalek, John F. *Commander of All Lincoln's Armies: A Life of General Henry W. Halleck.* Cambridge, MA: Harvard University Press, 2004.

Marvel, William. *Burnside.* Chapel Hill: University of North Carolina Press, 1991.

——. *The Great Task Remaining: The Third Year of Lincoln's War.* Boston: Houghton Mifflin Harcourt, 2010.

——. *Lincoln's Autocrat: The Life of Edwin Stanton.* Chapel Hill: University of North Carolina Press, 2015.

——. *Lincoln's Darkest Year: The War in 1862.* Boston: Houghton Mifflin, 2008.

——. *Mr. Lincoln Goes to War.* Boston: Houghton Mifflin, 2006.

——. *Radical Sacrifice: The Rise and Ruin of Fitz John Porter.* Chapel Hill: University of North Carolina Press, 2020.

——. *Tarnished Victory: Finishing Lincoln's War.* Boston: Houghton Mifflin, 2011.

Mason, Jack C. *Until Antietam: The Life and Letters of Major General Israel B. Richardson, U.S. Army.* Carbondale: Southern Illinois University Press, 2009.

Matsui, John H. *The First Republican Army: The Army of Virginia and the Radicalization of the Civil War.* Charlottesville: University of Virginia Press, 2016.

McClintock, Russell. *Lincoln and the Decision for War: The Northern Response to Secession.* Chapel Hill: University of North Carolina Press, 2008.

McPherson, James M. *Tried by War: Abraham Lincoln as Commander in Chief.* New York: Penguin, 2008.

McWhirter, Christian. *Battle Hymns: The Power and Popularity of Music in the Civil War.* Chapel Hill: University of North Carolina Press, 2012.

Michie, Peter S. *General McClellan.* New York: D. Appleton, 1915.

Miller, William J., ed. *The Peninsula Campaign: Yorktown to the Seven Days*. 3 vols. Campbell, CA: Savas Woodbury, 1997.

Miller, William Lee. *Lincoln's Virtues: An Ethical Biography*. New York: Alfred A. Knopf, 2002.

———. *President Lincoln: The Duty of a Statesman*. New York: Alfred A. Knopf, 2008.

Mitchell, Stewart. *Horatio Seymour of New York*. Cambridge, MA: Harvard University Press, 1938.

Moe, Richard. *The Last Full Measure: The Life and Death of the First Minnesota Volunteers*. New York: Henry Holt, 1993.

Murray, Williamson, and Wayne Wei-sang Hsieh. *A Savage War: A Military History of the Civil War*. Princeton, NJ: Princeton University Press, 2016.

Myers, William Starr. *A Study in Personality: General George Brinton McClellan*. New York: D. Appleton-Century, 1954.

Neely, Mark E., Jr. *Lincoln and the Democrats: The Politics of Opposition in the Civil War*. New York: Cambridge University Press, 2017.

———. *The Union Divided: Party Conflict in the Civil War North*. Cambridge, MA: Harvard University Press, 2002.

Nevins, Allan. *The War for the Union*. 4 vols. New York: Charles Scribner's Sons, 1959–71.

Nicolay, Helen. *Lincoln's Secretary: A Biography of John G. Nicolay*. New York: Longmans, Green, 1949.

Noe, Kenneth W. *The Howling Storm: Weather, Climate, and the American Civil War*. Baton Rouge: Louisiana State University Press, 2020.

Oberholtzer, Ellis Paxson. *Jay Cooke: Financier of the Civil War*. 2 vols. Philadelphia: George W. Jacobs, 1907.

Paludan, Philip Shaw. *The Presidency of Abraham Lincoln*. Lawrence: University Press of Kansas, 1994.

Pearson, Henry Greenleaf. *James S. Wadsworth of Geneso*. London: John Murray, 1913.

Perry, Bliss. *Life and Letters of Henry Lee Higginson*. Boston: Atlantic Monthly, 1921.

Picq, Ardant du. *Battle Studies*. Translated and edited by Roger J. Spiller. Lawrence: University Press of Kansas, 2017.

Pinsker, Matthew. *Lincoln's Sanctuary: Abraham Lincoln and the Soldiers' Home*. New York: Oxford University Press, 2003.

Potter, David M. *Lincoln and His Party in the Secession Crisis*. New Haven, CT: Yale University Press, 1942.

Powell, William H. *The Fifth Army Corps*. New York: G. P. Putnam's Sons, 1896.

Pryor, Elizabeth Brown. *Six Encounters with Lincoln: A President Confronts Democracy and Its Demons*. New York: Viking, 2017.

Rable, George C. *Fredericksburg! Fredericksburg!*. Chapel Hill: University of North Carolina Press, 2002.

Rafuse, Ethan S., ed. *Corps Commanders in Blue: Union Major Generals in the Civil War.* Baton Rouge: Louisiana State University Press, 2014.

———. *McClellan's War: The Failure of Moderation in the Struggle for the Union.* Bloomington: Indiana University Press, 2005.

Ramold, Steven J. *Across the Divide: Union Soldiers View the Northern Home Front* New York: New York University Press, 2013.

Randall, James G. *Lincoln the President: Springfield to Gettysburg.* 2 vols. New York: Dodd, Meade, 1945.

Randall, James G., and Richard N. Current, *Lincoln the President: Last Full Measure.* New York: Dodd, Mead, 1955.

Reed, Rowena. *Combined Operations in the Civil War.* Annapolis: Naval Institute Press, 1978.

Rhodes, James Ford. *History of the United States from the Compromise of 1850 to the Final Restoration of Home Rule at the South in 1877.* 7 vols. New York: Macmillan, 1892–1906.

Robertson, James I., Jr. *General A. P. Hill: The Story of a Confederate Warrior.* New York: Random House, 1987.

Ropes, John Codman. *The Story of the Civil War.* 4 vols. New York: G. P. Putnam's Sons, 1933.

Rowland, Thomas J. *George B. McClellan and Civil War History: In the Shadow of Grant and Sherman.* Kent, OH: Kent State University Press, 1998.

Salter, William. *The Life of James W. Grimes.* New York: D. Appleton, 1876.

Schutz, Wallace J., and Walter N. Trenerry. *Abandoned by Lincoln: A Military Biography of General John Pope.* Urbana: University of Illinois Press, 1990.

Sears, Stephen W. *George B. McClellan, the Young Napoleon.* New York: Ticknor and Fields, 1988.

———. *Landscape Turned Red: The Battle of Antietam.* New Haven, CT: Ticknor and Fields, 1983.

———. *Lincoln's Lieutenants: The High Command of the Army of the Potomac.* Boston: Houghton Mifflin, 2017.

———. *To the Gates of Richmond: The Peninsula Campaign.* New York: Ticknor and Fields, 1992.

Shankman, Arnold M. *The Pennsylvania Antiwar Movement, 1861–1865.* Rutherford, NJ: Fairleigh Dickinson University Press, 1980.

Shenk, Joshua Wolf. *Lincoln's Melancholy: How Depression Challenged a President and Fueled His Greatness.* Boston: Houghton Mifflin, 2005.

Silbey, Joel H. *A Respectable Minority: The Democratic Party in the Civil War Era, 1860–1868.* New York: W. W. Norton, 1977.

Slade, A. D. *A. T. A. Torbert: Southern Gentleman in Union Blue.* Dayton, OH: Morningside, 1992.

Slotkin, Richard. *The Long Road to Antietam: How the Civil War Became a Revolution.* New York: Liveright, 2012.

Smith, Adam I. P. *No Party Now: Politics in the Civil War North.* New York: Oxford University Press, 2006.

Smith, William Ernest. *The Francis Preston Blair Family in Politics.* 2 vols. New York: Macmillan, 1933.

Snell, Mark A. *From First to Last: The Life of Major General William B. Franklin.* New York: Fordham University Press, 2002.

Starr, Louis M. *Reporting the Civil War: The Bohemian Brigade, 1861–1865.* New York: Collier Books, 1962.

Starr, Stephen Z. *The Union Cavalry in the Civil War.* 3 vols. Baton Rouge: Louisiana State University Press, 1979–85.

Stearns, Frank Preston. *The Life and Public Services of George Luther Stearns.* Philadelphia: J. B. Lippincott, 1907.

Stoker, Donald. *The Grand Design: Strategy and the U.S. Civil War.* New York: Oxford University Press, 2010.

Stotelmyer, Steven R. *Too Useful to Sacrifice: Reconsidering George B. McClellan's Generalship in the Maryland Campaign from South Mountain to Antietam.* El Dorado Hills, CA: Savas Beatie, 2019.

Styple, William B. *McClellan's Other Story: The Political Intrigue of Colonel Thomas M. Key, Confidential Aide to General George B. McClellan.* Kearney, NJ: Belle Grove, 2012.

Symonds, Craig L. *Lincoln and His Admirals: Abraham Lincoln, the U.S. Navy, and the Civil War.* New York: Oxford University Press, 2008.

Taliaferro, John. *All the Great Prizes: The Life of John Hay from Lincoln to Roosevelt.* New York: Simon and Schuster, 2013.

Tap, Bruce. *Over Lincoln's Shoulder: The Committee on the Conduct of the War.* Lawrence: University Press of Kansas, 1998.

Tarbell, Ida M. *The Life of Abraham Lincoln.* 2 vols. New York: Macmillan, 1917.

Thomas, Benjamin P., and Harold M. Hyman. *Stanton: The Life and Times of Lincoln's Secretary of War.* New York: Alfred A. Knopf, 1962.

Thomas, John L., ed. *Abraham Lincoln and the American Political Tradition.* Amherst: University of Massachusetts Press, 1986.

Thompson, Jerry. *Civil War to the Bloody End: The Life and Times of Major General Samuel P. Heintzelman.* College Station: Texas A&M University Press, 2006.

Tidball, Eugene C. *"No Disgrace to My Country": The Life John C. Tidball.* Kent, OH: Kent State University Press, 2002.

Trefousse, Hans L. *Benjamin Franklin Wade: Radical Republican from Ohio.* New York: Twayne, 1963.

———. *The Radical Republicans: Lincoln's Vanguard for Racial Justice.* New York: Alfred A. Knopf, 1969.
Warden, Robert B. *An Account of the Life and Public Services of Salmon Portland Chase.* Cincinnati: Wilstach, Baldwin, 1874.
Waugh, John C. *Lincoln and McClellan: The Troubled Partnership between a President and His General.* New York: Palgrave Macmillan, 2010.
Weber, Jennifer L. *Copperheads: The Rise and Fall of Lincoln's Opponents in the North.* New York: Oxford University Press, 2006.
Weigley, Russell F. *A Great Civil War: A Military and Political History, 1861–1865.* Bloomington: Indiana University Press, 2000.
———. *Quartermaster General of the Union Army: A Biography of M. C. Meigs.* New York: Columbia University Press, 1959.
———. *Towards an American Army: Military Thought from Washington to Marshall.* New York: Columbia University Press, 1962.
Weisberger, Bernard A. *Reporters for the Union.* Boston: Little, Brown, 1953.
White, Horace. *The Life of Lyman Trumbull.* Boston: Houghton Mifflin, 1913.
White, Jonathan W. *Emancipation, the Union Army, and the Reelection of Abraham Lincoln.* Baton Rouge: Louisiana State University Press, 2014.
White, Ronald C., Jr. *A. Lincoln: A Biography.* New York: Random House, 2009.
Williams, Kenneth P. *Lincoln Finds a General: A Military Study of the Civil War.* 5 vols. New York: Macmillan, 1949–59.
Williams, T. Harry. *Lincoln and His Generals.* New York: Alfred A. Knopf, 1952.
———. *Lincoln and the Radicals.* Madison: University of Wisconsin Press, 1941.
———. *McClellan, Sherman, and Grant.* New Brunswick, NJ: Rutgers University Press, 1962.
Wilson, Douglas L. *Honor's Voice: The Transformation of Abraham Lincoln.* New York: Alfred A. Knopf, 1998.
———. *Lincoln's Sword: The Presidency and the Power of Words.* New York: Alfred A. Knopf, 2006.
Winslow, Richard Elliott. *General John Sedgwick: The Story of a Corps Commander.* Navato, CA: Presidio, 1982.
Zornow, William Frank. *Lincoln and the Party Divided.* Norman: University of Oklahoma Press, 1954.

Articles

Canfield, Daniel T. "Opportunity Lost: Combined Operations and the Development of Union Military Strategy, April 1861–1862." *Journal of Military History* 78 (July 2015): 657–90.

Davis, George B. "The Antietam Campaign." In *Papers of the Military Historical Society of Massachusetts,* 3:27–72.

Fishel, Edwin C. "Pinkerton and McClellan: Who Deceived Whom?" *Civil War History* 34 (June 1988): 115–42.

Fry, Zachery A. "McClellan's Epidemic: Disease and Discord at Harrison's Landing, July–August 1862." *Civil War History* 64 (March 2018): 7–29.

Grimsley, Mark. "Lincoln and Little Mac." *Civil War Monitor* 5 (Winter 2015): 26–27, 72.

———. "The Lincoln-McClellan Relationship in Myth and Memory." *Journal of the Abraham Lincoln Association* 28 (Summer 2017): 63–81.

———. "Little Mac Fauntleroy." *Civil War Monitor* 6 (Summer 2016): 26–27, 74.

———. "Overthrown: The Truth behind the McClellan-Scott Feud." *Civil War Times Illustrated* 19 (November 1980): 20–29.

Hagerman, Edward. "The Professionalization of George B. McClellan and Early Civil War Field Command: An Institutional Perspective." *Civil War History* 21 (June 1975): 113–35.

Haven, Franklin. "The Conduct of General McClellan during His Stay at Alexandria in August 1862." In *Papers of the Military Historical Society of Massachusetts,* 2:265–85.

Holden Reid, Brian. "General McClellan and the Politicians." *Parameters* 17, no. 1 (1987): 101–12.

"The Lost Order." *Civil War Monitor* 7 (Spring 2017): 4.

McSeveney, Samuel T. "Re-electing Lincoln: The Union Party and the Military Vote in Connecticut." *Civil War History* 32 (June 1986): 139–58.

Polsky, Andrew J. "'Mr. Lincoln's Army' Revisited: Partisanship, Institutional Position, and Union Army Command, 1861–1865." *Studies in American Political Development* 16 (Fall 2002): 176–207.

Pryor, Elizabeth Brown. "Conflict, Chaos, and Confidence: Abraham Lincoln's Struggle as Commander in Chief." *Virginia Magazine of History and Biography* 129. no. 1 (2021): 2–79.

Rable, George C. "McClellan Redux?: The Often-Reported, Imminent Return of Little Mac." *Journal of the Abraham Lincoln Association* 28 (Summer 2017): 40–62.

Rafuse, Ethan S. "McClellan and Halleck at War: The Struggle for Control of the Union War Effort in the West, November 1861–March 1862." *Civil War History* 49 (March 2003): 32–51.

———. "'Poor Burn?': The Antietam Conspiracy That Wasn't," *Civil War History* 54 (June 2008): 146–75.

———. "'The Spirit Which You Have Aided to Infuse': A. Lincoln, Little Mac, Fighting Joe, and the Questions of Accountability in Union Command Relations." *Journal of the Abraham Lincoln Association* 28 (Summer 2017): 1–39.

———. "Typhoid and Tumult: Lincoln's Response to General McClellan's Bout with Typhoid Fever during the Winter of 1861–62." *Journal of the Abraham Lincoln Association* 18 (Summer 1997): 1–16.

Ropes, John C. "General McClellan's Plans for the Campaign of 1862." In *Papers of the Military Historical Society of Massachusetts*, 1:61–87.

Rowland, Thomas J. "'Heaven Save a Country Governed by Such Counsels!': The Safety of Washington and the Peninsula Campaign." *Civil War History* 42 (March 1996): 6–17.

Sears, Stephen W. "The Curious Case of General McClellan's Memoirs." *Civil War History* 34 (June 1988): 101–14.

———. "The Curious Case of the Lost Order." *Civil War Monitor* 6 (Winter 2016): 30–40, 73.

———. "McClellan and the Peace Plank of 1864: A Reappraisal." *Civil War History* 36 (March 1990): 57–64.

Weld, Stephen M. "The Conduct of General McClellan during His Stay at Alexandria in August 1862." In *Papers of the Military Historical Society of Massachusetts*, 2:289–302.

Wilson, Charles R. "McClellan's Changing Views on the Peace Plank of 1864." *American Historical Review* 38 (April 1933): 498–505.

Winther, Oscar Osburn. "The Soldier Vote in the Election of 1864." *New York History* 25 (October 1944): 440–58.

DISSERTATIONS

Harsh, Joseph L. "George Brinton McClellan and the Forgotten Alternative: An Introduction to the Conservative Strategy in the Civil War: April–August 1861." Ph.D. diss., Rice University, 1970.

Johnson, Patricia Carley. "Sensitivity and Civil War: The Selected Diaries and Papers, 1858–1866, of Frances Adeline (Fanny) Seward." Ph.D. diss., University of Rochester, 1964.

INDEX